BIOGRAPHICAL DICTIONARY
of the Board of
Governors of the Federal
Reserve

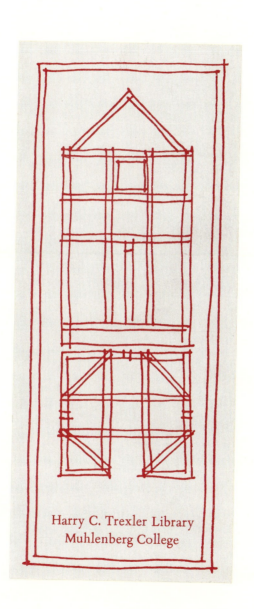

BIOGRAPHICAL DICTIONARY
of the Board of
Governors of the Federal
Reserve

EDITED BY

Bernard S. Katz

GREENWOOD PRESS
New York • Westport, Connecticut • London

Library of Congress Cataloging-in-Publication Data

Biographical dictionary of the Board of Governors of the Federal
  Reserve / edited by Bernard S. Katz.
     p.   cm.
  Includes bibliographical references and index.
  ISBN 0–313–26658–1 (alk. paper)
  1. Board of Governors of the Federal Reserve System (U.S.)—
Biography—Dictionaries. I. Katz, Bernard S.
  HG2563.B46 1992
  332.1'1'092273—dc20   91–11329

British Library Cataloguing in Publication Data is available.

Library of Congress Catalog Card Number: 91–11329
ISBN: 0–313–26658–1

First published in 1992

Greenwood Press, 88 Post Road West, Westport, CT 06881
An imprint of Greenwood Publishing Group, Inc.

Printed in the United States of America

The paper used in this book complies with the
Permanent Paper Standard issued by the National
Information Standards Organization (Z39.48–1984).

10 9 8 7 6 5 4 3 2 1

For my brother Sam

CONTENTS

PREFACE

The history of banking in the United States has been said to reflect the character of the nation—an attempt to come to terms with the need for a centralized system offset by a national suspicion of the concentration of power. The passage of the Federal Reserve Act of 1913 represented a middle ground between the competing forces of the bankers' need for private control and the populist call for governmental oversight. The act established a money and banking framework that may be considered the closest compromise the country could come to centralized banking and brought to an end the historical collage that represented the fragmented and erratic banking system that existed for the first 125 years of the nation's history. The creation of the Federal Reserve system can be considered the result of the financial panic of 1907 and the 1912 election year, which gave the presidency to Woodrow Wilson.

The demand for reform resulting from the 1907 money panic was fed by publicists and politicians, and the president-elect had publicly voiced his concern that the private banking interests of the city of New York were effectively exercising the powers of a central bank. Upon his assumption of the presidency, Wilson melded the competing needs of the bankers for private control of the money system and the public's fear of Wall Street. In seeking a comprehensive solution to the nation's monetary matters, Wilson accepted his adviser's recommendation to establish a series of reserve banks able to create money and to lend reserves to banks within their region; however, Wilson could not agree with the suggestion that the comptroller of the currency supervise the entire system. While providing the nation with a responsive money supply, the plan appeared to cater to the needs of the private banking community and not that of a competitive and populist society. Wilson's concern with centralized banking power and his sensitivity to the public's fear of a hegemony of monied interests, and his own political philosophy, resulted in his recommendation of a Federal Reserve Board to supervise the proposed system. The composition of the appointed board was to be primarily comprised of nonprofessional bankers, individuals who would not profit directly from their own policy decisions.

This supervisory board was to be appointed by the president, with approval by the Senate. The board would be the controllers and coordinators of the activities of the regional banks, while professional bankers would run the regional reserve banks. The control of monetary policy is today in the hands of the nonbanking professional, the six members of the board of governors of the Federal Reserve, and its chairperson.

Under the provisions of the original Federal Reserve Act, the Federal Reserve Board was composed of seven members: five appointive members, the secretary of the Treasury, who was ex officio chairman of the board, and the comptroller of the currency. The five original appointive members had terms of two, four, six, eight, and ten years, respectively. In 1922 the number of appointive members was increased to six, and in 1933 the term of office was increased to twelve years. The Banking Act of 1935, approved August 23, 1935, changed the name of the Federal Reserve Board to the Board of Governors of the Federal Reserve system and provided that the board should be composed of seven appointive members; that the secretary of the Treasury and the comptroller of the currency should continue to serve as members until February 1, 1936, or until their successors were appointed and had qualified; and that thereafter the terms of members should be fourteen years and that the designation of chairman and vice-chairman of the board should be for a term of four years.

Despite their important decision-making roles, the personal profiles of these men and women who control the national money supply have been cloaked in shadow. While the chairman of the Federal Reserve system must make periodic appearances before Congress, the remaining six still remain, largely unknown. Most policies of government officials have public hearings. The individuals who institute and argue national policy from the traditional three branches of government are flesh and blood before the public. Washington commentators give bell, book, and candle about their background, politics, and personalities, and the public makes their evaluations. The governors of the Fed, however, remain obscure, private people.

This remoteness has periodically given rise to the public's perception of sinister motives and objectives for these powered people. It is perceived that those who control money are monied individuals, who do not embrace the best interests of those outside the club. This conspiracy conception has filled university libraries with racks of periodic monographs and polemic paperbacks spreading the argument of banker cartels and the ruination of the domestic economy for the benefit of the already mighty. Helping to obscure a balanced perception of the board is the institution itself. The Federal Reserve is vitally important to the economic health of the nation, and while it is a public institution, it fiercely protects its independence and is legislatively permitted to work outside the normal checks and balance structure of the federal government. Constitutionally, it is, in the words of an outspoken fifty-year congressman, the late Wright Patman, "a pretty queer duck."

In the mercurial economic period of the early 1980s, Federal Reserve policy appeared to vie for the title of the nation's prime public enemy. By its restrictive monetary policy, interest rates soared, and the nation went into recession. The controllers of the money creation purse were perceived to be that single variable that was responsible for a rising unemployment unmatched since the Great Depression. The hardship and frustration of the nation galvanized to a single point, the Federal Reserve Board chairman. Criticism was ubiquitous.

In 1987 a local ceremony was taking place honoring Paul Volcker, the past chairman of the Fed. The service, however, was marred by the gathering of a local Common Citizens Panel protesting the event. Placards denounced the Fed and accused it of secret meetings and rapacious intent and of devastating the industrial base of the United States. That event was the genesis of this book.

This volume provides biographical profiles of all the members of the governors of the Federal Reserve system from its formation through January 1991. As a cross-referencing tool, asterisks will immediately follow the names of governors who are mentioned outside of their respective profiles. The entries give information on the backgrounds, training, politics, wisdom, and even the pettiness and insecurities of the lives of the men and women who have sat to influence the monetary direction of the United States. With an extended analysis of both the background and economic issues faced by each chairperson, the biographies consider the debates and controversies that flared with both heat and light within oak-paneled meeting rooms and with the presidents of the United States. What emerges from these essays are the independent turns of will of the governors as they seek to choose the correct money policy for the times, as well as to ensure the continued independence of the Federal Reserve system.

INTRODUCTION

George G. Sause

BOARD OF GOVERNORS OF THE FEDERAL RESERVE SYSTEM

The Board of Governors is the senior management group of the Federal Reserve system, which was established in 1913 to provide central bank services to the United States. The nation had existed without a central bank since 1836 when the charter of the Second Bank of the United States expired. The National Bank Act of 1863 attempted to create a uniform banking system, but this system had several serious defects. The two main deficiencies, a defective reserve system and an inelastic currency, led to recurring liquidity crises. The term *inelastic currency*, when applied to the national banking system, referred to the fact that the quantity of bank notes (currency) in circulation did not vary with the needs of business and the economy. Instead, the amount varied with the quantity of U.S. securities owned by banks, and this in turn depended on the size of the U.S. debt and the interest yield of the bonds. On a number of occasions, the quantity of bank notes declined during a period of rapid economic development.

The term *defective reserve system* refers to the fact that the banks, being profit motivated and competitive, tended to keep no more reserves than the minimum required by law. The problem thus created was complicated by the fact that some of the reserves of rural banks could be kept on deposit with central reserve city banks. A heavy demand for currency or bank credit led to a liquidity crisis since the banks, holding a bare minimum of reserves, could not satisfy the demand for money even though the business of an individual borrower was sound and the nation's economy healthy. Another defect, an absence of a central clearinghouse system for checks, was less serious. Money transfer (check clearing) was slow and very inefficient.

Congress took action to overcome these defects by creating the Federal Reserve system. The act establishing the system was signed by President Woodrow Wilson on December 19, 1913. The system began operating in December 1914. The nation is divided into twelve Federal Reserve districts, each of which contains a Federal Reserve bank. Thus, there is the Federal Reserve Bank of Boston, New York, Philadelphia, and so on. Each bank is a corporate entity; it has its own capital and its own officers and is governed by its own board of directors. The banks are not profit motivated and are therefore willing to keep reserves in excess of the legal minimum requirement. However, if revenues of a Federal Reserve bank exceed expenses, the bank adds 10 percent of this surplus to its capital reserves and pays the remaining 90 percent to the U.S. Treasury.

Commercial banks with national charters must belong to the system; that is, they must be member banks. State-chartered banks may be members if certain requirements are met.

The Board of Governors of the Federal Reserve system is the coordinating agency for the twelve Federal Reserve banks and the member banks.

MEMBERSHIP AND ORGANIZATION OF THE BOARD OF GOVERNORS

Section 10 of the Federal Reserve Act established the Federal Reserve Board (the name was changed to Board of Governors in 1935) of seven members. Five were appointed to ten-year terms by the president with the advice and consent of the Senate. In addition, the secretary of the Treasury and the comptroller of the currency were ex officio members. The secretary of the Treasury served as ex officio chairman. Section 10 noted that the president, in appointing members of the board, is expected to provide for a fair representation of the nation's financial, agricultural, industrial, and commercial interests.

The board was increased to eight in 1922, with the additional person being an appointed member. Another minor change came in 1933 when the term of office was increased to twelve years. The Banking Act of 1935 brought about more important changes. The secretary of the Treasury and the comptroller of the currency were removed from the board, whose title now became Board of Governors of the Federal Reserve system. There were to be seven appointed members, no two of whom could come from the same Federal Reserve district. The term was to be fourteen years, and a member who had served a full term could not be reappointed. Also, the president was to designate one member as chair and one as vice-chair, each to serve for four years. Thus, the term of the chair and the vice-chair is the same as the president's term of office. The terms of the chair and vice-chair, however, are not coterminous with that of the president except by coincidence.

SUPERVISORY POWERS OF THE BOARD

The Board of Governors has supervisory powers over both the Federal Reserve banks and the member banks. The board has a right to examine the reserve banks, to readjust the district boundaries, and to suspend or remove officers and directors. It must approve the establishment of any Federal Reserve branch bank or it may require a reserve bank to establish such a branch or to maintain accounts in foreign countries. The board appoints the class C directors, regarded as representatives of the general public, of each Federal Reserve bank. This is one-third of the total. Also, the act contains a blanket clause that gives the Board of Governors power to exercise general supervision over the Federal Reserve banks.

The Board of Governors exercises some supervision over member banks. It has the power to examine these banks but in practice has delegated this to the Federal Reserve banks. The bank has the power, subject to various legal safeguards, to remove the officers and directors of member banks.

STATUS OF THE FEDERAL RESERVE SYSTEM AND THE BOARD OF GOVERNORS

Upon the establishment of the Federal Reserve system of 1914, the attorney general of the United States described the Federal Reserve Board as an independent bureau or establishment of the government. It was therefore not under the jurisdiction of the Treasury Department. The Board of Governors has repeated this legal opinion on several occasions since then, reminding the nation of its independent status.

The Board of Governors is legally independent because of the acceptance of the opinion of the U.S. attorney general. This independence is effective for several reasons. The board levies semiannual assessments on the Federal Reserve banks in order to pay its expenses. This frees the board of congressional control through the budget. Board expenditures were audited by the General Accounting Office until 1933, when this practice was dropped. The board does submit an annual report to the Speaker of the House of Representatives, who publishes it for the information of Congress. The independence of the board is strengthened by the procedures for appointment of members of the board.

Because of the independent status of the board, it is not subject to restrictions that apply to federal civil service appointments. There is general agreement that this increases the board's ability to attract competently trained personnel. There is also general agreement that the process of appointment to staff positions and the conduct of these appointees is free of conventional political influence.

The independence of the board should not be overstated. It acts in accordance with its best judgment as it strives to achieve the economic goals prescribed by Congress, but it is, of course, subject to normal statutory restrictions.

CONTROL OF THE SUPPLY OF CREDIT

A commercial bank's ability to create credit, and therefore increase the money supply, is limited by bank reserves. The Board of Governors has the power to limit the creation of bank credit by setting reserve requirements for member banks within the maximum and minimum levels established by Congress. Currently this is an important control method.

Although relatively unimportant today, the setting of the discount rate is the one specific control included in the original Federal Reserve Act. Prior to the establishment of the Federal Reserve system, liquidity crises in the economy occurred when commercial banks were unable to extend credit because of inadequate reserves. Now member banks needing additional reserves may borrow from the Federal Reserve bank in its district. The member bank pays interest, which is known as the discount rate. The reserve banks set the discount rate, but this must be approved by the Board of Governors. The level of the discount rate encourages or discourages member banks from borrowing. The discount rate is relatively unimportant today because of the use of open market controls, but the announcement of an increase or a decrease in the discount rate has an effect on the attitude of the economic system.

The chief quantitative control in modern times is known as open market operations: the Federal Reserve banks may purchase or sell federal government securities on the open market. If the banks are net purchasers, member bank reserves increase. The reverse occurs if they are net sellers.

The twelve members of the Federal Open Market Committee make decisions concerning the purchase or sale of government securities. The committee consists of the seven members of the Board of Governors plus five other persons selected by the twelve Federal Reserve banks.

CONTROL OF THE USE OF CREDIT

None of the controls mentioned to this point influences the allocation of bank credit among the several sectors of the economy. Varying reserve requirements, changing the discount rate, and buying and selling on the open market control the amount of credit created but the allocation of this credit is left to market forces. This is consistent with the belief that a free market leads to an allocation of resources in the public interest. Occasionally, however, Federal Reserve authorities have felt that too much credit, causing undesirable results, was going to certain segments of the economy. In brief, they deemed improper the existing allocation of credit from the point of view of the public interest. Methods are available to modify the allocation.

MARGIN REQUIREMENTS

In 1929, speculators using bank credit in the stock market contributed to the rapid rise of security prices. The Federal Reserve authorities were unable to control credit in securities markets without hindering the other sectors of the economy. The Securities Exchange Act of 1934 gave the Board of Governors the right to set minimum margin requirements on loans made for the purpose of buying securities, thus restricting the allocation of bank credit to the securities market.

CONSUMER CREDIT CONTROLS

In emergencies, especially in a time of war, other selective controls have been employed by the Board of Governors. Controls were placed on credit used for the purchase of consumer goods. The board may restrict consumer credit by setting minimum down payments for various classes of goods, the same principle as margin requirements, and it may discourage borrowing for consumption purposes by limiting the time period allowed for repayment.

REAL ESTATE CREDIT

The Board of Governors has on occasion imposed controls on credit used for the purchase of real estate. As in the case of consumer purchases, these controls required minimum down payments and limited the length of time to maturity of the debt. These restrictions have varied according to the type and the value of the real estate purchase and were less severe on low-cost as opposed to high-priced houses.

MORAL SUASION

This is not a control but a method of persuasion. The Federal Reserve authorities try to persuade member banks to operate in a fashion that the authorities feel will further the public interest. Moral suasion may take an indirect form, such as providing member banks with up-to-date information concerning economic conditions in the nation, or authorities may use more forceful measures, such as appeals to reason, patriotism, and the need banks have for good public relations. It is difficult to assess the effectiveness of moral suasion. The prestige of the Board of Governors supports the program. Also, member banks are aware that these persuaders have the power to use more forceful measures.

In summary the Board of Governors has an important role to play in the American economic system, and the members of the board must be competent and public spirited.

BIOGRAPHICAL DICTIONARY
of the Board of
Governors of the Federal
Reserve

WAYNE D. ANGELL (1930–   )

Robert C. Winder

On February 7, 1986, Wayne D. Angell was sworn in as a member of the Board of Governors of the Federal Reserve system to complete the unexpired term of Lyle Gramley.* His tenure continues through January 31, 1994. Currently he is chairman of the board's Committee on Federal Reserve Bank Activities. Angell also serves as chairman of the Group of Experts on Payment Systems in Basel, Switzerland.

Angell's background and experiences bring to the Federal Reserve board new expertise and perspective, along with an unusually creative mind. He was born in Liberal, Kansas, on June 28, 1930, and although he is well traveled, Kansas has always been his home. Angell's family had moved to Kansas from North Carolina more than one hundred years ago when the post–Civil War deflation wrought havoc on his agricultural ancestors. His undergraduate degree was received in 1953 from Ottawa University in Ottawa, Kansas. His M.A. and Ph.D. degrees (in economics) are from the University of Kansas. They were awarded in 1953 and 1957, respectively. His Phi Beta Kappa key and his selection to *Who's Who in America* attest to his academic and professional success. Angell is married and has four children. He is a deeply religious man and has been active in the Baptist church, serving as a trustee of the Kansas Baptist Foundation and as president of the Kansas Baptist Convention, among other positions.

The breadth of Angell's professional background may be unmatched on the Board of Governors at the present time. He started his career in 1954 as an instructor of economics at the University of Kansas and by 1956 had become professor of economics at Ottawa University, where he stayed until 1985. At Ottawa University, Angell served as dean of the college from 1969 to 1972. In the years from 1971 to 1985, he served as an officer or a director for a number of banks in Missouri and Kansas. While developing his financial and banking credentials, Angell simultaneously was cutting his political teeth. From 1961 to 1967 he was a state representative in the Kansas House of Representatives, and in 1964 he served as vice-chairman of the Republican Legislature Campaign Committee in Kansas.

Angell's relationship with the Federal Reserve system dates back to 1972–1973, when he served on an advisory committee to the Board of Governors studying bank holding company legislation. From 1979 to 1985 he served as a director of the Federal Reserve Bank of Kansas City, thereby providing the critical experience as well as the stepping-stone to become a member of the Board of Governors. From 1981 to 1985 Angell also served as an economic consultant to banks and thrift institutions in Kansas, Missouri, and Colorado. And from 1950 to 1985, he was active and integrally involved in the operation of a 3,300-acre Kansas farm.

The fact that Angell was from Kansas and had been actively involved in farming since 1950 was critical in his nomination and subsequent confirmation. There was a sense in the Senate that the Federal Reserve board needed better balance in terms of both geographic representation and experience and interests. Angell was a true midwesterner, not an inside-the-beltway bureaucrat. More important, his lifelong experience and interest in agriculture could bring to the Board of Governors increased understanding and sensitivity to the problems experienced by the agricultural sector.

Angell was introduced at the U.S. Senate confirmation hearing on January 23, 1986, by a fellow Kansan, U.S. senator Robert Dole. In his remarks, Dole emphasized that Angell possessed outstanding qualifications and was a "real live farmer." The chairman of the confirmation committee, Senator Jake Garn (R, Utah), noted the "serious problems besetting American agriculture" and argued that Angell's practical experience in farming would help the Federal Reserve board deal with issues relating to agribusiness and agricultural banks.

While there was agreement on the desirability of Angell's farming experience, that consensus did not extend to the gamut of other issues discussed. Senator William Proxmire (D, Wisconsin) called into question Angell's commitment to balancing the federal government's budget, as well as his commitment to continuing the tight, anti-inflation monetary policy that seemed to be breaking the back of the inflation of the early 1980s. Proxmire's misgivings were serious and pervasive. He confessed his fear that Angell's policies "will cause superinflation and maybe worse." And, finally, Proxmire threatened that Angell's confirmation could create a new majority on the Federal Reserve board committed to radical and potentially disastrous economic policies. Proxmire's charge was as obvious as it was ominous. If both Wayne Angell and Manuel Johnson[*] (simultaneously being considered for membership on the Board of Governors) were confirmed, then along with Martha Seger[*] and Preston Martin[*] a majority of the Federal Reserve board would be appointed by President Ronald Reagan. The specter of a majority of the Board of Governors indebted to President Reagan and supportive of supply-side economic policies haunted the Democratic members of this Senate committee and raised partisan political eyebrows around the nation. Elements in the national media pursued this scenario, and stories of a "gang of four" dominating economic policymaking appeared.

Sensitive to Proxmire's charges and cognizant of the partisan undercurrents,

Angell proclaimed his commitment to follow a low inflation monetary policy, and on the issue of deficits, Angell was equally emphatic: "There's been no time in my entire adult life that I have ever advocated deficits" (U.S. Congress, 1986, 11).

The inquisition into Angell's views on inflation and monetary policy continued as he was grilled on a novel but controversial proposal that the Federal Reserve system should use an index of commodity prices as an indicator of inflation. The essence of Angell's position is that the traditional measures of inflation are obtained only with a significant time lag and as a result are not necessarily indicative of current economic conditions. But commodities, such as precious metals, oil, and wheat, are sold at auction every day and provide both timely and reliable information particularly useful for policymaking. In addition, Angell argues that because commodity prices are free to change immediately in response to supply and demand conditions, they provide a particularly sensitive and accurate measure of inflation. More traditional measures of inflation, such as the consumer price index (CPI), are not as sensitive to current conditions since they partly reflect production costs (especially wages), which are slow to adjust to a changing economic environment.

Angell's views on the potential advantages of employing a commodity price index as a guide to monetary policy have received attention by the financial community at large, and this may be his principal contribution to the economics discipline. In a widely read paper presented to the Lehrman Institute on December 10, 1987, Angell observed that the ability to achieve a stable price level by targeting monetary aggregates depends critically on the predictability of the income velocity of money. For most of the post–World War II era, the velocity of money was reasonably predictable. But since the 1970s, significant deregulation of the financial services industry, along with the transition from high inflation to disinflation, have led to instability of velocity and hence weakened this once reliable link between the money supply and economic activity. With this increased uncertainty, it is crucial, in Angell's view, for the Federal Reserve system to obtain accurate and immediate information about price movements.

Angell (1987) presents evidence that commodity prices have been an excellent indicator of changes (peaks and troughs) in consumer prices since the mid–1960s. The average lead time over this period is seven and one-half months. Interestingly, the robustness of this relationship is not particularly sensitive to the composition or weighting method of the commodity price index. On this basis, Angell recommends the use of a commodity price index "as a guide to adjusting short run money growth target ranges." Angell was careful to point out that he is not advocating a "commodity price standard." Specifically, he is not arguing that the commodity price index supplant or replace the monetary aggregates as an intermediate target. Rather, the index would simply be an indicator of inflationary pressure to assist the Fed in choosing optimal monetary targets. Reflecting his monetarist heritage, Angell confesses that "monetarism is correct in insisting that controlling inflation requires monetary restraint . . .

the proposal is designed to make monetary targeting more effective.''

In his short tenure on the Board of Governors, Angell has become deeply involved in the issue of banking and payment system risk. In a June 7, 1989, presentation to the International Symposium on Banking and Payment Services, Angell noted that because Federal Reserve banks typically credit accounts of commercial banks receiving funds before determining that accounts at paying banks are adequate to cover these payments, the Federal Reserve banks have become ''major unsecured intraday creditors.'' And, ultimately, it is the nation's taxpayers rather than the stockholders of depository institutions that bear the risk of loss from daytime overdrafts. A better system, in Angell's view, would be to develop a ''private intraday market for federal funds . . . where various market participants would be evaluated carefully and face differential risk premiums and credit limits.'' This would not only reduce the likelihood that the failure of one institution would lead to an ''unwind of payments'' and collapse of the system, but it would also result in a more efficient allocation of credit. In Angell's scheme, the Federal Reserve system would continue to supply credit only in emergencies, and even then it would require collateral and charge a rate above that which would be established in a private market.

Angell's bold proposals for reducing payment system risk are reflective of an open and creative mind and symptomatic of his willingness to discuss virtually any issue. Recently in the public press, he discussed developments in China, predicting that despite some recent setbacks, China would continue to develop its market sector and increase trade with the West. Regarding the economic integration of Europe in 1992, he was sanguine about the potential for increased international trade in manufactures and the potential benefits to midwestern U.S. companies. Angell visited the Soviet Union in September 1989 to give economic advice on how to jumpstart the Soviet economy with the advent of *perestroika*. In an exchange published in the *Wall Street Journal* (October 5, 1989) Angell urged a bewildered Gosbank representative to define the Soviet ruble in terms of a fixed amount of gold and maintain convertibility for Soviet citizens as well as the rest of the world.

These comments and others reveal Angell's unusual outspokenness and almost evangelical approach to policymaking. Angell accepted the nomination to become a member of the Board of Governors only after receiving private assurances from the Reagan administration that he would not be muzzled with respect to his views on economic and monetary policy.

BIBLIOGRAPHY

Angell, Wayne D. 1987. ''A Price Guide to Monetary Aggregate Targeting.'' Presented to the Lehrman Institute, New York, December 10.
———. 1989. ''Policy Response to Issues in Central Bank Payment Services.'' Presented to the International Symposium on Banking and Payment Services, Washington, D.C., June 7.

"Put the Soviet Economy on Golden Rails." 1989. *Wall Street Journal*, October 5, p. A28.

U.S. Congress. Senate. Committee on Banking, Housing, and Urban Affairs. 1986. *Nominations of Wayne D. Angell and Manuel Homan Johnson, Jr., to Be Members of the Board of Governors, Federal Reserve System.* January 23.

Who's Who in America, 1988–1989. Wilmette, Ill.: Marquis Who's Who.

C. CANBY BALDERSTON (1897–1979)

Nancy M. Thornborrow

C. Canby Balderston, who served on the Board of Governors of the Federal Reserve from August 1954 to February 1966, was born in Kennett Square, Pennsylvania, on February 1, 1897. The son of John L. and Anna E. Marshall Balderston, he received all of his formal education in Pennsylvania, attending the Westown School from 1912 to 1914 and Pennsylvania State College from 1915 to 1917. His original career goal was to become a chemical engineer; however, he interrupted his studies during World War I and served on the western front with the Friends Ambulance Service. After the war, he remained in Europe and worked with the Red Cross in Belgium. When he returned home, he resumed his formal education at the Wharton School of Finance and Commerce of the University of Pennsylvania, studying industrial relations and management. Balderston graduated with a B.S. degree in economics in 1921. He continued at Wharton for graduate training, receiving three additional degrees: an A.M. in 1923, a Ph.D. in 1928, and an LL.D. in 1955. He also received an LL.D. from Swarthmore College in 1965. On July 28, 1922, he married Gertrude Emery. They subsequently had two sons, Frederick E. and Robert W. Balderston's first wife died, and, on November 21, 1942, he married Ida Roberts Smedley. She had three children, Walter, Henry, and Alice, by a previous marriage.

Balderston joined the faculty of the University of Pennsylvania in 1925 and from then until 1931 served as assistant professor of industry. In 1931 he was promoted to the rank of professor of industry. At that time, Wharton, the oldest business school in the country, had a curriculum dedicated to the study and teaching of current business practices. In 1933 Joseph Willits, a faculty member in the Department of Industrial Research, became dean of the Wharton School. Willits saw the need for Wharton to become a leader in the research necessary to guide the country toward recovery from the Great Depression. While many of the Wharton faculty were comfortable teaching only courses in finance, accounting, transportation, insurance, and marketing, Willits believed that economic science and research would provide solutions to the country's economic crisis. He began curricular reform at Wharton, and one of his closest allies in the struggle was C. Canby Balderston.

Balderston's field of interest and expertise was industrial relations. Between 1929 and 1940, he authored five books covering such topics as profit sharing, executive guidance, wage setting, and management. He did not limit his scholarship to publishing his ideas; he also began what would prove to be a lengthy career of making public addresses. In September 1932, for example, while addressing the annual conference of the Life Office Management Association, he spoke against employee stock ownership plans, and in November 1940, while addressing the New York chapter of the Society for the Advancement of Management, he suggested that proper wage adjustment depended on systematic wage surveys and that wages should not be adjusted as a result of union pressure. During this period Balderston had his first contact with the Federal Reserve. Between 1939 and 1940, he served as a management consultant preparing studies on the compensation of Federal Reserve bank officers and on the selection and development of officers.

Having transformed Wharton into a more scholarly institution, Willits left in 1939 to become the director of the Social Science Division of the Rockefeller Foundation. He was replaced in the deanship by Alfred Williams, who left only two years later to become president of the Philadelphia Federal Reserve Bank. On July 10, 1941, Balderston, who was serving as chairman of the Geography and Industry Department, was appointed dean by Dr. Thomas S. Gates, president of the University of Pennsylvania. However, in 1941 the country was preparing for World War II, and the Wharton School effectively shut down as many faculty assumed positions in the federal government's war effort. Between 1942 and 1945 Balderston served as chief of both the War Department Wage Administration Agency, passing on wages for civilian employees of the department, and the corresponding Wage Administration Section of the Headquarters Army Service Forces. In 1944 he was the recipient of the War Department's Exceptional Civilian Award.

In January 1943 Wharton announced curricular changes to accommodate students whose college careers might be interrupted by military service. The school decided to stress ten specialized fields: accounting, economics, finance, government service, industrial management, industrial relations, insurance, marketing, statistics, and transportation. The curriculum thus returned to a pre-Willits content. While having been an admirer of Willits's new curriculum, Balderston himself was quite conservative. His basic goal seems to have been maintaining the traditions of the Wharton School.

Balderston's own reputation and responsibilities continued to grow over the next ten years. On April 8, 1943, he was named a director of the Federal Reserve Bank of Philadelphia, and, on March 18, 1949, he was named deputy chairman of the Philadelphia Fed, a position he retained until December 31, 1953. In April 1950 he became president of the American Association of Collegiate Schools of Business; in 1951 he became president of Leeds and Lippincott Company

(Chalfonte-Haddon Hall hotels); in December 1952 he was elected a director of the American Institute of Management; and in April 1954 he was elected chairman of the board of directors of the National Bureau of Economic Research. He also served as vice-president and director of the Philadelphia Chamber of Commerce; trustee of Industrial Relations Counselors; trustee of Bryn Mawr College; chairman of the Investment Committee, Westown School; and a member of the board of managers of Friends Hospital, Frankford.

Perhaps Balderston's most tangible contribution to Wharton during his deanship was the raising of $2.3 million for the construction of Dietrich Hall, the home of the Wharton School. Much of the research being done by Wharton faculty during this period was being conducted by various research institutes, which were funded by outside corporate interests. The Finance Department, with funding from the Merrill Foundation, established the Securities Research unit; the Insurance Department, in cooperation with Northwestern Mutual Life Insurance Company, set up the Pension Research Center. Unfortunately the Industrial Research Department (IRD) died when its Rockefeller grant ran out. The demise of IRD coincided with the departure of one of Wharton's leading scholars, Simon Kuznets.

On August 2, 1954, President Dwight Eisenhower nominated Balderston, a Republican, to be a member of the Board of Governors of the Federal Reserve system. He replaced Oliver S. Powell,[*] who had resigned in 1952, and was to serve out Powell's term, which began February 1, 1952. At the time of Balderston's appointment, the board had been short two members for several months. The board chairman, William McChesney Martin, Jr.,[*] a Democrat appointed by Truman in 1951, had suggested reducing the board membership from seven to five members, but Eisenhower decided to retain the seven members. Because Balderston was a Quaker, he was not required to take the usual oath, and no Bible was used in his swearing in. In March of the following year, Martin was redesignated chairman of the Board of Governors, and Balderston was designated vice-chairman for a term of four years beginning April 1, 1955. Both were reappointed by President Eisenhower in 1959 and by President Kennedy in 1963. It is reported that over the years, Martin and Balderston became close associates in spite of their political differences.

During the twelve years of Balderston's service on the Board of Governors, Federal Reserve policy was committed to steady economic growth and price stabilization. Throughout the 1940s, the Fed had agreed to supply the reserves necessary to finance World War II. The money supply was manipulated to keep rates of government securities constant. During that period, therefore, the Fed gave up its major instrument in the prevention of inflation. By 1953 this pegging policy was eliminated. The Eisenhower administration was concerned about a recession, and the Fed's Open Market Committee wanted to promote economic growth and full employment, so it expanded the money supply. In addition, reserve requirements for member banks were reduced, and there were two reductions in the discount rate; all of these actions combined to create the economic boom of 1955–1957. By 1957–1958, however, the economy was facing a recession. In spite of the fact that the Fed adopt a policy of "leaning against the wind" in an attempt to moderate business cycles rather than to eliminate them, the data suggest that between 1956 and 1961, the Fed allowed the money supply to move procyclically, worsening both the 1957–1958 and 1960–1961 recessions. From 1964 to 1971, the Fed appears to have continued to use a procyclical policy, which allowed excessive monetary expansion, thereby causing inflation.

Throughout his tenure on the Board of Governors, Balderston gave numerous public speeches discussing the importance of monetary policy in maintaining stable economic growth, full employment, and low inflation. He addressed such diverse groups as the American Bankers Association, the National Association of Real Estate Boards, and the New York Bond Club. He returned to Wharton on numerous occasions to give public lectures. Making public announcements about money came to be known as "jawboning." The Fed seems to have used this psychological technique to pave the way for policy changes, and Balderston appears to have been the Fed's principal public speaker. All of his speeches conveyed similar themes. He discussed the need for policy made at the federal level and then the importance of free markets in making allocative decisions. Economic health, he maintained, relied on the combined actions of government, business, labor, and consumers. He insisted that economic growth and price stability were not incompatible ideas and that inflation was not necessary to maintain full employment. He described the need to stabilize aggregate demand via fiscal policy and then to use monetary policy to stop inflation. Flexible monetary policy, he maintained, was the key to economic growth. In 1964 Balderston's comments about easy credit touched off a rally in the government securities market that was termed the Balderston bounce. And in 1965 he warned that a sharp decline in the liquidity of the nation's banking system was a cause for concern.

Balderston testified before the House Banking Committee on at least thirteen separate occasions. In addition, he wrote some fourteen letters that became part of the official congressional record. His testimony covered a wide range of issues: supporting a bill that would require companies trading securities over the counter to register them with the Securities and Exchange Commission, thereby making them subject to Federal Reserve margin requirements; supporting the Fed's request for greater flexibility in setting reserve requirements, thereby allowing banks to count vault cash as part of their required reserves; opposing an increase in the federal bank deposit insurance by saying it would lessen the public's interest in the stability of banks; opposing banks' underwriting of state and local revenue bonds because they were viewed as riskier than bonds backed by the taxing powers and financial resources of the state; and defending the right of the Fed to remain independent of the executive branch and to make policy in direct opposition to that desired by the president.

In December 1965, the Board of Governors voted to raise the discount rate. Balderston reportedly urged the increase, calling it necessary to curb inflation.

The Fed had simultaneously raised the rate that banks could pay on certificates of deposit from 4.5 percent to 5.5 percent. President Lyndon Johnson was reported to have opposed the discount rate increase; this was during the time of the Vietnam buildup, and he feared a recession. Many Democratic members of Congress were enraged at the Fed's independence. The Congressional Joint Economic Committee summoned the entire board to special hearings. Balderston attended the hearings, which took place in December. His term officially terminated on January 31, 1966; however, he continued to vote on some important issues until President Johnson appointed Andrew F. Brimmer* as his replacement on February 26, 1966. Balderston officially resigned as of February 28, 1966.

Balderston left the Federal Reserve board to become Regents Lecturer at the University of California, Berkeley. He subsequently returned to Washington, D.C., where between 1966 and 1977 he was adjunct professor of finance at American University. He continued to publish articles; one, "Fiscal and Monetary Policy," appeared in the September 1968 issue of *The Annals of the American Academy of Political and Social Science*. He remained president of Leeds and Lippincott Company until 1975, when he assumed the position of chairman for the years 1975–1977. From 1968 to 1973 he was a director of the Security National Bank in Washington; from 1972 to 1979 he was a director of Indiana Square Income Securities, Inc. He served as president of Temporary Investment Fund, Inc. (1973–1979), Federal Short-term Securities Trust (1975–1979), and Chestnut Street Exchange Fund (1976–1979). He served on the board of directors of the Sidwell Friends School. Balderston was also a member of numerous organizations and clubs. He died on September 9, 1979, at the age of eighty-two.

BIBLIOGRAPHY

Anderson, Clay J. 1965. *A Half-century of Federal Reserve Policymaking, 1914–1964*. Philadelphia: Federal Reserve Bank.

Balderston, C. Canby. 1928. *Managerial Profit Sharing*. New York: Wiley.

———. 1930. *Group Incentives*. Philadelphia: University of Pennsylvania Press.

———. 1935. *Executive Guidance of Industrial Relations*. Philadelphia: University of Pennsylvania Press.

———. 1959. "Monetary Policy and Inflation." *Annals of the American Academy of Political and Social Science* 326 (November): 116–25.

———. 1968. "Fiscal and Monetary Policy." *Annals of the American Academy of Political and Social Science* 379 (September): 78–82.

———, and Karabasz, Victor S. 1938. *Management of a Textile Business*. Washington, D.C.: Textile Foundation, 1938.

Bratter, Herbert. 1962. "Banking's Spotlight on—C. Canby Balderston." *Banking* (April): 82.

"Current Events and Announcements." 1954. *Federal Reserve Bulletin* (August): 835–36.

Eastburn, David P. 1965. *The Federal Reserve on Record: Readings on Current Issues from Statements by Federal Reserve Officials*. Philadelphia: Federal Reserve Bank.

Sass, Steven A. 1982. *The Pragmatic Imagination: A History of the Wharton School 1881–1981*. Philadelphia: University of Pennsylvania Press.

Who's Who in America, 1977–1981. Vol. 7. Chicago: Marquis Who's Who.

EUGENE ROBERT BLACK
(1873–1934)

Ogden O. Allsbrook, Jr.

Eugene R. Black served as governor of the Federal Reserve Board from mid-May 1933 to mid-August 1934. His term was unusually short because, at the outset, he believed his public service to be temporary, and he agreed to serve for three months, until President Franklin Roosevelt could select a permanent successor. Although short, his term nearly coincided with the trough of the great contraction of 1929–1933.

Eugene Black was born in Atlanta, Georgia, in 1873, the son of Eugene Pinckard and Zachariah Harriet Harmon Black. His father, a Confederate veteran, became the leading real estate dealer in Atlanta. Eugene Black graduated from Boy's High School in 1889 and from the University of Georgia at the age of twenty (1892), where he was a member of Phi Kappa (literary) and Chi Phi (social) fraternities. He attended Atlanta Law School and passed the bar examination in 1893. Although he had refused to study criminal law, in 1897 he was appointed solicitor of criminal court in Atlanta. As a lawyer, however, corporation law was his specialty, and the giant Southern Railway was a client. He practiced law almost continuously until 1921, when he became a commercial banker and president of the Atlanta Trust Company.

In 1897, Black married Gussie Grady, the daughter of one of the South's greatest journalists, Henry Grady. They had three children: Eugene R. Black, Jr., who became president of the International Bank for Reconstruction and Development; Julia (Mrs. Walter H. Wellborn); and Henry Grady Black. Governor Black's brothers were Judge William Harmon Black of the Supreme Court of the State of New York and Charles H. Black, an Atlanta realtor.

Black's career as a lawyer spanned a quarter-century until he switched careers in 1921. He accepted the presidency of the Atlanta Trust Company and served until 1928, when he was made governor of the Federal Reserve Bank of Atlanta. From then until May 1933, he watched from Atlanta as the U.S. monetary system lurched toward collapse.

During his governorship of the Atlanta Federal Reserve Bank, he gained a reputation for levelheadedness and inspiring confidence in the reserve district.

His contemporaries regarded him as the optimum choice for governor of the southeast district. His success in protecting the U.S. dollar in Cuba by injecting dollar reserves into Havana banks gained him international stature. He personally flew to Havana, first with $16 million and later with $9 million more. He also developed a friendship with the next president, Franklin D. Roosevelt, who had a home in Warm Springs, Georgia, which was known as the "little White House."

After Black became governor of the Federal Reserve system, his friendship served well in his opposition to Roosevelt's desire to have the Fed surrender its gold stock, then valued at $3 billion. After his resignation, their friendship enabled Black to act as informal liaison between Roosevelt and commercial bankers, an activity that doubtlessly strained his physical resources.

Before his term in Washington, Eugene Black was a civic-minded person, with many interests in the local community. An orthodox Baptist (and deacon), he aided the Billy Sunday crusades in Atlanta. During World War I, he managed the southern division of the American Red Cross. For three years, he held the Georgia agency for Prudential Insurance Company, and he was a director of the *Atlanta Constitution* as well. He was once president of the Atlanta Chamber of Commerce, and he actively pursued resolution of such problems as streetcar and railway employee strikes and city traffic regulations. When asked in 1901 by the alumni society of the University of Georgia of any writings, he responded in bold hand, "Not guilty." It appears that he remained innocent of this charge for the rest of his life. He preferred the speech as his method of addressing posterity.

Governor Black's brief presence at the Federal Reserve in Washington attests to his influence on the economy at its lowest turning point in early 1933. With the exception of erratic industrial production, the major indicators registered significant gains during his tenure. Although Black was a reluctant appointee to the top position at the Fed, his position was arguably the second most important position in U.S. political economy then.

When Black took a leave of absence from his leadership post at the Atlanta Fed, his reluctance was well founded. Financially it was a hardship, since he earned more than twice as much as governor of the Atlanta Federal Reserve Bank than he would earn as governor of the Federal Reserve Board. Professionally it was the greatest challenge of his life, since the economy was depressed and the Roosevelt administration was using unorthodox and controversial methods to resurrect the economy.

His experience in managing financial crises in Florida and Louisiana and then in Cuba from his post at the Atlanta Federal Reserve Bank no doubt attracted Roosevelt's interest. Roosevelt was interested in those who could get the job done, and Black came to Washington only two months after Roosevelt declared a bank holiday on March 6, 1933. Three days later, Roosevelt requested and Congress passed (on the same day) the Emergency Banking Act, allowing strong banks to begin reopening. It is noteworthy that Roosevelt had become president only five days earlier, so Eugene Black was made governor within two and one-half months of Roosevelt's accession to power.

The Emergency Banking Act created sweeping powers to commandeer all gold to the U.S. Treasury, license all banks, conserve all bank assets, issue preferred stock to raise bank capital, issue more Federal Reserve notes, enlarge Federal Reserve bank loans to member banks, and allow Federal Reserve banks to make direct loans to virtually anyone ("individuals, partnerships, and corporations"). In later testimony before the Senate Committee on Banking and Currency in 1934, Black was asked by Senator William McAdoo if the reserve banks were still making personal loans. Governor Black attempted to evade the question by responding, "Senator, you are discouraging me in my thoughts." Senator Hamilton Kean then jumped in to press the point: "In other words, you are discounting paper every day which is not in strict compliance with the law?" With typical wry response, Black responded, "Senator, I am not going to confess here about it."

During his early months, Black presided over the reopening of solvent banks. From no banks being open on March 9, 5,077 member banks had reopened by March 15, 12,469 member and nonmember state banks were open by April 12, and 14,016 were open on August 30. Black was convinced that stemming the depression meant that, first, banks must have excess reserves, and second, banks must make productive loans. He stated that the task required the close cooperation of the Fed, the Treasury, the comptroller of the currency, and the Reconstruction Finance Corporation (RFC).

One of the facets of the Roosevelt recovery program was to reflate prices in the economy. To sponsor inflation during depression is, today, a suicidal act in many ways. The nature of real money balances, then so scarce, was not increased by any inflationary pressures. In this, Black was correct. He opposed inflation, and he said so less than four months after his appointment.

But Black was also averse to deflation. He stated in September that the consequence of not reopening all banks would be deflationary, and that was a problem also. To Black, putting money in circulation and avoiding hoarding was the paramount objective. If the means of injecting money to farmers directly (outside of banks) also meant that crops were destroyed or prices were raised, then that was a secondary order of effect. In this case, the positive quantity of new money could exceed the negative effect of inflation. Black urged commercial banks to become just that once again: originators of commercial loans for production rather than collateral lenders only for capital investment.

To assess the impact of Black at the Fed, under the Emergency Banking Act that authorized increased Federal Reserve note issue and increased lending by reserve banks to member banks, a quantitative test (with primitive data) may be used. One method is the classical equation of nominal output, $MV = PQ$. During the two-year period from the second quarter of 1933 (when Black joined the board) until the second quarter of 1935 (seven months after Black had returned to Atlanta), M (as demand deposits) increased 50 percent, V (as velocity of deposits outside of New York) fell 25 percent, P (as wholesale prices) rose 27 percent, while Q (as real GNP) rose only 10 percent. Using these data, we see that the Fed did much to raise the basic money stock, but velocity offset that by one-half. Clearly the demand for money was not yet being utilized to buy additional goods or services. The inflation absorbed more than half of the increase in money, leaving only a small amount to spur real growth.

How did member banks behave during Black's tenure as governor? From the beginning, loans increased, but before 1933 ended, loan volume began falling once again. Instead of making loans, banks began purchasing securities, including governments, and holding excess reserves. Nevertheless, demand and time deposits rose consistently through 1934.

Later, after leaving Washington, Black attributed the decline in velocity (increased demand for idle balances) also to uncertainty over the currency. Remember that he opposed both inflation as a policy and deflation as an effect in restoring the economy to prosperity. Now, out of the top position at the Fed, he argued that currency uncertainty could return if the exchange rate of the dollar was fixed, while the exchange rate of the British pound was free to float. He likened this to the United States's being on a fixed gold standard, while the United Kingdom was off the gold standard.

In August 1933 Black and the rest of the Federal Reserve Board were charged with contributing to the decline in velocity. Senator Elmer Thomas of Oklahoma charged that the Fed actually was reducing the money stock, since he observed a reduction in credit extended by reserve banks to commercial banks. Black explained that these data were incomplete and did not reflect the substitution effect involved. What happened was that the financial panic precipitated large withdrawals of currency from commercial banks for hoarding at homes. During and after the bank holiday, reserve banks extended credit as currency to commercial banks to replace the currency withdrawals by the nonbank public. Now that the crisis had passed, the data showed a return to commercial banks of cash hoards and the subsequent return of the substitute emergency currency to the reserve banks. Thus, commercial banks were rebuilding reserves from which they could make loans and increase the money stock. In fact, the Fed was conducting open market operations to increase reserves, and, of course, the situation developed into one of excess reserves.

Excess reserves in a time of high unemployment was troubling to Black. In his last public address as governor of the Federal Reserve Board, Black told the Montana Bankers Association that they and he were both responsible for getting loans out to the public. The reserve banks were not lending money to commercial banks because commercial banks had excess reserves, but commercial banks were not making available loans for reasons that Black attributed to several causes.

Concern about loan quality is one reason, Black argued, but bankers have a social responsibility to make loans based not only on borrowers' credit statements but also on the character or quality of the individual. In this, Black seemed to urge an additional (or perhaps a lesser) degree of risk assumption.

Another reason for excess reserves was the absence of or gap in borrowing opportunity for small firms to capitalize assets. Large firms could borrow in the central capital markets, but small firms could not, nor could they borrow from commercial banks for the extended period required. Black proposed a solution to this gap within two months of his appointment, which is widespread today in other ways. He proposed that Federal Reserve banks be authorized to make loans to small firms if and only if commercial banks have declined the loan. And if commercial banks or any other financial institution made such loans, the reserve banks would be authorized to purchase such loans within five years and free member or nonmember banks or other lenders to make more loans.

It was Black who originated the legislation in testimony before the House Committee on Banking and Currency that provided for direct loans to firms by the reserves banks and the RFC. That also was within two months of his arrival in Washington.

The real problem Black and the rest of the board faced in these early months was the uncertainty facing commercial banks on the demand side. The reserve banks had, under Black's guidance, begun regular purchases of government bonds in the open market to create excess reserves within commercial banks, and that was successful. But commercial banks, replete with excess reserves on the supply side, were unwilling or unable to increase the basic money stock with new loans. Unfortunately, no one foresaw the negative impact that forthcoming Regulation Q would have on this impasse.

Instead, direct loans by reserve banks and the RFC to firms that had been denied loans by commercial banks was one way to raise the active money stock. Another way would be to assure commercial banks that loans they would make to firms that would become increasingly risky would be bought by reserve banks, thus reducing loan risk toward zero.

At this time, fiscal efforts to raise the active money stock took the shape of federal purchases of cotton (one-third of the crop was destroyed) for $120 million, and pigs and sows were purchased for $50 million. Obviously, these monies bypassed loan officers at commercial banks. In addition, $3.3 billion was authorized to build public works, such as roads, bridges, buildings, and monuments.

In order to discourage the most intense form of hoarding in monetized gold as well as bullion, the Emergency Banking Act was passed two months before Black arrived in Washington. The act required that all private parties surrender their gold coin, bullion, and certificates to the U.S. Treasury. Later, after Black arrived, the question of proper ownership of the Fed's gold was debated. Black stood firmly behind both the principle that the current law required the Fed to hold gold to endorse Federal Reserve notes and the desire by the administration to transfer the gold to the Treasury, devalue it, and use the surplus profit to finance a $2 billion emergency stabilization fund. The situation was resolved on

January 30, 1934, by the Gold Reserve Act. This act transferred gold from the Fed to the Treasury in exchange for gold certificates, and the weight of gold dollars at the Treasury was reduced by 40 percent (from 25.8 grams to 15.24 grams).

In a White House dinner shortly after the Fed transferred its gold to the Treasury, Black reported that President Roosevelt observed him pocketing the gold flatware from his table. The president asked the governor about this unusual behavior, and Black replied that he was only trying to get his gold back. Everyone appeared to enjoy Governor Black's point of view.

At the same time that the internal devaluation occurred, by executive order, Roosevelt devalued gold by raising its price to $35 per ounce. Actually, since September 1933, the gold price had been raised monthly from a low of $26.62 per ounce. Although Black was opposed to devaluation, this action was beyond the scope of his authority. He realized, however, that when England left the gold standard, remaining on a fixed value gold standard raised considerable difficulty for the United States.

Clearly Black's greatest contribution to monetary policy was the resumption of open market operations when he became governor in May 1933. During 1932 open market operations were, on balance, ineffective. From mid-May through June Black oversaw the injection of $150 million in reserves into the banking system. From July until mid-August another $60 million were added, and from then until mid-October another $280 million were added. Virtually a half-billion dollars of excess reserves were created, but the lack of loan generation from these reserves by commercial banks caused the Fed to reduce further purchases gradually. By November 8 the Fed held $2.43 billion in bonds, more than ever before in Fed history. From October until December 1933 excess reserves reached $800 million.

In September 1933, in a speech before the American Bankers Association annual meeting in Chicago, Black, only four months into office, began to receive indications that his policy of creating excess reserves would meet resistance. The meeting itself was described as one of the stormiest of its kind. Black attempted to support Roosevelt's decree that bank "loans can and will be made" when he stated, "We are trying to force money to seek investment." Unfortunately, the bankers did not cooperate fully to the extent that they amassed nearly $2 billion in excess reserves. They effectively trapped liquidity.

These excess reserves were a thorn in Black's policy. He confessed his grief over the slippage between the Fed's actions and commercial banks' responses. In a speech to the Montana Bankers convention, he pleaded with them to make use of their idle reserves to generate loans:

What are the Reserve banks doing? We are doing everything in God's name we know how, and everything the law will let us do to bring America back into her own. You have more deposits now than ever before in American history. You have in your vaults all the reserves the law requires you to have. In addition to that you have $1.8 billion excess reserves in your banks. I want to know what you are going to say when you are asked, "What have you done to help in the recovery program of America?" (Black 1934b)

The Fed's actions were probably having beneficial effects, however. From 1933 to 1934 the total of deposits plus currency outside banks rose. Indexes of industrial production, employment, and prices were rising during 1933 just as the monetary base rose. The greatest surge in output occurred during the second quarter, while greater surges in employment and prices were recorded one quarter later. The year 1934 marked further recovery, although the rate of recovery was smaller.

On August 10, 1933, the Fed enacted Regulation M, the formal establishment of the Federal Open Market Committee. Arguably this marked the beginning of the modern Fed. Under the board, this committee would centralize authority for controlling the injection and deletions of reserves in commercial banks. District reserve bank governors would control seven of the twelve votes, nonetheless.

Only nine days later, the board approved Regulation Q, which prohibited the payment of interest on demand deposits and limited the interest rate payable on time and savings deposits to 3 percent. The purpose of this regulation was to reduce competition among banks in attracting deposits (to make loans), and, in that, it may have been too effective. When competition is limited, elements of monopoly are introduced, and the reluctance of commercial banks to make riskier loans is reinforced. Since deposits cost much less, there is no great pressure to convert reserves into loans to service deposit costs. The excess reserves of 1933, which earned no interest, and the deposits, which required no interest payments, understandably caused banks to be reluctant to make loans. It seems that this regulation was, in part, the undoing of the open market purchases by the Fed.

In fact, Regulation Q raised the real possibility of a liquidity trap. Since reserves earned no interest from the Fed and now banks had to pay no interest on most deposits, no incentives existed to make loans of moderate or greater risk. Since the Fed was buying bonds to create excess reserves, interest rates were falling. And since commercial banks were neglecting opportunities to make more loans, excess reserves were accumulating. Without loans to earn interest, commercial banks could either hold excess reserves or buy bonds at higher prices set by the Fed in open market operations. Hence, interest rates would be very low, and large excess reserves would simulate an excess demand for money. For the nonbank public, an equivalent impasse would have been a period of deflation that induced an excess demand for money (the less risky alternative) as interest rates fell. Thus, while the central bank was increasing the monetary base, commercial banks were building an excess demand for money under the influence of an artificially low floor and ceiling rate of interest. In effect, the marginal cost of acquiring and maintaining excess reserves approached zero, while the expected marginal benefit of making loans was less certain, with one distinct possibility being a negative rate of return. In fact, on both ninety-day bankers' acceptances and short-term U.S. securities, yields fell from ½ of 1 percent to ¼ of 1 percent during Black's tenure.

In mid-November 1933 Black and the other members of the Federal Reserve Board took further action to cut the rediscount rate from 3 percent to 2.5 percent. Overall the board cut the discount rate three times.

On January 1, 1934, a major provision of the Banking Act of 1933 signed by Roosevelt on June 16, 1933, became effective. From now on, commercial bank deposits up to $2,500 would be insured by the newly created Federal Deposit Insurance Corporation (FDIC). Black's attitude to deposit insurance, unlike that of commercial bankers at the time, was completely supportive. Commercial bankers traced their aversion to deposit insurance from concern that it could reward bad banking by transferring risk premiums from depositors in sound banks to depositors in unsound banks. Whatever Black's private views on this issue, he supported the law for the confidence it inspired in the banking system as a whole.

Two months later, Black appeared before the House Committee on Banking and Currency to testify on the wisdom of creating a supermonetary authority (the Federal Monetary Authority), which could possibly have created a monetary supreme court (H.R. 7157). As Black skeptically testified, he described a replacement for the Fed that would take the place of Congress, the Treasury, and the Federal Reserve system. He had many reservations about such a superagency's concentrating power in the hands of a few. Vindication came with the death of this bill.

In an appearance on March 23 before the same House committee, Black restated a 1931 contracyclical recommendation made by the Federal Reserve Board to control velocity. He testified that the board should have authority to graduate the required reserve ratios of commercial banks over the course of a business cycle. In advocating an automatic rule for monetary policy, Black was a progressive. The idea was that as national income increased, minimum reserve ratios would increase; as national income decreased, minimum reserve ratios would decrease. Moreover, demand deposits would require initial rates of 7, 10, or 13 percent, depending on the location of the banks. Banks in financial centers (city banks) where speculative activities would begin would have higher minimum reserve ratios (13 percent). Banks elsewhere (country banks) would have lower reserve ratios (7–10 percent).

Black's testimony shows a prescience about monetary policy little understood at the time or perhaps even now. He implicitly went beyond the mere quantity of money (M) to the demand for that money ($1/V$). He thus distinguished between the money stock (M) and the money supply (MV), which is more important. If the Fed could control MV by automatically varying reserve requirements, then the rest of the formula (PQ) could be managed better.

As Black testified, if speculation began in financial centers where city banks are located, the already high minimum reserve ratio would be lifted still higher. But other country banks would not undergo a change in their minimum reserve ratios. Black maintained that this would help arrest speculation by denying additional loans "at the right time, in the right places, and to the right institutions." It is interesting now to speculate on why he did not add "and to the right degree." In his testimony, he proposed that reserve ratios be raised by applying an additional 5 percent of net deposits plus 50 percent of the change in average daily debits (velocity) in deposit accounts. Black confirmed that his beliefs and recommendations were based on data from 1928 and 1929 showing that while reserves and deposits increased slightly, debits increased rapidly during the stock market boom.

A supplementary recommendation made at this time was more widely accepted. Black proposed that vault cash held by commercial banks be counted as legal reserves. This had not been the case earlier. Obviously, as national income rose and loans increased, vault cash would decline, and banks would become more vulnerable if a run on banks developed. With vault cash eligible as reserves and with prospective automatic hikes in required reserve ratios, early stability over the cycle might be gained.

Time and again in testimony before the Senate and House committees on banking and currency, Black endorsed authority for the Fed to make loans directly to firms of the type that commercial banks could not make. These were longer-term loans of up to five years' duration. Black also wanted authority to be able to purchase illiquid capital loans from lenders to free their capital and prevent major losses. The only alternative the board had exercised was to buy bonds in the open market. But when excess reserves mounted and the RFC failed to approve loans rapidly enough to be of consequence, a liquidity trap could occur. When Congress finally enacted the legislation to enable the Fed to make individual loans, it wrote the legislation in such a way that these loans could scarcely be made. In any case, of the $600 million loan demand estimates Black perceived, the Fed could have provided only about half of that under the best of circumstances.

Clearly Black was citing a problem with velocity (V). If loans are made, demand deposits are created, and the cost of money ensures that it will be spent, usually in productive, profitable, and employment-creating ways. Hence, money is placed in circulation, and velocity, and thus the money supply (MV), rise.

In later testimony regarding the securities exchange bill Black argued that to have "such a recovery in the United States that none of us could dream of," we must "open the capital market." Even as the securities exchange bill increased the regulation of national securities markets and imposed margin requirements on securities purchases, Black believed that it would not prevent firms from gaining productive access to capital markets.

Since Congress was about to enact legislation regulating the securities industry (signed by Roosevelt on June 6, 1934), Black was called to testify also on the prospective role of the Fed as regulator. He appeared before the Senate Committee on Banking and Currency. In the preceding year, the Banking Act of 1933 had already prohibited commercial banks (member and nonmember alike) from underwriting security issues. Now Black argued that setting margin requirements for the purchase of stock on credit should be set by the Fed rather than any other agency. Black acknowledged that the Glass-Steagall Act had given the Fed the authority to restrict commercial banks' loans for security purchases but that authority was a less graduated power than control over margin requirements.

When asked if the new margin requirements would have halted speculative frenzy in the stock market of 1928 and 1929, Black responded negatively. He remarked that with gains of 20 to 40 percent per day, a gambling instinct pervaded, and the promise of quick returns would have overwhelmed the cost of making margin payments.

Curiously, the Senate committee asked Black whether the Fed practiced the policy of pegging interest rates on government securities. Black's response was that this would be an improper function for the Fed to perform. Unfortunately, Regulation Q became the tool to peg interest rates on sources of funds for commercial banks, and those effects may also be called improper. In these hearings, Black again raised the idea of a velocity control power being granted to the Fed. However, to avoid delay in passage of the Securities Exchange Act, he did not try to press his plan into that act.

Thirteen days later, Roosevelt signed an act enabling Federal Reserve banks to make loans to small and medium-size firms for working capital. Black had testified extensively and enthusiastically for this emergency measure, given the surplus in excess reserves currently in banks. This act further provided that the Fed could purchase commercial bank loans to firms in order to free those banks of most of the risk of default and allow them to make more loans. These "loan guarantees" obligated commercial banks to a maximum 20 percent of any loss that might be suffered by Federal Reserve banks.

Given the rapid pace of construction activity by the federal government to showcase federal agencies in Washington and elsewhere and to alleviate unemployment, it was natural that plans to provide a permanent and unique home for the Board of Governors commenced during Eugene Black's tenure. Black actively supported the construction of a building sufficient to bring all employees of the board under one roof. At this time, employees were housed in three floors of the U.S. Treasury building (scattered around the building) and in three floors of the Shoreham Building, which was separated from the Treasury building. This arrangement meant that the statistics group, Research Department, and Bank Operation Department were two city blocks from the Fed headquarters. Ultimately, Black's permanent successor, Marriner Eccles,* was able to carry this construction project toward completion.

When Black left Washington for Atlanta in August 1934, he fully expected to resume his work as governor of the Federal Reserve bank there and to serve as national liaison between the Roosevelt administration and the commercial banks. Interestingly, memoranda between offices at the Fed seemed to question that his expenses be paid by the Washington office. At last this bureaucratic snag was resolved favorably, and Black was to travel extensively among the districts to gather information and represent the administration.

Perhaps Eugene Black would have given us a written account of his years at the Fed if time had permitted. He suffered a fatal heart attack on December 19, 1934, only four months after leaving the Fed in Washington.

BIBLIOGRAPHY

Allsbrook, Ogden O. 1989. Conversation with Eugene R. Black, Jr. August 31.

Black, Eugene R. 1933a. "Looking Forward." Address to the American Bankers Association, September 5.

———. 1933b. Letters. In *Commercial and Financial Chronicle*, August 26.

———. 1934a. "We Can Build America Again." *Southern Banker* (September): 11.

———. 1934b. Testimony before the U.S. Congress, House, Committee on Banking and Currency. 73d Cong., 2d sess., May 2.

Federal Reserve Bulletin. February 1934. July 1934.

ANDREW FELTON BRIMMER (1926–)

Rexford Ahene

A respected member of the caucus of senior economists today, Andrew Brimmer was the first black named to the Federal Reserve Board. His selection in 1966 by President Lyndon B. Johnson was regarded by some as a brilliant and necessary move designed to add another liberal Democrat to the board and to help counteract the tight money strategies of the board's conservative chairman, William McChesney Martin.[*]

Brimmer arrived on the board with impeccable credentials. He had received his high school diploma in 1944 from Tensas Parish Training School in St. Joseph, Louisiana, before moving to Bremerton, Washington. He enlisted in the U.S. Army and served between 1945 and 1946 in Hawaii. Brimmer's tenure in the army made it possible for him to qualify for a federal educational subsidy, which paid for a substantial portion of his education at the University of Washington.

In his sophomore year at the University of Washington, Brimmer was enamored with the clarity, order, and logic of the economic way of thinking. He explained later that economics provided the tools for answering many of his questions about life in the United States during his formative years.

After earning a bachelor's degree in 1950, Brimmer received the John Hay Whitney Foundation fellowship to pursue a master's degree in economics at the University of Washington. His master's thesis, "Economic Aspects of Fair Employment," set the stage for Brimmer's extensive scholarship focusing on black economic problems in the United States. The period immediately following the completion of his master's degree was spent on a Fulbright fellowship at the Delhi School of Economics, University of Bombay.

Upon his return to the United States in 1952, he enrolled at Harvard and in 1957 earned his doctorate in economics with a concentration in monetary economics and economic development. Brimmer has since received numerous honorary degrees and despite an active career in the public and private sectors has maintained his affinity for scholarship and professional excellence.

A prolific writer, Brimmer has both the background and experience of a journalist. He started as a journalism major and worked during his college days as the assistant editor of the *Seattle Dispatch*. Some of his early publications include a monograph on the framework of industrial organization in India and several articles focusing on entrepreneurship, banking, and finance in India and Africa. Since 1954, however, Brimmer says of himself: "I've deliberately concentrated on my job as a professional economist."

After his studies in India, he returned in 1952 to accept a position as research assistant at the Center for International Studies at the Massachusetts Institute of Technology. In 1954–1955, he was a teaching fellow in economics at Harvard. Brimmer decided early in his career that the New York Fed, the Washington, D.C., Fed, the Brookings Institution, and the Rand Corporation were among the places he wanted to work as a professional economist. In 1955 he joined the Federal Reserve Bank of New York while writing his doctoral thesis on monetary policy, interest rates, and the investment behavior of life insurance companies. He resigned in 1958 in order to join the faculty at Michigan State University. Three years later, he joined the Wharton School as professor of finance and commerce. His first book, *Life Insurance Companies in the Capital Markets*, was published in 1962, and several articles published in the *Journal of Finance*, *Review of Economics*, and *Statistics and the Banker* were also written and published during this phase of his career.

Brimmer started work in government in 1963 as deputy assistant secretary for economic policy review in the Commerce Department. In 1964 he gained national prominence through the research he contributed to the U.S. Supreme Court ruling on the constitutionality of the public accommodation sections of the Civil Rights Act. His later duties after succeeding Richard Holton as the assistant secretary of commerce made him one of the key government spokesmen on such topics as the balance of payments, tourist travel, and U.S capital investment abroad. Brimmer was instrumental in persuading American business groups to postpone marginal overseas investments and to finance foreign projects by sourcing for funds abroad during the balance-of-payments crisis of 1965. In a presentation before the American Finance Association in December of that year, Brimmer reported the success of his strategy: a decrease in U.S. direct foreign investment from $1.159 billion in the first quarter of 1965 to $891 million and $515 million in the second and third quarters, respectively. He was also responsible for providing valuable statistical data to the public as the officer in charge of the Bureau of Census and the Office of Business Economics.

When Brimmer was invited to join the Federal Reserve board in February 1967, President Johnson, in his typical artful and expedient manner, wanted to fill the seat vacated by C. Canby Balderston.* Johnson's public characterization of Brimmer as "a man of moderation whose brilliance is combined with a sense of fair play" made Brimmer appear to be a fiscal liberal—someone who would side with J. Dewey Daane* and other liberals on the board. Those who knew of Brimmer's business-oriented philosophy, however, regarded him otherwise.

Brimmer himself announced that he planned only to "look at the issues in as clear-headed a manner as possible."

At the time Brimmer was appointed to the board, there was general agreement among members that a tight money policy was necessary to restrain domestic demand. The economic boom of 1964–1965, coupled with the escalation of the Vietnam War, caused the deficit to rise, fueling inflation. The board responded by tightening credit. The discount rate set by the New York Federal Reserve at 4.5 percent in 1966 was the highest since 1929. With the federal fund rate at 5.11 percent, the prime rate banks charged rose to 5.63 percent. As the economy began to feel the burden of these anti-inflationary policies, many on the board, including Brimmer, were criticized for bringing undue financial strain to bear on the banking system. By the fall of 1966, there were fears of panic on Wall Street. Brimmer found himself challenged to defend the policies of the board under circumstances similar to his 1965 Commerce Department experience.

Rather than supporting the call by the public for easy credit, Brimmer and Sherman J. Maisel[*] became the first members of the board to defend its policies publicly. Brimmer called on the administration to help in the fight against inflation by raising taxes. In a series of speeches, he admonished the commercial banks for endangering the viability of the banking system by expanding business lending at the expense of all other clients. In an era of the Federal Reserve's anti-inflationary tight money policy, Brimmer argued that intense competitive pressure to make business loans and the absorption of heavy capital losses through liquidation of securities amounted to poor judgment by the banks. Brimmer suggested that the banks cooperate with the Fed rather than blame it for refusing the credit demands of their clients. Furthermore, he favored the suspension of a 1962 law that allowed companies to deduct a maximum of 7 percent of the cost of new capital expenditure for income tax purposes as an additional disincentive to borrowing during this period.

By November 1967 Brimmer had explained the board's policies clearly to most of his audience. At the Arizona Bankers Association meeting that month, he repeated that the fear of financial panic perpetuated throughout the summer of 1966 by the financial community did not rest on a careful appraisal of ongoing events. He pointed out that, had there been any grounds that market pressure was moving to precipitate a panic, "the Federal Reserve would not have hesitated to inject whatever amount of bank reserves may have been required to avoid it." His call to the administration to help take responsibility for fighting inflation contributed, in part, to the passage of the 1968 tax surcharge law signed by President Johnson.

He was equally outspoken on the question of taxes. In the event of "a serious shortage of effective demand," Brimmer believed a tax cut would be needed to induce consumers to spend and to provide inducements to business firms to undertake fixed investments for this purpose.

Brimmer's tenure on the board was an active one. He was an outspoken defender of the Fed's independence and supported innovative banking practices. He opposed ceilings on interest rates for bank savings, preferring to rely on market forces for determining rates. On the question of introducing bank credit cards, Brimmer was quick in pointing out that the need to ensure a sound banking system should not discourage innovations that will "contribute to public convenience." In order to increase the competitive posture of savings and loan associations against the commercial banks and market securities, he suggested they should be allowed to lend widely to increase the availability of mortgage credit. Brimmer also proposed the introduction of a universal system of reserve requirements to replace the system that varied with geographic location. Brimmer's outspokenness did not always play well with the banking community. Some believed he had aspirations to be an "iconoclast." Others fumed that he was the "most doctrinaire" of all the economists on the Federal Reserve board.

Brimmer used his position to disseminate controversial but well-documented opinions on such diverse matters as wage and price controls, pollution, income maintenance, and the economic status of minorities and taxes. Although most of Brimmer's professional concerns have nothing to do with race, he assisted in the preparation of the Department of Commerce testimony on discrimination in interstate commerce in 1964. He was a member of the three-member federal delegation sent to investigate the Watts riots in 1965. He was also particularly interested in the impact of desegregation on members of the black middle class, particularly those who had built their careers in predominantly black neighborhoods by providing services not readily available under segregation.

Brimmer had a good deal to say about black economic development. He supported the need for a stated policy of fostering black businesses and lending support to black entrepreneurs during the Nixon administration. He argued that black banks were more a symbol of black achievement than a meaningful source of capital for economic development. Brimmer questioned how most black businesses could be expected to be successful in neighborhoods where most of the nation's poor were concentrated. During the Watts investigation, Brimmer instigated a survey that revealed that between 1960 and 1965, when the income of the typical American family had jumped substantially, the purchasing power of the average Watts family had declined by $400. In the ghetto, he argued, "self-employment offers a low and rather risky payoff."

Brimmer also favored some viable method of "moderating the rise of wages and other forms of labor compensation" to curb wage and price spirals. At the same time, he believed minimum wage laws worsened black unemployment by hindering the hiring of unskilled ghetto teenagers. In his view, the key to black economic advancement is better access to jobs as salaried managers and skilled workers with major corporations and the successful management of companies with the capital resources to command national attention.

Despite his accomplishments as a prominent black economist and public servant, Brimmer steered clear of writing for the *Review of Black Political Economy*.

To have done so during the period of his public career, in his opinion, would imply an endorsement of separatism. His professionalism, however, earned him the respect of his peers of all races. A former student referred to him as "one of the most brilliant professors I ever had." A close colleague who worked with him during the Johnson administration says: "Andy is very able, effective, and dynamic" (but wishes he were not "so damn conservative").

Brimmer was considered a fiscal liberal at the time of his appointment to the board. He was unanimously confirmed by the Senate on March 4, 1966, for a full term of fourteen years, ending January 31, 1980. His record indicates, however, that he neither joined nor escaped from any voting bloc during his eight years on the board. At the end of his fifth year, Brimmer felt he "still [had] a role to play" and was "reasonably content" in his job. When he resigned with almost six years of his term remaining, Brimmer stressed that his decision was not the result of "any policy disagreements with his colleagues." He was among the first to support a tight monetary policy to curb spiraling inflation. He also supported the slight loosening of the growth of money supply permitted by the board in the summer of 1974. The long-run view, according to Brimmer, is to counteract the weakening of demand by easing monetary policy without overreacting.

Following his resignation from the Federal Reserve board, Brimmer joined the corporate and academic world. He was immediately appointed the Thomas Henry Carroll Ford Foundation Visiting Professor at Harvard Business School and was elected the first black member of Du Pont's board of directors. During the same period, he founded and became the president of Brimmer & Company in Washington, D.C., a firm engaged in economic and financial consulting. He served as a director of Bank of America and was a member of the board of governors of the American Security Bank, International Harvester Company, and Gannett Company between 1974 and 1976.

Brimmer has received a long string of honors and awards. He has honorary doctorates from a number of colleges, including Oberlin College, Long Island University, Nebraska Wesleyan University, and Marquette University. His awards for excellence in public service include the Government Man of the Year by the National Business League in 1963; the Arthur Flemming Award in 1966; the Russworm Award by the National Press Club in 1966; the Golden Plate Award of the American Academy of Achievement in 1967; the Horatio Alger Award in 1974; and the Equal Opportunity Award by the National Urban League in 1974. Brimmer is active in a number of professional associations, including the American Economic Association, the American Statistical Association, the Interracial Council for Business Opportunity, the Association for the Study of Afro-American Life, and the National Economists Club of the Council on Foreign Relations.

A pleasant and always jovial gentleman, Brimmer married Doris Millicent Scott of New York in 1953 when she was a graduate student at Radcliffe. Their daughter, Ester Diane Brimmer, was born in 1962. His favorite pastimes include hiking and tennis on those rare weekends when he can spare some time away from the office.

BIBLIOGRAPHY

Brimmer, Andrew. 1962. *Life Insurance Companies in the Capital Markets*. East Lansing: Bureau of Business and Economic Research, Michigan State University, May.
———. 1966. "The Negro in the National Economy." In John P. Davis, ed., *The American Negro Reference Book*. Englewood Cliffs, N.J.: Prentice-Hall.
———. 1988. "Income, Wealth and Investment Behavior in the Black Community." *American Economic Review*, 78 (May):151.
———, with Allen Sinai. 1981. "Rational Expectations and the Conduct of Monetary Policy." *American Economic Review* 71 (May):259.
Current Biography. 1968. New York: H.W. Wilson.

JOSEPH A. BRODERICK (1881–1959)

Yale L. Meltzer

Joseph Broderick, who served on the Federal Reserve board from February 3, 1936, to September 30, 1937, was born on December 7, 1881, in New York City. While attending elementary school, he worked at night in a dry-goods store in New York City. After graduating from elementary school, he took a job as a messenger at the State Trust Company in New York City, where he soon became a bookkeeper.

During the period 1896 to 1910, Broderick held various positions at the State Trust Company and Morton Trust Company by day and studied at night at New York University's School of Commerce, Accounts and Finance, from which he graduated in 1906. After that he continued his studies in banking at the American Institute of Banking (1908–1909).

In 1910 he took a position as a bank examiner with the New York State Banking Department. In 1914, seeing an opportunity at the Federal Reserve system, which was starting up operations, Broderick took the position of chief examiner for the Federal Reserve Board, which he held until 1918. He became secretary to the Federal Reserve Board in 1918. He left that position in 1919 in order to become vice-president of the National Bank of Commerce in New York City, holding this position until 1928.

Broderick was active in many areas of banking and finance, and his expertise was highly respected. In 1926 he went to Poland as part of a special mission headed by Professor Edward Walter Kemmerer of Princeton University to give advice to the government of Poland about how it should organize and operate its banking, monetary, and financial system. Broderick served with such distinction that he was awarded the Order of Polonia in Restituta with the title of Knight Commander. He returned to the United States with an enhanced reputation.

Franklin D. Roosevelt, while governor of New York, appointed Broderick superintendent of banks for the state in 1929. Herbert H. Lehman, who succeeded Roosevelt as governor in 1933, greatly admired Broderick and reappointed him. He served in this position until 1934, an extremely turbulent period in banking.

In 1936 President Franklin D. Roosevelt appointed Broderick to be a member of the Board of Governors of the Federal Reserve system. He was confirmed readily by the Senate and became a Federal Reserve board governor on February 3, 1936. In this position, he continued to deal with the many banking problems of the Great Depression.

During the period of Broderick's tenure on the Federal Reserve board, the Federal Reserve pursued an easy money policy, considered necessary because the country was operating far below its full capacity level. During 1936 a growing increase in excess bank reserves was particularly disturbing to the Federal Reserve board. As a result, when Broderick joined the board, it raised margin requirements from 45 percent to 55 percent because of the relatively sharp rise in stock prices at the time. The board was exercising its new power, granted by the Securities Exchange Act of 1934, to set margin requirements.

As a means of reducing the excess reserves of member banks of the Federal Reserve, the board also raised legal reserve requirements in mid–1936 and mid–1937. Here it was using its new powers, granted under the Banking Act of 1935, to vary reserve requirements. In addition, during the period of Broderick's tenure, the board pointed out that U.S. government securities should become increasingly important as investment vehicles for bank funds.

Broderick resigned from the Federal Reserve board on September 30, 1937. The next day, he became president of the East River Savings Bank in New York City, a position he held until January 1952, when he became chairman of the board of the East River Savings Bank. He remained chairman until October 1, 1957, when he retired.

Broderick was a member of the Executive Council of the American Bankers Association from 1938 to 1939 and again from 1948 to 1949. He was made an honorary member of the National Association of Supervisors of State Banks and the American Institute of Banking. He served on the board of directors of the Bankers Club of America and was a member of the New York University Men-in-Finance Club. In 1948–1949 he served on the Council of New York University.

He married Mary Rose Lyons on August 2, 1915. They had three sons. He died on April 5, 1959.

BIBLIOGRAPHY

Federal Reserve System Board of Governors. 1936–1938. *Annual Report*. Washington, D.C.
Meltzer, Yale L. 1989. Correspondence with the Board of Governors, Federal Reserve System.

JEFFREY M. BUCHER (1933–)

Thomas J. Pierce

When in fall 1971 a Nixon administration official inquired of Jeffrey Bucher's interest in membership on the Federal Reserve board, the banker-lawyer was sufficiently surprised that he later had his secretary contact the White House to confirm the validity of the inquiry. Little in his background or experience suggested even remotely the likelihood of a presidential call to service as a central banker.

The son of a Chicago investment banker who moved west in the late 1920s, Jeffrey M. Bucher was born February 9, 1933, in Los Angeles. He attended preparatory school and completed his undergraduate education in southern California, earning a bachelor's degree in psychology from Occidental College in 1954. After graduating from Stanford Law School in 1957, he accepted a position in the law division of the Los Angeles–based United California Bank (UCB), a subsidiary of Western Bancorp, a multibank holding company. With the exception of a two-year stint with a private law firm, Bucher spent his entire working career prior to the Federal Reserve with UCB. He was vice-president of the law division and served as the bank's secretary-treasurer from 1960 to 1968. During the following four years, he was senior vice-president in charge of the bank's trust division. At the time of his appointment to the Federal Reserve board, UCB was the nation's fourteenth largest bank in terms of deposits and nineteenth among trust banks in terms of assets managed.

President Nixon nominated Bucher for board membership on April 27, 1972, as a replacement for Sherman Maisel,[*] a University of California, Berkeley, economist whose term had expired. During the ensuing confirmation hearings before the Senate Committee on Banking, Housing, and Urban Affairs, Senator William Proxmire (D, Wisconsin) launched what, in effect, was a one-person crusade against Bucher's appointment. Given the technical nature of monetary policy, he believed all board members should be professional economists. Accordingly, Bucher's lack of formal training in economics irritated Proxmire, particularly in the light of the February 1972 board appointment of another noneconomist, Louisville businessman John Sheehan.[*] Since four of the five

Federal Reserve board appointees during the Kennedy and Johnson years were economists and Nixon's first appointee was Arthur Burns,* Proxmire considered the Sheehan and Bucher appointments a "major leap backwards to the days when bankers and businessmen were calling the shots with tragic results for the economy" (*Congressional Record*, 1972, p. 19321).

In addition to his reservations regarding the nominee's monetary policymaking qualifications, Proxmire considered Bucher's trust department experience too narrow to qualify him as a banker. He also felt Bucher's employment with a bank holding company might constitute a conflict of interest in board regulatory deliberations. Finally, he raised questions about a commodities speculation scheme involving a Swiss subsidiary of UCB that had resulted in a $48 million loss, intimating that as an officer of the bank, Bucher could or should have known about the subsidiary's questionable activities.

Also testifying against the Bucher nomination was a retired California state superintendent of banks, William A. Burkett. Trust department officers, he claimed, were "not truly" bankers. They invested clients' funds but performed no typical banking functions. In addition, having passed judgment on qualifications of prospective state bank presidents during his tenure as superintendent, Burkett ventured that Bucher "would not qualify for appointment to the presidency of even the smallest bank in California because of his total lack of knowledge and experience in banking" (U.S. Congress, 1972, p. 33).

For the most part, the committee dismissed Burkett's testimony. Wallace Bennett (R, Utah) noted that Burkett had never met Bucher who, the senator contended, was merely Burkett's latest target in an ongoing vendetta against UCB. Senator Proxmire's campaign against the nomination fared no better. There was no demonstrable support for the idea of appointing only economists to the Federal Reserve board. In fact, the committee seemed to favor the presence of at least one banker on the board, and Jeffrey Bucher, contending his background in banking was "quite a bit broader than trust work," was judged suitably qualified. The fifteen-member committee voted 13–1, with one abstention, to confirm his nomination.

Undaunted, Proxmire arranged for inclusion of the entire transcript of the committee hearing in the *Congressional Record*, copies of which he subsequently disseminated widely among businessmen and economists in the hope of generating broader opposition to the Bucher nomination. Among the respondents were a former chairman of the Council of Economic Advisers, Leon Keyserling, and a future Nobel Prize winner, Robert Solow. Despite these efforts and a final plea before the full Senate, Proxmire cast the lone vote against Bucher's confirmation.

While Proxmire had failed to convince his colleagues that Bucher was unqualified to serve, it seems equally true that the full Senate, like the majority of its Banking, Housing, and Urban Affairs Committee, was generally opposed to appointing only economists to the Board of Governors. There was considerable sentiment for a banking representative on the board. Moreover, several senators expressed concern that delegating board responsibilities solely to economists would further isolate monetary policy considerations from the public domain. Economic experts or "technicians," John Tower (R, Texas) argued, tend to have fairly similar outlooks on matters by virtue of their similar education and professions. This, in turn, will bias their policymaking to a fairly narrow vein. A broader spectrum of opinion was necessary to ensure informed decision making. Furthermore, it was argued, with 250 economists on staff at the Fed, there would be plenty of advice available to board members lacking formal training in economics.

With the hubbub of the confirmation process behind him, Bucher took the oath of office on June 5, 1972. At thirty-nine years of age, he was the youngest appointee to the Federal Reserve board in its fifty-eight-year history. Despite his youth, Bucher gradually established an individual presence on the board. Proxmire's contention that chairman Burns's policy recommendations would be rubberstamped by this "inexperienced amateur" proved groundless. During Bucher's tenure from mid–1972 through 1975, external supply shocks and the dismantling of wage and price controls contributed substantially to the worst inflationary conditions in the United States during the post–World War II era. Stagflation worsened short-run policy trade-offs, creating enormous uncertainty for policymakers. Given the circumstances, there was remarkable consensus in monetary policy decisions. Federal Open Market Committee (FOMC) minutes reveal differences of opinion regarding the degree to which monetary and credit conditions should be eased or tightened in particular instances but indicate little disagreement regarding the general thrust of monetary policy. Within that context, Bucher's voting record reflects a tendency toward slightly easier monetary and credit conditions than that of his colleagues; he cast four of the FOMC's twenty-one dissenting votes in 1974 and 1975, always for less restrictive or more expansive policy. His dissenting statements, however, typically reflected due consideration of the potential long-run inflationary implications of the policy measures he espoused. In general, Bucher's voting record on monetary policy matters characterizes him as a team player, a label that also aptly describes his FOMC colleagues. Clearly, however, he was no lackey of the chairman.

The same conclusion emerges from an examination of his voting record on supervisory and regulatory matters. The board acted on hundreds of bank merger and acquisition applications annually during the mid–1970s, as well as on requests made by independent banks and bank holding companies (BHCs) seeking to expand operations into areas closely related to banking. Bucher typically voted with the majority; most decisions, in fact, were unanimous. Nevertheless, statements supporting his occasional dissenting votes reveal an advocacy of vigorous competition in banking activities. Both the Bank Merger Act of 1960 and the 1970 amendments to the Bank Holding Company Act directed banking authorities to consider the possibility of "undue concentration of resources" stemming from proposed activities and transactions. Interpreting concentration and competition in a conservative vein, Bucher generally did not support applications by large

BHCs to acquire banks in already concentrated markets, preferring de novo entry, which simultaneously increased competition and reduced concentration. Furthermore, he sometimes opposed mergers among banks in markets where little concentration currently existed on the grounds that future competition would be limited if the newly created entity appeared capable of eventually dominating the market.

In addition to monetary policy and bank supervisory and regulatory responsibilities, Bucher played a major role in developing regulations implementing the wave of consumer protection legislation enacted in the mid–1970s. With passage of the Truth in Lending Act of 1968, the board was directed to write regulations indicating the exact manner in which lenders must disclose credit costs so as to enhance consumer comprehension of credit terms. Board vice-chairman J. L. Robertson,[*] a lawyer, was assigned primary responsibility for overseeing that task. Upon Robertson's retirement in 1973, the reins passed to Bucher. Impending passage of legislation forbidding discrimination in the extension of credit on the basis of sex or marital status and numerous other consumer affairs measures added substantially to the Fed's regulations-writing burden. In response, a separate Office of Saver and Consumer Affairs was established within the Federal Reserve in July 1974. Accordingly, Bucher's oversight responsibilities expanded. His legal background was an obvious asset in these endeavors, and he frequently presented the Fed's views on proposed consumer and banking legislation to congressional subcommittees.

The board's burgeoning regulatory responsibilities in consumer affairs and banking eventually led Bucher to conclude that former governor Robertson's 1962 proposal to unify federal bank supervision under a federal banking commission ought to be reconsidered. Under that plan, the Fed would have been freed essentially of regulatory and supervisory responsibilities, enabling it to concentrate on monetary policy. The commission would have specialized in regulatory and supervisory matters as opposed to each of several agencies handling those chores on a part-time basis with significant duplication of task and resulting inefficiency.

Contributing to Bucher's interest in regulatory unification was the realization that board responsibilities were continually growing. Passage of the Bank Holding Company Act of 1956, in conjunction with related measures enacted over the following fifteen years, greatly increased the board's regulatory and supervisory workload. Regulations-writing chores associated with consumer affairs legislation of the 1970s added to that burden. While the macroeconomy became increasingly complex, board members necessarily spent less time considering monetary policy matters. Though this evolutionary path of board responsibilities may have been undesirable, Bucher's legal and banking experience became increasingly valuable in that environment.

Having served on the board less than four years, Bucher tendered his letter of resignation to President Gerald Ford in October 1975. The immediate financial penalty associated with leaving the private sector to join the Federal Reserve and the increasing opportunity cost of board service over time figured substantially in his decision. He left office January 2, 1976, at age forty-two, joining the Los Angeles office of the law firm Lillick, McHose and Charles as a senior partner specializing in bank regulatory matters. In addition, he has served as special counsel to the California superintendent of banks and as a member of the Federal Deposit Insurance Corporation Advisory Committee to the Task Force on State and Federal Regulations of Commercial Banks. From 1983 to 1987, he was chairman of the board, First Interstate Bank of Washington, D.C., N.A.

Bucher is divorced and has five grown children. He currently resides in Los Angeles.

BIBLIOGRAPHY

Bucher, Jeffrey M. 1975. "Federal Bank Regulatory Reform." Address to the Western Independent Bankers Association annual meeting, San Francisco. March 11.
———. 1989. Personal interview. Los Angeles, August 3.
Dowling, Robert. 1972. "Bucher, Trust Officer at UCB, Nominated to Replace Maisel at Fed." *American Banker*, April 28.
Federal Reserve System Board of Governors. 1972–1975. *Annual Reports.*
———. 1972–1976. *Federal Reserve Bulletin.*
U.S. Congress. *Congressional Record—Senate.* May 31, 1972.
U.S. Congress. Senate. Committee on Banking, Housing, and Urban Affairs. 1972. *Hearing on the Nomination of Jeffrey M. Bucher to Be a Member of the Board of Governors of the Federal Reserve System.* 92d Cong., 2d sess., May 12.

ARTHUR F. BURNS (1904–1987)

John P. Cullity

Arthur F. Burns, who served as chairman of the Federal Reserve board from 1970 to 1978, was born in Stanislau, Austria, in 1904. His family emigrated to the United States and settled in Bayonne, New Jersey, in 1910, where his father did home construction and repair work. He attended the local schools, earned excellent grades, and was awarded a scholarship to Columbia University. His original career objective was in architecture, but his studies in economics soon led him in another direction.

Burns received his bachelor's and master's degrees from Columbia in 1925 and his doctorate in 1934. While there he met and studied with Wesley C. Mitchell, who was responsible for hiring him to work at the National Bureau of Economic Research in 1930 while he was still pursuing his graduate studies. That same year, Burns married Helen Bernstein. Earlier, in 1927, Burns had joined the economics faculty at Rutgers University; he remained there until 1944, when he was hired by Columbia. Among the outstanding economists he taught at Rutgers were Milton Friedman, Geoffrey H. Moore, and Julius Shiskin. In the stimulating intellectual environments at the National Bureau, Rutgers, and Columbia, Burns matured as an economist. During this period, he published numerous papers dealing with trends and cycles in economic activity. His best-known monographs were *Production Trends in the United States since 1870* (1934) and the monumental *Measuring Business Cycles*, coauthored with Wesley Mitchell (1947).

When Mitchell stepped down as director of research at the National Bureau in 1945, he turned over this post to Burns. During his tenure as research director, in addition to his supervision of a vast number of enormously significant research projects, Burns wrote a series of reports on the theme that theorizing on the basis of an incomplete set of facts posed a serious danger to the development of an economic science. This theme provided him with a vehicle to express his skepticism about the Keynesian revolution, which was based on the tacit assumption that a stable consumption function existed and the idea that intended investment was independent of the adjustment processes of the free market.

Burns continued at his post of director of research until 1953, when he went to Washington to chair the Council of Economic Advisers in President Dwight Eisenhower's first administration. He remained there until 1957, when he returned to his teaching duties at Columbia University. At that time, he also became president of the National Bureau.

In 1959 Burns became president of the American Economic Association. The theme of his presidential address, "Progress towards Economic Stability," was that a conjuncture of structural changes in the economy had modified the business cycle. More specifically, these changes tended to make recessions shorter and more moderate.

In 1969 government service once again brought him to Washington as counselor to the president, a cabinet-level rank. Burns was one of the first to join President Richard Nixon's White House staff in 1969. He was charged with general responsibility for policy development in domestic and economic affairs. Although the position appealed to him, he actually wanted the chairmanship of the Federal Reserve. In fact, the president had promised him this post. However, William McChesney Martin* had no intention of resigning until his full term was up. Burns once put it at the time, "Martin will be sitting in that chair right up to midnight, Hawaii time, of his last day in office." His forecast turned out to be accurate and he needed to wait more than a year, but in 1970 he achieved his dream of chairing the Federal Reserve board.

Burns's term as chairman of the Federal Reserve board started in the midst of a mild recession that began in late 1969. The economic policy of the new administration was called gradualism. The administration was anxious to rid the economy of persistent inflation, which had started in the mid–1960s. It wanted to slow economic growth gradually to undernourish the inflationary tendencies. (In the late 1980s, such a policy would be called "engineering a soft landing.") The situation of 1970 turned out to be a mild recession of a special type: an inflationary recession, which presented a dilemma. If the Fed pursued an expansionary monetary policy to deal with the recession, this would push up inflation. On the other hand, if it pursued a restrictive monetary policy to stop the inflation, it risked turning a mild recession into a deeper one. In his search for a solution to this dilemma, Burns stressed that the answer was to pursue a middle course between the "policy of extreme restraint followed in 1969 and the policies of aggressive ease pursued in some earlier years" (Burns 1978, p. 110). Growth in the money supply averaged about 5½ percent in 1970, quite high by historical standards; nonetheless, Burns did not think it was too high because a high precautionary demand for liquidity existed at the time.

In large part, this high demand for liquidity resulted from the announcement of the bankruptcy of the Penn Central Transportation Company in June 1970. The firm, one of the nation's largest businesses, had large amounts of maturing commercial paper that could not be renewed, and it was unable to get credit elsewhere. There was considerable concern that similar developments might beset other major issuers of commercial paper and also seriously affect securities in other markets. In this environment, the Fed acted swiftly to assure the nation's banks that the discount window would be made readily available to meet unusual borrowing demands.

The recession came to a close in late 1970, in part the result of the more stimulative monetary policy initiated by the Fed during the course of the downturn. In the early months of the recovery period, growth in the monetary aggregates remained high as a result of concern that rising interest rates might abort the expansion. By mid–1971, however, the Fed started to slow the growth in the money stock because of concern about the persistence of inflationary forces at work in the economy. Wholesale and consumer prices advanced about 5 percent on an annual basis in the first half of 1971, when wages and salaries were growing at roughly a 7 percent to 8 percent annual rate.

Burns at this point had a dramatic change of mind about a serious matter of economic policy. In the mid–1960s, he had written with considerable eloquence about the dangers inherent in wage and price controls (Burns 1965). However, in mid–1971, he began stressing that the economy was no longer working the way it had in the past and that it needed an income policy to speed the transition from rapid inflation to general price stability. At a meeting of the top Nixon advisers at Camp David in mid-August 1971, a decision was made to change economic policy in a number of ways. One of the major decisions was to impose an immediate ninety-day freeze on price and wage increases, followed by a period of more flexible wage and price controls.

One aspect of Burns's involvement with the wage-price control program deserves comment. When President Nixon set up the program, he named Burns to head the Committee on Interest and Dividends, which was supposed to hold down, among other things, interest rates. Any such effort, however, implies an expansion of the money supply. In testimony before the Congress in his role as chairman of the committee, there is no explicit reference to the possibility that his responsibilities in the post might conflict with his responsibilities as chairman of the Federal Reserve board.

The early effects of the new wage-price program were positive. The objective of the strategy was to bring the growth in consumer prices down to a 2 to 3 percent annual rate by the end of 1972. Growth in these prices was slightly above the upper end of the range in the second half of 1972. Later, however, matters did not work out so well.

A careful reading of the minutes of the Federal Open Market Committee (FOMC) for 1972 discloses that the group was still considerably concerned about the high level of unemployment during the cyclical expansion. When the recession began in late 1969, the nation's jobless rate was 3.5 percent. At the recession trough in November 1970, the unemployment rate was 5.9 percent. Nineteen months later, in June 1972, the rate was 5.7 percent, only 0.2 percentage points below its trough level. The minutes of the FOMC during 1972 make repeated reference to the need for further expansion of monetary growth in order to remedy this sluggishness in the labor markets.

There was, to be sure, sharp growth in the money supply during this period.

Some critics of Burns's performance as chairman of the Federal Reserve have argued that he engineered the sizable expansion of the money stock in order to ensure the victory of President Nixon in the fall 1972 election. A *Fortune* magazine article charged that the Fed's performance in 1972 "baffles, indeed stupefies, monetary historians. . . . At the end of the first quarter, the economy had substantially recovered from its 1970–71 doldrums. . . . Yet the money supply grew by 7.9% during calendar year 1972, appreciably faster than the 6.6% of 1971'' (Rose 1974). The article alleged that at one meeting in 1972, the dispute between Burns and the FOMC majority became tense. In frustration because of his inability to convince the committee of the need to hold down interest rates, Burns, it claimed, left the meeting in anger. An hour later, the story went, he returned and announced that he had talked to the White House. The committee took the hint: the White House was determined to keep rates from rising.

Burns responded to the article with a terse note to the editor: "The July issue of *Fortune* . . . purports to describe certain events during the meeting of the Federal Open Market Committee. There is not one grain of truth in this report.'' Andrew Brimmer,[*] a member of the FOMC at the time, agreed: "These assertions are false in both the general and the particular. When the article was in preparation the author spoke to me by telephone seeking confirmation of the reported event. I told him no such episode took place.'' *Fortune* replied that "some others who attended that FOMC meeting recollect it differently.'' It never revealed the names of its anonymous informants.

Burns's well-known letter to Senator William Proxmire (D, Wisconsin) of November 1973 discussed the experience of 1972–1973. It noted that according to data available as late as January 1973, the rate of growth of the narrowly defined money supply (M1) during 1972 was 7.2 percent, while the real gross national product (GNP) increased 7.7 percent. Thus, on the basis of the data available, M1 was growing at a rate well below the increase in the physical volume of overall production. Burns suggested that the sharp upsurge of the inflation rate in 1973 was due to a series of special shocks, including a worldwide boom landing on top of the boom in the United States, critical shortages of basic materials, the escalation of farm product prices as a result of crop failures in many countries in 1972, sharp increases in fuel prices, and the depreciation of the dollar, which raised the prices of imported goods. Nonetheless, he also acknowledged that in retrospect "monetary policy should have been a little less expensive in 1972. But a markedly more restrictive policy would have led to a still sharper rise in interest rates and risked a premature ending of the business expansion, without limiting to any significant degree (the 1973) upsurge of the price level'' (Burns 1973, pp. 6–7).

Burns's defense of the Fed was evaluated by Nobel laureate Milton Friedman, who had long been critical of the Fed's discretionary actions. In his own letter to Senator Proxmire, Friedman argued that economic theory and empirical evidence combine to establish the strong presumption that the acceleration of monetary growth was largely responsible for the acceleration of inflation.

The Federal Reserve accorded top priority to the battle against inflation in

1973 and into 1974. Consumer prices rose 6.2 percent from 1972 to 1973 and then 11 percent from 1973 to 1974. The objective of the Fed's monetary actions, at least until late in 1974, was to moderate the growth of the money supply in order to slow the expansion of total spending in the economy. A policy of this sort would help to abate inflationary forces. The narrowly defined money stock, which had grown at a 7.7 percent annual rate from the fourth quarter 1971 to the fourth quarter 1972, advanced at rates of 6.3 percent and 5.1 percent over comparable periods from 1972 to 1973 and 1973 to 1974.

The oil embargo in the fall of 1973 led to a doubling of oil prices between October 1973 and January 1974. This compounded the problem of rising energy prices, which had already doubled between January and October 1973. These developments helped shape the pattern of economic activity in 1974.

In response to the slowing of the growth of the monetary aggregates during this period, the growth of the nation's economy also slowed. After a sizzling 9.3 percent annual rate of advance in real GNP in the first quarter of 1973, growth for the remainder of the year averaged only 2 percent. Not only that, there were sizable declines in the growth of physical output in 1974. To be sure, the embargo on oil shipments to the United States by Arab nations and the sharp increases in oil prices established by the Organization of Petroleum Exporting Countries (OPEC) made an impact. So too did the movement to a freely floating exchange rate regime, which led to a decline in the foreign exchange value of the dollar. To this must also be added the termination of the wage-price control system in April 1974, although there is some disagreement among observers concerning the significance of decontrol with respect to price acceleration. This was a tumultuous era in the economic and political life of the nation.

Burns and his associates at the Fed were operating in uncharted waters. In 1974, real GNP fell over four consecutive quarters while the GNP price deflator was advancing at a double-digit rate. Up to that time, the nation had never experienced an inflationary recession of this sort. The sharp increases in prices were obviously disguising the significance of many of the real changes occurring in the economy. As late as August 1974, Burns was not sure that the nation was in a recession.

President Gerald Ford convened a summit conference on inflation in September 1974 to which he invited the nation's leading business, financial, and labor leaders and economists. He solicited their views on appropriate policies to deal with the problems confronting the nation. There was a lot of criticism of the Fed's policy of moderation in the growth of the monetary aggregates. Burns responded to his critics by stating that he realized the Fed was not winning any popularity contest. Nonetheless, he assured his audience, the Federal Reserve would persevere in pursuing policies that were necessary to curb rampant inflation (Burns 1978, pp. 181–84).

In October 1974 the Franklin National Bank, one of the largest commercial banks in the United States, was declared bankrupt. As a result, the Fed put aside its monetary targets for a while to prevent a financial panic. It opened its discount window wide and modified its regulations so that commercial banks could raise funds in the open market to lend to firms that were unable to renew maturing commercial paper. It also lent Franklin National over $2 billion, and while these loans were outstanding, it arranged a takeover by another bank to protect the interests of Franklin's depositors and customers.

The 1973–1975 recession was one of the sharpest downturns in the post–World War II period in the United States. Real GNP fell 5 percent, and industrial production plummeted 15 percent. The nation's jobless rate increased 4.4 percentage points to 9 percent. There was an $82 billion decline in real GNP from the peak in the fourth quarter 1973 to the first quarter 1975. A decline in final sales to consumers and businesses accounted for a portion of this large fall in real output, but a reduction in inventories was responsible for more than half of the decline. Stocks were being built up at a $25 billion rate at the peak, whereas at the trough they were being liquidated at a $20 billion rate. The $45 billion change accounted for more than half of the drop in total output.

Burns was well aware of the importance of the changes in inventories at the time. He later commented on these changes in a speech designed to provide perspective on the recession:

One of the unfortunate consequences of inflation is that it masks underlying economic realities. As early as the spring of 1973, a perceptible weakening could be detected in the trend of consumer buying in the country. The escalating pace of inflation fostered expectations of still higher prices and persistent shortages in the years ahead, so that intensive stockpiling of commodities continued. Inventories increased out of all proportion to actual or prospective sales. (Burns 1978, p. 207)

The sharp recession finally ended in March 1975. The Fed authorities were, of course, aware that significant declines in the rate of inflation usually accompany economic slowdowns or recessions. In fact, the inflation cycle peaked in the United States in September 1974. At that time, the six-month smoothed change in the consumer price index was rising at a 12.4 percent annual rate. (A six-month smoothed change is computed by calculating the ratio of the current month to the average of the twelve previous months and expressing that at an annual rate.) By June 1976 consumer prices were rising at a 4.9 percent annual rate. The inflation rate had dropped almost 8 percentage points over a twenty-one-month period.

June 1976 was, however, the cyclical low in the inflation cycle. No further progress was evident in the months that immediately followed. Moreover, inflation made a slight comeback during 1977. The basic inflation rate hovered about 6 percent during this period, reflecting the difference between increments to the hourly compensation of labor of about 8 percent and productivity increments of roughly 2 percent.

Burns's second four-year term as chairman of the Federal Reserve board ended on January 31, 1978. In early January, President Jimmy Carter told him that he would not be reappointed and that he had selected G. William Miller* as his successor. The president asked Burns to stay on as one of the Fed's seven governors, a term that would not expire until 1984. Upon reflection, Burns decided against it. He had no desire to leave his post as chairman of the Fed but was at odds with the administration. His top priority was to rid the economy of inflation, and there was considerable concern about this inside the administration. For example, the prime rate rose almost one and a half percentage points between December 1976 and December 1977. President Carter's chief economic advisers' main goals were speeding up economic growth and reducing unemployment. Burns's concern about inflation was considered to be a stumbling block to the achievement of these goals.

In testimony before the Senate Committee on Banking, Housing, and Urban Affairs in November 1977, he argued that a determined effort to blunt any rise in interest rates in 1977 would have required a sharp increase in the money supply. The expansion in the money stock would practically destroy any hope of containing inflation and would transform the central bank into an engine for inflation. This testimony turned out to be his last appearance before congressional committees as Federal Reserve chairman.

When Burns left his post at the Federal Reserve board in February 1978, the economy was in the thirty-fifth month of economic expansion, real GNP was growing at a 3.6 percent annual rate, the unemployment rate was 6.3 percent, and the smoothed growth in the CPI was 6.2 percent.

Arthur Broida, FOMC secretary in the 1970s, labels the period as "a wretched decade." It contained an unprecedented series of adverse shocks that policymakers, economists, and the general public could not control because nothing in the monetary history of the United States bore any resemblance to them.

In the Per Jacobsson Lecture to the International Monetary Fund in Belgrade in September 1979, Burns attempted to convey the difficulty of formulating effective policy. The title of his lecture was "The Anguish of Central Banking." He posed an important question: Why do central bankers allow inflation to continue when it is well known that every long-run inflation is sustained by excessive growth in the money supply? His answer conceded that the Federal Reserve had the power to stop inflation in its tracks. It could have fashioned a sufficiently restrictive monetary policy that would have put enough strains in financial and industrial markets that the price advances would be ended. This was not done mainly because of changes in philosophical and political currents that were transforming American life and culture; the Federal Reserve itself was caught up in these currents.

In the 1960s philosophical and political thinking in the United States tended to stress the need for the government to address the unfinished business of our society. In the innocence of the time, many thought that the public sector could be an effective agent for dealing with high unemployment, poor housing, inadequate education, poverty, environmental pollution, crime, health care systems, discrimination, and other parts of an unfinished agenda. Moreover, it could

tackle and solve such problems while the nation was engaged in military operations in Southeast Asia and attempting to transport men to the moon and back.
All of these objectives required extensive funding, but each time the government
moved to enlarge the flow of benefits, there was an implicit assumption that
monetary policy would accommodate the action. Similar suppositions accompanied inflationary pricing decisions and wage bargains of businesses and trade
unions. However, if monetary policy was developed that was seriously inconsistent with the upward pressures on prices, serious difficulties would occur in
the economy. The Federal Reserve would be frustrating the intent of the Congress, to which it was responsible.

To be sure, the Fed stepped hard on the monetary brakes in 1966, 1969, and
1974; however, the restrictive policies were not maintained long enough to end
the inflation. Burns called this the anguish of central banking in a modern
democracy. At the same time, the central bankers themselves are not totally free
from responsibility for the inflation. The Fed had some room for discretion in
the 1970s, but while it was testing its freedom to undernourish inflation, it was
under strong pressure from both the executive branch and the Congress to accommodate their wills. In this hostile environment, it had to allocate a lot of
energy to warding off legislation that could destroy any hope of ending inflation.

In this contest of will with the executive branch and the Congress, the Fed at
times may well have underestimated the discretion at its disposal. That is, it
may have committed errors in political judgment. Nevertheless, Burns believed
that errors in economic and financial judgment were in practice a far more
significant problem for the Fed during his term than political errors. In his
apologia, he confesses that these include errors in the evaluation of unemployment statistics: the Federal Reserve was slow to recognize the growing importance
of structural unemployment and at times pushed expansionary policies too far.

When changes occur rapidly, the possibilities for making errors are legion,
and rapid changes were occurring in banking and financial institutions in the
1960s and 1970s. These rapid changes, which persisted into the 1980s, made
their imprint on monetary theory, which itself has always been a highly controversial subject. The Federal Reserve was confronted with difficult questions
about the relative weight to be accorded to different measures of money and
interest rates in the short and long runs; about the most significant concept of
money for policy purposes; about the length and the regularity of the lags between
changes in money growth rates and movements in economic activity and prices;
about the likely changes in the velocity of circulation resulting from institutional
innovations and cyclical fluctuations; and so on. Furthermore, there are other
problems of a fundamental character, such as potential conflicts between domestic
and international objectives, about the correct response to unique events not
treated by theory, and about the current relevance of any theory developed on
the basis of experience to an environment in which behavioral patterns are
continually evolving.

In Burns's view, the potential of central bankers to make mistakes becomes larger in an inflationary environment. High and rising interest rates are usually viewed as a restraining force on economic expansion. But when nominal interest rates contain an inflation premium, as long as the nominal rate stays below or only slightly above the inflation rate, it will probably have perverse effects on the economy. Specifically, it will increase the costs of doing business, but it will do little or nothing to restrain overall spending. Inflation tends to take the sting out of rising interest rates.

In "The Anguish of Central Banking," but also in much greater detail in *The Ongoing Revolution in American Banking* (1988), Burns stressed that changes in financial practices that began in the 1960s culminated in an explosion of financial innovations in the 1970s and 1980s. The innovations raised many questions for policymakers, not the least of which related to the meaning of particular growth rates of the monetary aggregates.

Regulatory activities and the development of computer technology were in part responsible for many of these changes. Sharply rising market interest rates also provided a powerful incentive for such innovations. These rising rates stimulated financial institutions and their customers to modify their procedures. Commercial banks reacted to rising rates by economizing on noninterest-bearing reserves; their customers reacted by reducing their noninterest-bearing demand deposits. Furthermore, banks and large corporations tapped into new sources of funds in the Eurodollar and domestic commercial paper markets. The potential of the federal funds market and the market for negotiable certificates of deposit were exploited. Savings banks, savings and loan associations, credit unions, and money market mutual funds began providing services on which they paid interest. Moreover, banks met this competition for transactions balances by providing to large depositors special services that reduced the average level of balances they carried and by employing ingenious means to pay interest on balances held in large part for transactions purposes.

The environment, which is of principal concern to the monetary policymaker, was profoundly influenced by these changes. In the 1950s and early 1960s, monetary restraint was channeled mainly by reductions in credit availability. In the 1970s, rising interest rates were the main channel of restraint. Thus, higher levels of interest rates were required to achieve a given level of restraint, quite separate from the effects of inflation premiums. But it was not always clear how much higher the rates needed to go to achieve the desired effect. Similarly, the relationship of changes in M1 (currency plus demand deposits) to transactions balances was reasonably well understood in the 1950s and early 1960s. However, with the development of new alternatives to bank demand deposits in the 1970s, a lower rate of growth in M1 was needed to achieve a given degree of restraint, but how much lower was not clear.

The technical tasks associated with the formulation of appropriate monetary responses are formidable. Some would argue they are insurmountable, and therefore such policy might be better conducted by using some mechanical rule relating to the growth of monetary aggregates. Burns always resisted this argument. His

position was that discretionary economic policy has surely at times been mistaken, but more often it was reasonably successful. He contended that the dis-
appearance of business depressions, which a couple of generations ago brought
mass unemployment for workers and mass bankruptcies for businesses, was
largely due to the stabilization policies of the post–World War II era.

On the prospects for future containment of inflation, Burns argued in his 1979
Per Jacobsson Lecture that that would require the development of new currents
in the political landscape, which would facilitate the difficult adjustments required
to perform the task. In fact, new currents were developing in the political environment in the United States as the 1970s came to a close.

Burns was seventy-four years old when he stepped down as chairman of the
Federal Reserve Board. He accepted a position as Distinguished Scholar in
Residence at the prestigious American Enterprise Institute, a Washington think
tank, and took on part-time teaching duties at Georgetown University. Moreover,
he continued lecturing on economic policy at other universities across the country.

In 1978 the American Enterprise Institute published his *Reflections of an
Economic Policymaker*, which consisted of speeches and congressional statements from 1969 to 1978. The critical reviews from both sides of the political
aisle were excellent.

For the first year and a half after he was removed as chairman of the Fed,
Burns maintained a discreet silence on most matters of economic policy. To be
sure, one could read between the lines in some of his speeches his growing
impatience with the lack of a firm policy to deal with quickening inflation. But
by mid–1979, he began once again to play a more active role in the public policy
debate. He joined the Committee to Fight Inflation, a bipartisan group in makeup,
whose membership included former secretaries of the Treasury, former chairmen
of the Federal Reserve board, a former chairman of the Council of Economic
Advisers, and a former under secretary of the Treasury.

Burns did not, however, forsake partisan political activity. During the presidential campaign of 1980, he served as chairman of Ronald Reagan's Task
Force on International Monetary Policy. Martin Anderson, who served on President Reagan's staff as chief domestic and economic policy adviser, writes that
there were eight people the president relied on most for economic advice: They
were Milton Friedman, Alan Greenspan,* William Simon, Paul McCracken,
George Shultz, Murray Weidenbaum, Caspar Weinberger, and Arthur Burns.

Anderson tells us that Burns strongly supported the suggestion to Reagan in
1979 that he make spending control and systematic tax cutting the centerpieces
of this economic program. Burns also endorsed the goal of a balanced budget,
plans for regulatory reform, and the development of a sound, predictable monetary policy. Burns was, of course, well aware of the need for close scrutiny of
the nuts and bolts of any program with such far-reaching implications. In 1981,
he cautioned, "Skepticism concerning the underpinnings of the Reagan program
is not confined to traditional liberals. It is also felt to some degree by economists,
businessmen, and others who are entirely sympathetic to the President's philos-

ophy that the restoration of a healthy economic environment requires much more reliance on the free market and less on government.'' In his view, ''the Reagan economic program is better viewed as an evolving plan for restoring the nation's economic health than as a static plan that warrants minute critical dissection'' (Burns 1981).

In 1981 President Reagan selected Arthur Burns as his ambassador to the Federal Republic of Germany. Burns hesitated before accepting the assignment. Although his health was good, he was already seventy-seven years of age. Furthermore, his professional career had been totally focused on economic and financial matters, and he was still engaged in the national debate on economic policy. On the other hand, a number of business, financial, and political leaders in the Federal Republic were acquaintances. Helmut Schmidt, then chancellor of the republic, was an old friend. The vision of starting out in a new career that might contribute to the preservation of peace and freedom was also appealing. Burns also felt that as a practicing Jew, ''there might be a certain moral fitness, perhaps a step toward further reconciliation, in becoming ambassador to a country that had perpetrated during the Nazi era unspeakable crimes against [his] co-religionists, including members of [his] own family.'' Burns served as ambassador from 1981 to 1985. During this period, there was a change of government in the Federal Republic, and Schmidt was replaced as chancellor. Nonetheless, he retained high respect with the new chancellor, Helmut Kohl, and other members of the government. Serious students of activities in Bonn on this side of the Atlantic and in Europe agreed that he did an outstanding job. In 1986 Burns delivered a series of lectures to the Council on Foreign Relations in New York, which were published under the title *The United States and Germany: A Vital Partnership*.

Burns, a hard worker all his life, also has had a rewarding family life. He has two sons: David, a lawyer, and Joseph, an economist. The family spent many summers at their farm in Vermont, where Burns built a separate cabin for use as a study. Geoffrey Moore and Milton Friedman were among the professional colleagues and friends who lived nearby.

After his return from Germany, he resumed his post at the American Enterprise Institute. He began work on a book dealing with the revolutionary changes that had taken place in American banking from the 1950s to the 1980s. He surely enjoyed the intellectual environment at the institute and the lively exchanges with colleagues and friends such as Gottfried Haberler, William Fellner, Herbert Stein, Thomas Johnson, and others. He agreed to give a series of lectures at the bicentennial celebration at the University of Pittsburgh in March 1987. These lectures were to form the basis for the book, *The Ongoing Revolution in American Banking*. In the course of the meetings at Pittsburgh, he became ill. In his last public statement on March 18, 1987, Burns shared his thoughts with his audience on a problem of worldwide dimension—the problem of apathy or indifference— indifference to violation of human life, human dignity, and human freedom. He concluded with this advice:

The moral and religious instruction that we derive from our parents is fundamental. Over two thousand years ago the Hebrew prophet Micah reminded the Israelites that all God required of them was "to do justly, and to love mercy, and to walk humbly with thy God." Notice that Micah did not speak of preaching about justice, or expecting justice from others; he spoke of *doing* justly; in other words, every one of us must act justly towards others. Notice again that Micah spoke of "loving mercy"—not just being merciful, compassionate, generous. . . . Notice finally that Micah counselled that we walk humbly with God. And by this he meant that we must avoid arrogance, that we must seek and practice tolerance, that we need to take a deliberately equitable attitude toward all faiths, all creeds, all peoples and nations.

Arthur Burns died on June 26, 1987.

BIBLIOGRAPHY

Anderson, Martin. 1988. *Revolution*. New York: Harcourt Brace Jovanovich.

Burns, Arthur F. 1934. *Production Trends in the United States since 1870*. Washington, D.C.: National Bureau of Economic Research.

———. 1954. *The Frontiers of Economic Knowledge*. Washington, D.C.: National Bureau of Economic Research.

———. 1965. "Wages and Prices by Guideline." *Harvard Business Review*.

———. 1969. *The Business Cycle in a Changing World*. Washington, D.C.: National Bureau of Economic Research.

———. 1973. "The Role of the Money Supply in the Conduct of Monetary Policy." *Federal Reserve Bank of Dallas Business Review* (December).

———. 1978. *Reflections of an Economic Policymaker*. Washington, D.C.: American Enterprise Institute.

———. 1981. *The Reagan Economic Program*. Washington, D.C.: American Enterprise Institute.

———. 1986. *The United States and Germany: A Vital Partnership*. Washington, D.C.: Council on Foreign Relations.

———. 1988. *The Ongoing Revolution in American Banking*. Washington, D.C.: American Enterprise Institute.

———, and Mitchell, Wesley C. 1947. *Measuring Business Cycles*. Washington, D.C.: National Bureau of Economic Research.

Rose, Sanford. 1974. "The Agony of the Federal Reserve." *Fortune* (July).

MILO D. CAMPBELL (1851–1923)

Jean-Claude Leon

Milo D. Campbell, who served as a governor of the Federal Reserve for but two weeks from January to February 1923, was born in Coldwater, Michigan, on October 23, 1851. He graduated from Michigan State University when he was twenty-one years old. Admitted to the Michigan bar in 1877, he practiced law in the early years of his professional life in Coldwater County and elsewhere in Michigan. He subsequently gave up the practice of the law to enter politics and public service.

He held various public offices. He was superintendent of schools of his home county for two years and later county school examiner for four years. He was a member of the Michigan legislature from 1885 to 1895 and later served as secretary to Governor Lute for four years. Subsequently he was a member of the state railway board for two years and state insurance commissioner for four years. In the latter capacity, he was credited with accomplishing a great reduction in the insurance rates in the state of Michigan and in forcing fraudulent concerns out of business.

Following his service in this position, he was appointed chairman of the State Tax Commission, which formulated legislation that increased the taxable property base of the state of Michigan by $300 million. The entire system of railroad taxation was reorganized in this period. Campbell served also as president of the State Board of Prisons and Reformatory Institutions. He had been mayor of his home town and was united marshal of the Eastern District of Michigan under the Taft administration. He had been a candidate for a position on the U.S. Interstate Commerce Commission and was the defeated Republican candidate for governor in his state in the 1920 campaign.

During all of his various activities, his chief interest was farming and legislation dealing with agriculture. He championed the cause of the farmers, as the title of a pamphlet he published in 1888, *The Evils of Free Trade*, indicates. From 1920 until his death on March 23, 1923, Campbell was president of the National Milk Producers' Association and was also prominent in other farmers' organizations. He was especially involved in developing programs of cooperative business organizations among farmers. He was an authority on agricultural matters related to the scientific operation of the modern farm as advanced by the Department of Agriculture. He was considered an expert in improvement of soils and all the arts of agriculture, horticulture, and kindred subjects. Campbell was a working farmer all his life; he personally managed his two productive and model farms on the outskirts of Coldwater.

He had become a national figure because of his activities on behalf of farmers, and President Warren Harding appointed him the "dirt farmer" member of the Federal Reserve Board in January 1923, a designation that raised some eyebrows in Washington. The *New York Times* sarcastically commented, "With all due respect, management of model farms end of a milk producers' association is not necessarily preparatory for practical banking." In fact, this constituted less an attack on Campbell than on the newly created position on the board. Campbell was appointed after the farm block had succeeded in getting the Federal Reserve Board enlarged in 1922. The original bill passed by Congress specified that a representative of the agricultural interests be named, but this was changed after President Harding had agreed that if the number of members of the board were increased, he would select a man familiar with the needs of the farmers.

"The Dirt-Farmer Banker Arrives" wrote the *Literary Digest* on January 27, 1923. "The hand that guides the plow is in a fair way to be the hand that guides our national finances." But in fairness to Campbell's background and experience, the *Literary Digest* added, "Americans of clear mind and sound business instincts are usually quick to master the problems of public offices of this kind when they are faced with their actual responsibilities."

Campbell's nomination came along with that of Daniel R. Crissinger[*] as governor of the Federal Reserve Board. President Harding had refused to renominate W. P. G. Harding[*] as governor. Faced with high inflation pressures in 1919, W. P. G. Harding and his colleagues at the board had increased the official bank rate in order to combat credit inflation, which threatened financial disaster. President Harding then declared publicly that the reserve board's "policy of drastic deflation" was "mistaken." Faced with declining prices in the early 1920s, the farmers in the Midwest were particularly affected. The Crissinger nomination was seen as the culmination of a long fight waged against the reappointment of former governor Harding whose deflation policy was attacked by farmer's organizations and southern and western senators.

As a member of the board, Campbell was to give representation to the West. It was argued that for good or evil, the Midwest held the balance of political power in the United States and that this had to be recognized in U.S. economic institutions. While the course of the reserve board would not be changed because of the presence of a "dirt farmer," at least the board would understand the opinions of the agricultural interests and perhaps the farmers would also understand the reasons behind the action of the board. It was believed that Campbell's appointment would be a gain for all concerned.

Campbell, however, did not have the opportunity to champion the cause of the farmers. He died of a cerebral hemorrhage while playing golf near Washington, D.C., only two weeks after being appointed to the Federal Reserve Board. He had attended a board meeting on the morning of his death, at which time "he showed his usual vitality and great interest in the deliberations of the board."

Campbell was described in the resolutions adopted after his death by the Branch County Bar Association of Clearwater as a man who began life poor and without means or opportunities. Through force of his energy, industry and application, he attained positions of unusual prominence and distinction. At the time of his death he had reached national importance.

BIBLIOGRAPHY

Campbell, Milo D. 1888. *The Evils of Free Trade, Effect upon Michigan Farmers and Laboring Men, Viewed in the Light of Facts and Statistics.* N.p.
"The Dirt-Farmer Banker Arrives." 1923. *Literary Digest*, January 27, p. 16.
Literary Digest. 1923. January 27, p. 16.
"The Reserve Board Nominations." 1923. *New York Times*, January 13.

LAWRENCE CLAYTON (1891–1949)

Philip Lane

Although Lawrence Clayton was a member of the Board of Governors for only a little less than three years (February 1947-December 1949), this short time period should not diminish his contributions to the Federal Reserve system.

Born in 1891 in Salt Lake City, Lawrence Clayton attended the University of Michigan (1911–1913), and the University of Utah (summer 1913). He received his A.B. in 1914 from Stanford University and was elected to membership in Phi Beta Kappa. Clayton continued his formal education at Harvard Law School, where he received his LL.B. In 1917, Clayton's career was placed on hold while he spent the next two years serving with the U.S. Army as an officer with the 102d Field Artillery. He advanced to the rank of major by 1919. After World War I, Clayton continued his association with the army as a reservist. By 1939 he had been promoted to the rank of colonel and continued on inactive duty.

Clayton returned to his native Utah, where he began his career in banking and finance. He married Ruth Dunn, and together they had three children: Sybella, Lawrence, and Barbara. His first job was with Clayton Investment Company of Salt Lake City as a manager and vice-president. He joined the First National Bank of Ogden, Utah, in 1924. Clayton rose through the ranks, becoming a vice-president in 1931. In 1934 he left First National Bank to begin his association with the Federal Reserve as the assistant to the chairman of the Board of Governors.

While it is difficult to document the exact impact of Clayton's role on Fed policy or other areas in his position as the assistant to the chairman, Marriner Eccles[*] (chairman, 1934–1951) recruited Clayton to join him in Washington. One biography of Eccles relates the role Clayton played as an adviser and a trusted friend. This work, by Sidney Hyman, cites two cases of Clayton's role as adviser to Eccles. First, Eccles relied on Clayton and one other adviser for guidance when working on the Banking Act of 1935. Two, before the invasion of Poland by the Germans, Eccles met with President Roosevelt to discuss and evaluate alternatives; the meeting was less than productive. Clayton provided Eccles with a humorous perspective to this incident. Clayton's role was important for the board and monetary policy for he served during two difficult times: the Great Depression and World War II.

He left the Federal Reserve in 1945 after eleven years of service and moved back to the private sector, this time in Boston. He served for two years as president of Clayton Securities Company. His home was now North Scituate, a suburb south of Boston, where he was a member of the Hatherly Country Club as well as the Algonquin Club.

In February 1947 Clayton was appointed a member of the Board of Governors from the First District. During his term of office, he represented the board in statements to Congress twice. One time dealt with a bill pending that would have had the effect of requiring all national banks in a territory to join the Federal Reserve within ninety days after the territory became a state. Hawaii was the state that would have to adjust if the bill was passed. The second time was before the Senate Committee on Labor and Public Welfare.

Clayton represented the board before trade associations and other groups. He addressed the American Bankers Association in January 1948 with a talk on the bank supervisory viewpoint. In April 1949 the Eastern Regional Clinic of the Mortgage Bankers Association, meeting in New York City, heard an address that examined some aspects of the mortgage interest rate structure. He spoke to the Virginia Bankers Conference on the relationship of the Federal Reserve to the dual banking system.

Clayton's record as a member of the board is similar to his record as the assistant to the chairman: he worked behind the scenes to effect change in monetary policy and other Federal Reserve policies. He was the good soldier, who rose to be an officer.

Lawrence Clayton died on December 4, 1949, at the age of fifty-eight of a heart ailment. He had played golf the previous day at Burning Tree Country Club in Washington, D.C.

BIBLIOGRAPHY

Hyman, Sidney. 1976. *Marriner S. Eccles.* Stanford: Stanford University.
Who Was Who in America, 1943–1950. Chicago: Marquis Who's Who.

PHILIP E. COLDWELL (1922–   )

David E. R. Gay and Thomas R. McKinnon

Philip E. Coldwell, a Democrat, was nominated by President Gerald Ford to complete the balance of Andrew F. Brimmer's[*] fourteen-year term, which began in 1966. Coldwell was the first Federal Reserve bank president appointed to the Board of Governors since 1927, when President Calvin Coolidge selected Roy A. Young[*] (1927–1930) from the Federal Reserve Bank of Minneapolis.

Born in Champaign, Illinois, on July 20, 1922, the son of Montgomery Ian and Donna Clare Rose Coldwell, Philip Coldwell married Norma Elaine Abels on June 1, 1942. They had two sons. Coldwell received his B.A. and M.S. degrees from the University of Illinois in 1946 and 1947, respectively. He received his doctorate in economics from the University of Wisconsin, Madison, in 1952. He was an instructor at the University of Illinois, 1946–1947; an associate professor at Southwestern Louisiana Institute, Lafayette, 1947–1948, and associate professor, 1950–1951; and an instructor at Montana State University, 1949–1950. Coldwell joined the Federal Reserve system in 1951 and remained until 1980. He was an associate economist at the Federal Reserve Bank of Kansas City (1951–1952) and moved to the Federal Reserve Bank of Dallas in 1952. He provided leadership as the director of research beginning in 1954, vice-president in 1960, first vice-president in 1962, and president from 1968 until his appointment to the Board of Governors in 1974.

Coldwell's civic interests have been varied. Among others, he was a director of the Dallas Council on World Affairs, a public councilor of the Texas A&M Research Foundation, a trustee of the Southwestern Legal Foundation at Southern Methodist University, a trustee of Austin College, an adjunct professor with the University of Texas at Dallas, and a director of the Diamond Shamrock Corporation. He also was a founder and first president of the Dallas Economists Club. He served as a lecturer in the Southwestern School of Banking.

At the time of his nomination and subsequent confirmation as the fifty-first member of the Board of Governors, there was speculation about his future role. Popular accounts indicated that chairman Arthur F. Burns[*] backed his nomination and was pleased about the appointment. But his public positions were inconsistent with the board's restrictive monetary policy. He was critical of budget deficits, citing them as a cause of inflation. In April before he was nominated, he indicated that fears of bank holding expansion were sometimes unjustified. His speech was well received by bank holding companies.

At confirmation, Coldwell was introduced and warmly endorsed by Senator John G. Tower (R, Texas), and his nomination also was endorsed by Senator Lloyd Bentsen (D, Texas). As a research economist at the Dallas Fed, he initially worked in industrial economics and later monetary policy and financial markets. As president of the Dallas Fed (1968–1974) he was a member of the Federal Open Market Committee. Senator William Proxmire (D, Wisconsin) recognized that the Fed was independent of the executive but was troubled by Coldwell's response that it was somehow independent of Congress. Proxmire pressed for an efficiency audit by the General Accounting Office (GAO), in addition to the regular financial audit. Coldwell's response—that the Fed should be independent on monetary policy— was quickly challenged by Senator Proxmire. He argued that there was no constitutional basis for any Fed independence from Congress. He argued that the GAO, as an agent of Congress, had every right to conduct an efficiency audit of another agent of Congress, the Federal Reserve board. Coldwell favored adjusting upward Regulation Q but not its abolition. In further discussion about bank management and solvency, Coldwell supported the role of the Fed as a lender of the last resort when a bank is illiquid, not insolvent.

Both senators were pleased with the Fed's interest in housing, particularly under chairman Burns, and its participation by purchasing Government National Mortgage Association (GNMA) mortgages. After fifty minutes of questioning, the hearing ended with the nominee's being supported by both senators.

Coldwell's efforts on the board, as reflected in his speeches, included a policy debate on targets versus indicators of monetary policy. In 1975 he favored a policy of action and reaction to short-run economic considerations involving interest rates. Due to the variability of monetary aggregates, the emphasis on long-run considerations, and the neutered role for the board with a monetary rule, he was critical of monetarists and skeptical of their ability to implement a long-run policy. He claimed that monetarists ignored foreign balances that affect the money supply. Actually he focused on changes in the money supply or changes in interest rates as policy targets without reference to the indicators of a successful monetary policy.

By late 1975, he focused on inflation in his public speeches. He asserted that inflation was the central policy issue of the government since it distorted the economy and led to recession and unemployment. Inflation was caused by deficits aimed primarily at help to the poor and unemployed. Unexpectedly it also decreased the incentives to work. International markets, with flexible exchange rates, contributed to inflation, he argued. Also higher prices for imported oil, along with higher grain prices, were "inflationary." Union power led to higher wages; such cost-push factors were not only a cause of inflation but also a result of inflation. Business inefficiencies and "overregulation" led to additional inflationary pressure, he argued.

On the bicentennial of the American Revolution, Coldwell characterized the previous 200 years as being typically credit shy but with overspending by government and having an imbalance between credit supply and demand. Credit also was attracted from abroad. He lamented that lack of credit slowed the growth of the nation. His remarks may have reflected the sentiment of the time. Clearly more investment would have yielded a higher level of growth but such arguments ignore the rationing function of prices, which keep one from being credit shy or eliminating imbalances in markets. The problems that he identified were largely price dependent also. His explanation of the founding of the Fed was that it was due to "inelasticity of the currency, inflexibility of its supply, and the mismatched location of available credit relative to demands." Deficits led to increases in the money supply and thus caused inflation. He overlooked any possible role that the Fed played in inducing or prolonging the Great Depression. His speech had no analysis of the implications of the nation's moving from a gold standard to arbitrary changes in the money supply, risk spreading through national branch banking such as Canada's free banking and the absence of bank panic during the Great Depression, or that Americans have always had interdependent markets. Instead, reliance on foreign markets was alleged to be detrimental.

Coldwell in 1987 forcefully argued for required membership in the Federal Reserve system. In effect, he argued that monetary policy was not just for members but for the general public good. Fearing private competition, the Fed intended to keep private firms from dominating services being provided by the Fed. By its activities in currency and coin distribution, check collection, transfer of funds, and transfer of U.S. government securities, the Fed implements mechanisms for payments. By pricing some of the Fed's services, it can provide basic services nationally, with some cross-subsidies. He fully intended to have the Fed price some of its services "as long as we do not allow private concentrations to be substituted for the Federal Reserve." Seeking hegemony, or monopoly, he favored continued domination by the Fed.

In the area of monetary and fiscal policy, Coldwell favored fighting inflation with spending cuts. Monetary policy should not be tied to a growth rule. The government keeps aggregate supply reduced through regulations that maintain higher costs such as minimum wages, delayed impact of excessive environmental impediments, and the cost of reporting and monitoring compliance for OSHA, Equal Credit Opportunity, and so forth. Inflation has to be fought (as it increased from 6 to 7 percent) by the breaking of inflationary expectations.

Policy options, Coldwell believed, ruled out mandatory wage and price controls as ineffective and distortive, but voluntary wage and price controls may help, he argued. The more fundamental problem was an inadequate savings rate due to a negative real rate of interest (without reference to his preference to focus on interest rates in monetary policy). With larger investment tax write-offs and higher capital gains tax credits, the savings rate could increase. Tariff barriers would be counterproductive also. Instead he favored negotiating entry for U.S. products while keeping its own market free and open.

In other housekeeping matters, Coldwell testified for a three-year or five-year waiting period before releasing the Federal Open Market Committee minutes. He spoke in favor of the Fed chairman's four-year term being appointed a year after the U.S. president took office but the maintaining of continuity with the vice-chairman's term. An increased number of directors at Federal Reserve banks also would be acceptable. In 1979 he testified regarding the problems and limitations of House resolution 2364 and its sunset provisions.

Coldwell's public speeches (1975b, 1979a, 1979b) frequently reflected an understanding of the political processes without the analysis exemplified by public choice. He referred to individuals as the forces that could shape aggregate magnitudes without his inquiring about incentives to do that. The different incentives and returns from free riding in a large or small group were ignored. In 1979 he discussed a series of issues, primarily to congressional committees and subcommittees, on monetary control, Fed membership, equity in reserves, and pricing of Fed services. He learned that it is easier to block than to propose legislation. New legislation had a political dimension that he did not recognize. Compromise was a necessity. Also, new initiatives must be approved by those who oppose the proposals. Finally, each participant will favor short-run self-interest.

In one of his last speeches, Coldwell applauded the monetary reforms illustrated by the one-dollar coin and the two-dollar bill. As many others did, he argued that the potential savings in production as well as efficiency of use meant that their usage should be encouraged. He predicted that by early 1980, the supply of one-dollar coins would be sufficient to quit printing one-dollar bills.

In addition to his monetary policy duties, Coldwell concentrated on three other areas. First, he was chairman of the board's Committee on Reserve Bank activities, where helped to develop budget measurements and personnel estimates. From 1974 to 1980, there was an almost 15 percent decrease in Fed personnel. He argued that this led to pricing of Fed services, as requested by Congress, and permitted the reallocation of resources into regulatory efforts. Second, he served on various committees to assess regulatory effects and the reformulation of rules for compliance with Congress. Finally, his interest in international aspects of monetary policy led to his representing the board at meetings of the Western Hemisphere Governors Conference and sometimes to the Bank for International Settlements.

BIBLIOGRAPHY

American Banker. 1974. September 27.

Coldwell, Philip E. 1975a. "Have We Learned from Our Mistakes?" Spring semester seminar, Rice University, March 24.

————. 1975b. "Public and Private Responsibilities for Economic Stability." Texas Rose Festival Distinguished Guest luncheon, October 17.

————. 1975c. "The Struggle for Economic Stability: A Bicentennial Opportunity." Lamar University Bicentennial Distinguished Lecture series, December 7.

————. 1977. "The Supply and Cost of Money—As Guides to Monetary Policy." Twenty-sixth Annual UCLA Business Forecasting Conference, December 8.

————. 1978a. "Statement" before U.S. Congress, House, Committee on Banking, Finance, and Urban Affairs, July 31.

————. 1978b. "Are We Really Serious about Fighting Inflation?" Conference on Economic Development, Troy, Michigan, October 19.

————. 1979a. "The Economy and Banking in 1979." Atlanta Chapter of the Bank Administration Institute, Atlanta, February 15.

————. 1979b. "The Ball Is in Your Court." ABA's Senior Correspondent Banking Forum, Atlanta, March 29.

————. 1989. "The Fed's Role in Defining the Payments System." Bank Administration Institute conference, New Orleans, September 13.

U.S. Congress. Senate. Committee on Banking, Housing, and Urban Affairs. 1974. *Nomination of Philip E. Coldwell. Hearing.* 93d Cong., 2d sess., October 8, pp. 1–14.

Wall Street Journal. 1974. September 27.

Who's Who in America, 1966–1967. Chicago: Marquis Who's Who.

DANIEL RICHARD CRISSINGER
(1860–1942)

James W. Schmotter

In March 1923 Benjamin Strong, the powerful governor of the New York Federal Reserve Bank, expressed outrage about the Federal Reserve Board's dissolution of the committee of governors of the system's individual banks that had been meeting regularly since the year before. This action, he declared, constituted "actual management" of the banks' activities "by a political body." Strong's comment reflected the ongoing tension between professional bankers and political appointees over the direction of the Federal Reserve Board's policies in the 1920s, a tension that is perhaps best exemplified in the career of the man who on January 12, 1923, had become its governor, Daniel Richard "Dick" Crissinger of Marion, Ohio.

Neither contemporary observers nor later historians have been kind to Crissinger. Both judged his initial appointment to the Federal Reserve Board as comptroller of the currency and his later elevation to its governorship as some of the worst of the many embarrassing political patronage appointments that Warren G. Harding made after his arrival in the White House in 1921. The journalist and historian Samuel Hopkins Adams commented that "friendship and the fact that they used to steal melons together aside, there had been no discernible reason for the appointment of neighbor Daniel R. Crissinger to be Comptroller of the Currency," and went on to blame the excesses of the bull market of the late 1920s on Crissinger's ineptitude. Strong's biographer, the economist Lester V. Chandler, observed, "The most charitable thing that can be said about President Harding's appointments to the board is that they were unsuitable." This especially held for Crissinger, whom Chandler contended "knew almost nothing of economics and finance, learned little, was incompetent as an administrator and ineffectual in personal relationships." Unlike others of Harding's weekly poker circle, Crissinger was never charged with any crimes while in office, and evidence suggests that he approached his duties on the board with seriousness. But the lasting impression that remains is of a personal friend of the president elevated to positions above his intellectual capacity.

Daniel R. Crissinger was born on December 10, 1860, in Tully Township, outside Marion, Ohio. His father was a farmer and keeper of a rural store and sawmill in the hamlet of Caledonia, where Crissinger grew up and did indeed engage in youthful pranks such as stealing watermelons with his close boyhood friend Warren G. Harding. Later observers noted that he might have remained a farmer or manual laborer had not an accident in his father's sawmill crippled one of his hands, which turned him toward more bookish pursuits. He was educated in a one-room rural school and at Buchtel College (later the University of Akron), from which he graduated in 1885. After reading law with Judge William Z. Davis at the University of Cincinnati, he was admitted to the Ohio bar the next year.

The ambitious young Crissinger returned to Marion determined to make his mark and soon did. By 1888 he had developed a successful law practice and had been elected prosecuting attorney; later he served three terms as city solicitor. At the same time, he was acquiring farmland and developing a successful live-stock breeding business. In 1898 he became attorney for the Marion Steam Shovel Company, the city's most prominent business, and a nationwide leader in the construction equipment industry. Even before his college graduation, he had married Ella Frances Scranton of Concord, Michigan, and was the father of two daughters, Donna Ruth and Beatrice Elizabeth.

Crissinger's early career was the model of the up-and-coming young man of the late nineteenth-century American heartland, and in that regard it paralleled the rise of his townsman Warren Harding, who lived only a block away and with whom he had remained a close friend. By the 1890s Harding was a successful local journalist, the owner-editor of the *Marion Star*. He and Crissinger were active fellow members of the Elks and Masons, served on many local boards together, and were frequent poker and billiards companions. Both also had political ambitions, and it was only here that their paths diverged. Unlike Harding, Crissinger was a Democrat, and, unlike the future president, he seemed unable to attain elective office outside the city of Marion. While Harding was winning a seat in the U.S. Senate, Crissinger was twice running unsuccessfully for Congress. These results, as well as his friendship with Harding, were no doubt factors in his switching of party affiliation after 1910.

Not surprisingly, Crissinger was an enthusiastic supporter of Harding's 1920 presidential bid, organizing a Make Marion Unanimous for Harding committee, a bipartisan Harding for President club, and ceremonies on Notification Day that brought 150,000 visitors to the small Ohio city. (He warned that any restaurant caught overcharging would be shut down.) For this loyalty as well as his longtime friendship, Harding rewarded him with the appointment of comptroller of the currency. Public eyebrows were naturally raised, for although Crissinger was a successful businessman within the admittedly limited sphere of Marion County, Ohio, his only banking experience had been a short stint as president of one of the local banks. Nonetheless, even his critics came to admit that he performed capably as comptroller, extending branch banking within cities and seeking to include more state banks in the national banking system.

His elevation in early 1923 from the seat he held on the Federal Reserve Board as comptroller to its governorship caused considerably more controversy. Secretary of the Treasury Andrew W. Mellon strongly opposed the appointment and counseled the president against it, but Harding was determined, for political as well as personal reasons. The press generally viewed Crissinger's promotion as a triumph for the rural political and economic interests that favored a policy of easy and expanding credit. Beyond representing the environment from which both Harding and Crissinger had sprung, agricultural interests were an important part of the Republican political coalition of the day. Crissinger's appointment was, in fact, widely praised in most of the nation's press save that of the industrial Northeast. *Literary Digest* called him a ''Dirt Farmer'' and able representative of the West. Other observers expressed confidence that the solid, small-town American values he had learned in Marion were more than adequate compensation for his lack of direct banking experience. A *Current Opinion* article, ''Crissinger: A Graduate of the Little Red School House,'' declared, ''He has a natural, shrewd intelligence as a foundation and, to build on this, a well-educated trained mind.'' To those who challenged the new governor's lack of experience, the author pointed out that his predecessor, W. P. G. Harding[*] (no relation to the president), had been only a bank president in Birmingham, Alabama, a city not much larger than Marion. Further, Crissinger, as attorney for Marion Steam Shovel, had direct knowledge about business conditions throughout the United States, for ''Marion shovels are almost as universally used as cotton gins and harvester machines.''

Those on the nation's farms and in regional banks who looked to Crissinger for support in providing easier credit through lower interest rates were not disappointed. Throughout his tenure as governor, he gave consistent advocacy to this position and so became the spokesman for one side in the most debated monetary question of the day: the role of the Federal Reserve in controlling credit. Early in the Harding administration, business interests led by Mellon had, thanks to the postwar recession, succeeded in establishing a tight credit policy. Mellon and Crissinger had in fact clashed several times at Federal Reserve Board meetings over this issue, with the former and like-minded colleague governor Harding carrying the day. However, with prosperity returning in 1922 and with Harding's departure changing the balance of power on the board, such a policy became increasingly difficult to maintain. Lower interest rates were an issue that played well in many legislative districts, and this fact was forcefully communicated to the Federal Reserve Board.

In fact, after Crissinger's ascendancy, the board established a general policy of easing credit through the establishment of lower interest rates, which continued throughout the 1920s. This policy, which was only mildly inflationary in the middle of the decade, accelerated after the Wall Street bulls began to gallop in 1927. With hindsight, many of those seeking to unravel the causes of the crash of 1929 and the economic catastrophe that followed returned to this shift in policy as the beginning of trouble and found Crissinger culpable. In reality, however, it appears that he acted far more for narrow political reasons than for philosophical ones—either about economic theory or about the role of the Federal Reserve system in the nation's polity. Others far more experienced in economics advocated the same policies, and by 1928 Crissinger himself had left the board to pursue the surging bull as an investor.

Yet this position had been the issue that brought him into public, and fatal, conflict with Benjamin Strong. In September 1927 he led the board in demanding that the Chicago Federal Bank lower its prime discount rate from 4 to 3.5 percent. Most of the system's other banks had already taken this step, but when Chicago balked, the board reverted to naked political pressure, ordering the bank with the force of law to comply. This action particularly troubled Strong not because of the economic implications of continuing easy credit but because of the threat it posed to the independence of the individual Federal Reserve banks. The New York governor charged that Crissinger deliberately withheld from the board the word of Mellon's opposition to this policy and so was "disloyal to both the Secretary of the Treasury and the Board." And he agreed with the equally outraged Senator Carter Glass of Virginia that the board's action went beyond its constitutionally mandated authority.

Faced with what one observer called a "veritable storm of protest," Crissinger attempted to defend his actions, but with his friend Harding dead for three years and a less supportive Calvin Coolidge in the White House, he soon withdrew from the fray. He resigned in November, allegedly to "enter a Washington securities firm and make some money." His replacement, Roy Young[*] of the Minneapolis Federal Reserve Bank, concurred with Strong and Glass, and in early 1928 the board set aside the Chicago decision. The general trend of easy credit continued after Crissinger's departure, however, demonstrating that the Chicago rate controversy was really much more about internal Federal Reserve politics than about economic principles.

Certainly Crissinger could identify sensible rationales for the actions taken by the board in the Chicago controversy. In July 1927 the central bankers of England, Germany, and France had visited with the board and urged a reduction of the discount rate at all Federal Reserve banks. Strong had, in fact, speedily accomplished a reduction of the rate at the New York bank identical to the one the board was forcing on Chicago. And at the height of the public controversy, Crissinger produced an embarrassing 1919 letter from Carter Glass, then secretary of the Treasury, arguing that the board had legal authority to control the individual banks.

These were convincing reasons, but they did not address the basic problem that had plagued the board throughout his tenure: its subordination to the prestige and power of the New York bank as an institution and to Benjamin Strong as an individual. Crissinger had seldom taken on Strong in head-to-head controversy. When he did, as in the Chicago case, he lost badly. As the institutional economist William O. Weyforth observed in 1933,

In practice the Board has suffered a marked derogation of its prestige. Treated at the outset as a sort of subordinate bureau of the Treasury Department, compelled during the period of war finance to accept practically the complete domination of that department, and destined thereafter to find the control over open-market operations centered in a committee of the regional banks, the conduct of foreign relations entrusted to the Federal Reserve Bank of New York, and its one attempt to assert its reputed power to initiate rate changes subjected to violent criticism, the Board has by one means realized that position, which initially in some quarters it was expected to occupy, of a supreme court of finance.

Clearly, Dick Crissinger seemed to possess neither the skills nor the inclination to attempt to alter this reality.

Perhaps it was a knowledge of this power relationship that led in part to Crissinger's frequently noted lack of effectiveness as a Federal Reserve governor. Strong was, after all, one of the most imposing figures of the business and financial world of his day. Well connected, self-confident, and hard working, he was the consummate professional. Others who engaged him in dispute found fates similar to Crissinger's. Further, the institution he directed was by the consensus of all the most important bank in the nation. The Marion lawyer was overmatched in this arena and probably had the good political sense to recognize the fact. But a less favorable interpretation of the languor that characterized the Federal Reserve Board under Crissinger was also frequently voiced by Strong and others. Put simply, the governor was an appallingly poor manager and incapable of leading the board in any direction. Long before the Chicago controversy, Strong observed that the board "was further reduced by internal bickering and disorganization. Governor Crissinger was too ineffectual to maintain satisfactory working relationships within the Board or to keep even the routine work of the Board flowing."

The history of the Federal Reserve Board under the leadership of Daniel Richard Crissinger is hardly its finest hour. Beyond the continuing advancement of an easy credit policy, it accomplished little, leaving the most delicate negotiations with foreign bankers to Strong and the governors of other individual banks. To the results of these negotiations it reacted after the fact, as it generally did, as well to the pressures for easy credit that came its way from Capitol Hill. Much of this lethargy must be charged to Crissinger.

After his resignation from the Federal Reserve Board, Crissinger joined the mortgage loan firm of F. H. Smith Company in Washington, D.C. In 1929 he and six other officers of the firm were indicted for using the mails to defraud, but the charges were dropped three years later. In 1934 Crissinger retired and returned to Marion, where he pursued various business interests until his death from pneumonia in 1942.

Benjamin Strong and his colleagues never permitted the Federal Reserve system to be controlled by a political body or by its leader, even if he were the president's boyhood friend. In that respect, the brief and undistinguished career of Daniel R. Crissinger as a central banker represents an early example of the institutional independence that would characterize the Federal Reserve system in the years to come.

BIBLIOGRAPHY

Adams, Samuel Hopkins. 1939. *Incredible Era: The Life and Times of Warren Gamaliel Harding*. Boston: Houghton Mifflin.

Chandler, Lester V. 1958. *Benjamin Strong: Central Banker*. Washington, D.C.: Brookings Institution.

"Crissinger: A Graduate of the Little Red School House." 1923. *Current Opinion* 74, no. 9 (March): 283–84.

Francis, Russell. 1968. *The Shadow of Blooming Grove: Warren G. Harding in His Times*. New York: McGraw-Hill.

Murray, Robert K. 1969. *The Harding Era: Warren G. Harding and His Administration*. Minneapolis: University of Minnesota Press.

Weyforth, William O. 1933. *The Federal Reserve Board: A Study of Federal Reserve Structure and Credit Control*. Baltimore: Johns Hopkins University Press.

EDWARD H. CUNNINGHAM
(1869–1930)

Ronald Robbins

Farmer, local and state politician, cofounder and leader of the Iowa farm bureau movement, Edward Henry Cunningham served as the "dirt farmer" member of the Federal Reserve Board from May 5, 1923, until his death on November 28, 1930.

Cunningham was born in Burlington, Wisconsin, on December 14, 1869, to P. H. and Hannah Cunningham. His education was limited to the elementary and high schools of his home county. A farmer's son, he moved to Manson, Iowa, in 1889 to take a job as a farm hand. By 1892 he had advanced to manager of a large livestock farm near Newell, Iowa. After several years as a farmer, he successfully entered the real estate business in Newell. In 1917 he returned to farming by buying a farm near Cresco, Howard County, Iowa.

A Republican, Cunningham became active in local politics and was elected mayor of Newell in 1902. He was reelected to the position in 1904 and 1906. Moving from local to state politics, he was elected to the Iowa House of Representatives in 1908. Reelected in 1910 and 1912, he served as the Speaker of the House of the Thirty-fifth General Assembly in 1913.

In addition to his political activities, Cunningham was active in the farm bureau movement. As cofounder of the Iowa Farm Bureau in 1913, he directed the membership drive that resulted in a membership of over 110,000 by 1919. He served as secretary of the organization from 1920 to 1923. In addition to his state positions, he was active in the national farm bureau movement.

Cunningham's farm bureau activities led to his appointment to the Federal Reserve Board. The deflation of 1920, with its disastrous effect on farmers, led to pressure by farm organizations and the midwestern congressional farm bloc to secure a "dirt farmer" position on the Federal Reserve Board. Their feeling was that the farm community had no voice in the monetary decision-making process and that a working farmer would promote the interests of the farm community before the board, preventing another agricultural depression such as that of 1920. When President Warren Harding's initial appointment to the position, Milo Campbell[*] of Michigan, died shortly after taking office in March

1923, Harding appointed Cunningham to an interim position on the board on May 5, 1923. In December President Calvin Coolidge nominated Cunningham to a ten-year term as governor representing the Chicago district. Cunningham's nomination was confirmed by the Senate in January 1924.

Cunningham's appointment was a result of political good fortune. When Campbell died, President Harding and Secretary of Agriculture Henry Wallace looked to Kansas to supply his successor. However, when Kansas's U.S. senators could not agree on a candidate, Wallace and Harding moved on to neighboring Iowa to supply the nominee. Iowa's senators quickly united behind Cunningham, and Wallace officially nominated him for the position on April 17.

During a speech at a testimonial dinner prior to his taking office, Cunningham pledged not to be the representative of one bloc; however, his actions clearly showed that he saw himself as the advocate of the farmer and small businessman. He consistently opposed any action that he viewed as making the board a vehicle to aid "big speculation and big eastern business."

Financially harmed by the deflation of 1920, Cunningham was a persistent opponent of direct action by the board. Instead, he preferred a policy of persuasion. He was especially opposed to adjustments in discount rates, which he saw as protecting the stock market at the expense of the farmer and small businessman. Throughout his tenure, Cunningham was often with the minority on major votes by the board and on several occasions was the only negative vote.

In November 1925 he was the only board member to oppose the Boston Federal Reserve Bank's application to increase its rediscount rate from 3.5 percent to 4 percent. When the stock market suffered a sharp decline in 1926, he opposed a resolution to increase the investment account to $300 million, which had been proposed to ease the money market. In January 1928 he was so opposed to the Chicago bank's request for a rate increase that he not only voted no but asked for the privilege of filing a statement where he stated that he did not wish business penalized by the excesses of the stock market, which had been caused to no small extent by the system's open market policy. In 1929 his advocacy of Adolph Miller's[*] policy of moral suasion or direct pressure instead of open market activities led E. A. Goldenweiser, director of the Division of Research and Statistics, to state that Cunningham "makes the best statement for moderation, because he frankly thinks in terms of the hardship of high rates for the small businessman. He refuses to attack the problem from any point of view except that." Even in 1930, Cunningham maintained his position by voting against the New York bank's request for a reduction in the minimum buying rate for bills.

In failing health for several years, Cunningham suffered a heart attack on November 28, 1930, while walking through the halls of the Treasury building. Taken to his nearby office, Cunningham died within twenty minutes. He was survived by his widow, Ida E. Scoval, and their son, Lloyd. In its November 29 obituary, the *Des Moines Register* wrote that Cunningham's staunch belief in the importance of agriculture and the long-term stability of farmland was best summed up by a quotation from a discussion of farmland values when he admonished, "Don't sell Iowa short."

BIBLIOGRAPHY

The Annals of Iowa. 1931. 3d ser. 17: 638.
Des Moines Register. 1930. November 29, p.1:8.
Who Was Who in America, 1937–1942. Chicago: Marquis Who's Who.
Wicker, Elmus R. 1966. *Federal Reserve Monetary Policy, 1917–1933*. New York: Random House.

J. DEWEY DAANE (1918–   )

Yale L. Meltzer

J. Dewey Daane, who was a governor of the Federal Reserve board from 1963 to 1974, was born on July 6, 1918, in Grand Rapids, Michigan. He attended Duke University, where he graduated magna cum laude (Phi Beta Kappa) with an A.B. degree in 1939. From 1945 to 1947, he attended Harvard University as a Littauer fellow at the Harvard Graduate School of Public Administration, where he received an M.P.A. in 1946 and a D.P.A. in 1949.

From 1939 to 1960 Daane held various positions at the Federal Reserve Bank of Richmond. He was appointed monetary economist in 1947, assistant vice-president in 1953, and vice-president in charge of research in 1957. He also served as consultant to the bank's president, was associate economist on the Federal Open Market Committee, and was an adviser to a number of Federal Reserve system committees. In addition to his numerous activities at the Federal Reserve, he found time to be an instructor in economics at the University of Richmond Evening School of Business Administration (1941–1945, 1947–1959).

On May 1, 1960, Daane went to the Federal Reserve Bank of Minneapolis as vice-president and economics adviser to the president. He remained there only until July 15. Later that year, he took a position at the U.S. Treasury as assistant to the secretary of the Treasury for debt management. Subsequently he served as deputy under secretary of the Treasury for monetary affairs and then acting fiscal assistant secretary.

On November 29, 1963, Daane was appointed to the Board of Governors of the Federal Reserve system and remained a governor until March 8, 1974. While on the board, he was a member of the Federal Open Market Committee and the Fed's Steering Committee on International Banking Regulation.

At the Federal Reserve board, Daane performed several particularly important functions. He represented the United States from 1963 to 1974 as one of the two U.S. deputies of the Group of Ten (G–10) (deputies to the finance ministers and central bank governors of the ten leading industrial countries). He was involved with the studies and negotiations regarding the new reserve assets, the SDRs (special drawing rights in the International Monetary Fund). The creation of the SDR (referred to as IMF money or, more popularly, as paper gold) involved the creation of new money in the world—money to supplement gold and the U.S. dollar (the key international currency) in the international monetary system. The negotiations on the SDR required Daane to attend almost monthly meetings in Europe.

He also represented the United States in the G–10 meetings dealing with international monetary crises. From 1972 to 1974 he represented the United States as one of the two U.S. deputies on the Committee of Twenty of the Board of Governors of the International Monetary Fund on Reform of the International Monetary System. He regularly attended monthly meetings of the central bank governors of the Bank for International Settlements (Basel, Switzerland) and also participated in meetings of Working Party 3 of the Organization for Economic Cooperation and Development (OECD), which dealt with the balance of payments and related problems.

On March 8, 1974, Daane ended his tenure as a member of the Federal Reserve board and became a consultant to the board in that same month. He continued to serve as a consultant until June 1974 and then assumed new positions of authority and responsibility. He became vice-chairman of the board of the Commerce Union Bank and Tennessee Valley Bancorp, Inc., in Nashville, Tennessee (May 1975-December 1977); served as a director of the Commerce Union Bank of Memphis, Tennessee (September 1974–1985) and as a director of the Commerce Union Corporation and Commerce Union Bank of Nashville, Tennessee (September 1974-April 1988); was section leader of the Graduate School of Banking of the University of Wisconsin (August 1975–1983); and served as a member of the Panel of Economic Advisers of the Congressional Budget Office in Washington, D.C. (November 1976-June 1987). Daane was also a director of the Chicago Board of Trade (February 1979–1982) and chairman of the International Policy Committee of the Commerce Union Corporation in Nashville, Tennessee (January 1978-April 1988).

Since September 1974 Daane has been the Valere Blair Potter (formerly Frank K. Houston) Professor of Banking at the Owen Graduate School of Management of Vanderbilt University in Nashville, Tennessee. He has remained a director of the Whittaker Corporation since July 1974, as well as a member of the board of advisers of the Patterson School of Diplomacy and International Commerce of the University of Kentucky in Lexington, Kentucky. He also remains a director of the National Futures Association (since February 1983), a director of the Sovran Bank/Central South in Nashville, Tennessee (since April 1988), and chairman of the Money Market Committee of the Sovran Bank/Central South in Nashville, Tennessee (since April 1988).

Daane has written numerous articles for various professional journals and for the Federal Reserve Bank of Richmond's *Monthly Review*. He is a member of, among others, the following organizations: American Economic Association; American Finance Association, Bretton Woods Committee; Global Economic

Action Institute; John F. Kennedy School of Government Alumni Association, Harvard University; and the Vanderbilt Institute for Public Policy Studies.

In 1963 he married Barbara W. McMann. They have three daughters.

BIBLIOGRAPHY

Bowsher, Norman, N.; Daane, J. Dewey; and Einzig, Robert. 1958. "The Flow of Funds between Regions of the United States." *Journal of Finance* 13 (March): 1–20.

Bowsher, Norman N.; Einzig, Robert; and Daane, J. Dewey. 1955. "Task Force Report on Interregional Flows of Funds and District Member Bank Reserves." Paper presented at Federal Reserve System Conference on the Interregional Flows of Funds, Washington, D.C., April.

Daane, J. Dewey. 1949. "The Fifth Federal Reserve District: A Study in Regional Economics." Ph.D. dissertation, Harvard University.

Federal Reserve System Board of Governors to Yale L. Meltzer, 1989.

CHESTER CHARLES DAVIS
(1887–1975)

Jack B. White

The life of Chester C. Davis would be worthy of note even if he had never been a member of the Board of Governors of the Federal Reserve system. Indeed, he is best remembered as the director of the Agricultural Adjustment Administration, one of the New Deal programs of the mid–1930s. In addition, he served as president of the Federal Reserve Bank of St. Louis for ten years. When these accomplishments are considered, a picture evolves of a multifaceted individual. Even after he had retired, Davis traveled to India for the Ford Foundation.

Davis's connection to agriculture was natural, having been born on a tenant Iowa farm in 1887. He had a deep concern for the plight of the farmer, the result of the struggle he and his five siblings had to help their father pay the mortgage despite the setbacks caused by weather and insects. Because all hands were needed in the fields, Davis's early education was sporadic, occurring mostly in the winter when farm demands were lighter. In spite of the spotty educational background, he was admitted to Grinnell College in 1906. No stranger to hard work, Davis paid his own way through college. During his senior year, he took a year off from his studies, moved to South Dakota, and ran two weekly newspapers. He returned to college and graduated Phi Beta Kappa in 1911.

As a new college graduate, Davis decided to travel to the West Coast. The trip made two lasting changes in his life. While traveling through Montana, he met Helen Smith. They were married in 1913, a union that would last until his death and produce two sons. He was also introduced to Joseph Dixon, a progressive reformer who would have a great deal of influence on Davis's life.

Drawing on his journalistic experience, Davis stayed in Montana and became editor of the *Montana Farmer* in 1917. During his tenure as editor, the paper became known as a force not only for the farmer but also for good government. In 1921 Joseph Dixon was elected governor of Montana, and Davis was named state commissioner for agriculture and labor. When the Dixon team was defeated in the subsequent election, Davis moved to Illinois, where he used his experience while working as the director of grain marketing for the Illinois Agricultural Association.

Dixon's defeat did not deter Davis's political activities. Although he had earlier supported Republican candidates, he helped manage the agricultural issues for Alfred E. Smith's presidential campaign in 1928 and supported Franklin D. Roosevelt in 1932. Roosevelt recognized Davis's expertise in agricultural matters and selected him to help write the Agricultural Adjustment Act. With the act's passage, Davis was selected to direct the production division. In 1933 Davis became the administrator of the Agricultural Adjustment Administration (AAA). A drought welcomed him to his new post, but Davis proved equal to the task. As head of the AAA, Davis enacted several programs to control farm production and increase farm income. The programs were largely successful, increasing total farm income by 50 percent from 1934 to 1936. In 1936 the Supreme Court declared the AAA, as well as the National Recovery Act and other New Deal programs, unconstitutional. Davis's response to the setback was to tailor the subsequent Soil Conservation Act as an acceptable replacement for the AAA by emphasizing soil conservation as opposed to market intervention.

In 1936 Davis was appointed to the Board of Governors of the Federal Reserve system to fill out a term nominally representing farm interests. Although he was no banker, Davis accepted the post. He mistakenly thought that the position would be more peaceful than those connected with the struggling farm sector. However, the recession of 1937, perhaps caused by the Fed's increase in reserve requirements, thrust the board into the bright light of criticism. Appointed to a full fourteen-year term in 1940, Davis resigned in 1941 to accept the position of president of the Federal Reserve Bank of St. Louis. Thus, his voice was heard in the Federal Open Market Committee until 1951, when he resigned from the St. Louis bank.

Although he had left the board, Davis was called back to Washington a number of times. During 1943 the pressures of a wartime economy began to be reflected in the inflation rate. Davis was summoned to Washington to serve as war food administrator. He also served the Truman administration as a member of the advisory board of the Office of War Mobilization and Reconversion in 1945 and 1946, as well as the chairman of President Truman's Famine Emergency Committee in 1946.

After resigning from the St. Louis Federal Reserve Bank, Davis was named a director of the Ford Foundation. He recognized the pressing food needs of the Third World countries and was instrumental in developing foundation programs in India and Pakistan. He retired in 1953 but remained a consultant until 1954, visiting India and observing the results of the programs he help institute.

Davis died in 1975 six weeks shy of his eighty-eighth birthday. To say that it was a full eighty-eight years is an understatement. When his accomplishments are examined in the light of his background, they become even more impressive. Davis was not one of Roosevelt's Ivy League brain trust. Rather, the son of a tenant farmer who graduated with honors by the sheer force of his own determination, he went on to serve two presidents and become world renowned for his knowledge of agriculture and agricultural programs.

BIBLIOGRAPHY

Current Biography. 1940. New York: H. W. Wilson Company.

National Cyclopedia of American Biography. 1984 Vol. 62. Clifton, N.J.: James T. White and Company.

New York Times. 1975. September 26, col. 1, p. 76.

Schapsmeir, Edward L., and Schapsmeir, Frederick H. 1975. *Encyclopedia of American Agricultural History*. Westport, Conn.: Greenwood Press.

FREDERIC ADRIAN DELANO
(1863–1953)

Juli Cicarelli

In 1914 Frederic Adrian Delano was fifty years old and the president of the Chicago, Indianapolis & Louisville Railway when he was named by President Woodrow Wilson as vice-governor of the newly formed Federal Reserve Board. He would resign as vice-governor in 1916 but stayed on the board until 1918, when he enlisted in the U.S. Army Corps of Engineers.

Delano's four-year tenure on the reserve board came at a time when the board was still in its formative period. When President Wilson chose the first members of the board, he selected individuals who would represent a balance between those who feared the newly organized system would be controlled by the "money people" (eastern bankers or the financial community) and those who feared it would be controlled by the government. During his tenure, Delano represented and shared the view of the members of the financial community, who would have preferred a more centralized body under private control. In the seven-member voting board, he voted in a bloc with Adolph C. Miller,[*] a prominent economist, and Paul M. Warburg,[*] a Wall Street banker. All three feared Treasury Department control.

This anti-Treasury bloc was matched against the pro-Treasury bloc of Assistant Treasury Secretary Charles S. Hamlin,[*] governor of the board, Treasury Secretary William G. McAdoo, and Comptroller of the Currency John S. Williams, all of whom served as ex officio members of the board. The two opposing blocs would often be offset by the swing vote of Alabama banker W. P. G. Harding,[*] who would later replace Hamlin as governor. In the early days, these two opposing factions clashed in meetings that were so hostile that it was thought that the system would not survive.

In November 1915, less than one year after the Federal Reserve banks were organized, Delano, along with Warburg and Harding, proposed the elimination of the reserve banks at Kansas City, Minneapolis, Atlanta, and Dallas and deferred for later study the elimination of the Richmond and Boston banks. This proposal represented the last gasp of those who favored a more centralized banking system and felt the board had the power to set the number of Federal Reserve banks. Rumors about this proposal had been reported in the press and caused much controversy. Because of the controversy, Delano was courteous enough to send a copy of the proposal to Senator Carter Glass, author of the Federal Reserve Act. Glass replied immediately that he felt such a step would be illegal, adding that the Federal Reserve system was at the weakest period of its existence and such a proposal would lead to its undoing.

President Wilson, who had been informed of the proposal, was exasperated, feeling that such action by the board would constitute an intolerable usurpation of power, without legal or implied sanction, and he was considering a reorganization of the board. The governors had been intending to vote immediately on the proposed bank elimination but on the advice of Glass and others deferred their vote for one week in order to get legal advice from Thomas W. Gregory, the U.S. attorney general. Gregory subsequently ruled that the proposed elimination was in fact illegal.

Glass noted that Delano was not as fervent as others on the board who pushed for a more centralized system. When the attorney general ruled the matter illegal, the proposal to abolish the banks was dropped. Yet this suggested elimination had provoked bitterness at a time when the board was in a fragmented and weakened state, and it had threatened the very structure of a system born in a fragile compromise. Over time, the bitterness eased, but the fights between the warring factions begun in Delano's time would go on long after he resigned.

Another overwhelming problem faced by Delano and the other newly appointed governors was their inexperience. Benjamin Strong, governor of the Federal Reserve Bank of New York from 1913 until 1928, said of the group that he and they were simply "greenhorns," with no guide or compass, no experience, or cohesion, adding that they had everything to learn and everything to lose as the result. Strong would go on to say that the Federal Reserve governors were responsible men who stood the strain of criticism and abuse, staying with the job because of a real spirit of public service. This spirit could be seen in Delano, who when he was nominated for the board said he would accept the nomination because he felt it was his duty to do so. But as the country became involved in World War I, he saw his duty elsewhere, and in July 1918 he resigned the board to join the U.S. Army Corps of Engineers.

With his railroad experience, the army sent him to France, where he was eventually named deputy director of transportation in Paris. After the war, he would devote himself largely to public service.

Given his lifetime accomplishments, Delano's four-year service on the Federal Reserve Board could be seen as a mere footnote in a long and varied career. During his life, he would be known as a member of a famous American family, a railway executive, an army officer, a banker, a government official, and a pioneer in city planning. His many accomplishments, and his influences on the very texture of American life as we know it today, can be traced to a combination of his own personal values and his birth into a famous American family—the influential, colorful, and wealthy Delanos.

Frederic Adrian Delano was born in Hong Kong on September 10, 1863, and died on March 28, 1953, in Washington, D.C. He was the eighth of nine children of Warren and Catherine (Robbins) Delano, who traced their roots back to William the Conqueror. The American branch of the Delanos descended from Phillipe De Lannoy (Delano), the first French Huguenot to settle on American soil. The Delano men had traditionally been sea trading merchants, and Warren, Frederic's father, was no exception. He was a merchant in what was politely called the China trade (family detractors would later note that the Delano family fortune had been made in the illegal opium trade).

The Delanos were a patrician, close-knit clan and became close friends to another aristocratic family, the Roosevelts. Frederic's older sister, Sara, married James Roosevelt and gave birth to Franklin Delano Roosevelt.

Frederic, like his older brothers and sisters, was brought up in a proper Victorian household. He received his preparatory education at Adams Academy in Quincy, Massachusetts, and went on to graduate from Harvard University in 1885. When he was twenty, he was sent by his father to Colorado, where he began his railroad career as an assistant in the engineering department of the Chicago, Burlington, & Quincy Railroad Company. There he would learn rail-roading from the tracks up. By 1888 he was in Chicago, where he met and married Matilda Annis Peasley, a daughter of railroad executive James Carr Peasley. The couple had five daughters: Catherine, Louise, Laura, Matilda, and Alice (the last two died in childhood). Mrs. Delano, know as Aunt Tilly, died in 1943 after a long illness.

Delano was called a conservative businessman by Eleanor Roosevelt, and his views about fiscal responsibility would always follow the family line: he worked hard and did not squander resources. He was seen as an astute businessman and, like the other men in his family, was responsible for maintaining the family fortune and for looking after the female relatives.

He worked his way up through the Burlington railroad and during 1901–1905 served as the railroad's general manager. In 1905 he became president of the Wheeling & Lake Erie Railroad Company and the Wabash Pittsburgh-Terminal Railroad Railway Company. He later became president of the Wabash Rail Company and then president of the Chicago, Indianapolis & Lousiville Railway Company.

After World War I Delano served as chairman of the board of directors of the Metropolitan West Side Elevated Railroad Company in Chicago and a director of the Union Mining Company of Maryland. From 1932 until 1936 he was chairman of the board of the Federal Reserve Bank of Richmond. In 1933 he demonstrated his inventive abilities by patenting a one-way window glass. But increasingly, Delano devoted less time to business and more to promoting the emerging field of urban planning.

In a lifetime spanning eighty-nine years, Frederic Delano was able to bridge the gap between the noblesse oblige aristocratic attitudes of the Delano family and the democratic ideals and public empowerment views expressed by his nephew Franklin in the 1930s. Frederic Delano's social and political values differed from earlier Delano males, including his father, Warren, who voted Republican and prayed Episcopalian. Warren Delano may have admitted that all Democrats were not horse thieves, but it did seem to him that all horse thieves were Democrats. Frederic disagreed; he became a Democrat and an advocate of governmental programs geared to the less fortunate.

In his later years, Delano became the titular head of the extended Delano family and young Franklin Roosevelt's favorite uncle. Uncle Fred advised Franklin Roosevelt in FDR's youth, and he would be a trusted adviser during his nephew's presidency. As far back as 1912, Delano had had experience with public policy matters, having been appointed by President William Taft to the Commission on Industrial Relations.

Delano was an early advocate of resource planning and a pioneer in urban planning. In the 1920s he settled in Washington, D.C., where he organized a committee to create the National Park Commission. He also played an influential part in early development plans for Chicago and New York City.

In 1927 he became chairman of the Washington, D.C., Committee on Unemployment. In 1929 he was a founder and served as the first president of the Washington Community Chest, a volunteer community funding program now known as the United Way.

When his nephew became president during the depression, Delano's pioneering work in resource planning led him to become an active participant in Roosevelt's New Deal. He served on the National Planning Board of the Public Works Administration, a federal agency set up to get the unemployed to work in public works projects.

In 1934 President Roosevelt decided to put the physical development of the country on a planned basis. He put his uncle Fred in charge of what would become the National Resources Planning Board (NRPB). Like Delano, Roosevelt envisioned resource planning as covering many aspects of national life: land, water, forests, dams, power, poverty, and politics. With the NRPB, Delano said he was doing the kind of work he enjoyed: conserving national resources in the aid of human welfare. He would serve as chairman of the NRPB until 1943, when the board submitted to the president a 721-page plan that projected a ten-year New Deal focusing on economic and social planning for postwar America. This ambitious plan generated a great deal of controversy in the press and received a cool reception in Congress. Delano, who was cited as one of the chief architects of the report, was known to be shy of the press; he avoided public contact and said little about the controversy. He was then seventy-nine years old and had spent a lifetime in public service. He would leave it to others to carry on his views.

Throughout his lifetime, Delano had expressed his views through his writings, in both scholarly journals and the popular magazines of the day. He was known as an expert in banking and finance and wrote in those fields. His writing also focused on his other interests: taxation, transportation, urban planning, and the preservation of natural and community resources.

In Washington, D.C., he served as chairman of the executive committee of the Smithsonian Institution; trustee and later chairman of the board of the Brookings Institution; a member of the advisory council of the Stable Money Association; a director of the Carnegie Institution of Washington; and a trustee of the Russell Sage Foundation and the Carnegie Endowment for International Peace.

He was honored many times for his lifetime of service. For his services during World War I, he was made a chevalier of the French Legion of Honor and was awarded the U.S. Distinguished Service Medal. The American Institute of Mining and Metallurgical Engineers named him to its Legion of Honor in 1937, and he was decorated with the Order of Sheng Li by the Chinese government in 1948. In 1949 he received medals from the Société des architectes and the American Railway Engineering Association.

Frederic Adrian Delano died in Washington, D.C., on March 28, 1953, at age eighty-nine. He was survived by his daughter, Mrs. James Lawrence Houghteling of Washington; a sister, Mrs. Price Collier of Tuxedo Park, New York; eleven grandchildren; and twelve great-grandchildren.

BIBLIOGRAPHY

Chandler, Lester V. 1958. *Benjamin Strong, Central Banker*. Washington, D.C.: Brookings Institution.

Church, Allen. 1965. *The Roosevelts, American Aristocrats*. New York: Harper & Row.

Glass, Carter. 1927. *An Adventure in Constructive Finance*. Garden City, N.Y.: Doubleday, Page.

National Cyclopedia of American Biography. 1967. Vol. 40. Clifton, N.J.: James T. White and Company.

"National Planner." 1937. *Scholastic*, January 30, p. 21.

Schlesinger, Arthur M., Jr. 1958. *The Age of Roosevelt*. Vol. 3, *The Coming of the New Deal*. Boston: Houghton Mifflin.

"They Stood Out from the Crowd." 1934. *Literary Digest*, December 15, p. 10.

ERNEST G. DRAPER (1885–1954)

Philip Lane

Ernest Draper served for twelve years as a member of the Federal Reserve's Board of Governors before retiring at the end of his term in 1950. He was born in 1885 in Washington, D.C., to Professor Amos G. Draper of Gallaudet College and the former Bell Merrill. Ernest received his B.A. from Amherst College in 1906, graduating Phi Beta Kappa. He began his career as a clerk in New York City after graduation. By 1912 Draper was the president of American Creosoting Company. In 1911 he married Mary W. Childs. They raised three children: William H. Childs, Doris Bartlett, and Mary. He maintained his job at American Creosoting until 1920, when he became treasurer and vice-president of the Hills Brothers Company, packers of Dromedary dates and other food products. Before joining Hills Brothers, however, Draper served in the U.S. Navy during World War I. He was a lieutenant and served as a navigator on the U.S.S. *Sierra*. These experiences were reported in his book, *Navigating the Ship* (1920). His relationship with ships continued for a good part of the remainder of his life. While an executive at Hills Brothers, Draper was a member of several commissions in New York State. From 1931 to 1935, he was a member of the Commission on Unemployment and also served on the Advisory Commission on Minimum Wage and the New York City Art Commission.

He left Hills Brothers in 1935 to go to the Commerce Department, where he served as the assistant secretary of commerce. Draper represented the Department of Commerce on several boards or commissions. He was appointed a member of the National Labor Board and the Business Advisory Council of the Department of Commerce, for which he was later a member of the executive committee on commercial policy. The President's Commission on Crop Insurance was his other major outside assignment. Ernest was a joint author of *Can Business Prevent Unemployment* (1935) with Sam Adolph Lewisohn, John R. Commons, and Don D. Leschohier.

In March 1938 Draper was appointed a member of the Board of Governors from the Second District. During his term of office, he represented the board in statements to Congress at least four times. On one occasion, the subject concerned suggestions for improving the Mead bill, before the Subcommittee of the Senate Banking and Currency Committee, which dealt with the provision for the insurance of loans to business. Near the end of World War II, Draper spoke before the Committee on Post-War Economic Planning and Policy on the issue of supplying credit for business during the transition and early postwar years. He returned to this topic later but with a focus on small businesses and the role of the Federal Reserve in assisting them.

Draper represented the board before trade and other groups on several occasions. He addressed the School of Business Administration, University of Minnesota, in 1939 on the Federal Reserve's role in a changing world. In April 1940, he addressed the Economic Club of Detroit on the Federal Reserve's role in the time of a European war. The New School of Social Research was the location of a 1941 address on the impact of defense, production, and on small business. In less academic or regulatory areas, Draper spoke several times promoting savings bonds. He was the chair of the government unit of the American Red Cross War Fund Drive in 1944.

During his tenure with the board, Draper had two publications: "Small Business and its Credit Problem," published in the *Washington Post* in 1939, and, with Walter Gardner, "Goods and Dollars in World Trade," in the *Federal Reserve Bulletin* in 1944.

Draper's time as a member of the board was characterized by three distinct periods: the end of the Great Depression, when he focused the credit problems of small business; the years during World War II, when the members of the board focused their attention on the war effort and finding ways the Federal Reserve could support that effort; and after World War II, dealing with the transition to a peacetime economy. Draper continued to focus on the special place of small business, in large part because of his background before joining the board. Much of Draper's contributions to the board are not easily documented for he, like most other members of it, worked behind the scenes to affect monetary policy and other Federal Reserve policies.

Ernest Draper died on April 30, 1954, after a long illness. He was survived by his second wife, the former Theodora Trowbridge Elliman. He was a member of the American Economic Association and the Academy of Political Science. He contributed to *Outlook* and the *American Management Review*.

BIBLIOGRAPHY

Draper, Ernest. 1920. *Navigating the Ship*. New York: D. Van Nostrand.

Draper, Ernest; Commons, John; Leschohier, Don; and Lewisohn, Sam. 1935. *Can Business Prevent Unemployment*. New York: A. A. Knopf.

Draper, Ernest, and Gardner Walter. 1944. "Goods and Dollars in World Trade." *Federal Reserve Bulletin* (November).

Hyman, Sidney. 1976. *Marriner S. Eccles*. Stanford: Stanford University.

Who Was Who in America, 1943–1950. Chicago: Marquis Who's Who.

MARRINER STODDARD ECCLES (1890–1977)

William J. Barber

Marriner Stoddard Eccles must surely qualify as one of the most colorful figures in the annals of American central banking. He was the major architect of the Banking Act of 1935, which restructured the Federal Reserve system along its current lines. His leadership of the system was coterminous with turbulent episodes in twentieth-century economic history: the struggle against mass unemployment during the Great Depression and the mobilization of the economy for war and its reconversion after 1945. In the final phase of his career as a central banker—from 1948 to 1951 (when he continued as a member of the board, though not as its chairman)—he was a strong advocate of the independence of the Federal Reserve from the Treasury. In his view at that time, the commitment of the Federal Reserve to support the government bond market, a residue from financing practices developed during World War II, was no longer appropriate. By the time of the Korean conflict, he was persuaded that the Federal Reserve could conduct counterinflationary policies responsibly only when "liberated" to use its instruments of control of the money supply and interest rates autonomously.

But perhaps Eccles's most significant contribution was the role he played in conditioning official Washington in the 1930s and 1940s to a Keynesian style of thinking about macroeconomic management. Throughout his years in public life, he was a consistent champion of policies designed to control the level of aggregate demand. The federal government, in his view, had a primary responsibility to manage purchasing power in the interests of achieving full employment and price stability. Though there was a singular convergence between many of the policies he pressed for and those recommended in John Maynard Keynes's *General Theory* (1936), Eccles arrived at his position quite independently. He was untutored in technical economic theory. With a note of pride, he asserted in his memoirs, "The concepts I formulated, which have been called 'Keynesian,' were not abstracted from his books, which I had never read. My conceptions were based on naked-eye observation and experience in the inter-mountain region. Moreover, I have never read Keynes's writings except in small extracts up to this day'' (Eccles 1951, p. 132). Eccles was an American original, and his influence was the greater because of that.

Marriner Stoddard Eccles was born on September 9, 1890, in Logan, Utah, and was eldest son by the second wife of David Eccles (a Scottish immigrant who had been brought to the Utah Territory as a child). By twentieth-century standards, the young Marriner would be judged as the issue of a polygamous arrangement. His parents, however, were married five years before the Mormon church banned plural marriages. Marriner was thus to have eight full siblings and twelve half-siblings.

Though the senior Eccles had prospered as a self-made man—by the turn of the century, he had put together an impressive empire in the upper mountain states that included interests in lumbering, railroading, sugar processing, and banking—he insisted that the young Marriner learn the disciplines of thrift and industry, as well as fealty to the doctrines of Mormonism. As the father had taken his first job at the age of eight, so also should the son. Marriner entered the labor force at this point in his life as a summer employee in a box factory with the remuneration of five cents per hour for a ten-hour day. In 1909 he graduated from high school, an event that was to mark his last contact with formal education. For the next two years, he served as a Mormon missionary in the slums of Glasgow, Scotland.

Upon his father's death in 1912, it fell to Marriner to manage the portion of the assets allocated to his mother and his eight brothers and sisters (who were then minors). He quickly demonstrated his business acumen and by the mid–1920s had organized the largest bank holding company in the intermountain region. Meanwhile he had established a family of his own: in 1913, he married May Campbell Young, whom he had met during his missionary tour in Scotland, and she was to bear him four children. (This marriage was terminated in 1950; he married Sara Madison Glassie in 1951.)

The events following the crash of 1929 reoriented Eccles's activities and his thinking. In company with fellow members of the banking fraternity, he was engaged in a desperate struggle to forestall bank runs. Unlike many of his colleagues, Eccles succeeded in keeping his banks open, and none of his depositors lost a penny. In his memoirs, he wrote about these episodes:

We kept our banks open through these and other crises. But to do so, we had to adopt a rough and distasteful credit and collection policy. Living with oneself was not a pleasant experience under those circumstances. In whatever quiet moments were available I began to wonder whether the conduct of bankers like myself in depression times was a wise one. Were we not all contributing our bit to the worsening of matters by the mere act of trying to keep liquid under the economic pressures of deflation? By forcing the liquidation of loans and securities to meet the demands of depositors, were we not helping to drive prices down and thereby making it increasingly difficult for our debtors to pay back what they had borrowed from us? By our policies of credit stringency in a time of drastic deflation, were we not throwing a double loop around the throat of an economy that was already gasping for breath? (Eccles 1951, p. 70)

In 1931 and 1932 Eccles elaborated on these themes in a series of speeches delivered in Utah. Conventional views about the way out of depression, he argued, should be rejected. There was no foundation for the conclusion that the economic system would correct itself if left to its own devices. Nor should one anticipate that efforts to balance the federal budget—allegedly to restore investor "confidence"—would be successful. Deficits were the result, not the cause, of depressed national income. What was needed was more spending, not less. "The difficulty," as he diagnosed it in an address to the Utah State Bankers Convention in June 1932, was "that we were not sufficiently extravagant as a nation" (Eccles 1951, p. 83). It was the task of government to direct its economic policies to guarantee opportunities to work for all who sought them.

A chance meeting with Stuart Chase, a nationally prominent publicist who had been invited to speak in Salt Lake City, was to bring Eccles to the attention of a wider audience. In the ensuing conversation in February 1933, Chase suggested that Eccles share his views about the requirements of the economic situation with Rexford Guy Tugwell, one of President-elect Franklin D. Roosevelt's leading brain trusters. A meeting between Eccles and Tugwell was arranged for later that month in New York. Although Tugwell expressed surprise that a banker could be associated with such "radical" views, there was no immediate follow-up. In October 1933, however, Tugwell invited Eccles to visit Washington. By this time, Eccles had refined his views. As he expressed them that month in an address to the Utah Educational Association:

The question is not how bankers and those who have idle money and credit can bring about recovery, but why they should do so, so long as there is no incentive offered in any field of profitable investment. A bank cannot finance the building of more factories and more rental properties and more homes when half of our productive property is idle for lack of consumption and a large percentage of our business properties are vacant, for want of paying tenants. The government, however, can spend money, because the government, unlike the bankers, has the power of taxation and the power to create money and does not have to depend on the profit motive. The only escape from a depression must be by increased spending. We must depend upon the government to save what we have of a price, profit, and credit system. (Eccles 1951, p. 130)

Eccles's November 1933 visit in Washington was to lead to greater things. Tugwell arranged appointments with a representative cast of New Deal luminaries, including Henry Wallace, Harry Hopkins, Harold Ickes, and Henry Morgenthau, Jr. He was then offered a post as special assistant to the secretary of the Treasury for monetary and credit affairs. He accepted, with the expectation that he would stay in Washington no longer than a year and a half. When the senior position on the Federal Reserve Board, then styled as "governor," fell vacant, Eccles's name was brought forward as a candidate for this post. President

Roosevelt formally announced his decision to appoint Eccles on November 10, 1934.

Marriner Eccles had risen to become the nation's premier central banker but by a most unlikely route. No doubt senior officials in Roosevelt's New Deal found his attacks on economic orthodoxy to be appealing; after all, there were few bankers in the land who shared his sympathies for an active role for government in economic experimentation. At the same time, Eccles was short on the credentials that would typically be associated with this post, at least in normal times. He lacked a college education. His banking experience, though acknowledged to be successful, was limited. His operations had been confined to a parochial mountain region, remote from the East Coast financial establishment, thought to be the standard breeding ground for central bankers. At least nominally, he was not a member of the president's political party (although he had voted for Roosevelt), and he was identified with a religious sect that was distinctly a minority.

Although flattered to be Roosevelt's choice for the job, Eccles still insisted as a condition of acceptance on the president's support for legislation to reform the Federal Reserve system. In Eccles's judgment, the authority of Washington, as opposed to that of the regional Federal Reserve banks, was altogether too weak. The original Federal Reserve Act of 1913 had conveyed effective day-to-day control of operations to the officers of Federal Reserve district banks, who were themselves selected by the private commercial bankers who formed their membership. In this arrangement, the head of the Federal Reserve bank in New York, situated in the nation's financial capital, was much the first among equals. Amendments introduced in the Banking Act of 1933 had created a committee composed of one member from each of the Federal Reserve district banks to formulate recommendations on the conduct of open market operations. The board in Washington, though empowered to approve or disapprove those recommendations, had no authority to initiate action. In Eccles's judgment, a coordinated monetary policy was impossible in such circumstances when decision making was so fragmented.

The Eccles bill was a matter of high controversy in congressional hearings, as well as in banking circles, in 1935. Although Eccles did not get everything he wanted when the Banking Act of 1935 emerged from the legislative pipeline, he still reached most of his objectives. The Washington arm of the system, which had been titled the Federal Reserve Board, was renamed as the Board of Governors of the Federal Reserve system. The board's membership was reduced from eight to seven, and the ex officio places formerly allocated to the secretary of the Treasury and comptroller of the currency were eliminated. More important, the weight of the Open Market Committee was shifted to the center: in the new dispensation, the committee was composed of the seven members of the Washington-based Board of Governors and five representatives of the twelve district banks. The 1935 legislation extended the authority of the system in other important ways as well: the discretionary power of the Board of Governors in

Washington to change required reserve ratios was enlarged. In addition, the range of assets against which the system could lend to member banks was broadened.

All of this represented a major achievement, but a hurdle remained: Eccles still had to go through the Senate confirmation process before taking on the duties of chairman of the reconstituted Board of Governors of the Federal Reserve system, scheduled to commence operations with its enhanced empowerments on February 1, 1936. Senate confirmation came but only at the eleventh hour. The delay was largely attributable to the recalcitrance of Senator Carter Glass of Virginia, then chairman of the key subcommittee of the Senate Committee on Banking and Currency. Glass regarded himself as the principal author of the Federal Reserve Act of 1913. He could never quite forgive those who would undo much of the decentralization he had built into the original system.

Although Eccles was preoccupied with restructuring the Federal Reserve system when he donned the mantle of a central banker, he remained active in urging a stimulative fiscal policy on the Roosevelt administration. Formally, his official duties were concerned with the management of monetary policy, but he regarded this instrument of policy as ineffective in the search for solutions to the depression. To be sure, he stood for easy money in these circumstances. Nevertheless, the active ingredient in the policy mix should be deficit spending, and he called for more of it than the president was willing to endorse. In his memoranda to the White House, he reiterated the case for more aggressive expenditures on public works. He also went public with the message that the expansion of the national debt need not be burdensome when ''we owe it to ourselves'' and that the real burden facing the nation was the production lost from the waste arising from involuntary unemployment. In late 1935 some members of Roosevelt's staff were dismayed when Eccles curtailed his speaking engagements out of fear that his pronouncements might intensify the opposition of Senator Glass to his confirmation as chairman of the Board of Governors. As Stephen Early, the president's press secretary, put it in December 1935: ''Eccles now is as quiet as a clam. He is refusing all kinds of invitations, some of which if accepted would do us a world of good. We are under attack with our best gun silenced.''

At a number of moments in 1936 and early 1937, it appeared to some observers that Eccles had lapsed in his commitment to cheap money in an underemployed economy, though he resolutely denied this to be so. The momentum of recovery then seemed to be established; 1936 was the best year for the economy since 1929. Meanwhile, the banking system was awash with excess reserves in unprecedented volume. In the view of a majority of the members of the Federal Open Market Committee, the Federal Reserve should exercise its newly acquired powers to raise reserve requirements. Such action, it was held, would be a useful precaution in the interests of increasing the system's leverage should it later wish to restrain the lending powers of member banks in the event of inflationary pressures. Increases in required reserve ratios were scheduled in three installments: August 1936, March 1937, and May 1937. The insider view at the time was that the banks would still have more than adequate lending capacity to sustain recovery, even after this program had been implemented. (Eccles, it should be noted, did not support the third round of increases in reserve requirements in May 1937 but was outvoted in the Federal Open Market Committee.) In his public statements, he insisted that even after the full increase in reserve requirements had taken effect, "the supply of money to finance increased production at low rates [was] ample" and that he had not retreated from his advocacy for an easy money policy. He attributed price rises then observable in some sectors to nonmonetary factors, such as "strikes and monopolistic practices by certain groups both in industry and organized labor," and argued that these "unwarranted price advances" had to be treated by measures other than a "restrictive monetary policy" (Eccles 1937b).

Meanwhile, Eccles insisted on the primacy of a correct fiscal policy in engineering a securely grounded recovery. His memoranda of April 1937, written when the president was anticipating that the elusive goal of a balanced budget would be achievable in the next fiscal year and was calling for retrenchments in federal spending, gave a new twist to the argument. He urged the president to resist "conservative pressures" that "aim first at reduced spending and next at reduced taxes on the rich." This course, he maintained, would be a fundamental mistake. Government expenditures needed to continue without reduction, and their stimulus to national income would generate increased revenues that would bring the budget into balance within a few years. When that happened, tax rates should not be reduced. The problem then would be to ensure an adequate volume of spending from the private sector. This could be accomplished through a combination of progressive taxation of incomes and programs to redistribute income to the poor. He summarized his case as follows:

Continuation of present tax rates as recovery progresses will help prevent oversaving . . . and so will defer future depressions or lessen their intensity. At the same time, continued Federal spending, both for transfer of incomes to low-income groups and for service for their use, will directly increase their ability to consume. Both the policy of taking income from the top, and the policy of injecting income at the bottom, contribute to stability and tend to prevent or moderate depressions. (Eccles 1937a)

This concern about the development of fiscal strategies for the longer term was soon dominated by a more immediate problem. No one in official Washington anticipated the recession that began in August 1937 and brought a downturn in employment and industrial production more severe than the one immediately following the stock market crash of October 1929. This phenomenon introduced a new analytic puzzle: why should it have occurred when the economy was still far short of full employment? Critics of the Roosevelt administration tended to read this turn of events as demonstrating the bankruptcy of the New Deal's deficit spending programs and as proving conclusively the futility of heterodox governmental intervention. The very survival of the Eccles style of Keynesianism was in jeopardy.

Eccles and his staff at the Federal Reserve—most notably, Lauchlin Currie (later designated the economic adviser to the president)—offered a different interpretation of the puzzle. The recession of 1937–1938, in their view, was not a challenge to their analysis of the impact of government spending on the behavior of national income but a confirmation of it. The "net contribution of government to spending" had shifted from expansionary in 1936, when the final installment of the World War I veterans' bonus was distributed, to contractionary in 1937, when social security payroll taxes began to reduce private purchasing power. This finding appeared to establish a direct causal linkage between changes in government outlays and changes in the level of economic activity. What, then, should be the remedy for rising unemployment? The answer seemed obvious: an aggressive program of enlarged deficit spending.

By April 1938 Eccles and other senior officials had managed to convert Roosevelt to this point of view. Then, for the first time, the president embraced deficits as a positive good in stimulating a depressed economy. Up to that point, he had always apologized for the red ink accumulated during his years in the White House. Eccles, though not alone, made a significant contribution in generating the arguments to justify this fiscal revolution in American economic policymaking.

After Pearl Harbor, the challenge to economic policymakers took a different turn. The issue was no longer the adequacy of aggregate demand to achieve full employment; the problem instead was to suppress private demand. This was essential if the war effort were to be conducted successfully with minimal inflationary pressure.

The tools of Keynesian-style demand management, though devised in the context of underemployment, were thus invoked to provide strategies for economic mobilization in a fully employed economy. Eccles and others, particularly the economists at the Bureau of the Budget and the Office of Price Administration, called for stringent fiscal disciplines. They sought major tax increases and a program of universal compulsory savings. Strict wage and price controls were also part of their policy packages, but they argued that the effectiveness of these interventions would ultimately depend on the success or failure of measures to drain off private purchasing power and to suppress consumption.

Eccles was acutely disappointed that the hard-line anti-inflationary program he espoused was not fully adopted during the war. Secretary of the Treasury Henry Morgenthau, Jr., was firmly opposed to taxation that appeared to be regressive and to savings programs that were nonvoluntary. The result was that the war was financed much more by borrowing and much less by current tax revenues than Eccles would have preferred. He recognized, however, that war expenditures could not be totally financed on a current basis and that some debt financing was inevitable. To assist the Treasury in placing bond issues, he agreed to an arrangement whereby the resources of the Federal Reserve would be deployed to support the government bond market. This meant that the wartime Federal Reserve was committed to create enough liquidity to ensure that the

Treasury's bond issues were fully subscribed and at low interest rates. Eccles was uncomfortable about the extent to which government securities were bought by banks rather than by the general public, and he anticipated that this arrangement would bring troubles later. Nevertheless, in the context of national emergency, he went along.

The Federal Reserve's commitment to support the government bond market meant, in effect, that the central bank had sacrificed its autonomy. Moreover, it had lost much of its control over the money supply; commercial banks, holding large quantities of government debt, could readily augment their reserves by selling bonds to the Federal Reserve. Similarly, the central bank's influence over interest rates had been compromised by its undertaking to support the government bond market at par. As an instrument for economic stabilization, monetary policy had been paralyzed.

The federal government was thus not well armed to fight postwar inflationary pressures. Characteristically Eccles called for tight fiscal policies in this economic environment. He believed further that monetary restriction should play a part in countering inflation. This was not an option so long as the Federal Reserve remained subservient to the Treasury's debt managers. The immediate postwar years witnessed some unseemly episodes of intragovernmental infighting between Eccles's Federal Reserve (which sought liberation to tighten interest rates and to restrict the money supply) and the Treasury (which had an obvious stake in keeping interest rates low to minimize debt servicing charges). Because the Federal Reserve was responsible to the Congress and not to the president, the system was technically empowered to operate independently and to ignore the wishes of the executive branch. But a political reality also had to be reckoned with. The president retained the power of appointment to positions on the Board of Governors, and Eccles's term as chairman was due to expire in 1948. For his part, President Harry Truman had made clear the priority he attached to low interest rates and to pegs supporting the prices of government securities.

Eccles chafed against these restrictions and was not reappointed as chairman. He did, however, remain a member of the Board of Governors until 1951 and in this capacity spoke out more vigorously against Treasury hegemony. The so-called accord between the Federal Reserve and the Treasury announced in the spring of 1951 provided that the central bank would discontinue support for government securities after April 15. With the autonomy of the Federal Reserve system reestablished, Eccles resigned from office soon after. He resumed his banking and business career in Utah, with a brief interruption in 1952 for an unsuccessful campaign for the Republican nomination for a seat in the U.S. Senate. He died on December 18, 1977, in Salt Lake City.

BIBLIOGRAPHY

Early, Stephen. 1935. Memorandum, December 13. Franklin D. Roosevelt Presidential Library, Hyde Park, N.Y.

Eccles, Marriner. 1937a. "How to Prevent Another 1929 in 1940." April. Franklin D. Roosevelt Presidential Library, Hyde Park, N.Y.

———. 1937b. Press release, March 15. Franklin D. Roosevelt Presidential Library, Hyde Park, N.Y.

———. 1951. *Beckoning Frontiers: Public and Personal Recollections*. Edited by Sidney Hyman. New York: Alfred A. Knopf.

——— et al. 1944. *Curbing Inflation through Taxation*. New York: Tax Institute of America.

Blum, John Morton. 1959–1967. *From the Morgenthau Diaries*, 3 vols. Boston: Houghton Mifflin.

Hyman, Sidney. 1976. *Marriner S. Eccles: Private Entrepreneur and Public Servant*. Stanford: Graduate School of Business, Stanford University.

Stein, Herbert. 1969. *The Fiscal Revolution in America*. Chicago: University of Chicago Press.

Tugwell, Rexford Guy. 1957. *The Democratic Roosevelt*. Garden City, N.Y.: Doubleday.

RUDOLPH MARTIN EVANS (1890–1956)

Donald R. Wells

Rudolph Martin Evans, who served on the Board of Governors of the Federal Reserve Board from February 1942 until March 1954, was born November 4, 1890, in Cedar Rapids, Iowa, the son of Martin Evans and Margaret (Ganshorn) Evans. He graduated from Cedar Rapids High School and from Iowa State College at Ames, Iowa, earning a B.S. degree in civil engineering in 1913.

After working with a New York construction company for a short time after graduation, Evans became associated with the export business of the Allied Machinery Company of America in 1916. In 1918 he enlisted in the U.S. Army, serving ten months with the 116th Engineers. On his discharge from the army, he rejoined Allied Machinery, married Lenore Marguerite Allen on April 15, 1919, and went to Australia of behalf of Allied Machinery. He and his wife had two daughters, Lenore Marguerite and Nancy Lee.

In 1921 Evans left Allied Machinery and moved with his family to Laurens, Iowa, where he became a livestock farmer for twelve years. A Democrat, he was appointed regional representative of the Corn-Hog Section of the Agricultural Adjustment Act in 1933 and later became chairman of the Iowa Corn-Hog Committee in Des Moines. In 1936 he became special assistant to the secretary of agriculture in Washington, D.C., and in October 1938 was appointed administrator of the Agricultural Adjustment Administration. He held this position until appointed to the Board of Governors of the Federal Reserve system by President Franklin Roosevelt in February 1942 to replace Chester C. Davis.[*]

During Evans's tenure on the board, the United States was involved in World War II and then, after a five-year interval, the Korean conflict. This was the period when the Federal Reserve's monetary policy was subordinated to the Treasury's goal of keeping interest rates on government bonds low. The Fed was forced to purchase all government bonds at par that the private sector did not want to hold in order to keep the yields fixed. The main anti-inflation tool the Fed used in this period was raising reserve requirements, but it also relied on a selective tool, Regulation W, which limited the terms of consumer credit. On the subject of controlling consumer credit R. M. Evans was a tiger.

Consumer credit controls, which were in effect during World War II, were allowed to lapse in November 1947, but Evans testified before Congress that month for their reinstatement—if not permanently, at least for three years. He was back before Congress in August 1948, again asking for permanent legislation to allow the Federal Reserve board to set minimum down payments and a maximum number of monthly payments for consumer durables. Evans revealed his philosophy on consumer credit in his speeches before the Consumer Installment Credit Conference of the American Bankers Association in St. Louis on March 30, 1949, and before the Tri-State Convention in Atlantic City on October 13, 1950. In Evans's view, the greater the stock of durable goods a nation has, the more unstable its economy will be. He believed that consumer credit can get the seller, as well as the buyer, in an overextended position and that sellers should refrain from competing on the basis of generous credit terms. He argued that credit was more than a private deal between two parties because of its impact on the whole economy. Evans was alarmed about the inflationary potential of putting additional purchasing power in the hands of the public when the economy was already operating at full capacity.

Even before the Korean conflict began, Evans stated his own personal philosophy, which reflected his stand on consumer credit. He distanced himself from rugged individualism, which he characterized as holding that it is not the government's business to protect people from their own folly. Instead, he stated that regulations that help to bring about greater economic stability are entirely consistent with democratic and capitalistic institutions and with the overall objective of the greatest good for the greatest number. As further evidence of his position on this subject, when the Board of Governors voted on February 21, 1951, to exempt from the down payment restriction any credit contract of less than three months' duration, Evans was the only member to vote against it.

Other than that one vote, Evans was a team player on the board. Most decisions were unanimous during the pegging period and during the famous accord with the Treasury when pegging was ended. During the Korean conflict, Evans and the board voted not only for consumer credit controls but also for higher margin requirements under Regulations T and U and for real estate credit controls under Regulation X. The votes of the board throughout 1951, 1952, 1953, and up to March 1954, which was Evans's last meeting, were all unanimous except one, and he was not the dissenter.

Another matter that put Evans in the limelight between 1949 and 1952 was his role as the Federal Reserve's hearing officer in the antitrust case against Transamerica Corporation filed under the Clayton Act. The board charged Transamerica with creating a credit monopoly in five western states because of its stock holdings in 600 banks. These hearings lasted over two years before Evans ruled that Transamerica would have to divest itself of forty-seven banks. The board adopted Evans's findings in March 1952 but with two dissenting votes; James K. Vardaman[*] accused Evans of arbitrarily and unfairly discriminating against Transamerica in his conduct of the hearings and of excluding material evidence offered by Transamerica, and Oliver S. Powell[*] disagreed about how many banks it takes to monopolize credit.

Evans moved to Arnolds Park, Iowa, after leaving the board in March 1954. He died on November 21, 1956.

BIBLIOGRAPHY

New York Times. 1956. November 22.
"The Reminiscences of Rudolph M. Evans: Columbia University Oral History Project."
        1972. Glen Rock, N.J.: Microfilming Corp. of America.
Who's Who in America, 1952–1953. Chicago: Marquis Who's Who.

STEPHEN SYMMES GARDNER (1921–1978)

Neela D. Manage

Stephen Symmes Gardner, a leading Philadelphia commercial banker and deputy secretary of the U.S. Treasury since 1974, was appointed by President Gerald Ford in 1976 to a fourteen-year term as a member of the Federal Reserve board. Gardner was sworn into office on February 13, 1976, and was designated vice-chairman for a four-year term that began February 1, 1976.

Stephen Gardner was born December 26, 1921, in Wakefield, Massachusetts, to George F. and Mildred (Edmands) Gardner. His father was an investment banker in Boston, and Stephen Gardner, even when he was a young boy, found his father's work fascinating; he always wanted to be a banker. After high school graduation, he went to work for Boston's First National Bank as a messenger. His college education was interrupted when he joined the U.S. Army in 1942 during World War II. He served in Europe for three years until 1945 and did not complete college until after World War II. During his service in the army, he attained the rank of captain and won the Bronze Star. Married to Consuelo Andonegui on May 15, 1943, he had five children: Susan, Seth, Hilary, Pierce, and S. Symmes, Jr.

Gardner attended Harvard College in 1946–1947 and then joined Harvard Graduate School of Business Administration, where he received a master's of business administration degree in 1949. His concentration of study was finance and banking. In 1949 he was hired as a credit trainee in the banking department of the Girard Trust Bank, the third largest bank in Philadelphia. Shortly after that, he moved into lending as the assistant of the senior lending officer and then became operations officer. He spent his entire career prior to coming to Washington in 1974 with the Girard Bank. During his career at this bank, Gardner was vice-president in charge of branches, senior vice-president and head of the banking department (which handles all the commercial lending and the bank's investment policy), executive vice-president, and director prior to becoming president in 1966 and chairman of the board in 1971.

Gardner's aim was to ensure that the Girard Bank provided services and extended opportunities to the entire community. He emphasized minority employment and opened branches not only in the opulent suburbs but in ghetto areas as well. During his career at the Girard Bank, Gardner participated in several cultural, civic, and conservationist projects in Philadelphia. He was a director of the YMCA Foundation, the Philadelphia Orchestra Association, and the Philadelphia College of Art; a trustee of the United Fund; and a member of the World Affairs Council and the Wilderness Club.

Gardner was also a leading member of Philadelphia's financial community, serving as chairman of the Greater Philadelphia Movement and the Mayor's Advisory Committee. He was the Metro chairman of the National Alliance of Businessmen. He was a member of the Pennsylvania Economy League, Reserve City Bankers, and the Philadelphia Committee on Foreign Relations. He also served as director of several national corporations, including the INA Corporation, Narco Scientific Industries, the Budd Company, and the Amstar Corporation.

In August 1974 Gardner was appointed deputy secretary of the Treasury, a position held by William E. Simon, who became Treasury secretary. As deputy secretary he had direct responsibilities for a wide variety of Treasury activities concentrating on tax matters and tax policy. He was appointed in February 1975 to the President's Commission on Personnel Exchange, established by President Ford to provide an exchange program for federal executives and those in the private sector. He was the coordinator on behalf of the administration for bills introduced in Congress dealing with bank lending and investment powers. Congressional leaders often described him as a fair, open-minded, and straightforward individual who was able to encourage people with conflicting views to come to a consensus and adopt responsible positions on any issue.

When Gardner joined the Federal Reserve board as vice-chairman, the Fed faced many challenges, both with respect to its monetary policy as well as its bank regulatory function. The U.S. economy had just started recovering from a recession following a severe period of inflation.

At the Federal Reserve, chairman Arthur Burns's[*] predominant concern was inflation. His monetary policy strategy consisted of providing sufficient money to support a modest recovery without generating any inflationary pressures. Burns was frequently criticized by Congress and the Carter administration for maintaining a tight monetary policy that was inhibiting the economy's growth and preventing further declines in the unemployment rate. Gardner was a soft-spoken and congenial person and during his tenure as vice-chairman did not challenge Burns on his monetary policy approach. Gardner usually voted with the majority in supporting the trend toward higher interest rates resulting from the Fed's monetary policy during that period.

Gardner's major contribution at the Fed was in the area of bank regulation. He was the expert on regulatory matters at the Fed and was the lead person on bank regulatory reform. He had twenty-five years of banking experience at the Girard Bank, mainly in the areas of lending and bank branching. He had a keen insight into the banking system and a detailed knowledge of how banks operate and respond to bank regulations. He had worked closely with bank regulators and examiners during his career at Girard. Although not a trained economist, he had practical experience. His opinion was that a banker, especially in the commercial lending field, becomes a sort of grass-roots economist. He came to the Fed with a clear understanding of the needs of banks and the improvements in banking regulation that would benefit the industry.

The industries that were hit the hardest by the 1974–1975 recession were construction and housing. Banks that had made substantial loans in these areas were experiencing problems managing their loan portfolios. At that time, a few large banks had failed, and others had tremendous difficulties with bad loans. Newspapers were reporting some banks to be on so-called problem lists that were compiled and maintained by the Federal Reserve and other bank regulatory agencies.

In such an environment, there was tremendous pressure for regulatory reform. There was widespread dissatisfaction about the adequacy of the existing regulations governing banks and growing concern over the soundness of the banking system. Pressures for regulatory reform were mounting in four general areas: tighter bank examination procedures so that any bank problems could be identified and bank failures prevented; increased public disclosure of banks; insider loans, overdrafts, and correspondent banking practices by insiders; and the overlapping of regulatory authority and the possible restructuring of the regulatory agencies with respect to the bank supervision process.

Recognition of these problem areas led the regulatory agencies, primarily the Federal Reserve board, to initiate some changes in their bank examination and supervision procedures. At the Fed, Gardner chaired the Committee on Bank Regulation and Supervision and was also a member of the Inter-Agency Coordination Committee on Bank Regulation. The publicity received by the banking industry in the light of the recession-related problems it faced also resulted in the introduction of several reform legislative proposals in Congress. Gardner was the Fed spokesman on regulatory matters and testified before congressional committees on several bank regulatory matters.

He was a proponent of increased competition in the banking system. He viewed government regulation as essential for monitoring the safety and soundness of the system but was against excessive regulations that could substitute some of the free market decisions in the industry. Gardner believed that in spite of the banking problems caused by the recession and a few cases of bank fraud, the U.S. banking system was basically sound. Although bank examination procedures could be improved in some areas, he perceived the supervisory structure as essentially effective. Gardner believed that the system could be improved by increasing the enforcement powers of bank examiners.

Gardner provided a clear perspective of the highly publicized issue of some banks being on so-called problem lists. He claimed that some banks may be identified as needing more than average monitoring and supervision when they experience some difficulties. The number of institutions on these lists and the length of time such attention is given was, in Gardner's view, an indication of the supervisor's alertness rather than a measure of supervisory performance. Furthermore, he maintained, since these troubled institutions also provided essential services to the public, the close scrutiny maintained by supervisors to ensure the safety of these institutions also represented responsible public policy.

Gardner maintained that bank examination and supervision should not only be aimed at obtaining compliance with regulations and ensuring the safety of the public's deposits but should also serve the public interest in a broader sense by fostering competition, which would ultimately result in a strong and sound banking system. He warned of the social costs and the economic risks of a bank regulatory system that goes beyond these goals. Gardner firmly believed that it is not the job of the supervisor to determine whether specific loans or types of loans should be extended or even how a bank's resources should be used except when such actions violate laws and endanger the soundness of the bank.

Although Gardner was against excessive regulation of banks, he was fully aware of the complex structure of banking institutions, especially that of bank holding companies, which control banks and nonbank subsidiaries. Gardner pointed out that a more systematic monitoring of nonbank subsidiaries was needed to evaluate the true financial condition of banks controlled by bank holding companies. These banks accounted for roughly two-thirds of the total deposits in the banking system. In November 1977 the Fed voted to extend bank-style examination and evaluation procedures to nonbanking affiliates. Although the vote was unanimous, some Fed governors were troubled by the philosophical implications of the increased scrutiny of the nonbank subsidiaries by the Fed. They thought it was a step in the direction of Fed regulation of nonbanking companies. Gardner also thought it was a difficult issue but believed such procedures were necessary to protect the banks controlled by holding companies.

The case in favor of greater bank disclosure was that it would increase the public's awareness of the conditions at banks and the discipline at banks since they would be aware of the disclosure of their activities. The process would thus allow market forces to monitor the system. Gardner was aware of the trend toward increased disclosure of banks, especially the disclosure requirements of bank holding companies by the Securities and Exchange Commission. But he advised caution in implementing greater disclosure of bank operations for two reasons. He noted that such disclosures could jeopardize the bank if it resulted in mindless bank runs on the basis of information that was not recent or in some cases even subjective and that they could compromise the bank examination itself if examiners did not give a frank and objective appraisal fearing that their report might destroy a bank.

Stephen Gardner was an important witness during congressional hearings to determine the extent to which unsound banking practices were widespread in the U.S. banking system. He explained that there were some instances of unsound banking practices but that there were adequate safeguards within the regulatory structure to avoid an extensive occurrence of these practices. He testified that the Federal Reserve board had taken action to terminate excessive salaries and dividends paid to directors and controlling shareholders by bank holding companies and that regulatory agencies had adequate powers to deal with overdraft policies and preferential loan treatment given to bank officials.

Two other areas in which Gardner made significant contributions during his tenure at the Fed were the payments mechanism and the regulation of foreign bank operations in the United States. He was the Fed representative on issues involving electronic funds transfer systems and related consumer protection issues. He warned of the antitrust implications of shared systems and the potential antitrust violations resulting from cooperation among financial institutions in order to take advantage of the electronic technology. Gardner firmly believed that vigorous competition among financial institutions is ultimately the best form of consumer protection. The Federal Reserve first proposed some formal regulation of foreign bank operations in the United States in 1974. These proposals went through extensive revisions, and when Gardner joined the Fed, he stressed the importance of placing foreign bank operations under federal banking and monetary regulation similar to domestic commercial banks. At the time the United States was the only country among the major industrialized economies without a national banking law governing foreign banks. He strongly supported the International Banking Act, which put foreign and domestic banks on a more equal footing. Gardner clearly saw the procompetitive advantages of such legislation as well.

Gardner was aware that it was becoming more difficult to manage monetary policy because of the changing infrastructure of the economy and because monetary policy was not independent of fiscal policy, which was then characterized by increasing budget deficits. He was concerned with the size of the budget deficits and did not adhere to the view that Treasury debt is not important. He considered the national debt to be a serious issue because of the increasing share of interest payments in the budget deficit and the rise in the purchase of Treasury debt by foreigners. With respect to the structural aspects of inflation and the proposals for incomes policies to hold down wage and price increases, Gardner was interested in supporting the free market mechanism in the economy. He thought businessmen were predicting price rises in 1976 because of a quadrupling of energy costs and because manufacturing firms faced high environmental cleanup costs. The underlying basic causes of price increases at the time, according to Gardner, were actually technical in nature. He placed great emphasis on the private sector to offset rising wages and prices through competitive means wherever possible.

Stephen Gardner died of cancer in his Washington, D.C., home, on November 19, 1978, at the age of fifty-six. He was survived by his wife, three sons, two daughters, two sisters, and eight grandchildren.

Gardner had begun a distinguished career at the Fed and during his short tenure made important contributions to the Federal Reserve's bank regulatory programs.

His untimely death does not enable us to determine the total impact of the regulatory programs he initiated and directed at the Fed. His strong views on the importance of competition in the banking industry, the need for a balanced approach toward bank supervision and regulation, and his warnings about the ramifications of rising interest payments on the public debt and the dependence on foreign financing of budget deficits are a few notable examples of how he shaped the regulatory and monetary policy approach at the Fed. In the light of the importance of these issues in the last ten years, characterized by deregulation in the banking industry and the huge budget deficits of the 1980s, it is easy to envisage the enormous influence he could have had on the Fed had he served his full fourteen-year term.

BIBLIOGRAPHY

Gardner, Stephen S. 1977a. "Statement to Congress." *Federal Reserve Bulletin*, pp. 116–19.
———. 1977b. Testimony in hearings before the Committee on Banking, Housing, and Urban Affairs of the U.S. Senate, September.
———. 1977c. "Statement to Congress." *Federal Reserve Bulletin* (July): 651–54.
———. 1978. Testimony in hearings before the Committee of Finance of the U.S. Senate, February.
U.S. Congress. Senate. Committee on Banking, Housing, and Urban Affairs. 1976. *Hearing on the Nomination of Stephen S. Gardner*. 94th Cong., 2d sess., January.

LYLE E. GRAMLEY (1927–   )

Marie McKinney

Lyle E. Gramley was no stranger to the Federal Reserve system when he was nominated by President Jimmy Carter to join the Board of Governors in 1980. Except for a tour of duty as a member of Carter's Council of Economic Advisers (CEA) between 1977 and 1980, Gramley had worked in Washington as an economist at the Fed since 1964. During this period, he had earned a reputation as an eclectic economist, one who combined theory and reality to produce a practical, commonsense approach to formulating economic policy. As an economist Gramley has never believed in a doctrinaire approach to policy. He cautions against relying on simple rules, especially where monetary policy is concerned, but he has not allowed popular sentiment to force him to abandon the basic tenets of economic theory as a guide to action.

Although he has spent much of his working career in the nation's capital, Gramley lived in the Midwest in his early years. He was born in Aurora, Illinois, a small city about 40 miles southwest of Chicago. Illinois ranks among the leading agricultural states, and during his high school days Gramley worked on a farm where he cared for horses and learned to shuck and thrash oats. He can still milk a cow by hand or machine, no mean set of accomplishments for a professional economist.

Gramley's educational roots are also in the Midwest. In 1951 he received a B.A. from Beloit College, where he was elected to Phi Beta Kappa. He traces his interest in economics as a profession back to his undergraduate days, when he was enrolled in an economic principles class taught by a woman who truly impressed Gramley to the extent that he changed his intended major from engineering to economics. He pursued his interest in economics at the graduate level at Indiana University, where he received his Ph.D. At Indiana his major fields of concentration were business cycles and monetary economics.

Gramley's interest in business cycles and monetary theory led him to the Federal Reserve system, where he has spent most of his career as a professional economist. In 1955 he joined the staff at the Federal Reserve Bank of Kansas

City as a financial economist, thus beginning his commitment to public service. At the bank he was introduced to economic forecasting and devoted his research and writing to commercial banking, capital markets, and monetary policy. In 1962 he was appointed to the faculty of the University of Maryland, where he taught monetary theory to graduates and undergraduates. At Maryland he became acquainted with Charles Schultze, who was later to become chairman of the CEA under Jimmy Carter.

After leaving the University of Maryland, Gramley rejoined the Fed, this time on the staff of the Board of Governors in Washington, D.C. In 1977, at the time of his appointment to the CEA, he was serving as director of the Division of Research and Statistics, responsible for economic forecasting, analysis of financial markets, and advising on monetary policy—solid preparation for his work with the CEA. Gramley served on the council until 1980, when he was appointed a governor of the Federal Reserve system.

In the position of governor, he has a major influence on the direction of monetary policy. Gramley feels that he brings not only the training of an economist into this responsibility but, because of his roots in the Midwest, a strong empathy with broad sectors of the U.S. economy. He has expressed special concern over the plight of those sectors hit hardest by restrictive monetary policy, such as agriculture, small business, and residential housing.

Gramley has published many articles in the fields of banking and monetary policy and has stressed the importance of money as a tool of economic policy but cautions against the use of simple growth targets for monetary aggregates. His other publications include many that were written while he was with the Federal Reserve banks. In his capacity as representative of the Federal Reserve system, Gramley has made many speeches to professional business and banking organizations.

Gramley describes the three and a half years he spent as a member of the CEA as the most exciting of his professional career. On March 18, 1977, he joined Charles Schultze and William Nordhaus as a member of the CEA. Nordhaus, a professor from Yale University, assumed the role of chief theoretician. Gramley undertook the responsibility for economic forecasting and macropolicy and, later, labor policy.

Although the Carter years are remembered for the monumental battle against inflation and unemployment (stagflation), the administration began its tenure in an atmosphere of mild optimism. In 1977 the economy was entering its third year of recovery, and, although still a threat, the rate of inflation had receded significantly from its high level earlier in the decade. The economic priorities of the early Carter days were to stimulate economic growth, increase employment, and extend the benefits of a productive society to its less fortunate members. Although the energy problem surfaced early in the administration, the full extent of its economic consequences was not realized until much later.

The Carter administration ended during troubled economic times. Inflation, interest rates, and unemployment—the so-called misery index—were well above traditional levels. Gramley, in reflection, has recognized the limitations of demand management in a complex economy and the limited goals that it can achieve.

When Gramley left the council in 1980 to rejoin the Federal Reserve system as a governor, he brought with him a healthy respect for the destructive potential of inflation and a commitment to avoid policies that would lead to increased inflationary pressure.

Of the issues that absorbed Gramley's attention in his role as governor of the Federal Reserve system, the need to combat inflation continued to have a high priority. He brought up the subject frequently when speaking to professional financial associations. His concern also extended to the other issues that influence the implementation of monetary policy, including the impact of federal deficits on interest rates and the effect of high interest rates on the American economy. He was concerned with the effect of high interest rates on the exchange value of the dollar and its relationship to the trade deficit and to domestic industries that face increased import competition. Finally, he was concerned with the changes in the financial sector that followed deregulation.

All these issues are related. It was inflation and inflationary expectations that led originally to higher interest rates. High real interest rates had been sustained, in part, by the need to finance the federal deficit. Never had the need for coordination of fiscal and monetary policy been greater than during Gramley's years on the Fed's Board of Governors. Yet during that period, mounting federal deficits kept interest rates high, forcing some sectors of the economy out of the credit markets. High interest rates also meant that the United States was less competitive in the field of international trade, as well as posing a threat to the economic stability of developing countries that sell goods to the United States.

Deregulation and the restructuring of the financial sector created further problems in implementing monetary policy by reducing the control of monetary authorities over the financial sector. Deregulation was necessary to permit banks to compete for deposits on an equal footing with other financial institutions. But by reducing the distinction between savings and transactions balances and banking and nonbanking institutions, pursuit of monetary policy was been made more difficult. Finally, the Federal Reserve board itself switched its operational target from control of interest rates to control of monetary aggregates.

The new, freer environment created new challenges and responsibilities for central bankers. Although the positions he presents are usually his own and not necessarily those of the Fed, as a governor of the Federal Reserve system, Gramley had an excellent forum to bring these issues before a concerned public. He has always been concerned with the impact of restrictive monetary policy on vulnerable sectors of the economy. He has reason to believe that these sectors are subject to increasing vulnerability. Because the Fed targets monetary aggregates and not interest rates, interest rates have become more volatile, reaching higher levels when heavy demand pressure is put on credit markets by the government or the private sector or when monetary policy grows restrictive.

Because interest rates are allowed to float, these rates, not credit availability, serve as the transmission mechanism for monetary policy. The shift means that it has grown more difficult to protect interest-sensitive sectors of the economy, such as residential housing and small business, from credit shortages. In the past, Gramley was more optimistic regarding the ability of the banking authorities to allocate credit to these sectors. In the early 1980s they were priced out of the credit market when interest rates rose.

Providing a wholly acceptable monetary policy for the 1980s proved to be as controversial as providing fiscal policy during the Carter administration. In each case, Gramley encountered a new generation of problems, problems that had been unanticipated just a few years ago. He examined those problems with great care, and his pragmatic solutions contained equal amounts of economic theory, practical good sense, and concern for the individuals and institutions affected by policy. He recognized the complexity of the problems and never suggested popular but simple solutions. Before offering a solution, he examined all of its ramifications—immediate and long term, desirable and disagreeable.

In 1985 Gramley resigned from the Fed after serving for five years as a member of the Board of Governors. These were dramatic years for monetary policy. Under the leadership of Paul Volcker[*] the Fed took bold moves to break the back of inflation, even at the cost of one of the deepest recessions since the 1930s.

After resigning from the Fed, Gramley was named chief economist and senior staff vice-president for the Mortgage Bankers Association of America, where he can devote his efforts to studying the impact of monetary policy on the residential and commercial housing sector. From that position, he can keep a close watch on the impact of economic conditions on housing markets.

Late in 1987 Gramley correctly predicted that the stock market crash of that year would not have a major negative impact on the economy; he was even able to see a silver lining in the aftereffects of the crash. Interest rates, including mortgage rates, declined following it. The result, he predicted, would be a healthier housing market for the United States. In addition, the postcrash reduction in consumer spending moderated inflation and also led to lower nominal interest rates. The big gainers, he felt, were the low- to moderate-income buyers who were less likely to have been affected by the drop in stock prices.

As a former insider, Gramley continues to comment on the conduct of Fed operations, and his opinion on these issues is sought after. In a 1988 article in *Mortgage Banking*, Gramley gave Fed chairman Alan Greenspan[*] high marks for his conduct of monetary policy during his first year in office. Gramley was especially impressed by Greenspan's skillful handling of the aftereffects of the stock market crash. Greenspan prevented what could have been a serious liquidity crisis and maintained the public confidence that the Fed would be a dependable supporter of strained credit markets.

In over a quarter of a century of service to the public sector, Gramley has provided thoughtful and prudent advice to policymakers. In this role, he has not pursued his own agenda; rather he has attempted to clarify the merits and short-comings of the policies being evaluated.

Gramley is well liked by his associates, who describe him as unfailingly courteous. He was also known by his colleagues at the Fed as a hard worker who was always prepared for meetings.

He is married to the former Evelyn Wachtel, and for many years they have lived in Potomac, Maryland, just outside Washington, D.C.

He is a member of the National Association of Business Economists and the American Economics Association.

BIBLIOGRAPHY

Gramley, Lyle E. 1974. "Guidelines for Monetary Policy—The Case against Simple Rules." In *Readings in Money, National Income, and Stabilization Policy*. 3d ed. Edited by Warren L. Smith and Ronald L. Teigen. Homewood, Ill.: Richard D. Irwin.

———. 1980. "Supply-Side Economics: Its Role in Curing Inflation." Speech delivered to community leaders in Seattle, Washington, September 11.

———. 1981. "Financial Innovation and Public Policy." Speech delivered at the Financial Innovation Conference, Northwestern University, Evanston, Illinois, April 22.

———. 1982. "Financial Innovation and Monetary Policy." Speech delivered at the Nineteenth Meeting of Governors of Central Banks of the American Continent, Quito, Ecuador, March 22.

———. 1984a. "The Outlook for Economic Expansion in 1984." Speech delivered at the Thirty-ninth Annual Senior Executive Economic Outlook Conference of the Mortgage Bankers Association of America, New York, January 12.

———. 1984b. "Our Internal and External Deficits and the Relationship between Them." Speech delivered to the Twin Cities business community, Minneapolis, June 14.

———. 1988. "Happy Anniversary Alan Greenspan." *Mortgage Banking* (July): 38–42.

"Lyle Gramley Goes Home." 1980. *New York Times*, May 25.

"Stock Market Plunges! What Happens Next?" 1987. (Interview with Lyle Gramley.) *Mortgage Banking* (December): 13–14.

U.S. Congress. House. Committee on Banking, Housing, and Urban Affairs. 1977. *Nomination of William D. Nordhaus and Lyle E. Gramley*. 95th Cong., 1st sess., January 26.

———. Senate. Committee on Banking, Housing, and Urban Affairs. 1980. *Nomination of Lyle E. Gramley. Hearings*. 96th Cong., 2d sess., April 15, 16.

ALAN GREENSPAN (1926–)

Thomas Havrilesky and Bernard S. Katz

It is doubtful when Alan Greenspan left the Julliard School of Music to play in a big band that he envisioned his future in the highest offices of public service. From musician to the chairmanships of the President's Council of Economic Advisers from 1974 to 1977 and then of the Board of Governors of the Federal Reserve in 1988 is, indeed, a splendid, if not remarkable, journey.

Born March 6, 1926, Greenspan was the single child of Herbert and Rose (Goldsmith). After the divorce of his parents in 1926, Greenspan lived with his mother's sister in the Washington Heights section of Manhattan. The young Greenspan substituted tenacity for gregariousness, a tendency evident today. Raised in a household steeped in religion and music, Greenspan still assigns priority to Mozart as well as Friedman.

Attending and graduating from New York's George Washington High, Greenspan considered serious music as a career and enrolled in Julliard. This, like his dance band stint, was short lived. His love of books and learning drew him back to formal education. Attending New York University, he majored in economics and graduated summa cum laude in 1948. Greenspan stayed on at NYU and obtained his M.A. in economics in 1950. While in graduate school, he married Joan Mitchell. The marriage was annulled after one year but not before his wife introduced him to Ayn Rand. This meeting strongly influenced Greenspan's views on political economy.

Ayn Rand was a leading spokesperson for objectivism, or rational selfishness, which extols the virtues of unfettered laissez-faire capitalism. This market approach to human behavior is exemplified in Rand's novels *The Fountainhead* and *Atlas Shrugged*.

Greenspan's association with Rand welded his thoughts on the linkage between efficiency (of capitalism) and morality. In early issues of the *Objectivist*, a Randian periodical, Greenspan's writing championed capitalism and scored the inequities and inefficiency of the welfare state. He described the welfare state as a mechanism to confiscate the wealth of the productive members of society and of deficit spending as a scheme to hasten this process. Greenspan advocated

monetary rules and decried consumer protectionism. These were not simply the
musings of a young man; Greenspan has sustained these beliefs throughout his
professional career.

After completing his M.A. degree, Greenspan enrolled in the doctoral program
at Columbia University. His studies were initiated under the tutelage of Arthur
Burns,* a past chairman of the Federal Reserve board (1970–1978). Greenspan
left Columbia in 1973 before finishing the program for, in his own words, the
work became "less and less interesting." Nevertheless, by 1977 Greenspan was
granted a Ph.D. in economics by New York University.

Greenspan's professional career began primarily as that of economic consultant
and forecaster. Except for an occasional foray as an instructor in economics at
the Nathaniel Branden Institute in New York City, a forum for Ayn Rand
followers, and for New York University from 1953 to 1955 and again after his
chairmanship of the Council of Economic Advisers, Greenspan's activities have
focused on the private sector.

Greenspan's first position was with the National Industrial Conference Board,
a nonprofit research organization supported by business subscriptions and do-
nations. His work at the board was to estimate the demand for steel, aluminum,
and copper. He stayed with the board until 1953, at which time he joined up
with William Townsend to form the consulting firm Townsend-Greenspan and
Company. Upon the death of Townsend in 1958, Greenspan assumed the firm's
presidency.

The firm's expansion was slow and controlled, in part due to Greenspan's
firm hand. He ran "a one-man band," using his staff primarily for research. By
1974 the Greenspan-Townsend firm represented over 100 major industrial and
financial institutions, embracing the nation's leading banks. The success of the
firm has been attributed to Greenspan's skill in taking fragmented numbers and
composing a general picture of the movement of the economy.

Greenspan's interest in public service began with a series of political associations. By 1968 he had become Richard Nixon's director of domestic policy
research. He was also the president-elect's transitional representative to the
Bureau of the Budget, as well as his chairman of the Task Force on Foreign
Trade Policy. Greenspan was appointed to the Task Force on Economic Growth
(1969), the Commission on an All-Volunteer Armed Force (1969–1979), and
the Commission on Financial Structure and Regulation (1970–1971). President
Nixon nominated Greenspan to chair his President's Council of Economic Advisers in August 1974. With Nixon's resignation at the end of August, Greenspan
was to serve throughout the presidency of Gerald Ford.

Greenspan's appointment made him the first business economist to serve as
chairman of the council. Reflecting Gerald Ford's economic conservatism,
Greenspan was a strong advocate of private enterprise. The extent of his convictions can be garnered from his testimony during the hearings before the Ninety-
third Congress.

One of the strongest tenets held by Greenspan, one that he continually iterated, regards the damage done to the economy through deficit spending. Deficits bring government into private capital markets, and this, he asserts, crowds out private borrowers. The traditional crowding-out problem has a series of adverse effects; one is that private investment will lose out to government borrowing, and the deprivation in private capital formation erodes the nation's economic strength.

Greenspan argued regularly that within a free society, the claim of government on a person's income is not unqualified. Moreover, he asserted that the principal form of taxation, the progressive income tax, defies the rules of equity and also threatens the total amount of taxes collected through its disincentive effects. In response to this view, Senator William Proxmire (D, Wisconsin) of the Senate Banking Committee, upon reviewing the appointment of Greenspan, remarked that Greenspan had an "incredible posture for an economic realist"—one of opposing the progressive income tax.

Greenspan inveighed against the mixed economy, an incomes policy, antitrust legislation, wage and price controls, subsidies, import quotas, government-guaranteed loans, and consumer product safety laws, among others. He advocates free and competitive markets.

Once sited at the council, Greenspan's unassailable reputation as an economic forecaster was put in jeopardy. Having taken office in August 1974, he inherited an economy that was faced with a rising and disturbing rate of inflation. In his role as chairman, forecaster, and policy strategist, Greenspan ran into some difficult times. In September at an economic conference meeting to discuss inflation, Greenspan spoke about the essential health of the economy. Accordingly, he counseled President Ford to ask Congress for a counterinflationary tax surcharge. By the end of 1974, Greenspan's words and recommendation were completely out of phase with an economy that was experiencing its largest decline in output in any peacetime year since the early post–World War II period. Another forecasting error took place in April 1975. While Greenspan was maintaining that the worst was yet to come, the economic decline had actually flattened out. From that low point, his forecasting performances improved impressively.

When Greenspan assumed office, the unemployment rate stood at 5.5 percent and inflation at 12 percent. By December 1977 the unemployment rate, after climbing to a high of 8.5 percent in 1975, had fallen to 6.3 percent, and inflation, as measured by the consumer price index, had fallen to 6.1 percent. Whereas Greenspan had misread the strength of the economy when he had become chairman, by the end of his tenure, both inflation and unemployment had fallen significantly from their previous highs.

Public sector employment did not change Greenspan's work habits. At his desk from 7:30 A.M. until the late evening hours carried through from New York to Washington. Greenspan had little interest in either money or what it could buy, and in social Washington, Greenspan exhibited the same diffidence of his youth.

Greenspan's unaggressive manner allowed him a good deal of acceptance among philosophically diverse associates. Carrying his 180 pounds comfortably on a 6-foot frame, Greenspan speaks softly but candidly in a quiet baritone. His renowned command of the numbers of his trade is accompanied by wit and reason. Reputedly ill at ease with smalltalk or gossip, Greenspan is far more comfortable in the discourse of economic analysis. His occasionally singular diction has been dubbed "Greenspanese" by insiders.

At the council, Greenspan earned credibility not only with fellow economists but with the president. While his early political gaffe that inflation hit the wealthier harder than the poor may not have won him broad accolades, it did suggest a hard-core conservatism that endeared him to the right. Thus, Greenspan did not have to play the Washington political game. He saw his function as advising the president as to the state of the economy. Where it had been argued that the Nixon council was weakened by its political maneuvers, Ford's council won respect for its firm attitude toward analyzing the facts.

With the end of the Ford administration, Greenspan returned to private life and reassumed the headship of his consulting firm. By the end of 1984 his firm employed almost forty professionals and had revenues approximating $3 million. Nevertheless, upon leaving the council, Greenspan did not leave public service. He served out his appointment to the National Commission on Supplies and Shortages (1974–1977) and in December 1981 was appointed chairman to the controversial National Commission on Social Security Reform. In this function it was suggested by Congressman Willis Gradison (R, Ohio) that if Greenspan could succeed in bringing about agreement on the commission, "he should get the Nobel Peace Prize." While forging consensus among the warring parties on the commission in early 1983, the prize still awaits.

By 1984, relations between Federal Reserve chairman Paul Volcker[*] and President Ronald Reagan had become strained. Reagan was rankled over the heroic accolades that Volcker, a Democrat, had received for what Reagan believed was his own administration's success in reducing inflation. Then, in 1985–1986, after James Baker became treasury secretary, disagreements became more intense over currency intervention, the persistent budget deficit, and the failure of the Fed to satisfy the administration's desire for more rapid monetary growth in order to try to reduce interest rates and the value of the dollar in international currency markets. The strain became more apparent with the increase in the number of ease-oriented supply-side appointees to the board in 1985–1987. The crisis reached its apogee when in 1987, for the first time in history, the Federal Reserve chairman dissented from the majority of the Federal Open Market Committee (FOMC) in a formal vote on a directive that had called for further easing the discount rate. This singular event greatly reduced Volcker's ability to speak for the board, and, under such stressful circumstances, it became increasingly difficult for him to advance his objective of moderate money growth. In August 1987 Volcker handed in his resignation, and Reagan was left with the decision of who would follow him.

The president wanted someone who would be more in tune with contemporary Republican economic principles. In this respect Alan Greenspan ranked favorably but not ideally. True, Greenspan was opposed to higher tax rates, which he viewed as a disincentive to productive effort. But he was also in favor of less government regulation, as evidenced by his vocal support of banking deregulation. In these areas Greenspan and Reagan were in accord. A major area of disagreement, however, was that Greenspan tacitly disagreed with the Baker-Reagan supply-side bias in favor of monetary ease.

Another key concern of Reagan was to please the financial community. Volcker was held in exceedingly high esteem by the financial sector, and Reagan's appointee would have to impart confidence that the rapport between the chairman and the private financial sector would continue. Greenspan, with his private sector experience as well as his reputation as a Washington heavyweight, seemed to fit the bill. He was as respected as Volcker by financial sector leaders in every area (with the possible exception of his limited experience in international financial diplomacy).

More important than ideology and private financial sector reputation, Reagan wanted to head the Fed with a Republican. Greenspan's strong ties to the Republican party led the president to believe that he would be a team player and would yield to the administration's desires on monetary policy.

With these criteria in mind, the president appointed Alan Greenspan to the helm of the Federal Reserve. The historic record, however, shows that Federal Reserve chairmen are usually much more than cookie-cutter figureheads for the administration that appointed them. Over the past forty years, Fed chairmen have been able to imbue the organization with their own values. Alan Greenspan proved no exception. Before we establish his imprint on the central bank that he heads, it is important to understand the political and economic forces that have impinged on monetary policy over the past forty years.

As the redistributive policies of government have grown in the past four decades, monetary policy, employed to camouflage the effects of these redistributions, has become more politicized. In exchange for having to deal with a higher degree of political influence, the Federal Reserve has demanded from politicians their tacit acceptance of a greater degree of central bank autonomy. Since anti-inflationary monetary policy and autonomy go hand in hand, there has also occurred an increase in anti-inflationary militance at the Federal Reserve. Because political pressures on monetary policy are usually ultimately inflationary and Fed demands are anti-inflationary, it is necessary to examine this subtle trade-off in greater detail and then apply the resulting insight to analyzing the evolution of the Fed chairmanship.

The evolution of monetary policy toward higher levels of external pressure and visibility is reflected in subtle changes in the elaborate symbiosis between the Federal Reserve, the administration, Congress, and the private financial services sector. Since its inception, politicians have granted to the Federal Reserve a certain degree of immunity from outside pressure on its monetary policy decisions, as well as a certain amount of regulatory domain and budgetary autonomy—that is, Federal Reserve independence. In exchange, they have always had their way with monetary policy if need be and periodically were able to bash their Fed whipping boys whenever anything went wrong and they needed to let off political steam. The routes by which politicians have influenced the Fed vary, ranging from making reliable appointments to the board through a spectrum of increasingly overt means of signaling, ranging from casual hints to outright support of legislation that would reduce Federal Reserve powers. Federal Reserve leaders, in turn, have always been obliged to receive the signals and accede dutifully to the bashings, even as they played their roles as oracles of sound money and sound banking.

There are formidable indications that political pressure on Federal Reserve officials has grown increasingly intense in recent decades. The Banking Act of 1935 set the stage for the political pressures to come by increasing the power of the Federal Reserve board and the FOMC at the expense of the Federal Reserve banks. Constraints on monetary excesses were weakened with Congress's enjoinder to the Fed to promote high employment under the Full Employment Act of 1946. Further erosion of monetary discipline occurred when Congress abolished the ratio requirement of gold certificates to bank reserves in 1966 and to Federal Reserve notes in 1968. The Depository Institutions Deregulation and Monetary Control Act of 1980 extended central bank control over the entire financial services sector. The centralization of monetary power is further reflected in the steady erosion of private sector influence within the FOMC. This is revealed, for example, in the trend in the private-versus-public sector career characteristics of FOMC members. Over the 1960–1988 period, the average years in private banking and private industry of FOMC members had negative trend coefficients that were significant at the .01 level. The upshot of all these changes is that the politicization of monetary policy has been coextensive with the trend toward an all-powerful Federal Reserve board and, more important, an all-powerful chairman.

There is considerable evidence that informal political and private pressures on Federal Reserve officials have intensified in recent decades (Havrilesky 1988). In addition, on more formal levels there are also indications of increased pressure. As an example, formal interest group presence within the Federal Reserve has risen, reflected most strikingly in the stipulations of the Federal Reserve Reform Act of 1977. As another example, the scale of formal interactions between political principals and their central bank agents has greatly expanded, highlighted not only by the requirements of the Full Employment and Balanced Growth Act of 1978 but also by the growing input of Fed officials in practically all aspects of government economic policy.

Private bankers, for their part in the symbiosis, receive favorable regulatory treatment from politicians and their Federal Reserve overseers and can also influence monetary policy if necessary but, given the popular aversion to bankers in politics, must avoid the appearance of doing so (Havrilesky 1990a). They also must come to the defense of the Fed whenever it is politically beleaguered. Bankers are, of course, also expected to make generous campaign contributions to politicians, especially those involved with monetary and financial regulatory policy (Havrilesky 1991).

These arrangements have been widely discussed. What is of interest here is the slow but subtle changes that have occurred in the terms of trade between politicians and the Fed. The more that politicians have wanted to have their way with monetary policy, the more they have exposed monetary policy to public scrutiny. Given the symbiosis discussed, greater political pressure upon and greater public exposure of Federal Reserve officials is not costless to politicians. In exchange, they have had to make greater compensating concessions to Federal Reserve autonomy. Empirical studies suggest that the more autonomous is a central bank, the more anti-inflationary is its monetary policy. Therefore, given the institutional arrangements that overlay American monetary policy, the greater the political and private pressure on the Federal Reserve and the greater its concomitant exposure to public scrutiny, the greater are the tacit concessions to Federal Reserve autonomy and the greater its concomitant anti-inflationary militance. Of course, the inflationary demands of politicians contrast rather starkly to their anti-inflationary concessions to Fed autonomy, chronically placing Fed officials in the discomfiting position of having to reconcile contradictory policy objectives.

Next, we apply this insight to a comparative evaluation of the Federal Reserve chairmanship. The behavior of four successive Federal Reserve chairmen corroborates the pattern. William McChesney Martin, Jr.,[*] Arthur Burns, and Paul Volcker were each greater devotees of Federal Reserve independence and anti-inflationary militance than their predecessors. Alan Greenspan represents an even higher level on this trend line.

William Miller's[*] tenure at the Federal Reserve was too brief to warrant inclusion. Indeed, the disaster that arose from Miller's exceptional political pliability testifies as to the wisdom of the trends discussed here. Chairmen prior to Martin, Thomas McCabe[*] and Marriner Eccles,[*] were not included because prior to 1951, the Federal Reserve was subordinate to the U.S. Treasury, even though provision for titular Fed independence dates from the Banking Act of 1935.

The first chairman in the post-accord era, while an exemplar of conservative deportment, was less than stalwart in resisting political pressure. Although he was the key negotiator for Federal Reserve independence in the Accord of 1951, William McChesney Martin regularly succumbed to administration influence, first under the thrall of John Kennedy's romantic economic activism and then under the strain of Lyndon Johnson's legendary arm twisting. Martin also evinced a well-known disdain for economic theory and economists. Consistent with the atheoretical spirit at the Fed at the time, he believed that the central bank could and should manipulate interest rates. This generated a deluge of criticism from researchers that gave birth to the insistence that the Federal Reserve pay more attention to the monetary aggregates.

Arthur Burns, while periodically posturing in the cause of Federal Reserve independence, was about as pliable as Martin. In 1972 Burns ignited the quintessential spate of preelection monetary ease that to this day represents one of the few supporting instances of a traditional political business cycle. He also advocated easy money during the early days of the Carter presidency, in order, it is reported, to curry administration favor and win reappointment. While an academic economist and a conservative, Burns was a sophisticated inductivist of the American institutionalist school and not a macroeconomic theorist. By the end of his tenure, his credentials as an economic policy conservative had tarnished rather badly. Burns's support of countercyclical tax cuts and price controls was anything but neoclassical, and his attempts to keep interest rates low during Richard Nixon's experiment with price controls, as well as during the early Carter years, were inconsonant with neoclassical precepts.

Paul Volcker, in contrast, set a considerably higher standard for Fed autonomy. His sound money resolve contributed to Jimmy Carter's nightmare on Constitution Avenue. During the Reagan era, Volcker was under continual pressure, first over 1981–1984 from traditional monetary conservatives on the council and at the Treasury for tighter monetary policy and, then, after 1985, from supply siders in the administration and on the board for easier money. To these pressures he ultimately succumbed, as any Fed chairman must, but in resisting, his deportment was splendid. While careful to avoid the theorist label and even more careful to avoid the embrace of the official enemies of the realm, the monetarists, Volcker skillfully invoked neoclassical analysis whenever he was confronted with congressional demands that he control interest rates. Volcker also used a neoclassical demeanor to resist the easy money pleas of his supply-side-dominated board after Treasury Secretary Baker's quiet palace coup of 1985 (Havrilesky 1988, 1990b).

Alan Greenspan represents the high-water mark of the forty-year tide toward greater Federal Reserve autonomy and monetary policy conservatism. After only three years in office, he has overcome the White House's good cop–bad cop rap, risen above Beryl Sprinkel's sound money criticisms from the Council of Economic Advisers, and successfully deflected the easy money persuasions of James Baker, a prominent player in the supply-side coup of 1985–1986. The proper test of Greenspan's mettle will occur when pressures for monetary ease mount, as they inevitably must in the face of economic crises.

Over the past forty years, monetary policy has become increasingly politicized. This has required a weakening of formal institutional restraints on monetary excesses, namely, the elimination of the gold reserve ratio and the reduction of reserve bank and private sector authority within the Federal Reserve system. As a consequence, over this forty-year span, power within the system has devolved to the Federal Reserve board, particularly to its chairman. Discipline against monetary excesses therefore rests, almost exclusively in the strength of the anti-inflationary persona of the chairman.

Given the symbiosis that exists between politicians, the Federal Reserve, and the financial services community, if politicians are more frequently to have their way with monetary policy, they must grant more autonomy to the chairman. Since autonomy and anti-inflationary monetary policy are highly correlated, this realignment would lead one to predict that over the past four decades, successive Federal Reserve chairmen will have become greater devotees of central bank independence and anti-inflationary militance.

In his conservative demeanor, Alan Greenspan represents the apotheosis of this trend. Although his anti-inflationary authority will be exposed to bashings from politicians, it is difficult to envision a more appropriate chairman.

BIBLIOGRAPHY

Havrilesky, Thomas. 1987. "A Partisanship Theory of Monetary and Fiscal Policy Regimes." *Journal of Money, Credit and Banking* (August).

———. 1988. "Monetary Policy Signaling from the Administration to the Federal Reserve." *Journal of Money, Credit and Banking* (February.)

———. 1989. "A Compassionate Solution to Distributional Conflict." *Challenge* (March-April).

———. 1990a. "The Influence of the Federal Advisory Council on Monetary Policy." *Journal of Money, Credit and Banking* (February).

———. 1990b. "The New Political Economy of Monetary Policy." *Public Budgeting and Financial Management* (August).

———. 1990c. "A Public Choice Perspective on the Cycle in Monetary Policy." *Cato Journal* (Winter).

———. 1990d. "Distributive Conflict and Monetary Policy." *Contemporary Policy Issues* (April).

———. 1991. "The Causes and Consequences of Big Bank PAC Contributions." *Journal of Financial Services Research* 3, no. 1.

———, and Gildea, John. 1991. "Reliable and Unreliable Partisan Appointees to the Board of Governors." *Public Choice*.

CHARLES SUMNER HAMLIN (1861–1938)

Michael Connell

Charles Sumner Hamlin was an influential figure in the early life of the Federal Reserve Board. He served as the first governor of the Federal Reserve Board from August 10, 1914 to August 9, 1916. His primary contributions as governor were organizational and diplomatic. As governor, he developed a workable organizational structure that enabled the first board to perform its functions. His skills as a diplomat were essential to help the board through early power struggles and philosophical differences concerning the day-to-day operation of the board and its role in the economy. Following his brief tenure as the governor, he was twice appointed to full ten-year terms (1916–1926 and 1926–1936) as a member of the board. Following the completion of his second ten-year appointment on February 4, 1936, he served as special counsel to the board until his death on April 24, 1938.

The young Hamlin was an idealist and a reformer with a special interest in international trade and tariffs. These qualities attracted him to the 1888 political campaign of Grover Cleveland, for whom Hamlin campaigned vigorously. Despite his defeat in 1888, Cleveland did not forget the young Boston attorney. Following Cleveland's reelection in 1892, Cleveland appointed Hamlin assistant secretary of the Treasury in charge of customs. During his four-year tenure in this position, Hamlin devoted his efforts to the efficient collection of taxes. His attention to detail and organizational skills were well suited to this type of task, and Hamlin enjoyed marked success in this position. At the urging of the newly elected president McKinley, Hamlin remained as assistant secretary of the Treasury briefly in the new Republican administration in 1897.

In the sixteen years of Republican presidency from 1897 to 1913, Hamlin remained in the private sector. Following the resignation of his Treasury position in 1897, he returned to Boston to resume his law practice. Although he did not hold a formal government position during this period, he remained interested in public affairs. He served as an arbitrator in several industrial disputes and on several international commissions. In 1897, as a special commissioner to Japan, he represented the United States at talks between the United States, Japan, and Russia to study the fur seal fishery problem. The following year, he represented the United States in similar talks with the British. In 1908 he was decorated by the Japanese emperor for his work on the Japanese Famine Relief Commission in 1906. He was a delegate to international peace conferences in 1907, 1908, and 1911. He was a member of the executive committee of the 1899 Indianapolis Monetary Convention and a delegate to the Democratic National Convention in 1904. In 1910 he declined a unanimous nomination for Congress.

During the presidential campaign of 1912, the lifelong Democrat was the president of the Woodrow Wilson League of Massachusetts. Following Wilson's election, Hamlin was appointed to the Treasury position that he had previously held during the Cleveland administration. He served as an assistant secretary of the Treasury until his appointment to the Federal Reserve Board in 1914. His capable performance in this position did not go unnoticed by Wilson's secretary of the Treasury, William G. McAdoo.

Following the passage of the Federal Reserve Act on December 23, 1913, President Wilson began to consider appointments to membership of the first reserve board. Although the spirit of the act would have called for professional monetary expertise as a prerequisite for membership, contemporary press opinions were that the new board should represent a diversity of professional interests and geographic regions. The extent to which President Wilson subscribed to the popular diversity theory is unknown; however, the initial board members (a Boston lawyer, a Wall Street executive, an Alabama banker, a Chicago railroad executive, and a University of California professor of economics) would appear to conform to the diversity theory.

Although Hamlin would become the first governor of the Federal Reserve, he was not President Wilson's first choice for that position. Richard Olney of Boston, a distinguished Massachusetts Democrat who had served as secretary of state under President Cleveland, was Wilson's first choice as the New England representative and governor. Olney declined Wilson's invitation to accept the appointment, citing his age. Secretary of the Treasury McAdoo suggested to President Wilson (who had recently become McAdoo's new father-in-law) that Hamlin be appointed as the New England representative and serve as the board's first governor. McAdoo was familiar with Hamlin's character, views, and work ethic from his position in the Treasury. Following McAdoo's suggestion, Wilson nominated Hamlin for board membership in the spring of 1914. In order to maintain continuity when terms expired, each of the new board members was appointed to a different length term, ranging from two to ten years. On August 10, 1914, Hamlin was sworn in as the first governor of the Federal Reserve Board, with the shortest of the five terms (two years).

Although Hamlin's position of governor evolved into the position of chairman, the initial governorship of the board was not the powerful policymaking post that the chairman is today. The initial board had five appointed members and two ex officio members, the secretary of the Treasury and the comptroller of the currency. The original Federal Reserve Act called for the secretary of the Treasury to preside at meetings of the Federal Reserve Board; the governor was to exercise power only in the secretary's absence. Therefore, the power of the initial governorship depended directly on the involvement of the secretary of the Treasury. In the early years of the board, Secretary McAdoo took a direct and frequent interest in the affairs of the board, thus relegating Hamlin to a subordinate position, which he appeared quite willing to accept. (Recall that McAdoo had also been Hamlin's superior in the Treasury Department.)

Hamlin possessed the intellectual and educational qualifications for the post, and his diplomatic skills were well suited to the position of governor; however, he was not a particularly dynamic or innovative leader. The power to be exercised by the new board and the role that the new board was to play in national monetary affairs were not readily apparent. Congress had set the new board members' salaries equal to those of cabinet members, suggesting that the board members were to assume powerful leadership positions. Congress, however, had also given a substantial amount of the control of the new board to the secretary of the Treasury, suggesting a subordinate position to existing monetary authority. Since the operation and functions of the new board were not rigidly defined by Congress in the enabling legislation, the role that the new board would assume would be determined by its future actions. The initial days of the board would become a feeling-out process in which it would develop its internal and external procedures, outline an organizational structure, and search for its proper place in the financial arena. The role that the new body would assume in its early years was influenced significantly by Hamlin.

Hamlin's study of the Federal Reserve Act convinced him that Congress had included in the legislation a theoretical outline of the organizational structure of the board. Thus, he entered the position of governor with a distinct theory of the functions and organization of the new board. Under Hamlin's view of the Federal Reserve Act, the board was comprised of five equal members, each of whom had an equal right and responsibility to determine national monetary policy and to administer the board's powers. Under this organizational theory, Hamlin viewed his own role as governor as a discussion leader and agenda setter for an essentially democratic body. This view made him a weak executive who refused to make even minor decisions without consulting the full board. Under his direction, early board meetings were long and consumed with the discussion of details since Hamlin was unwilling to exercise an authority independent of the other board members.

Under Hamlin's leadership, the early board developed a cumbersome system of committees, used during the first two years of the board's life. Since the number of board members was small (five), each member was required to serve on several committees. This system of administration necessitated many meetings and double consideration of every matter to come before the board because the issues were addressed in both committee and the full board by essentially the same individuals. Using this organizational structure, the board was able to establish procedures for technical matters, such as check clearing and eligibility requirements, but was not able to announce and enforce any cohesive national monetary policy. It is not clear if the board's failure to effectuate monetary policy during Hamlin's two-year governorship resulted from a lack of board desire to pursue policy or a lack of power to effectuate policy goals. The board's cumbersome organizational structure and its lack of an aggressive executive are one potential explanation for the lack of policy. An alternative explanation would be the weakness of the member banks relative to the ongoing economic expansion.

One of the first issues to be addressed (implicitly if not explicitly) by the board under Hamlin's leadership was the scope of its powers. While a strict reading of the Federal Reserve Act might lead one to conclude that the board was authorized to act only in emergency situations, Hamlin and the other early members did not perceive the role in this fashion. Although the board was not able to implement monetary policy effectively during this period, Hamlin's board believed that the administration of an ongoing nonemergency monetary policy was a legitimate function. This view of its powers influenced the organizational structure of the board. Following this view, the board developed the administrative mechanisms that would allow it to engage in day-to-day operations and to effectuate ongoing implementation of policy in the future. This organizational structure allowed the board to develop into the hands-on policy body that it is today.

Another aspect of the new board's powers involved the types of financial instruments that would be regulated. On this issue, Hamlin did believe that the actions of the board were bound to only those types of bills specified in the language of the act. In an address delivered before the New York Chamber of Commerce on December 3, 1914, Hamlin maintained that two of the act's basic principles were ''that commercial paper must be turned from the non-liquid investment into a quick liquid asset; that commercial paper based on the trade and commerce of the people is the best self-liquidating asset that can be had.''

Hamlin's tenure as governor was marked by weak executive leadership and a subordination of Federal Reserve Board power to U.S. Treasury power. In an early board versus Treasury squabble, Secretary of the Treasury McAdoo was able to prevent the board from establishing separate offices outside the Treasury building. Some of the first board members felt that McAdoo had an unstated agenda to keep the new board subordinate to the existing Treasury and that Hamlin's leadership facilitated that agenda. Hamlin's personal subordination to Secretary McAdoo is demonstrated by the following incident. An early board committee, comprised of Paul Warburg,* Frederic Delano,* and William Harding,* was studying the optimal number of districts for the reserve system (Federal Reserve Act language implies that the board has the power to adjust and create districts but limits the number of districts to a maximum of twelve). This committee was prepared to recommend the combination and elimination of some existing districts. When the committee first raised the subject at a meeting of the full board, Secretary McAdoo was not present due to illness. Hamlin objected to the preliminary discussion of the report and delayed discussion until the following week. When the issue was raised again, Hamlin further delayed the discussion, citing the absence of McAdoo:

When the Board reassembled and the Committee expected the subject to be taken up, it found itself confronted with a legal opinion of the Attorney General, which Governor Hamlin, acting without authority from the Board, in conjunction with, and at the insistence of, Mr. McAdoo, had requested President Wilson to secure. The Attorney General's opinion was to the effect that the Reserve Board had no power to abolish any reserve bank. Thus, while the Board had deferred discussion out of courtesy to Mr. McAdoo, the latter, together with the Board's Governor, and the President, had combined, without the knowledge of the four appointive members of the Board, to forestall any debate by securing this opinion of the Attorney General. (Warburg 1930, p. 430)

These actions are indicative of early board subordination to the Treasury (and Hamlin's personal subordination to McAdoo). The Treasury/non-Treasury split of the board that developed during Hamlin's governorship severely limited the ability of the board to effectuate policy.

Hamlin's perception of his role as governor is further demonstrated by his refusal to exercise his executive authority aggressively. The manner in which he dealt with the Conference of Governors, an informal group of bankers and financiers representing the interest of larger banks, is illustrative. In late 1914 this group began to hold meetings in reaction to the Federal Reserve Act discussions in Congress. Henry Parker Willis, an early board member, described the conference as an effort to create an interbank board of control not subject to law or administrative regulation. The group elected a chairman and a paid secretary and conducted periodic meetings that had the effect of usurping reserve board power. Willis adds,

The attitude of the council and its representatives grew more and more peremptory and domineering. . . . There was a growing disposition among the membership [of the Governor's Council] to think and act as if this council were the real arbiter and final authority in all system matters—the Board becoming only a ratifying body. For this point of view and for the tendencies evidenced in the Governor's Council, the Federal Reserve Board had only itself to thank. . . . There existed a sharp division of opinion in the Board itself respecting the place to be taken by the Governor's Council and the attitude to be assumed with regard to it. Governor Hamlin, although perceiving the dangers and possible outcome of the council, was not prepared at that time to raise any sharp issue with its members and thus the organization continued. (Willis 1923, pp. 703–6)

Hamlin's refusal to assert aggressively executive authority allowed a continuation of a situation that was in direct opposition to the performance of his duties as governor. (Upon taking control of the board, Harding, who succeeded Hamlin, acted quickly to restrain the power and influence of the Governor's Council.)

Hamlin's initial two-year appointment as governor expired on August 9, 1916. The two years of his governorship had led to a Treasury/non-Treasury split among the board membership. The Treasury faction was comprised of Secretary of the Treasury McAdoo, Comptroller of the Currency Williams, and former Treasury assistant Hamlin. Miller, Delano, and Warburg resented what they believed to be Treasury domination of the board and voted and acted as a group against what they perceived to be board domination by McAdoo. Harding did not side with either group and held the balance of power on the board with his swing vote. Upon the expiration of Hamlin's short two-year term as governor, the non-Treasury group attempted to get President Wilson to appoint Warburg as governor of the board. Wilson, however, appointed Harding to succeed Hamlin as governor and reappointed Hamlin to a full ten-year term as a member of the board. With this change in leadership and the outbreak of war in 1917, the role of the board changed dramatically. Harding proved to be a much stronger executive than Hamlin had been, and wartime concerns turned McAdoo's attention elsewhere. This combination of events allowed the board to operate more independently of the Treasury and was an important step in the evolution of the board.

It is unclear whether McAdoo suggested Hamlin for the position as governor because he could foresee that the primary task of the board's early years would be organizational and administrative or because he (McAdoo) wished the board to assume a secondary financial role to his own role as secretary of the Treasury and thought that Hamlin's leadership would facilitate that goal. As later events revealed, Hamlin did possess strong organizational skills, but under Hamlin's leadership, the board was not innovative and Hamlin sided with McAdoo, his former boss, on a significant number of issues addressed by the board. In the opinion of Willis, the board's first secretary:

The choice [of Hamlin as the board's first governor] was wise. Many of the more difficult problems to be met by the Board at the outset were those of personal relationship, choices of men, and settlement of organizational questions. Mr. Hamlin was essentially a diplomat in the best sense of the word, tactful, gracious and considerate of the feelings and opinions of his associates. He was peculiarly well qualified for the first problems that grew out of Reserve Board organization. (Willis 1923, p. 667)

However, Willis follows these laudatory comments with observations about Hamlin's inability to exercise executive authority and the need for new leadership when Hamlin's initial term as governor expired.

During World War I, Hamlin was chairman of the Capital Issues Committee (this committee was not associated with the Federal Reserve Board), created by the War Finance Corporation Act for the purpose of determining if proposed new issues of securities were considered essential to the war effort since nonessential enterprises and securities would divert capital from the war effort. The committee did not have the power to prohibit the issuance of any proposed security but merely relied on the patriotic cooperation of issuers to refrain from issuing nonessential securities. Hamlin's committee considered the proposed securities issues and announced the degree to which they considered the issues worthy of support.

Hamlin's ten-year term on the board (1916–1926) is remarkable only by his absence of any policymaking initiative. He moved from a cautious leadership role to nearly invisible follower role. Lester Chandler's biography of Benjamin Strong, the dynamic head of the New York Federal Reserve Bank, contains the following anecdotal evidence, which is characteristic of Hamlin's personality and board activity. While discussing the board's lack of expertise and leadership in the early 1920s resulting from unqualified appointees of President Harding, Chandler reflected on the possibility that some existing board member might take control of the board. He noted that Hamlin was still a member of the board and described him as intelligent and possessing a thorough understanding of the reserve system's operation. But he then added that Hamlin was a quiet note-taking sort of fellow, quite unlikely to undertake anything on his own initiative, thus, dismissing the possibility that Hamlin might take control of the board in a time when a need for leadership existed.

Upon the expiration of his full ten-year term in 1926, Hamlin was reappointed to a second ten-year term. Again Hamlin's influence and activity during this period are minimal. In the famous 1927 incident where the board ordered the Chicago Federal Reserve Bank to lower its rate, Hamlin voted in the minority against the action, reflecting his lifelong position of caution, nonintervention, and reluctance to exercise control.

During the stock market crash of 1929 and the ensuing depression, Hamlin believed that the board should follow a passive, noninterventionist role. In 1931 he was called to testify before the Senate committee investigating the board's activity during 1929 prior to the crash. At the time of the crash, the New York Reserve Bank had wanted to raise the discount rate in order to discourage speculation, but the board opted to follow a more passive policy of moral suasion. Hamlin was a strong supporter of the board's policy, which he believed had been effective in reducing the number of loans. In his Senate testimony, he stated that he believed that it was wrong to raise rates in order to discourage speculation if the rate increase would adversely affect commercial business. He also testified that he did not support increased rates because he feared that any resulting financial panic would be blamed on the board. Although these two reasons seem mutually inconsistent, each alone is consistent with Hamlin's demonstrated caution, refusal to intervene in the economy, and unwillingness to take a firm policy or leadership role.

When Hamlin's third appointment to the board expired on February 3, 1936, he became a special counsel to the board. He remained in this position until his death two years later. Thus, Hamlin was associated with that board for the last twenty-four years of his life (two years as governor, two ten-year terms as a member, and two years as special counsel). He did not appear to have the desire to pursue other career goals or disassociate himself from the activities of the board. His extensive personal diaries offer an inside view of the early board and its activities. It seems inconsistent that he would document so fully and devote himself so completely to a regulatory agency that he believed should take a passive, secondary role in financial affairs.

Hamlin was the author of *The Interstate Commerce Act Indexed and Digested* (1907), *The Index Digest of the Federal Reserve Act* (1916), and *The Index Digest of the Federal Reserve Bulletin* (1921). He received honorary LL.D. degrees from Washington and Lee in 1895 and Columbia in 1930. He married Huybertie Lansing Pruyn in 1898, and they had one daughter, Anna. He died on April 24, 1938, in Washington D.C., of chronic kidney inflammation.

Hamlin was a cautious, intelligent, tactful man who was reluctant to intervene in the affairs of others. His personality and training as a lawyer were reflected in his legalistic mind, his ability to organize, and his attention to detail. These qualities led to his success as an attorney, an assistant secretary of the Treasury, and an architect of organizational structure of the Federal Reserve Board. These same qualities, however, limited his performance as the first governor and later as a member of the Federal Reserve Board. His weak executive style and passive board membership were characteristic of his overall approach to issues. Given these personal and professional qualities, he would appear to be an ironic choice as a member of a new federal regulatory agency whose function was to intervene in monetary markets and set national policy.

BIBLIOGRAPHY

Chandler, Lester. 1958. *Benjamin Strong, Central Banker*. Washington D.C.: Brookings Institution.
Hamlin, Charles S. 1907. *The Interstate Commerce Act Indexed and Digested*.
———. 1916. *The Index Digest of the Federal Reserve Act*.
———. 1921. *The Index Digest of the Federal Reserve Bulletin*.
Harding, W. P. G. 1925. *The Formative Period of the Federal Reserve*. Cambridge, Mass.: Riverside Press.
McAdoo, William G. 1930. *The Crowded Years*. New York: Macmillan.
Warburg, Paul. 1930. *The Federal Reserve System*. New York: Macmillan.
Who Was Who in America, 1986. Chicago: Marquis Who's Who.
Willis, Henry Parker. 1923. *The Federal Reserve System*. New York: Ronald Press.

WILLIAM PROCTOR GOULD HARDING (1864–1930)

Geofrey T. Mills

William Harding served as a governor of the Federal Reserve from August 1914 to August 1922. He was educated at the University of Alabama. Upon graduation, he entered the world of finance as a bookkeeper in a bank in Birmingham, Alabama, and in quick order became the president of the Berney National Bank of Birmingham. By the early years of the twentieth century, Harding's expertise and acumen were becoming known on a regional scale, and in 1908 he assumed the presidency of the Alabama State Bankers Association. By 1913 he was elected president of the Birmingham Chamber of Commerce. At this juncture in his career, Harding was rapidly accumulating a reputation as a bright young man who could serve the nation in some capacity as a financier. As a result, in 1914 he was appointed as the southern member of the Federal Reserve Board. This appointment, as deserving as it was, in all likelihood probably would not have been made had not the enabling legislation for the Federal Reserve system mandated regional representation. At that time, much more so than today, the business, commercial, and financial life of the nation was heavily concentrated in New York and, to a lesser extent, in Boston. It would have been remarkable for a southern banker, with no reputation or expertise beyond that of the immediate region, to earn such a position without a New York base. Nonetheless, it was an excellent appointment, and in August 1916 Harding was made the second governor by the board itself.

His years as governor were tumultuous and exciting, covering some of the most interesting and important events in twentieth-century financial history. Any pro-active governor directing these years would have found himself embroiled in controversies, and when his official term ended in August 1922, Harding was not reappointed despite a heavy lobbying effort by his supporters. After his years as Federal Reserve governor, he became a financial adviser without portfolio to foreign nations. His two most noteworthy engagements in this period were as a financial adviser to Cuba in 1922 and to Hungary a year later. The new League of Nations asked that he become the financial administrator to Hungary, but Harding preferred the role of a visiting expert to that of an onsight administrator.

This reluctance on his part to become an overseas bureaucrat was probably due to his newly elected position as governor of the Federal Reserve Bank of Boston in 1923. Harding no doubt saw this position as a fitting conclusion to a distinguished career in banking and one of greater relative importance as a League of Nations functionary, no matter how highly placed. In this judgment he was correct, especially given the deteriorating influence of the league in the 1920s. There is, therefore, a touch of irony in Harding's career path. He concluded his career as the ultimate financial insider, the governor of what was then the second most important Federal Reserve bank. That he was able to achieve so much in an era of financial concentration in New York from a southern background is quiet testimony to his character and abilities. Harding will not be remembered as one of the more brilliant or innovative of Federal Reserve leaders, but he was intelligent and competent and gave the country commonsense leadership during a period of great uncertainty.

The Federal Reserve system, much like the Treasury, is a fixture of American finance and economic policy. But given the poor state of instruction regarding the history and evolution of this institution, we are in danger of simply assuming that the institution has been around forever. This is an ironic happenstance since, outside of perhaps the Treasury, there is no other institution of the federal government that has been so heavily documented and researched. Any reasonably sized library will devote hundreds of linear feet of shelf space to titles on the Federal Reserve. Its history, functions, leadership, influence, mistakes, and powers are all chronicled, one title after another stacked like soldiers at attention. The problem is that no one, except a narrow range of experts and a few dilettantes, ever reads the material. The net result of this process is that the early history, authority, and influence of the Fed is lost in the mists of history, clouded by the larger events of World War I, the League of Nations, and the roaring twenties.

Typically the first individual of any consequence from the Federal Reserve a serious student will meet is Benjamin Strong, who was a president of one of the regional banks, that in New York. Strong is important as the discoverer, some say inventor, of open market operations, his position slightly elevated as the last strong monetary leader before the 1929 collapse. The early leaders of the Fed are obscured for a number of reasons. Of primary importance is the fact that they all did, fundamentally, a good job. There were no unsolvable problems or huge crises to contend with—and as a result nothing to mark their path. The war was fought and won in good order, the immediate postwar period was punctuated by a sharp credit inflation, followed by a crash, but a very short one, and the succeeding decade was generally one of economic prosperity. History tends not to remember so well those who presided over periods of peace and tranquility. If one is to be vividly remembered, it is much better to rule in a period of controversy and turmoil. Sandwiched as he was between World War I and the Great Depression, the career of William Harding, no matter how noteworthy, was bound to be less newsworthy than those who came later.

Another reason for this diminutiveness of Harding has to do with the origins of the Federal Reserve itself. It has been only a relatively recent development that the chairman of the Fed has achieved the level of a sort of cult figure. In the years before 1960, the individuals who led the nations central bank were anonymous individuals who had carved out careers relying on narrow expertise, a core knowledge, and political connections. Since this time, they have become more public figures. The Federal Reserve in its early years was an institution unsure of its role in the nation's economic life and invested with formal authorities more appropriate to the Bank of England than the U.S. central bank. Heavy reliance on the discounted note did little to secure the Fed's role as an economic force, which had to await the refinement and perfection of open market operations. The fact that the Federal Reserve was itself a new, haltingly imperfect, and remarkably uninformed institution meant that its leaders would not be able to break out of this institutional environment until the organization itself changed.

William Harding therefore found himself in 1916 to be the titular leader of a new financial organization with unproved authority, designed to be a central bank in a country with a strong tradition of regional independence in financial matters, in a nation on the brink of war. That he did as well as he was able to in this situation is testimony to both the system and the man. Furthermore, the Federal Reserve was not really on its own to make and implement monetary policy due to the war effort. From approximately April 1917 through the end of 1919, the focus of financial effort and activity was on the Treasury and its efforts to finance the war. The main source of federal government revenue was from the sale of government bonds, and in this the Federal Reserve was destined to play a major role. The Federal Reserve system had to keep its discount rates low to help hold down interest payments on federal debt, accomplished primarily at the direction of Treasury officials. This decision, fundamentally political in nature, was made in the best interest of war finance as then understood and placed the Federal Reserve in a subordinate position to the Treasury. These actions would be repeated, although somewhat differently, in World War II as the prime function of the Fed once again became that of maintaining low interest rates on government-issued debt.

The history of the Federal Reserve system dates at least to the Civil War and the efforts of the Union administration to rationalize and stabilize the financial and economic side of the Civil War. In some respects, the National Banking Act of 1863 can be seen as an antecedent of the Federal Reserve Act. For our purposes here, the proximate cause of the Federal Reserve system is the panic of 1907 and the legislation for monetary reform that it brought in its train. Breaking the so-called money trust and protecting the financial system from periodic panics were major goals of this reform effort. The decade 1900–1910 was littered with commissions, legislative proposals, hearings, laws, investigations, and other efforts to reform the nation's monetary system. Only a detailed analysis of this era can make sense out of these various initiatives. However, it would be safe to say that the Fowler bill, the Aldrich-Vreeland Act, and the National Monetary Commission were the more important efforts of the decade.

Through a consolidated series of events, personalities, and politics, the Glass bill was introduced to Congress in 1913. This bill emerged, altered and amended to be sure, and was signed into law in December. Thus, on the very eve of World War I, the nation finally had a central bank. However, having a central bank in law and having one able to function as a true stabilizer of the financial system in fact were two different things. By dint of inexperience, lack of resources, and the overwhelming pressure of the war, the new Federal Reserve system was not able to function independently of Treasury operations until the termination of hostilities. This was the environment in which W. P. G. Harding took the reins as governor of the Federal Reserve.

Unlike other monetary systems, the Federal Reserve was created as a creature of Congress but uniquely independent of congressional influence and oversight. The Federal Reserve has both political and financial independence. The governors are appointed by the president but serve for long fixed terms, and the Fed's funding is supplied by member banks, not congressional appropriations. This situation is unique to the U.S. federal system. Furthermore, the charge of the Federal Reserve is vague and open-ended. This is both a blessing and a curse, but it does potentially provide the Fed with a great deal of latitude.

This, then, is the environment in which Harding found himself in 1916. The situation in those early years was such that the Federal Reserve was unable to function as a central bank. During the war years of 1917–1919 the U.S. Treasury and its policies toward government debt and interest rates held the Fed captive. This situation made a lie out of the notion of an independent Fed. One of the most important outcomes of this captivity was Federal Reserve dealing in government debt, albeit at once removed via discounting from the regional banks. This peculiar form of credit established one of the most important and lasting legacies of this era, although almost no one recognized it at the time. In fact, it went almost unnoticed. This was the mechanism of which Federal Reserve credit and influence was based on Treasury debt. Today it is automatic that open market operations consist entirely of short-term government debt bought and sold by the open market window in New York. In World War I, it was extraordinary and thought to be an ugly but necessary by-product of the war effort.

Financing the war through a combination of higher taxes (the income tax had been made constitutional immediately before the United States entered the war) and large issues of Treasury debt helped to create a situation where the basic operations of the Federal Reserve were to undergo radical change.

One of the major problems with the pre–Federal Reserve monetary system, in addition to a regional, specifically eastern orientation, was the unfortunate habit of a severe tightening of credit in time of recession or financial crisis. The economic thought of the time was that the intelligent application of the real bills doctrine would prevent this contraction. The Federal Reserve was then charged with implementing a variant of this doctrine in its operations. The first annual report of the Federal Reserve made it clear that the Fed's role was to stabilize economic activity by prevention, not simply react to emergencies with a curative of some sort or another. It should be underscored, however, that this view was not universally held. In the transition from a pre–Federal Reserve situation, there were those who felt that the Fed should be as passive as possible in normal times and step in only when there was a clear need. This debate on the role of monetary policy has been with us ever since.

To the extent that we are aware of Harding's views on monetary policy, it would be fair to characterize him as pro-active. He believed that the Federal Reserve was invested with a trust to help maintain economic stability and that the best vehicle was an intelligent application of the real bills doctrine. Monetary theory—specifically, the relation between money and economic activity—had not progressed beyond this point, and Harding was typical of other bankers of his era. There is some irony, therefore, in Harding's stewardship of the Federal Reserve in the war period. It would not be safe to say that monetary policy, as conducted in World War I, was countercyclical. Instead, the policy was one of accommodation of Treasury demands to maintain an adequate flow of credit to the government at acceptable levels of interest rates. Second, Harding's Federal Reserve was responsible for establishing a huge market in both short- and long-term government debt. This debt laid the foundation for the open market operations that were to follow in later years and certainly had little to do with the application of the real bills doctrine.

An evaluation of the monetary policy in the war years, and Harding's role in it, will have to be written elsewhere. However, it is difficult to be too critical of the Harding leadership given a number of considerations. First and foremost was the war itself and the unprecedented demand it placed on the government for men and material. In this environment, it is difficult to conceive of the Federal Reserve's doing anything to hinder the Treasury's need for cash. Second, it is important to remember that in 1917, the Federal Reserve was a very young institution. It had no history or traditions, was still short of resources, and had no clear guide on how best to behave in the wartime economy. It is little wonder that it was willing to follow the Treasury's lead. Finally, we can point to approximately identical Federal Reserve behavior in World War II as evidence that, in wartime at least, the Treasury assumes supremacy, for in that war, Fed behavior was just as accommodating to Treasury's demands for debt sales and low interest rates. Given these circumstances, we can hardly have expected Harding and his policies to vary from what the Treasury demanded.

It was also Harding's fate to be in the long shadow of Benjamin Strong, president of the New York Federal Reserve Bank in these years. As Lester Chandler has pointed out in his excellent biography of Strong, in many respects, it was Strong who was the de facto leader of the Federal Reserve. From his position in New York, Strong was always able to second-guess and to provide active leadership on his own. Harding admits as much in his own book on the early years of the Federal Reserve. One example of Strong's influence in these matters was his desire to end the dependence on real bills and use bankers' acceptances to create a situation where the Federal Reserve could control money and credit. No such ideas or leadership came from Harding's office. And Strong's influence only rose, if anything, after the war.

In December 1919 the Treasury finally allowed the Federal Reserve to elevate the discount rate and thereby terminated the Fed's role as a mere supporter of Treasury wishes. The Federal Reserve was now free to chart its own course with regard to monetary policy and immediately ran into a controversy regarding the feasibility of the use of the real bills doctrine as a policy guide. Harding addresses this issue in his book, as does every other scholar who investigates this period. This debate over the real bills doctrine in theory was counterbalanced by a boom-and-bust cycle of economic activity from which Harding was unable to escape, although the blame was not entirely that of the Federal Reserve.

In brief, what happened is this. Through 1919 the Federal Reserve banks had been asking for increases in the discount rate in order to stem a rising inflation. The Treasury was unwilling to yield on this point, and it was not until late 1919 and early 1920 that the discount rate was allowed to increase. Although not entirely at fault, the Federal Reserve was caught up in a cycle of easy credit, followed by a sharp tightening of credit policies, via the discount rate. The crash in commodity prices and subsequent reduction of economic activity was then laid at the doorstep of the Fed. In a sense, Harding was lucky that the crash of 1920–1921, while very sharp, was also brief, and general economic prosperity returned for the remainder of the decade. Harding was hard-pressed to explain Federal Reserve activities to an angry public. He was even accused of engaging in speculation for his own benefit when commodity prices fell. This was an absurd charge, as anyone who was familiar with events and Harding's character knew, but the perception of a flawed policy persisted. No doubt, this episode helps to explain why Harding was not reappointed to the Federal Reserve when his term was officially over in August 1922. It was at this point that Harding became involved in various international financial activities, and he eventually ended up at the Boston Federal Reserve Bank.

The debate over the real bills doctrine, and a plausible substitute for it, if any, confirmed that Benjamin Strong was the focal point in a movement to establish other monetary policies to fulfill the Federal Reserve's charge. And although it was to take a while longer to end the real bills theory fully, it was clear by 1922 that a substitute would be developed. This substitute would be open market operation in short-term government debt, and Strong would claim the majority of credit for its implementation.

An evaluation of William Harding's stewardship of the Federal Reserve is remarkably easy to determine. In one sense, his tenure was governed almost entirely by the circumstances of the environment. And in another sense, he was probably the perfect person for this period in the Federal Reserve's history.

Harding's ability to strike an independent course in monetary policy before December 1919 (early 1920 really, for an effect to be felt) was nil. Had the Federal Reserve been unwilling to follow the lead of the administration, the Overman Act could have been invoked to strip it of what authority it did possess.

Harding was a team player and certainly willing to go along with executive wishes regarding war finance. He was also effective in creating consensus within the board itself and among the regional ranks. After the war, when discount rates were advanced, the Federal Reserve was blamed for the crash of 1920–1921, and while it cannot be argued that the Fed was blameless in pursuing this course of action, it is not the case that it was alone. The timing of the increase in rates, coupled with the rapid fall of government expenditures on the war, would have provoked a recession in any event. Furthermore, the Federal Reserve was still in the evolutionary stage of developing appropriate monetary tools. The passing of the real bills doctrine, lack of a suitable replacement, and institutional constraints all conspired to render the Federal Reserve to a diminutive role in economic affairs, at least for a few years.

Lest this judgment seem too negative, it needs to be said that Harding's situation was probably inevitable given the circumstances and that he personally was an outstanding choice for this period. Honest, prudent, and above reproach and an effective advocate of administration policies, it is difficult to imagine another individual doing a better job with the tools and situation presented to Harding over 1916–1922.

BIBLIOGRAPHY

Anderson, Clay J. 1965. *A Half-Century of Federal Reserve Policymaking, 1914–1964*. Philadelphia: Federal Reserve Bank of Philadelphia.

Burgess, W. Randolph, ed. 1930. *Interpretations of Federal Reserve Policy in the Speeches and Writings of Benjamin Strong*. New York: Harper.

Chandler, Lester V. 1958. *Benjamin Strong, Central Banker*. Washington, D.C.: Brookings Institution.

Dictionary of American Biography. 1946. Centenary ed. Vol. 8. New York: Charles Scribner's Sons.

Harding, W. P. G. 1925. *The Formative Period of the Federal Reserve System*. Boston and New York: Houghton Mifflin.

Harris, S. E. 1933. *Twenty Years of Federal Reserve Policy*. 2 vols. Cambridge, Mass.: Harvard University Press.

Taus, Ester Rogoff. 1943. *Central Banking Functions of the U.S. Treasury, 1789–1941*. New York: Columbia University Press.

Wicker, Elmus R. 1966. *Federal Reserve Monetary Policy, 1917–1933*. New York: Random House.

HEINZ ROBERT HELLER (1940–   )

Bernard S. Katz

H. Robert Heller became the sixty-sixth appointed governor of the Federal Reserve on August 19, 1986. He served four years of his appointed ten-year term, resigning in July 1989 to join VISA International. While at the Fed, Heller was the chairman of the Committee on Banking Supervision and Regulation and served as the administrative governor. He also served on several interagency committees, such as the Federal Financial Institution's Examination Council and the National Advisory Council on International Monetary and Financial Policies, and was a delegate to the Organization for Economic Cooperation and Development. In 1991 Heller became president of VISA U.S.A. Heller points out that there are similarities between the Fed and VISA; the Fed runs the payment system in the United States, and VISA plays an important role in the worldwide payments system.

Born to H. K. W. and Karin (Hermann) Heller in Cologne, Germany, on January 8, 1940, Heller's parents, now deceased, resided in Germany, where his father was an executive at Lufthansa, the German national airline. Heller came to the United States as a college student in 1960. Finding a fondness for the country, Heller continued with his education and stayed on to achieve his notable career. Heller became a naturalized citizen in 1970 and married Emily E. Mitchell on December 5, 1970. They have a daughter, Kimberly, and a son, Christopher.

After arriving in the United States in 1960, Heller graduated from Parsons College, Iowa, with a B.A. in 1961. From Parsons he went to the University of Minnesota, graduating in 1962 with an M.A. in economics. Heller then attended the University of California at Berkeley, where he earned the Ph.D. in 1965. (While at Berkeley Heller was an acting instructor in economics.) From Berkeley, Heller went to the University of California at Los Angeles as an assistant professor in 1965 and was promoted to associate professor of economics in 1968. During the time Heller was at Los Angeles, he also held a Ford

Foundation fellowship. In 1968 Heller's text, *International Trade Theory: Theory and Empirical Evidence*, was published. While at Los Angeles Heller also took a year's leave of absence to be visiting professor at the Universitaet des Saarlandes, the Universitaet Goettingen, and an exchange visitor at Nagoya City University in Japan.

Heller left Los Angeles for the University of Hawaii in 1971 as professor of economics and later served as chairman of the department until his departure in 1974. (During 1973–1974 Heller also held a North Atlantic Treaty Organization fellowship.) During Heller's tenure at Hawaii, he published three additional books: *The Economic System* (1972), *Japanese Investment in the United States*, (1974), and *International Monetary Economics* (1974). At that point in his career Heller left academia and joined the International Monetary Fund (IMF) in Washington, D.C.

At the IMF, Heller assumed the position of chief of financial studies, where he was in charge of basic research on monetary and fiscal policy. Heller left the IMF in 1978 for the Bank of America headquarters in San Francisco, as senior vice-president and director of international economic research. While at the bank, Heller made a number of appearances before Congress, giving testimony on a wide range of international economic subjects, such as the debt problems of the developing countries, the U.S. trade deficit, IMF quota increases, and the balance of payments. Heller's interest in public service was heightened during the early years of the Reagan administration, and after eight years at the Bank of America, he returned to Washington. Heller's nomination for the Federal Reserve board by President Ronald Reagan was to fill the unexpired term of former Fed vice-chairman Preston Martin,[*] whose term was to end January 31, 1996.

As is so often the case, at the announcement of his nomination, interested observers were quick to pin an ideological stripe to Heller's banker suit. In quick order, he was labeled a supply sider, an eclectic, a moderate, and a gold bug. An economic adviser to Congressman Jack Kemp (R, New York), an advocate of supply-side theory, praised Heller as a pragmatist, "but not a pragmatist of the wrong ideological bent." Heller prefers the pragmatist label without the additives.

Heller's German birth is only occasionally carried in his speech; his conversation flows easily and is combined with an easy sense of humor and an easy laugh. Heller states that he has friends in both the supply-side and monetarist theory camps. While willing to take sensible ideas from either school, his overriding belief is in the free market. He argues that if "left free to assert itself, the invisible hand of the marketplace will guide people's actions toward fostering overall economic welfare." While there was concern among some congressmen that upon his appointment Heller would align himself with the Reagan administration's desire for an easing of the Fed's tight money policy, Heller gave high marks to Paul Volcker's[*] restrictive monetary policy and then served on Alan Greenspan's[*] board, which continued a strong concern for a noninflationary growth path. Heller notes that in all his Federal Open Market Committee votes, he never dissented from the majority consensus.

Heller's philosophy is not one of artificial or quick fixes. In a speech given to the Nineteenth World Management Congress where indexation for inflation was under discussion, he argued that indexation would place an economy in a "straight jacket without hope for adjustment or ultimate improvement in performance." For Heller, economic growth was achieved by hard work and the proper utilization of economic resources. The Fed's role was to provide a proper environment for this to take place.

While at the Fed, Heller's main concern was international issues. He sought to promote fair competition and global capital standards for financial institutions. He also argued for an environment that would promote the internationalization of the American banking system. In his 1987 *World of Banking* journal article, "Future Directions in the Financial Services Industry: International Markets," he argued that a comprehensive overhaul of the U.S. financial system was needed if the nation was to remain the world's leading financial power. He pointed out that American banks are more specialized and less diversified than they would be if interstate banking was allowed. Along these domestic lines, Heller was the swing vote in the Fed that permitted banks to engage in securities activity.

The extent to which Heller devoted himself to international concerns is summed up by a Washington banking lobbyist who stated that he did not have many dealings with Heller because "he always seemed to be giving speeches overseas." Heller's writings also followed his international travels. One of his main concerns was the further monetary integration of the European Community (EC) as well as further central bank cooperation. He cautioned that the forming central bank would work well only if all regional and special interests were represented in the institution; any premature establishment of a European central bank could place the institution under grave strains and policy conflicts that would endanger its proper functioning. Whenever the opportunity arose, Heller championed for the removal of barriers to nationwide banking to foster U.S. competitiveness in world markets from both a financial and export perspective. In this respect, he cautioned the EC not to limit the ability of foreign banks to compete in those countries after economic and financial integration planned to take place in 1992.

In reflecting over his professional career Heller has stated that he was content and challenged in every position he held. This attitude extends to his leisure activities; Heller is an avid sailor and a member of the San Francisco Yacht Club and enjoys the physical challenges of skiing.

Heller has served on the editorial board of the *International Trade Journal*, as well as an associate editor of the *Journal of Money, Credit, and Banking*. He is currently on the boards of the U.S. Council on International Business, BMW of North America, the National Center for Financial Systems Research, the Institute for International Financial Diplomacy, the Institute of International Education, and the San Francisco World Affairs Council, and he is director of the American Institute for Contemporary German Studies of John Hopkins University, Washington, D.C.

BIBLIOGRAPHY

Contemporary Authors. 1988. New Revision Series, Vol. 22. Detroit: Gale Research Company.

Heller, H. Robert. 1968. *International Trade Theory: Theory and Empirical Evidence*. Englewood Cliffs, N.J.: Prentice-Hall.

———. 1972. *The Economic System*. New York: Macmillan.

———. 1974a. *International Monetary Economics*. Englewood Cliffs, N.J.: Prentice-Hall.

———. 1974b. *Japanese Investment in the United States*. New York: Praeger Publishers.

———. 1987. "Future Directions in the Financial Services Industry: International Markets." *World of Banking* (May-June): 18–21.

———, and Rhomberg, R. 1977. "The Monetary Approach to the Balance of Payments: Introductory Survey." In IMF, *The Monetary Approach to the Balance of Payments*. Washington, D.C.: IMF.

U.S. Congress. Senate. Committee on Banking, Housing, and Urban Affairs. 1986. *Hearing*. 99th Cong., 2d sess., August 5.

ROBERT C. HOLLAND (1925–   )

Penny Kugler

With the resignation of J. L. Robertson* from the Board of Governors of the Federal Reserve on April 30, 1973, President Richard Nixon was faced with the difficult task of appointing a replacement to fill Robertson's unexpired term, which was to end January 31, 1978. On May 16, 1973, President Nixon announced that he intended to nominate Robert C. Holland, a Republican. The Senate confirmed the nomination on June 1, and Holland, at the age of forty-eight, took the oath of office on June 11, 1973; he was the first Fed staff member ever to be appointed to the board. With Holland's appointment, five of the seven men on the board were economists.

Robert Carl Holland was born in Tekamah, Nebraska, to Carl Luther and Gretchen (Thompson) Holland on April 7, 1925. He spent his childhood in the small town of about 2,000 and during those depression years ''learned the value of hard work, commitment and the importance that economics plays in personal as well as national life.''

Holland graduated from Tekamah High School in 1942 and then attended the University of Nebraska at Lincoln for one year. His academic career was interrupted in 1943 by World War II at which time he served with the 96th Infantry Division in the Philippine invasion campaign as an amphibious infantryman. Holland was at Leyte when Douglas MacArthur returned. He attended the U.S. Military Academy at West Point from 1944 to 1945 ''before deciding not to become a general'' and was honorably discharged from the army in 1945.

Holland returned to college in 1946 at the University of Pennsylvania's Wharton School of Finance and Commerce in Philadelphia. He graduated in 1948 with a B.S. degree in finance, receiving the Herbert S. Steuer Memorial Prize as the outstanding graduate. While working on his M.A. degree in economics, Holland acted as an instructor in money and banking at Wharton. He received his master's degree from the University of Pennsylvania in 1949. From 1951 to 1954 he attended the University of Chicago on a part-time basis and in 1959 received a Ph.D. in economics from the University of Pennsylvania. His dissertation was entitled ''Bank Lending to Sales Finance Companies, 1951–1954.''

At the University of Pennsylvania, Holland studied under Professor C. Canby Balderston,* "who had also served as a member of the Federal Reserve board. Also at the university at the same time was Karl Bopp, who later served with the Philadelphia Fed, and Charles E. Walker, who served as executive vice-president of the American Banking Association.

Holland had numerous articles published while at the University of Chicago. From 1951 to 1955, his articles were published in *Business Conditions*, a review of the Federal Reserve Bank of Chicago. In 1952 his article "Role of Monetary Policy in Fighting Inflation" was published in *Social Education*.

Characterized as easy-going and articulate, Holland started with the Federal Reserve Bank of Chicago in 1949 as a financial economist in the research department, a position he held until 1957. While working at the Chicago Fed during the day, Holland taught economics at the American Institute of Banking in the evenings. He served as assistant vice-president in research at the Chicago Fed from 1957 to 1959 and vice-president (loans) and chief lending officer in charge of the discount window from 1959 to 1961. While at the Chicago Fed (1954–1955), Holland also served as secretary to the Conference of Presidents of the Federal Reserve banks.

Holland joined the Board of Governors of the Federal Reserve in 1961 as an adviser in the Research and Statistics Division. He argued that an adviser must serve two masters—that of his own intellectual honesty as well as the philosophy and demands of the board members. The adviser must provide the information they want and any contrary evidence.

Holland must have been successful in acting on his philosophy because he moved rapidly through the Federal Reserve system. In *Nation's Business* (April 1967), Holland, along with Daniel H. Brill and Robert Solomon, were described as "the newest, and most influential brain trust in Washington. They are, in summary, a top-notch team of research economists, the catalysts, the implementors, and to some degree the innovators of, and for, the Federal Reserve Board."

Rarely did Holland spend more than two or three years at a position before advancing. The positions he held included: associate economist, Federal Open Market Committee (FOMC) (1962–1966); associate director, Division of Research and Statistics (1964–1965); adviser to the board (1965–1967); FOMC secretary (1966–1973); secretary of the board (1968–1971); finally reaching executive director, Board of Governors (1971–1973), the top staff position at the Fed.

Although he is not classed as a monetarist, few others had more to do with the wedding of basic Friedmanian doctrine to the actual practice of central banking. While on the board, he worked with monetary policy options for the FOMC. He has been credited with turning the Fed's main concern to monetary aggregates (primarily reserves for private deposit) and away from interest rates to control growth in the money supply. Holland's major time on the board was spent in three major multiyear system projects: a reappraisal of the discount mechanism, the application of economic analysis to the structural changes in the banking system resulting from the expansion of bank holding companies, and the adapting of modern business planning and management techniques to Federal Reserve business.

Holland resigned from the Board of Governors on May 15, 1976. According to the *American Banker*, Holland resigned because his salary of $42,000 was insufficient: "I can't afford to stay. I'm about to pay three college tuitions this fall and I can't afford in good conscience to make my family put up with this." David Lilly,* a former chairman of the board of directors of the Minneapolis Federal Reserve, was nominated by President Gerald Ford to fill the vacancy left by Holland's resignation.

After leaving the board, Holland accepted the position of president of the Committee for Economic Development (CED) and currently holds that position. The CED consists of a board of trustees composed of 250 university presidents, board chairmen, and presidents of major corporations. It researches serious long-run economic problems facing the nation and then publishes the results in policy statements. Holland oversees economic research projects and supervises the organization's education outreach to community leaders, government, and business.

Holland holds memberships in a wide range of organizations, including the American Economic Association, American Finance Association, Beta Theta Pi fraternity, St. Paul's Lutheran church in Washington, D.C., the Cosmos Club, and the Kenwood Golf and Country Club.

Over the years, he has given his time to serve on numerous committees and task forces: National Bureau of Economic Research Advisory Committee of Exploratory Study of Banking Markets and Bank Structure (1965); National Council of Churches, Commission on Church and Economic Life; Labor-Management Advisory Committee (1965–1966); Program Committee on the Church and Economic Life, National Council of Churches (1967–1968); Task Force on Finance, Lutheran Church of America (1971); and Finance Department Advisory Committee, the Wharton School of Finance and Commerce, University of Pennsylvania (1973).

On September 7, 1947, Robert Holland was married to DeEtte Harriet Hedlund, a teacher from Osceola, Nebraska. They have three children: Joan DeEtte Holland Geltz (born 1953) of Centreville, Virginia; Nancy Gretchen Holland Kerr (born 1956) of Newport Beach, California; and Timothy Robert Holland (born 1958) of Baltimore, Maryland. Holland and his wife currently live in Bethesda, Maryland.

BIBLIOGRAPHY

"Banking's Spotlight on Three Young Men at the Fed." 1966. *Banking* (February): 46–47.

Fedgram 7. 1976. Federal Reserve Bank of Chicago. April 30.

Holland, Robert Carl. 1952. "Role of Monetary Policy in Fighting Inflation." *Social Education* 16, no. 3 (March): 121–22, 124.

———. 1964. "Research in Banking Structure and Competition." *Federal Reserve Bulletin* 50, no. 11 (November): 1383–99.

———. 1970. "The Federal Reserve Discount Mechanism as an Instrument for Dealing with Banking Market Imperfections." *Journal of Money, Credit, and Banking* 2, no. 2 (May): 138–46.

———. 1974. "Saving: An Old-Fashioned Virtue in a New Fangled World." *New England Economic Review* (November-December): 20–23.

———. 1975a. "Banking Holding Companies and Financial Stability." *Journal of Financial and Quantitative Analysis* 10, no. 4 (November): 577–87.

———. 1975b. "Monetary Policy as a 'Social Science.' " *Ohio State University Bulletin of Business Research* 50, no. 3 (March): 1–2, 6.

———. 1989. Biographical summary.

U.S. Congress. Senate. Committee on Banking, Housing, and Urban Affairs. 1973. *Hearing*. 93d Cong., 1st sess., May 31.

PHILIP CHAPPELL JACKSON, JR. (1928–   )

Kathie S. Gilbert

The turmoil the economy faced as it made extensive readjustments in a post-OPEC (Organization of Petroleum Exporting Countries) marketplace and a growing problem with bank failure related to risky investment portfolios set the stage for the selection of a Federal Reserve Board of Governors' member who had a special understanding of the housing and mortgage finance market. Chairman Arthur F. Burns[*] found that person in Philip Chappell Jackson, Jr., who had extensive experience in housing and the mortgage banking field. Jackson was sworn in as a member of the Board of Governors on July 14, 1975, to complete the unexpired term of John E. Sheehan,[*] a Kentucky businessman who retired from the board on June 1, 1975, to become president of White Motor Company. Although eligible to serve until January 31, 1982, Jackson stepped down from the position on November 17, 1978.

When Jackson arrived at the Federal Reserve, it was under attack from both the academic and political communities. The academics accused the Fed of holding back the nation's economic recovery, and Congress was unhappy with the Fed's willingness to exert stronger influences through monetary policy. Congressman Wright Patman (D, Texas) had introduced a bill to submit the Fed to a congressional audit; a study by the congressman accused the Fed of spending money frivolously. The public sentiment against the Fed was growing sufficiently strong that President Gerald Ford, in an effort to shore up the importance of an independent policy body, made an unusual appearance at Jackson's swearing-in ceremonies. Ford made a strong appeal for independence for the Fed: ''I think it is highly important for all of us to emphasize now—as it has been in the past and I trust it will be in the future—that the Federal Reserve Board is an independent institution, a very vital, integral part of our total government setup, but one that occupies a very unique part in the workings of the Federal Government'' (*Wall Street Journal*, July 18, 1975). Ford made the first presidential appearance at the Fed since Franklin D. Roosevelt attended the dedication of its building on October 20, 1937.

Jackson credits Arthur Burns for his appointment to the Fed. Burns had a very close relationship with President Ford and in essence was able to name his own appointees. Burns first mentioned the possibility of appointing Jackson in the summer of 1974. His interest in Jackson stemmed from his strength in the housing and mortgage finance fields given the growing severity of credit problems related to these areas. Jackson saw these bank failures as the result of banks' investing too largely in highly speculative assets representing situations where the banks were not prudent in making investments and loans. In May 1975 Jackson visited with Burns about the possibility of service on the board. His family's business had just been sold, and he was willing to consider public service, promising Burns an answer within twenty-four hours if the president was willing to appoint him. During the interview with Jackson, Burns apologetically inquired whether Jackson was a Democrat or a Republican, while simultaneously indicating that the answer was immaterial. Jackson's tact can be seen in his answer: "Everyone in Alabama is a Democrat."

Jackson was born October 27, 1928, to Philip C. Jackson and Margaret Ellen Maddox Jackson in Birmingham, Alabama. He married Barbara Ellis Ritch in 1954, and they had three children: Virginia Ellen, Philip C. III, and Florence Jean. He attended Phillips High School and Birmingham Southern College before completing a B.S. degree in commerce and business administration at the University of Alabama's Tuscaloosa campus. Later he attended the School of Mortgage Banking at Northwestern University.

Jackson, whom President Ford characterized as "a person who has spent his life in the mortgage field," joined the Jackson Company, a mortgage banking company in Birmingham upon his college graduation. He served the family firm as mortgage vice-president and director. He was a contributing author to a textbook on mortgage banking and a past president of the Alabama Mortgage Bankers Association and the Mortgage Bankers Association of America. Jackson credits his work with trade associations for providing irreplaceable training in developing collegiality and team management skills.

Jackson, while recognizing his ability to understand the problems of real estate finance and the complications that legal restrictions initiated in the housing market, made it clear upon his appointment that he did not intend to be an advocate for any sector of the economy, including housing. That he had been in the thrift or housing side of the market was an advantage in his view because he "could participate in the discussions at least from the standpoint of understanding the ramifications of the decisions the Board might make."

Inflation was relatively high, and significant idle capacity was present in the economy when Jackson was named to the Board of Governors. Jackson's concern with real estate holdings' proving a problem for many banks was to "let the banks know there's no pressure to liquidate these assets . . . [and], if a bank needs advances for normal commercial purposes, recognize that real estate has value" (*Washington Post*, September 6, 1975). In the Senate confirmation hearings, he stated that "it's extremely important that we recognize the difference between a non-earning asset . . . versus an asset that represents total loss." In his view, patience to work out the problem was the "more prudent course of action" to "help extricate banks from the potential impairment of their assets" (U.S. Congress 1975).

Jackson was the first governor to be confirmed after Senator William Proxmire (D, Wisconsin) took over the Committee on Banking, Housing, and Urban Affairs from Senator John Sparkman (D, Alabama). Jackson, who had a strong practical background in financial matters, approached the hearings from the viewpoint that it was prudent not to be perceived as committed to a particular point of view. Thus, his answers to committee questions during the first confirmation hearing were bland and noncommittal general statements. Proxmire took offense with the degree of response Jackson gave to the questioning and recessed the first committee meeting without approving Jackson's confirmation. Senator Sparkman, anxious for Jackson's success, urged Jackson to tell Proxmire something, no matter how foolish or unrealistic it might appear later on. Jackson heeded that advice and was much more definitive during the second hearing.

Jackson addressed his reticence to provide specific prescriptions by stating that he felt it appropriate to enter the policymaking arena

with no bias, no personal prejudice, anything of that sort. . . . I was concerned that the committee might properly question the candor of my original remarks if I answered the question one way today and find that proper and better facts produce a better conclusion later. Finally, . . . if I am to have influence on that committee [Federal Open Market Committee] beyond the 8 ⅓ percent vote that I'd have, those members of that committee have got to feel confident that I don't take positions unless I have done my homework and done the job in the manner that they think appropriate before arriving at conclusions. (U.S. Congress, pp. 44–45)

Jackson saw the banking system as the means through which the economic and personal resources of the country could be utilized and developed. His experienced and thoughtful approach added a forceful, pragmatic view to the Federal Reserve board. At the time of his appointment, Jackson was the only governor who had ever made a loan or collected a payment.

As president of the Mortgage Bankers Association of America, Jackson frequently testified before the congressional Subcommittee on Housing and Urban Affairs. He was regarded as a strong and effective advocate of mortgage credit policies helpful to the housing industry. Chairman Arthur Burns recognized Jackson's experience in legislative relationships and his ability to articulate a position effectively. He gave him many assignments on Capitol Hill to represent Federal Reserve positions. Jackson's ability to spin a great story, his honesty, and his good-old-boy manner helped him build and maintain good working relationships within Congress and the federal bureaucracy.

Jackson was an ardent admirer of Burns. He viewed Burns as an extraordinary teacher who maintained a close personal relationship with the people with whom he worked. Although characterized as a Burns devotee, Jackson retained his independence and often took the chairman on in meetings. Burns, in return, respected Jackson's independence and became furious when *Time* magazine characterized Jackson as better known for his hunting prowess than his skill as a monetary scholar. He felt Jackson was someone who presented reasoned judgments that forced others to listen and respond.

In Jackson's view, regulation could not overcome the mistakes of "stupid management decisions." He was a firm believer in fostering incentives that make the market work and minimizing the temptation to demand that government solve everything. Impatience to get quick results led only to more government intervention:

Our economic system has been constructed on the concept of private ownership of property and on economic freedom of choice in the use of property. The aggregate free choices, and differentiation of our people have been the means by which our resources are allocated and our potential developed. Let us never lose sight that this capacity to discriminate— in the nonsocial meaning of that word—has been one of the means by which the country has become great. [Speech, 16 June 1977]

Jackson adhered to the adage that the best government is that which governs least. His experience with the Federal Reserve reconfirmed this. Regulation should be a last resort and implemented only when there were enough problems from the free marketplace to merit a restraint on everyone else's freedom: "We must have the national courage to endure small evils or small catastrophes without putting massive constraints on the freedom of the citizens to solve the problems. The resulting evils of using massive constraints are much greater than enduring the abuses of a few individuals" (Jackson 1979). Regulation tended to follow regulation as impatience for a quick solution grew. Court decisions followed regulations until things became so complicated that understanding was impossible, cutting down on the competitiveness in the economy and making the consumer the loser. Jackson strongly supported the private sector's freedom to fail, for without that there would be inadequate freedom to succeed.

Jackson was quick to point out that it was not just labor, consumers, or educators who pushed strongly for government intervention. His experience proved that business and professional people were "equally guilty of turning to government quickly the minute their own ox gets into a ditch." In his work to simplify the Truth in Lending Act of 1968, legislation intended to help the public understand the true cost of and use of credit, Jackson sought a bill that limited the regulatory aspects while emphasizing the most significant disclosures and making credit information more readable and usable.

Congressional members, Jackson observed, often take a public stand that they privately discount. Much of this posturing relates to the rhetoric of whether the Congress should have a more active role to play in monetary policy. Governors were apolitical, Congress political. Scathing diatribes toward the Fed were often for the public; privately, congressional members indicated that their outbursts should be discounted.

Jackson's biggest frustration while on the board was in how political responses often got in the way of what was the best economic policy or the most rational approach. His broad knowledge of the pragmatic aspects of lending or running a business often were frustrated by new regulations or regulations that did not fit well with the essential operational activities of businesses.

Congress also had a tendency to throw to the Federal Reserve difficult economic issues related to tax structure or budget that were well outside the realm of monetary policy and action. The business of the Fed should have been, in Jackson's view, the economic welfare of the country.

One weakness Jackson noted was the temptation within the board to rely on only traditional data sources when analyzing the economy. He encouraged the board to talk with financial industry leaders to uncover trends that data were slow to pick up. For example, the staff predicted an increase in long-term interest rates, but, when the major life insurance companies told the board that they had large amounts of money in their portfolios and were desperately looking for investment opportunities, evidence shifted from the view that long-term rates would rise. History showed that the insurance experience was more accurate than the Fed-generated data. Another example Jackson cited was when Donald Regan, then chief executive officer of Merrill, Lynch, Pierce, Fenner and Smith, called and requested an opportunity to visit with the board. He wanted to alert them to the rapid and large growth in the firm's newly created money market mutual funds. A new intermediary, which we now call M2, had surfaced. The importance of tempering leading indicators data with familiarity with actual happenings in business and industry was critical, in Jackson's view, if the Board of Governors was to assess economic situations accurately. Jackson supported citizen involvement in government. He advocated expressing one's views to both elected and appointed officials. His advice in addition to getting involved was to have the personal courage to seek solutions without turning to the government for help and to live in the heat of a tough, competitive, unsheltered environment. Finally, he advocated concern and compassion for one's country, state, city, neighborhood, fellow citizens, and family such that one becomes compelled to respond personally to needs: "Resist the temptation to hope that someone else will do it."

Jackson's fondness for tennis created a stir in Washington when he reserved the William McChesney Martin[*] Memorial Tennis Court for use every morning for an hour's play. Trophies of his hunting success adorned the walls of his board office. His interest in big game hunting, particularly wild sheep, remains a vital part of his life, and he can still be found traveling the world as he attempts to hunt every species of wild sheep known.

After experiencing the bureaucratic ways of the federal government, Jackson decided it was time to move on to another career, especially since he was already in his fifties. He left the Federal Reserve board on November 17, 1978, for personal reasons. Reinforcing his decision that this was the appropriate time to step down was his knowledge that his replacement should serve long enough to be taken seriously.

Jackson believed that no member should use his or her Federal Reserve position as a stepping-stone to a new job. Thus, he resigned and left the board before opening discussions about his next career. Initially he chose to serve as an outside professional corporate director for seven different public companies; however, when this did not prove to be as rewarding and stimulating as he had hoped, he joined the Central Bank of the South as the second in command. He continued his career in banking with the same company until he retired in 1989.

Much of Jackson's life was intertwined with education. As an active member of trade associations, he had participated in many continuing education programs. With retirement, he returned part time to the teaching profession and simultaneously rejoined the full-time student ranks at Birmingham Southern. When he is not studying for or attending his music history courses, he can be found teaching in the Business and Economics Department.

BIBLIOGRAPHY

Battey, Phil. 1978. "Jackson Cites Fed Frustration, Opposes 'Massive Constraints.' " *American Banker*, October 23, p. 23.

"Ford Watches as Jackson Is Sworn In." 1975. *Washington Post*, July 15, p. D1.

Holusha, John. 1977. "Business Profile (Philip C. Jackson, Jr.): Obscure, Nevertheless Important." *Washington Star*, May 29, p. C1.

Hutnyan, Joseph D. 1975. "Washington Bank Notes: Ford's Trip to the Fed More Than Just Birthday Greetings." *Wall Street Journal*, July 18, p. 4.

Jackson, Philip C. 1977. "In Defense of Discrimination." Remarks presented to the American Bar Association National Institute on Consumer Credit, New York, June 16.

———. 1978. "Addresses, Essays, Lectures of Philip C. Jackson, Jr." Mimeographed. Federal Reserve Library, Washington, D.C.

———. 1979. "Real Estate: Can We Afford Not to Own It?" *American Banker*, May 15, pp. 25–26.

———. 1989. Personal interview. September.

Mandala, Andrew. 1975. "New Fed Governor Avoids Role as Housing Advocate: Philip C. Jackson Speaks Out." *Washington Post*, September 6, p. E45.

U.S. Congress. Senate. Committee on Banking, Housing, and Urban Affairs. 1975. *Nomination of Philip C. Jackson, Jr.* 94th Cong., 1st sess., June 9, 20.

GEORGE ROOSA JAMES (1866–1937)

Jean-Claude Leon

George Roosa James, who served as a governor of the Federal Reserve from April 1923 to February 1936 was born in Memphis, Tennessee, on September 12, 1866, to Henry and Caroline (Roosa) J. James. Educated in public schools, he married Elizabeth Carpenter on January 12, 1888. Before being appointed a member of the Federal Reserve Board, his professional background had been in manufacturing and merchandising. In 1886 he was secretary of the James & Graham Wagon Company located in Memphis. In 1889 he was appointed president of the company. In 1910 he was president of the State National Bank of Memphis and later served as vice-president of its successor, the Central State National Bank, after being consolidated with Central Bank & Trust Company in 1912. In 1915 he was president of the William R. Moore Dry Goods Company.

James also held various public offices. From 1892 to 1893 he was a member of the Memphis City Council. During World War I, he served as chief of the Cotton and Cotton Linter Section of the War Industries Board and later as a member of the Industrial Board of the Department of Commerce.

On April 29, 1923, President Warren G. Harding appointed James, then fifty-six years old, as a member of the Federal Reserve Board. He succeeded John R. Mitchell[*] of Saint Paul, who had resigned. The appointment of James, a Democrat, was in line with the White House policy of placing a member from the South on the board. President Herbert Hoover reappointed him in 1931 for a term of ten years, but he served only until February 3, 1936, when President Franklin Roosevelt decided not to reappoint him during the reform of the Federal Reserve system in 1936, enacted by Congress the previous year.

The Banking Act of 1935 brought major changes to the Federal Reserve system. The governors of the twelve reserve banks were given the new title of president. More important, the Open Market Committee ceased to be an advisory body and acquired genuine authority over the Federal Reserve system's buying and selling of government and other paper. On the committee, representation of the reserve banks was cut from twelve to five members. Of the board, two members, the secretary of the Treasury and the comptroller of the currency, automatically lost their ex officio jobs. The other six members also lost their positions unless reappointed by President Roosevelt. This was the case for George R. James.

As a member of the Federal Reserve Board, James developed a reputation of a man of strong ethics and technical expertise. He came from Memphis to Washington in 1917 as a dollar-a-year man in President Woodrow Wilson's wartime organization. He was listed as a Democrat, but his party affiliation was not strong. He served under three Republican administrations (Harding, Coolidge, Hoover) and received appointments from two of them, in 1923 and 1931. At the time of his reappointment in 1931, James, a former manufacturer, merchant, and banker, weighted heavily the duties of a public official member of the Federal Reserve Board paid only $12,000 a year.

His tenure at the Federal Reserve Board undoubtedly resulted in private financial sacrifice. *World's Work* noted,

The man who goes on the reserve board must give up his regular work, move to Washington, and devote his full time to the board. While he will be voting salaries of from twenty to fifty thousand dollars to executive officers of the reserve banks, and passing upon matters vital to the welfare of member banks whose officers in some instances receive compensation running into six figures and beyond, his own salary will be but twelve thousand dollars a year. If he is the type of man who has had much larger earnings, his reserve-board appointment for the ten-year term will "cost" him around half a million dollars. (Deiger 1931)

James's voting record during his thirteen years of tenure as a member of the Federal Reserve Board indicates an inclination for an easy money policy to stimulate business, a position he reversed after the crash of the stock market in 1929.

In 1925, some Federal Reserve officials expressed concern about stock market speculation. In this context, the Federal Reserve Bank of Boston applied in early October 1925 for an increase in the rediscount rate. The directors of the New York bank opposed any increase in rates. They preferred to use direct action, or moral suasion, to reduce stock exchange loans. James agreed with the New York directors and opposed a rate increase.

In March 1926 the stock market suffered a sharp setback. Benjamin Strong of the New York bank indicated that a business recession had started and that the Open Market Investment Committee ought to be prepared to purchase government securities if required. James introduced a resolution at a meeting of the board to give the committee the authority to increase the investment account.

In 1927, the international situation was a major reason for an easy money policy. Following a July meeting of the Open Market Investment Committee, discount rate reductions were announced by the Federal Reserve banks except by the Chicago Federal Reserve Bank, which refused to reduce its rate. James joined a majority vote of the board to force Chicago to reduce its rate.

During the stock market mania of 1928, the monetary authorities wanted to control stock market speculation by controlling the flow of bank credit through the sales of securities and increases in the rediscount rate, without adversely affecting output. Adolph Miller,[*] a member of the board, considered those tools too blunt. With Charles Hamlin,[*] another board member, they persuaded the board to adopt in January 1929 a policy of direct pressure, that is, moral suasion to prevent further increase in lending by member banks for the purpose of increasing stock speculation. The board was sharply divided over the merit of this policy. Some members believed that this policy was ineffective and resulted in increasing the discount rates. James was a strong supporter of the policy of direct pressure. However, when opposition within the board to the Miller-Hamlin policy for direct action developed, James voted with the majority in favor of rate increase, expressing in effect the doubt that moral suasion could work alone.

Federal Reserve policy notwithstanding, the stock market collapsed in October 1929, and the economy slipped into a deep recession. In the aftermath of the stock market collapse, James, together with two other board members, Edward Cunningham[*] and Miller, formed a strong minority who consistently opposed easing action through the purchases of government securities as a stimulus to business activity.

During his long years in Washington, James's rewards were to be found in the satisfaction provided by the experience of public service. In 1935, *Time* noted, "Next year George Roosa James will be seventy years old and though he has the crotchets that go with age, he is crammed full of useful technical information." James died on March 9, 1937.

BIBLIOGRAPHY

"Business and Finance." 1935. *Time*, December 30, pp. 27–28.

Deiger, J. M. 1931. "Wall Street or Washington, Which Shall Rule the Federal Reserve?" *World's Work* (August): 49.

Wicker, Elmua R. 1966. *Federal Reserve Monetary Policy, 1917–33*. New York: Random House.

MANUEL H. JOHNSON (1949–   )

Robert C. Winder

Manuel Homan Johnson was confirmed by the U.S. Senate to serve a full fourteen-year term as a member of the Board of Governors of the Federal Reserve system. His tenure began February 7, 1986, three days before his thirty-seventh birthday. Few other people have come to the Federal Reserve system with such great promise as Manuel Johnson. The quality of his academic and professional background along with the force of his personality give him the potential to be a leading and even dominating force in the Federal Reserve system. Johnson's swift selection to serve as vice-chairman of the Board of Governors beginning in August 1986 is evidence of his ability and ambition.

Johnson was born on February 10, 1949, in Troy, Alabama. He received his undergraduate degree in economics from Troy State University in 1973. His M.S. and Ph.D. degrees in economics were received from Florida State University in 1974 and 1977, respectively. Upon graduating from Florida State University, Johnson accepted a position at George Mason University; he had obtained the rank of associate professor by 1980. In 1982 Johnson left academia to serve in the U.S. Department of Treasury as deputy assistant secretary for economic policy. He was promoted to assistant secretary by 1982 and continued in that position until his move to the Federal Reserve board in 1986.

While at Treasury, Johnson provided counsel and support to the secretary of the U.S. Treasury on economic policy issues and was the Treasury Department's liaison in formulating presidential forecasts and positions on budgetary issues. In addition, Johnson served on a wide range of committees and task forces dedicated to economic policymaking and actively participated in policy briefings to senior members of the White House staff.

Johnson was equally active as a member of the Board of Governors of the Federal Reserve system. As vice-chairman, he assisted in directing the formulation of monetary and credit policy for the domestic economy and was integrally involved in the coordination of the Federal Open Market Committee's operations. In the absence of the chairman, Johnson served as the Fed's chief officer. Beyond these responsibilities, Johnson was in charge of the Federal Reserve system's international affairs. Accordingly, he was the Fed's representative to both the International Monetary Fund and the Group of 10 Central Bank Governors, which meets monthly in Basel, Switzerland. He also chaired the Fed's Committee on International Finance, the Committee on Payment System Policy, and the Committee on Research and Statistics.

Throughout his professional career, Johnson has remained an active scholar, publishing over sixty articles, books, and monographs. Many of his articles have appeared in juried (refereed) journals, including the *Cato Journal*, the *Journal of Contemporary Policy Issues*, *Economic Inquiry*, and *Public Choice*. Not surprisingly, he has won numerous awards and honors. In 1986 he won the Florida State University Distinguished Alumni Achievement Award and received an honorary doctor of laws degree from Troy State University. In the same year, he received the U.S. Treasury Department's Alexander Hamilton Award for outstanding leadership. Johnson has received numerous other awards from his alma maters, including Florida State University's Honor Award for Outstanding Contributions to Public Policy (1985) and Troy State University's Alumnus of the Year Award (1982). In addition to a litany of accolades and honors from both the Treasury Department and various academic institutions, Manuel Johnson's achievements have been recognized by the Center for the Study of Public Choice and the Nuclear Regulatory Commission, as well as other organizations. He is listed in *Who's Who in America*, *Who's Who in Finance and Industry*, and *Who's Who in American Politics*.

Manuel Johnson is married and has two children. His frequent twelve-hour workdays leave him little idle time. He plays golf only infrequently, and as a result his scores have soared to the high eighties. Johnson is a veteran of the U.S. Army Special Forces (1968–1971), serving as an elite Green Beret in Korea.

During the U.S. Senate hearings on Johnson's nomination to the Board of Governors, Democratic senators treated the highly regarded nominee with deference but did not pull any punches. Johnson, if confirmed, would be the fourth appointee of President Ronald Reagan, thereby giving the Republican administration a majority of the governors. The fear of a "gang of four" on the Board of Governors supportive of President Reagan's supply-side economic policies gave the Democratic members of the Senate committee great concern. Senator Donald Riegle (Michigan) asked Johnson, "Do you consider yourself a supply-sider?" Johnson, most likely anticipating this question, responded that he is a supply sider in the sense of believing in the efficiency of free markets but not in the sense of believing that tax cuts will "pay for themselves overnight." Continuing this line of questioning, Riegle asked, "Do you believe in the Laffer Curve?" Johnson answered that although a cut in the capital gains tax would probably lead to additional revenues, the evidence is that a general cut in tax rates would "not lead to a full recovery of revenue."

During the Senate hearing, Johnson was also grilled on studies he supervised while at the Treasury Department that seemed to conclude that higher federal budget deficits do not necessarily raise real interest rates or drive up the international value of the dollar. Sensing the importance of this issue to his credibility, if not his confirmation, Johnson was precise and thorough in his explanation. According to Johnson, an expanding federal deficit can be expected to raise real interest rates if all other economic variables are held constant. However, because a variety of variables are likely to change in response to an expanding deficit, the studies he performed while at Treasury were "not able to pick up this systematic relationship that commonsensical reasoning comes up with."

As an example, Johnson noted that an increase in the deficit typically elicits an inflow of foreign capital, which tends to dampen any rise in the interest rate. Furthermore, an expanding deficit resulting from a cut in the marginal tax rate on saving would result in an increase in the level of saving, thereby providing an offset to the additional government borrowing. Taking another tack, Johnson pointed out that the money households use to buy government bonds might have been spent on consumption rather than saved, so that one cannot conclude that deficits always reduce the amount of private saving for other uses.

A well-prepared and forceful Manuel Johnson successfully defended his position on deficits and interest rates and on a variety of other issues and was easily confirmed by the full Senate to serve as a member of the Board of Governors of the Federal Reserve system. In his brief tenure, Johnson's natural political savvy and southern wiles made him an influential and highly visible figure at the Federal Reserve system. Federal Reserve chairman Alan Greenspan,[*] like his predecessor Paul Volcker,[*] trusted and relied on Johnson.

Johnson's expertise and interests are diverse, and his professional career is an odyssey still unfolding. Fresh out of graduate school, Johnson went to George Mason University in 1977 primarily as a labor economist. Following a brief but prolific stint in academia, he was brought to the U.S. Department of Treasury in 1982 by the noted supply-side economist Paul Craig Roberts. At the Treasury Department, the young Johnson became a platoon leader in the supply-side revolution, arguing for lower tax rates to spur economic growth.

Johnson's essential views on tax policy are revealed in his 1985 *Cato Journal* article, "President Reagan's Modified Flat Tax: Analysis and Comparison," where he advocated a more neutral tax structure with lower marginal tax rates. Johnson noted that when taxes are "levied unevenly" across different types of goods or across the types of labor or capital, relative prices are altered and the ability of the price system to allocate resources efficiently is impaired. Firms are led to combine labor and capital in the production process in suboptimal ways, resulting in a reduction in national output. Consumers purchase combinations of goods that do not maximize their satisfaction in relation to resources employed. In addition, Johnson discussed tax-induced distortions involving work effort and saving. Taxing earned income reduces the (after-tax) return to working and therefore results in a substitution of leisure for work. Taxing interest income and dividends reduces the (after-tax) return to saving, resulting in less saving and a higher level of consumption. While admitting that it is a fantasy to hope for a tax system that is entirely neutral with respect to economic decisions, Johnson seems firmly entrenched in the supply-side camp.

During his tenure at the Treasury Department, Johnson, like other supply siders, had been critical of Paul Volcker's tight money policies as a threat to economic growth and to the Reagan fiscal revolution. Not surprisingly, when Johnson joined the Fed in 1986, he was viewed with some suspicion by chairman Volcker and by monetarists in general. But at the Fed, he surprised many observers by seeming neither evangelical nor ideological. Despite his supply-side pedigree, Johnson was easy to work with and was clearly committed to a level monetary growth consistent with stable prices and reasonably calm financial markets.

While a member of the Board of Governors, Johnson contributed to the debate over the implementation of monetary policy. In a second *Cato Journal* article (1988), he described the limitations of the strict monetarist approach to policymaking, which prescribes constant growth in the monetary aggregates. Because of the volatility in the velocity of money, the predictability of the relationship between the money supply and nominal gross national product has been weakened, calling into question the usefulness of the monetary aggregates as an intermediate objective. While Johnson confessed that it was "probably too early to conclude that the monetary aggregates will not be useful in the future as policy indicators or targets," he believed it was important to develop additional measures as guides to decision making. Accordingly, Johnson supported using information obtained from the yield curve, the foreign exchange market, and indexes of commodity prices as signals as to the tightness or ease of monetary policy. Data on all three variables are available on a daily basis and can be accurately measured. Because these are market-determined prices, they reflect the expectations of a large number of individuals and in general tend to lead movements in the consumer price index. When used in conjunction with each other, they can provide insight to policymakers. For example, if the value of the U.S. dollar is depreciating internationally, commodity prices (in terms of dollars) are rising, and the yield curve is upward sloping, this composite picture suggests that monetary policy may be overly expansive. A rising dollar internationally along with falling commodity prices and a downward-sloping yield curve may signal a monetary policy that is excessively tight.

Governor Johnson also advocated using relative interest rate movements as a guide to monetary policy. In *Monetary Policy in an Era of Change* (1989), he observed that "banks are profit maximizing institutions" and that they base their decisions on the spread between the cost of funds (indicated by the federal funds rate) and the return on assets rather than on reserve levels. If this spread is wide, even banks lacking excess reserves can obtain additional reserves in the federal funds market in order to make loans and purchase assets, thereby expanding the money supply. This assumes that the Federal Reserve system accommodates the increased demand for reserves. If the spread between the cost of funds and the return on assets shrinks, the incentive is for banks to call in loans and sell assets in order to lend reserves in the funds market. The effect is to reduce demand deposits and the money supply. In this way, adjustments in the federal funds rate relative to other interest rates become the key to the money creation process and to the Fed's control over credit conditions.

In addition to domestic monetary and fiscal policy, Johnson has a demonstrated interest in international economics. Because of the significant volatility in the international value of the dollar experienced in the 1980s, in his article "Reflections on the Current International Debt Situation" (1987), Johnson advocated better coordination of domestic policies across countries. With reference to the multifaceted and seemingly intractable international debt crisis, he encouraged the industrial nations to pursue pro-growth policies and to maintain open markets for the exports of the developing world. In particular, industrial countries currently enjoying trade surpluses should adopt trade policies enabling debtor nations to earn hard currency to help pay international loans. At the same time, the debtor nations in Latin America and elsewhere should undertake domestic reforms promoting saving, investment, and growth in order to reduce the burden of debt repayment. Since these and other reforms will ameliorate the debt problem only over time, it will be necessary for both the World Bank and the money center commercial banks to continue to restructure the debt in the interim.

Johnson has won plaudits from Fed watchers and economists of virtually all persuasions. His professional credentials, personal attributes, and relative youth made him a formidable and potentially dominant force at the nation's central bank. However, Johnson unexpectedly announced his resignation effective August 3, 1990. He planned to return to George Mason University and assume the Koch Chair in International Economics and become director of the Center for Global Market Studies.

BIBLIOGRAPHY

Johnson, Manuel H. 1985. "President Reagan's Modified Flat Tax." *Cato Journal* (Fall): 499–520.
———. 1987. "Reflections on the Current International Debt Situation." *Economic Review* of the Federal Reserve Bank of Kansas City (June).
———. 1988. "Current Perspectives on Monetary Policy." *Cato Journal* (Fall): 253–60.
———. 1989. "Perspectives on the Implementation on Monetary Policy." In William S. Haraf, ed., *Monetary Policy in an Era of Change*. Washington, D.C.: American Enterprise Institute for Public Policy Research.
U.S. Congress. Senate. Committee on Banking, Housing, and Urban Affairs. 1986. *Nominations of Wayne D. Angell and Manuel Homan Johnson, Jr., to Be Members of the Board of Governors, Federal Reserve System*. January 23.
Who's Who in America, 1988–1989. Wilmette, Ill.: Marquis Who's Who.

EDWARD W. KELLEY (1927–   )

Jack B. White

Edward W. Kelley joined the Board of Governors of the Federal Reserve system on May 26, 1987, filling the unexpired term of Emmett J. Rice.* Initially his desire was only to serve out the two years remaining on Rice's term. However, Kelley was persuaded to accept a full term and was sworn in for a fourteen-year term on April 20, 1990. Assuming he serves his entire term, Kelley will be part of the dramatic changes that take place in the financial market as we move into the twenty-first century. Kelley has had significant experience in the business world, having been associated with several industries, including construction, plastic and metal fabrication, trucking, and computer services. The diversity of this background makes him aware of how changes in the financial markets affect diverse businesses.

Born in Eugene, Oregon, on January 27, 1927, Kelley grew up in Houston, Texas. Staying close to home, he attended Rice University and graduated with a degree in history in 1954. Following service in the U.S. Navy, he enrolled in the Harvard Business School. He received his M.B.A. in 1959.

Kelley then returned to Houston to run the family business, Kelley Manufacturing, a fabricator of sheet-metal products used in construction. He not only increased the scope of the company to include consumer products but also expanded it to market its products nationwide. He sold Kelley Manufacturing in 1981 and affiliated with Investment Advisors Incorporated, a firm that serves institutional investors. He was chief executive officer of Investment Advisors when he was nominated to the Board of Governors.

While Kelley's background is primarily that of a businessman, his connection to banking came shortly after his departure from Harvard. In 1961 he became a director of Southern National Bank and except for a brief lapse from 1972 to 1974 served until 1984. He thereby gained invaluable insights into the banking regulatory process from the perspective of the regulated entity.

Kelley's Houston background served him well in two ways. First, James A. Baker, also from Houston, has known Kelley since childhood (they attended the same schools). Baker was President Ronald Reagan's secretary of the Treasury when Kelley was selected and no doubt presented his friend as a possible candidate for the empty governor's chair at the Fed. Second, Lief Olsen, an economist at Citicorp, was also mentioned as a possible successor to Emmett Rice. However, federal law prohibits two members of the Board of Governors from representing the same Federal Reserve district. Since Alan Greenspan* was representing the Second Federal Reserve District (New York) then, Olsen could not be allowed to represent New York. (This fact did not necessarily preclude Olsen; he could have claimed to represent the district of his birth or even where he attended school.) Kelley, on the other hand, could represent the Eleventh District (Dallas), which lacked representation at that time. However, a more plausible explanation of why Kelley, a nonbanker and noneconomist, received the nomination over Olsen is that Olsen is a more doctrinaire monetarist. Kelley, on the other hand, bears no ideological allegiance.

Kelley's business background has inclined toward increased deregulation and competition in banking. During confirmation hearings in 1987, he could not specify what determined the optimal balance between competition and bank safety but held that each issue should be decided on its own merits. Such a pragmatic point of view was accepted by the Senate, and Kelley's confirmation did not generate any significant opposition.

Kelley's views on monetary policy also lacked any strident ideological perspective. He testified that changes in the money supply should be permitted to occur without attempts to fine-tune trends. He added, however, that he would favor some sort of monetary intervention when those trends become disruptive to the economy.

Although Kelley lacks formal training as an economist, this does not mean that he is an observer in the discussions at the Fed. Prior to his confirmation, those who knew him were confident that he would be able to understand and contribute to the discussions on monetary policy and the regulation of financial markets. In addition, the staff at the Federal Reserve provide any background information a governor needs in order to be fully versed on an issue. Each member also maintains contacts with a number of professional economists, providing insights from several sources. (Formal training in economics is not a prerequisite for serving in a position of economic adviser. Alan Greenspan, chairman of the Council of Economic Advisers to President Ford, did not receive his Ph.D. until 1977.) However, Kelley knows there is no substitute for first-hand information. "We [board members] talk around the country to gather as much anecdotal evidence as we can, and just plain old sit quietly, looking out the window and thinking about it," he reports. Such "plain old sitting and thinking" served him well in business and provides the insight of an experienced practitioner to the discussions at the Fed.

There have already been signs that Kelley's opinions are well respected within the government. When illness forced Henry Wallich* to resign in 1986, Kelley suggested that his successor should be someone with experience in banking. Knowing that many of the issues that would be facing the board would relate to banking deregulation, Kelley considered a banker to be an excellent addition to the board. Not surprisingly, the eventual appointee, John LaWare,[*] had been a banker for his entire professional life.

BIBLIOGRAPHY

"Balancing Act at the Fed." 1987. *Time*, January 26, p. 3.

Rehm, Barbara. 1987. "Federal Reserve Nominee Kelley Faces Senate Panel." *American Banker*, May 6, p. 2.

———. 1988. "Kelley Says a Banker Would Be a Good Addition to the Fed." *American Banker*, March 7, p. 15.

———. 1989. "Kelley Reported Ready to Accept Another Fed Term." *American Banker*, December 15, p. 3.

GEORGE HAROLD KING, JR. (1920-   )

Kathie S. Gilbert

George Harold King, Jr., millionaire lumberman and rancher, arrived at his Federal Reserve Board of Governor's position in a distinctive manner. At the time of his appointment, King was primarily known for his purebred Hereford cattle and his contributions to cattle breeding. King himself said he rode a white-faced Hereford yearling to the Fed. Only thirty-eight at the time of his appointment, King was the youngest man ever to have been appointed to the Federal Reserve Board of Governors. He served from March 1959 to September 1963.

King was born in Oakdale, Louisiana on August 18, 1920 to George Harold and French Freeman King. He was an outstanding athlete at both Glenmora (Louisiana) High School where he graduated in 1937 and at Louisiana State University where he played football between 1937 and 1941. He received his bachelor's degree in accounting from Louisiana State University in 1941. Within a year of graduation, he entered active duty as an ensign in the United States Naval Reserve. When he left active duty in February 1946 it was at the rank of lieutenant. He maintained inactive status with the United States Naval Reserve.

In May 1942, King married Daudrille Elaine Hollaway of Melville, Louisiana. After World War II, the Kings, and their children, Linda Elaine born November 1944 and George Harold III born November 1945, moved to Canton, Mississippi where King was employed at King Lumber Industries, a company founded and headed by his father. A third child, Lisa Hollaway was born in February of 1955. The Kings divorced in the spring of 1963. At King Lumber Industries King served as treasurer (1946–1949), executive vice president (1950–1958), and president (from 1958 until his appointment to the Federal Reserve board).

King held great respect for his father whose picture proudly graced his Federal Reserve office. Although encouraged by his father to play a major role in the family's lumber business, King had the dream of owning a cattle ranch. His dream soon became a reality and in 1957 his ranch produced and exhibited the champion Hereford bull, T. R. Zato Heir 74th, at the National Western Livestock Show in Denver.

King identified himself as a Republican, a rarity in the deep South of his day, and served as county chairman of the Citizens for Eisenhower. This activity did not go unnoticed and he was recommended to Eisenhower for consideration to a Board of Governor's appointment.

King had very limited banking experience. He characterized his background as being mainly that of a depositor and credit user; however his business and ranching activities gave him some firsthand knowledge of how vital credit was to a growing business.

Largely because of his influence as a businessman and rancher, he was appointed as a director of the New Orleans branch of the Federal Reserve Bank of Atlanta in January 1956. In 1958 he was elected chairman of the New Orleans Branch Board, and just prior to being nominated to the Board of Governors, King was reappointed to a second term on that board.

When Eisenhower's staff called to invite King to visit with the president about the Federal Reserve appointment, King, who had been up all night with a newborn calf, was skeptical about the legitimacy of the call. Finally convinced, he flew to Washington to visit with the president but remained lukewarm to the idea. Washington was a far cry from the ranch that he dearly loved. When he told his wife that he wanted to get out of it, she provided little consolation, noting that he was "stuck with it."

After a perfunctory nomination hearing held on Wednesday, March 11, 1959, King was appointed to the Board of Governors of the Federal Reserve to fill the ten months remaining in the term of Governor James K. Vardaman, Jr.,[*] a fellow Mississippian, who had resigned. A second, more extensive hearing was held on February 4, 1960 when Governor King was confirmed for a full fourteen-year term to the board.

King did not demonstrate a high level of sophistication at his confirmation hearings or in the board position. He was not familiar with the monetary views of any of the leading academics or private sector economists. He chose to rely largely on his own, rather limited, personal experience when confronted with setting new policy. He believed the Federal Reserve should access as many tools as possible and should not resort to a monetary rule. Monetary policy was too complex an activity to be set by a formula; it was better to temper factual data with responsible judgement, especially since lags in transmitting information in the economy made precise forecasting impossible.

King did not have the reputation of being an independent thinker; rather he was recognized as an ingrained supporter of Chairman William McChesney Martin, Jr.[*] He became a predictable member consistently voting with the board majority on the side of restraint and "tight" money. Governor King disliked the term "tight money," feeling it was a misnomer that must have been thought up by "someone who felt that perpetual inflation was a good thing for the country." A more appropriate term, in King's view, was a "sound money" program. Likewise, for clarity, "easy money" should be retitled as "printing press money."

When King arrived at the Federal Reserve, the world's dependence on U.S. benevolence was ending. Countries were again able to stand on their own economic feet. This growing economic strength abroad placed new pressures on the U.S. dollar, and led to expanding gold flows from the United States to the industrial nations of Western Europe. New challenges had to be faced as the

Fed dealt with a domestic economy that needed expansion and an international economic situation that called for greater restraint.

Changes in the discount rate and open market operations were stressed, while the reserve requirement was deemphasized. Interest rate stability became fashionable, becoming a key variable after the Council of Economic Advisors questioned the Fed's emphasis on tight money, especially since rates were the highest they had been since the 1920s. In King's view, it was essential to maintain tight money if the economy was to achieve a balanced budget and stable dollar.

The conservatives, of which King and Chairman Martin were supporters, felt that tighter money would help stem the flow of dollars abroad and provide additional funds for domestic expansion. The liberals felt that tighter money had little impact on the flow of dollars abroad but was capable of doing serious damage to domestic expansion. Tight money coupled with the "bills only" doctrine, which ended following Kennedy's inauguration, was used to support a large gap between short-term and long-term rates.

King and his fellow conservatives supported the view that monetary management alone was insufficient to maintain economic stability; however, any supplemental governmental actions should interfere as little as possible with the workings of the free market. Economic growth should be achieved through a climate of as much freedom as possible. Fiscal actions that encouraged individuals to expand their investments and their plant and operations should be fostered. King was a strong believer in free markets and in the view that encouraging individual responsibility served the public interest effectively. King's homespun and down-home philosophy—he spoke proudly of being called a "cracker-barrel philosopher"—was an integral part of his speeches. He credited the philosophical ideas of Socrates, Plato, and Aristotle, among others, as the light that illuminated the way for him in his travel through life. Thomas Jefferson's philosophy of government was a special favorite of the governor. He preached eloquently that faith in the nature and destiny of the individual was at the heart of democratic theory. As the United States dealt with the growing Communist threat the nation would gain by stopping to examine its own weaknesses more closely than might otherwise be the case. "We must intensify our efforts to invade men's minds with the principles of democracy and freedom . . . but much more important, we must instill in men's minds the religious and spiritual bases of democracy" (Charlottesville, Virginia, 1962).

King supported open discussion of controversial issues. However, Americans seemed reluctant to speak out for the dreams of a democratic society. King chastised such views saying that to voluntarily impose censorship is to strike at a fundamental principle of democracy.

King also felt that as a nation we were reluctant to curb our apparently insatiable desire for more money and less work. This seriously contributed, in his view, to our international imbalance position. King was fearful of the growing search for economic security. Americans were bartering away their heritage to gain "cradle to the grave" security that "cannot even come near perfection without robbing us of the remainder of our freedom."

King's many speeches while governor espoused two favorite themes—the inappropriateness of the term "tight money" and the virtues of free enterprise. To whomever he was addressing, King made no claims of being an expert on money or monetary policy.

King represented the Federal Reserve at the 1961 meeting of the Bank for International Settlements where he supported the removal of the ceiling on interest payable by member banks on foreign government and central bank time deposits. Domestically, he voted against raising the ceiling imposed by Regulation Q on domestic accounts because savings seemed adequate to meet domestic growth needs.

King believed monetary policy was limited in its scope and impact. Naively, he felt that the Federal Reserve system did not really lead or follow in issues of economic policy. Instead, he saw the Fed "dealing with [economic] developments on a day-to-day and a month-to-month basis with the decisions made in the best interest of the country as a whole" (February 4, 1960 *Hearing*, p. 13). The critical ingredient for King was the need for monetary policy to maintain the integrity of the currency.

King's announcement of his resignation on September 21, 1963 came as a surprise to Washington. King stated that he was increasingly uncomfortable on the board because of the complex matters with which it dealt. King had proposed when nominated to do only the best he knew how to do and to try to continue to learn. He never presented himself as an expert. He stated that his main interest in being on the board was to help make decisions that would promote sustainable growth as much of the time as possible and to minimize the ups and downs of the economy that had "very terrible effects on business and . . . on unemployment."

J. Dewey Daane,[*] Deputy Undersecretary of Treasury for Monetary Affairs, who was viewed as more moderate, was named on October 30, 1963 to replace King. King returned briefly to his Canton, Mississippi home to which he had returned frequently during his Federal Reserve board tenure. The King Ranch had been dismantled several years earlier, however, and King's attention once again turned toward his lumber, oil, and gas interests, which led him to resettle in the Baton Rouge, Louisiana area.

BIBLIOGRAPHY

Bratter, Herbert. "*Banking's* Spotlight on—George Harold King, Jr." *Banking* 55:54.

King, George Harold, Jr. "Bank Credit in an Expanding Economy." Remarks presented at Jekyll Island, Georgia to the annual convention of Georgia Banker's Association on April 26, 1962. Mimeographed. Washington, D.C.: Federal Reserve Library, 1962.

King, George Harold, Jr. "Democracy versus Communism." Remarks presented at Charlottesville, Virginia to the School of Consumer Banking on August 18, 1961. Mimeographed. Washington, D.C.: Federal Reserve Library, 1962.

Poe, Edgar. "G. Harold King, Jr." *New Orleans Times-Picayune*. December 6, 1962.

U.S. Congress, Senate, Committee on Banking and Currency, *Nominations of George H. King, Jr., and Karl Brandt: Hearing*. 86th Cong., 1st sess., March 11, 1959.

U.S. Congress, Senate, Committee on Banking and Currency, *Nomination of George Harold King, Jr.: Hearing*. 86th Cong., 2d sess., February 4, 1960.

JOHN P. LAWARE (1928–   )

Jack B. White

John P. LaWare, appointed to the Board of Governors in 1988, has had a long and distinguished career in banking. He joined Chemical Bank in 1953 and spent the next twenty-five years there, rising to senior vice-president. He left Chemical Bank in 1978 to become chairman of Shawmut Corporation in Boston, the second largest bank holding company in New England at the time.

Born in Columbus, Wisconsin, on February 20, 1928, John LaWare did not intend to become a banker. He attended Harvard University with the initial goal of a career in medicine. Although he received his bachelor's degree from Harvard in biology in 1950, medicine had lost its allure for him. The machinations of government had captured his interest instead. This interest in government and politics caused him to alter his career objectives. He earned a master's degree in political science from the University of Pennsylvania and had every intention of teaching at the college level. However, the outbreak of the Korean War led to LaWare's service in the air force and to a thirty-five-year postponement of applying his knowledge of governmental interaction. After his stint in the air force, LaWare was offered a teaching position at the University of Pennsylvania. The only drawback to the position was that it would not begin for several months. Being twenty-five years old and married, LaWare did not want to wait for employment. At LaWare's request, his father suggested several industries that offered good prospects for the future. Banking, he contended, offered the most possibilities because so few people had entered the field during the 1930s and the 1940s. This would produce a significant shortage in management and make advancement quite rapid.

LaWare ended up at Chemical Bank almost by accident. He had been interested in a job offer from J. P. Morgan and Company, only to discover that it too would not begin for several months. At a friend's suggestion, he approached Chemical Bank. As LaWare recalled, "I'd never even heard of Chemical Bank. But I found it down there in the bowels of Wall Street and I gave their personnel guy the same snowjob [as given to the personnel officer at J. P. Morgan], and he bought it."

After twenty-five years at Chemical Bank that included serving as a vice-president and senior lending officer, as well as directing the marketing division, LaWare became chief executive officer at Shawmut, a bank that was well positioned and of good size (assets approximately $3 billion in 1978) but that generated lackluster earnings. Its return on assets was a disappointing 0.4 percent, while return on equity was in the 8 percent to 9 percent range. Most discouraging of all, the bank's stock was selling for only 50 percent of book value. When LaWare left Shawmut to join the Fed ten years later, the return on assets had risen to 0.87 percent, and the return on equity was a respectable 14.62 percent. The market recognized the reversal, and Shawmut stock began to sell at 115 percent of book value.

This solid turnaround was the result of LaWare's tireless efforts to transform Shawmut into a bank where the emphasis was on the bottom line. By dividing the holding company along business lines instead of legal definitions, Shawmut was able to improve performance and efficiency. For instance, the community banking segment allows the holding company to have a uniform pricing structure among all of the subsidiary banks. In the financial services area, trust fees were raised to make the division profitable. Since the trust department was generating returns in excess of its competitors, LaWare saw no need for the division to be a loss leader.

While chairman of Shawmut, LaWare was elected chairman of the Association of Bank Holding Companies and testified before Congress on numerous occasions regarding deregulation of the banking industry. As a banker, LaWare favored an approach that would place all companies that were financial in nature on an equal footing. Thus, banks and savings and loans would be able to enter into insurance, investments, and real estate. While this may seem like a dramatic departure from traditional definitions of banking services, LaWare argued that many of these nonbank financial companies were entering banking by purchasing nonbank banks and providing many, but not all, banking services. LaWare's contention was that removing artificial restrictions would allow companies that are essentially financial in nature to merge and efficiently provide a full range of financial services.

Despite LaWare's experience (which also included being a director of the Federal Reserve Bank of Boston), events nearly conspired to deny him the appointment to the Board of Governors. President Ronald Reagan had already appointed six of the seven members of the Board of Governors when the seventh position was vacated by the resignation of Henry Wallich.[*] Reagan's choice of LaWare, a Democrat from Massachusetts, was politically astute. Ironically, Senator William Proxmire (D, Wisconsin), chairman of the Senate Banking Committee, threatened to not consider LaWare's nomination in order to give Reagan's successor an opportunity to nominate a board member. In the end, Proxmire relented, and LaWare was confirmed.

As a member of the Board of Governors, LaWare was forced to shift his focus from a profit-oriented businessman to a regulator concerned with industry safety and soundness. His position on bank expansion into real estate reflects that shift. Real estate brokerage is essentially a financial transaction. However, real estate development is more closely akin to retailing and commerce, and as such, LaWare would resist allowing banks into development.

Another issue facing bank regulators in the 1990s is that of risk-based capital. LaWare acknowledges that it will be difficult to identify the appropriate weights that should be assigned to the various asset groups. However, he points out that asset risk is only one of the several types of risks banks face. Interest rate risks and liquidity risks also need to be considered when attempting to ensure bank stability. Dealing with these risks is much more difficult than assigning capital weights to asset structure. However, with a pragmatism that comes from years of business experience, LaWare concedes that "we're going to have to come to grips with them."

Perhaps the biggest adjustment LaWare has had to make in his move from Shawmut's CEO to a member of the Board of Governors was one of committee dynamics. As CEO, LaWare comments, "There was only one vote that counted, and that was mine." As a member of the Fed, he must work to convince six other highly knowledgeable colleagues that his opinion is the correct one.

BIBLIOGRAPHY

Cocheo, Steve. 1989. "From Regulated to Regulator." *ABA Banking Journal* (February): 29.

Helm, Leslie, and McNamee, Mike. 1988. "Why Democrats Don't Want This Democrat at the Fed." *Business Week*, June 6, p. 32.

"John LaWare's Priorities at Shawmut Corp. 'Put Profitability First, Expansion a Distant Second.' " 1986. *American Banker*, January 22, p. 24.

Rehm, Barbara. 1988a. "LaWare Transforms Quickly into a Central Banker." *American Banker*, August 29, p. 9.

———. 1988b. "No Roadblocks for LaWare." *American Banker*, July 1, p. 3.

DAVID MAHER LILLY (1917–   )

Neela D. Manage

David M. Lilly, a manufacturing executive from Minnesota with extensive business experience, was nominated by President Gerald Ford in April 1976 to
become a member of the Federal Reserve board. Lilly was sworn into office on
June 1, 1976, to fill an unexpired term ending January 31, 1978, resulting from
the resignation of Robert C. Holland* in May 1976.

David Lilly was the first business executive on the seven-member board since
the departure of John Sheehan* from the Fed in May 1975. When he was
nominated as Fed governor, he was chairman of the board and chief executive
officer of the Toro Company, where he had held several positions since 1945.
But Lilly was not without ties in the public sector and in the world of banking.
At the time of his Fed appointment, he was a director of the First National Bank
of St. Paul and the First Bank System, an association of Minneapolis–St. Paul
banks. He had begun his working career in private banking as a clerk at the First
National Bank of Minneapolis in 1940–1941 where he later served as a member
of the board of directors from 1957 to 1968. He was a former chairman of the
board of directors of the Federal Reserve Bank of Minneapolis from 1971 to
1973 and served as a member of this same board in 1969–1970. He was also
assistant to the under secretary of the U.S. Treasury during 1941–1942.

David M. Lilly was born June 14, 1917, in St. Paul, Minnesota, to Richard
Coyle and Rachel Cunningham Lilly. He graduated from Saint Paul Academy
in 1935 and received an A.B. degree in economics from Dartmouth College in
1939. Married to Perrin Brown on December 5, 1946, he has three children:
David Maher, Jr., Bruce, and Susanne. Lilly entered the U.S. Army in 1942,
was awarded the Bronze Star for his military service, and held the rank of major
when he was discharged in 1945.

In 1945 Lilly joined the Toro Company, a major producer of lawn and turf
maintenance equipment, as vice-president and general manager and was also
elected a director. He was associated with Toro for most of his professional
career prior to his presidential appointment to the Federal Reserve board. He
was named president of Toro in 1950 and chairman of the board in 1968.

Lilly has served on the board of directors of various corporations and educational institutions. When he was appointed as Fed governor, he was chairman of the board of trustees of Carleton College, a member of the visiting committee to the Graduate School of Education at Harvard University, a member of the Council of the Alumni of Dartmouth College, and a member of the University of Minnesota College of Business Administration's Consultative Council. He was also a director of several corporations, including General Mills, Dayton Hudson Corporation, the St. Paul Companies, and Honeywell.

Lilly was treasurer of the Minnesota Republican State Central Committee for three years until 1966, after which he became chair of the Minnesota Republican Finance Committee (1966–1968). In 1968 he was a delegate to the Republican National Convention.

Lilly's attributes as a business leader, community leader, and an individual were best described by former senator Walter Mondale (D, Minnesota) when he introduced Lilly at the Senate confirmation hearings. He described Lilly as a remarkable leader in Minnesota and an outstanding citizen and business statesman who was highly respected in the community. Mondale noted that Lilly always insisted that businessmen should be more than profit makers; they should also be community leaders who are deeply concerned about the future of their community, their state, and their country. Lilly represented precisely this mixture of a successful businessman with a distinguished career and a highly respected community leader.

Lilly resigned as chairman of the board and chief executive officer of the Toro Company to accept his Federal Reserve appointment in June 1976. At that time, the U.S. economy was entering the second year of its recovery from what was then considered to be the most severe recession in the post–World War II period. The rate of inflation measured by the consumer price index had dropped to 6.1 percent during the twelve-month period ending April 1976. Real gross national product grew at an annual rate of 7 percent in the first quarter of 1976. Long-term interest rates and the unemployment rate had also declined. The unemployment rate, however, was still above 8 percent at the beginning of 1976, a level considered too high for robust economic growth.

At the Federal Reserve, chairman Arthur Burns's[*] primary concern was inflation. His monetary policy strategy consisted of providing sufficient money to support a modest recovery without reigniting inflation. The economic priorities of the Carter administration at the time, however, were to stimulate economic growth, lower the unemployment rate, and address the relevant social issues.

The administration and several congressional leaders did not always approve of what they considered to be the tight-fisted reign of Arthur Burns. The years during which Lilly served on the Board of Governors thus were politically turbulent and economically challenging times for the Fed.

Concern over the experience of the board members was publicly expressed during the Senate confirmation hearings for David Lilly. Senator William Proxmire (D, Wisconsin), chairman of the Senate Banking Committee, spoke of the

Fed's "revolving door" and its "rookies." House Banking Committee chairman Henry Reuss (D, Wisconsin) was reported by the *Wall Street Journal* as criticizing the "rent-a-governor basis" on which the Fed was operating. It is important to put such concerns about the expertise of the Fed governors in perspective. Although the length of their service on the board was limited, their experience in the field was extensive: Philip Coldwell* was a former president of the Federal Reserve Bank of Dallas; Philip Jackson,* a mortgage banker, was a past president of the American Mortgage Bankers Association; J. Charles Partee* was the Fed's managing director for research and economic policy; Stephen Gardner,* a Philadelphia banker, joined the Fed after serving as deputy secretary of the U.S. Treasury for two years; and Henry Wallich* was a distinguished academic economist. David Lilly, the most recent appointee, was a former chairman of the Minneapolis Federal Reserve Bank and an experienced business executive with a vital understanding of labor markets and the business sector.

The issue of independence of the new members from the chair was a more valid concern. Chairman Burns, being a veteran, was in a position to exert profound influence over the new members of the board. Since most of the Fed members had served for less than two years, congressional leaders were disturbed by the enormous power Burns was likely to exercise in the monetary policy decisions at the Fed. As their presence on the board increases, they are in a position to form their judgments more independently of the chair. As the public record shows, Lilly has exhibited that independence on several occasions.

Lilly came to the Fed with valuable insights and views of the business community. He recognized that the Fed has a monetary policy function and a bank regulatory function, but he also viewed it as a large organization that, like any corporation, has to be managed well. He was actively involved in extending the management concepts he had implemented at the Minneapolis Fed to the other regional Federal Reserve banks.

As a business executive, Lilly was interested in labor markets and how regulations such as minimum wage laws affect inflation. In a speech (Lilly 1977c) to the Virginia Council on Economic Education, he suggested that the government require inflation impact statements just as it requires environmental statements on new programs. He suggested that the government should file impact statements when there are changes in programs such as minimum wage or import restrictions. According to Lilly, the greatest threat to the economy was inflation, which could change the entire fabric of the economy unless it was brought under control.

Lilly also had a balanced view of how monetary policy influences the economy. During a conversation, he told me that, in his view, the most important challenge facing the Fed during his tenure was to avoid inflation without creating a recession. He held the view that the amount of money and credit had a profound influence on the performance of the economy. If too much money was available, it would increase the risk of inflation, whereas too little money would slow the pace of economic activity. Although the inflation rate for 1976 was 5.8 percent, consumer prices increased at an annual rate of 10.0 and 8.1 percent in the first and second quarters of 1977, respectively. Starting in mid-July 1977, the money supply also began to grow rapidly, and the Fed voted to raise short-term money market rates during several Federal Open Market Committee (FOMC) meetings in the second half of 1977. Lilly did not consider this monetary tightening the appropriate policy response in the face of a slow-growing economy with very little improvement in unemployment. During this time, he exhibited his independence and voted against the majority decision to push interest rates up. At the September 20, 1977, FOMC meeting, the Fed voted to raise the range for the federal funds rate to 6 to 6.5 percent. Lilly and Wallich dissented and thought the FOMC's policy called for "somewhat more firming in the money market conditions" than they thought appropriate. They also felt that rapid growth in the monetary aggregates might represent an increase in the public's demand for money in relation to growth of the gross national product, which they thought should be accommodated. Lilly also believed that such monetary tightening would not be effective in treating the underlying structural inflation.

In January 1978 the Fed raised the range for the federal funds rate to 6.5 to 7 percent. Lilly and J. Charles Partee[*] voted against this action because they did not believe that the interest rate hike could be justified by the performance of the domestic economy. That same month, the Fed announced an increase in the discount rate to 6.5 percent in order to prop up the sagging dollar in foreign currency markets. Lilly and Partee opposed the discount rate increase on the grounds that it was risky for the domestic economy and that it would not be very effective in helping the dollar.

Lilly firmly believed that the federal government plays a major role in determining the price level and its rate of change. During a congressional hearing on anti-inflation proposals (1978), Lilly testified that the government contributes to the inflation problem in two ways. First, it affects inflation through stimulative fiscal policies and their accompanying large deficits. Second, government regulations impede market performance, adversely affect the price structure, and thereby result in inflation. Based on this view of the cause of inflation, Lilly believed that the solution would be to lower deficits and to alter the structure of markets in ways that avoid higher prices. Some regulations, such as minimum wage laws and agricultural price supports, raise prices directly, whereas others limit the ability of the economy to absorb an increase in the price of some factor of production. Environmental standards raise costs of activities that could otherwise lower inflationary pressures. Lilly also argued that wage and price controls and tax-based incomes policies would not be effective in solving the inflation problem because they were aimed at the wrong sector. Since such policies are aimed at a single factor, labor, he warned that market forces may push the allocation of resources in the wrong direction.

When asked to describe the two years he was at the Fed relative to the rest of his professional career, Lilly said that his time at the Fed was spent largely on bank regulatory matters relating to bank holding companies and consumer credit as opposed to monetary policy matters. He thought these regulatory aspects of the job were not as exciting as the monetary policy aspects.

There were two major changes that Lilly considered desirable within the Fed. First, he thought that the Federal Reserve bank president should go through the public selection process and Senate confirmation hearings, especially because they serve on the FOMC on a rotating basis. Second, the results of the FOMC deliberations should be immediately made available to the public. Although he conveyed his views on these matters to congressional leaders, no changes have been made.

Although his official term expired January 31, 1978, Lilly served as a member of the board, awaiting the appointment of his successor, until February 24, 1978. After returning to Minnesota from Washington in March 1978, Lilly was re-elected to the Toro Company Board and was chairman of its Organization and Compensation Committee. In December 1987 he retired from the Toro board of directors. He was also appointed dean of the School of Management of the University of Minnesota in June 1978, where he was later named vice-president for finance and operations in 1983. He retired from the University of Minnesota on June 30, 1988, and currently resides in St. Paul. Lilly is a trustee on the board of trustees of Carleton College and continues to serve the community.

BIBLIOGRAPHY

Lilly, David M. 1977a. "Statement to Congress." *Federal Reserve Bulletin* (May): 468–72.
———. 1977b. *Federal Reserve Bulletin* (April): 366–70.
———. 1977c. "The Threat of Inflation." Speech to the Virginia Council on Economic Education, Richmond, Virginia, September 23.
———. 1978. Congressional testimony published in *Anti-Inflation Proposals*, Hearing before the Committee on Banking, Housing, and Urban Affairs of the U.S. Senate, May, pp. 30–39.
U.S. Congress. Senate. Committee on Banking, Housing, and Urban Affairs. 1976. *Hearing on the Nomination of David M. Lilly.* 94th Cong., 2d sess., May 17.

THOMAS BAYARD MCCABE
(1893–1982)

Earl W. Adams

Thomas Bayard McCabe was the chairman of the Board of Governors at one of its pivotal moments. Although both Marriner Eccles[*] and William McChesney Martin,[*] whose long chairmanships bracket his, were well known as active participants in the Fed's struggle for independence, McCabe was the head when the accord between the Treasury and the Federal Reserve actually was achieved.

The following joint statement, issued for release on March 4, 1951, by the secretary of the Treasury and the chairman of the Board of Governors appeared in the *Federal Reserve Bulletin* for March 1951:

The Treasury and the Federal Reserve System have reached full accord with respect to debt management and monetary policies to be pursued in furthering their common purpose to assure the successful financing of the Government's requirements and, at the same time, to minimize monetization of the public debt.

Neither the drama leading up to the appearance of this statement nor its significance is apparent in the moderation and vagueness of its language. That McCabe should have participated in a struggle to determine the nature of our central bank was in some ways a logical culmination of his heritage and earlier career.

Thomas B. McCabe was born on July 11, 1893, in Whaleyville, Maryland. His mother's family (Whaley) had been among the early settlers in Maryland; his father's, in Delaware. As a child, the young McCabe lived in West Norfolk, Virginia, and then in Selbyville, Delaware. He once described his roots in the following terms: "My father was a little country banker. I lived across the street from the bank. So I saw the problems of the littler banker. . . . He was also banking commissioner of the state [Delaware]. So I had a chance to observe the manner in which the banks were examined" (U.S. Congress, 1948, p.201). His father, in addition, had tried his hand at elective politics; at one point he served as Speaker of Delaware's legislature.

Having completed his early education at Wilmington Conference Academy in Dover, Delaware, McCabe enrolled in Swarthmore College, where he majored in economics and received the A.B. degree in 1915. His alma mater was later to award him an honorary LL.D., as were twelve other colleges and universities.

McCabe claimed that his background was training in connection with a small bank and a small business. In fact, upon graduating from college, he secured a job as a $15-a-week salesman for a small paper company with one mill and 500 employees in Chester, Pennsylvania. This was in 1916. The following year the United States entered World War I, and McCabe left civilian life to serve in the U.S. Army, first as a private but advancing to captain by 1919.

After the war he returned to the paper company but as assistant sales manager. A year later he was sales manager, and the following year he was named a director of the firm at the age of twenty-eight. By the time he was thirty-four, he was president and chief executive officer, positions he held for thirty-nine years. During his stewardship, that small paper company, the Scott Paper Company, grew to become a multinational firm with more than sixty plants, over 40,000 employees, and multibillion dollar annual sales. At the time of his confirmation as chairman of the Board of Governors, he held 86,574 shares of its common stock, valued then at more than $3.7 million.

He married Jeanette Laws on February 28, 1924. The McCabes made their home in Swarthmore, Pennsylvania. They had three sons: Thomas Bayard, Jr., who died in 1977, Richard Whaley, and James.

As early as 1937, Thomas McCabe was associated with the Federal Reserve system. Appointed a class C director of the Federal Reserve Bank of Philadelphia in that year, he became the chairman of its board and Federal Reserve agent in 1939. He served in that capacity until his move to the Board of Governors. He was proud of his service on the board of the Philadelphia Federal Reserve Bank and spoke in his confirmation hearings of his view of the relation between the Board of Governors and the regional Federal Reserve banks:

I think that what we have is excellent. That is we have . . . in Washington a Board of Governors who are devoting most of their time to problems of central banking. You have 12 regional banks that are close to the grass roots, that are studying the problems of finance and commerce, the problems of industry, agriculture, in their area.

I feel that it is very helpful to the Board of Governors . . . to have the advice, counsel, and opinion of the directors of these 12 regional banks, . . . because they are close . . . to the people and close to industry.

I think the more that the Board of Governors can receive the opinions and the counsel of these 12 banks and their branches, the better. In doing that, . . . I don't think for one moment that the Board of Governors should ever relinquish any of their authority or their responsibilities. . . . My feeling is that having been a director of a regional bank and the chairman of its board, and having been connected with that bank for some 10 or 11 years, I think I have a feeling for the part that those directors can play. . . . I am like a sales manager that has come to the home office after he has been in the field. That is always a healthy thing because the sales manager has an understanding of the territory that I think is of value to the home office. (U.S. Congress, 1948)

McCabe had also served the system as chairman of the Chairmen's Conference of the Federal Reserve system and, for two years, of the special committee to study executive officers' positions and salaries in the twelve Federal Reserve banks.

His public service was not limited to bank-related activities. He was a member and chairman of the Business Advisory Council for the U.S. Department of Commerce, and as the United States prepared for and then entered World War II, his public involvement accelerated. He served in a series of increasingly important positions related to the war effort: executive assistant to Edward Stettinius on the Advisory Commission of the Council for National Defense, deputy director of the Division of Priorities (Office of Production Management), and deputy Lend Lease administrator.

From its establishment, McCabe had been a trustee and member of the research and policy committee of the Committee for Economic Development (CED). In 1945 he resigned from the CED in order to become army-navy liquidation commissioner, then foreign liquidation commissioner, and in 1946, in addition, special assistant to the secretary of state. His job was to direct the disposal of army and navy war surplus property overseas. The controversy that surrounded McCabe's sale of surplus transportation and construction equipment to China (one headline of the day read, "China got the Boodle, the American Taxpayer the bill") returned to haunt him during the hearings for his confirmation as a member of the Board of Governors.

While McCabe was serving his country, the Federal Reserve system was facing some challenges of its own. During World War II, the Fed was pledged to aid in the financing of the defense effort. This was accomplished by keeping interest rates on U.S. Treasury securities of different maturities in an agreed-upon pattern via Federal Reserve purchases of government issues at fixed prices if the public did not buy them. This policy, known as "pegging" or "the peg," assured the Treasury of its funding at low (and known) interest rates and guaranteed the success of each Treasury offering. It also guaranteed that the Fed had virtually given up control of the money supply since its open market operations were dictated by the financing needs of the Treasury. Thus, reserves of the banking system would change in response to those needs, not the needs of the economy.

Because interest rates, especially those on ninety-day bills, were so low and the Fed was committed to purchase them, the Fed owned most of these short-term Treasury securities by the end of the war. After the war, continued purchases added reserves to the banking system, and Fed officials, especially chairman Marriner Eccles,* began to warn the administration and the public of the dangerous inflationary policy that was being pursued. The Fed argued that interest rates ought to be allowed to rise to alleviate the pressure toward higher prices.

Eccles's term as chairman (though not on the Board of Governors) was to expire on February 1, 1948. President Harry Truman, sufficiently agitated by the stance of Eccles in opposition to the administration's support of the pegging scheme in the bond market, announced that he would not reappoint him. The death of Ronald Ransom[*] in January had created a vacancy on the board; Truman named McCabe to fill this vacancy and indicated his intention to appoint him chairman.

It took more than two months for McCabe's appointment to be approved by the Committee on Banking and Currency and confirmed by the Senate. The opposition to McCabe's confirmation (led by Senator Charles Tobey of New Hampshire, chairman of the committee) centered around two issues. The first concerned the alleged irregularities in McCabe's sale of war materials to China at the close of the war. These charges ranged from general doubts that the sales were in the best interest of the United States to more specific complaints, such as that eleven operable B–25s with very low flying hours were sold to a Chinese firm owned by the premier's brother but that when the story broke in the newspapers, McCabe had ordered that the planes be destroyed by having their tails cut off. The second was that opposition to pending restrictive bank holding company legislation, especially from the Transamerica Corporation, lay behind the McCabe nomination. Neither allegation, in the end, was substantiated to the satisfaction of the committee's majority. McCabe finally took over on April 15, 1948.

During the reign of Eccles, the battle lines had been drawn between the Fed and the Treasury concerning support of the government bond market; now the conflict resumed. The Treasury, to enhance its position, began to announce its offerings weeks rather than days ahead, thus committing the Fed to support the market lest an offering were to fail to be sold. The Treasury seemed to be asserting that it needed to have access to a low interest rate regardless of conditions in the economy.

On June 28, 1949, the Federal Open Market Committee (FOMC) announced a new policy "to direct purchases, sales, and exchanges of Government securities . . . with primary regard to the general business and credit situation" (*Federal Reserve Bulletin*, July 1949). McCabe later indicated just how significant he believed this new stance to be; he believed it signified the removal of the straitjacket in which monetary policy had been operating for nearly a decade.

Actually, freedom from the straitjacket in 1949, a recession year, meant that responding to the general business and credit situation required the Fed to allow interest rates to fall. Indeed, the June 1949 policy statement argued that the maintenance of a relatively fixed pattern of rates absorbed reserves from the market at a time when the availability of credit should have increased. Allowing rates to fall was a policy that would get no argument from the Treasury.

The real test with respect to monetary policy was whether it would become flexible. Did the 1949 announcement mean that the Fed would also push interest rates up during a period of inflationary pressure even if there was a federal government deficit to be financed? When Senator Paul Douglas (D, Illinois) put this question to McCabe in hearings before his committee, McCabe answered that he would go to extraordinary lengths to convince the Treasury of his view.

When the United States entered the Korean conflict the following year, the

Fed was presented with the opportunity to demonstrate its resolve. From the Fed's perspective, there was a growing pressure for price inflation due to the imposition of increased defense spending on an already expanding economy. The Treasury, on the other hand, now had, in addition to the refunding of the debt remaining from expenditures during World War II, also the financing of new defense expenditures over which to agonize. A confrontation was inevitable.

In mid–1950 the Fed began to tighten credit by raising the discount rate. It was the only policy instrument the Fed could freely use since reserve requirements were near their legal limit and open market operations were, in principle, supporting the peg. The secretary of the Treasury was not only astonished but publicly protested the move. The Fed clearly was asserting its independence and was beginning to loosen the peg.

Skirmishes continued through 1950 and into 1951 when Secretary of the Treasury John Snyder declared in a public speech that the long-term Treasury bond rate would continue at 2 ½ percent and that he had the assurance of chairman McCabe that new Treasury issues would be financed at that rate. McCabe and the FOMC, which had not authorized the statement, countered by allowing the price of the 2 ½ percent Treasury bond to fall (increasing its yield).

For the first time in its history, the entire FOMC was called to the president's office on January 31, 1951. This meeting led to the final round in the battle.

President Truman released to the press a letter to chairman McCabe on the following day asserting, ''I have your assurance that the market on government securities will be stabilized and maintained at present levels.'' As he put it in his memoirs (1956), ''I was given assurance at this meeting that the Federal Reserve Board would support the Treasury's plans for the financing of the action in Korea.'' McCabe and the others present had no recollection of giving this assurance. Indeed, the minutes of the meeting, leaked to the press, contained no assurance either.

McCabe, speaking for the FOMC, confronted the president in a letter suggesting that a policy of keeping rates low would actually undermine public confidence during inflationary times and could work against the policy of financing the war effort. The secretary of the Treasury was notified that the Fed would no longer allow itself to be committed to policies whose wisdom it questioned.

A truce was called. Truman formed a committee to forge a compromise between what was euphemistically called ''stability in the government securities market'' and credit restraint. McCabe, Secretary Snyder, and the chairman of the Council of Economic Advisers were among its principal members. Meanwhile, William McChesney Martin,* then under secretary of the Treasury (representing Secretary Snyder, who was in the hospital), and Winfield Reifler, McCabe's closest economic adviser and assistant, were meeting to negotiate the details of a formal agreement. The accord emerged on March 3, 1951. The Fed was free to pursue an independent monetary policy.

Throughout this period McCabe had tried to act as a mediator. Although perhaps not so committed as Eccles, in all his public statements McCabe was a supporter of a strong and independent Federal Reserve system. For example, he consistently urged that reserve requirements should apply to all commercial banks, not just members—an idea not implemented until 1980.

He was not successful in avoiding the conflict and public airing of rather bitter differences and opposing points of view, which were a source of embarrassment to him and to the president. However, at the end of this difficult time, a new era emerged featuring the possibility of a strong central bank with a flexible, independent monetary policy, although it would be many years before the implications of the accord would be understood.

McCabe had submitted his resignation on February 26, 1951, upon being informed by President Truman that his services were unsatisfactory. The formal announcement came just after the accord on March 9. The *Federal Reserve Bulletin*, which announced the accord, was to be the last published over McCabe's signature. He had lost a battle with Truman and Snyder, but his side had won the war.

McCabe, who described himself as a middle-of-the-road Republican, was a great admirer of Dwight D. Eisenhower. After leaving the Board of Governors, McCabe devoted himself to helping Eisenhower to be elected president in 1952. Later in the 1950s he chaired a committee that prepared *The Challenge to America: Its Economic and Social Aspects,* a Rockefeller Brothers' Fund report.

He retired from the board of Scott Paper Company in 1980 over sixty-four years after he had started as a salesman with the company. He was a "perennial salesman." A friend said in the 1980s, "He's still selling. He could sell anybody anything, he's so heart and soul in it."

On May 27, 1982, at the age of eighty-eight, he died at home in Swarthmore. Full of years and honors, he had served his company and his country in many ways.

The principles of central banking that he supported are summarized in two statements to congressional committees he made while chairman:

The Federal Reserve System was established to provide for flexibility in our monetary system. It was not designed to make available any amount of money that borrowers might demand without regard to the productive capacity of the economy and the speculative nature of the commitments. The System would be derelict in its duty if it did not exercise a proper measure of restraint. (Fforde, 1954, p. 269)

I would be the last to want government to have power and authority merely for the sake of having power and authority. In the complex and fluid monetary field, however, the timeliness of policy moves is of critical importance. That is why . . . in the interest of a stabilized progressive economy, it is essential that our monetary machinery be prepared in advance to adapt itself to changing economic needs. (U.S. Congress, 1949, p. 356)

Thomas B. McCabe's legacy is the part he played in establishing what was to become the stance of monetary policy during much of the post–World War II period.

BIBLIOGRAPHY

Clifford, A. Jerome. 1965. *The Independence of the Federal Reserve System*. Philadelphia: University of Pennsylvania Press.

Fforde, J. S. 1954. *The Federal Reserve System, 1945–1949*. London: Oxford University Press.

Kettl, Donald F. 1986. *Leadership at the Fed*. New Haven: Yale University Press.

Truman, Harry S. 1956. *Memoirs*. Vol. 2. *Years of Trial and Hope*. Garden City, N.Y.: Doubleday.

U.S. Congress. Joint Committee on the Economic Report of the President: Hearings before the Committee on the Economic Report. 1949. 81st Cong., 1st sess. February 8, 9, 10, 11, 14, 15, 16, 17, 18.

U.S. Congress. Senate. Committee on Banking and Currency. 1948. *Confirmation of Thomas B. McCabe: Hearings*. 80th Cong., 2d sess. March 3, 10, 11, 24, 30.

JOHN KEOWN MCKEE (1891–1977)

Nancy M. Thornborrow

John Keown McKee served on the Board of Governors of the Federal Reserve Bank from February 1936 to February 1946. In 1936, a newly reorganized Federal Reserve system was confronting numerous challenges. McKee's appointment to the board was a result of his effective performance as a bank examiner. In fact, his entire career was in the field of banking; therefore, he brought to the board a practitioner's perspective and familiarity with many facets of the banking system.

McKee was born in Pittsburgh, Pennsylvania, on November 19, 1891. The son of Mr. and Mrs. James McKee, he received his education in Pittsburgh, attending Allegheny Preparatory School and the University of Pittsburgh Night School. While at Pitt, McKee specialized in banking and commercial law. He joined the People's National Bank of Pittsburgh as a messenger in 1907. During World War I, McKee interrupted his banking career to serve overseas with the Heavy Tank Corps of the U.S. Army. Upon his return to civilian life, McKee rejoined the People's Bank and was promoted to assistant cashier in 1919. When the First National Bank and the People's National merged in 1922, he went with First National, representing the institution in receiverships and supervising doubtful loans.

On June 18, 1918, McKee married Bessie Belle Lewis of Steubenville, Ohio. They subsequently had three children: John Keown, David Lewis, and Bessie Jane. Between 1923 and 1928 McKee developed oil properties inherited in Kansas, and between 1928 and 1931 he managed family real estate holdings.

The 1929 crash of the stock market was a forerunner of the lengthy and severe depression of the 1930s. International panic brought on by the declining world economy forced the United States to give up more than one-quarter of its gold holdings. The gold outflow combined with domestic hoarding of currency to threaten the solvency of every bank, insurance company, and fiduciary agent in the land. Many banks were forced to close as citizens attempted to withdraw their deposits. The situation was so desperate at the federal level that President

Herbert Hoover supported emergency legislation in the form of the Glass-Steagall Act of 1933 which authorized the substitution of government bonds for commercial paper under the Federal Reserve circulation. Congress was convinced that, without this provision, the United States would be forced to default on gold demands. It was during the turbulent years of 1931 and 1932 that McKee returned to banking. This time he represented the U.S. comptroller of currency as receiver for insolvent banks in Ohio and Pennsylvania.

During this same period, it became obvious to President Hoover that in order to save the industrial base of the United States—manufacturing, railroads, and so forth—that new lending agencies would have to be created. One such agency was the National Credit Corporation (NCC) organized in October 1931. The NCC was based on the idea that stronger banks should help weaker ones. A second and subsequently more effective agency, the Reconstruction and Finance Corporation (RFC), was created in January 1932 to make government loans to hard-pressed banks and other financial institutions in an attempt to slow the number of bank failures. McKee moved his family to Washington and in 1932 became an examiner for the RFC in charge of bank reorganizations. In 1933 he became chief of the examining division of the RFC, a post which he held until his appointment to the Board of Governors of the Federal Reserve in 1936.

One of McKee's first responsibilities as chief examiner of the RFC was to attempt to save the Michigan banking system. His examination showed that the system was dominated by the First National Bank Group, which had received no RFC loans, and the Guardian Trust Group, which had borrowed $15 million from the RFC and was applying to borrow $50 million more to stabilize the Union Guardian Bank. The Hoover administration attempted to save Union Guardian because it feared that if the bank closed the entire state would be caught up in a bank panic. McKee was dispatched to Detroit and from February 11 to 13, 1933, he tried to work out a plan to save the banks. McKee estimated that the amount of money needed was $49.6 million. The RFC was prepared to advance the money provided they could secure satisfactory collateral. Unfortunately only $37.72 million security was offered and, when Henry Ford refused to ''freeze'' the $7.5 million he had on deposit at Union Guardian, the RFC had to abandon its plan. The inability of the bankers and of Detroit industrialists Walter Chrysler, Alfred P. Sloan, and Henry Ford, to resolve the financial crisis in Michigan brought Governor William Comstock into the fray. He proclaimed a 10-day ''bank holiday,'' thereby undermining Washington's attempt to stabilize the situation. A year later, on January 15, 1934, McKee appeared before the Senate Committee on Banking and Currency and testified about both the role of the RFC in the Michigan bank crash and the subsequent plans for reorganization of the Michigan banks.

Much of the inability of the administration to establish effective monetary policy during this period appears to have been a result of the fact that Hoover, a Republican, had been defeated by Franklin D. Roosevelt in the 1932 election. Roosevelt was to assume the presidency on March 5, 1933; and therefore, the banking community was in limbo awaiting the new administration's policy announcements.

McKee, himself a Republican, continued his work with the RFC even as the country moved from the Hoover administration to the New Deal policies of Roosevelt. When the financial crisis of the depression was over, the Federal Reserve system underwent some major changes to help regulate credit and bank reserves. These revisions were incorporated in the Banking Acts of 1933 and 1935, the Securities Act of 1933, and the Securities Exchange Act of 1934. The Banking Act of 1935 replaced the smaller Federal Reserve Board with an expanded group of seven to be called the Board of Governors of the Federal Reserve System. The Act further expanded the powers of the central bank to increase its effectiveness in dealing with fluctuations in the economy and its flexibility for emergency action. The Act also sought to centralize more of the system's power in Washington and reduce the autonomy of the twelve regional banks. The new board was to have a majority voice in directing the open-market policies of the system, that is, the extent to which Regional Reserve banks buy and sell government securities, thereby reducing or increasing the volume of money available on the market. Formerly the heads of the regional banks made the open-market decisions; under the new act the Board of Governors, along with five selected regional bank presidents, would make those decisions. It also removed both the secretary of Treasury and comptroller of the currency from board membership, thereby strengthening the independence of the Federal Reserve from the executive branch. In essence, the Fed was given sweeping powers over the country's currency and economic life. The newly appointed members were charged to think of the banking system in those terms. The normal length of office for the new board members was to be fourteen years; however, the first group of appointments was made for staggered times allowing for terminations of office every two years. In recognition of his effective service at the RFC, President Roosevelt appointed John McKee to a ten-year term commencing February 1, 1936.

When McKee became a member of the board, the major problem facing the Federal Reserve system was the large and growing volume of excess reserves which were depriving the Fed of its ability to regulate credit and the money supply. The Fed's challenge was to attempt to restore its control over credit without adversely affecting business recovery. The board decided that rather than selling government securities to absorb excess reserves it would raise the reserve requirement. And they began to use open-market operations to maintain stability in the government securities market. By the end of the decade, fiscal policy had largely replaced monetary policy in terms of controlling money and credit. The Fed's efforts went mainly toward regulating prices in the government bond market.

In 1938 attention turned to determining what the Fed's role and policies would be should war break out in Europe. It was determined that the Federal Reserve and the Treasury would cooperate in stabilizing the government securities market.

After Japan attacked Pearl Harbor, the Fed made it clear that its primary objective was to facilitate financing of the war. Preventing inflation was of secondary concern. In April 1942, McKee, along with fellow Board of Governors members Eccles[*] and Draper,[*] was appointed as a member of the War Loans Committee. The committee's function was to supervise the activities of the Fed and to act as fiscal agent for the United States in connection with war production. Ultimately changes in business, banking, and credit demonstrated the need for more information on the economy and encouraged research cooperation among all the regional banks and the Board of Governors in looking at policies used to finance the war, potential postwar problems, and policies for dealing with the war's aftermath.

The war economy created a new dilemma: either low rates which facilitated financing the war would result in inflation as postwar demand soared *or* credit restriction from high rates would make financing the war more difficult and would mean losses for those holding government securities. In a special report to Congress, the Board of Governors requested that commercial banks be required to hold a special reserve of government securities against net demand deposits. This special reserve would enable the Fed to maintain a pattern of rates and still exercise control over reserves. Many in Congress believed existing powers to be sufficient and argued that no new requirements were necessary.

This view of the Fed was reflected in testimony given by McKee to the House Committee on Banking and Currency in December 1944. He had once previously testified before that committee in September 1940 regarding the assignment of claims under public contracts. His testimony in 1944, however, related to the absorption of exchange charges. The Fed in 1944 was eager for the Congress to enforce Regulation Q which prohibited interest payments on demand deposits. McKee alleged that large city banks were essentially violating the law by offering to absorb the exchange charges of their small, rural correspondent banks in return for their establishment of balances with the large banks. This absorption of charges associated with bank transactions was viewed by the Fed as analogous to paying interest on those deposits—a violation of Regulation Q. In addition, McKee expressed alarm that small banks—by locating their demand deposits in larger banks—would be at the mercy of the larger banks' loan policies and might be unable to meet their customers' requests for withdrawals should events of the early thirties repeat themselves. McKee suggested that, if Congress curtailed the absorption practice, rural banks would be encouraged to help their own communities by making local deposits available for local loans. Additionally he suggested that rural banks should invest their excess deposits in government securities rather than entrusting them to big city banks.

As McKee neared the end of his term on the Board of Governors he exchanged correspondence with Woodlief Thomas, head of the division of research and statistics at the Fed. In a letter dated February 1, 1946, Thomas commended McKee for his "practical horse-sense questions" and added:

We shall miss the opportunity of drawing upon your fund of facts. . . . We feel that you represent and have presented to us a point of view which is most important for us to keep in mind in appraising the economic situation. It has helped to take us out of our ivory towers and put us among the people who really make the decisions and determine the trends that we attempt to analyze.

McKee's term expired on February 1, 1946. He assumed the presidency of the Continental Bank & Trust Company of New York on September 1, 1946. Less than a year and a half later, on February 14, 1948, the *New York Times* carried a story alleging that the Chemical Bank and Trust Company was seeking to absorb the Continental Bank & Trust Company. The report indicated that McKee would be invited to become a senior officer of Chemical Bank when the two merged. Continental Bank had been established in 1870 and appeared to be in sound financial condition at the time of the suggested merger. Within two weeks a second merger offer was made by the New York Trust Company. The airing in the newspaper of the two offers and the tension surrounding them flouted a long tradition of secrecy in the banking community concerning such mergers. On March 3, 1948, McKee, in a statement to the press, protested the use of his name in connection with the board of directors' statement concerning their acceptance of the sale of Continental to Chemical Bank. The news of the bank's sale did not sit well with numerous stockholders, some of whom threatened to sue the board of directors. On April 5, 1948, McKee expressed his own views concerning the sale:

I have always felt that the proposed sale and liquidation of the Continental Bank and Trust Company, on the basis of the existing offer of the Chemical Bank and Trust company, is not in the best interest of our stockholders for the reason that in my opinion the premium offered to purchase the Continental is grossly inadequate to offset the expense at this time of liquidating a thriving institution which is in sound condition and enjoying good earnings. I therefore opposed the proposal of the Chemical Bank and voted against the acceptance of that proposal. I have not altered my views on this subject. (*New York Times*, April 5, 1948, 30:6)

In spite of some legal maneuvering by several stockholders, the majority voted to sell the bank to Chemical Bank on April 14, 1948. Controversy continued to surround the bank's sale throughout the following year. Eventually stockholders were paid $15 per share, an amount which was $10 less than original projections. In retrospect, it appears McKee's analysis of the situation was sound.

McKee did not assume a position with Chemical Bank, but instead returned to Washington where he continued to manage his own investments. In 1951, he was named to the board of trustees of George Washington University; he was trustee emeritus at the time of his death. McKee was a member of the Duquesne Club in Pittsburgh and of the Metropolitan Club in Washington. He also was a member of the Burning Tree and Columbia country clubs. McKee died on

Thursday, December 15, 1977, of an apparent aneurysm. He was eighty-six years old.

BIBLIOGRAPHY

Anderson, Clay J. 1965. *A Half-Century of Federal Reserve Policymaking, 1914–1964*. Philadelphia: Federal Reserve Bank.
Eastburn, David P. 1965. *The Federal Reserve on Record: Readings on Current Issues from Statements by Federal Reserve Officials*. Philadelphia: Federal Reserve Bank.
Jones, Jessee H., and Edward Angly. 1951. *Fifty Billion Dollars*. New York: Macmillan.
The New York Times. January 16, 19, 28, 29, 31, 1936; February 1, 2, 4, 1936; August 9, 1946; February 14, 26, 29, 1948; March 1, 3, 16, 1948; April 2, 5, 10, 22, 1948; January 15, 20, 1949.
Prochnow, Herbert V., ed. 1960. *The Federal Reserve System*. New York: Harper & Brothers.
Sullivan, Lawrence. 1936. *Prelude to Panic: The Story of the Bank Holiday*. Washington, D.C.: Statesman Press.
Time. 1936. "Banks and Brakes; New Federal Reserve Board," February 10.
Washington Post. 1977. Obituary of John Keown McKee, December 16.

WAYLAND WELLS MAGEE
(1881–1970)

Cynthia Saltzman

Wayland Wells Magee served as a member of the Federal Reserve Board from May 18, 1931, to January 24, 1933. He was appointed by President Herbert Hoover to fill the vacancy created by the death of Edward H. Cunningham.[*] Hoover referred to Magee as the farmer director of the Federal Reserve Board, noting that Magee had been endorsed by farm and financial interests throughout the West.

Magee was born in Chicago on September 24, 1881. He received a bachelor of science degree from the University of Chicago in 1905. His junior year was spent at the University of Bonn, Germany, where he studied under Strausburg, the famous botanist. He studied law at Harvard and Northwestern University in 1907 and 1908, respectively.

In 1908, Magee embarked on a trip around the world; his travel included Japan, Korea, Manila, India, and Cairo. Along the way he engaged in various odd jobs. While in the Philippines he spent several weeks driving steam automobiles filled with mail, passengers, and freight between Manila and Baguio. The highway, which he called the "Banquet boulevard," was a road of two hundred bridges. In Ceylon he found employment checking in ship cargos, in Burma he worked on the oil pipelines, and in Cairo he ran a milk route. He was known to advise young men to "go west and keep on going until you're back where you started from."

Prior to his appointment to the Federal Reserve Board, he served as president to the Nebraska Crop Growers Association, a director and member of the executive committee for the Nebraska Dairy Development Society, and a director of Ak-Sar-Ben Live Stock Show from 1929 to 1931. During the years 1927 to 1930, he was a board member of the Omaha branch of the Federal Reserve Bank of Kansas City. He served as a director to the Kansas City Fed from 1930 to 1932.

On January 10, 1933, President Hoover submitted Magee's name to the Democratically controlled Senate for reappointment. As a Republican, there was little chance that Magee would be reappointed by President-elect Franklin Roosevelt. His term expired on January 24, 1933.

The expiration of Magee's term, because it left only four members, prohibited the board from making advances to member banks on their promissory notes. An emergency measure within the Glass-Steagall Act allowed any reserve bank, with the consent of at least five board members, to make advances on the promissory notes of member banks with less than $5 million capital when these banks did not have adequate assets to obtain credit from the reserve banks. With only four members, the board could not act.

In 1910 he gave up his Chicago law practice and moved to Summer Hill farm, a corn farm in Nebraska established by his grandfather, Colonel James H. Pratt. Magee was proud to boast that Summer Hill used only certified seed, whose purity was attested to by the National Crop Growers Association.

Magee married Marion Edith Thomas on October 24, 1916. Widowed in 1920, he married Harriet Gage on May 20, 1922. They had four children: Marion, Louise, Wayland, and Kimball.

Magee was a member of Alpha Delta Phi, a Mason, and an Elk. He belonged to the Cosmos Club in Washington and the Union League in Chicago.

BIBLIOGRAPHY

New York Times, May 6, 1931, p. 13; May 24, 1931, p. 8; January 10, 1933, p. 2; January 26, 1933, p. 25.
Who Was Who in America. 1976. Vol. 6. Chicago: Marquis Who's Who.

SHERMAN J. MAISEL (1918–   )

Jane M. Simmons

In April 1965, at the ceremony for the swearing in of Henry Fowler as secretary of the Treasury, President Lyndon B. Johnson announced the nomination of Sherman J. Maisel, economist and educator, of the University of California at Berkeley, to the Board of Governors of the Federal Reserve system. The nomination was a surprise since most rumors as to potential appointees carried the names of various bankers as candidates for the chair just vacated by A. L. Mills,[*] a banker from Oregon. The selection of Maisel marked the first time an academic economist had been appointed to the board since the nomination of Adolph Miller,[*] who was also a University of California at Berkeley professor and appointed to the first board in 1914. President Johnson's decision, with the concurrence of the board chairman, William McChesney Martin,[*] to appoint an academic economist as a governor was made because of their recognition of the value of a board member with expertise in macroeconomic forecasting, modern monetary theory, and real estate finance.

At the time, Maisel was serving on a team, established by the Social Science Research Council (SSRC) under the leadership of Lawrence Klein and James Duesenbery, that was constructing the first large-scale econometric model of the U.S. economy. The model, published in 1965, made use of the rapidly developing ability of computers to solve a large number of equations simultaneously. Involving over twenty-five experts, the SSRC group developed both the theories and techniques that provided the basis of most large-scale forecasting over the next twenty-five years.

Maisel's appointment to the board ensured that modern economics would have a voice in its deliberations. His previous research in the areas of housing, consumer expenditures, and real estate finance also brought other desirable areas of expertise to the board. During that period, President Johnson and his advisers were sensitive to the potential problems within the savings and loan industry and to the adverse cyclical impact of interest rates on housing production and availability.

Maisel's tenure on the board (April 1965–May 1972) covered a period of major debate and rapid development in the concepts of monetary policy. The Federal Reserve moved from an emphasis on conditions in the money markets (primarily short-term interest rates and borrowing at the discount window) to greater use of quantitative measures of bank reserves and the money supply. It also shifted from policies based primarily on reacting to money markets to policies based on forecasts of the economy and its probable reactions to alternative changes in the money supply and interest rates. In 1965 and most of 1966, the Federal Reserve made policies in accordance with its traditions. During December 1965, the board made one of its most critical decisions. By a 4–1 decision, it voted to increase the interest rate on savings and certificates of deposit. This vote was viewed by the administration and Congress as going contrary to the administration's policies of voluntary wage and price controls. Prior to the board's action, speculation around Washington was that Johnson's advisers wanted a tax increase and were using his well-known antipathy to higher interest rates as a lure to convince him to propose a tax increase to help pay for military expenses in Vietnam. The president's advisers had urged the board to delay action until after the budget was finalized. As a result of the board's decision not to follow this advice, interest rates rose, and President Johnson presented a budget without a tax increase.

In the following eight months, while interest rates rose, the amount of money and credit also rose at a rapid rate. In September 1966 the Federal Reserve invoked moral suasion for the first time since World War II. It issued a letter to member banks stating that banks that continued to expand loans rapidly might find it more difficult to borrow at the discount window. Although the reactions of the large commercial banks were extremely negative to this use of pressure, the policy was successful in limiting new loans to a desirable level.

As a result of the divergent movements between interest rates and money and credit in the first half of 1966, the Federal Reserve reexamined its operating procedures. Maisel chaired a system-wide committee charged with developing new methods under which the Open Market Committee would debate policies and instruct the manager of its open market account.

The major recommendations of this committee on open market operations were gradually implemented. The culmination of the changes occurred at meetings in January and February 1970 when the committee adopted new procedures that placed primary emphasis on the use of quantitative measures of reserves and money in setting and implementing monetary policy.

During his tenure on the board, Maisel served on both intragovernmental committees on housing finance and on a special White House task force to recommend new housing finance procedures to the president. Maisel played a prominent role in moving the government's housing policies toward a greater use of market mechanisms. The Federal National Mortgage Association (FNMA) was changed to a government-sponsored agency outside the budget so that it would no longer be constrained to curtail lending at the times when its aid was most necessary. Until that time, purchases of mortgages by FNMA raised the budget deficit. When FNMA became a privately funded government-sponsored agency, it could borrow and purchase mortgages on the basis of the needs of the market rather than on the size of the federal deficit.

Two other significant policies that Maisel recommended and helped to implement were the development of the GNMA (Government National Mortgage Association) pass-through certificates and the use of adjustable rate mortgages (ARMs). The development of the GNMA pass-through certificates, along with similar certificates issued by FNMA and then by the Federal Home Loan Mortgage Corporation, led to the use of mortgage-backed securities as a major source of housing credit. The adoption of ARMs was, however, delayed for over ten years. As a result, savings and loans were squeezed and suffered major losses when their costs of short-term deposits shot through the revenues that they received from their holdings of long-term fixed-rate mortgages.

Maisel's education and work experience prepared him for the challenges he faced as a member of the Board of Governors. He was born in Buffalo, New York, to Louis and Sophia Maisel on July 8, 1918. He married Lucy Cowdin on September 26, 1942, and they had two children, Lawrence and Margaret, and a grandchild, Nicholas Grant Maisel.

After he was graduated from the Nichols School in Buffalo, Maisel attended Harvard University, where he received his bachelor of arts degree in economics in 1939 and was inducted into Phi Beta Kappa honor society. He began his career in Washington as an intern with the National Institute of Public Affairs in the same year. Perhaps prophetically, his first job was on the economic research staff of the Board of Governors of the Federal Reserve.

Maisel served in the armed forces from 1941 to 1945, advancing from the rank of private to captain. During that time, he was graduated from the U.S. Command and General Staff School at Fort Leavenworth, Kansas.

When World War II ended, Maisel served as an economist and foreign service reserve officer in the Department of State. He worked on problems related to reparations, restitutions, and the reconstruction of Western Europe. He then resumed his education at Harvard, receiving master's degrees in economics and public administration, as well as a doctorate in economics, which was granted in 1949.

His teaching experience began at Harvard as a teaching fellow from 1947 to 1948 while he completed his Ph.D. He then joined the faculty of the School of Business Administration at the University of California at Berkeley. He rose in position from assistant professor to professor and served the school as a faculty member until 1986. During that period, he took time from teaching for public service, including the Board of Governors, and a series of fellowships. At Berkeley, he also served as a research associate and rotating chair at the Center for Research in Real Estate and Urban Economics. He was a fellow of the Fund for the Advancement of Education in 1952–1953, a fellow at the Institute of Basic Mathematics with Application to Business in 1959–1960, and a fellow at the Center for Advanced Study in the Behavioral Sciences in 1972.

Following his tenure with the Board of Governors, Maisel returned to the University of California at Berkeley. He also served from 1972 until 1979 as a member of the senior research staff and codirector-West of the National Bureau of Economic Research. He undertook and was the principal investigator for a major project for the National Science Foundation. The project focused on the problems faced by the federal deposit insurance agencies due to the opportunities given to insured institutions with little or no capital. It paid these insured institutions to bet wildly on unusually risky loans since they were given a "heads I win, tails you lose" proposition. A failure of the Federal Savings and Loan Insurance Corporation to grasp this fundamental principle was a key factor in the recent savings and loan debacle.

In 1986 Maisel received emeritus status and the Berkeley Citation from the University of California at Berkeley. He continues active participation in the economic field as a senior research economist at Berkeley's Center for Real Estate and Urban Economics while operating a consulting firm engaged with both private businesses and the government in the spheres of macroeconomics, forecasting, and finance.

Maisel's research interests and publications include the field of monetary and fiscal policy, forecasting, business economics, the housing and construction industry, and real estate finance. Included among his thirteen published books and monographs are *Real Estate Finance* (1987), *Macroeconomics: Theories and Policies* (1982), *Risk and Capital Adequacy in Commercial Banks* (1981), *Managing the Dollar* (1973), *Fluctuations, Growth and Forecasting* (1957), and *Housebuilding in Transition* (1953).

Maisel's contributions to the economic literature include numerous articles and published speeches covering related areas in monetary theory, finance, and macroeconomics. Most of these writings sought to develop the theories while applying them empirically to specific problems.

In keeping with his commitment to the community in which he lived, Maisel served as a member of the board and vice-president of the Berkeley Unified School District. He was a member of the City of Berkeley's Planning Commission, its Urban Renewal Committee, and its City-University Liaison Committee. Maisel also served as a director of the Consumers Cooperative of Berkeley.

Among his other forms of public service, Maisel participated in advisory committees to the Federal Housing Administration, the U.S. Bureau of Census, the State of California, the Social Science Research Council, and the Building Research Advisory Board of the National Research Council. He has been called upon frequently for expert testimony by committees of Congress and the California legislature. From 1985 to 1988 he served as chair of the board of directors of the Farmers Savings and Loan Association, one of the new institutions established by the Federal Home Loan Bank Board to help untangle the savings and loan catastrophe.

Maisel has also served as a trustee of the Population Reference Bureau, a trustee of the World Affairs Council of Northern California, and was on the board of advisers for the National Association of Retarded Children. His professional memberships include the American Economic Association, the Econometric Society, the Regional Science Association, and the American Finance Association, of which he was president in 1973.

Both of Maisel's children became lawyers. His son, Lawrence, chose to focus on corporate law with particular emphasis on economic aspects. His daughter, Margaret, became involved in public interest law primarily. She worked for the Consumer Product Safety Commission and the Legal Services Corporation. She has taught in law schools while practicing mainly with nonprofit law firms.

BIBLIOGRAPHY

Maisel, Samuel. 1965a. "Banking's Spotlight on S. J. Maisel." *Banking* 57 (June).

———. 1965b. "Fed Line-up Veers to the Liberal Side." *Business Week*, September 11, pp. 146, 148, 150, 153.

———. 1965c. "Pressure Goes on Fed Not to Tighten Credit." *Business Week*, November 13, p. 40.

———. 1966. "Where the Fed Gets Its Bold New Ideas." *Business Week*, December 10, pp. 101-2, 104.

———. 1967a. "Keeping the Fed on Middle Ground." *Business Week*, February 25, pp. 36–37.

———. 1967b. "Monetary Policy and the Residential Mortgage Market." *Federal Reserve Bulletin* 53 (May): 728–40.

———. 1967c. "Waiting for Fanny." *Fortune* 76 (August): 176, 178.

———. 1967d. "The Worst Is over in Housing." *Business Week*, January 21, p. 27.

PRESTON MARTIN (1923–   )

Annette E. Meyer

Preston Martin, a governor of the Federal Reserve board from March 1982 to March 1986, is currently chairman and chief executive officer of WestFed Holdings, H. F. Holdings, SoCal Holdings, and Wespar Financial Services. The last is a jointly owned service corporation. The three holding companies were formed to acquire two savings and loan subsidiaries and a savings bank.

Preston Martin was born in Los Angeles on December 5, 1923. He began acquiring business experience at approximately thirteen years of age when he worked a paper route in Los Angeles and handled complaints against other paperboys. Martin attended the University of Southern California and paid his way by teaching and working the late shift at a Lockheed plant. At the university, he earned a B.S. and an M.B.A. in finance by 1948. After army service, he went to Indiana University for his Ph.D. in monetary economics, which was completed in 1952. Between 1954 and 1966, he devoted his time to developing real estate projects and organizing an economics research group specializing in savings and loan matters. In each case, he served in the capacity of proprietor or principal.

It was during this period that his book, *Real Estate Principles and Practices* (1959), was published. In the preface, he indicates that the purpose of the book was to emphasize "real estate finance, real estate development within the new patterns of metropolitan areas and federal housing policy." At the time of its publication and until 1963, Martin was a professor of finance and director of executive programs at the University of Southern California. He was a visiting professor at universities in Italy and Pakistan and established a business school in Turin. When he returned to the United States, he revived his entrepreneurial activities in real estate and finance and as a consultant gave speeches concerning the slow pace of development of the savings and loan industry.

Ronald Reagan, then the governor of California, appointed Martin as the new state savings and loan commissioner in 1967. From 1967 to 1969 the new commissioner facilitated the mergers of two large savings and loan institutions now known as American Savings and Loan Association (of California) and Great Western Savings and Loan Association. Another institution, now called First

Nationwide Savings, was converted from a mutual savings and loan to a stock form.

In 1969 Martin was appointed chairman of the Federal Home Loan Bank Board by President Richard Nixon. His activities concerned deregulation of the savings and loan industry, improving credit functions of the Federal Home Loan Bank (FHLB), setting up the Federal Home Loan Mortgage Corporation (FHLMC), and aligning the time durations and terms of assets and liabilities for these institutions.

Martin resigned his Washington job in 1972 to found PMI Mortgage Insurance Company. The following year, lacking capital for expansion, he sold the company to Sears Roebuck's Allstate Insurance subsidiary. He continued to manage PMI for six years after that and then moved to Chicago to head Sears's new financial services group. He founded, organized, and staffed Seraco Enterprises, a holding company for Sears Allstate Companies. He remained chairman and chief executive officer from 1980 until its merger into Coldwell Banker in 1982. In January 1982 the Reagan administration nominated him for vice-chairman of the Federal Reserve board (FRB). He was a member of the President's Commission on Housing at the time.

At the beginning of his term on the Fed, Martin voted consistently with the majority on the Federal Open Market Committee (FOMC), the group that buys or sells U.S. government securities to affect bank reserves and the nation's money supply. But in 1984 the economy slowed, and Martin dissented five times, urging greater money growth. Even if greater money growth had been accepted by the board, Martin admitted limitations to its success in an article in *Bankers Monthly* (May 1984). Although monetary policy can provide the appropriate expectational environment for a decline in interest rates over time and hence the possibility of new investment, it cannot ensure increased productivity, investment, and balanced growth.

Maxwell Newton (1983) claimed that Martin was a "career businessman" and not familiar with the inner workings of the Fed from a professional point of view. He argued that Martin, and Frederick H. Schultz,[*] whom he replaced in 1982, were on the board principally to give it balance and thus represented no threat.

During his four years on the board, Preston Martin spoke before numerous congressional committees on activities ranging from development of the Eurodollar market, to financial and options markets, to merger and buyout activity. The topics that received the most frequent attention were the agricultural sectors and the mortgage markets. For example, in June 1983, Martin spoke before the Subcommittee on Domestic Monetary Policy of the House Committee on Banking, Finance, and Urban Affairs concerning home and farm foreclosures and measures for financially troubled home owners and employment. In his remarks, he emphasized the boundaries of monetary policy. It can be a contributing factor to the rate of growth of nominal income, but that does not reveal its effect on real economic activity and unemployment, if any, in the long run. If there is structural unemployment in the economy, it is not likely that monetary policy or fiscal policy will be useful. Rather, monetary policy should foster a lasting noninflationary expansion of business activity, sound financial markets, and a strong international financial system. The major role of fiscal policy at this time should be the reduction of huge budget deficits.

In September 1983 Martin presented his view of two Senate bills addressed to widening and deepening the secondary mortgage market before the Subcommittee on Housing and Urban Affairs of the Senate Committee on Banking, Housing, and Urban Affairs. While recognizing the outstanding accomplishments of the Federal National Mortgage Association (FNMA) and the Federal Home Loan Mortgage Corporation and the contributions of the Government National Mortgage Association (GNMA) in furthering home ownership and residential financing, the time had come, he said, for the private market to take over mortgage-based securities.

Martin recommended several ways to bolster private security markets, including removing any constraints introduced by federal or state laws on private mortgage securities and removing statutory limitations on investment in mortgage-related securities.

At the time of Martin's statement, the two government-sponsored enterprises, FNMA and FHLMC, provided some benefits in this area that he felt could not be provided by private alternatives. Because of their federal connections, they can ensure that benefits accrue to the most needy borrowers as identified through the political process. Martin made similar statements in an article in *Savings Institutions* in January 1984. Public policy to further home ownership and residential financing needs measures to stimulate private market institutions. Since then, totally private firms issuing mortgage-backed securities in competition with FNMA and FHLMC have developed.

By March 1986, the agricultural sector was having more serious problems than any others encountered since the 1930s. Farms had been accumulating large amounts of debt, said Martin in his statement before the Senate Committee on Banking, Housing, and Urban Affairs. The board considered favorably the proposal of voluntary debt restructuring according to generally accepted accounting principles and made other recommendations as well.

After Martin left the board, Congress passed the Competitive Equality Banking Act of 1987, which included some of the board's recommendations. For example, rules for acquisition of failed savings institutions were relaxed (Title I), and so were rules for closing troubled savings institutions (Title IV).

Martin, spent his leisure time bicycling, playing tennis, or operating his personal computer. He and his third wife, Genevieve DeVere, lived in Georgetown during his second stay in Washington. His son, Pier Preston, was living in Tucson, Arizona, at the time.

At the office, Preston Martin attended meetings of the board at which chairman Volcker* presided. Volcker, a former under secretary of the Treasury and a former president of the Federal Reserve Bank of New York, was a cautious and deliberative person who disagreed with some of Martin's comments to the press.

The first involved a linguistic squabble over Martin's use of the term *growth recession*, quoted in *Business Week* (May 5, 1985), to portray the predicted path of the economy for the coming period based on existing data. Volcker disliked the term, arguing it was contradictory. A second incident was recorded in *Fortune* magazine (September 6, 1985) and referred to Martin's comments to reporters in New York on the international debt crisis after he had addressed a group of international business representatives. Martin stated that more study of plans for handling the international debt crisis, including a debt-equity swap arrangement, was needed. In fact, the Fed had studied these plans already, and Volcker had rejected them as unrealistic. Now he rejected Martin's remarks, as reported, as unintelligible. Nevertheless, Martin later explained that he believed that the diverse views of board members should be aired.

One primary conviction that Martin had in common with Volcker and most other individuals associated with the Fed was the need to preserve the Fed's autonomy. Therefore, he was pleased to learn shortly after his appointment to the board that monetary policy continued to be exempted from regulatory reform. "The proper conduct of monetary policy requires a high degree of discretion and a minimum of complex procedural rules that could delay and frustrate timely and effective action responsible to the changing needs on the economy." The balance of his statement before the Subcommittee on Administrative Law and Governmental Relations of the House Committee on the Judiciary (July 14, 1983) listed operations of the discount window, rules concerning reserve requirements, margin credit, and interest on deposits as examples of items to be exempted from regulatory reform. He recommended that Congress consider exemptions to regulations applying to the safety and soundness of banks and thrift institutions also. It was Martin's contention that "there is an inherent link between the central bank's responsibility for the stability of the financial system and the conduct of monetary policy."

On the international scene and with respect to the rise in the value of the dollar, Martin addressed the Subcommittee on Economic Stabilization of the House Committee on Banking, Finance, and Urban Affairs (July 18, 1985). The rise in the value of the dollar had contributed to rising trade and current accounts deficits. He emphasized that reducing the federal budget deficit was essential for dealing with both deficits. Curbing spending would reduce government demand for resources and saving, and upward pressure on the dollar would be halted.

In addition to Martin's contributions to international monetary affairs as a member of the Federal Reserve board, he also represented the United States at the Bank for International Settlements at Basel and has served on the Group of Experts on Payment Systems.

Delayed availability of deposit funds was a practice that gained increased attention in 1985 as bills concerning it were introduced in the Congress. Martin expressed the views of the board concerning deposit availability in a statement before the Subcommittee on Financial Institutions Supervision, Regulation, and

Insurance of the House Committee on Banking, Finance, and Urban Affairs (October 10, 1985). He identified alternative methods for dealing with the problem but indicated that the board does not favor nationally imposed availability schedules; state action may be more appropriate. More recently, one of the provisions of Title VI of the Competitive Equality Banking Act of 1987 required that, by September 1990, depositories must make funds available to customers within one business day.

At other times Congress and the Federal Reserve board sought different solutions to a problem. For example, Martin announced in an interview for *U.S. News & World Report* in January 1983 that disinflation was the primary goal and furthering recovery the second. The Fed had succeeded in bringing down inflation by reducing the money supply, but, said Martin, the board's control was limited. When asked if targeting interest rates might be a better method, he responded that targeting rates is not a practical way to implement monetary policy, particularly because of the relative ease of international capital movements to offset it. Nevertheless, Congress tends to prefer the use of the technique and, conversely, tends to respond quickly to high interest rates. The reaction was evident in the early 1980s when many bills and resolutions were introduced in Congress to regulate the conduct of monetary policy by the Federal Reserve.

John T. Woolley (1984), claimed that Congress was often disturbed at high interest rates and high unemployment. It appears that whenever interest rates are high, serious challenges to the conduct of monetary policy are raised by the Congress, such as proposing audits by the General Accounting Office or suggesting alteration of the composition of the Federal Open Market Committee. Prominent debates on monetary politics, explains Woolley, have not been in terms of Republican or Democrat but rather in terms of monetary economist or mainstream Keynesian. The monetarist is primarily concerned with the money stock and holding down inflation, while the Keynesian is primarily concerned with holding down interest rates.

Preston Martin can be counted within the monetarist group, but it can be argued that his approach is eclectic in that he does not subscribe to any one camp within that group. For example, in an article in the *Economic Review* (FRB of Kansas City) in 1986, he mentioned not only monetary and reserve aggregate targets for fighting inflation but other monetary policy targets such as relating policy to the growth of total debt, targeting nominal gross national product or nominal income directly, and addressing the dollar's exchange value.

Martin's public and private service records have earned him several awards over the years, including two from the home building industry, two alumni awards from the University of Southern California (one of these in 1988), and two White House awards for Governmental Organization Management Excellence.

Preston Martin tendered his resignation from the Board of Governors of the Federal Reserve system by letter to the president dated March 21, 1986, effective the end of April 1986. He expressed his regret at leaving after forty-eight months on the board but declared that it was a personal decision based on his goals and objectives. At a press conference held on the same day, Martin was asked about the possibility of a future role as chairman of the Fed; Martin declined "to pursue that line of hypothetical thinking."

BIBLIOGRAPHY

Martin, Preston. 1959. *Principles and Practices of Real Estate*. New York: Macmillan.
———. 1983a, 1985, 1986a. "Statements to Congress by Preston Martin, Vice Chairman, Board of Governors of the Federal Reserve System." *Federal Reserve Bulletin* 69:177–81, 411–15, 595–99, 697–701, 769–76; 71:508–17; 937–41; 72: 312–15, 382–89.
———. 1983b. "Fed's Strategy for Spurring Recovery." Interview with Preston Martin, vice-chairman, Federal Reserve board. *U.S. News & World Report*, January 10, pp. 38–39.
———. 1984a. "The Business Outlook Now." *Bankers Monthly*, May 15, pp. 4–6, 19.
———. 1984b. "Who Will be the Future Players in the Market." *Savings Institutions* 105 (January): S12–13.
———. 1986b. "Monetary Policy over the New Decade." *Economic Review* (FRB of Kansas City) 71 (January): 3–10.
Newton, Maxwell. 1983. *The Fed—Inside the Federal Reserve*. New York: Times Books, Inc.
Woolley, John T. 1984. *Monetary Politics*. New York: Cambridge University Press.

WILLIAM MCCHESNEY MARTIN, JR. (1906–   )

Daniel Vencill

William McChesney Martin, Jr., chair of the Federal Reserve for nearly nineteen years (1951–1970), was to the banking and financial world what J. Edgar Hoover was to the FBI. He was appointed chair by a fellow Missourian, President Harry Truman, and reappointed by Presidents Dwight D. Eisenhower (twice), John F. Kennedy, and Lyndon B. Johnson.

In the five administrations between Truman's and Nixon's, Bill Martin was the most influential economic policymaker in Washington. He served out the remaining four-and-one-half-year term of Thomas McCabe,* who resigned in a policy disagreement with the Treasury secretary. Truman then appointed Martin to the $16,000-a-year job for his own fourteen-year term. President Richard Nixon once asserted that no other economic policymaker in the United States since Alexander Hamilton had had an influence as considerable as chairman Martin's over such an extended period of time. After hearing that comment, Martin allegedly began posing for pictures under a portrait of Hamilton.

Martin avoided being too specific about the Fed's methods and goals, choosing instead to cloak its operations in a mystique that left him freedom for manuevering. He took the stance that experience and discretion were the key rather than reliance on formal theories and set targets. The need for discretion was essential. Martin lived and breathed the themes of maneuverability and intuition. The most Martin would reveal about the Fed's objectives was that it would "lean against the winds of inflation and deflation with equal vigor." Also, observers sometimes said that Martin once reportedly likened the Fed to someone who removes the punch bowl just as the fun begins. Critics said the Fed had come to function like a chaperone at a fraternity party. It legitimizes the process without changing it very much at all. Martin's method of figuring out which way the wind was blowing was to stick his finger in the air. Another interpretation might be a reliance on commonsense empirical evidence. One Fed staffer related that if Martin were told that figures showed retail sales were off, he would go to Macy's see for himself, and tell his staff they were all wrong.

Over the years, the practical demands of presidents forced the Fed and the

White House to forge close, if sometimes reluctant, partnerships. Martin proved to be the consummate politician. It has been claimed that he built a strong foundation for the Fed's policymaking by institutionalizing the Fed's power in the chair's position so it would outlive his tenure. Martin is said to have firmly established the Fed's independence, a term that continues to create considerable controversy. As Kettl notes,

Martin firmly cemented the Fed's independence. He not only established the rhetoric of operating flexibility, but he also demonstrated that the Fed reserved the right to take independent action when the economy threatened to overheat. Despite occasional disputes, however, the presidents during Martin's tenure usually got what they wanted; monetary policy was typically characterized by accommodation. Martin rarely strayed far from presidential policy, and on those occasions when he did, it was for a common reason: inflationary pressures were mounting and the reserve banks were pressing for tighter money. (1986, p. 111)

On the afternoon of January 30, 1970, his last offical day on the job, Martin greeted in his office, one by one, the nearly 900 reserve board staff members who worked in the white marble building on Constitution Avenue. It was his wish to express his thanks to the staff in that manner rather than at the traditional (and stuffy) staff reception that other board members proposed to hold in his honor.

Martin was born December 17, 1906, the son of William McChesney Martin and Rebecca Woods. When he was seven years old, his father became governor and later president of the Federal Reserve bank in St. Louis. His father was called upon by President Woodrow Wilson and Senator Carter Glass of Virginia to help in the drafting of the Federal Reserve Act. William and his younger brother, Malcolm Woods, were brought up with strict Presbyterian principles; after graduation from the St. Louis Country Day School, William enrolled at Yale University.

Martin gave consideration to the ministry but thought better of it. Instead he majored in English and Latin but indulged an interest in economics that had been kindled by discussions between his father and Harvard professor Oliver Sprague. He made the tennis team and served as associate editor of the *Yale Daily News*. Self-effacing and studious, he refused to join a fraternity.

After graduating from Yale University and working toward a law degree at Columbia University, he joined the small stock brokerage firm of A. G. Edwards in 1929. He became a partner within two years. The head of the firm, also a member of the New York Stock Exchange, wished to divest himself of his eastern responsibilities and suggested sending Martin to Wall Street as the firm's representative. Martin agreed and purchased Edwards's seat, thus becoming a member of the exchange as of June 1931. He made the move partly to continue at Columbia University the studies he had begun at the Benton School of Law in St. Louis. In New York, he managed to attend Columbia intermittently for the next six years, although he apparently never graduated. Martin meanwhile operated his firm's membership on the New York Stock Exchange floor for seven years.

He made quite an impression. He was named a governor of the exchange in 1935 and earned the title "Boy Wonder of Wall Street" when he became the first full-time paid president earning $48,000 in 1938 at age thirty-one. His mission was to restore public confidence in the stock market and clean up the mess left by predecessor Richard Whitney, who had been jailed for embezzling the funds of customers and exchange members.

A voter for Franklin D. Roosevelt in the 1932 election, Martin quickly aligned himself in the exchange with a group of liberal leaning members. He teamed with Frank Vanderlip in founding the quarterly *Economic Forum*, of which he was co-editor over 1932–1934.

Martin was drafted into the army in 1941, trading his NYSE president's salary for the $24 a month pay of a buck private. In his Wall Street days, one of Martin's prime interests was tennis, and he was a good enough player to reach the second round of the Men's Nationals three times. It was through this sport that he met his future wife. On April 3, 1942, he married Cynthia Davis, daughter of Dwight Davis, the donor of the international tennis trophy, the Davis Cup; they have one son and two daughters, William III, Cynthia, and Diana. World War II interrupted his banking career but did not break his boy wonder pattern of rapid promotion. By the end of the war, he was a full colonel—and fellow Democrat Harry Truman's choice to head the Export-Import Bank. Martin remained at Ex-Im until 1949; then he took another pay cut to become assistant secretary of the Treasury for international affairs, where he played the central role in crafting that department's famous 1951 accord with the Fed. When Fed chair Thomas McCabe quit in April 1951, the job belonged to Martin.

During his reign at the Fed, Martin was described as tall, spare, peering through gold-rimmed glasses—a man who looked more like a folksy, small-town businessman than the boss of the world's most powerful central bank. He would hoist his legs onto a marble table when he chatted with visitors. He spoke softly, smiled often, and sprinkled his conversation with anecdotes. At the Fed, he played tennis almost daily with vice-chairman James Robertson[*] in the courts across from the Fed building on Constitution Avenue. He could be seen playing table tennis in the basement of the Fed. After a long day, he would roar out of the underground parking lot, like a comic book superhero, in his 1951 Cadillac convertible. One visitor stepped away from his office and proclaimed, "That man exudes power."

As head of the Fed, Martin worked twelve-hour days of puritan dedication, broken only by frequent sets of tennis on the clay courts that he conveniently set up on the Fed's former parking lot. On Washington's active social circuit, the teetotaling, nonsmoking Martin was noted for his dry wit and charm, but he was hardly a lion. As the number one central banker, however, Martin succeeded in serving and occasionally defying five presidents of widely differing philosophies and economic agendas—and winning grateful praise from all of them. His first months as chair were to be prophetic. Martin's predecessor had resigned in protest of the easy money policy pressures of President Truman. But Martin was not the president's man. Almost immediately under Martin, the Fed imposed precisely the same tight money policies that McCabe had pushed. And when reporters confronted Truman over his new appointee's intransigence, the feisty president said meekly that Martin was "doing the best he can."

Martin found a Fed badly in need of rebuilding, a task that was to become his major preoccupation. The Fed of 1951 was a sorry, dowdy operation. For a decade it had done little more than peg the price of Treasury securities in the open market, thus abrogating its central bank function of controlling the growth of the money stock. Moreover, control of the Fed, and the policy shaped by the Federal Open Market Committee (FOMC), was divided between Washington and the powerful Fed of New York, which conducts the Fed's all-important securities dealings in the open market. Opposing newcomer Martin was the New York bank's president, Allan Sproul, then rated as the nation's most skilled and experienced central banker.

Martin quickly won the fight with New York for control as Sproul retired in 1956. Just as quickly, he turned monetary policy from a passive to an active tool. Martin's management style was diametrically opposite to his most famous predecessor, Marriner Eccles.[*] Whereas Eccles in his twelve-year tenure spoke first in meetings and then literally dared colleagues to disagree, Martin listened carefully to the views of others first and then spoke his own mind. He was low key. "Everyone speaks his piece," he often said. "I want to be convinced before I take the plunge. The man I distrust is the man who is certain he knows the answer." Staff members reported that once everyone had spoken, the chair conciliated and pacified. "Martin tried to separate issues and find the common denominator. He influenced the board, of course—but he didn't drive it." His plan was to run the Fed with a low profile and high principle. His former colleague, Sherman Maisel[*] wrote:

Martin likes people and has the ability to put others at ease. His interest in individuals he felt to be a significant part of his job. He enjoyed talking to people in depth, trying to obtain a better feel for the economy and an understanding of the problems faced by people in every walk of life. In addition, he believed his job required interpretation of the Federal Reserve to others. One can truly say, in a slight alteration of Will Rogers's statement, that no man who really knew Bill Martin disliked him. Whenever I traveled throughout the world, people would make a point of meeting me in order to be remembered to Bill Martin. They wanted to express their great fondness for him. (1973, p. 114)

Martin's monetary philosophy was pragmatic, utilitarian, and evolutionary, and his policy implementation was intuitive. His economic model was a homely variant of the quantity theory of money, with a predilection for real bills doctrine and a conservative notion of efficient markets and the "little guy." It is hard to understand how one can hold the quantity theory and the real bills doctrine at the same time. He pushed for more statistics, more staff research into the basic workings of monetary policy. Economists (Martin himself was certainly not one) were a necessary evil. He distrusted economists, whom he thought presented simple solutions to inherently complex problems. He was against the theories of a constant-growth-rate rule for the money supply, no matter what slack or overheating existed, as espoused by Milton Friedman, then a University of Chicago professor. Friedman argued that the Fed should stop leaning against the economic winds and simply pay attention to keeping the stock of money in the economy growing at a steady, say 4 percent, rate. One has the impression that under the Martin board, research dealt with institutional trivia, and was not allowed to consider policy until the mid–1960s.

Martin envisioned the role of monetary policy in this way: "We have a moving stream—the money stream. We want the money in the stream to grow as the river bank can hold it. We don't want it to overflow the banks" (*U.S. News & World Report*, February 11, 1955, p. 56). But the stream did overflow with regularity in the postwar years and forced the Fed to keep applying tight money policies. Martin often related that the famous economist, John Maynard Keynes, had warned him long ago that the biggest problem of the postwar world would be coping with inflation.

Martin's monetary policy has been described as consistently pragmatic and clearly calling for discretionary control of the money supply. Yet closer examination indicates that Martin was also an agnostic about monetary theory and always stressed the limits of the Fed in either controlling the economy or forcing it off its natural, market-determined path. He believed that economics was more art than science; too many economists in the Fed kitchen could also spoil the soup.

Looking back, Martin in a December 10, 1985, *New York Times* interview, claimed he told himself when he took office,

My gracious, here I am the new chairman of the Fed and I'm doing my best—I'm not the brightest fellow in the world but I'm working hard on this—and I haven't the faintest idea of how you figure the money supply. Yet everybody thinks I have it at my fingertips. They don't really know what the money supply is now, even today. They print some figures—I'm not trying to make fun of it—but a lot of it is just almost superstition.

Martin knew enough about monetary policy to know how little he understood and how ready he had to be to change his mind, "but I also knew that most outside theoreticians knew even less, had less practical grasp of all the problems, and I spend a good deal of my career fighting off simplistic theories."

Fed insiders were quick to point out that Martin's role was seen as consensus builder. By allowing others to be heard and then articulating a position on which almost everyone could agree, he was often able to produce unanimous votes on policy issues.

At his 1956 nomination hearings in the U.S. Senate, Martin repeated his famous metaphor about the Fed's number one job: "Our purpose is to lean against the winds of deflation or inflation, whichever way they are blowing." Leaning against the wind was the primary justification for discretionary policymaking (as opposed to monetary rules or other partisan expedients) because the Fed first had to determine which way the wind was blowing, when to move, and how far to lean against it. This led to the independence issue, for to lean against the wind, the Fed must be unfettered by partisan politics, short-run constraints, or political pressures, such as the Treasury's pegging goals.

Martin always conceded his strong anti-inflation bias. He did not discuss the relative social costs of inflation versus unemployment, and he minimized the possibility that there were some sort of Phillips curve policy trade-off. At that time there was, however, no definitive empirical work on the redistributive effects on the welfare of, say lower-income blacks, as a result of moderate inflation. He was not insensitive to complaints that he was too quick to react to hints of inflation (a "hair trigger") even at the risk of stifling economic growth.

Martin complained that monetary policy was often oversold and asked to do too much. Monetary policy is only one of several tools at the government's command. Others include direct controls (which he opposed), fiscal policy, debt policy, and wage-price guidelines. At other times, though, Martin acted as though the Fed were the only game in town; it was called upon "to be the chaperon at the party who must take away the punch bowl just as the party gets going."

Martin was often modest, although he certainly characterized himself as skilled in interpreting financial markets. He reiterated the inability of staff, including himself, to explain movements in the money supply. For this reason, he put his confidence in intuitive or qualitative indicators, such as the "tone" and "feel" of financial markets.

An insight was provided by former governor Sherman Maisel, an economist and careful student of the Fed. Maisel worked side by side with Martin and often disagreed with his position; however, Maisel objects to the stereotype of Martin as a narrow deflationist who, robotlike, pursued tighter money throughout his career. As Maisel says, he was probably consistently less expansionist than the administration, and although a convert to the New Economics of Keynesian demand management, he continued to believe that currencies lose value because of budget deficits.

Martin made it clear in interviews and speeches that he was concerned when ordinary people began to buy stock, fearing that this signaled irresponsibility, financial manipulation, and a return to the 1929 scenario of uninformed speculation and ultimate collapse.

Martin under several administrations was officially committed to multiple policy goals and often maintained that any action taken to achieve any one high-level goal did not conflict with the achievement of the other goals. Naturally, this placed him under considerable pressure to be vague and mysterious in his statements, thinking, and testimony at times. As long as Martin's Fed did not have a single goal, critics attempting to evaluate its record of accomplishments would face an exasperating job.

Because Martin and the Fed in general have rejected the view that it should confine itself to the pursuit of a single goal, it has focused on the interrelatedness of objectives and therefore the need to examine the behavior of the whole economy rather than any single indicator in isolation. Since many factors, including exogenous variables or policy not under its control, can influence the price level or any other criterion, it cannot guarantee stability of prices or the ability to prevent variance of any other single index. It should be noted that using a single indicator is not necessarily inconsistent with having many goals.

Martin was always more comfortable with a board consisting of fewer economists and more businessmen and bankers. Much of the time, the board had few, or no economists. It was surprising that he opposed the appointment by President Johnson of the first black to the Board of Governors (Andrew F. Brimmer[*]). The ostensible reason was that Brimmer was an economist, and so were John Mitchell,[*] J. Dewey Daane,[*] and Maisel, who were already on the board. He believed the board was overbalanced toward professional economists. Martin argued that Brimmer, a fourth economist, would not preserve the required balance of interest specified in the law, and this would damage confidence and gravely impair the ability of the Federal Reserve to carry out functions of vital importance to the economy and the government alike. Surprisingly, rumors and warnings were relayed to the president that highly placed members of the financial community objected to Brimmer's appointment, and such a move might provide Martin's resignation from the board.

As we now know, Brimmer was ultimately appointed, and he proved to be effective; but this was only after Lyndon B. Johnson was privately informed that Martin would not resign or publicly fight the Brimmer appointment. However, Martin did tell Brimmer that he would be considered a "junior appointee." Evidence indicates that Johnson strongly wanted to make a symbolic gesture early in his administration by appointing a black to a high government post. Skeptics believed that with the same appointment, the president would be able to get revenge on Martin for his defiant decision to raise the discount rate over White House objections a few weeks earlier.

The media often reported Martin's dismay over the number of economists appointed to the board, although under his leadership, the economists on the research staff increased dramatically to more than 300 in the research and statistics department. Martin was fostering a new cutting edge in research on the workings of monetary policy.

In reality, the relationship between the board and the Fed staff was of the love-hate variety. Martin maintained an acid opinion of the professional staff's capabilities. "I rely on my staff," he would declare, "the way a drunk relies on a lamppost: for support, not for illumination."

Martin always believed that the economy was far too complex to model in detail (a point also made by Friedman and the monetarists who argued for simple reduced-form models of the economy [with few equations] rather than large structural econometric models). Martin evidently opposed the nomination of Arthur Burns[*] as his replacement on the ground that Burns would bring to the job the baggage of the academic economist rather than the necessary broad vision of the generalist who understood real market behavior.

It has been argued that because Martin served during the administrations of Eisenhower, Kennedy, and Johnson, Federal Reserve power was more formidable than it was in the 1940s. By cooperating a good percentage of the time, the Fed was able to exert a noticeable influence on government policy formation. As Martin discovered, however, to make the Fed completely independent of and operationally separate from the administration is likely to result in less, rather than more, economic power.

Martin had a somewhat undeserved reputation as an inflexible champion of hard money. He astutely flexed his policies according to his view of current conditions. When President Kennedy and economist Walter Heller brought the New Economics to Washington, Martin's board supported maximum growth by allowing a record expansion of credit. When Lyndon Johnson shied away from higher taxes to pay for the Vietnam War and tried to pull off a guns-and-butter fiscal policy, Martin correctly sensed the inflationary dangers. He not only persuaded the Fed board in 1965 to raise interest rates and shrink the supply of money but refused to back down despite LBJ's personal and public protests. Though furious, Johnson reappointed Martin to his fifth term as chair. Later, the Fed's clumsiness in fighting inflation tarnished Martin's stature. The Fed constricted the money supply so sharply in 1966 that the move almost caused a financial panic and helped precipitate the 1967 minirecession. In 1968 Martin admitted that the board had erred by relaxing credit restraint in the mistaken, albeit widely held, belief that the income tax surcharge would quickly cool the economy. It is evident that as chair he had influence beyond his one vote on the seven-member board, and Martin disarmingly accepted blame for the erratic Fed policies that permitted the inflation of the late 1960s. He said that he left "a legacy of errors" and "the worst inflation since the Civil War."

Martin strongly supported the recommendation that the term of office of the chair of the Fed board should be made roughly coterminous with that of the president. This change would enable each new president to nominate his own Fed chair. To insist that a new president accept a Fed chair to whom he seriously objects would serve little purpose and most likely reduce the effectiveness of the Fed rather than increase it. Kennedy and Johnson would have liked to appoint replacements for Martin, but Martin's high standing in domestic and international financial and business circles made this unfeasible as a practical matter. Martin felt it was so important to avoid even the suspicion that monetary policy had partisan motivations that during his tenure, the Fed attempted to avoid any change in monetary policy before a presidential election. This seems to be the policy under any chairman.

Martin's operating style was different from that of Marriner Eccles. Martin was calm, persuasive, and low key. Under Martin's management, all reserve bank presidents, not merely the board members and those presidents who were formally members of the FOMC, participated regularly in FOMC meetings, which were usually held every three weeks. Although only the twelve FOMC members could vote, all present were free to express their opinions. Partly because of his skill in shaping a consensus that met his own views, Martin for many years was as successful as Eccles in achieving unanimous votes on the FOMC.

Policy decisions were inevitably compromises. No one always got what he wanted, including the chair. Martin was the master politician—someone who, in the words of one governor, "would sort of wheedle everybody into a consensus." For Martin, sharp public differences of opinion and split votes were anathema; if he sensed that he lacked "sufficiently broad" (which for Martin meant complete) support for a major change in course, he would put it off until the next meeting of the FOMC. FOMC policy directives to the New York trading desk in these days were notoriously vague: "err on the side of ease," "continue a moderate restraint," or "maintain the existing degree of restraint with lesser restraint possible if conditions warrant it."

But during the 1960s, Kennedy-Johnson appointees were not always Martin men (a luxury he enjoyed in the Eisenhower years), and sharper differences began to develop among board members. Split votes in board and FOMC meetings became more frequent, though invariably Martin was on the side of the majority.

Martin's leadership externally was perceived to be as strong as Eccles's. Martin spoke for the system in negotiations with the president and other top government officials, in testifying before congresssional committees, such as Wright Patman's, and in reporting to the public through speeches. Increasingly, other board members and bank presidents also added their voices yet it was Martin as Fed chief executive who had the dominant voice. An examination of the voting procedures at the Fed in the 1950s and 1960s does not indicate a clear leadership by Martin but is not consistent with Patman's "dictator" accusation or domination by any particular bloc on the FOMC. Martin's consistent role in voting with the majority may be explained by his noted skill in smoothing over differences so as to obtain unanimous or nearly unanimous votes. As Martin's influence over new appointees weakened in the 1960s, voting differences continued to follow no consistent pattern that reflected difference among the Fed bank presidents and board members or among newly and previously appointed board members.

In 1956 the Fed faced a test in its resolve to oppose the Treasury on its financing needs. The Fed at that time viewed inflation as a clear danger and was moving to tighten bank credit. In April, despite the open opposition of the secretary of the Treasury, the secretary of commerce, and the chair of the Council of Economic Advisers, the Fed approved an increase in the discount rate.

Congressional watchdog committees leaped into action. Martin explained the circumstances as follows:

Pursuing our method of cooperation, I began discussions with [Treasury] Secretary [George] Humphrey. In February of that year, Governor [C. Canby] Balderston and I had a meeting with Secretary Humphrey and there was a disagreement as to the nature that the economy was developing. We were so convinced; we discussed it with various people, and in a series of meetings from about the middle of February until the last week in March. By the last week in March the position of the Federal Reserve . . . was that it would be wise for us to go up in the discount rate. . . . We finally reached a point where there was no meeting of the minds that could be had, and there was nothing for the Federal Reserve to do except to go and act. And we acted. (U.S. Congress 1957)

It was this episode that Martin used to prove that the Fed was "independent within the government"—but, he added, not independent of the government, by which he meant that this independence does not allow the Fed to pursue a policy course contrary to basic national economic policies, but it does provide freedom for the Fed to exercise considerable independent judgment in the complicated field of monetary and credit policy. Martin continued:

We feel ourselves bound by the Employment Act and by the Federal Reserve Act. And in the field of money and credit . . . we consult with them [the administration] but feel that we have the authority, if we think that in our field, money and credit policies, that we should act differently than they, we feel perfectly at liberty to do so.

During this period, as well as later, Congress was jealous of its prerogative to control the Fed. Sometimes congressional leaders were not convinced that Martin paid much attention to their views. In 1956, when Martin had made the point that the Fed was responsible not to the president but to Congress, Senator Paul Douglas grilled him:

Senator Douglas: Do you regard the Federal Reserve Board as an agent of the Executive or an agent of Congress?

Mr. Martin: I regard it as an independent agency of the government.

Senator Douglas: To whom is it responsible? To the Executive or the Congress?

Mr. Martin: It is responsible to Congress. . . .

Senator Douglas: Mr. Martin, I have had typed out this little sentence which is a quotation from you: The Federal Reserve Board is an agency of Congress. I will furnish you with scotch tape and ask you to place it on your mirror where you can see it as you shave each morning, so that it may remind you. (U.S. Congress 1956, pp. 23–25)

Indeed, the Fed did "stand before the bar of public opinion": the press and public opinion in 1956 played the role Martin ascribed to them. They followed administration-Fed differences avidly and were quick to criticize.

To give an independent Fed the power to negate at will the basic policies of the federal government would be intolerable for any administration, Republican or Democratic. But independence is a matter of degree. Independence to Martin could not mean isolation. The real question for Martin concerned the terms on which the Fed participated in government policymaking and execution.

In his nineteen years as chair, Martin was criticized by liberals for his tight money, but they could not accuse him of being manipulated by incumbent Republicans. All three recessions in the 1950s occurred in election years. The slack and unemployment above the natural rate helped Democrats unseat Republicans in Congress and, ultimately, the White House.

It is argued that Vice-President Nixon pushed the Eisenhower cabinet to apply political pressure on Martin to ease credit during Nixon's 1960 campaign for president. After the election, it is reported that Nixon telephoned Martin at the Fed, lambasted him, and blamed him and the Fed for his defeat. At critical times the Fed took action which the administration opposed, clearly a reaction to the previous period when the Treasury dominated the Fed's actions.

Martin resisted any pressure to peg government bond prices, a sentiment that goes back to the Fed-Treasury Accord of 1951. To understand the debate, we must go back to World War II when the United States sold roughly $200 billion in bonds to finance the war effort without raising taxes, which have labor market disincentives. In fact, taxes were raised slightly, but not enough to balance the budget.

To accomplish this job, the active support of the Fed was required. The Treasury in effect printed money by selling bonds to both the Fed and the public at artificially high prices. After the war, the Fed and Treasury were faced with the problem of what to do about the huge overhang of government debt. The answer was to get the Fed to "peg" Treasury bonds at par, which involved artificially high prices. This meant that the Fed had to buy all bonds that were offered to it at fixed prices. It was argued that the Fed lost all control of the money stock because it had to stand ready to provide cash for all government bonds offered; the Fed had become an engine of inflation. The accord purportedly ended this practice, which was anathema to discretionary monetary policy.

Newly inaugurated President Kennedy and Treasury Under Secretary Robert V. Roosa opposed the central bank's bills-only doctrine. (In the spring of 1953 the Open Market Committee adopted the policy of confining its operations to short-dated securities, namely Treasury bills. The decision to operate in short maturity securities came to be known as the bills-only doctrine.) This set up a major confrontation that Martin was to lose. Prior to Kennedy's inauguration, rumors were flowing fast in the capital that Martin would be asked to resign as chair because Kennedy did not have confidence that the Martin Fed would support the New Economics and lower interest rates. Kennedy denied the rumors, and after Martin and Kennedy's first meeting in February 1961, it was reported that they had "a mutually satisfactory discussion." Kennedy was quite persuasive; Martin announced the abandonment of the cherished doctrine on February 20.

Martin has always denied that Kennedy pressured him into operating directly in the long-term Treasury bond market.

Since 1953 Martin had favored a policy of dealing almost exclusively in ninety-one-day Treasury bills, the shortest-term government security, when the Fed entered the open market to sell (which soaked up bank reserves, decreased deposits, and raised rates) or buy (which expanded reserves and raised the growth rate of money) securities.

Just before the November election, on October 25, and a few days after the price of gold had soared to $40 per ounce in London, Martin abandoned bills only and in his open market operations began trading in securities with maturities of up to fifteen months. Under the Kennedy policy, Martin moved to direct action to influence the long-term rate by buying bonds. In adopting Operation Twist, Martin reinforced the Kennedy administration's attempt to bring down the long-term rate while holding short-term rates stable or increasing them. The administration felt that the short-term rate should be held up to help stem the outflow of dollars to higher-yielding money markets in Europe. The aim was to twist the term structure of interest rates to achieve a downward-sloping yield curve. Lower long-term rates were designed to stimulate domestic business borrowing, a higher investment rate, and ultimately a higher rate of economic growth. The Treasury helped by dumping a huge short-term offering on the market, timed with the Fed's policy. The Fed could execute Operation Twist by selling short-term T-bills from its existing portfolio and use the funds obtained to simultaneously enter the long-term government T-bond market and buy securities to add to its portfolio.

Privately, Martin insisted that he would have resisted the policy change if the White House had "ordered him to buy long-term Treasury bonds." Martin decided to run to the goal Kennedy set and go along with the program because he was not entirely confident that his own policy was correct, and he was willing to give his critics a chance to see if they were right. Government bond dealers, financiers, and bankers had urged Martin to stick to his guns on bills only; they regarded this as a minimum interference with the overall supply and demand for funds. They regarded Martin's decisions as a capitulation but claimed the policy would make it exceedingly difficult to achieve a smooth reversal from easy to tight money. Dealers also liked the greater predictability of interest rates that resulted under bills only. A major argument for bills only was that it protected dealers from capital losses.

The results of Operation Twist were mixed. The short-term rate was maintained above 2 percent throughout 1961. But the long-term rate did not drop significantly, partly because the Fed started to relax its buying of bonds in June as the economy itself recovered. But the Fed managed to keep credit easier during the 1962 recovery than it did during the 1950s when bills only was the doctrine.

But the New Economics worked. The Kennedy-Johnson tax cuts and spending increases raised aggregate demand and eliminated the full employment gap. There was also a higher monetary growth rate. It seemed that fine tuning had arrived and the business cycle was dead. For 106 months, from February 1961 until December 1969, the nation enjoyed its longest period of uninterrupted economic expansion. The stocks enjoyed a long bull market, unemployment fell, and real per capita income rose. As the country approached full employment, a discreet combat developed between Martin and the White House. There was a clash over the question of the economy's capacity to continue to grow so rapidly without kindling the inflation fires, and Martin publicly objected to the guns-and-butter policy of the Johnson administration.

When LBJ was thinking of replacing Martin in 1967, Gardner Ackley of the Council of Economic Advisers (CEA) sent the president a reassuring memo. Ackley had conferred privately with other governors who assured him that "Bill was increasingly becoming a follower of the 'New Economics.' Now that the 'New Economics' is firmly in the saddle in both places (the Fed and the Treasury), Bill can be counted on to cooperate."

In December 1965 there was a much ballyhooed dispute between the Fed and the president over raising the discount rate, which would signal to financial markets a switch in policy direction. The Fed, in a clear rejection of administration preferences, raised the discount rate. President Johnson was furious and summoned Martin to his Texas ranch for some old-fashioned brow beating. This is perhaps the best-known example of Fed conflict with the executive branch. Martin saw this as an issue of the limits of presidential power.

Many times during that year, there was tension between the administration and Martin over Martin's freedom to speak publicly about economic policy without prior clearing or coordination with the administration. The Quadriad (the secretaries or chairs of the Treasury, the Council of Economic Advisers, and the Office of Management and Budget) was reactivated by the Johnson administration in the spring of 1965 as a forum where negotiations over macroeconomic policy could take place. Johnson and his officials hoped that by involving Martin further, they could get him on the team so that he would "run to the right goal when the president called the play." This would keep him from taking a public position that was at odds with the administration, and thus a public embarrassment.

Early in 1965, Johnson's economic advisers started to worry that their ambitious employment goals would not be achieved. This was when the war on poverty was declared. The administration was anxious to ensure that monetary policy accommodated its efforts to stimulate growth, and hence it was keenly alert for any early warnings of monetary policy constriction.

Via a series of meetings in the beginning of October, administration economists made sure that Martin was apprised of their preference on monetary policy. Despite these overt pressures, Martin informed the Business Council, with Gardner Ackley, CEA chair, present, that he believed interest rates should be raised. Ackley recognized that this constituted a declaration of Fed independence.

Why did Martin defy Johnson and run to the other goal? We know that on other occasions Martin used references to the White House to influence FOMC actions. The FOMC's decisions on the federal funds rate and how much money to feed into the money market, or take out, often set the stage for decisions taken by the full board on the discount rate of interest. This was the setting on December 5, 1965. At that time, commercial banks were in a position to borrow from the twelve Federal Reserve district banks at 4 percent—the discount rate then in effect—and lend at 4 ½ percent or better. It was on the recommendation of two of the twelve Fed banks (New York and Chicago) that the Fed board approved a boost in the discount rate to 4 ½ percent to restrain the demand for money for business loans and further credit expansion.

Martin was firmly convinced that the problem facing the Treasury was also to be accorded primary consideration. Most of the analysis of the period ignores Martin's sound reasoning. If the Vietnam War escalation were to continue, then Treasury Secretary Fowler would be looking to the Fed to make a market for about $10 billion in new debt during 1966. Martin did not want to monetize this unprecedented amount of government bonds—printing new money in the process, which would obviously set demand inflation in motion: resulting from too much money chasing too few goods, in his words. In the view of Martin and those on the board who voted with him, the move to raise interest rates was needed, in part, to make that market for heavy government financing. Martin correctly felt that rates had to be at a level where new Treasury bonds coming on the market (to finance the two undeclared wars) would find a ready market among individuals, corporations, and foreign investors.

The increase in the discount rate to the highest level it had reached in more than thirty years (and the increase in the Regulation Q ceiling on deposits to 5 ½ percent was also the highest since the regulation was established thirty years prior) set the stage for a clash between Martin and LBJ. Johnson expressed "regret" and on December 6 brought Martin and Fowler by Air Force One to Johnson's ranch in Texas for a conference.

Some observers considered Martin's stand at this time as the Fed's finest hour for asserting its independence in the face of President Johnson's vigorous opposition. Martin was summoned to the LBJ ranch in Texas for barbecued steaks, presumably smothered with blandishments, but he was not tempted to change his mind. One top LBJ official recalls that the president was "literally exploding" over the Fed's raising of interest rates. Later the former aide said, "I wouldn't say the President was exactly mollified, but Martin must have handled the situation pretty well. He was far calmer when Martin left."

More important, Martin had made his peace with Johnson while still sticking to his own tight money guns. That meeting closed on a rather quiet note. Johnson claimed that he had not tried to change Martin's mind. Martin announced that the board still wanted to work as closely as possible with the administration and intended "no defiance." Martin had won this round; he saw the coming disaster resulting from the twin problems of managing the boom and financing the war. The fact was that as the war continued and government deficits grew, monetary policy took on increasing importance.

Toward the end of Martin's tenure, the Fed probably became too flexible. Between late 1966 and mid–1967, for example, it took its foot off the brakes and hit the accelerator: the money growth rate went from a 1 percent annual rate to a 13.5 percent annual rate; then the Fed tightened again. The last loosening under Martin occurred in the summer of 1968, and he admitted later that it was a mistake that gave a large impetus to inflation.

What may be concluded about the Fed's independence in the Martin years? I agree with Seymour Harris (1964a) that there "are degrees of independence." As he points out, when the chair goes along with the president, a modus vivendi prevails. But the Fed is one of the primary agencies contributing to the formulation of policy, and when it expresses fears of an expansionist policy, it contributes to this formulation. Once the president has determined a policy, however, the Fed is likely to cooperate:

Besides, to satisfy the demand for an independent board, on the part of financial men in particular, it is important for the Federal Reserve to give an impression of a degree of independence that does not in fact prevail. Chairman Martin is an able and intelligent central banker, and knows only too well how much discretion the FRB in fact has, and the extent to which it can deviate from providing monetary policy consistent with the growth, employment, and stability goals of the administration. (Pp. 117–18)

Besides, independence is an attribute that might be justified only while the Fed's powers were limited.

On June 1, 1965, Martin delivered an address entitled, "Does Monetary History Repeat Itself?" His answer to this rhetorical question jolted Wall Street. Stock prices skidded when the top man in the Fed asserted, "We find disquieting similarities between our present prosperity and the fabulous 20s." The speech was a pointed warning to the government and the country against excesses that could repeat the cycle of boom and bust. As a result of the speech, Martin was soon being referred to as "William McChicken Little Martin," after the barnyard character who, being struck on the head by an innocently falling acorn, ran around the farm yelling that the "sky is falling" and instilling panic among the other creatures.

Martin was perplexed by the reaction his speech received, especially the hostile reception in the White House and Congress. In particular, he had included in his remarks the fact that if some of the similarities seemed menacing, "we may take comfort in important differences between the present and the inter-war situation": a better distribution of national income, a smaller increase in stock market credit, stability in wholesale prices, an improved structure of commercial and investment banking and business, and a better understanding of "the potentialities of monetary and fiscal policies."

Martin spent much of his time in the 1960s worrying about the balance-of-payments deficit and defending the dollar. He attended many monthly central bankers' meetings in Basel, Switzerland. In 1969, discussions turned on the skidding price of gold. By 1970 Martin was shooting down the notion that central bank intervention could hold the market price of gold at $35 an ounce. (The price of gold was $39.27 per ounce in 1968, $35.45 in 1969, and reached $186.75 by 1974.) Martin has proposed the notion of a world central bank and was one of the earliest backers of "paper gold" to meet the world's growing needs for liquidity. Paper gold, or special drawing rights (SDRs), was to supplement gold and dollars in settling international payment balances.

In the late 1960s some observers in the United States and abroad had come to the conclusion that an increase in the official price of gold would be desirable (or inevitable). Martin firmly believed that a higher gold price was neither necessary nor desirable. At one time, he held the view that requiring gold backing for currency disciplines the money-supply process. By 1968 Martin was against this same requirement; he had apparently changed his mind.

Martin lost points a number of times with congressional critics, particularly when he altered course and tightened. In discussing his reluctance to honor administration overtures for a delay in tighter money until January 20, 1966, when the administration's budget for the next year would go to Congress, he said, "I happen to be a money-market man, not a great economist," and he conceded another time that he could not class himself or anyone else on the board as a great student on the balance of payments. The Fed's relations with the Congress that created it and oversees it were more muddled than ever. Johnson was able to reappoint Martin for his fifth consecutive four-year term as chair only over the strident objections of such notables as Senate Finance Committee chair Russell Long (D, Louisiana) and House Banking Committee chair Wright Patman (D, Texas).

Patman authored a forty-seven-page attack on Martin, whom he charged held the "all-time record for waste—$200 billion worth" of allegedly needless interest costs paid by American taxpayers since President Truman made Martin head of the "money dictatorship" in 1951. Patman found a "startling" parallel between the workings of the system's FOMC and fascist implications in the way the "Gestapo is put out in the hall" to ensure secrecy during the FOMC meetings.

Martin favored a tax increase—even greater than the proposed 10 percent Johnson administration surcharge—as necessary to eliminate the inflationary budget deficit that was engendered by the Vietnam buildup. This was a quite unpopular position. Senator Jacob Javits (R, New York) cited "enormous opposition" by the public to higher taxes. "I get mail, too," Martin smiled, reporting that he did not like a tax boost either.

Patman also reacted strongly, almost irrationally, to Martin's June 1, 1965, speech referring to the similarities between the period preceding the 1929 stock market crash and the mid–1960s. Patman, a perennial critic of Martin and the Fed and a long-time friend of President Johnson, launched an attack in a June 10 speech. Patman asserted that Martin "is advocating . . . policies that will bring about the disaster he seems eager to foster." He suggested that Martin had outlived his usefulness as a public servant in charge of America's central bank.

Inflation inevitably produces speculators; if people act on inflationary expectations, the result is a self-fulfilling prophesy. Expecting higher stock prices in the future, agents buy to get a quick profit, but in the process they bid up prices. Martin thought there was too much speculation in the late 1960s and early 1970s. He saw inflation as eroding the store-of-value function of money while provoking a get-rich-quick mentality and reducing incentives to save and invest in real productive capital. He wrote a famous report on reforms for the securities market (1971), designed to correct the market breakdown that was engendered by the great inflation that began in 1965.

Martin believed that a lot of institutions were speculating at that time; they were not investing but were turning over securities at a rate that was unwarranted by any real standard of investment analysis. The institution of the stock market was designed, in Martin's view, so that the little men could diversify and get investment counsel service they could not otherwise afford. It was not designed for fairly large agents to buy large blocks of institutional securities and get the same sort of position in securities that the old pool operators had.

Many of the reforms Martin called for in his report and testified about in Congress have become standard features of today's securities markets. He had a vision of what the future was to hold, which included such computerized innovations as the National Association of Securities Dealers Automated Quotations (NASDAQ).

Today Martin has given up most of his twenty-four directorships, which included serving on the boards of American Express and U.S. Steel. He has continued to work part time as adviser to the Riggs National Bank in Washington, D.C., and is a director of the National Geographic Society and president of the National Tennis Foundation.

He is still convinced of a principle that guided his long and impressive career in public service: "Good credit policy is not a partisan issue. It doesn't matter if you're a Democrat or a Republican. Creating too much money or perpetual government deficits is inflationary." When Martin started his career over forty years ago, the Treasury bill rate was one-quarter of 1 percent. "People don't believe that, but it is absolutely true. And now it's in the teens. This is a moving train rushing basically in the wrong direction, and without sounder policies we will never stop it." Martin was a money moralist who did more to establish Fed independence than other chairmen, with the exception of Marriner Eccles and Paul Volcker.[*]

Martin reminisced a few years ago and provided a performance appraisal of his stewardship of the Fed (*Newsweek*, January 12, 1981): "I knew enough about monetary policy to know how little I understood, and how ready I had to be to change my mind. But I also knew that most outside theoreticians knew even less, had less practical grasp of the problems, and I spent a good deal of my career fighting off simplistic theories" (p. 13). The dominance of Martin and Eccles is illustrated by the remark current in Washington during much of their tenures that the Fed consisted of the chairman and six random nonentities.

Martin is a type of person sorely missed in Washington today. Public servants of his integrity indeed may be endangered species. Many managers with his skills would be lured away by the much higher salaries of the private sector yet Martin chose to accept a much lower salary and life-style for nearly twenty years in order to serve the public and community. Today he looks forward to competing in tennis tournaments for seniors. "There are tournaments for over 70, over 75 and even a new category for over 80. I'd like to last long enough to play in one of those!" For services rendered to his country, he without a doubt deserves to play perpetually in tennis heaven.

BIBLIOGRAPHY

Brunner, Karl, and Allan H. Meltzer. 1964. *An Alternative Approach to the Monetary Mechanism*. Prepared for the Subcommittee on Domestic Finance of the House Committee on Banking and Currency. 88th Cong., 2d sess. Washington, D.C.: Government Printing Office.

Clifford, A. Jerome. 1965. *The Independence of the Federal Reserve System*. Philadelphia: University of Pennsylvania Press.

Dale, Edwin L. 1967. "Johnson Renames Martin as Federal Reserve Head." *New York Times*, March 30, p. 1.

Friedman, Milton, and Schwartz, Anna Jacobson. 1963. *A Monetary History of the United States, 1867–1960*. Princeton: Princeton University Press and the National Bureau of Economic Research.

Harris, Seymour E. 1964a. *Economics of the Kennedy Years and a Look Ahead*. New York: Harper & Row.

———. 1964b. "Monetary Policy under Two Administrations." *Challenge* (February).

Havrilesky, Thomas. 1988. "Monetary Policy Signaling from the Administration to the Federal Reserve." *Journal of Money, Credit and Banking* 20, no. 1 (February): 83–101.

Hearings, 1957. U.S. Senate Finance Committee, 85th Cong., 2d sess. Washington D.C.: Government Printing Office.

Kettl, Donald F. 1986. *Leadership at the Fed*. New Haven: Yale University Press.

Maisel, Sherman J. 1973. *Managing the Dollar*. New York: Norton & Company.

Martin, William McChesney, Jr. 1953. "The Transition to Free Markets." Address to the Economic Club of Detroit, April 13.

———. 1955. "Don't Be Afraid of Prosperity." *U.S. News & World Report*, February 11.

———. 1963. Speech to the American Economic Association, December 1962. Reprinted in *Federal Reserve Bank of New York Monthly Review*, January.

———. 1965. "Does Monetary History Repeat Itself?" Address to Columbia University, New York, June 1.

———. 1971. "The Securities Markets: A Report with Recommendations." Submitted to the Board of Governors of the New York Stock Exchange, August 5.

Mayer, Martin. 1974. *The Bankers*. New York: Weybright and Talley.

Mayer, Thomas. 1968. *Monetary Policy in the United States*. New York: Random House.

Nomination of William McChesney Martin, Jr. 1956. Hearings before the Senate Committee on Banking and Currency. 84th Cong., 2d sess. Washington D.C.: Government Printing Office.

Recent Federal Reserve Action and Economic Policy Coordination. 1966. Hearings before the Joint Economic Committee. 89th Cong., 1st sess. Washington, D.C.: Government Printing Office.

Rossant, M. J. 1964. "Mr. Martin and the Winds of Change." *Challenge* (January).

Stein, Jeremy C. 1989. "Cheap Talk and the Fed: A Theory of Imprecise Policy Announcements." *American Economic Review* 79, no. 1 (March).

Woolley, John T. 1984. *Monetary Politics: The Federal Reserve and the Politics of Monetary Policy.* New York: Cambridge University Press.

EUGENE MEYER (1875–1959)

James N. Marshall

Eugene Issac Meyer was born on October 31, 1875, in Los Angeles and died on July 17, 1959, in Washington, D.C. His working years encompassed three careers. He organized his own Wall Street investment firm and was a successful broker and investment banker. He then entered a long period of government service in a variety of posts in the administration of every president from Woodrow Wilson to Franklin Roosevelt. His tenure as governor of the Federal Reserve Board was from September 16, 1930 until May 10, 1933. Finally, with his purchase of the *Washington Post*, he became the owner and publisher of a major newspaper.

Meyer's father was an adventuresome man. Eugene Meyer, Sr., was a native of Strasbourg, a city in the French province of Alsace. He was born to a family that had achieved some prominence; his grandfather had been made a chevalier of the Legion of Honor by Napoleon I. In 1859 he crossed the Atlantic and made his way to the isthmus of Panama. He then traveled up to California by pack mule, settling in Los Angeles, where he met and married Harriet Newmark, the daughter of a prominent rabbi.

In 1884 the Meyers moved to San Francisco, where Eugene Meyer, Sr., had been engaged to manage a commercial banking enterprise. Eugene, Jr., was educated in the public schools of San Francisco and then attended the University of California at Berkeley (1892–1893). His studies were interrupted when his father accepted employment with the French investment banking firm of Lazard Frères in their New York City office. Young Eugene resumed his studies at Yale, graduating one year early in 1895 with a bachelor of arts degree and membership in Phi Beta Kappa. He spent 1896–1897 in Europe, studying languages, foreign banking, and international finance. He lived in Paris, London, and Frankfurt and briefly attended the University of Berlin. He used his family connections to get employment with some of the great counting houses of Europe.

Upon his return to the United States, Meyer accepted a position as a clerk with Lazard Frères in New York. Despite his father's wish that he remain permanently with the firm, he decided in 1901 to strike out on his own. He formed his own brokerage firm, Eugene Meyer, Jr., & Co. His personal plans called for becoming independently wealthy by age fifty, at which time he would devote ten years to public service and then retire. He became wealthy far beyond what he ever dreamed, gave sixteen years of public service, and never did retire.

By a careful husbanding of his resources, Meyer was able to buy a seat on the New York Stock Exchange for $50,000, and his years on Wall Street were handsomely rewarded. Surpassing the goals he had set for himself, his personal fortune was variously estimated at between $40 million and $60 million by his fortieth birthday. Meyer considered himself an innovator in the investment world and believed his firm the first to have a serious research department. He developed what he claimed to be a "scientific" approach to investment decisions based on statistical analysis. He had also devised a method for using estimates of freight car loadings to forecast general business trends. His firm published a report on United States Steel in 1909 that estimated a value for the company's shares for several possible economic scenarios. Success fostered a broadening of his interests. His firm became active in the investment banking field, and he was instrumental in the development of the railroad, oil, copper, and automotive industries. He figured importantly in the organization of the Allied Chemical Company and served as a director on many corporate boards. In 1913 he was elected to the board of governors of the New York Stock Exchange. He established many valuable and lasting associations with other men of affairs, most notably Bernard Baruch, Louis Brandeis, and Felix Frankfurter.

Changes in Meyer's personal life kept pace with those in his public life. On February 12, 1910, he married Agnes Elizabeth Ernst, the daughter of a New York attorney and self-styled author. Agnes had spent a brief time as a newspaper reporter. After her marriage, she became active in the promotion of modern art through acquisitions, the organization of shows, and the operation of an art gallery. Eugene and Agnes Meyer had five children, two of whom achieved their own prominence. Their daughter Katharine married Philip L. Graham, who assisted in the management of the *Washington Post* and took full charge of the newspaper upon Meyer's death. When Graham committed suicide in 1963, Katharine assumed the leadership of the *Post*. Under her command, the *Post* became increasingly influential in national affairs and from 1972–1974 played a pivotal role in exposing the Watergate scandals. Dr. Eugene Meyer III was a noted authority in the psychiatric field and a faculty member at the Johns Hopkins Medical School until his death in 1982.

By late 1916 Meyer became increasingly convinced that the United States would be drawn into the world war. He felt that his long-anticipated entry into government service was nearing. It had been his intention to leave his firm in the care of his beloved younger brother, Edgar, who had been made a partner in the business in 1908. With the loss of Edgar in the sinking of the *Titanic* in 1912, Meyer decided that when the time came to withdraw from business, he would liquidate his Wall Street firm. Meyer was a lifelong Republican, and his hopes for a government post temporarily dimmed with the reelection of President

Woodrow Wilson. Despite this apparent setback, he continued the gradual liquidation of his Wall Street business and began to resign his corporate directorships. Desperate for some kind of role in the coming war, he sought active service in the armed forces, only to find himself ineligible due to color blindness.

In October 1916 the U.S. government created the Council of National Defense, an agency made up of several cabinet secretaries and charged with mobilizing the country's industrial might for entry into the war. This council was supported by a civilian advisory commission made up of businessmen and financiers. This civilian body's Committee on Raw Materials was headed by Bernard Baruch. In March 1917 Baruch's committee was attempting to secure a vast supply of copper for the armed services. The price of copper was three times its prewar level. Aware that Meyer had been involved in the financing of the copper industry, Baruch enlisted his aid. Meyer's contacts in the industry enabled him to procure the copper at half the market price. Meyer was subsequently invited to join the advisory commission as a member of its Committee on Finished Goods, and his career as a "dollar a year" public servant began. Meyer soon joined Baruch's Committee on Raw Materials as an adviser on nonferrous metals and was later made a member of the National War Loan Savings Committee. In late 1917 Meyer was selected to head the nonferrous metals section of the War Industries Board. In January 1918 Secretary of War Newton Baker appointed Meyer as his special consultant to investigate the problem of lagging aircraft production.

In April 1918 Congress established the War Finance Corporation (WFC) to provide financial assistance to essential industries experiencing difficulties due to the war. Meyer was nominated to be one of the five directors of the WFC. At the conclusion of the war, the WFC began to wind down its operations. Meyer argued that the end of the war would lead to an economic downturn, and the WFC should be restored to its full powers in order to ease the painful reconversion back to a peacetime economy. He was instrumental in drawing up the legislation that modified the War Finance Act, reauthorizing the WFC as an agency to facilitate the financing of American exports, mainly agricultural products, to Europe. In early 1919 Meyer was elected managing director of the WFC, though his hopes for a revitalized WFC were to go unfulfilled. In the immediate aftermath of the war, serious inflationary pressures had developed. Treasury Secretary David Houston felt demand needed to be restrained and that the credit expansion promoted by the WFC was not consistent with price stability. In May 1920 Houston suspended the export lending operations of the WFC, and Meyer resigned his position. In March 1921 President Warren Harding reappointed Meyer as a director of the WFC, and he was subsequently elected its managing director.

The WFC obtained a new legislative mandate in the Agricultural Credits Act of 1921, a law written by Meyer that called for relief for the producers of and dealers in agricultural products. Loans were extended to sugar beet, cotton, and wheat growers, as well as the livestock industry. By the time the authority for the WFC expired at the end of 1924, Meyer was convinced that its mission had been accomplished. He was reappointed to head the WFC by President Calvin Coolidge to preside over its liquidation, which began in earnest in January 1925 and ultimately returned nearly $500 million in capital stock and over $64 million in accumulated profit to the U.S. Treasury.

Meyer was appointed in 1926 to chair a four-member commission created to handle a crisis that had developed in the cotton industry. A bumper crop threatened domestic cotton prices, and his commission took action to remove the surplus from the marketplace. Then, in March 1927, Treasury Secretary Andrew Mellon recommended to President Coolidge that Eugene Meyer be made commissioner of the Federal Farm Loan Board. There were opponents to the nomination of Meyer, most notably Republican senator Smith Brookhart of Iowa, who disapproved of Meyer's Wall Street background and regarded him as less than fully sympathetic to the problems of the American farmer. Meyer was generally credited with the rehabilitation of the land bank system and the program of agricultural loans it supported. His tenure did add to his list of political enemies, including vocal critic Senator Huey Long. In May 1929 he resigned as commissioner.

In September 1930, with the Congress out of session, President Hoover gave Meyer a recess appointment as governor of the Federal Reserve Board, which allowed him to serve until the Senate reconvened and conducted its formal confirmation proceedings. The nomination was complicated from the start. A position for Meyer was originally thought to be provided by the resignation of board governor Roy Young,* who had accepted the governorship of the Federal Reserve District Bank of Boston. But a technicality in the Federal Reserve Act was discovered that stipulated that no Federal Reserve district could have more than one member on the board. The incumbent vice-governor of the Federal Reserve Board was Edmund Platt,* who was also from the same Federal Reserve district as Meyer. When Platt announced his resignation to take a job with a private banking concern, the way was cleared for Meyer's nomination. Some claimed that Platt's departure had been forced. This charge provoked vociferous denials and was to figure importantly in the stormy confirmation hearings.

The Hoover administration was dissatisfied with the Federal Reserve Board's failure to act promptly and decisively to rein in the stock market speculation of 1928 and 1929. In the economic collapse that followed the stock market crash, a change in leadership was thought necessary. Meyer had long been interested in the job. He had shared in the concerns expressed by many over the speculative frenzy in the stock market. The crash and the ensuing depression troubled him deeply. But long before these events transpired, Meyer had expressed alarm about the weaknesses in the banking system. He viewed his appointment as an opportunity to press for fundamental reform. Though the choice of Meyer was widely hailed in banking circles and in the financial press, it provoked opposition from the usual quarters. The nomination had been favorably reported to the full Senate by its Committee on Banking and Currency in early December. Louis

McFadden, chairman of the House Committee on Banking and Currency, urged the Senate to reject Meyer, claiming that Young and Platt had been forced out to make room for a governor whose allegiance was to Wall Street and foreign banking interests. Senator Smith W. Brookhart (R, Iowa), a member of the committee considering the Meyer appointment, charged that he had been denied sufficient opportunity to question the nominee and demanded that the nomination be recommitted. He engaged in the same demagoguery as McFadden, calling Meyer "the Judas Iscariot to cooperation throughout the United States" and "one who has worked the Shylock game for the interests of big business." Brookhart's invective is a reminder of how much the standards for acceptable public discourse have changed; thinly disguised anti-Semitism was once fair play in the American political arena.

The campaign Brookhart and McFadden organized led to the recommittal of the Meyer nomination in late January 1931, and the Senate Committee on Banking and Currency formed a subcommittee to hold hearings. Even in the face of stern criticism from President Hoover, McFadden was unrelenting in his attacks on Meyer in public speeches and in testimony delivered at the confirmation hearings. The nominee was characterized as an inveterate job seeker, who not only secretly controlled the chemical industry but intended to enslave the Federal Reserve system to the demands of the Bank of International Settlements and the interests of international financiers. His rantings included the accusation that Meyer's brother-in-law, Alfred Cook, had negotiated the resignations of Young and Platt, and he claimed that Platt's new job at the Marine Midland Trust had been orchestrated by its president, George Rand, to facilitate the nomination. McFadden did succeed in forcing the subcommittee to call Cook, Young, Platt, and Rand to testify. All four denounced him and flatly denied all of his allegations. Senator Brookhart was no kinder. In the hearings, he quizzed Meyer repeatedly about his associations with the large investment houses. Meyer was portrayed as a tool of Wall Street, who was unsympathetic to agriculture and had wrecked the Federal Joint Stock Land Banks during his tenure as commissioner of the Federal Farm Loan Board. Brookhart charged that Meyer had attempted to influence the indictments that grew out of the land bank scandals. Meyer responded by describing himself as a friend to agriculture, pointing out that during much of his government service, farm prices actually improved. The major confrontation of the hearings arose from Brookhart's insistence that Meyer state in advance the policies he would pursue as governor of the Federal Reserve Board, especially in connection with the prevention of a recurrence of stock market speculation. Meyer was adamant in refusing to respond, saying that he would prefer to be denied confirmation than be forced to reveal prematurely what actions he might advocate.

As the hearings began to wind down, McFadden made a last-ditch effort to prevent confirmation. He announced that he had been informed that two Republicans in the New York State Senate had joined with the Democratic opposition in voting down a proposed investigation of alleged illegal activities on the part of Tammany Hall Democrats in New York City—allegedly in exchange for the support of New York's two Democratic U.S. senators in the vote on Meyer's confirmation. Senator Copeland of New York spoke for himself and for Senator Robert Wagner in denouncing the charges on the Senate floor. McFadden had made sure to place his accusations in the *Congressional Record*, but the House quickly voted to have his remarks stricken from the record.

Serious observers never thought Brookhart had any realistic chance of blocking the Meyer nomination. Rather than face the inevitable, he chose to complain to the end that he was not given ample time to examine the nominee. Before the full Senate in the final debate, Brookhart argued one last time that Meyer was not qualified to lead the Federal Reserve but was fit only to be "a stock gambler." While a protracted debate had been anticipated, it did not materialize. The debate had run its course a full hour and a half before the scheduled time of the confirmation vote. The Senate decided to turn to other business until the time of the vote arrived. On February 25, 1931, Meyer was confirmed by a vote of 72 to 11.

The economic downturn that began in June 1929 became a deep and protracted slide, in large part as a result of the unprecedented monetary contraction of 1929–1933, a period during which the money stock declined by one-third. This contraction is difficult to ignore in assessing the success of Meyer's tenure as governor of the Federal Reserve Board. Whatever talents he had, they were not adequate to the task of devising a monetary policy that could restore some semblance of prosperity. But the fault is not wholly his. The institutional arrangements that governed the operation of the Federal Reserve system at the time made such a policy difficult, if not impossible. The Federal Reserve Act was passed in 1913 and implemented in 1914. In its formative period, the system was dominated by the New York district bank, its importance deriving from its location in the financial center of the United States and its role in handling the nation's international monetary affairs. The governor of the New York bank from its inception until his death in 1928 was Benjamin Strong, a man of extraordinary ability who was held in the highest regard throughout the system. When he departed, there was no one of his stature to fill the void, and a power struggle ensued within the system. The Federal Reserve Board in Washington had tired of its role as a largely supervisory and review body and moved to assert its control over the system. It attempted to extend its authority by insisting on greater centralization of the system's decision-making process. The struggle was intensified by policy disputes over how best to contain the stock market speculation of late 1928 and 1929 and actions to be taken to offset the effects of the crash in October 1929. The New York bank had raised its discount rate and sold government securities in order to combat the speculation. The Federal Reserve Board did not agree with this approach and sought to end the speculation by direct warnings that threatened the revocation of the discount privileges of member banks that engaged in excessive lending for speculative purposes. In its confrontation with the New York bank, the board was joined by the eleven other Federal Reserve district banks, which were suspicious of the New York bank, resentful of its dominance, and supportive of a power shift that would increase their influence. The system's policymaking body had been the Open Market Investment Committee, consisting of five reserve bank governors, with the New York governor as the first among equals. In March 1930 this committee was replaced by the Open Market Policy Conference. Under this new arrangement, membership on the conference was granted to all twelve reserve bank governors. This effectively ended the hegemony long enjoyed by the New York bank but made policy deliberations more cumbersome since many bank governors arrived at meetings bound by the instructions of their bank directors. As Meyer assumed his post, conditions within the system bordered on institutional paralysis as the nation faced its gravest economic crisis.

When Meyer received his recess appointment in September 1930, the first banking crisis of the depression years was taking shape. A wave of bank failures emanating from the agricultural regions swept the country in October and November, culminating in December with the failure of the Bank of United States, a large commercial bank located in New York City. In the face of increased bank suspensions, currency hoarding, and an overall contraction of credit, George Harrison, Strong's successor at the New York bank, urged a policy of monetary expansion through the open market purchase of government securities. Meyer enthusiastically endorsed Harrison's recommendation and generally advocated open market purchases throughout his tenure. At the time of his appointment, Meyer probably did not fully appreciate the very limited nature of the powers exercised by the governor of the Federal Reserve Board. His predecessor as board governor, Roy Young, had been a determined foe of open market purchases and a proponent of reining in the power of the New York bank. From early to mid–1930 he was able to convince the reserve board to disapprove discount rate reductions and open market purchases proposed by the New York bank. It was believed by some observers at the time that his test of wills with the New York governor had in part led to his removal as board governor. If true, it is ironic indeed that he was then appointed as governor of the Boston reserve bank. With that position came membership on the Open Market Policy Conference, where his opposition to open market purchases was all the more effective and surely served to offset Meyer's support for them. In a meeting held in January 1931, Meyer had his first serious encounter with those in the system who favored a tight money policy. The conference had voted to sell government securities, and he was strongly opposed, saying that a program of sales would lend credence to charges that the Federal Reserve system was "pursuing a deflationary policy." The other governors, though impressed by Meyer's conviction, were not moved to vote his way. Harrison's campaign of persuasion had failed, and the policy stalemate continued. The New York bank, by then unwilling to pursue its own independent policy course, was becoming more timid in its advocacy of open market purchases given the resistance of the other reserve banks.

The banking crisis had eased by early 1931 amid some signs of a developing recovery, but Federal Reserve policy offered little encouragement. By March 1931 a second and more severe banking crisis was underway, and economic decline resumed with a vengeance. Harrison again began to urge open market purchases. No purchases actually took place until after a meeting of the executive committee of the Open Market Policy Conference held on June 22, at which Meyer said that the board preferred "a larger program of purchases." Shortly after, Harrison, concerned over the financial situation abroad, halted the purchases despite Meyer's objections. In August Meyer and Harrison again joined in urging purchases. Meyer argued that system policy was too passive and had, perhaps unintentionally, permitted credit to contract. At a subsequent meeting of the conference, Meyer's call for a new and substantial program of purchases was rejected. His opponents thought purchases were futile, convinced as they were that the banking system was unwilling to employ any additional reserves. In his disappointment, Meyer demanded a change in operating procedure. At his insistence, the board would thereafter meet with the conference before, not after, it made its policy recommendation. Meyer began to see Harrison as ineffectual in presenting the case for open market purchases. He felt the participation of the board in the policy deliberations of the conference would win over the bank governors. To streamline policy implementation, the board gave Meyer the authority to approve conference recommendations for open market purchases.

In his first year in office, Meyer faced several international issues. To reduce the strain on the system of international payments, he advocated a reduction in German reparations, as well as cuts in the war debt repayments of the British and French. At the same time, he carefully guarded Federal Reserve prerogatives by resisting pressure from the Hoover administration to make lending commitments to Germany during its banking crisis in 1931. Frequent disagreement with administration initiatives led to an increasingly strained relationship with President Hoover. In September 1931 Great Britain abandoned the gold standard. The widespread belief that the Hoover administration would follow the British example put pressure on the dollar and provoked a large gold outflow from the United States. The Federal Reserve response was to stem the gold outflow by following the orthodox policy of raising the discount rate, though the domestic repercussions would be adverse since no offsetting credit expansion was pursued. Meyer was fully supportive of this policy. As a result of Britain's departure from the gold standard and the Federal Reserve's policy reaction to it, the new procedures Meyer had pushed through never had a chance to influence the conduct of policy. Purchases were abandoned and discount rate increases instituted in their stead by the system. Policy had but one aim—to stem the flow of gold out of the United States—and Meyer concurred.

The policy of tightness put renewed strains on an already beleaguered banking system. President Hoover called for the organization of a private voluntary association of commercial banks to provide credit relief to troubled banks. Known as the National Credit Corporation, it was unequal to the task, and the banking community quickly called for government intervention, a move long urged by

Meyer but one Hoover had been unwilling to make. His reluctance gave way under the press of events and Meyer's constant prodding. What emerged was a legislative proposal, written largely by Meyer, that led to the creation of the Reconstruction Finance Corporation (RFC).

Meyer's disenchantment with monetary policy grew as the Federal Reserve system remained deadlocked. To end the depression, he believed that an agency along the lines of the WFC was needed with the authority to take action on a far broader front. Under his direction, the staff of the Federal Reserve Board drafted a bill calling for the creation of the RFC, which would be given broad authority to extend emergency financing to banks, financial institutions, and railroads. Congressional hearings began on December 18, 1931, and Meyer appeared as the first witness called by the Senate Banking and Currency Subcommittee.

The legislation passed by Congress was a modified version of the Meyer proposal but retained many of the essential features of his original plan. It was signed into law by President Hoover on January 22, 1932, giving the RFC authorization to lend up to $2 billion. On February 2 the RFC board of directors elected Meyer as its chair. He began the practice of devoting his mornings to the affairs of the Federal Reserve Board and his afternoons to those of the RFC. Currency hoarding and bank failures eased in the months following the start of the RFC. Over 5,000 financial institutions had been lent more than $1 billion. RFC president Charles Dawes resigned in June 1932 to return to the management of his troubled Chicago bank, which then applied for and received a substantial RFC loan. This hint of impropriety resulted in legislation in July 1932 that required monthly reports to the president and the Congress on all RFC loans, including names of borrowers and the amounts. In August House Speaker John Nance Garner ordered that the reports be made public. While Democrats claimed that public disclosure would prevent favoritism in the granting of RFC loans, it was widely believed that Garner's action was in retaliation for Meyer's failure to keep Democratic members of the RFC board fully informed of the agency's activities. This disclosure seriously impaired the effectiveness of the RFC, since potential borrowers, fearful of the consequences of exposing their weakness in public, became reluctant to borrow. This reluctance was heightened in January 1933 when RFC loans made before the previous August became public.

Harrison had urged Meyer not to accept the RFC post. Once on the job, Meyer's colleagues on the Federal Reserve Board began to complain of his inattentiveness to his duties. It was also rumored that serious policy differences had developed between Meyer and Treasury Secretary Ogden Mills, an ex officio member of the RFC board. Finally, the physical strain of the two jobs began to take its toll on Meyer. On July 11, 1932, President Hoover cited "overwork" and the "danger of a physical breakdown" in announcing his recommendation to Congress that the Federal Reserve Board governor and the Farm Loan commissioner be eliminated as members of the RFC board of directors. Meyer resigned as RFC chair on July 31.

By the middle of 1932, signs of a cyclical revival began to appear. Lending by the RFC, the passage of the Glass-Steagall Act in February, and the beginning of a large-scale program of open market purchases in April by the Federal Reserve combined to bring some economic improvement. The Glass-Steagall Act introduced much-needed reforms that facilitated open market operations. One section of the act, inserted at Meyer's insistence, permitted government bonds to serve as collateral for the issue of Federal Reserve notes. The system made use of its new operating procedures by approving massive open market purchases. This renewed interest in monetary expansion was in large measure a result of political pressure. Meyer used the threat of some ill-advised congressional action to prod the system into a new round of open market purchases. Senator Carter Glass was contemplating reform of the banking laws to discourage lending for speculative purposes. Some members of Congress wanted to restore some purchasing power to the economy through the passage of a bonus bill for veterans. Meyer noted that some senators favored a resolution requiring the Federal Reserve to state its policy program publicly. Continued inaction would ensure its adoption and could lead to other unwarranted intrusions into the policy arena. Treasury Secretary Mills supported Meyer's view, saying that many in the Congress believed the Federal Reserve had done virtually nothing to arrest the business decline. Governor Harrison was greatly alarmed by the introduction of the Goldsborough bill in the House. If enacted, it would direct the Federal Reserve to adopt policies to restore the wholesale price index to its 1926 level. Harrison had been called to testify before the House committee considering the proposal. He argued before his conference colleagues that he had to be able to promise major Fed action during his House appearance if passage of the Goldsborough bill was to be forestalled. Fear of congressional retribution got the better of conviction, and on April 12, 1932, the Open Market Policy Conference reluctantly acquiecsed to the demands of Meyer and Harrison. It gave approval for the open market purchase of $500 million in government securities, with another $500 million in purchases authorized on May 17. With the passage of time, however, opposition to purchases resurfaced within the conference. As congressional adjournment approached, the Federal Reserve lapsed back into inaction, and the additional authorization was never fully executed. Meyer said that the system risked the full fury of Congress; if it could not carry out the full purchase program and was unable to enact an "effective united system policy," the centralization it dreaded would be forced upon it. But once again policy drift ensured another missed opportunity.

In the fall of 1932, new banking difficulties emerged in the Midwest and Far West. The campaign rhetoric of the 1932 presidential election created uncertainty over the future course of economic policy. Especially uncertain were the intentions of the incoming Roosevelt administration with respect to the gold standard. Fears of a dollar devaluation led to a gold drain. This resulted in a tightening of monetary policy, as discount rates were increased to stop the gold outflow. The signs of economic recovery that had briefly appeared in midsummer vanished, and the downturn resumed. RFC lending activity offered little hope. Since the previous August, all such loans were required by law to be disclosed publicly, and this greatly inhibited borrowing by distressed banks. Meyer had devised the RFC as a way to take decisive action given the inaction and timidity of the Federal Reserve system. Now the RFC had been rendered useless. Meyer's disillusionment with the system as a force for economic recovery is clear in remarks he made at a conference meeting in December 1932. The opponents of open market purchases had often pointed to the large volume of reserves held by the banking system in excess of the legal requirements as proof of the futility of such a policy. Meyer believed that this large reserve position was the understandable response of a banking system trying to cope with massive failures in the face of erratic and unpredictable monetary policy. Meyer felt that the benefits which would normally follow from an expansion of reserves failed to materialize in 1931–1932 "because of uncertainty as to our future policy." In a January 1933 meeting of the conference, both Meyer and Treasury Secretary Mills warned that continued Fed inaction could lead to the passage of some inflationary measures by Congress. Though bolder action by the Fed was surely in order, it is difficult to appreciate their fear of inflation, given the economic circumstances of the early 1930s.

As 1933 began, the banking system was headed for its final agony. Currency hoarding and monetary contraction took hold with unprecedented force. Fed policy drifted between neutrality and tightness right up to the climax of the banking panic in early March. Statewide bank holidays were a commonplace, and the use of scrip became widespread. By the middle of February, bank holidays had been declared in Nevada, Iowa, Louisiana, and Michigan. By early March there were holidays in half the states. The pressure was now on the large New York City banks as banks in states with holidays tried to improve their financial position by making heavy withdrawals from the accounts they maintained in New York banks. On March 3 Harrison told Meyer that because of the gold drain it had experienced, the New York bank was in violation of its legal reserve requirements and that its directors favored a nationwide bank holiday. The board in Washington granted an immediate suspension of reserve requirements for a period of thirty days. Meyer and Mills thought it unlikely that a nationwide holiday could be arranged that day. Meyer suggested that Harrison prevail upon the governor of New York State, Herbert Lehman, to declare a bank holiday in his state. Harrison was initially opposed. When it became clear that President Hoover would not declare a national holiday, he relented and paid a visit to Governor Lehman, who agreed to a state bank holiday effective March 4. Illinois, Massachusetts, New Jersey, and Pennsylvania immediately followed. The Federal Reserve system had become a willing participant in bringing about the very thing it was established to prevent: the collapse of the banking system. On March 6 President Roosevelt suspended gold payments and proclaimed a national bank holiday until March 9. Since the presidential authority to call a bank holiday was based on a dubious interpretation of the

Trading with the Enemy Act, emergency legislation passed in 1917 during World War I, a special session of Congress met on March 9 to enact more explicit powers. Roosevelt then extended the holiday, which lasted until March 15 in some parts of the country. Many banks never reopened.

Meyer's role in the events leading up to the banking collapse is complicated. He met with Mills and the incoming Treasury secretary on February 27 concerning a Treasury refunding issue that was imperiled by the banking crisis. The board was asked to inject reserves through open market purchases to ensure that the banks could absorb the issue. Meyer said that such a move was impossible given the need to tighten policy to stop the gold outflow, and the independence of the Federal Reserve might be brought into question if such a request were granted. President Hoover had written to the Federal Reserve Board on February 28 to ask whether any new actions seemed advisable, with specific mention made of the desirability of deposit insurance and measures to facilitate the use of scrip in areas hit hard by the panic. Meyer dismissed both ideas without offering any constructive alternatives. By March 2 Meyer and the rest of the board were inclined to favor a national bank holiday, but they could not get a firm commitment from Hoover, who continued to prefer the more limited measure of placing restrictions on withdrawals of gold and currency. Roosevelt remained unwilling to take part in any joint action. In the waning hours of the Hoover administration, the Federal Reserve Board finally made a formal recommendation calling for a national bank holiday. One of Hoover's last official acts was to send a letter to Meyer in which he rejected the board's recommendation. Hoover felt he was ill-served by the board and Meyer during the banking crisis. He wrote in his *Memoirs, The Great Depression, 1929–41* (1952) that the board "was indeed a weak reed for a nation to lean on in time of trouble." In an odd footnote to a very strained relationship, Meyer declined to follow Hoover's call for all high officials, including Meyer, Chief Justice Charles Evans Hughes, and others, to resign as the new administration took power.

Although Roosevelt had asked Meyer to stay on as board governor, at least temporarily, he never intended to remain for long under a Democratic administration. He took care not to be too closely identified with Democratic actions, declining to participate in the reopening of the banking system. Some of the policy positions adopted by the new administration also convinced him that a prompt departure would be best. He believed that the gold standard should be maintained and had misgivings about the direction Roosevelt seemed to be taking on the dollar. Meyer also disagreed with administration support of an amendment to a Senate banking bill that would have granted to state chartered banks borrowing privileges at the Federal Reserve without imposing any membership requirements. In early March press accounts mentioned that Meyer had made his intention to resign known at the White House, and some speculated over his supposed annoyance at Roosevelt's failure to consult him concerning an appointment to fill a board vacancy. By late March he had tendered his resignation and was asked to remain until a successor was chosen. Editorial comment was generous to Meyer. In an editorial dated April 13, 1933, the *New York Times* attributed the resignation to either the physical strain on Meyer or his desire to give the new president the chance to have someone of his own choosing in so sensitive a position and went on to note the wide regret with which the resignation was met. In a letter dated May 8, Roosevelt officially accepted the resignation effective May 10. Eugene R. Black* was sworn in as Meyer's successor on May 19, 1933.

Meyer did not bring any strong ideological convictions with him to the board. He thought of himself as a man of action, a problem solver. Though a loyal Republican and very sympathetic to the needs of business, he had rejected the uncompromising laissez-faire taught him at Yale by William Graham Sumner. But his view of himself as defender and savior of free enterprise was not wholly compatible with the technocratic tinkering that characterized his government service. His was a public career built on government intervention. When the Wilson administration decided to dissolve the WFC and put an end to the wartime government interference in business, it was Meyer, champion of market capitalism, who successfully fought to revive the WFC and expand its powers. Once Meyer came to believe that monetary policy was of limited usefulness in a deep depression, he pushed for the RFC as a superior, though more intrusive, alternative. These seeming inconsistencies are easily understandable given the nature of the Great Depression and may be a virtue in someone holding an important policy position. But the contradictions cannot be overlooked. In testimony delivered in Senate hearings in 1931, he was unsympathetic to a proposal to establish a council that would institute and coordinate national economic planning. Yet in 1932, in his official capacity, he personally orchestrated a move to buy up surplus cotton to support cotton prices. Since he believed economic recovery possible only if there was a revival of commodity prices, Meyer had proposed, unsuccessfully as it turned out, a commodities corporation that could support raw materials prices through the extension of credit. Meyer was very disturbed by the direction of New Deal economic policy. After leaving the Federal Reserve Board, he publicly criticized the Roosevelt administration on numerous occasions for reckless and unwarranted interventions in the economy. Strangely for Meyer, it was the despised New Deal that enacted into law some of his most cherished ideas, including the Commodities Credit Corporation and major banking reforms.

Meyer's singular regret as he left the board was that he had been unable to reform the banking system. This was high on his agenda as he took office, but the unremitting crises of the depression years constantly drew his attention away from his reform initiatives. The dual banking system, which allowed both state and nationally chartered depository institutions, was in his view an abomination and had done much to deepen and prolong the depression. A unified banking system, with all banks under the regulatory control of the Federal Reserve system, would end the ''competition in laxity'' that had long characterized the relationship between state and federal bank regulatory bodies and, according to Meyer, could do more than any other reform to prevent future depressions. He had formed study groups within the system to examine the matter and had delivered recommendations to the Senate Committee on Banking and Currency calling for a unified commercial banking system in which banking privileges would be extended only to nationally chartered institutions. Since Meyer envisioned a banking structure in which state control was effectively eliminated, concerns over the constitutionality of such a system were raised. Legal counsel at the board was of the opinion that a unified system could pass constitutional muster. By November 1932 the system had agreed on a banking reform proposal that it would recommend to Congress, but it never received any formal consideration, since the incoming Roosevelt administration chose to draft its own banking reform legislation.

On June 1, 1933, Eugene Meyer bought the *Washington Post* at a bankruptcy sale from Edward McLean for a reported $825,000 and became its publisher. For many years he had harbored ambitions for a career in the newspaper business. In the 1920s the management of the *New York Times* had suggested that he might take a position with their paper in a business capacity, but Meyer's interests were more in an editorial and journalistic direction. It is claimed that in 1929, before the onset of the Great Depression, his offer of $5 million for the *Post* was turned down. He said that his operation of the *Washington Post* would be guided by a strict devotion to the public good and that partisan politics would have no place at his paper. The financial condition of the *Post* during the first years of his ownership was precarious, with substantial losses sustained for several years. In 1940 Meyer became both publisher and editor, and the *Post* by that time was flourishing, with circulation tripled to 170,000 and advertising revenue much increased. The editorial page was internationalist in tone and very supportive of Roosevelt's foreign policy. In domestic matters, it was generally hostile to the New Deal and disapproving of the "leftward" turn its policy initiatives were alleged to have taken. Economic policy was routinely attacked, and a campaign of unusual ferocity was mounted against Roosevelt's Supreme Court packing scheme.

Meyer targeted New Deal economic policies not only in *Post* editorials but in his public speeches as well. He was critical of Roosevelt's housing policies, especially in connection with its alleged failure to provide low-cost housing. In late 1937 Meyer delivered a speech in which he deplored what he described as a policy of "excessively easy money." In remarks that seem intemperate given the steepness of the 1937 business downturn, he said that such a policy risked inflation, and he complained that too much emphasis had been placed "on reform and not enough on recovery." Roosevelt was willing to ignore the sharp and frequent attacks on his domestic programs, for he was deeply appreciative of the editorial support Meyer had given to his foreign policy. By March 1941 the two men felt sufficiently reconciled for Roosevelt to appoint Meyer to the National Defense Mediation Board, a panel formed to settle labor disputes that might disrupt defense work. In April 1944 Meyer was named to the War Production Board's advisory committee for civilian policy, which was created to study the problems of converting the wartime economy back to civilian production. By this time, Meyer had become an enduring fixture on the Washington scene. On the occasion of his seventieth birthday on October 31, 1945, a celebration in his honor was attended by cabinet members, Supreme Court justices, diplomats, and newspaper officials. Meyer held firmly to his internationalist views. He endorsed the United Nations and was a strong advocate of postwar assistance to Great Britain. He supported American participation in world hunger relief and was a member of President Truman's Famine Emergency Committee, which he had been instrumental in organizing in response to the food shortages that developed in Europe at the end of the war.

Meyer's last major government post came in June 1946. With President Truman's approval, he was elected to be the first president of the International Bank for Reconstruction and Development. Better known as the World Bank, it was established under the 1944 Bretton Woods agreement to provide long-term loans for reconstruction in war-damaged areas and development in member nations. Meyer resigned his positions as editor and publisher at the *Post* and named his son-in-law, Philip Graham, as acting publisher. In accepting the presidency of the World Bank, he had promised to stay just long enough to oversee the hiring of a competent staff, establish operating procedures, make the preparations for raising funds in the capital markets, and begin the formal review and processing of loan applications. Believing those modest ends to have been accomplished and tiring of the bureaucratic infighting over personnel matters and policy, he resigned effective December 18, 1946. Upon his return to the *Post*, Meyer created the position of board chairman for himself and permanently relinquished his former duties as editor and publisher, with Philip Graham succeeding him as publisher.

Meyer's public service extended beyond the numerous posts he held with the federal government. As a result of his interest in crime prevention and concern for juvenile delinquency, he became president of the Washington Criminal Justice Association in 1936, a position he held until 1945. Meyer maintained a lifelong interest in psychology and psychiatry, which, combined with his involvement in the problems of returning veterans, led in 1944 to his selection as the first lay president of the National Committee for Mental Hygiene, and he served in that capacity until 1946. In 1945 he was appointed chair of the postwar planning committee of the Washington Board of Trade, as well as the District of Columbia chair of the Committee for Economic Development. In the late 1940s, he was occasionally involved in the mediation of labor disputes. Appointed by President Eisenhower, he served on the Committee on Purchases of Blind-Made Products from 1953 to 1956. In recognition of his dedicated service and philanthropic work, Meyer was the recipient of many awards and honors, including honorary degrees from Yale University (1932), Syracuse University (1934), and the University of California at Berkeley (1942).

On July 17, 1959, after a remarkably full life, Eugene Meyer died, survived by his wife and five children.

By any standard, Eugene Meyer was supremely successful as an investment broker and newspaper publisher. One of his greatest regrets was that success did not follow him to the Federal Reserve Board. It was his misfortune to arrive at the central bank not only at a time of profound economic distress but when the institution itself was crippled by its own vacillation. He personally advocated a policy of expansion, but his views did not prevail within the system. Instead, he was forced to preside over one of the most notorious and damaging monetary contractions in American economic history. The inaction of the Federal Reserve and the perversity of the policies that it adopted during his tenure so thoroughly discredited monetary policy that it took decades for it to be fully rehabilitated. In the one office that he had truly coveted, he became a victim of events as well as a victim of the timidity and intellectual poverty of those within the system on whom he relied. He would always look back in frustration at his days on the Federal Reserve Board with one solemn conviction: he did not "believe in monetary manipulation as a method of recovery."

BIBLIOGRAPHY

Friedman, Milton, and Schwartz, Anna J. 1963. *A Monetary History of the United States: 1867–1960*. Princeton, N.J.: Princeton University Press.

Goldenweiser, E. A. Goldenweiser Papers. Manuscript division, Library of Congress.

Hamlin, Charles S. Diary: 1887–1937. Hamlin Papers, Manuscript division, Library of Congress.

Harrison, George L. George L. Harrison Papers on the Federal Reserve System. Columbia University Library.

Hoover, Herbert. 1952. *Memoirs, The Great Depression, 1929–41*. New York: Macmillan.

Jones, Jesse. 1951. *Fifty Billion Dollars*. New York: Macmillan.

"Meyer, Eugene." 1941. In *Current Biography: Who's News and Why, 1941*. Edited by Maxine Block. New York: H. W. Wilson Company.

Pusey, Merlo J. 1974. *Eugene Meyer*. New York: Alfred A. Knopf.

————. 1980. "Meyer, Eugene Issac." In *Dictionary of American Biography, Supplement Six, 1956–1960*. Edited by John A. Garraty. New York: Charles Scribner's Sons.

Rothbard, Murray. 1975. *America's Great Depression*. 3d ed. Kansas City: Sheed and Ward.

U.S. Congress. Senate. Subcommittee of the Committee on Banking and Currency. 1931. *Hearings on the Nomination of Eugene Meyer to Be a Member of the Federal Reserve Board*. 71st Cong., 3d sess., January 27, 28, 31, February 2, 3, 5, 6, 7.

Washington Post. 1959. "Publisher Eugene Meyer Dies at 83; His Life Spanned Three Careers." July 18, pp. 1, 10.

Who's Who in America, 1960–61. Chicago: Marquis Who's Who.

Woolf, S. J. 1932. "A Leader in the War on the Depression." *New York Times Magazine*, August 21, pp. 3, 15.

ADOLPH CASPAR MILLER
(1866–1953)

Robert Stanley Herren

Adolph Caspar Miller, who served on the original Federal Reserve Board of Governors from 1914 to 1936, was born in San Francisco on January 7, 1866, to Caspar and Fredericka Miller. He earned a B.A. from the University of California, Berkeley, in 1887 and an M.A. from Harvard in 1888. During the next decade, he held a number of academic jobs: instructor of political economy at Harvard (1889–1890), assistant professor of history and politics at the University of California (1890–1891), associate professor of political economy and finance at Cornell (1891–1892), and professor of finance at the University of Chicago (1892–1902). He studied at universities in Paris and Munich (1895–1896). He married Mary Sprague, a daughter of a wealthy Chicago merchant, on October 7, 1895. His academic research centered around issues of public finance; he published articles in the *Quarterly Journal of Economics* and the *Journal of Political Economy*.

In 1902 University of California president Benjamin Wheeler recruited Miller to be chair of the Economics Department and Flood Professor of Economics and Commerce. One of Miller's first acts as chair was to recruit Wesley C. Mitchell, a former student at Chicago, to join the Berkeley department; in 1912, Mitchell became Miller's brother-in-law when he married Lucy Sprague. Although Miller did not publish much in the next decade, he forged a reputation as an excellent instructor who captivated and influenced many undergraduate students. Wesley Mitchell wrote in 1945 that Miller "had the finest gift of exposition of any academician I have ever listened to at length" (Mitchell 1953, p. 86). In addition to his academic interests, Miller enjoyed music, traveling, horse racing, and farming (he owned a farm outside Santa Cruz).

The 1912 election of Woodrow Wilson resulted in Miller's leaving academic life and entering the hectic world of a government official in Washington, D.C., because Wilson appointed Franklin K. Lane as secretary of interior. Lane, who had been Miller's close friend when both men had been undergraduates at Berkeley, appointed Miller as an assistant secretary of interior in 1913. Miller's primary responsibility was to reform the system of national parks.

With his substantial experience as an academic economist and his more recent work within the Wilson administration, Miller was a logical choice to represent the West Coast on the Federal Reserve Board. At the suggestion of his aide, Colonel House, President Wilson nominated Miller for the ten-year term. The Senate quickly confirmed Miller, who never even testified. Miller and the rest of the board began work on August 10, 1914.

Miller and several other appointive members (Frederic Delano,[*] W. P. G. Harding,[*] and Paul Warburg[*]) considered themselves to be nonpartisan neutral experts who had responsibility for running the monetary system for the public good and not necessarily for the needs of specific private bankers or the Treasury Department. Because the Federal Reserve Act had only vaguely defined the lines of authority within the system, Miller's faction often became embroiled in controversy with the ex officio members (secretary of Treasury and comptroller of the currency), the district banks, and Congress over the board's precise role in the system.

Miller's group ignited a political firestorm in 1915 when they discussed the possibility of merging Federal Reserve districts. The Federal Reserve Act had provided for "not less than eight nor more than twelve" districts; Congress also established an Organization Committee that decided on twelve reserve banks. Miller's group wanted large districts so that each district bank would possess enough capital to meet its responsibilities. Politicians throughout the United States and in Congress, the board's ex officio members (who had been members of the Organization Committee), and district bank officials immediately protested even discussing the issue (no formal plan of reorganization was ever submitted). The U.S. attorney general effectively ended the debate by ruling in November 1915 that the board could not reduce the number of district banks and, in April 1916, that the board could not change the location of bank reserve cities. For Miller, this dispute concerning the board's relationship with the district banks foreshadowed his disputes with the Governors' Committee during the 1920s.

The board's appointive members were already involved in another organizational dispute: the independence of the board from the Treasury Department. Secretary of Treasury William McAdoo always considered the board to be subservient to the Treasury Department and constantly attempted to reduce the status of board members. Although today the disputes over location of meetings (the board met in the Treasury building until 1935 when the Fed obtained its own building) and over the social status of board members may appear petty, Miller's faction wanted to become more independent from the Treasury and they believed that the higher their status was, the more independent of political influences they could be. The first governor, Charles Hamlin,[*] had previously served in Treasury under McAdoo and was personally loyal to him. Although the other appointed members personally liked Hamlin, they advocated regular rotation in the offices of governor and vice-governor to maintain the board's independence. After much controversy, President Wilson, in August 1916, appointed Harding as governor and Warburg as vice-governor.

The U.S. entry into World War I intensified the dispute over monetary policy between McAdoo and the board. Miller disliked McAdoo's policy of financing war borrowing at interest rates below those existing in the bond market; Miller generally favored higher discount rates than did the Treasury Department. However, he refused ultimately to vote against Treasury's position; both contemporaries and later writers criticized Miller for his "capitulation" to the Treasury Department on this issue.

A more generous view of Miller's voting record would emphasize his belief that during wartime, monetary policy could not reallocate resources without seriously damaging the business sector. In "War Finance and Inflation" (1918), he argued that the government must reduce private consumption spending to prevent excess demand from resulting in inflation; relying exclusively on tighter monetary policy to prevent inflation would result in higher interest rates—so high, he contended, that they would more likely reduce productive business investment than consumption. Moreover, he considered the Treasury's policy of relying on calls for patriotism to reduce consumption spending to be ineffective. Instead, Miller preferred a policy of increasing taxes or, second best, a policy of direct controls over consumption.

Before the board and Treasury could agree on wartime policy, the war ended and the board faced a new set of economic problems. During the next several years, Miller struggled to develop an overall view of monetary policy. His view of stabilization policy included the idea that monetary policy could not prevent business recessions; recessions resulted from businesses' working down excess inventories and from a lack of business confidence, resulting in reduced investment spending. The Federal Reserve, by providing an elastic currency, could prevent a recession from causing a financial panic and general depression. Miller argued that only as the recession's momentum ceased could expansionary monetary policy stimulate the economy.

Miller therefore believed that the Fed would have to tolerate some deflation. He also thought that the Fed should accept (temporary) inflation when the economy had unused capacity so that price increases would stimulate production, thereby being self-liquidating. On the other hand, when the economy reached productive capacity, he considered further price increases to be undesirable; the Fed's role was to prevent such inflation.

Because the idea of productive capacity formed a prominent part of his view on proper monetary policy, Miller actively worked to improve the available information on the economy's performance. He was a driving force behind the formation and continued improvement of the Federal Reserve's Division of Research and Statistics. Because he realized that the available data were fragile and that lags existed, he often hesitated in voting for substantial changes in monetary policy.

During the early 1920s, Miller formed his view regarding the role of open market operations in monetary policy. He quickly realized how open market operations could change reserves within the banking system. He and several other board members, however, incorrectly concluded that rediscounting commercial bills would result in banks' making more loans for productive and less for speculative purposes than would purchases of government securities. In other words, they mistakenly thought that the methods by which reserves were injected into the system would determine how those reserves would be used ultimately.

Miller's views concerning open market operations brought him into conflict with his former friend, Benjamin Strong. Primarily because the Treasury Department was concerned about the lack of coordination of district banks' open market operations, the system in spring 1922 established the Committee of Governors on Centralized Execution of Purchases and Sales of Government Securities by Federal Reserve Banks. Strong, through this committee, dominated the coordination of open market policies. Miller infuriated Strong by convincing the board in March 1923 to place jurisdiction over open market operations with the board; Strong was in the West for health reasons, fighting his losing battle with tuberculosis. The board dissolved the existing Governors Committee and established an Open Market Investment Committee with the same membership as the Governors Committee. Although individual banks still legally could buy and sell securities without this committee's approval, this action temporarily enhanced the board's power. Although Strong vigorously protested this action, it probably did not reduce his influence on policy and indeed may have increased it because the change reduced the influence of other district banks. Miller advocated this action because he believed the board worked toward the overall good of the economy and banking system, while district banks' actions were often just motivated by desire for earnings.

By the end of Miller's first decade on the board, he had seen, and had been partially responsible for, the board's increase in stature and power, although disputes concerning responsibilities and control continued among the board, Treasury, and district banks. Miller's ideas on monetary policy had formed the basis of the Fed's policy as outlined in the *Tenth Annual Report* (1924). The Washington establishment respected Miller's work enough that a Republican president, Calvin Coolidge, appointed him in 1924 for another ten-year term; family wealth allowed Miller to continue serving the public rather than having to accept higher-paying jobs in the private sector.

Miller's recommendations during the 1927–1929 period proved to be controversial. In 1927 Strong convinced the system to adopt an easier money policy designed to reduce interest rates, in large part to stem the inflow of gold from Europe. Miller and Strong both accepted the same theory concerning how domestic monetary policies affected gold flows; they also agreed that following World War I, the United States needed to adopt policies that would result in gold flowing from the United States to other countries. In 1927, however, they disagreed on monetary policy because Miller did not believe that European countries were still deficient of gold reserves. Moreover, Miller contended, easy money policies would fuel too much stock speculation.

Miller continued to present a minority point of view within the system until

Strong's death in November 1928. At the time, Miller believed the economy faced two problems: the economy was operating at less than full capacity, and the speculative frenzy on the stock market had reached a dangerous level. He opposed the purchases of government securities because he believed that this would increase speculation in stocks without increasing productive investment. At the same time, he opposed raising the discount rate because business investment was still too weak and a higher rate probably would not discourage the flow of funds into stock speculation. Miller later wrote, "Control by rate action in a speculative gale of such fury as swept the United States in 1929 is a good deal like spitting against the wind"(1935, p. 456).

Miller desired a method to control credit selectively, that is, to direct credit toward "productive" uses and away from the stock market. In this situation, he considered the use of either open market operations or changes in the discount rate to be too blunt of a tool. With the board's not having legal authority for selective credit controls, Miller joined with Hamlin in persuading the board to adopt in January 1929 a policy of "direct pressure"—moral suasion to prevent any further increase in lending by member banks for use of financing stock purchases. Other board members and district banks believed that the policy of direct pressure was ineffective and called for hikes in the discount rate. Miller's adversaries finally prevailed in August 1929; both Miller and Hamlin believed that the policy of direct pressure had succeeded.

Federal Reserve policy did not prevent the stock market from collapsing in October 1929 or the economy from slipping into a recession. During 1930 Miller consistently opposed purchases of government securities for three reasons: his mistaken belief that banks would use reserves acquired that way in speculative activities, concern that high interest rates were necessary to stem gold outflow, and his lack of confidence that monetary policy could prevent an ordinary business recession.

By 1931 Miller came to believe that this was not a typical economic downturn and thus the Fed needed to take a bold stroke. But he was unable to exert enough leadership to convince the board and Open Market Policy Committee to follow his suggestion to increase open market purchases substantially. The economic situation worsened throughout 1932; by early 1933, a nationwide banking crisis threatened. Miller suggested to both the board and Herbert Hoover, a friend and former neighbor, that clearinghouse certificates should be issued and a moratorium or banking holiday should be imposed; the board did not favorably act on these recommendations.

The inauguration as president of Franklin Roosevelt marked the beginning of drastic financial reform within the United States. After Roosevelt's bank holiday restored some stability to the banking system, Congress enacted reform legislation such as the Banking Acts of 1933 and 1935 and the Securities and Exchange Acts of 1933 and 1934. Although Miller had been a friend of Roosevelt since Roosevelt's stint as naval secretary, apparently Miller did not play a direct role in the formulation of Roosevelt's reform efforts. On the other hand, many reforms were consistent with Miller's long-held beliefs of creating a strong, central bank. The newly formed Board of Governors did not include the ex officio members; it did control district banks. The Open Market Committee controlled all purchases and sales of securities for the entire system. Congress also provided the board with several selective credit controls, such as the ability to set margins on loans for stock purchases.

Having served for over two decades on the board, Miller was not appointed to the new Board of Governors. Although Roosevelt was inclined to appoint his old friend, Roosevelt's choice for chair of the board, Marriner Eccles,[*] convinced the president that the only procedure fair to all members of the previous board was not to appoint any of them to the new board.

After retirement, Miller and his wife continued to live in Washington and to play an active role in the city's cultural life. He served as a member of the building committee for the Federal Reserve Building and on the board of the Library of Congress Trust Fund. In 1940 the University of California gave him an honorary LL.D. degree. Adolph C. Miller died in Washington on February 2, 1953. His wife died four years later.

Adolph Miller was actively involved in the development of monetary policy between 1914 and 1935. He was influential in providing institutional content to the newly formed Federal Reserve system. His logical and analytical approach contributed much to the discussions of monetary policy.

It is more difficult to obtain a clear picture of Adolph Miller the person, in part because most of the existing portraits were drawn by his critics, such as Hamlin, McAdoo, and Strong. Even these men conceded that Miller was intelligent, a "capable critic and consultant," and charming outside the Federal Reserve's boardroom. They contended, however, that he lacked leadership abilities and tended to be verbose and inconsistent. Felix Frankfurter, the Supreme Court justice, more warmly remembered his long-time friend and fellow patron of the arts:

He infused private lives with his own high standards and his feeling for the arts, our public affairs with his disinterestedness and courage. A man of wide reading and avid learning, he knew the difference between knowledge and wisdom. . . . As such, he served under five presidents. . . . With at least three of these he was on intimate personal terms; they drew upon his counsel in good season and bad. To all he gave that rarest aspect of devotion to the presidential office—courageous candor. To each he told, with surgeon-like truthfulness, exactly what he believed, however, unwelcome his analysis and explication of complex issues may have been, and of course always with exquisite courtesy. (Frankfurter 1956, pp. 323–24)

BIBLIOGRAPHY

Federal Reserve Board. 1924. *Tenth Annual Report of the Federal Reserve Board*. Washington, D.C.: Government Printing Office.

Frankfurter, Felix. 1956. *Of Law and Men*. New York: Harcourt.

Miller, A. C. 1895. "National Finance and the Income Tax." *Journal of Political Economy* (June): 255–88.

———. 1902. "Fiscal Reciprocity." *Journal of Political Economy* (March): 255–58.

———. 1908. "The Conversion of the English Debt." *Quarterly Journal of Economics* (July): 437–48.

———. 1918. "War Finance and Inflation." *Annals of the American Academy of Political and Social Science* (January): 113–34.

———. 1919. "After War Readjustment: Rectifying the Price Situation." *Annals of the American Academy of Political and Social Science* (March): 306–22.

———. 1935. "Responsibility for Federal Reserve Policies: 1927–29." *American Economic Review* (September): 442–58.

Mitchell, Lucy Sprague. 1953. *Two Lives: The Story of Wesley Clair Mitchell and Myself*. New York: Simon and Schuster.

G. WILLIAM MILLER (1925–   )

Marie McKinney

On December 8, 1977, President Jimmy Carter surprised many Washington insiders by nominating G. William Miller to replace Arthur Burns* as chairman of the Board of Governors of the Federal Reserve system. The announcement was greeted with enthusiasm by labor leaders and the business community where, as chief executive officer of Textron, Miller enjoyed a reputation as a dynamic and capable corporate leader. Other constituencies questioned the president's choice. They cited as liabilities Miller's lack of experience in the conduct of monetary policy and his eagerness to stimulate the economy. As 1977 drew to a close, inflation threatened to swamp a foundering business recovery, while unemployment remained uncomfortably high at almost 7 percent. Critics cautioned that an unseasoned, pro-growth chairman was the wrong person to guide monetary policy prudently through the remaining years of the Carter administration.

Miller responded to his critics with élan. He was confident he would be able to learn the ropes quickly enough to ensure economic stability. As testimony concluded on January 24, 1978, the first day of the Senate confirmation hearings, Miller declared that his goal as chairman of the Federal Reserve board was to be named Rookie of the Year. Miller's goal was never realized. When he left the Fed to become Treasury secretary in July 1979, after slightly over a year in office, inflation measured by the consumer price index had reached double-digit levels and threatened to accelerate. Miller's policies were felt by many to be too soft on inflation and had been challenged at Federal Open Market Committee meetings by several fellow committee members, including Paul Volcker,* then president of the New York Fed and soon to be named chairman of the Board of Governors to replace Miller. Most seriously, many accused Miller of sacrificing Fed independence to accommodate the political priorities of the Carter administration.

In retrospect, an examination of Miller's historic positions reveals a distinct bias toward expansionary policies and a deep suspicion regarding the pernicious effects of tight money on financial markets. Clearly any expectations that Miller would be a serious inflation fighter while chairman of the Board of Governors were bound to be disappointed.

Based on his past record of success, Miller had reason to be optimistic regarding his ability to promote economic growth through his position as a member of the Washington economic policymaking establishment. By 1977 Miller had accumulated a strong record of personal and business achievement. At the time of his nomination, he was the chairman of the board of the Textron Corporation, a large manufacturing conglomerate headquartered in Providence, Rhode Island, where he was known as an able administrator and an astute corporate strategist. In his private life, he played an active role in public sector employment initiatives, and he had the enthusiastic support of the Rhode Island business and political communities.

Although Miller spent most of his adult life on the East Coast, he grew up in the Southwest. He was born on March 9, 1925, in Sapula, Oklahoma, to James Dick and Hazel Deane (Orrick) Miller. Soon after his birth, the family moved to Borger, Texas. Like many other teenagers during the depression, Miller often worked to supplement the family income. He attended Amarillo Junior College and then was appointed to attend the U.S. Coast Guard Academy in New London, Connecticut, where he earned a degree in marine engineering. He served a four-year tour of duty as a line officer in the Far East with assignments in Okinawa and Shanghai. It was in Shanghai that he met his wife, the former Ariadna Rogojarsky. They were married in December 1946.

When he returned to the United States, Miller enrolled in law school at the University of California at Berkeley where he graduated at the top of his class in 1952. He was an editor of the *California Law Review* and was described as an outstanding student. Success followed Miller to New York City, where he began his corporate career at Cravath, Swaine, and Moore, a Wall Street law firm.

After spending several years at the law firm, Miller joined Textron. Originally the company had been a producer of textiles. Its chairman, Royal Little, had initiated a program of diversification and acquisition that transformed a local firm into a Fortune 500 company. Miller was introduced to Little and Textron in the mid–1950s when Miller was working for Cravath, Swaine, and Moore, which had been engaged by Textron to help fight a proxy battle over the American Woolen Company. Shortly after, in 1956, Miller joined Textron and rose rapidly in the corporate organization. By 1977, under Miller's stewardship, Textron had become the eighty-third largest company on the Fortune 500 list, with 65,000 employees and $2.6 billion in sales.

Miller believed that commercial success brought social obligations. To Miller a business organization was more than a profit-making endeavor. As he told the National Council on the Humanities in 1967, it was the responsibility of business leaders to promote human and spiritual values to improve the community in which they live and work. Miller followed up on his commitment by participating in many public and private initiatives to foster these values. His special concern

was in the area of promoting meaningful employment opportunities for the
disadvantaged. He served on John F. Kennedy's Committee on Equal Employment Opportunities and later chaired the National Alliance of Businessmen, an
organization concerned with providing jobs for minorities. He also worked in
the Labor Department's Help Through Industry Retraining and Employment
(HIRE) program, designed to provide jobs for 100,000 returning Vietnam
veterans.

His leadership and contributions extended to the political sphere. Miller was
active in Democratic politics. He was an enthusiastic supporter of Rhode Island
senator Claiborne Pell. In 1966 he chaired Pell's reelection committee and in
1968 served as the chairman for Businessmen for Humphrey-Muskie. Many
Rhode Islanders felt he would have made an excellent governor for the state,
but the job never interested him. While a resident of Rhode Island, Miller served
on the board of the Rhode Island Hospital Trust Company and as a class B
director for the Federal Reserve Bank of Boston.

With this background, it would appear that Miller had demonstrated the potential for becoming a valued public servant. The chairmanship of the Fed offered
him the opportunity to use his administrative skills to make a valuable contribution to the public sector. As events unfolded, however, it proved difficult for
Miller to fulfill these expectations. The issues appeared early as observers questioned his economics training, and in the first day of confirmation hearings,
questions were raised concerning his personal and business ethics.

The nomination itself was interpreted by political observers as a sign that
Carter was looking for a Fed chairman who would be soft on inflation. As 1977
drew to a close, it had become clear to observers that Fed chairman Arthur
Burn's* anti-inflation policy initiatives increasingly conflicted with the expansionary policies of the Carter administration and that it was unlikely that Carter
would reappoint Burns for another term as chairman. Despite an uncomfortably
high unemployment rate, gross national product continued to grow steadily
throughout the year, and new jobs were being created. Despite several years of
economic growth and steady increases in total employment, the unemployment
rate was above 6 percent as the country neared the peak of the business cycle.
The administration did not want to threaten the continued expansion with tight
money, anti-inflation measures that Burns suggested before "full employment"
was reached. In a speech delivered on October 4, 1977, Charles Schultz, chairman of the president's Council of Economic Advisers, openly criticized Burns's
tight monetary policy.

The announcement that Burns would be replaced came as no surprise; what
was surprising was the appointment of Miller, an outsider. Press speculation had
focused on names such as Paul Volcker,* president of the New York City Federal
Reserve Bank and a long-time member of the Federal Open Market Committee;
Andrew Brimmer,* a former Fed governor and a respected economic consultant;
and Arthur Okun, a well-known economist and adviser to several Democratic
presidents. Instead President Carter choose G. William Miller, a corporate ex-

ecutive, a noneconomist from outside the traditional Washington circles, a man likely to be sympathetic to Carter's pro-growth policies.

Despite the surprise, reaction to Miller was largely favorable, although a few questioned his lack of economic training and policy experience. As chairman of Textron, Miller had a reputation as an able and forward-looking leader in the business community. Over the years, his economic views had appeared in the business press in periodicals such as *Forbes*, *Fortune*, and *Business Week*. His opinion was respected by the readers of those periodicals. Miller had also been active in public service, especially in programs to promote employment among the disadvantaged, minorities, and Vietnam veterans. Although some labeled him a rookie, others, like Senator Pell of Rhode Island, felt his practical experience in business and his reputation for excellence would help him overcome this handicap.

The honeymoon was brief. The Senate Banking Committee opened the confirmation hearings on January 24, 1978, and the hearings lasted for an unprecedented five weeks. The opening questions dealt with Miller's economic philosophy and potential policy positions. The experience issue surfaced early in the proceedings as Senator William Proxmire (D, Wisconsin) expressed concern that Miller's lack of experience with monetary policy would mean that there was too much learning on the job to be done. Miller would quickly have to become knowledgeable about a wide spectrum of issues: how the economy responds to credit expansion and contraction; the mechanics of international monetary policy; bank and bank holding company regulations; and consumer credit regulations. Proxmire said he wanted a man capable of moving right into the job, a man who would not have to learn from his mistakes. Others, such as John Anderson, chairman of the House Republican Conference, raised the issue of Fed independence. He noted that although Miller generally gave lip-service to the idea of Fed independence, on several occasions he had also expressed the view that there should be a congruence of fiscal and monetary policies. Anderson found these positions inconsistent. Congruence could easily be interpreted to mean capitulation.

Miller was questioned regarding his statement that the Federal Reserve could fight unemployment and inflation simultaneously. Exactly how he would accomplish this feat Miller would not or could not say. In the hearings, Miller admitted he was not an expert on the Fed. Further, he believed that the most effective tools for fighting inflation were outside the Fed's control: capital investment, reduced federal deficits, and lower energy costs. The role of monetary policy in combating inflation was not clearly defined in Miller's mind.

Even with these major questions regarding the adequacy of Miller's experience and his positions on policy left unanswered, the committee shifted focus and zeroed in on a $2.9 million payment that Bell Helicopter (a Textron subsidiary) had made to a sales representative from Iran. The payments were linked to an Iranian military official and member of the Iranian ruling family. Miller firmly maintained that he was unaware of the payment, but the introduction of this line of questioning permanently shifted the focus of the hearings from economic issues to Miller's integrity and ethics as a businessman.

Three volumes and 2,932 pages of testimony later, Miller's nomination was cleared by the committee on March 2. The final vote was 14 to 1. Of the members of the Senate committee, only Senator Proxmire withheld his support. On March 8, 1978, Miller was sworn into office to succeed David M. Lilly* as a member of the board and Arthur Burns as chairman.

Senator John Sparkman (D, Alabama) described the committee's work as one of the toughest investigations he ever witnessed. To Senator Don Riegle (D, Michigan), it was a no-holds-barred investigation that failed to produce any evidence to contradict Miller's assertions that he knew nothing about the payments.

Although Miller emerged with his integrity intact, the diversion may have served as a smokescreen, obscuring the issues of experience and economic objectives. At a time when inflation threatened to undermine the economy, it appeared that the Senate received no clear idea about how the country could expect Miller to conduct monetary policy. Like the captain of a spacecraft or the pilot of an airplane, the director of monetary policy must understand the internal workings of his vehicle. The Senate failed to follow up on these questions in favor of those concerning suspected payments to foreign officials. The result was that they never resolved the question of how Miller would conduct monetary policy or, indeed, whether he could conduct monetary policy effectively.

In earlier speeches and interviews, Miller had given every indication that he would avoid policies that inhibited economic expansion, even at the cost of inflation. He said he believed that the inflation-unemployment trade-off could be managed to achieve both stable prices and lower unemployment. During the hearings, however, he avoided any specific commitment relative to how he would conduct monetary policy in specific situations.

Although Miller's views were not established with certainty at the time he assumed office, his past public statements indicated he would want to shift the Fed role from one of inflation fighter to promoter of long-term economic growth. In 1974 Miller had been highly critical of Arthur Burns's policy of restraint (considered excessive restraint by some). In the light of this position, it seems obvious that Miller would be unlikely to wage a strong battle against inflation if the result threatened substantial job loss or a reversal in national income growth. These views were confirmed in his early statements to Congress. In the spring of 1978, Miller predicted continued moderate expansion of economic activity. Although he recognized the existence of inflationary pressures, he implied he would not use restrictive or rigid monetary policy directives to threaten the long-run performance of the economy. According to Miller, an overly restrictive monetary policy would run the risk of "serious market disruption and economic dislocation."

This position is unusual among central bankers who, in the words of an earlier Fed chairman, had the responsibility for taking away the punch bowl just when the party gets going. In contrast, Miller personally felt the nation's strongest inflation-fighting tools lay outside the province of the Federal Reserve. In his opinion, the Fed should pursue policies to encourage investment while other, more appropriate, means should be used to fight inflation. He saw the causes of inflation in the spiral of rising unit labor costs driven up by higher wages (including a raise in the minimum wage) and higher employer costs for social security. Other causes he cited included farm price supports, import restrictions, a decline in the dollar (which caused import prices to rise), and finally inflationary psychology. He saw these as the causes of inflation, not their manifestations, and therefore did not feel monetary policy presented an effective tool for fighting inflation. He was highly suspicious of monetarists and their recommendations for the conduct of monetary policy. Instead he suggested cuts in government spending, reduction of social security taxes, and restraint in the growth of federal salaries. He rejected measures that would result in credit shortages. In the words of one business publication, he chose to protect credit markets rather than use them as vehicles to slow inflation.

Even with high nominal interest rates and a shortage of mortgage money, in mid–1978 it appeared that Miller and his colleagues at the Fed might take a firm stand against inflation, even if it meant a slight recession. Carter was encouraged to trim and postpone his proposed tax rebate on the grounds that it might fuel further inflation.

At the same time, however, Miller warned the Senate Budget Committee that a more restrictive monetary policy would jeopardize private financial markets and risk serious market dislocations. Miller stated that private capital spending must be encouraged in order to promote employment and productivity and to ensure American competitiveness. Reduction of the federal deficit and implementation of appropriate investment tax policy would channel private saving into capital investment and encourage firms to expand. As late as May 1978, Miller was predicting an inflation rate of about 6 percent for the coming year.

On April 25, 1978, Miller addressed the Senate Committee on Banking, Housing, and Urban Affairs. Despite the fact that he recognized the inflationary threat and believed there was little reason to be optimistic about reducing inflation in the near future, he felt restrictive monetary policy should be used only with great caution to ensure that credit remained in reasonably good supply. Inflationary pressures, he explained, were embedded in the structure of the economy. Monetary policy, he reasoned, could attack these "causes" only at a great social cost, if at all.

Miller's approach to monetary policy was unorthodox, as was his approach to management of the Board of Governors and the Fed bureaucracy. As the public spokesman for the Fed, the chairman plays a substantial role in determining the direction of monetary policy. He sets the agenda, structures the conduct of meetings, and ultimately fashions the motions that are subject to vote. Unless there exists substantial disagreement, the Fed governors and other members of the Federal Open Market Committee (FOMC) follow his lead.

Miller attempted to introduce a more efficient corporate style of management to the conduct of Federal Reserve meetings. Scholarly debates were discouraged in favor of the swift completion of business. Meetings became shorter. There were more charts and fewer detailed documents. The number of regular weekly meetings was reduced from three to two. Miller also wanted to delegate more authority to the regional banks. Not all of these innovations were greeted with enthusiasm by his fellow policymakers at the Fed.

On the whole, Miller enjoyed amicable relations with Congress except for one run-in over exercise of Fed authority. During the 1970s the Federal Reserve system was increasingly concerned with attrition of member banks; member banks were leaving the Fed in alarming numbers (sixty-nine banks in 1977 alone), and new banks were failing to join. The reason for the decline in membership centered around the requirement that member banks keep substantial reserves in the form of vault cash on noninterest-bearing accounts at the Fed. As rising interest rates increased the opportunity cost of idle assets, member banks began to feel they operated at a competitive disadvantage with other nonmember depository institutions and withdrew from the Fed in increasing numbers. Miller concluded that one solution to the problem would be to pay interest on the deposits of Fed member banks. This remedy had been suggested before but faced stiff opposition in Congress. Miller proposed that the Fed sidestep Congress and change the rules on its own authority. This stance negatively affected Miller's heretofore congenial relations with Congress and was ultimately abandoned.

Meanwhile, there were strong indications that Miller's cautious efforts at restricting money growth were inadequate to stop price increases. During the year that followed his appointment, inflation continued to accelerate despite a steady rise in the targeted federal funds rate (from 6 ½ percent in February 1978 to 10 ½ percent in May 1979) and the announced intentions to slow the rate in money supply growth. In retrospect, it is clear that the rising interest rates were in nominal terms only and that, in fact, during portions of the period, real interest rates were negative.

Monetary growth regularly exceeded the Fed's monetary targets during this period by over 15 percent (the discrepancy was in part disguised because the Fed systematically adjusted the base from which it calculated the increase). On the surface, there was an appearance of a contractionary monetary policy, but this belied the substance of expansionary monetary policy. During the spring of 1978, for example, bank loans were rising at an annual rate of 22.5 percent. This anomaly was recognized by some FOMC members such as John Wiles who, as early as May 1978, voted against policy recommendations on the grounds that slowing inflation required more rigorous actions to restrain monetary growth. Wiles later would be joined by other board members as the rate of inflation increased and the time of Miller's departure from the Fed drew near.

By late summer 1978, growing U.S. inflation threatened to sink the dollar. World currency markets, alarmed by the central bank's lukewarm efforts to restrict inflation, added to the Fed's dilemma. In response, Miller proposed voluntary wage and price guidelines to slow inflation and stabilize the dollar, again symptomatic of his reluctance to use monetary policy to fight inflation. The dollar continued to fall.

In October 1978 the Fed raised the discount rate from 7 percent to 7 1/4 percent. Miller voted against the measure. He intended to keep a firm control on interest rates and speculated that if the Fed had relinquished control over interest rates in 1974, rates would have risen to 20 percent. Miller was not about to sabotage credit markets during his tenure in office.

In November 1978 the discount rate was increased by an additional 1 percent. Michael Blumenthal, the Treasury secretary, not Miller, made the announcement. In his testimony before the Senate Committee on Banking, Housing, and Urban Affairs on November 16, Miller noted that real interest rates were still not high and that credit remained adequate, and he stated that the intention of the Fed was to work for gradual change. He pointed out that a significant change in growth rates would require substantially higher interest rates, which would unacceptably risk damaging the financial markets. At this point his inflation estimate for 1979 was low, at 6 3/4 to 7 1/2 percent.

By year end, it was recognized by many that William Miller was not going to convert from his pro-growth economic philosophy to the religion of tight money (and become a serious inflation fighter). Miller himself told a *Fortune* reporter that he would run the Fed for human beings and would not use monetary policy to create a recession. Early in 1979 he told Congress that growing inflation was an urgent concern, but he favored a policy directed at fostering slow and steady economic growth as most appropriate to fight inflation in the long run. He recommended ''patience'' and ''prudence'' to guide policy initiatives.

As inflation continued to surge in 1979, more FOMC members voted against Miller's policy recommendations. Even members of Carter's own economic team of advisers suggested a tougher stand, especially Treasury Secretary Michael Blumenthal, who was concerned with continued erosion of the value of the dollar. Meanwhile, Miller continued to demonstrate sympathy with Carter's no-recession position, engendering talk of too much cooperation between the Fed and the White House. Rumors surfaced that Miller himself would seek the Democratic nomination for president in 1988.

In his final report to Congress as Fed chairman on July 17, 1979, Miller continued to advise against strong anti-inflationary measures and conceded that economic slowdowns meant that any progress toward price stability would be delayed.

Lack of consensus on economic policy in the Carter administration was obvious. During a much-publicized weekend at Camp David, Carter engaged in a soul-searching reevaluation of his agenda. The result was the firing of four cabinet secretaries, including Secretary Blumenthal. Reportedly Blumenthal was not regarded as a team player by many in the administration, who felt that he had been too aggressive in his criticism of administration actions to control inflation and shore up the dollar. On July 19, 1979, Miller resigned from the Fed to become Carter's Treasury secretary.

With Blumenthal's portfolio, Miller inherited his position as the official economic spokesperson for the administration. At this time, Charles Schultz, chairman of the Council of Economic Advisers, and Otto Khan, head of the Wage and Price Administration, were silent regarding policy. It became Miller's job to step in, put the team back together, and lead it. One suspects Miller felt more at home in this role. His first attempt at leadership involved the Chrysler bailout. He proposed that the government guarantee private sector loans instead of the tax relief plan originally proposed.

Miller faced many problems during his tenure at Treasury, including worsening inflation accompanied by high unemployment and rising oil prices. He was the administrator who impounded Iranian assets in U.S. banks and later worked with Carter for the release of the American hostages being held in Iran.

When one compares Miller's record of achievement in the private sector with what must have been a challenging but ultimately disappointing term in the public sector, one wonders if perhaps he was placed in the wrong position at the wrong time. Miller was in a job that failed to take advantage of his strengths. A careful examination of his record should have made it clear to Congress that his economic philosophy would make it impossible for him to be an inflation fighter. Miller advocated pro-growth policies when he was nominated and remained an advocate of growth during his tenure in office.

In order to understand Miller's policy positions as Fed chairman, it is helpful to examine his economic philosophy—the views he held on economics and the economy as he entered the job. These views were well formed and generally accessible before his nomination. Some appeared in print, and others were outlined in several speeches that gained him national recognition. By examining these records in the context of Miller's business and public sector experience, we get a clear picture of his philosophy.

During the first stagflation crisis, *Business Week* published an article under Miller's byline describing his views on the government's role in reducing inflation (October 5, 1974, p. 16). Miller seriously questioned the efficacy of the traditional tools of monetary and fiscal policy (control of the monetary aggregates and reduction of government spending) to reduce inflation. He felt that the resultant unemployment and economic hardship were too high a welfare cost to pay for stable prices. He rejected any kind of general credit control in favor of selective measures such as a surcharge on loans for low-priority purposes.

In January 1977 he delivered a much-quoted speech before the Traffic Club of Pittsburgh in which he discussed the simultaneous attainment of full employment and price stability. In this speech, he rejected the notion of a trade-off between inflation and unemployment. He stated his belief that accepting higher rates of unemployment would not lower the inflation rate. Because of transfer payments such as welfare benefits and unemployment insurance, individuals were insulated and would not accept lower wages if threatened with job loss. Thus, a recession, he reasoned, would not be effective in reducing inflation. Further, transfer payments would prop up aggregate demand levels and counteract any reduction in demand caused by reduced economic activity.

Miller believed strongly in the free enterprise system. The government, he believed, should play only a limited role in the economy, mainly to create a stable and supportive environment for business where it could operate with a minimum of uncertainty. These influences resulted in an economic philosophy that was unorthodox by textbook standards. Miller's priorities were directed toward long-term growth and job and capital creation. He viewed policy as the aggregate of individual actions.

When comparing the welfare losses attributable to unemployment and inflation, Miller firmly believed that the losses due to unemployment were a more serious threat to welfare. If a policymaker were forced to take a risk with respect to the economy, Miller felt he should favor the risk of inflation over the risk of unemployment. He believed the nation should not have to suffer to control inflation. He also believed that such methods were not politically viable.

Miller was an optimist who felt the nation did not have to choose between inflation and unemployment. With sufficient capital investment and employee training, increased production could be achieved at lower costs as opposed to increased costs, which would translate to inflation. Perhaps his ideas came from his experience with the individual firm as it experienced economies of scale. Miller was also a believer in cost cutting through increased investment. These principles may not be transferable to the aggregate economy as it reaches high levels of capacity utilization. Backlogs and capacity restriction are most often seen in the very industries that supply capital equipment; labor shortages are first experienced in highly skilled professions where training of additional workers takes a long time. Although, in principle, Miller conceded that these bottlenecks must be addressed, he did not describe how this could be done.

Miller was only the second businessman to occupy the position of Federal Reserve board chairman. He viewed the economy from the eyes of a businessman with a concern for productivity, growth, and expanded employment opportunities. He believed that economic policy should focus on the parts, not the aggregate. The whole would automatically improve—a modern invisible hand, as it were.

In retrospect, Miller lacked the instincts of a true disciple of the dismal science. He was unprepared to accept responsibility for the trade-offs involved in carrying out anti-inflationary economic measures. He did not acknowledge the need for a unifying theory of economic behavior and activity, which would have been required for him to implement effective aggregate policies. Because he failed to distinguish between the symptoms of inflation and its underlying causes, he was unable to formulate a comprehensive and effective Federal Reserve strategy to fight inflation.

Miller's lack of experience in the field of economic policy was raised as an

issue at his confirmation hearings but brushed aside in favor of questions regarding his personal integrity and business ethics. The deciding issue became
integrity rather than appropriate economic experience. Miller's unwillingness to
deal firmly with inflation should have been clear at the hearings and his actions
as chairman of the Federal Reserve board predictable.

After leaving government service, Miller remained in Washington, where he
became active in the venture capital industry. He is a founder and partner in G.
William Miller & Co. Inc., a venture capital firm that specializes in corporate
turnarounds focused on firms in declining industries. Miller's firm provides
assistance in obtaining financing for troubled companies, and he serves as a
management consultant in exchange for equity positions.

BIBLIOGRAPHY

Miller, G. William. 1974. "A Businessman's Anti-inflation Formula." *Business Week*,
    October 5.
————. 1977. "The Not Impossible Goal." *Vital Speeches of the Day*, March 15. Speech
    delivered before the Traffic Club of Pittsburgh, January 27, 1977.
Moritz, Charles, ed. 1978. *Current Biography Yearbook*. New York: H. W. Wilson
    Company.
U.S. Congress. Senate. Committee on Banking, Housing, and Urban Affairs. 1978.
    Nomination of G. William Miller. 95th Cong., 2d sess., January 24.

PAUL EMMERT MILLER (1888–1954)

Bernard S. Katz

Appointed as a governor of the Federal Reserve board by President Eisenhower in July 1954, Paul E. Miller took the oath of office on August 13, 1954. His appointment was to fill the remainder of the unexpired term of Rudolph M. Evans,* who left the Fed after some twelve years of service. After being in office for only a little more than two months, the new governor passed away in his home in Montgomery County, Maryland, on the morning of October 21, 1954, from an apparent heart attack.

Born in Cedar Rapids, Iowa, on October 30, 1888, the son on Jacob Kurtz and Ida M. (Bluebaugh), Miller attended Iowa State College, graduating with a B.S. degree in 1911. Upon graduation, he joined the faculty of the University of Minnesota West Central School of Agriculture and Experiment Station in Morris, Minnesota, as an instructor in agronomy. While teaching at the university, Miller married Margaret Jones on June 23, 1914, in Manchester, Iowa. They were to have three sons: John, Edward, and Paul.

In 1917 Miller was appointed professor and superintendent of the West Central School in which he began his teaching career. While at West Central, Miller also attended Iowa State College. He graduated in 1921 and was granted a master of science degree in agriculture. He was to attain one more degree, an honorary doctor of economic science in 1951 from the National University of Ireland, undoubtedly the result of his activities as agricultural consultant for the Organization for European Economic Cooperation in 1950 and as chief of the Economic Cooperation Administration Special Mission to Ireland (1950–1951).

While at the West Central School in the 1930s and during the drought and depression that severely affected the farming community at that time, Miller took an active interest in farm credit. This concern culminated in his appointment as Minnesota's drought relief chairman in 1934.

In 1938 Miller was appointed professor and director of the University of Minnesota's Agricultural Extension Service in St. Paul. In 1943 he was appointed a director of the Federal Reserve bank in Minneapolis. (He also served as a member of the board of directors of the Federal Land Bank of St. Paul from

1946 to 1949.) By 1954, the year of his appointment to the Board of Governors, Miller had risen to become chairman of the Minneapolis Fed.

While central banking was not a part of Miller's early life or plans, his extensive agricultural education and experience, his expressed interest in farm credit, and his years in government service and at the Federal reserve bank all combined to groom him for the nomination to the position of governor to the Federal Reserve board. Another reason that may have supported his nomination, aside from his lifelong Republican party affiliation, was that at the time of his nomination during the Eisenhower administration, the board lacked an expert in agriculture, which it must have as mandated by law. Miller's nomination and appointment filled this gap.

Miller was by no means a partisan political appointment. He was, by training and nature, an agriculturist with a strong concern for the well-being of farmers. This was clearly pointed out in his nomination hearings.

The Committee on Banking and Currency, the committee that would pass on Miller's nomination, met on August 2, 1954. The first question posed to Miller by the committee's chairman, Senator Homer E. Capehart, was quite pointed: "What is your position on bank holding company legislation?" Miller's answer was similarly open, honest, direct, and in keeping with his strict agricultural background: "Mr. Chairman, I don't believe—it may be foolish to say this—I have any." The committee shortly went into executive session, and Miller's appointment was passed.

Miller's death in October 1954 ended a successful career as educator, agriculturist, and banker, a career expressly concerned with the well-being of small farmers and of the nation.

BIBLIOGRAPHY

U.S. Congress. Senate. Committee on Banking and Currency. 1954. *Nomination of Paul E. Miller. Hearing*. 83d Cong., 2d sess., August 2, pp. 1–3.

U.S. News & World Report. 1954. August 6, p. 14.

Who's Who in America, 1954–55. Vol. 28. Chicago: A. N. Marquis.

ABBOT LOW MILLS, JR. (1898–1986)

Thomas J. Pierce

Abbot Low Mills, Jr., a governor of the Federal Reserve from February 1952 to February 1965, was born at the close of the nineteenth century to a Portland, Oregon, family prominent in local banking, civic, and political circles. His father was a Brooklyn native who had moved west after earning a bachelor's degree from Harvard in 1881. With a business associate, Mills, Sr., formed a private banking firm in Colfax, Washington, in 1885. Disposing of that interest in 1890, he relocated to Portland, where he continued his banking career, becoming president of the First National Bank of Portland in 1903, an office he held for twenty-four years. As one of the leading bankers in the Pacific Northwest, Mills, Sr., was a director of the Portland branch of the Federal Reserve Bank of San Francisco in 1917–1918 and served on the regional committee of the Federal Reserve Board's Capital Issues Committee, which was established during World War I to ensure adequate supplies of credit to war-related industries. He also was the Twelfth District's representative to the Federal Advisory Council from 1919 to 1921. In addition to his banking pursuits, Mills, Sr., was a prominent Republican, elected to the Oregon House of Representatives in 1904 and serving as Speaker of the House in 1905.

Given his father's banking endeavors, Abbot Mills, Jr.'s, career path, in retrospect, is not surprising. After spending his childhood years in Portland, Mills attended Middlesex School in Concord, Massachusetts, and later enrolled at Harvard. He served briefly in the U.S. Army during World War I as a second lieutenant stationed in Georgia. His bachelor's degree from Harvard was awarded in 1921. Mills, Jr.'s, banking career commenced in October 1920 when he accepted a messenger's position at his father's bank. Moving through the ranks, he subsequently served as assistant cashier and vice-president, developing expertise in credit.

In 1924 Mills married Katherine Ainsworth. They raised two girls and two boys. Theirs was also a marriage of banking interests. Katherine's father was president and then chairman of the board of the U.S. National Bank of Portland. In 1933 Mills left First National for an assistant vice-presidency at U.S. National, becoming a vice-president two years later. He was first vice-president at the time of his appointment to the Federal Reserve Board.

On January 23, 1952, President Harry Truman nominated Mills for appointment to the Board of Governors to complete the unexpired portion of Marriner Eccles's[*] fourteen-year term, which began February 1, 1944. Amid the Treasury-Fed controversy regarding interest rate pegging in the wake of World War II, Eccles's push for Fed independence appears to have been a major factor in Truman's decision to deny his reappointment as chairman in 1948. Eccles continued as a board member until July 1951, a few months after the announcement of the Treasury–Federal Reserve Accord. His replacement was confirmed by the Senate without objection on February 6, 1952. Mills took the oath of office on February 18, beginning his six-year term at an annual salary of $16,000.

The February 1 confirmation hearings before the Subcommittee on Federal Reserve Matters of the Senate Committee on Banking and Currency, at which James L. Robertson's[*] nomination also was considered, were brief and uneventful. The only substantive question asked of Mills was whether he looked upon the Fed as a government agency that should work in cooperation with, not subordinate to, the Treasury in managing the national debt. He responded affirmatively. Senator Paul Douglas, noted University of Chicago economist-turned-politician, grilled Robertson on the same issue, given the latter's nineteen years of experience at the Treasury Department, but asked nothing of Mills. Aside from Douglas's concerns about Robertson's ability to exercise independent judgment on monetary matters, the subcommittee seemed satisfied, if not enamored, with the nominees' qualifications. Capturing the subcommittee's sentiments, chairman A. Willis Robertson remarked that the president's nominations were "better than usual."

In serving the remaining six years of Marriner Eccles's term through early 1958, there is little direct evidence of Mills's performance. Minutes of 1953 Federal Open Market Committee (FOMC) meetings indicate his advocacy of the bills-only policy, which limited Fed intervention in the government securities market to transactions in short-term Treasuries. Doing so, the majority of FOMC members contended, would focus open market operations on the objectives of monetary policy as opposed to achieving a specific pattern of interest rates in the government securities market. As the "nearest thing to money," Treasury bills were deemed the appropriate object of the Fed's attention. With the exception of the bills-only controversy, there was a remarkable degree of unanimity in board and FOMC voting on monetary policy matters during the mid–1950s. Thus, the record tells little of Mills's individual contribution to Fed decision making.

The February 1958 confirmation hearings following his nomination by President Eisenhower for a new fourteen-year term as governor, however, provided clear evidence of on-the-job training in monetary theory and policy during the previous six years. When Senator William Proxmire of Wisconsin asked why prices continued to rise rapidly in the presence of contractionary measures by the Fed, Mills noted that households had accumulated large stocks of liquid assets over the past decade, which fueled consumer demand despite credit tightening efforts by the Fed. In response to Paul Douglas's inquiry as to why prices had not fallen in 1957 when the economy grew faster than the money supply, Mills discussed the behavior of velocity. When Douglas questioned the efficacy of expansionary monetary policy, citing the 1930s as a time when reserve expansion and interest rate reduction produced little new lending, Mills explained that expansionary measures work "as long as there is a spirit of confidence and a reasonable willingness for venture-taking," conceding that public attitudes and psychology affect the outcome of discretionary policy measures.

In addition to explaining capably the theoretical underpinnings of Fed policy as understood at the time, Mills also emphasized the responsibility of board members to approach monetary policymaking in an objective, nonpartisan manner when Senator Richard Neuberger, a fellow Oregonian, made an unscheduled appearance to discuss with Mills their home state's 12.8 percent unemployment rate, the nation's highest. Noting the widely held conception that Federal Reserve policies were substantially responsible for Oregon's plight, Neuberger asked if Mills felt any special responsibility to devise policies that would mitigate the situation. Mills responded that a Federal Reserve board governor's duties "must be performed and fulfilled without . . . favoritism to any particular geographic area or to any particular sector of economic activity no matter how sentimentally dear or close it might be to you" (U.S. Congress 1958, p. 14).

Since commitment to independent judgment has traditionally been a key element of the Federal Reserve's persona, Mills's testimony to that effect might be considered a pat restatement of standard party line. His voting record from 1958 to 1965, however, shows he was indeed a strong-willed, independent thinker. From November 4, 1959, through February 9, 1960, he cast the only dissenting votes at six consecutive FOMC meetings, always favoring easier monetary and credit conditions. At the seventh meeting, the committee voted unanimously to ease, though that action subsequently proved insufficient to avoid recession. Between November 1963 and March 1964, Mills again crusaded for easier policy, voting against the majority on seven of nine occasions and abstaining twice. In several other instances, Mills opposed efforts to stem capital outflows through credit-tightening measures, which he felt might retard domestic economic growth. While casting dissenting votes in favor of tighter policy on isolated occasions, Mills's voting record during his final seven years on the board revealed a greater tendency toward easing than his colleagues. In the absence of more detailed information regarding his monetary philosophy, however, his performance as a policymaker is difficult to assess. He appears to have been as well versed in monetary theory as his peers, though board members during his tenure typically had little formal training in economics. His was a reasoned, studious approach to monetary policymaking. Most of all, however, he trusted his own judgment, a trait as evident in regulatory and supervisory matters as in monetary policy deliberations. Pursuant to passage of the Bank Holding Company

Act of 1956, the Federal Reserve issued Regulation Y to assist in implementing the new legislation. Among the board's responsibilities was evaluation of both applications for bank holding company (BHC) formation and requests by existing BHCs to acquire stock in existing or new banks. While the board was to consider numerous factors in considering these requests, the most controversial by far proved to be the criterion concerning maintenance of competition in banking. Specifically, the Fed was charged with determining whether proposed transactions would extend the size or extent of BHC systems ''beyond limits consistent with adequate and sound banking, the public interest, and the preservation of competition in the field of banking.'' While often disagreeing with and being outvoted by fellow board members, Mills's ability to articulate his view of the nature of competition and its application in a banking environment assisted the board in developing a consensus view of appropriate competitive behavior.

In essence, Mills did not believe big was necessarily bad, nor did he believe that competitive behavior required the presence of large numbers of firms. Consequently, he often voted for approval of transactions that would have permitted a large BHC to enter a new geographic market if it would provide competition for an existing BHC already serving the same market. Such transactions, he argued, promoted ''competition among equals,'' thereby promoting the public interest. He was not unconcerned with the viability of smaller banks, however, typically voting against applications of large BHCs to enter markets already served adequately by smaller institutions. Also, in geographic areas characterized by significant concentration of deposits within few institutions, he tended to favor de novo entry to the expansion of BHCs already participating in the local market. From Mills's perspective, neither size nor numbers per se necessarily promoted or discouraged competition. The vigor and intensity of competition could be assessed only through investigation of banking practices on a case-by-case basis in individual markets.

Having spent forty-five years in private and central banking, Abbot Low Mills, Jr., resigned from the board in March 1965 at the age of sixty-six. During thirteen years of service, he complemented earlier practical banking experience with competency in monetary theory and policy matters. Regarding supervisory and regulatory issues, he played a significant role in defining appropriate competitive behavior in the banking environment. And his unfettered opinion figured substantively in board deliberations. Mills retired to Medford, Oregon in the late 1960s and later returned to Portland. He died there on May 19, 1986, at the age of eighty-seven.

BIBLIOGRAPHY

Federal Reserve System Board of Governors. 1952–1965. *Annual Reports*.
————. 1952–1966. *Federal Reserve Bulletin*.
Greider, William. 1987. *Secrets of the Temple*. New York: Simon and Schuster.

National Cyclopedia of American Biography. 1937. Vol. 26. New York: James T. White and Company.

Prochnow, Herbert V., ed. 1960. *The Federal Reserve System.* New York: Harper & Brothers.

U.S. Congress. Senate. Subcommittee on Federal Reserve Matters of the Committee on Banking and Currency. 1952. *Confirmation Hearings of Abbot L. Mills, Jr., as a Member of the Board of Governors of the Federal Reserve System.* 82d Cong., 2d sess., February 1.

————. 1958. *Confirmation Hearings of Abbot L. Mills, Jr., as a Member of the Board of Governors of the Federal Reserve System.* 85th Cong., 2d sess., February 7.

GEORGE WILDER MITCHELL
(1904–   )

Mary Murphy

George Wilder Mitchell brought to his post of Federal Reserve board governor (August 1961–February 1976) a wealth of knowledge concerning the Federal Reserve—its policies, administration, and execution. An economist by training, he started his career as the director of research at the Illinois Tax Commission (1933–1939, 1941–1943). During the interim period (1939–1940), he was a member of the commission. In 1943 he served as an assistant to the director of the Department of Revenue in Illinois. From 1944 to 1948 he was a tax economist at the Federal Reserve Bank of Chicago. For the period 1949–1950, he became the director of the Department of Finance for Illinois. In 1951 he became the vice-president of the Chicago Federal Reserve Bank and was in that post for the ten years prior to his appointment to the Board of Governors. In August 1961 he was first appointed to serve the unexpired term of Menc S. Szymczak,[*] who had resigned. He was reappointed for a fourteen-year term beginning February 1, 1962.

During his years at the Chicago Fed, Mitchell had several leaves of absence. During the first, he acted as director of finance for Illinois. His duties included the preparation of the state budget and the determination of fiscal policies for the state government. On his second leave, he worked for the Civil Aeronautics Administration on a study of multiple taxation of air carriers. A third leave was spent as a member of a committee appointed by the Joint Committee of Internal Revenue Taxation to investigate the administration of the Bureau of Internal Revenue.

Mitchell majored in economics at the University of Wisconsin and received his B.A. in 1925. He started graduate work at the University of Iowa in 1927 and published *Business Activity in Iowa* (1930) and *Assessment of Real Estate in Iowa and Other Midwestern States* (1931). In 1930 he started teaching at Northwestern and enrolled in the graduate program at the University of Chicago. He continued his studies until 1933, when he was appointed director of research at the Illinois Tax Commission.

In Illinois Mitchell was considered a tough but fair and respected tax official expecting first-rate performance. He was not at all new to the Washington Federal Reserve since he had attended the Washington meetings of the Federal Open Market Committee as an associate economist. Others have portrayed him as articulate in getting his views known, reflecting the prize-winning debater he was at the University of Wisconsin. He has been described as talking in straightforward English colored with illustrations, but it was noted that he had difficulty in phrasing technical problems in lay terms.

He is a past president of the National Tax Association and also a member of the American Economic Association, the American Finance Association, the National Committee on Government Finance, Brookings Institution, Institute International de Finances Publiques, Regional Science Association, Delta Sigma Rho, and Phi Kappa Phi.

Mitchell is a staunch Democrat and proclaims the fact. The press has called him "an orthodox economist." Acquaintances have said that he is "more liberal in economic thinking than Chairman Martin." As an associate of Governor Adlai Stevenson, it was assumed that had Stevenson won the presidential election in 1952, Mitchell would have followed him to Washington. Some speculation existed in 1960 that President John Kennedy might name him as secretary of the Treasury.

Mitchell was first nominated to the board in August 1961. During his confirmation hearing, he was asked to state his philosophy of the Fed's independence from the Treasury, an important issue at the time. He replied that the Federal Reserve system operates to accommodate the entire economy—agriculture, business, commerce, and government—and that it cannot ignore the Treasury and the Treasury cannot ignore the Fed. Neither, however, should be tied to the other's decision. He testified that he would not feel bound out of loyalty or other considerations to follow the desires of the Treasury if he believed economic policy called for some other decision.

At the end of his appointment, he was hailed as a singularly gifted and dedicated public official with seemingly inexhaustible energies, ever-fresh ideas, and infectious enthusiasm. He was a moving force behind many of the Federal Reserve system's new activities over recent years. One of his major efforts has been to improve the nation's payment system. He prodded bankers to install and accept the innovative electronic system of payment and record keeping in the early 1970s and expressed concern that the failure to adopt such a system could result in a paper blizzard. The federal government, he pointed out, already used electronic input for paychecks at this time.

His other interests focused on credit, specifically automobile installment and consumer credit. As chairman of the Fed committee concerned with this issue, he helped prepare *Automobile Installment Credit Terms and Practices* and *Consumer Installment Credit* (1957). The following year he chaired the Fed's committee of survey of credit and capital sources, which wrote *Financing Small Business* (1958).

Mitchell played a major role in the area of bank supervision and in the efforts to improve regulation of foreign bank activities in the United States and of American bank operations abroad. His main contributions, nonetheless, were in monetary policy, where his knowledge and experience as an economist and tax expert enabled him to exert a persuasive influence on the country's financial system. Upon his retirement, William Proxmire and Adlai Stevenson stated that his forward-looking ideas and sound judgment would be missed by the Federal Reserve, Congress, and the rest of the nation.

Mitchell was born in Richland Center, Wisconsin, on February 23, 1904, to George Ray and Minnie (German) Mitchell. He was first married to Grace Marion Muir on August 30, 1927. They had four children: Marilyn Anne (Hagberg), Bruce William, Judith Nancy (Rediehs), and Margery Grace (Curtiss). Mitchell was later divorced and subsequently married Mary Toft Petty on November 14, 1964.

BIBLIOGRAPHY

Federal Reserve Board of Governors. 1985. *Biography*. Washington, D.C.: Federal Reserve Board of Governors.

———. 1989. *Biography*. Washington, D.C.: Federal Reserve Board of Governors.

Kutler, Jefferey. 1988. "Clearing House Group Cites Mitchell for Role in Payment Systems Industry." *American Banker*, March 28, p. 30.

Mitchell, George. 1930. *Business Activity in Iowa*. Ames: College of Commerce, State University of Iowa.

———. 1931. *Assessment of Real Estate in Iowa and Other Midwestern States*. Ames: College of Commerce, State University of Iowa.

———. 1976. "Mitchell Sees Toughest Competion for Banks from Credit Unions." *American Banker*, May 25, p. 1.

———. 1980. "Electronic Fund Transfer Act." *Computer-Law Journal* (Winter): 1–5.

———. 1986. "Similarities and Contrast in Payment Systems. (International Money Transfers Governored by the Bank for International Settlements.)" *Journal of Bank Research* (Winter): 175.

U.S. Congress. Senate. Committee on Banking and Currency. 1961. *Hearing on the Nomination of George W. Mitchell*. 87th Cong., 1st sess., August 15, pp. 1–15.

Who Was Who in America, 1976. Chicago: Marquis Who's Who.

JOHN R. MITCHELL (1868–1933)

Paul J. Kubik

John Raymond Mitchell, governor of the Federal Reserve from May 1921 to May 1923, was born on January 9, 1868, in Franklin, Pennsylvania, to Scotch-Irish parents. After his graduation from Phillips Academy, he attended Yale University, graduating with a Ph.B. in 1889. Before settling down permanently in Minnesota, Mitchell moved about the country, taking a number of varied positions. He was employed as a civil engineer in Seattle, Washington; a clerk in the Exchange Bank in Franklin, Pennsylvania; and a realty operator in the Pennsylvania oil fields. In 1897 Mitchell, whose father was a banker, settled in Winona, Minnesota, taking a position as vice-president of the Winona Deposit Bank. He resigned this position in 1906 to become president of Capital National Bank in St. Paul, a post he held until 1921. During this period he also acted as vice-president of the the Capital Trust and Savings Bank of St. Paul, second vice-president of the Twin City Rapid Transit Company, president of the Duluth Savings Bank, trustee of the Minnesota Mutual Life Insurance Company, and a Ninth Reserve District member of the Federal Advisory Council of the Federal Reserve system during 1917–1918.

A Presbyterian and member of the Metropolitan Club of New York and University Club of Chicago, Mitchell was married twice. On January 29, 1896, he was wed to Mary Ella Lamberton, the daughter of a Winona banker. The couple had three children before Mary's death in 1909: John Lamb; Eleanor, wife of William H. Kennedy; and Raymond Otis. Mitchell was married again, ten years later, to Adelia Sanders, the daughter of George W. Sanders of San Antonio, Texas.

In 1921 Mitchell resigned from his numerous private positions to take an appointment on the Federal Reserve Board. His appointment was confirmed by the Senate on April 29, 1921, and he assumed his office on May 12, 1921. Mitchell succeeded David C. Wills,[*] a Republican appointed on an ad interim basis by President Woodrow Wilson. The appointment of Mitchell, a Republican, was one in a series of steps taken by Republican presidents—in this instance,

President Warren Harding—to place Republicans on the Federal Reserve Board. Although Mitchell was given a ten-year term, he remained on the board for only two years, resigning May 12, 1923. After a brief return to the private sector, Mitchell was called back to public service. On September 8, 1924, he became Federal Reserve agent and chairman of the board of directors at the Federal Reserve Bank of Minneapolis. Mitchell remained at the Minneapolis bank until his death on January 31, 1933. He was succeeded by George R. James,* a Memphis businessman.

John Mitchell was a member of the Federal Reserve Board from May 12, 1921, to May 12, 1923. During this period, the principal policy tool of the system was the discount rate. A number of Federal Reserve bank requests to change their discount rates were considered during Mitchell's tenure. The first adjustment in rates came in July 1921 when the discount rate on commercial paper was reduced from 6 to 5 ½ percent at the New York, Boston, Philadelphia, and San Francisco reserve banks and from 6 ½ to 6 percent at the Chicago bank. Mitchell voted with the majority in approving the reduction. This rate reduction was one in a series of reductions that began in April 1921 and continued through July 1922. Although discount rates varied from bank to bank in this period, they typically moved together within a fairly narrow band. In the wake of World War I, discount rates at the principal reserve banks had been moved up to 7 percent in an effort to control the postwar inflation. Rates were then reduced, beginning in April 1921, in six steps until they reached 4 percent at the New York reserve bank.

Mitchell voted consistently with the majority of the board in approving these rate reductions (with the exception of November 1921, when he was absent). Unfortunately, the minutes from this period do not include even a summary of the discussion among board members preceding each rate vote. Since Mitchell voted consistently with the majority to reduce rates, it is likely that he agreed with the public argument of the board that lower rates were justified by the improved reserve position of the reserve banks (attributed to the substantial gold inflows that began in late 1920) and easier money market conditions. One indicator of conditions in the money market utilized by the board was short-term interest rates, such as the commercial paper rate in the New York market. The June 1922 reduction in the discount rate charged by the New York and Boston reserve banks from 4 ½ to 4 percent, for example, was a response to the reduction in the commercial paper rate below the reserve bank discount rate.

In early 1923 the easing policy of the previous two years was temporarily halted when the discount rate on commercial paper was raised from 4 to 4 ½ percent at the New York and Boston reserve banks. Mitchell again voted with the majority in approving the rate increase. The board cited an increase in speculation and overexpansion of credit as justification for its actions.

Policymaking was particularly difficult in the years of Mitchell's tenure on the board. First and foremost, the gold standard, with its attendant prescriptions for credit policy, was inoperative as a policy guide. The real bills doctrine, which underlay the Federal Reserve Act, had been discredited in the course of the brief postwar expansion, an expansion based largely on the restocking of inventories. Federal Reserve officials at both the Federal Reserve Board and reserve bank of New York, recognized that this inventory expansion, which was supported by so-called real bills, discredited the notion that credit would respond automatically to the legitimate needs of trade if reserve banks confined discounting to eligible bills.

In the period 1921–1923, Federal Reserve officials, particularly those at the reserve banks of the principal money centers, were developing an understanding of how operations in the market for government debt affected monetary and credit variables and could be used to effectuate policy. The development of open market operations was one of the most significant developments of the interwar period, but the Federal Reserve Board played only a limited role in this process.

BIBLIOGRAPHY

Federal Reserve Board. 1921–1923. Minutes of meetings.

Goldenweiser, E. A. 1925. *Federal Reserve System in Operation*. New York: McGraw-Hill.

West, Robert C. 1977. *Banking Reform and the Federal Reserve*. New York: Cornell University Press.

HENRY A. MOEHLENPAH
(1867–1944)

Shiva Sayeg

Born on March 9, 1867, in Juliet, Illinois, Henry Moehlenpah began a life that was to become highly involved with banking in the agricultural sector and gave him a brief term as a governor of the Federal Reserve from November 1919 to August 1920. The pursuit of higher education took him to Northwestern University in 1890. In 1893 he moved to Clinton, Wisconsin, where, three years later, on October 15, 1896, he married Alice Hartshorn. The marriage produced a son, Frederick, and a daughter, Elizabeth (Brady) Moehlenpah.

Moehlenpah's banking career, which started in Juliet in 1988, led him to the position of president of the Wisconsin Bankers Association in July 1913. Although the appointment lasted through 1914 only, he was reinstated in 1935 and retained that title until his death. His 1914 move to Milwaukee coincided with his being named president of the Wisconsin Mortgage and Securities Co.

In 1918 Moehlenpah became the president of the Bankers Joint Stock Land Bank and also ran as the Democratic nominee for state governor. This was only one of his bids for election to various state offices; he ran, unsuccessfully, in the capacity of the Democratic nominee for Congress, First District, Wisconsin, in 1906, for lieutenant governor in 1908, and for presidential elector in 1916.

The next significant phase of Moehlenpah's career came on September 5, 1919, when President Woodrow Wilson nominated him as a member of the Federal Reserve Board to complete the unexpired term of F. A. Delano.[*] The nomination was confirmed by the Senate on September 23, and Moehlenpah took office on November 10, remaining on the board until the expiration of the term on August 9, 1920. At the time of his appointment, Moehlenpah was president of the Citizens Bank of Clinton, Wisconsin; president of the Wisconsin Mortgage and Security Co., Milwaukee, Wisconsin; and director of the Rock County Savings and Mortgage Co.

His final banking position, which he accepted in 1921, was the presidency of Bankers Finance Corporation. The last twenty-four years of his life were spent in association with the Aetna Life Insurance Company, for which he served as supervisor of the eastern district. Over his life, he held memberships in a number of organizations, such as Phi Kappa Sigma and Knights of Pythias, as well as the City and Kiwanis clubs. Moehlenpah died at the age of seventy-seven on November 9, 1944, in Milwaukee.

Moehlenpah, who came from an agricultural state, placed himself as the representative of farming communities and consequently focused his banking and financial activities on farmers. He was especially concerned about the welfare of farmers and addressed their reduced purchasing power in the post–World War I economy. He argued that the erosion of their purchasing power would lead to a reduction in over half of the producing power of the country, a process that he claimed would undermine the health of the economy. He couched his concerns in the more appealing argument that the process of recovery from war depended on the production of real output and the encouragement of saving out of that output. He strengthened his argument by asserting that provision of support to farmers would allow the typical urban citizen to escape a further increase in the high cost of living.

Moehlenpah identified a severe shortage of credit in the agricultural sector, which he considered to be the weakest part of the postwar economy. He attributed the problem partially to the isolated state of farmers and country bankers in contrast to the organized, and thus more effective, nature of urban borrowers and bankers. He condemned the large city banks for their discriminatory attitude toward farmers as opposed to manufacturing and merchant customers. According to his argument, large city bankers exercised leniency toward their delinquent urban borrowers while forcing correspondent country bankers to pay their debts. The country bankers, in turn, had to force farmer borrowers to pay their debts even if it entailed the sale of livestock and other farm assets at figures well below the purchase price.

Moehlenpah also protested against lending of money for speculative purposes. He pointed out the necessity of savings to meet the government debt needs and encouraged any additional credit to be channeled toward production of real output, such as agricultural products.

His advocacy of the farming community was extended to the government by stressing that the Federal Reserve system was created for the purpose of stabilizing the agricultural as well as the industrial sector of the economy. He believed that the Federal Reserve Act should be amended so that it would provide more help to farmers. In particular, he proposed abolishing section 19 of the Federal Reserve Act, which prohibited country bankers from using member banks of the system to rediscount notes of farmers at reasonable rates at the central bank.

To address the credit needs of farmers and in view of the shortage of farm labor, Moehlenpah advocated mobilization of money and credit to the agricultural sector. With that in mind, he championed the creation of an entity that would make organized credit available to farmers for the purpose of purchasing machinery and increasing farm output. He claimed that six-month loans were too short for farmers and should be replaced by one-, two-, and three-year well-secured loans against which notes and debentures could be issued. Moehlenpah also advocated the popularization of federal farm loan bonds as collateral for commercial loans. In the hope of creating a long-term flow of credit to the agricultural sector and based on his high regard for the financial responsibility of farmers, he argued that these bonds were as secure as government bonds.

Despite his criticisms related to the shortcomings of the Federal Reserve system where the farmer was concerned, Moehlenpah encouraged state bankers to join the system. He claimed that the foregone interest on the reserves that they would have to keep at the central bank would be more than offset by the privilege they would gain through their access to the services of the Federal Reserve system. The most important of the benefits, in the view of Moehlenpah, was the opportunity for country bankers to rediscount farm notes at advantageous rates through the central bank instead of resorting to city banks on less advantageous terms. He believed this to be the main incentive for the country bankers to join the Federal Reserve system.

Moehlenpah's career was highlighted by his concern for the credit needs of the agricultural communities after the war and his frequent attempts to stress the importance of the state banker to the farming sector and, ultimately, to the welfare of the entire economy.

BIBLIOGRAPHY

Moehlenpah, Henry A. 1919. "An Address by Henry A. Moehlenpah." Delivered to the Convention of the Oklahoma State Bankers' Association, Oklahoma City, December 10.

———. 1920. "An Address by Henry A. Moehlenpah." Delivered to the Convention of the Dallas Group of the Texas State Bankers' Association, February 11.

———. 1922a. "Financing the World's Greatest Industry." *Banker-Manufacturer* (March): 11, 51.

———. 1922b. "Moehlenpah Urges Third Financial System." *Banker-Manufacturer* (June): 63–64.

New York Times. 1944. November 11, p. 13.

U.S. Congress. Joint Committee on Short-time Rural Credits. 1921. *Hearing on Short-time Rural Credits*. 67th Cong., 2d sess., December 28.

U.S. Congress. Senate. Committee on Banking and Currency. 1913. *Testimony of H. A. Moehlenpah. Hearings*. 63d Cong., 1st sess.

Who's Who in America, 1936–1937. Vol. 19. Chicago: A. N. Marquis Company.

Who Was Who in America, 1943–1950. Vol. 2. Chicago: A. N. Marquis Company.

RALPH W. MORRISON (1878–1948)

David E. R. Gay and Thomas R. McKinnon

The appointment of Ralph Morrison to the Federal Reserve board was in conjunction with the reorganization of the Federal Reserve system, which underwent major revisions that added powers to regulate credit and banking reserves. These changes were incorporated in the Securities Act of 1933, the Securities Exchange Act of 1934, and the Banking Acts of 1933 and 1935.

These acts overhauled the Federal Reserve system. They broadened the power of the system to deal with economic fluctuations. The system was empowered to change the reserve requirement up to twice the level currently in effect, make loans to member banks on the security of all "satisfactory" assets rather than just eligible paper for rediscount, and more easily engage in the buying and selling of government securities in the open market. Other provisions of these acts created the Federal Deposit Insurance Corporation, prohibited banks from paying interest on checking accounts, and empowered the system to set margin requirements of stock purchases.

The organizational framework of the Federal Reserve system was revised to consolidate more power in Washington. The Federal Open Market Committee was transformed from an informal group of reserve bank representatives to a formal statutory committee to guide monetary policy. The committee was thereafter composed of five reserve bank presidents and the seven members of the Board of Governors, giving the board a clear majority. In a move to increase the independence of the board from the executive, the secretary of the Treasury and the comptroller of the currency were removed from membership. A less obvious move to centralize power in Washington was to give the Board of Governors bureaucratic control over the twelve reserve banks.

The Banking Act of 1935 changed the name from the Federal Reserve Board in Washington to the Board of Governors of the Federal Reserve system. Members were required to come from different Federal Reserve bank districts and be broadly representative of industry, commerce, and agriculture. Terms were lengthened to fourteen years, and new appointments were to be staggered so that a term would expire and a new member take office every two years. Provision was made for a new board to displace the old board on February 1, 1936. Because of the requirement for staggered terms, the new board had initial appointments ranging from fourteen years to two years. Ralph Morrison received the two-year term.

The restructuring of the Federal Reserve system was controversial. Chairman Marriner Eccles,* strongly backed by President Franklin Roosevelt, was the primary architect of these changes. Reserve bank presidents, generally, and Wall Street bankers in particular, fought the changes but were unable to muster sufficient support in Congress. Darryl Francis, formerly president of the St. Louis Fed, observed that the consolidation of authority and the modern operation of the Fed began in 1935.

Born in Howell County, Missouri, on September 7, 1878, the son of Joseph and Julia McCann Morrison, and educated in public schools and West Plains College, Morrison married Leo Louise Chartrand of St. Louis in March 1903. He was the foreign sales manager of the St. Louis Car Company, 1903–1911; was employed by Central Power and Light, 1911–1925; and in investments, ranching, and banking, 1925–1934; president of the Texas-Mexican Railway Company, 1939–1948; president of the Pan American Hotel Company; and owner of the Saint Anthony Hotel in San Antonio. He also reported that he was a member of the Council on Foreign Relations and a 32-degree Mason. He was a member of the U.S. delegation to the World Monetary and Economic Conference in London in 1933.

The records in the library of the Board of Governors of the Federal Reserve system indicate only Morrison's reluctance to sign the approval of the February 20, 1936, minutes of the board because he was absent. A note indicated that approval of the minutes did not mean approving the actions of the board but merely routinely approving the record of the actions. Other reports indicated he disagreed substantially with Roosevelt's policies.

Morrison, a Democrat, was appointed for a two-year term to succeed J. J. Thomas.* He was sworn in on February 10, 1936, and resigned May 20, 1936. Reportedly he had policy disagreements with President Roosevelt and Fed chairman Eccles. Some sources indicated that Morrison was upset that he had been described as a political appointee for having been a financial supporter of the Democratic party. His resignation was accepted on July 9, 1936, with "real regret" by President Roosevelt after a delay for reconsideration. He served the briefest term from appointment to resignation in the history of the Federal Reserve.

He died on April 8, 1948, and left a substantial part of his estate as a charitable foundation. Former Baylor University president Abner McCall reported that part of the estate continues to be used at Baylor for a course required of all undergraduates on the U.S. Constitution since its inception. Initially, the course was to cover the 125 years since 1789, stopping before the Roosevelt administration. The Baylor Law School is housed in R. W. Morrison Constitution Hall.

BIBLIOGRAPHY

Francis, Darryl. 1989. Interview with the authors, Fort Smith, Arkansas, September 6.

McCall, Abner. 1990. Interview with the authors, January 15.

Morrison, Ralph W. 1936. Correspondence. March 9.

New York Times. 1936a. January 28, p. 25.

———. 1936b. May 21.

Who's Who in America, 1936–1937. Vol. 19. Chicago: A.N. Marquis.

———. *1948–1949.* Vol. 25. Chicago: A.N. Marquis.

DAVID W. MULLINS, JR. (1946–   )

Bernard S. Katz

On May 21, 1990, David W. Mullins, Jr., became the seventieth member of the Board of Governors of the Federal Reserve system. His appointment by an 18–0 vote of approval by the Senate Banking Committee filled a ten-month vacancy created by the resignation of H. Robert Heller,[*] whose term of office was to expire on January 31, 1996. The only point of controversy surrounding Mullins's appointment was that of his place of residency. The Senate questioned the fact that he resided in the Boston Federal Reserve District but was appointed from the St. Louis District.

Mullins, tall, slender, and currently unmarried, was born on April 28, 1946, in Memphis, Tennessee. He responded to the residency question by pointing out that he still had strong relationships with his home state of Arkansas, where his father had been president of the University of Arkansas. He indicated that he had been brought up in the St. Louis Federal Reserve District, that his family still resided there, that he still had business in the district, and that he had been a voting resident through graduate school. He argued that the only blemish on his record was that he had spent fifteen years as a professor at Harvard, and as he jested, "no one's perfect."

Mullins attended the University of Arkansas for one year before transferring to Yale University in 1964. After receiving a B.S. degree in administrative sciences in 1968, he went on to obtain an S.M. in finance from the Sloan School of Management at the Massachusetts Institute of Technolgy (MIT) in 1972. He continued his education in finance and economics at MIT and earned the Ph.D. in 1974. While a student at MIT, Mullins taught part-time at Bentley College in Waltham, Massachusetts.

After leaving MIT, Mullins joined the faculty at the Harvard University Graduate School of Business Administration, where he taught corporate finance and capital markets in the M.B.A. and doctoral programs. Mullins also served as the faculty chairman of Harvard's corporate financial management program for senior financial officers of major corporations.

Mullins was a faculty member at Harvard from 1974 to 1988. In 1987 he went to Washington to work on the presidential task force investigating the October stock market crash, where he was one of the panel's two top staffers. Nicholas F. Brady headed the task force, and when Brady became Treasury secretary, Mullins later joined him in Washington.

While at Harvard Mullins jointly authored a number of financial research papers that established his expertise on bonds, equity securities, and the stock market. In his 1989 paper, "Original Issue High Yield Bonds: Aging Analysis of Defaults, Exchanges, and Calls," he concluded that there was clear evidence that default rates were lower immediately after issue and rose over time. The paper earned him the Smith-Breeden Award given by the American Finance Association for the best finance article for 1989.

His research on equity issues also provided him with insight into the security markets. In "Signalling with Dividends, Stock Repurchases, and Equity Issues" (1986a), Mullins concluded that financial decisions that affect equity cash flow are interpreted by outside investors as signals reflecting inside management's appraisal of the firm's future cash flows. The paper concluded that cash outflows, stock repurchases, and increases in dividends are seen as positive signals and are accompanied by rises in stock prices. Another paper, "Equity Issues and Offering Dilution" (1986b), reaffirmed the hypothesis that large equity offerings are regarded as negative signals by investors.

Upon joining the Treasury Department in 1988 as assistant secretary for domestic financial policy and the later assistant secretary for domestic finance, Mullins became one of the principal architects in fashioning the Bush administration's solution of the savings and loan crisis. With this initial foray into the corridors of Washington politics, Mullins was at a disadvantage. While found to be intelligent and sensitive, he was inexperienced with the political traps of Washington. It was granted, however, that he apparently was a quick read. Despite an initial gaffe in recommending a 25 cent fee for each $100 held in a federally insured bank as an element to resolve the savings and loan crises, he did become the prime author of the Bush administration's final savings and loan bailout plan.

Mullins's responsibilities at the Treasury also encompassed financial institutions policy, securities market regulations, and corporate financial policy. He represented the Treasury on the board of directors of the Securities Industry Protection Corporation, the Pension Benefit Guarantee Program, and the Farm Credit Assistance Board. Mullins's two years of service at the Treasury were recognized with the presentation of the Treasury Department's highest honor, the Alexander Hamilton Award.

Mullins's two-year stint at the Treasury provided him with the necessary political experience to walk more comfortably in the hallways of Washington. He was no longer a political newcomer and developed the ability to talk at length without arriving at a specific conclusion. For example, at his Senate hearings, Mullins argued his belief that financial institutions should be "permitted to apply their expertise to a wide range of financial activities," while at the same time it was important for them "to live up to the standards of safety and soundness and to limit their exposure to the federal safety net."

His experience at the Treasury seasoned his political abilities but also provided him with a certain amount of baggage. The Senate Banking Committee had reservations that Mullins's association with the Treasury may have made him a Treasury man. At the time of his hearings, the Bush administration was pushing for the Fed to take an easier money stance. The chairman of the Senate committee, Donald W. Riegle (D, Michigan), expressed concern that Mullins was going to the Fed as "a White House crusader for easier monetary policy." Mullins replied that he would express his independent judgment on matters that come before the board. His response had precedence; there is ample evidence to support the argument that appointment to the Fed tends to make the governors creatures of the institution.

Mullins brought to the board experience with the financial services industry. At the Treasury, he helped to restructure the savings and loan industry, and he was on the Treasury task force that studied the 1987 stock market crash. Additionally, he aided in the Brady plan to find solutions to the Third World debt problem.

At his Senate hearings, Mullins presented detailed responses to his views on financial matters. With respect to deposit insurance reform, Mullins called for a limit on deposit insurance to a single deposit account. He also recommended that the Fed rethink the idea that a bank holding company be considered a source of strength for its insured bank subsidiaries. He further recommended a relaxation of the "firewalls" the Fed had set up to isolate insured deposits from risky underwriting of new loans, arguing that the buffer produced inefficiencies in the delivery of financial services. Along the same lines, Mullins argued that the competitive position of U.S. banks would be improved if restrictions on securities activities and interstate banking were removed.

Mullins's position on monetary policy have not yet been tested. His background, writings, and experience have not provided a basis to forecast his philosophy with respect to monetary matters. Mullins brought a theoretical background in financial structure more so than in monetary theory. Accordingly, he is expected to be active in securities and banking regulation, as well as fostering global interconnections of financial markets. He has until 1996 to make changes, in either policy or philosophy.

Mullins is a member of the Harvard Club of Boston, the Harvard Club of New York, the Yale Political Union, and the Society for the Advancement of Management. He is the recipient of Sloan and National Science Foundation fellowships and the MIT Bates Prize for the best master's thesis. He received an honorary A.M. degree from Harvard in 1984.

BIBLIOGRAPHY

American Banker. 1989. February 13, p. 7.
———. 1990a. March 26, p. 2.

————. 1990b. May 18, p. 2.

Federal Reserve Board of Governors. 1990. "Members of the Board of Governors of the Federal System." July.

Mullins, David W., Jr., and Asquith, P. 1986a. "Signalling with Dividends, Stock Repurchases, and Equity Issues." *Financial Management* 15, no. 3 (Autumn).

————. 1986b. "Equity Issues and Offering Dilution." *Journal of Financial Economics* 15, nos. 1–2 (January–February).

Mullins, David W., Jr.; Asquith, P.; and Wolff, E. 1989. "Original Issue High Yield Bonds: Aging Analysis of Defaults, Exchanges and Calls." *Journal of Finance* 44, no. 4 (September).

Mullins, David, and Homonoff, R. B. 1975. *Cash Management: Inventory Control Limit Approach.* Lexington, Mass.: Lexington Books.

U.S. Congress. Senate. Committee on Banking, Housing and Urban Affairs. 1990. *Hearing.* March 23.

EDWARD LEE NORTON (1892–1966)

Anne R. Hornsby

Edward Norton, governor of the Federal Reserve from September 1950 to January 1952, one of seven sons, was born in Blountsville, Alabama, to Reverend John and Martha (Maddux) Norton on June 13, 1892. He received a B.S. degree from Birmingham-Southern College in 1913 and an LL.D. from the University of Alabama in 1940. He married Jessie Stead on June 15, 1922 (deceased), and Corrine Richards in 1952. These two unions produced no children.

Shortly after finishing undergraduate school, Norton enlisted in the U.S. Navy during World War I and served as an ensign, ultimately working in the office of Assistant Secretary of the Navy Franklin D. Roosevelt. At the time of his enlistment, the navy had two branch openings: hospital service and the "black gang." He opted for hospital work and indicated his pleasure in that choice because he later learned that the "black gang" were the "boys who stayed below decks and stoked the furnaces." His hospital duty, however, was not at all glamorous; he worked as an orderly and engaged in hospital construction employed as a carpenter, hod carrier, and ditch digger. The drudgery of these tasks while stationed in Washington, D.C., was somewhat relieved when he acquired the assignment of writing a hospital gossip column for a local newspaper (as a youth, he had worked with the *Birmingham Ledger*).

Norton has been described as one of the outstanding businessmen in the Southeast. His business interests were varied, including the areas of finance, communication, and manufacturing. In the financial circle, he served as executive vice-president of Munger Mortgage Company (1926–1939), chairman of the board of First National Bank of Birmingham (1936–1950), chairman of the board of the Birmingham branch of the Federal Reserve Bank of Atlanta (1939), and member of the Board of Governors of the Federal Reserve system (1950–1952).

Norton was recommended for the Board of Governors of the Federal Reserve system by Frank Neely, chairman of Rich's (a local retail department store) of Atlanta, Georgia. At the time Neely was also chair of the Federal Reserve Bank of Atlanta. His recommendation was looked upon favorably by President Harry S. Truman, who appointed him to the board. It was said that President Truman wanted a businessman from the Sixth Federal Reserve District to fill a vacancy. The *New York Times* reported, however, that Norton's appointment was a result of political patronage; the president was seeking to reward Alabama senators Lister Hill and John J. Sparkman "for their efforts in preventing the States Right party from gaining control of the regular Democratic organization in their home state." Justice Hugo Black (an Alabama native) administered his oath of office. Norton did not serve long on the board. Within two years, he tendered his resignation in a letter to President Truman, citing personal business obligations as the reason.

In the area of communication, Norton was chairman of the board of Florida Broadcasting Company (WMBR, WMBR-TV), Jacksonville, Florida (1934–1952), and chairman of the board of Voice of Alabama (WAPI-WAFM-TV), Birmingham (1936–1950).

In manufacturing, he was chairman of the board of Royal Crown Cola Company, director of Louisiana Delta Offshore Drilling Company, director of Avondale Mills, and president and later director of the Coosa River newsprint plant. Constantly seeking to expand his business interests, in 1958, Norton purchased 100,000 shares of stock in the Nehi Corporation of Columbus, Georgia (the third largest soda firm in the nation and the largest in the softdrink canning business) for a reported $1.5 million, making him its largest shareholder. At the time of this transaction, he had been a director of the company for ten years.

In other areas, he was executive vice-president of Munger Realty (1924–1937) and president of the Birmingham Baseball Club (1930). His involvement and interest in these enterprises stemmed from his participation in college baseball. He was captain of the baseball team at Birmingham-Southern College and a star athlete in this sport. Munger, an avid sports fan of the college, became interested in Norton and offered him a summer job in his company. Norton accepted and worked most of his college summers with Munger enterprises. After college, Norton was faced with two major career choices: to accept a contract extended to him by the Mobile baseball team of the Southern League or to accept an offer of employment with Munger enterprises. He chose the latter and was affiliated with the Munger group throughout his career. He credits baseball with "directly determining the course of his career"; he said that it gave him the chance to meet the person (Munger) who would play a most influential part in his life. Thus, when he was given the opportunity to become president of the Birmingham Baseball Club (Barons), his life, one could say, came full circle; two loves of his life were united—business and baseball.

Though prolific in business matters, Norton, who was elected to Phi Beta Kappa, also left his mark in education. He was a great promoter and supporter of education, having served on numerous boards on the secondary as well as the postsecondary level. His involvement on the college level crossed color lines and was somewhat uncharacteristic of southern white behavior considering the hostile racial climate in Birmingham at the time. In addition to being chairman of the board of trustees of his alma mater, Birmingham-Southern College, as early as 1930 and serving on that board until his death in 1966, in 1943, he began serving as a member of the board of trustees of Miles College, a historically black college in Birmingham. At Miles he served as chairman of the executive committee.

As a benefactor of both of these institutions, buildings have been erected bearing his name: the Edward L. Norton Student Union at Miles College and the Edward L. Norton United Methodist Center at Birmingham-Southern. Many believe the latter is a fitting memorial to Norton, whose paternal forebears extended to three generations of Methodist ministers (his great-grandfather, grandfather, and father). Norton, an active Methodist layman for most of his life, joined the Methodist church at the age of thirteen. Another building that bears his name at Birmingham-Southern is the Edward L. Norton Center for Continuing Education in Business, which houses the Southern Trust School and the Executives in Residence program at the college.

Other educational interests saw Norton serving as a member of the Jefferson County Board of Education (1930–1940), trustee of the Eisenhower Fellowship foundation, trustee of the General Education Board of New York (1944–1952), and director of the Social Research Institute.

Norton's educational and business interests spurred him to become a world traveler. He made some seven trips abroad, primarily in Europe. On one of these European visits in 1958, Norton was impressed with the different types of manufacturing in the various countries, especially the ones in Italy. He said Italy "can give the United States competition in the sale of typewriters and sewing machines." This trip also helped him to formulate his opinion on American foreign aid. He said that the United States should expand its business interests abroad rather than "give money to assist foreign countries." In this way he perceived the United States as helping people to help themselves by providing jobs for them. He also advocated allowing foreign countries and individuals to buy stock in "U.S.-sponsored companies," which he said would eradicate "their distaste for anything 'foreign.'"

On this same trip, Norton let a comment slip that could be interpreted as being insensitive to racial and/or ethnic groups. At the World's Fair in Brussels, he indicated that he was not very impressed with the U.S. exhibitions, particularly the art display, which was heavily weighted with Indian pieces. He said, "You would think we were nothing but Indians over here." Nevertheless, Norton has demonstrated his concern for ethnic and racial groups through his support for historically black Miles College and by serving as a member of the national executive committee of the National Conference of Christians and Jews.

Upon his death at age seventy-three (April 12, 1966), Norton left an estate purportedly valued at several million dollars, with approximately half designated for Birmingham-Southern College.

BIBLIOGRAPHY

Birmingham News. 1958. July 24, November 22. 1966. April 13, June 18.
Birmingham News-Herald. 1938. March 27.

Corley, Robert G., and Stayer, Samuel N. 1981. *View from the Hilltop*. Birmingham-Southern College.

New York Times. 1950. May 27.

Who's Who in Methodism. 1952. Chicago: A. N. Marquis.

Who's Who in the South and Southwest. 1956, 1967–1968. Chicago: A. N. Marquis.

Who Was Who in America, 1961–1968. Chicago: A. N. Marquis.

JOHN CHARLES PARTEE (1927–   )

Anne R. Hornsby

John Charles Partee, appointed governor of the Federal Reserve in January 1976, was born in Defiance, Ohio, to Lauren W. and Florence (Paxton) Partee on October 21, 1927. He received his B.S. and M.B.A. from Indiana University in 1948 and 1949, respectively. He did additional graduate work at the University of Chicago (1952–1953). Partee married Gail Voegelin in 1946, and they have three children.

Partee has worked in various capacities in the financial services industry, first in the public sector and then in the private. Between 1949 and 1956, he was an economist at the Federal Reserve Bank of Chicago and, from 1956 to 1961, an associate economist and second vice-president of Northern Trust Company Bank of Chicago. With this wealth of experience of some twelve years in banking, Partee's career path saw him leave the private sector and return to the public arena. In 1962 he began working with the Federal Reserve board in various capacities: as adviser in 1964, director of research from 1969 to 1973, and managing director for research and economic policy from 1973 to 1975. After twenty-six years in the banking field, public and private, Partee was elevated to the Board of Governors of the Federal Reserve system in 1976, where he served as a member until 1986.

During his tenure with the Federal Reserve board, Partee made many presentations before various committees and subcommittees of the U.S. Congress, including the Subcommittee on Domestic Monetary Policy of the Committee on Banking, Finance, and Urban Affairs of the U.S. House of Representatives; the Committee on Banking, Housing, and Urban Affairs of the U.S. Senate; Subcommittee on Telecommunication, Consumer Protection and Finance of the Committee on Energy and Commerce of the U.S. House of Representatives; Subcommittee on Agriculture and Transportation of the Joint Economic Committee; Subcommittee on Financial Institutions, Regulation and Insurance of the Committee on Banking, Finance, and Urban Affairs of the U.S. House of Representatives; and Subcommittee on Financial Institutions of the Committee on Banking, Housing, and Urban Affairs of the U.S. Senate.

From 1977 to 1985, Partee addressed a number of issues at meetings of these governmental units: the role of open market operations in Treasury cash and debt management, potential insider loan abuses of financial institutions, the role of the Federal Bank Examination Council, centralization of bank supervision, evolving changes in the structure and functions of financial institutions, regulation of money market mutual funds, interest rate ceiling, and intrastate and interstate acquisitions of failed depository institutions.

On the issue of Treasury cash and debt management, Partee argued that the board supports extension of the direct borrowing authority, by which the Federal Reserve purchases U.S. obligations directly from the Treasury, in order to aid the Treasury in the management of its cash and debt positions. This would ensure the Treasury's ability to meet "its obligations without delay in the event of temporary need." Direct borrowing is valuable in periods of discrepancies between the Treasury's income receipts and expenditures. The Treasury has not abused this authority over time, and there are established safeguards on such borrowing in the form of a congressionally imposed debt ceiling. Partee argued for the extension of the direct borrowing authority without fear that such activity would generate undesirable cyclical fluctuations.

On another occasion, Partee allayed the concerns of Congress regarding the result of a survey that showed potential for abuse in the areas of bank stock loans, insider loans, and overdrafts. He questioned the shortcomings of the quality of the data used in the survey and concluded that "these dubious practices do not appear to be widespread or to involve quantitatively large commitments of available funds." Furthermore, he said, although the data reveal that approximately 90 percent of the credit extended to insiders of reporting banks was made to the directors or their business interests, the bulk of these loans represents normal commercial transactions made to credit-worthy bank customers where each type of loan was assessed interest rates at or above the prime rate. Nevertheless, because the potential for abuse appeared imminent, Partee indicated the board's support for legislation (which was passed by the Senate and introduced in the House of Representatives) designed to restrict extension of credit to insiders.

On the issue of consolidation of the three Federal Reserve bank regulators, Partee advocated maintenance of the status quo. He presented the board's view opposing pending legislation that would bring under one umbrella the regulatory functions of the comptroller of the currency, the Federal Reserve system, and the Federal Deposit Insurance Corporation. There has been much speculation in the banking community that these agencies perform overlapping and often conflicting functions. Partee argued, however, that monetary policy and supervision and regulation of banks are closely intertwined, and separation of these functions would lead to frustration of monetary policy objectives. He stated that the current structure of the three regulatory agencies "worked reasonably well" through continuous consultation and cooperation that serve as checks and balances eliminating potential conflicts and that "public confidence in the banking system has been maintained . . . because of the combined efforts of the three Federal Reserve Bank regulatory agencies.''

Though in opposition to centralization of the functions of the three regulatory agencies, Partee did give the board's support for a legislative bill establishing the Federal Reserve Bank Examination Council for purposes of developing uniform standards and procedures for bank examinations. This legislation would apply to Federal Reserve bank examiners, as well as state bank examiners, with the goal of "fostering more coordination between state and federal supervisory agencies.''

With evolving changes in the financial structure that increasingly blur the distinction between deposit institutions and other financial entities, Partee expressed his concern over the concept of the "nonbank bank.'' He said that the Federal Reserve has consistently supported separation of banking activity from commerce. This separation is lost, however, when the nonbank bank's proprietor is an industrial or financial parent that is not a bank holding company (thus rendering the firm free of Federal Reserve regulation). As a result, under the concept of nonbank bank, Partee argued, we find other financial institutions accepting transaction deposit accounts (an activity once considered the exclusive domain of commercial banks). Consequently, this may give rise to conflict of interest between banking services and nonbank activities. Although this financial evolution may possibly lead to abuse, Partee said that the board can also see benefits accruing from the practice as economies and increased competition emerge in the financial market. Therefore, he said, the situation should be watched closely and safeguards pondered "to eliminate potential for abuse.''

On another recent innovation in the financial market, Partee expressed the opinion of the board on the effect of the growth of money market mutual funds on commercial banks and thrift institutions and whether there is a need for the Federal Reserve to impose an interest rate ceiling and/or reserve requirement on money market mutual funds. Money market mutual funds are places where the small saver can earn interest rates competitive with those paid at commercial banks and thrifts. Since commercial banks and thrifts are regulated and (at the time) had interest rate ceilings, Congress wondered if the same restrictions should apply to money market mutual funds. Partee testified that the board was not in favor of imposing an interest rate ceiling or reserve requirement on money market mutual funds. He said that these entities are regulated by the Securities and Exchange Commission and do not pose a threat to monetary policy since their transactions are very small.

In a similar vein, Partee gave the board's support for other evolving changes in the functions of financial institutions. He testified that the board favors congressional legislative proposals advocating the gradual phasing out of an interest rate ceiling, nationwide issuance of NOW accounts, and the "widening of asset powers of thrifts'' (permitting federally chartered thrifts to acquire assets in the form of consumer loans and commercial papers, for example). In order for these changes to be compatible with the monetary policy objective of the Federal

Reserve, Partee said that the board endorses interest payments on transaction accounts at all depository institutions and recommends a system of "universal mandatory reserve requirement" applicable to all depository financial institutions (that is, these institutions would abide by the Federal Reserve system's reserve requirement).

With regard to bank mergers, Partee presented the view of the board on banks in agricultural regions and on interstate acquisitions. He argued that because of the poor economic state of farmers, there has been a large number of bank failures in rural areas. Since the board does not perceive any future improvement in the farm situation, it proposes bank mergers (the emphasis is on intrastate acquisition). Preferably, Partee said, weak agricultural banks should be allowed to merge with stronger banks situated outside the agricultural community that do not have many farm loans. And on interstate acquisitions, Partee testified that the board favors out-of-state mergers of "large failed depository institutions in certain emergency situations" for four reasons: (1) it would increase the number of potential bidders, enhancing the chance for a buyer; (2) in the absence of a buyer, liquidation of a bank implies loss of bank service in the community, and the uninsured depositor loses; (3) purchase by a bank within the state may violate antitrust legislation, leading to monopoly; and (4) to ensure domestic bank purchase and avoid the possibility that a foreign bank may make the acquisition. "Such preferential treatment of foreign banks seems . . . unfair."

Partee seized every opportunity to present the views of the Board of Governors of the Federal Reserve system before the U.S. Congress. These views allayed the concerns of Congress regarding current practices and evolving changes in financial institutions and markets and supported congressional proposals and legislation that fostered and accelerated the pace of these financial developments.

Partee's career has also influenced his professional and community involvement. He has served as director of the Neighborhood Reinvestment Corporation, chairman of the Federal Institution Examination Council, and member of the Conference of Business Economists.

BIBLIOGRAPHY

Federal Reserve Bulletin (September 1977): 817–22; (April 1978): 285–89; (July 1978): 542–43; (February 1980): 130–32; (March 1980): 221–25; (June 1980): 465–68; (June 1985): 409–12; (August 1985): 614–18.

Who's Who in America, 1982–1983. Chicago: A. N. Marquis.

EDMUND PLATT (1865–1939)

Edmund Platt, a governor of the Federal Reserve from June 1920 to September 1930, was born in Poughkeepsie, New York, on February 2, 1865. He attended Riverview Academy and Eastman Business College in Poughkeepsie before attending Harvard University. After graduating from Harvard in 1888, Platt went back to Poughkeepsie to teach history and English at the Riverview Academy while studying law. In 1890 he moved to Superior, Wisconsin, where he served as an editorial writer for the *Superior Evening Telegram*. He returned again to Poughkeepsie in 1891 to work for the *Poughkeepsie Eagle*, a family-owned newspaper. He married Adele Innis on June 23, 1892, with whom he had one daughter, Catherine. When his father died in 1907, he became editor and half owner of the *Eagle* with his brother, John.

Platt was elected to Congress in 1912 as a Republican representing the Twenty-sixth District of New York. The election was marked by the death of his Democratic opponent, incumbent R. E. Connell, on October 30. The mayor of Poughkeepsie, John Sague, was nominated to replace Connell on the ballot. Even so, the election was close because of the Democratic tide at the top of the ticket that year, with Platt receiving 20,618 votes to 20,191 for Sague, and 4,418 votes going to a Progressive party candidate. He ran successfully as the incumbent through the 1918 election.

Platt's first terms in Congress leave little public record. He spoke little on the floor in his first year in Congress. One notable exception was an exchange with Carter Glass, the primary sponsor of the Federal Reserve Act, near the end of the debate on that bill. Platt took Glass and the Democrats to task for switching their position concerning the extension of the Aldrich-Vreeland Act. That act provided for the issuance of currency in an emergency by groups of banks to provide for a more elastic currency. This, of course, became one of the major provisions of the Federal Reserve Act. Ironically, Platt voted against final passage of the Federal Reserve Act. The rest of his record until 1919 consists primarily of routine business, such as bills to increase an individual's pension. In 1919 he became chairman of the House Committee on Banking and Currency. In this capacity he guided several amendments to the Federal Reserve Act through the House to ultimate passage. Most notable were amendments to section 25, which allowed national banks to invest in subsidiaries engaged in the financing of foreign trade.

Platt resigned from Congress on June 7, 1920, in order to accept the nomination by President Woodrow Wilson to be a member of the Federal Reserve Board. He was sworn in the next day, June 8, 1920. On July 23, 1920, he was named vice-governor of the board (now called vice-chairman) and served in this capacity until his resignation from the board on September 14, 1930.

Platt's public record at the Fed is as lean as his record in Congress. What there is indicates that he was very much a tight money man. He tended to oppose discount rate cuts and in general any attempt to make credit easier to obtain. His appearance before the Senate Committee on Banking and Currency on January 26, 1931, just a few months after his resignation from the board, sums up his philosophy: "I may say that it was my impression during most of the time I was a member of the Federal Reserve Board, that the rate policy was too low." Indeed, he goes on to state that in 1920 (before he joined the board), he felt it was necessary to raise the discount rates to prevent credit from becoming too easy. This view is interesting in light of the fact that the country was in a depression at the time. Despite being a Republican, he tended to oppose the positions of President Warren Harding's appointees to the board, who tended to be in favor of much easier credit policy.

In September 1927 he was on the losing end of a series of 4–3 votes of the board reducing the discount rates for the Chicago and San Francisco banks. Some critics claim these actions were the seeds of the easy money policies that led to the crash in 1929. Throughout 1928 and into 1929, he continued to push for higher discount rates to curb the speculative fever in the financial markets.

After leaving the board, Platt became a vice-president of Marine Midland Corporation, the parent corporation for several banks in the Buffalo, New York, area. He served in this capacity until his death on August 27, 1939.

BIBLIOGRAPHY

Biographical Directory of the American Congress, 1774–1971. 1971. Washington, D.C.: U.S. Government Printing Office.
New York Times. 1939. August 28, p. L–18.
Official Congressional Directory, May 1920. 1920. Washington, D.C.: U.S. Government Printing Office.
U.S. Congress. Senate. Committee on Banking and Currency. 1921. *Hearings on the Nomination of Edmund Platt*. 71st Cong., 3d sess., January 26.

OLIVER S. POWELL (1896–1963)

Cynthia Saltzman

On July 12, 1950, Oliver S. Powell was nominated by President Harry Truman to serve the remaining term of the late Lawrence Clayton[*] on the Federal Reserve board. Powell was sworn in on September 1, 1950, by Judge George P. Boise of the municipal court. At the time of his appointment, he was first vice-president and secretary of the board of the Federal Reserve Bank of Minneapolis.

Powell was born on September 17, 1896, in White Rock, South Dakota. He received a bachelor of arts degree from the University of Minnesota in 1917, graduating with honors in economics. During his last two years of study, he spent his summers as a foreign service scholar to the National City Bank of New York. Upon graduation, he accepted a position with the bank at its Russian branch in Petrograd (now Leningrad). While there, he witnessed the outbreak of the Bolshevik revolution, with the massacre in Petrograd Square. He was able to escape through Siberia, spending three months in Japan before finding passage to America. In August 1918 Powell entered the U.S. Navy, acting as supply officer on troop transports and destroyers. He served until August 1920, when he joined the Federal Reserve Bank of Minneapolis as a clerk in the business research division.

Prior to his appointment to the Board of Governors, Powell spent thirty years at the Minneapolis Federal Reserve. In July 1927 he became head of the research department, editor of the *Monthly Review*, and alternate for the Federal Reserve agent in currency duties. In September 1933 he added secretary of the board of directors to his titles. On July 18, 1936, he was elected a vice-president, and on November 19, 1936, he was appointed a first vice-president. Given his long tenure at the Minneapolis district bank, it was not surprising that he resigned from the Board of Governors, effective June 30, 1952, to become president of the Federal Reserve Bank of Minneapolis. In his resignation letter to President Truman, he wrote, ''Having served for thirty years as an employee and officer of that Bank, I have a natural strong desire to serve as its President.''

When he served as a Federal Reserve governor, Powell was best known for his role as chairman of the National Voluntary Credit Restraint Committee, established by the Board of Governors to try to alleviate inflationary pressures that were being fueled by the Korean conflict. It was comprised of the national committee and forty-three regional committees with representatives from commercial banks, life insurance companies, investment banks, savings banks, and savings and loan associations. The goal was to reduce significantly credit commitments for nondefense purposes. In support of this goal, Powell traveled across the county giving speeches to regional committees and prominent bankers, stressing that under the program, the test "is not whether a loan is a good credit risk, but whether it is inflationary." In retrospect, it is generally believed that the program had a degree of success, much more so than a similar program established in the 1960s. At the time of the program, there were reports of some banks turning down as much as $10 million to $27 million in loans.

Powell is known for his dissenting opinion in the Transamerica Bank Holding Company antitrust case. The majority of the board held that Transamerica's control of 40 percent of the banking offices in a five-state area, under section 7 of the Clayton Act, had the effect of restricting commerce and tending to monopoly. Transamerica was ordered to divest itself of all capital stock in twenty-six California financial institutions, sixteen in Oregon, three in Nevada, one in Arizona, and one in Washington. In his written dissent, Powell stated that the case was tried too narrowly. He felt that statistics alone would not answer the question posed in the Clayton Act regarding the restriction of commerce. It was his opinion that factors such as the remaining competition and the probable development of consumer demands needed to be considered.

During his years in the Federal Reserve system, Powell sat on various committees involving operational issues. While on the Board of Governors, he chaired two special committees studying the check collection system. In 1937 he was chairman of the system committee studying uniform member bank reserve ratios. From 1930 to 1932 he was a staff member on the Federal Reserve committee on branch, chain and group banking for which he wrote "Causes of Failure of 225 Member Banks 1920–1931."

Throughout his career, Powell was concerned that the public should be educated about the banking system. His goal was to "spell out banking so that the man on the street can understand it." He was responsible for making the Minneapolis Federal Reserve's first motion picture, *Back of Banks and Business* (1935), and *The Federal Reserve Bank and You* (1950). He conceived the picture book *Your Money and the Federal Reserve System* (1941) and is the author of the booklet *Questions and Answers on Gold*.

He was involved in many educational activities outside the reserve system as well. He was the education director and instructor in banking and economics for the Minneapolis Chapter of the American Institute of Banking (1923–1927). In 1933–1934 he served as the institute's president. He spent eleven years as a lecturer for the Graduate School of Banking at Rutgers University and five years as a lecturer for the Central State School of Banking at Madison.

In a professional capacity, he served outside the reserve system as a consultant to the Committee on Economic Security in 1934, consultant in the statistical office of the Federal Deposit Insurance Corporation in 1934–1935, and chairman of the research committee for the Northwest Shippers Advisory Board in the 1930s. He served two years as an adviser to the Bank of Korea after his retirement in 1957 from the Minneapolis Reserve Bank. He was also active in the YMCA and the Boy Scouts of America. He was an honorary member of Beta Gamma Sigma and Delta Sigma Pi. On his death on July 26, 1963, he was survived by his widow, Ada, his two daughters, and a son.

BIBLIOGRAPHY

New York Times, July 13, 1950, p. 42; August 4, 1950, p. 4; September 2, 1950, p. 21; March 15, 1951, p. 43; April 1, 1951, p. 31; October 18, 1951, p. 47; October 31, 1951, p. 41; November 10, 1951, p. 22; November 23, 1951, p. 42; December 6, 1951, p. 54; December 8, 1951, p. 17; December 30, 1951, p. III–5; January 23, 1952, p. 37; March 26, 1952, p. 48; April 2, 1952, p. 40; July 1, 1952, p. 6.

Powell, Oliver S. Addresses and statements. Board of Governors Library, Washington, D.C.

U.S. Congress. Subcommittee on General Credit Control and Debt Management of the Joint Committee on the Economic Report. 1952. *Hearings*. 82d Cong., 1st sess.

RONALD RANSOM (1882–1947)

Jack B. White

What type of background would prepare one to serve on the Board of Governors during the latter years of the Great Depression and the no less trying years of World War II? For Ronald Ransom, the vice-chairman of the Board of Governors of the Federal Reserve system from August 6, 1936, until his death on December 2, 1947, the preparation came in the form of education, experience, and public service.

Ransom was born in Columbia, South Carolina, on January 21, 1882. He attended the University of Georgia, studied law, and received his LL.B. in 1903. Admitted to the Georgia bar the same year, Ransom practiced law in Atlanta until 1922.

He married the former Mary Brent Hoke of Atlanta in 1908. Their union produced one child, Barbara. In World War I, he contributed to the war effort not only with the American Red Cross but also with the U.S. Army, where he served as a first lieutenant in the chemical warfare service.

After the war, Ransom returned to the practice of law for four years. In 1922 he joined the Fulton National Bank of Atlanta as a vice-president, a position he held until 1933. He was promoted to executive vice-president of the bank, which he held until his appointment to the Board of Governors.

Ransom was a notable member of the banking community. He served as president of the Atlanta Clearing House Association in 1929, and was a member of the Georgia Bankers Association, serving that body as president in 1931. Nationally, he was a member of the American Bankers Association, where he served on a number of important committees. Notable among these were the Bank Management Committee, which he chaired, and the Bankers Committee of the National Recovery Act.

Ransom was involved in significant public service during the Great Depression. He was a member of the Special Relief Committee for the Atlanta area in 1932 and 1933. His excellent performance was recognized in 1933 when he was selected as chairman of the Georgia Relief Committee.

Ransom's tenure at the Fed included two episodes that continue to be studied today. The first deals with the recession of 1937. By 1933, the Great Depression was at its height. Over four thousand banks had closed their doors. Those that remained had accumulated over $3 billion of excess reserves. These reserves were excess only by definition, however. The banks had willingly built up these reserve levels as an insurance against bank runs. As long as the economy was in the throes of a recession, the Fed was content to ignore the fact that these excess reserves would support a monetary expansion of over $20 billion. Considering that the total money supply (M1) in 1935 was only $25.6 billion, this potential addition is significant indeed.

In 1936 industrial production rose, along with wholesale prices. With the economy expanding, the Fed now considered the excess reserves to be inflationary. Despite the fact that unemployment continued to hover at 14 percent, the Fed moved to remove the inflationary threat of the excess reserves by increasing bank reserve requirements. The first increase, in July 1936, reduced excess reserves to $1.5 billion. Subsequent gold imports raised that figure to $2 billion by year end, which the Fed still viewed as excessive. In January the Fed announced that the reserve requirements would be increased further in March and May. These increases would essentially convert all of the remaining excess reserves to required reserves. The month following the announcement, bond prices fell sharply. The recession began in earnest in the second quarter of 1937; the economy did not recover its 1937 production level until 1940.

By 1941, when the United States mobilized for World War II, interest rates had fallen as low as 0.5 percent on short-term government debt and only 2 percent on its long-term debt. The Treasury, realizing that the war would be financed largely with borrowed funds, desired to maintain these low interest rates. The Fed agreed to purchase the new debt issues at the current interest rate levels. By agreeing to maintain a given interest rate, the Fed relinquished control of the money supply. Since wartime price controls and rationing were in effect, however, the increase in the money supply accompanying the Fed bond purchases did not have an immediate effect on the price level. The war's end saw most of these controls lifted. The Fed, however, continued to accommodate the Treasury. Not surprisingly, without the price restraints in place, prices began to rise sharply in 1946. This increase in the price level was cooled only by a recession in 1948.

Ransom did not live to see the Fed reassert its independence with respect to the money supply or witness the postwar economic expansion. He died in 1947 at the age of sixty-five.

BIBLIOGRAPHY

Luckett, Dudley. 1984. *Money and Banking*, 3d ed. New York: McGraw-Hill.
Who Was Who in America, 1943–1950. Vol. 2. Chicago: A. N. Marquis Company.

EMMETT J. RICE (1920–   )

Jane M. Simmons

Emmett J. Rice commented on being a Federal Reserve board member to *Institutional Investor* in 1984, "From many points of view, it's not really a very good job. One would wonder why somebody would take it." From Rice's education and experience, one would not wonder why he was nominated to the board on April 12, 1979, by President Jimmy Carter, confirmed by the Senate on June 12, and appointed to the office on both June 20 and June 26. One would wonder about the timing of his appointment from his standpoint with the economic problems of inflation and high interest rates along with the election of a Republican president in 1980 whose subsequent nominations to the board splintered the members and caused much of the board's conflict to be aired in the media.

Born in Florence, South Carolina, in 1920, Rice's educational experiences began at the City College of New York, where he was graduated with the bachelor's degree in business administration in 1941. He continued his education at City College and earned his master's of business administration in 1942. After serving the U.S. Air Force from 1942 to 1946, his education was continued at the University of California at Berkeley, from which he was graduated with a Ph.D. in economics in 1955. While pursuing his Ph.D., he was a research assistant in economics and was selected as a research associate at the Reserve Bank of India as a Fulbright fellow in 1952.

Rice's academic experiences were brief. He was a teaching assistant from 1953 to 1954 at the University of California at Berkeley while completing his Ph.D. and then accepted a position as assistant professor in economics at Cornell University until 1960.

Rice devoted a significant portion of his time to civic organizations, such as the Federal City Council, the Greater Washington Business Resource Center, the D.C. Chapter of the American Red Cross, the Center for Municipal and Metropolitan Research, the Washington Performing Arts Society, and the Consortium of Universities, and he served as president of the Federal City Housing Corporation.

While Rice was quoted by *Black Enterprise* (Poole 1979) as having said, "I consider luck a very large element in my own personal success. There's a large element of luck in anybody's rise to an important position," it was more than luck that guided his career. His professional experiences in banking began when he took a leave in 1960 from Cornell to work as an economist for the Federal Reserve Bank of New York. He held that position until 1962 when he became adviser to the Central Bank of Nigeria in Lagos.

From 1964 to 1966 Rice was deputy director and then acting director for the U.S. Treasury Department's Office of Developing Nations. During the period from 1966 to 1970, Rice became the U.S. alternate executive director for the International Bank for Reconstruction and Development for the World Bank, the International Development Association, and the International Financial Corporation. He was appointed to the position by President Lyndon Johnson in October 1966. At the agency, he helped to establish the Central Bank of Nigeria.

While on leave from the Treasury Department, Rice served for one year (1970–1971) as the executive director of Mayor Washington's Economic Development Committee in Washington, D.C. In 1972 he was appointed senior vice-president of the National Bank of Washington, which at that time was the third largest bank in the Washington, D.C., area. He held the position of senior vice-president until his appointment to the Board of Governors in 1979. In June 1979 the *Banker* suggested that Rice's appointment to the board was political in two senses: he was viewed as a moderate Democrat, and he was the first black member of the board since Andrew Brimmer[*] resigned.

Soon after his appointment, Rice was interviewed by *Black Enterprise* magazine (Poole 1979). He was challenged by the reporter about what his position would mean for minorities in America. Rice replied, "The way monetary policy operates and the way it affects the economy doesn't allow for making a differential impact on certain sectors, population groups, or industrial groups. . . . There is very little scope for protecting the interests of black people. It's not that kind of job." He did indicate to the reporter that he hoped to push for more representation of minorities among the high-ranking employees in the reserve headquarters. He commented, "So far as I have seen, there is to my knowledge only one black officer, and that is the Equal Employment Opportunity officer. This is not a very healthy or satisfactory situation so far as employment of blacks is concerned. I would have thought that by this time there would have been more blacks at high officer staff levels at the Federal Reserve Board."

G. William Miller[*] chaired the board when Rice became a board member. On July 25, 1979, President Carter announced that Paul Volcker[*] would be the new board chair. The board faced double-digit inflation and the value of the dollar falling on the world market. When questioned about his liberal or conservative stance in terms of monetary policy, Rice would reply that he was an eclectic and a pragmatist, and that he didn't place himself on the spectrum as if he did he would confuse people. Rice sided with Volcker, who labeled himself a pragmatic monetarist and almost immediately introduced a monetarism measure aimed at controlling the money supply through changes in bank reserves.

In March 1980 the board still faced an 18 percent annual inflation rate and introduced a credit control aimed at curbing consumer credit, which seemed to have the desired effect. In early July inflation seemed to be slowing, but by February 1981, inflation remained at 11.5 percent, and the board had a new administration with which to deal. Throughout the changes, Volcker seemed to generate the most press. In May 1984 the *Institutional Investor* (Reich 1984) commented on Rice's performance as a board governor: "As the board's lone black member, he has been wrongly categorized, in his opinion, as an ultraliberal. He can almost invariably be counted on to vote with Volcker."

As the Reagan appointees began to join the board, Volcker needed all of the allies he could muster against what became known as the gang of four: Preston Martin,* Martha Seger,* Wayne Angell,* and Manuel Johnson.* Much of the media's attention focused on the clashes between Reagan's administration and Volcker. Much of the conflict centered on Volcker's decision-making ability, which may have undermined his credibility and have led to the dissenting vote in 1986 against Volcker on lowering the discount rate. Through all of this turmoil, Rice seemed to side quietly with Volcker.

In November 1986 *Dun's Business Month* announced that Rice had resigned from the Board of Governors effective December 31, 1986. *Jet Magazine* (October 1986) stated that Rice had quit the board with more than four years left in his term and quoted Rice as indicating that his decision to resign was personal and "was reached after serving many years in public life, the last seven and a half as a member of the board." A short caption in *Institutional Investor* suggested that Rice experienced conflicts with the Federal Reserve staff. "Of all of the board members, he has the worst relations with the Fed staffers: They accuse him of not working hard enough; he accuses them of trying to 'program' him" (Glynn 1986).

Rice is retired and currently living in the Washington, D.C., area. He occasionally does consulting work.

BIBLIOGRAPHY

"Emmett J. Rice: Appointment as a Member of the Board of Governors." 1979. *Federal Reserve Bulletin* 65 (July): 545.
"Emmett Rice Steps Down from Federal Reserve Post." 1986. *Jet*, October 20, p. 12.
Glynn, Lenny. 1986. " Turmoil at the Fed." *Institutional Investor* 20 (April): 71–78.
"New Fed Governors." 1979. *Banker* 129 (June): 179–80.
Poole, Isaiah J. 1979. "Emmett Rice: New Man at the Fed." *Black Enterprise* 10 (October): 50–52.
Reich, Cary. 1984. "Inside the Fed." *Institutional Investor* 18 (May): 137–50.
"Rice Quits Fed; Volcker Weakened." 1986. *Dun's Business Month* 128 (November): 14.

JAMES LOUIS ROBERTSON (1907–)

Penny Kugler

"I reviewed my life from beginning to end—or nearly end—and I have enjoyed it"—an extraordinary statement, but James Louis Robertson is an extraordinary man. Born in the small central Nebraskan town of Broken Bow (population 3,500) on October 31, 1907, he became one of the country's most respected banking authorities and was appointed to the Board of Governors of the Federal Reserve in 1952.

The youngest of five children, Louis arrived at the same time as the panic of 1907. His father, Andrew J. Robertson, then in banking, lost everything except the family home. Three years later, the senior Robertson suffered a stroke, which left him totally paralyzed for eight years. He died in 1918 when Louis was ten.

Louis was a janitor at a church, ran paper routes, and worked at his Uncle Ed's drugstore. By age fifteen he was a ranch hand receiving a dollar a day, a man's wages.

He entered Grinnell College after graduating from high school. His greatest love was not his studies but rather football and a young girl named Julia Jensen. Nebraska senator George W. Norris offered him a job in the Senate Post Office after his sophomore year. He left Grinnell and Julia behind and headed for Washington, D.C. By this time, Robbie (as he was now called) had decided he wanted to be a lawyer and enrolled in George Washington University. He was promoted to chief clerk at the Senate Post Office, which allowed him to schedule his own work hours. By working more hours on the weekends and fewer hours during the week, he could attend law school during the day and liberal arts school at night. Although this schedule was extremely difficult, Robbie was able to complete an A.B. degree along with his LL.B. degree. He was then admitted into Harvard Law School to begin graduate work. He did, however, take enough time off to marry Julia.

In 1931 he was admitted to the bar of the Court of Appeals for the District of Columbia, but in 1932, jobs, even for soon-to-be Harvard graduates, were few. The Federal Bureau of Investigation offered Robertson a job as a special agent; however, the position was to begin before the end of the school year.

Robertson began work with the FBI on the appointed date and was allowed time off from his new job to take final exams under Professor Operheim of George Washington University. Robbie assumes that the Harvard professors "felt sorry" for him and gave him the LL.M. degree.

The bank holiday of 1933 brought with it a career change for Robertson. The Office of the Comptroller of the Currency was in need of lawyers and conservators to determine which banks could be reopened and which would be liquidated. The job offered more money than that of an FBI agent, so Robertson accepted the position. He spent the next nine years handling legal problems concerning bank reorganization and eventually became the head of bank supervision. Robertson worked full time with bank supervisory problems as a deputy comptroller and in 1935 was admitted to the bar of the Supreme Court.

During World War II, he served as legal counsel to under secretary of the Navy James Forrestal. He returned to the comptroller's office at the war's end and was soon appointed first deputy, a position that gave Robertson the responsibility of national bank supervision.

Late in 1951 the recently appointed chairman of the Federal Reserve board, William Martin,* asked Robertson if he would consider an appointment to the board. Although Robertson informed Martin that he was content with his present position, Martin apparently pushed his name forward because Robertson tells that "out of the clear blue sky came word that the President wanted to appoint me as a Democrat to offset his appointment of Abbot Mills* as a Republican. I immediately sent back word that I could not accept the appointment for the simple reason that I was not a Democrat and had never been associated with any political party."[1] Shortly after, President Truman sent for Robertson and told him, "Mr. Robertson, I don't care what your politics are. I am told that you know more about bank supervision than any one else and that is exactly what the Federal Reserve needs right now. I want you to take this appointment."[2] The president guaranteed Robertson that he would never attempt to influence his vote. Robertson accepted the appointment given that condition and was sworn in as a governor in February 1952. Rarely had lawyers been appointed to the board, and at that time he was the only lawyer serving on the board. However, he had been associated with bank supervision for over twenty years.

The conscientious Robertson was faced with a dilemma in this new position. Although he was well versed in law and banking supervision, he had no formal training in economics. To be able to analyze the date that crossed his desk daily, he found it necessary to be tutored each day in economics for a year, until he felt as capable as his fellow board members.

While in office, Robertson gained the reputation of being extremely independent and outspoken—a strong but reasonable man. He was known for his dissenting point of view and often found himself on the minority side of the vote.

He was known for his easy money policy votes during the latter part of his first term in office. In early 1963 Robertson spoke out against the credit policy that he felt would cause short-term rates to rise, a position in which he found himself alone.

In May 1963 Robertson again was in the minority of a 6–5 vote of the Federal Open Market Committee to tighten money because he felt the unemployment rate was too high. Twice in July of that same year, he voted against any increase in monetary tightness. The easy money policy he advocated during his first term in office, along with his expert knowledge of bank supervision, may have been the reason he was reappointed to the board in March 1964. President Lyndon B. Johnson also favored an easy money policy, and since Robertson had been appointed for his first term in February 1952 and as such had not served a full fourteen-year term, he was eligible for reappointment.

When Robertson's term expired on January 31, 1964, however, President Johnson did not immediately reappoint him. Robertson's friends and colleagues were advising him to seek reappointment, but he refused. He was under the impression that his point of view was well known by those who would be advising the president concerning the appointment and that others would push in his behalf; moreover, it was not in his nature to seek a job.

Although Robertson was not officially reappointed until March 1964, he remained on the board while his reappointment was being considered. Two years later, in March 1966, he was elected vice-chairman, a position he would hold until his resignation from the board seven years later.

During his second term in office, Robertson proposed that the banking supervision system be changed. In the article, "Federal Regulation of Banking: A Plea for Unification"(1966), Robertson pointed out the waste and confusion brought about by the use of three separate agencies to perform relatively the same work that a single agency could do. The proposed agency, the Federal Banking Commission (FBC), was not a new idea; he himself had proposed the commission in 1962, and other unification proposals had been made as early as 1919. Robertson believed that the lack of unification created conflicts among the agencies, confusion to banks, and inequalities in classes of banks because of competition. He felt that layers of laws had piled up over the years that now were causing problems in bank supervision. He argued that the establishment of the FBC would allow the Federal Reserve board to concentrate on monetary policy—"the most vital function" of the board, according to Robertson. He pleaded that the proposal be ratified before a catastrophe occurred—a catastrophe much like the savings and loan problem facing the economy in the early 1990s. For Robertson, the failure to adopt this proposal was one of the most disappointing moments he faced while on the board.

Robertson was not simply concerned with banking supervision. In May 1969 he gave a speech in Omaha, Nebraska, before a group of bankers and businessmen. He talked as a "concerned citizen" about the country's youth and the need for them to be taught values by their parents. He spoke on the violence being seen on college campuses across the country and was concerned that campuses had become a place for "mass teenage temper tantrums." He felt some young people had lost respect for the rights of other citizens and the liberty that many Americans had fought so hard to obtain. The fact that some of America's youth were unhappy with the system was not the issue to Robertson; the problem was the way in which the students protested. He argued that it was not his desire to stifle dissent or discourage involvement by concerned people; he had been brought to Washington more than forty years previously by one of the greatest of liberal dissenters, the late senator George W. Norris, and his own role as a dissenter was fairly well known, at least in financial circles. To Robertson's surprise, the speech was printed in the June 9, 1969, edition of *U.S. News & World Report*. Mail flowed, and this encouraged Robertson to write *What Generation Gap?* (1970), which included many of the letters he had received, along with a response to each.

Robertson's outspoken nature sparked controversy and severe criticism in the banking industry in early 1970. As early as 1965, in an article entitled "The Changing World of Banking" (1965), Robertson condemned the techniques banks were using to obtain funds. In the late 1960s and early 1970s, as inflationary pressures mounted and the Federal Reserve tightened the "monetary screws" and interest rates were at record highs, banks began borrowing in the Eurodollar market as well as acquiring funds in the commercial paper market. In an attempt to circumvent Regulation Q and avoid reserve requirements, banks began issuing what they called unsecured short-term promissory notes. This practice, which began as early as September 1964, according to Robertson tended to undermine the effectiveness of the Federal Reserve to control the money supply in the economy. Not only were banks paying interest on such notes to attract funds, these notes were exempt from the reserve requirement mandated by section 19 of the Federal Reserve Act.

Robertson criticized banks' inventing a new name to disguise what were in reality demand deposits in order to weaken the Federal Reserve's authority. He was concerned that many of these new funds were more volatile than traditional sources, and banks could face solvency and liquidity problems down the road.

In May 1970 Robertson gave a speech in Phoenix, Arizona, to the directors of the San Francisco Federal Reserve, as well as area bankers and businessmen. He criticized the banking industry for attempts made to get around the Federal Reserve's measures to curb inflation. His speech caused controversy in the banking community and specifically with the president of the American Bankers Association, Nat S. Rogers. Rogers denied Robertson's accusation that "commercial banks were frustrating the objectives of monetary policy through money market devices." He felt that Robertson had attempted to remove the Federal Reserve's responsibility of controlling inflation to commercial banks and went on to say that attempts to secure lendable funds had not created new money sources but had only rerouted existing funds.

Robertson had strong anti-inflationary beliefs. According to Edwin L. Dale, Jr., of the *Washington Daily News* (May 20, 1973), "Robertson was a member of the William McChesney Martin School of Central Banking, which emphasized interest rates and did not fear aggressive use of tight money, even if some people went broke as a result. Indeed, this school has always felt that some people ought to go broke as part of the process of stopping what Martin used to call 'inflationary excess.' ''

He was referred to as the ''pro-crunch man'' and felt that just before his leaving office, the Federal Reserve had gotten soft in its approach to inflation. This may have been due to the fact that the board had focused mainly on the money supply as well as monetary aggregates and not on interest rates. Robertson was convinced that money crunches were effective measures in fighting inflation and that the 1966 and 1969 crunches, although devastating to some, had accomplished their task. He also believed that the Federal Reserve could use the threat of another crunch as its ''stick in the closet'' in case of future inflationary threats. He criticized the board's policy as too ''chicken-hearted'' and called the anti-inflationary policy too weak; however, he conceded on his retirement from the board that it appeared that the board was ''on the right path.''

Robertson submitted his letter of resignation from the Board of Governors of the Federal Reserve system on March 29, 1973, before the end of his term in office because of a health problem known as Tic douloureux. Talking became difficult for Robertson, and he felt his ability to serve on the board and Open Market Committee would be hampered. He had been in public service for over forty-two years, and although he believes the decision was the right one, it was also very difficult. Robert Holland,[*] a native of Nebraska, was appointed to fill Robertson's unexpired term.

Robertson lives with his wife of more than sixty years in Bethesda, Maryland. They had three sons, two of them deceased.

NOTES

J. L. Robertson contributed the information concerning his family history as well as some events of his life. I greatly appreciate his help and support.

1. Written correspondence with J. L. Robertson, March 14, 1989.
2. Robertson quoting President Truman, March 14, 1989.

BIBLIOGRAPHY

Bratter, Herbert. 1962. ''Banking Spotlight on James Louis Robertson.'' *Banking* (July): 55, 111.
Dale, Edwin L., Jr. 1973. ''Pro-Crunch Man Leaves Fed.'' *Washington Daily News*, May 20, p. A–12.
Federal Reserve. 1973. Press release, April 19.
Flor, Lee. 1970. ''A Result of Coincidences.'' *Washington Sunday Star*, March 1.
''Freedom Foundation Honors 5, Picks Leader.'' 1971. *Washington Star*, February 10, p. B–4.
Robertson, J. L. 1965. ''The Changing World of Banking.'' *Banking* (March): 45, 122.

————. 1966. "Federal Regulation of Banking: A Plea for Unification." *Banking*, pt.
    I, 673–95.
————. 1970. *What Generation Gap?* Washington, D.C.: Acropolis Books.
Rubenstein, James. 1970. "Robertson Criticized by Rogers for Remarks on Bank Evasion
    Tactics." *American Banking*, June 16, pp. 1, 24.

FREDERICK H. SCHULTZ (1929–   )

Gregory A. Claypool

Frederick Henry Schultz, who served as a governor of the Federal Reserve from July 1979 to February 1982, was born January 16, 1929, in Jacksonville, Florida, to Clifford G. and Mae (Wangler) Schultz. Raised in the Jacksonville area, he attended the Bolles School in Jacksonville from 1942 to 1946 before spending the academic year 1946–1947 at Lawrenceville School in Lawrenceville, New Jersey. From 1947 to 1950 he attended Princeton University. He spent the academic year 1950–1951 at the University of Kentucky before returning to Princeton in 1951 to complete his degree. He was graduated from Princeton in 1952 with an A.B. degree, majoring in history.

Just prior to his return to Princeton, in August 1951, he married Nancy Jane Reilly. They would eventually become the parents of four children; a daughter, Catherine, and three sons, Frederick H. Schultz, Jr., Clifford G. Schultz II, and John R. Schultz.

After graduation Schultz served with the U.S. Army in Korea. He served with such distinction that he was awarded the Bronze Star, in addition to the Korean Service Medal and the U.N. Medal.

Upon his return to civilian life in 1954, he entered the University of Florida Law School in Gainesville, Florida, where he completed two years of work before accepting a position with the Barnett National Bank in 1956. In 1957 he opened his own investment firm, Schultz Investments, which he currently operates in Jacksonville, focusing on the securities markets and providing venture capital to new and expanding business enterprises.

In the 1960s Schultz became deeply involved in Florida politics. After serving on the Jacksonville Expressway Authority from 1961 to 1963, he was elected to the Florida House of Representatives in 1963. He retained his seat in the House until 1970 and was elected Speaker of the House for the period 1968–1970. He was the recipient of numerous awards during this decade, including the Jacksonville Junior Chamber of Commerce Award for Outstanding Young Man, 1964, the Allen Morris Award for Outstanding Legislator for the years 1968 and 1970, the Louis Brownlow Prize given jointly by the American Association of Public Administration and the Council of State Governments for the best published writing in the area of state government during 1969, and the Jacksonville Junior Chamber of Commerce Good Government Award in 1969.

Upon leaving the Florida House of Representatives, Schultz continued to operate his investment company, and he became more involved in the banking community. He had become a member of the board of directors of Barnett Banks of Florida in 1968, when he remained until 1979. He also was on the board of directors of American Heritage Life Insurance Company for a little over two years, and he was chairman of the board of Barnett Investment Services, a subsidiary of Barnett Banks of Florida.

In addition to his business interests, Schultz maintained an interest in education. He was a member of many statewide committees concerned with education, including serving as chairman of the Citizen's Committee on Education, a two-year study of education in Florida. He developed a reputation for expertise in funding formulas and other innovations for financing quality education. This reputation led to his first federal appointment in 1978 as a member of the National Council on Educational Research. His nomination to this council was highly praised by the members of the Senate's Committee on Human Resources.

A little over a year later, on April 12, 1979, President Jimmy Carter announced his intention to appoint Schultz as a member and vice-chairman of the Board of Governors of the Federal Reserve system. This nomination was not greeted with overwhelming praise from members of Congress. Because he lacked a high-powered background in the field of economics, questions were raised concerning his ability to be an effective member of the board—understandable concerns given the state of the economy at the time of his nomination. Inflation was rampant, and there were very real doubts that the Federal Reserve could bring it under control. Several concerned legislators could not understand how Schultz's presence on the board would add to the Fed's expertise in the fight against inflation. Furthermore, because of Schultz's political background and support for President Carter during his campaign in 1976, the Senate Committee on Banking, Housing, and Urban Affairs raised the issue of whether Schultz could maintain the traditional independence of the Federal Reserve from the executive branch. In spite of these concerns, Schultz's nomination was confirmed by the Senate on July 18, and he took the oath of office on July 27, 1979.

As it turned out, Schultz's political experience was the perfect background for the events about to unfold at the Federal Reserve. He had been in office less than three months when the Board of Governors, under the chairmanship of Paul Volcker,* decided that drastic action was necessary to get control of inflation. On October 6, 1979, the Fed announced a change in operating methods. No longer would it attempt to control inflation through direct control of interest rates. Instead, it would attempt to control inflation by focusing on the aggregate measures of money supply and allow interest rates to fluctuate accordingly. Schultz supported Volcker in this decision on the grounds that something drastic needed to be done in the fight against inflation. He had told the Senate committee at his confirmation hearing that he would like to get to the point where the Fed could deal with the aggregates but also said he felt that point was not in the near future because of the uncertainty that surrounded the volatility of money.

Many of Schultz's subsequent activities on the Board of Governors would revolve around the economic effects of this so-called Saturday night massacre. He was called to testify before various congressional committees several times to explain the Fed's new policy and its effects on different sectors of the economy, specifically, small businesses, the banking industry, and agriculture.

Throughout the details of his testimony before these different committees, two principal themes recurred. First, Schultz argued that the negative consequences that were being experienced in the short run were more than outweighed by the long-run benefit of gaining control over inflation. In support of this argument, he frequently noted that small business owners were among the most ardent supporters of policies designed to combat inflation. The second theme in Schultz's remarks was that the negative impact of sharply rising interest rates could be considerably softened if government would adopt a sensible fiscal policy, namely, a balanced federal budget. It could be argued that these two themes were merely the party line of the Federal Reserves as it implemented this controversial change in operating methods. It is only fair to note, however, that Schultz had mentioned these same two points in his confirmation hearing, so while he may have been helping the Fed to maintain a united public front, he clearly believed that the change in policy was necessary.

Schultz's term on the Board of Governors expired on January 31, 1982. While the law provides that a governor should continue service until a successor is sworn into office, rules of ethics require that no participation in board meetings can occur within thirty days of involvement in activities in the private sector. Therefore, he submitted his resignation effective February 11, 1982. Schultz was eventually succeeded by Preston Martin.[*]

BIBLIOGRAPHY

"A Conversation with Mr. Schultz of the Fed." 1982. *Wall Street Journal*, January 15.
"A Look inside Paul Volcker's Fed." 1981. *New York Times*, May 3.
Schultz, Frederick H. 1969. "Legislative Modernization—The Florida Experiment."
    State Government 42 (Autumn).
U.S. Congress. Senate. Committee on Banking, Housing, and Urban Affairs. 1979
    *Hearing on the Nomination of Frederick H. Schultz to Be a Member and Vice
    Chairman of the Board of Governors of the Federal Reserve System*. 96th Cong.,
    1st sess., June 25.

MARTHA ROMAYNE SEGER
(1932–   )

Robert C. Winder

Martha Romayne Seger, who has served as a governor of the Federal Reserve since July 1984, was born in Adrian, Michigan, on February 17, 1932. She has received three degrees from the University of Michigan: a B.A. in 1954, an M.B.A. in finance in 1955, and a Ph.D. in finance and business economics in 1971. Seger has devoted herself to her career which began interestingly, in 1964 with a four–year stint as a financial economist with the Federal Reserve board in Washington, D.C., where she specialized in money and capital markets and financial institutions. In 1967 Seger left central banking for private banking, becoming the chief economist for the Detroit Bank and Trust Company. In 1974 she became vice-president for economics and investment for the Bank of the Commonwealth, also in Detroit.

Having worked in both government and private business, Seger's career took another turn in 1976 when she became adjunct associate professor at the University of Michigan and lecturer in finance at the University of Windsor. In 1980 Seger went to Oakland University as associate professor of economics and finance, but she was not destined to remain in the ivy-covered towers of academia. In a critical and formative career move, Seger served as commissioner of financial institutions for the state of Michigan in 1981–1982. As commissioner, she was the principal regulator of the state's financial institutions—both banks and thrift institutions. This tour of duty as a regulator developed and defined her views on the regulatory process and gave her critical experience and stature.

Seger returned briefly to academic life in 1983 as professor of finance at Central Michigan University, but within a year she was called on by President Ronald Reagan to become one of the seven members of the Board of Governors of the Federal Reserve system. She was sworn in to this position on July 2, 1984.

Seger has received numerous awards throughout her varied and successful career. In 1976 she was chosen by *Business Week* as one of the Top 100 Corporate Women in America. In 1986 she was selected as Michigan Woman of the Year and won the Kappa Kappa Gamma Alumnae Achievement Award and the New

Mexico School of Banking Leadership Award. She has been awarded several honorary doctorates in law and in management. Seger is active in a variety of professional organizations, including the National Associate of Business Economists, the Women's Economic Club, and the Economic Club of Detroit and has served on the boards of directors of several organizations.

As a young girl growing up in Michigan, Seger enjoyed mathematics and dreamed of becoming an engineer, but because of the realities and constraints of the time, she viewed this as impractical: "I grew up when women did certain things, and men did certain things." As an undergraduate, Seger initially bowed to convention and pursued a liberal arts curriculum; however, to satisfy an area requirement in social science, she randomly chose an economics course. This led to a second economics course and ultimately to two advanced degrees in economics and finance. During her graduate training, Seger was a research assistant to Paul McCracken, who was chairman of the Council of Economic Advisers during the Nixon administration.

Seger's decision to switch from liberal arts to economics and finance revealed a fiercely independent, even defiant personality, and, with the benefit of hindsight, was a harbinger of things to come. The Senate confirmation hearings on Seger's nomination to serve on the Federal Reserve Board of Governors were partisan, protracted, and often contentious. She was closely identified with the Republican party, having served in 1983 as chairman of the Economic Advisory Council of the Michigan Senate's Republican Caucus. In 1984 she served as chairman of a Michigan political action group supportive of supply-side economics. And she commented publicly that she "supports everything he [Reagan] is doing" upon being introduced by President Reagan as his nominee to fill the open slot on the Federal Reserve board. The partisan nature of the Senate hearing was aggravated by the timing of the nomination, which came on the eve of the 1984 presidential election, pitting the incumbent Reagan against the Democratic challenger, Walter Mondale.

The Senate hearing on the Seger nomination got off to a rocky start as Senator Donald Riegle (D, Michigan) noted that despite Seger's background, both in and out of academia, she had done virtually no publishing and her views on economics and monetary policy were not known. As a result, Riegle indicated, the Senate committee would have to "take whatever time is necessary" to develop and explore Seger's positions on these issues. Senator Riegle also expressed surprise that Seger did not choose to make an opening statement to the Senate committee to give some sense of her general view of Fed policy and the economy in general. Republican members of this committee fought back in what became an increasingly rancorous discussion. Committee chairman Jake Garn (R, Utah) noted that previous nominees had won Senate approval despite an absence of writings and publications and pointed out that Paul Volcker,[*] Nancy Teeters,[*] Preston Martin[*] Frederick Shultz,[*] and Emmett Rice,[*] had all been approved by the Senate and none chose to make an opening statement.

Senator William Proxmire (D, Wisconsin) expressed concern that Seger was so closely linked to Republican politics and causes that her confirmation might enable the "Reagan White House to seize the reins of monetary control." He grilled her about a story in the press that she was nominated, at least in part, for expressing to former Federal Reserve governor Preston Martin her desire to "follow a Reaganite growth path for monetary policy." Seger denied making such a remark. Proxmire asked Seger about her own position on whether monetary policy should be used in a countercyclical and discretionary way or whether she advocated the use of a monetary rule regardless of current economic conditions. Seger disavowed the use of a strict monetary rule and protested that "I am not a monetarist." In subsequent testimony Seger recalled that during her pren-omination interview with Donald Regan, then serving as President Reagan's chief of staff, she refused to be characterized as a Keynesian, monetarist, or supply sider. She recalled telling him, "I call myself a garbage collector, because I think I have picked up bits and pieces from all of these areas."

During the course of the Senate hearings, Seger was grilled on a wide variety of monetary, financial, and regulatory issues. On the exploding federal deficit, she indicated serious concern about the effect of the deficit on investor confidence, interest rates, and inflation but, when prompted, refused to subscribe to a tax increase to close the budget gap. In a recurring theme and consistent with the denial that she is a monetarist, Seger argued that too much emphasis is placed on short-term movements in the M1 measure of money. She also expressed interest in further deregulation of the financial services industry to allow banks to underwrite municipal revenue bonds and commercial paper and to participate in discount brokerage. According to Seger, banks already have similar powers and clearly have the knowledge and expertise to be successful in these new areas. Furthermore, as a matter of equity, banks should not be subject to constraints that put them at a competitive disadvantage compared to nondepository financial institutions. Also with reference to regulatory issues, Seger expressed support for the dual banking system but argued that the responsibility for regulating and supervising the commercial banking system should reside with the Federal Reserve system, along with the individual state agencies, while the Federal Deposit Insurance Corporation should concentrate exclusively on its insurance function.

Finally, after fourteen hours of testimony over four day's, Seger was approved by the Senate Banking Committee by a narrow 10–8 vote. The full Senate subsequently recessed without acting on the nomination, and on July 2, 1984, President Reagan used his power to appoint to put Martha Seger on the Federal Reserve board for a one-year term. One year later, Seger was approved by the Senate Banking Committee for a second time and without any debate passed the full Senate on a voice vote.

Seger's penchant for independence is the watermark of her career. At a regular meeting of the Federal Reserve board on February 24, 1986, Seger engaged in a shootout with Fed chairman Paul Volcker that shocked the investment community. Along with vice-chairman Preston Martin (also a Reagan appointee), Seger forced a formal vote to lower the discount rate. The powerful and imposing

Volcker, who had never lost a monetary policy vote, was absolutely opposed to such a cut. When the dust settled, Seger, with the support of the newest Federal Reserve board members Wayne Angell* and Manuel Johnson,* had won. Volcker was furious and, according to some reports, threatened to quit before the end of the day. In the end, Volcker did not resign but accepted a face-saving compromise whereby the cut in the U.S. discount rate was delayed until the Japanese and West Germans cut theirs. In a curious and ironic turn of events, it was vice-chairman Martin who resigned from the board just weeks later on March 21. Martin's surprise resignation left Seger "devastated" by some reports, and the larger-than-life Volcker was, seemingly, back in charge following the attempted coup.

As a member of the Board of Governors of the Federal Reserve, Seger has had a special interest in structural and regulatory issues. In a November 29, 1984, speech to the Association of Bank Holding Companies on "Interstate Banking: Prospects and Problems," Seger was characteristically forthright about her position on this issue:

As an economist, I welcome the removal of restrictions on entry into new markets. Entry restrictions often serve only to perpetuate the existing division of market shares, regardless of how well or how poorly the market is being served. While we all may prefer to operate . . . without the threat of competition, no better force has yet been devised to assure good performance.

In a subsequent speech to the New Mexico Bankers Association, "The Transition to Interstate Banking" (June 8, 1985), Seger indicated that interstate banking is already a reality despite a number of statutes prohibiting it. According to Seger, "The statutes simply force banks to conduct this interstate activity through a variety of alternative channels, some of which may be less efficient than full interstate banking." These alternative channels include Edge Act corporations, loan production offices, nonbank subsidiaries, automatic teller machines, and credit card services offered across states and the establishment of "nonbank banks," which are able to operate across state lines. According to Seger, the current pressure to permit interstate banking is derived primarily from increased competition between banks and nonbank financial services companies and the migration of the American population to the South and West. Regarding the latter point, it is understandable that northern and eastern banks desire to follow their customers to the Sunbelt.

Seger does not believe that a move to full interstate banking would significantly jeopardize the safety or soundness of the private banking system, nor would interstate banking threaten small, local banks or the degree of competition in local markets. But she does express concern about the degree of national concentration that could result from uninhibited interstate banking. Although competition from nonbank financial services providers could ameliorate this potential problem, Seger argues that reasonable merger restrictions on the largest banks should be part of any interstate banking law.

Seger in various speeches and presentations has indicated support for expanding the product line of banks in order for them to remain competitive with other segments of the financial services industry. This includes possible repeal of the Glass-Steagall Act of 1933, which separated commercial banking from investment banking. Seger also supports consideration of risk-based deposit insurance premiums (and possibly risk-based capital requirements) to provide the necessary incentives for prudent risk taking in a deregulated environment. In general, she supports less regulation but better supervision of the banking system. In a September 1985 interview with the *ABA Banking Journal*, she is on record as favoring a "less legalistic" system, with "fewer explicit thou shalt and thou shalt nots." According to Seger, the role of regulators is not to manage banks but, to identify problems and "see that they are solved by the people who are paid to manage." It is fair to say that Seger believes in the magic of the marketplace and supports a market approach consistent with the safety and soundness of the banking system.

Seger's tenure on the Board of Governors of the Federal Reserve system continues until January 31, 1998. If she chooses to stay, she will continue to be independent, forthright, and contentious.

BIBLIOGRAPHY

"Fed's Seger Picks on Regulation." 1985. *ABA Banking Journal* (September): 43–45.
Seger, Martha R. 1984. "Interstate Banking: Prospects and Problems." Presented to the Association of Bank Holding Companies, Baltimore, November 29.
———. 1985. "The Transition to Interstate Banking." Presented to the New Mexico Bankers Association, Albuquerque, New Mexico, June 8.
U.S. Congress. Senate. Committee on Banking, Housing, and Urban Affairs. 1984. *Hearings on the Nomination of Martha Romayne Seger to Be a Member of the Board of Governors of the Federal Reserve System.* 98th Cong., 2d sess., June 14.
Who's Who in America, 1988–1989. Wilmette, Ill.: Marquis Who's Who.

JOHN EUGENE SHEEHAN (1929–   )

Yale L. Meltzer

John (Jack) Eugene Sheehan, who served as a governor of the Federal Reserve board from 1972 to 1974, was born on December 11, 1929, in Johnstown, Pennsylvania, in a neighborhood where he strongly felt the impact of the steel industry. At an early age, he became aware of the importance of employment in the steel and related industries.

Sheehan attended the U.S. Naval Academy and graduated with a bachelor of science degree in engineering in 1952. In that same year, he was commissioned as an ensign in the U.S. Navy. Serving as a naval aviator with the U.S. Atlantic and Pacific fleets, he rose to the rank of lieutenant. In 1958 Sheehan resigned his commission to attend Harvard Business School, where he excelled in his studies and was elected a George F. Baker Scholar for academic excellence. He received the M.B.A. degree (with distinction) in 1960. From 1960 to 1963 Sheehan worked in the New York City office of the management consulting firm of McKinsey & Co.

In 1963 Jack Sheehan joined Martin Marietta Corporation, which only two years before had been formed by the consolidation of American-Marietta and the Martin Company. Sheehan subsequently became vice-president of Martin Marietta's Cement and Lime Division. He remained with Martin Marietta until he joined Corhart Refractories Company, a subsidiary of Corning Glass Works, on January 15, 1966, as president and chief executive officer.

At Corhart, Sheehan became involved with its operations in the manufacture and marketing of high-temperature materials and processes, primarily refractory materials used in the manufacture of steel and glass. Thus, he was able to apply his engineering and technical expertise.

Sheehan remained at Corhart until January 3, 1972, when he joined the Federal Reserve and was subsequently appointed by President Richard Nixon to become a member of the Board of Governors upon the recommendation of board chairman Arthur Burns.[*]

Sheehan's nomination was considered by the Senate Committee on Banking, Housing, and Urban Affairs on January 27, 1972. Senator William Proxmire

(D, Wisconsin) raised strong objections to Sheehan's nomination on the grounds that Sheehan was not a professional economist. Excerpts from the hearings before the committee bring out Sheehan's concepts regarding the Federal Reserve board and monetary policy:

I wouldn't neglect, Senator, the notion that I presented to you just now, that we operate a very large banking system, that there are 23,000 people, and I would submit that when you have a Board of seven Governors you ought to have one man experienced in management.

Further, this is a day of automation and computers. We have billions—23, I think— of checks to process in our system. We are moving dramatically toward automation and computerization of the checking system in this country. I think that 23 billion, if that is an accurate number, is going to double over the next 10 years.

Now the creation and the supervision of that system, it seems to me, takes some business management competence on the Board of Governors.

[On monetary policy] I don't come to this Board with fixed views on how monetary policy should be formed or executed. It seems to me that there is a great deal of controversy among leading academic scholars in the field as to the importance of monetary policy as an economic stabilizer and how monetary policy should be executed. Because this is the case it would seem to me to be foolish for me, a newcomer to the Board and to the field, to take any firm position before weighing the evidence very carefully, and I intend to do that.

[On monetary and fiscal policy] Well, I doubt that I will ever become associated with an extreme or rigid or fixed position on monetary policy. It seems to me impossible, for example, that the effects of monetary policy on economy are the same under all conditions. The world does change, and I think monetary policy has to adapt to the circumstances as they develop.

There may be times when the growth rate of the money supply is the more important thing we have to look at in effecting the health of the economy.

But there are other times, I am sure, when fiscal policy or the state of confidence of consumers or businessmen, or a major war on the coast of Asia, or the application of a national effort to control wages and prices directly looms larger in importance than monetary policy. I pledge to you that I intend to—I will keep as open a mind as I can so that I can apply the relevant considerations toward achieving the best solution to a problem rather than being committed to any single thought or rigid theory.

[On the function of the Fed] The function of the Federal Reserve Board and the System [is] to promote the expansion of the economy as briskly as possible, such that we can have full production and full employment at all times being consistent with a stable dollar. And I intend to act in the interests of the American people, not in the interest of some thoughts or prejudice I bring.

[On profits] We have profits in the American system that are as low as they have been as a percentage of the gross national product in 30 years. In order for business to expand and to create jobs profits are fundamental. When profits are low, people are nervous.

Workmen are concerned about their continued employment. Consumers will not spend with confidence, and businessmen tend to lack confidence; and so I think it compounds the inflationary problem.

[On steel] The major industry that our company served was the American [steel] industry. That industry earned a return on capital invested last year of 2½ percent, which is about half of what one can earn on a tax exempt municipal bond. The steel industry suffered in this country last year. The Nation imported $1,900 million worth of steel. We have a trade deficit this year of about $2 billion that would almost have been eliminated if we had been in an export position in steel as we were some 10 years ago. The cost increases incurred by the American steel industry in recent years have been dramatic, the most significant of which is cost of labor.

The primary problem in the American society in the sense of its inflation in my judgment is productivity or lack of it. This morning's newspaper reports that we have a productivity increase in recent months, I believe in the past year, of about 3.6 percent or so. It surprises me a little bit that it was that high for the year. However, on reflection, it is not surprising in view of the industrial situation. When factories are operating at 70 percent you get productivity at a rapid rate as you proceed from 70 to 90 percent or so.

But I think we have a fundamental productivity problem which involves the cooperation of management and organized labor in increasing the output of our factories.

Sheehan was confirmed by the U.S. Senate and took his oath of office on January 4, 1972, joining the Federal Reserve board under the chairmanship of Arthur Burns.* Just as the United States was beginning to come out of the recession that had set in during 1974, he decided to leave the board, resigning on June 1, 1975.

Prior to becoming a governor of the Federal Reserve board, Sheehan had been a director of the Louisville branch of the Federal Reserve Bank of St. Louis, a director of the Louisville Fund, a director and executive committee member of the Kentucky Center for the Performing Arts, and a director of the Orion Broadcasting Company (in television and radio). In 1975, after leaving the Federal Reserve board, he became president and chief operating officer of White Motor Corporation. He also became chairman and chief executive officer of Reading Industries, as well as chairman of Bristol Corporation, Mored, and Excelsior Brass Works.

Sheehan married the former Jean McEvers of Kansas City, Missouri, on September 8, 1956. They have two daughters and one son. Sheehan is a member of the Harvard Club (New York City), the Army and Navy Country Club (Washington, D.C.), the Duquesne Club (Pittsburgh, Pennsylvania), and the Pendennis Club (Louisville, Kentucky).

BIBLIOGRAPHY

Federal Reserve System Board of Governors. 1972–1975. *Annual Reports.*
———. 1989. Correspondence with Yale L. Meltzer.
U.S. Congress. Senate. Committee on Banking, Housing, and Urban Affairs. 1972. *Hearings on the Nomination of John E. Sheehan.* 92d Cong., 2d sess., January 27, pp. 5–21.

CHARLES NOAH SHEPARDSON (1896–1975)

David E. R. Gay and Thomas R. McKinnon

The appointment of Charles Noah Shepardson to the Board of Governors of the Federal Reserve system illustrates well the effort to make the board representative of diverse sectors of American society. He came to the board from Texas A&M College, where he was dean of agriculture and totally immersed in the discipline by education, experience and interest. It was evident from the confirmation hearing that Shepardson's knowledge of Federal Reserve policy was extremely limited and that his selection was based solely on his expertise in agriculture. This concern for broad representation on the board no longer seems to be a significant consideration in the selection of new members.

Charles Noah Shepardson was born January 7, 1896, in Littleton, Colorado, to Noah and Mary Margaret Chatfield Shepardson. His education included a B.S. from Colorado A&M College in 1917 and an M.S. from Iowa State College in 1924. He was first married in 1917 to Nellie V. Trammel, who died on August 17, 1920. In 1923 he married Florence Redifer. They had no children. Shepardson served in the U.S. Army during World War I (1917–1919), achieving the rank of captain in the infantry.

Shepardson's entire career prior to his appointment to the Board of Governors was spent in the field of agriculture. He began as an extension animal husbandman at the University of Wyoming in 1919 and then moved to Colorado State College in 1920, where he was associate professor of agriculture for eight years. In 1928 he moved to Texas A&M College and served as head of the Dairy Husbandry Department until he was appointed dean in 1944.

The organizations in which Shepardson participated reflect his interest in agriculture and education. He was a U.S. delegate to the World Dairy Congress in Berlin in 1937; a member of the American Jersey Cattle Club, serving as director three years; a member of the Texas Dairy Products Association, serving as president for two years; a member of the Inter-American Committee for the Dairy Industry; a member of the American Dairy Science Association; and a member and president of the Association of Southern Agricultural Workers. His educational affiliation included Resident Instruction Section, Association of Land

Grant Colleges and Universities, chairman, 1947; National Education Association; American Association for the Advancement of Science; and Texas State Board of Examination for Teacher Education.

Shepardson's only banking experience prior to his appointment to the board was his serving as a director of the Houston Branch of the Federal Reserve Bank of Dallas. He was a member of the Disciples of Christ church, a Mason, a member of Rotary International, and a lifelong Republican.

Shepardson's confirmation hearing clearly revealed that he was selected for his expertise in agriculture rather than banking. Senator Paul Douglas of Illinois sharply questioned the new nominee. When Shepardson expressed uncertainty as to whom the board owed allegiance, Senator Douglas admonished, ''I urge you to read the statute very carefully and to place on your mirror before which you shave in the morning the statement, 'The Federal Reserve Board is the agent of Congress and not the Executive.' If you read that every morning as you shave, either before or after you say your prayers, you will be in a much better position to help administer the affairs of the Board'' (U.S. Congress 1955, p. 3). Shepardson's subsequent speeches reflected that he learned the lesson.

When Shepardson was unable to answer who manages the Federal Open Market Committee and the proper action of the committee to alter the money supply, Senator Douglas quipped, ''It is terrible for a college professor to be asked questions.'' On further questioning, Shepardson admitted that he was not acquainted with the Full Employment Act of 1946 and that he did not think it the responsibility of the Federal Reserve board to maintain maximum employment. At this point Senator Douglas asked that Shepardson study the matter and send a letter stating his point of view within a month. After Shepardson admitted that there was a tremendous amount to be studied and learned, Senator Douglas offered to outline a reading course that would include a list of books and pamphlets that every member of the Federal Reserve Board should know.

Senator Allen Frear of Delaware, another member of the committee, defended the nominee by suggesting that Shepardson was selected for his expertise in agriculture, not banking. Despite the rocky beginning, Governor Shepardson became an effective and respected member of the Board of Governors.

During Shepardson's twelve years on the board, the national administration went from the conservative policies of the Eisenhower administration to the relatively liberal stance of the Kennedy-Johnson years, and the board generally reflected the trend. Shepardson maintained a preference for tight monetary policy throughout his tenure because he viewed inflation as the greatest threat to the economy. This consistent position took Shepardson from the mainstream of board policy to that of being its staunchest conservative. As the board became heavily weighted with Kennedy and Johnson appointees, Shepardson became less in tune with his colleagues and expressed misgivings about the board's focusing on economic trends at the expense of attention to banking industry matters. His infrequent speeches as a board member indicated a continuing interest in farm finance, and a colleague stated that his primary effort on the board was on internal administrative matters.

In a 1957 speech, Shepardson analyzed aggregate output and prices. Inflation occurred when aggregate spending in excess of income exceeded saving. If aggregate spending in excess of income was less than saving, then prices and output declined. Equilibrium occurred when the excess equaled saving. In his view, the aggregate fiscal policy was not suited to dealing with short-run fluctuations.

Instead of watching the money supply, he said the Fed adjusted the rate of growth of money and credit. Thus, one of the culprits leading to inflation was increasing wages in excess of productivity. Higher costs meant inflation. He forecast increased productivity due to higher population, atomic energy, and automation. The role of the Fed was to provide price stability and to restrict fluctuations in growth.

Economic growth depended on many factors, he recalled in 1959. One was the freedom of opportunity to employ new technologies. Sustainable growth was limited by immobility of labor. The national income was growing and its distribution was acceptable; he claimed growth was dependent on capital investment.

Shepardson emphasized the opportunities and perils of federal lending to farmers. Prudent loans, he argued in 1965, could be as profitable as nonfarming loans. Banks needed trained agricultural staffs. Along with the substitution of capital for labor in farming were increased demands for larger financing. Traditionally farmers avoided debt and were poor record keepers, but if private banks were reluctant to lend to farmers, then they might eventually be replaced by government agencies that would loan money. He was opposed to such state intervention.

President's Johnson's desire to tailor the board to his expansionary policies led to the retirement of Shepardson before his full fourteen-year term was completed. An obscure law, said to be discovered by chance, made retirement mandatory for persons who were more than seventy years old and who had fifteen years of government service. Shepardson was seventy-one, and his military service in World War I added to years spent on the board totaled fifteen years. Although a presidential waiver could have allowed him to complete his term, he was retired on April 30, 1967. He was immediately appointed a consultant to the board, a position he held until his death in 1975.

The retirement of Charles Noah Shepardson completed the board's metamorphosis that had been underway for seven years. The tradition of agricultural representation on the board was broken. More significantly, the board had become liberal, concerned with broad policies for the economy, and dominated by professional economists.

BIBLIOGRAPHY

Shepardson, Noah. 1957. "Some Factors Affecting Monetary and Credit Policy." Presented to the Pacific Northwest Conference on Banking, State College of Washington.

————. 1959. ''Economic Growth.'' Summer commencement address, Colorado State
      University.
————. 1965. ''Agriculture and the Commercial Banks.'' Presented to Banker's Summer
      School, Ontario Agricultural College, Canada.
U.S. Congress. Senate. Committee on Banking and Currency. 1955. *Nomination of
      Charles Noah Shepardson. Hearing.* 84th Cong., 1st sess., February 25.
Wall Street Journal. 1955. March 1, p. 4.
————. 1967. February 17, p. 18.
Who's Who in America. 1940–1941. Vol. 21. *1968–1969.* Vol. 35. Chicago. A. N.
      Marquis.

WILLIAM WAYNE SHERRILL
(1926–   )

David E. R. Gay and Thomas R. McKinnon

A man for all factions was the way that William W. Sherrill was described when he was appointed to the Board of Governors of the Federal Reserve system in 1967. When nominated by President Lyndon Johnson, he was a member of the board of the Federal Deposit Insurance Corporation (FDIC). He succeeded Charles N. Shepardson.[*] His confirmation was endorsed by Congressman Wright Patman (D, Texas), the most severe critic of the Federal Reserve system, William McChesney Martin,[*] chairman of the Federal Reserve system, who at the time was having a dispute with President Johnson, and the American Bankers Association. His term proved to be equally noncontentious.

William Wayne Sherrill was born on August 23, 1926, in Houston, to Harry C. and Ina Haywood Sherrill. With the outbreak of World War II, he joined the Marine Corps at the age of fifteen. He was wounded in action at the Battle of Iwo Jima and decorated with the Purple Heart. Like thousands of other GIs after the war, he entered college, but unlike the others, he was still in his teens. Sherrill received a B.B.A. with honors from the University of Houston in 1950. While attending college, he was employed by Southwestern Bell Telephone Company, where he became commercial department manager. He went on to receive an M.B.A. with distinction in finance from the Harvard Graduate School of Business Administration in 1952. He was married on June 18, 1948, to Marilyn Sue Poer, and they had three daughters: Cynthia Lee, Sandra Lynn, and Suzanne Elisa.

Sherrill entered public service in 1954 with the city of Houston. He began as the administrator of the city court system and went on to serve as executive assistant to the mayor, chief administrative officer, and city treasurer. Sherrill left public service briefly from 1963 to 1966 to take a variety of positions in finance. He was president of the Homestead Bank, at the time the nation's sixth largest; executive vice-president of the Jamaica Corporation, a Houston real estate firm; director of Colonial Saving and Loan Association; an administrator of three pension funds; and a private financial analyst. In 1966 he reentered public service when he was appointed a member of the board of directors of the FDIC and served until his appointment to the Federal Reserve board in 1967.

Sherrill's civic and fraternal positions included port commissioner, committee assignments for the Boy Scouts of America, the YMCA, and the Political Science Faculty Advisory Committee of the University of Houston. He was active in the Houston Alumni Association, serving as director and treasurer. In 1955, only five years after graduation, he was honored with the University of Houston Outstanding Alumnus Award. In 1967 Sherrill was appointed by the secretary of state as a member of the U.S. National Commission for the U.N. Educational, Scientific, and Cultural Organization.

At the time of Sherrill's appointment, a controversy was brewing between President Lyndon Johnson and the chairman of the Board of Governors, William McChesney Martin, over monetary policy. Johnson favored an easy money policy, while Martin wanted a tighter policy. Kennedy-Johnson appointees had come to dominate the board, and with the retirement of Charles Shepardson,* a frequent ally of Martin and the board's most conservative member, Martin would be increasingly isolated unless a like-minded governor were appointed. Martin had let it be known that he would consider resigning, and his strong support in the financial and business community presented a political problem for the president.

Sherrill was the ideal compromise. He was not a professional economist, as were four other members of the board, and his background in banking, business, and government pleased Martin. His private views were said to be closely in line with those of the president's Council of Economic Advisers, but his policy approach while at FDIC was pragmatic rather than doctrinaire. His nomination seemed to please all factions from populist Texas Democrat Wright Patman to the conservative American Bankers Association. At Sherrill's nomination hearing, a member of the Banking and Currency Committee, Senator William Proxmire (D, Wisconsin) observed that if Sherrill would continue with that kind of support over the next year or two, he would be not only remarkable but astonishing. Sherrill's initial appointment was to fill the year remaining on the term of his predecessor, and the ease of his reappointment to a full fourteen-year term indicated that he did continue to receive that support at least for a year. However, he was to serve only four years of that fourteen-year term.

Records at the Library of Congress indicate that he made only nine public speeches during his term—two of them statements before congressional committees and the other remarks via a telephone hookup to the American Bankers Association meeting in 1971.

One of the public policy issues that Sherrill debated was the extent to which the Fed uncovered evidence of organized crime or the extent to which organized crime could penetrate the banking industry. In his 1963 testimony, Sherrill argued that the Fed's primary responsibility was achieved through bank examination in order to ensure prudence. Most evidence of criminal activity was from internal sources such as "embezzlements, defalcations, and fraudulent and unlawful loans," rather than from external activity such as "armed robbery, theft and burglary," which are reported to the Federal Bureau of Investigation and the Department of Justice. The Fed examiners were "not aware of penetration of its state member banks by organized crime."

Of course, the Fed examiners were not trained for law enforcement, and their conclusions were based on apparently unrelated crimes. "The minimal extent, if any, to which organized crime has attempted penetration of our banks" is limited by several factors. First, large deposits in a bank would be suspicious and detected, he said. Second, other business ventures are more profitable than banking. Third, recent laws like Public Law 88–593 required notification of changed bank ownership and the nature of the new owners. The Federal Financial Institutions Supervisory Act of 1966 provided statutory authority "to institute cease and desist proceedings to remove directors or officers of banks under clearly prescribed circumstances." Fourth, coordinated activities of federal and state regulators and law enforcement personnel had deterred bank machinations by organized crime.

In his public remarks to the 1971 American Bankers Association, Sherrill praised the revamping caused by the 1970 amendments to the Bank Holding Company Act. He forecast "that the nation, the economy, and the public will be well served" by the new remolding of bank holding companies. In his view, the legislation increased competitiveness in banking and thereby increased overall competitiveness, which would encourage "high and rising productivity," thereby controlling inflation and unemployment.

He reiterated support for the demarcation of banking activities and commercial activities embodied in the Bank Holding Company Act of 1956. Otherwise bank managers could have a conflict of interest when lending and thereby jeopardize prudent bank management. He contended that the loophole in the 1956 act resulted by 1969 in twenty-three of the fifty-one billion-dollar banks (including the six largest banks) being owned by one bank holding company. Also, non-banking companies were acquiring banks and further blurring the distinction between banking and commercial activities. In a more competitive market, banks will survive by developing financial services rather than by lending alone. The Fed favored de novo enterprises by banks as a means of increased competition instead of bank expansion into areas by acquisition. He said that more firms meant more competition.

For regulatory agencies such as the Fed, banking competitiveness must be maintained as banks expand into banking-related activities, he said. The criteria would be "competition, public convenience, efficiency, and the effects on banking practices." The new procedures of the Fed would be to scrutinize proposals for banking-related activities to determine if they "pass the tests of net favorable effect upon competition and other public interests."

Sherrill's resignation in 1971, only forty-four years old, and four years after his appointment to a fourteen-year term, came as a surprise to most observers. Although he generally kept a low profile as governor, he had become openly critical of the Nixon administration for failing to adopt an income policy to counter wage-price inflation. According to the *Wall Street Journal* (1971b), friends said that Sherrill would not have considered leaving the board if a divorce from his wife of twenty-three years were not pending. After his divorce, he married Sharon J. Blansfield on October 28, 1972. He moved to South Bend, Indiana, and entered private business.

Sherrill was a noneconomist on a board dominated by economists. There were four economists on the seven-man board when he joined and five when he resigned. That trend has continued.

BIBLIOGRAPHY

Sherrill, William Wayne. 1968. Statement, to the Legal and Monetary Affairs Subcommittee, House Committee on Government Operations, February 7.
———. 1971. "Some Reflections on the New Bank Holding Company Legislation." Presented to the National Public Affairs Conference of the American Bankers Association, Washington, D.C., March 16.
U.S. Congress. Senate. Committee on Banking and Currency. 1967. *Nomination of William W. Sherrill. Hearing.* 90th Cong., 1st sess., April 25, pp. 1–6.
Wall Street Journal. 1971a. April 24, p. 2.
———. 1971b. July 7, p. 2.
Who's Who in America. 1970–1971. Vol. 36. *1980–1981.* Vol. 2. Chicago: A.N. Marquis.

ALBERT STRAUSS (1864–1929)

Robert Metts

Albert Strauss was appointed as a member and vice–chairman of the Federal Reserve Board on October 26, 1918, to succeed Paul M. Warburg.* He resigned his post on March 15, 1920. At the time of his appointment, Strauss was serving on the War Trade Board, established during World War I to supervise and control U.S. international economic relations during the crisis. During his tenure as a member of the Federal Reserve Board, Strauss continued his service on the War Trade Board and also participated in the Paris Peace Conference as a representative of the U.S. Treasury and as an adviser to President Woodrow Wilson on financial matters related to the transition to peace.

Strauss's service on the Federal Reserve Board, as well as his other public service during World War I, earned him great praise for his handling of the complicated problems the U.S. government encountered with respect to wartime and postwar international finance. He was held in such high esteem in Washington that President Woodrow Wilson, in accepting Strauss's resignation from the board in 1920, wrote, ''For nearly three years you have served the Government with singular distinction. You rendered equally fine service to the nation for several months in Paris as one of the financial advisors to the Peace Conference. Your withdrawal will be a distinct loss to the public service.''

In addition to his distinguished career in public service, Strauss established himself as an extremely succesful banker and businessman, serving as a member and leading partner in the banking house of J. and W. Seligman and Company. During his long and distinguished financial career, Strauss was officially connected with a number of corporations and at the time of his death was a director of the Pierce Arrow Motor Car Company, Cuba Cane Sugar Corporation, Manati Sugar Company, Cuban Tobacco Company, and Brooklyn-Manhattan Transit Corporation. He accomplished this record in both business and public service without ever having earned a college degree.

Strauss was born on October 26, 1864, in New York, the son of Philip and Anna (Rohman) Strauss, both German immigrants. In about 1848 Philip had come to New York, where he became the cofounder of the candy manufacturing firm of Greenfield and Strauss.

Strauss received his primary and secondary school education in the New York City public school system. In 1879, at the age of fifteen, he enrolled at the College of the City of New York, where he engaged in course work for three years. He discontinued studies in 1882 to accept employment at J. and W. Seligman, one of the oldest banking houses in New York City, which conducted its business in both America and abroad. Strauss advanced rapidly within the firm and was admitted as a member in 1901. Later he was to gain recognition as a full partner in the firm.

On June 9, 1896, Strauss married Lucretia Mott, daughter of George W. Lord, a merchant of New York City, and granddaughter of Lucretia Mott, the noted philanthropist, abolitionist, and pioneer exponent of woman's sufferage. Together they had three daughters: Marjorie Lord, Anna Lord, and Katharine Lord.

While in the employ of J. and W. Seligman, Strauss became an ardent student of every aspect of the banking business. He was particularly interested in international banking and ultimately became an authority on world trade, international relations, and foreign exchange. It was his expertise in these areas that caught the attention of the Wilson administration and led to his appointment to the War Trade Board. His prudent and conservative handling of the unique problems associated with wartime foreign trade, including the issue of the appropriate U.S. response to European embargos on the export of gold, won Strauss further recognition in Washington and led to his appointment, while still a member of the War Trade Board, as a special adviser to the U.S. Treasury on matters relating to gold and currency. His outstanding service in both of these capacities won him his 1918 appointment to the Federal Reserve Board. During his short tenure on the board, Strauss specialized in matters related to wartime and postwar international finance and in this capacity advised President Wilson during the Paris Peace Conference.

In 1920, after the crisis had passed, Strauss resigned his position on the Federal Reserve Board. He returned to J. and W. Seligman on January 1, 1920, and remained active in the firm until his death on March 28, 1929. Throughout his career, Strauss enjoyed the esteem of the banking fraternity and was known as a man of high principles and ideals. A Republican interested in community affairs, Strauss was a member of a number of clubs, including the India House, Recess, Broad Street, Army and Navy, City, Midday and Automobile of America clubs, of New York; the Buffalo Club, of Buffalo; the Cosmos and Riding and Hunt clubs, of Washington; and the Seawanhaka-Corinthian Yacht, Piping Rock, Huntington Country, and Beaver Dam Sports clubs.

BIBLIOGRAPHY

National Cyclopedia of American Biography. 1932. "Albert Strauss." Vol. 22, pp. 246–47.

Strauss, Albert. 1921. "The Federal Reserve System and the Foreign Exchanges." Address to the Students of the Department of Economics of Princeton University, January 21. Library, Board of Governors of the Federal Reserve System, Washington, D.C.

"Strauss Resigns His Post." 1920. *New York Times*, March 4.

"Wilson Praises Strauss." 1920. *New York Times*, March 5.

MENC STEPHEN SZYMCZAK
(1894–1978)

Gregory A. Claypool

Menc Stephen Szymczak, who served as governor of the Federal Reserve board from 1933 to 1961, was born August 15, 1894, in Chicago to Stanley and Magdalena (Werner) Szymczak. On January 15, 1916, he married Chicago native Helen Marie Lappin. They had two daughters, Helen Josephine and Mary Elizabeth. In addition to beginning his family life, Szymczak devoted himself to obtaining an education as preparation for his life's work.

His early adulthood education included work at St. Mary's College (Kentucky), extension work in commerce through New York University, graduate study at Mount St. Mary's Seminary in Cincinnati, Ohio, and studies at DePaul University. He received A.B. and A.M. degrees from both St. Mary's College and DePaul University, earned between 1914 and 1918. Later he obtained the LL.D. from three different universities: DePaul (1936), Fordham (1947), and Georgetown (1965).

Szymczak's studies led him initially to an academic career. He served as an instructor in mathematics at St. Mary's College from 1913 to 1914. In 1916 he became an instructor in mathematics and history at the DePaul University Preparatory School and served in this capacity until 1919, when he became an instructor in logic and public speaking in DePaul University's College of Commerce. In 1923 he was made professor of ethics, logic, and psychology in business administration and economics at DePaul and retained this position until 1933.

During the 1920s and early 1930s, Szymczak became prominent in Chicago-area banking and civic circles. In 1925 he was an organizer of the Ridgemoor Building and Loan Association, where he served as director until 1928. From 1926 to 1928 he also was superintendent of the Cook County Forest Preserve District. He was vice-president of Hatterman and Glanz State Bank in 1929 and 1930 and vice-president and director of Northwestern Trust and Savings Bank from 1930 to 1931. From 1931 to 1933 Szymczak was comptroller of the city of Chicago.

On June 14, 1933, he was appointed to the Federal Reserve Board, an appointment that lasted until January 31, 1936, when the Federal Reserve Board was abolished by the Banking Act of 1935. This act created a new Federal Reserve system to be governed by the Board of Governors, with its members appointed by the president of the United States. Szymczak was so highly regarded by this time that only he and Marriner Eccles[*] were reappointed to the newly constituted Board of Governors. Szymczak's appointment by President Franklin D. Roosevelt has been called the most significant federal appointment of a Polish-American to that time. His appointment was for a twelve-year period, effective February 1, 1936. Other appointees who joined Eccles and Szymczak on the newly constituted board were Joseph A. Broderick,[*] superintendent of banks of New York; John K. McKee,[*] chief of the examining division of the Reconstruction Finance Corporation; Ralph W. Morrison,[*] a Texas rancher and former utilities executive; and Ronald Ransom,[*] an Atlanta banker.

During his tenure on the Board of Governors, Szymczak was known as an opponent of unrestrained expansion of the money supply, a position not always popular in the difficult economic times of the late 1930s. It was a position, however, that made him a strong ally of Eccles and, later, William McChesney Martin.[*]

Szymczak was regarded as the board's resident expert in international economic affairs, especially concerning Europe. He was called upon several times to play a significant role in international economic problems brought about by World War II. From July through September 1944 he served as chairman of the mission to London for the Foreign Economic Administration for the reconstruction needs of Belgium. Also during 1944 he was U.S. adviser to the International Monetary and Financial Conference held at Bretton Woods, New Hampshire. This famous conference produced a wide range of practical rulings designed to establish an orderly international payments system in the postwar world. The best known of these rulings was the fixing of currency parities against gold. The provisions of the Bretton Woods agreement dominated international monetary policy until 1971.

In 1946 President Harry Truman persuaded Szymczak to accept the important job of U.S. director in charge of the rehabilitation of the German economy and granted him a leave of absence from the Board of Governors for this purpose. His objective as director was to restore Germany to as close to a self-sustaining economic basis as possible. The three major tasks that he faced in accomplishing this objective were fighting inflation with rationing and price controls, reestablishing German internal commerce and trade, and helping to revive Germany's foreign trade. Szymczak's task was called the key to achieving the objectives of the United States in Germany. He successfully served in this capacity from July 1946 to June 1947.

As Szymczak's twelve-year term was due to expire in early 1948, President Truman reappointed him to a full fourteen-year term. The Banking Act of 1935 had limited all appointees to one fourteen-year term. Because Szymczak's position on the original Board of Governors had been for a twelve-year period,

Truman argued that Szymczak was eligible for a full fourteen-year term. Three members of the Senate Banking Committee opposed his nomination. Their opposition was based on what they felt was the intent of the Banking Act of 1935, not on Szymczak's competence. The Senate Banking Committee voted 7 to 3 to recommend confirmation, and his appointment was confirmed by voice vote in the Senate on February 20, 1948.

Perhaps the one public event that most embroiled Szymczak in controversy during his tenure on the Board of Governors occurred in 1959. In early March of that year, he made a speech in which he indicated that the Fed was concerned about the level of unemployment. The financial community interpreted his remarks as indicating there would be no increase in the discount rate. However, the next day, four Federal Reserve banks increased the discount rate from 2 ½ to 3 percent.

Szymczak's term was to expire in January 1962; however, he decided to retire from the board early and did so effective June 1, 1961. In an article reviewing Szymczak's career on the Board of Governors, the *New York Times* referred to him as "the dean of the Federal Reserve System's board of governors," an obvious reference to his longevity on the board. Given the provisions of the law, his service of twenty-five years is likely never to be exceeded. His resignation provided President John F. Kennedy with his first opportunity to place a person on the Board of Governors. Kennedy used this opportunity to appoint George W. Mitchell.[*]

BIBLIOGRAPHY

"Dean of Reserve May Leave Board." 1961. *New York Times*, April 20.
Renkiewicz, Frank. 1973. *The Poles in America, 1608–1972: A Chronology and Fact Book*. Dobbs Ferry, N.Y.: Oceana Publications.
"Reserve Governor Warns of Temptation to Adopt Chronic Deficit Financing Policy." 1949. *New York Times*, May 10.
"U.S. Puts Szymczak in Key German Job." 1946. *New York Times*, July 25.

NANCY HAYS TEETERS (1930–   )

Juli Cicarelli

On August 28, 1978, President Jimmy Carter announced the appointment of Nancy Hays Teeters as a member of the Board of Governors of the Federal Reserve system. President Carter, anxious to advance the opportunities for women and minorities, had insisted on finding a woman to serve on the board. When Teeters took her oath of office in a White House ceremony on September 15, she became the first woman governor of the sixty-five-year-old Federal Reserve board.

Teeters's appointment to the Fed was something of a homecoming; she had worked there as a staff economist from 1957 to 1966. With her appointment as governor, she brought with her high professional credentials and a reputation as a liberal Democrat. She was a veteran of two decades of government service, and former Fed member Andrew F. Brimmer* noted that until Teeters's appointment, no Fed governor in recent years had had congressional experience. Before her Fed appointment, Teeters was assistant staff director and chief economist for the U.S. House of Representatives Budget Committee, where she had served for four years

At the time of her appointment, Teeters defined herself as a middle-of-the-roader on economic policy and considered herself an eclectic; she was, she said, for what worked, even if it was ideologically unpure. She was seen as a natural for a liaison role at the Fed, able to understand the complex issues the board dealt with and at the same time provide a bridge to the other major centers of Washington's economic policymaking machinery, the White House and Congress.

She had worked at the old Budget Bureau from 1966 to 1970 with Charles L. Schultze, who would go on to become chairman of President Carter's Council of Economic Advisers. Assistant Treasury Secretary Daniel H. Brill and Council of Economic Adviser member Lyle E. Gramley had both worked with Teeters when she was a staff economist at the Fed. In 1962 she had taken a year's leave from the Fed to serve on the Council of Economic Advisers with Paul A. Sarbanes under Walter W. Heller. Sarbanes, a Democrat, was later elected to the Senate and was a member of the Senate Banking Committee that confirmed Teeters. On the Republican side of the aisle, Senator Richard G. Lugar, another Banking Committee member, was Teeters's cousin.

Given her experience, Teeters was seen as a liberal who would attempt to keep monetary policy from turning overly restrictive. In fact, during her two decades of government service, she called economic shots as she saw them, stepping on both liberal and conservative toes. Yet it was said of her that she would never run out of friends in Washington. Recalling her varied jobs, she took pride in her four years with the House Budget Committee, where she had worked to make the federal budget controllable. She also took pride in a similar role for the Brookings Institution, where she had worked with Charles S. Schultz, Edward R. Fried, and Alice M. Rivlin and coauthored Setting National Priorities, the think tank's annual counterbudget.

Teeters started her years at the Fed under the chairmanship of G. William Miller[*] during a time of economic unheaval. The cartel of oil-producing nations, the Organization of Petroleum Exporting Countries, had roughly quadrupled oil prices in 1973–1974 and in 1978–1979 had more than doubled them again. This "oil shock," as economists called it, automatically caused price increases in every product Americans bought and sold. Long gas lines at the gasoline pump made people angry, and high gasoline prices fueled that anger. In the first three months of 1979, the government's index of consumer prices had risen at an annual rate of nearly 11 percent. Miller had been a corporate manager, not a banker or economist, before he replaced Arthur Burns[*] as Fed chairman in 1978. Miller's stewardship at the Fed had been widely criticized by Wall Street professionals who complained that Miller was much too cooperative with Carter's economic advisers and too timid about raising interest rates to lower inflation.

As a member of the Fed, Teeters was aware of the conflicting pressures faced by the board. She saw herself as a lightning rod between the demands of consumer groups and credit-granting groups, and in these difficult economic times, she expected to get blasted from both sides. She said her goals as a member of the Fed were the basic ones: high employment and low inflation. She noted that the Fed had two major instruments to reach those goals, fiscal policy and monetary policy, and she felt the Fed had been using them knowingly. Yet she recognized that the government sector was only 35 percent of the economy, and the Federal Reserve was only a small part of the government. The Fed could not solve economic problems by itself, she noted, stressing the need for cooperation on the part of the private sector to make the economy function properly.

In the meantime, President Jimmy Carter was scrambling to solve the nation's growing economic problems and to calm Wall Street jitters. In July 1979 he announced a major shakeup of his cabinet. One of these changes had Miller leaving the Fed chairmanship he had assumed only seventeen months earlier to become Treasury secretary. On August 6 Paul A. Volcker[*] was sworn in to replace Miller at the Fed. For the rest of her term on the Fed, Teeters would serve under the chairmanship of the strong-willed Volcker.

When Volcker took over, inflation was hovering around 14 percent. Volcker's job was to bring down this inflationary spiral and reassure the financial markets that the Fed would restrain the growth of money and credit. As a governor of the Fed, Teeters was concerned about inflation, but she was also concerned about the trade-off between inflation and unemployment. She understood the need for higher interest rates to slow the economy, but she was also acutely aware of the damage high interest could bring to the economy by destroying jobs and businesses, especially in the automobile and housing industries, which were highly influenced by interest rates.

In the early days of Volcker's chairmanship there were underlying tensions in the Federal Reserve's deliberations. Borrowing terminology used during the Vietnam War, the Fed was divided between the hawks—those members who believed the Fed had to raise interest rates and stabilize the dollar—and the doves—those who believed that inflation lubricated the economy and it was better to have low unemployment. During her tenure on the Fed, Teeters would always seen as a dove by the other members.

The first approaches by Volcker and the rest of the board to control inflation were cautious and involved gradual increases in the federal funds rate and the discount rate. Politicians were in favor of this gradual approach, but academic economists, market analysts, and bankers argued that the Fed's actions were too little and usually too late. In response to continuing inflation, Volcker adopted a new operating system at the Fed, using the theories expounded by University of Chicago economist Milton Friedman. The monetarist approach to controlling inflation is based on the notion of limiting the money supply itself and the level of reserves. Under this new system, interest rates would be allowed to rise or fall automatically in response to conditions in the money market. Teeters voted with Volcker for this new system, saying that the governors were concentrating on the monetary aggregates, but it seemed obvious to her that if the Fed set the money growth too low, interest rates would rise. It was clear to her and the others on the board that the Fed had to hold money and credit tight in order to control the inflation rate.

By the summer of 1980, the economy had contracted and expanded in a dizzying fashion. The money supply growth rose and fell like a rollercoaster, and the same zigzag had been visible in interest rates. The Fed members realized the monetarist system produced too much volatility in the economy. The money supply often jumped, resulting in a whipsawing of interest rates and a growing instability in the financial markets. This bred uncertainty, reduced the credibility of the Fed's policy, and raised inflationary expectations. In order to correct for this uncertainty, the Fed was forced to abandon the monetarist experiment and voted to tighten reserves and raise interest rates sharply. In the middle of the 1980 presidential election, the country was faced with double-digit inflation and rising unemployment at the same time.

In the years that followed, whenever money signals became confusing and the forecasts unclear, governors of the Fed would look back and remember the monetarist approach of 1980 as a fiasco. In reaction to this, a consensus was formed by the policymakers on the Fed. Whenever interest rates headed upward, the Fed's policy was not to ease up, no matter what the money aggregates signaled. In this consensus, there was one persistent dissenter, Nancy Teeters.

Teeters argued time and time again that the higher interest rates the Fed was authorizing were risking a major contraction in economic activity with a substantial rise in unemployment. She dissented five times in all as the Fed pushed the federal funds rate to 19.8 percent.

Teeters's views were out of step with the majority. She believed a more gradual approach would take longer but could still be effective. As always, Teeters continued to be concerned about the rising unemployment rate and continued business failures. She understood that once a consensus was formed on the board, there was a strong temptation for the members to fall into line, but she felt strongly about her position. She thought the rates had gone too high, and she wanted to say she voted against these stringent measures. In retrospect, Teeters would say she was not wrong. Month after month as the economy spiraled downward, she urged her colleagues to back off. By 1982 she warned they were pulling the financial fabric of the country so tight that it was going to rip. If the Federal Reserve did not swiftly ease up, she felt, it might lead to an unraveling of the financial system and a crisis of much larger dimensions. Several other governors came to share Teeters's alarm about the deteriorating economy, but none of them would vote against Volcker's views.

The incoming economic data reflected Teeters's view. While many forecasters, including the Federal Reserve, predicted a recovery, the data showed a continuing economic downturn, a shakiness in the domestic banking system, and a looming crisis in Third World debt. In July 1982 the Federal Reserve finally eased credit conditions. As soon as the money markets realized the Fed was easing credit, interest rates fell. By 1983 the American economy was prospering again, yet Volcker and the majority on the board continued to worry about inflation. For the next year until her term of office ran out in June 1984, Teeters continued to argue against Volcker's continuing tight rein.

Teeters was born July 29, 1930, and was forty-eight when she joined the Federal Reserve board. She grew up in Marion, Indiana, and received an A.B from Oberlin College in 1952. She received an M.A. from the University of Michigan in 1957. She was married to Robert D. Teeters in 1952 and has three children: Ann, James, and John.

She was a teaching fellow at the University of Michigan from 1954 to 1955 and from 1956 to 1957. From 1955 to 1956 she was an instructor at the University of Maryland overseas division, in Stuttgart, West Germany. In 1957 she joined the Fed as a staff economist. After nine years at the Fed, she left to work as a fiscal economist in the Office of Management and Budget. From there she went on to become a senior fellow at the Brookings Institution, where she served until 1973. From 1973 to 1975 she was a senior specialist of the Congressional

Research Service, Library of Congress. From there she joined the House Budget Committee as chief economist.

Teeters's published research is an outgrowth of her government work and her studies at Brookings. It focuses on forecasting, budget priorities, and the fiscal implications of the social security system.

She has served as vice-president, president, and chairman of the board of the National Economists Club. She has been a member of the Committee on the Status of Women of the American Economic Association and the board of the American Finance Association. She holds memberships in the American Economic Association, the Council on Foreign Relations, the National Association of Bank Women, the National Economists Club, and Women in Management. She is a member of the board of governors of the Horace H. Rackman School of Graduate Studies of the University of Michigan. She is also a member of the board of directors of the Prudential Bache Mutual Fund, the Technical Consultants to the Business Council, and the Conference of Business Economists.

Teeters has been awarded the Comfort Starr Award and a doctor of laws from Oberlin College. The University of Michigan has given her a Distinguished Alumni Award, the Athena Award of Alumnae Council, and a doctor of laws. She also has honorary degrees from Bates College and Mount Holyoke College. She was the recipient of the National Association of Bank Women's Industry Achievement Award in 1985. In 1987 she was elected to the YWCA's Academy of Women Achievers.

When Teeters left the Fed in June 1984, she became vice-president and chief economist for IBM Corporation. She remembers the board as a collegial group who respected one another and became good friends. After she left, her views were furthered by Preston Martin,[*] a conservative Republican who said not having Nancy Teeters around made him the expert on unemployment. He felt, as Teeters did, that there were real social costs to unemployment that the Federal Reserve board often ignored.

BIBLIOGRAPHY

Greider, William. 1987. *Secrets of the Temple: How the Federal Reserve Runs the Country*. New York: Simon and Schuster.
"Lady Governor." 1979. *Bankers Magazine* (March): 61–62.
"Natural for a Liaison Role at the Fed." 1978. *Business Week*, September 25, p. 46.
Teeters, Nancy Hays. 1988. Letter to author, September 29.
"Thoughtful Answers from New Fed Governor." 1979. *ABA Banking Journal* (May): 96–102.

JOHN JACOB THOMAS (1869–1952)

Donald R. Wells

John Jacob Thomas, who served on the Federal Reserve Board from June 1933 until February 1936, was born in Hancock County, Illinois, on January 1, 1869, the son of John C. Thomas and Anna Catherine (Luft) Thomas. He earned an LL.B. degree from the University of Michigan Law School in 1890 and was a student at the University of Nebraska from 1891 to 1892. He was admitted to the Michigan bar in 1890 and to the Nebraska bar in 1891. Thomas married Gertrude M. Kerrihard on December 19, 1906, and they had one son, John Justin Thomas. He was a member of the American Bar Association and the Nebraska Bar Association, becoming the president of the latter in 1933. He practiced law at Seward, Nebraska, served as county attorney of Seward County for 1895–1896, became county judge from 1898 to 1901, and was a member of the law firm of Thomas and Vail. He was known as Judge Thomas throughout the remainder of his professional life.

Thomas was active in Democratic party politics in Nebraska and served as chairman of the Democratic State Central Committee. In 1924 he ran unsuccessfully for the U.S. Senate against the incumbent, Senator George W. Norris. He was an active campaigner for Franklin D. Roosevelt in Nebraska in 1932 and a self-proclaimed friend of the farmer. He owned over a thousand acres of farmland in Nebraska at the time of his appointment to the Federal Reserve Board in 1933, plus a large farm in Oklahoma. Thomas asserted that farmers needed a larger share of the national income in order for the country to pull out of the depression. He stated that the drought that the country was experiencing then might be a blessing in disguise if it reduced supply and increased farm prices.

FDR appointed Thomas to the Federal Reserve Board in June 1933, and in August 1934 he was named vice-governor when Eugene R. Black* resigned. Thomas had been on the board's Executive Committee. During his short tenure, the Banking Act of 1935 changed the structure of the Federal Reserve system, creating the Board of Governors, giving these governors power to change member bank reserve requirements, and making them a majority on the Federal Open

Market Committee, and removing the secretary of the Treasury and the comptroller of the currency as ex officio members of the board.

Thomas was very much a team player while on the board; he denied that any conflict with the Treasury existed and testified before the Senate Banking Committee in June 1935 in favor of the administration's version of the amendment to the 1935 Federal Reserve Act. He agreed with board member Charles S. Hamlin,* and against Senator Carter Glass's view, that the board should have total control over open market operations, that reserve requirements should remain fixed and not be subject to variation by the board, and that there should be seven members of the board, not six; he was for removing the comptroller of the currency from the board but for retaining the secretary of the Treasury on it. Thomas was on the board when it was given the power to set margin requirements on stock purchases, Regulations T and U, with which he concurred. Another new power given the Fed at that time was section 13b, an amendment to the Federal Reserve Act, that permitted business firms to borrow directly from a Federal Reserve bank or with a commercial bank in conjunction with the Fed if this firm could not obtain credit elsewhere. These loans were for working capital for a period not to exceed five years. The law made a maximum of $280 million available, of which $84 million was approved by May 8, 1935. One measure studied but not adopted in Thomas's time was setting bank reserve requirements according to their velocity of turnover.

The one incident that cast Thomas into the limelight occurred in September 1934. The Federal Advisory Council issued a statement advocating that the United States return to the gold standard. Thomas and other board members were anxious to distance themselves from this view, but it was Thomas who wrote the letter to Walter Lichtenstein, secretary of the Advisory Council, strongly rebuking the council for taking a position that was not within its jurisdiction. On November 21, 1933, the Advisory Council made a similar statement on gold and Eugene Black said nothing, but Thomas was an FDR man and backed the administration's position. Thomas said that monetary policy was not discussed at the joint session of the board and the Advisory Council; the only issues covered were loans to industry under section 13b, the capital of banks coming under Federal Deposit Insurance Corporation coverage, clarification of emergency banking legislation, and if reserve requirements should be based on velocity. This strong rebuke led some writers to question the independence of the board from administration control.

The most significant measure taken by the board while Thomas was on it was the doubling of reserve requirements in 1936, which Thomas agreed to and which the board surprisingly called a policy of ease. This was done in two steps, and Thomas was there for only the first of these moves. In January 1936 the board unanimously agreed to increase margin requirements. The only time Thomas voted against the majority (and he was the only dissenting vote) occurred on January 4, 1936, when the board voted to revise Regulation R, permitting interlocking directors between commercial banks and government bond dealers.

Thomas left no written comment for his reason for opposing this measure. The last meeting of the board that he attended was on January 31, 1936, and he chaired that meeting because M. S. Eccles[*] was absent. The board voted unanimously to keep credit unchanged but to reduce excess reserves but did not specify how these excess reserves were to be reduced.

Thomas, though a strong supporter of FDR, was jettisoned by him in February 1936 along with three other members of the old Federal Reserve Board when the new Board of Governors was established. On February 10, 1936, Thomas became chairman and Federal Reserve agent for the Federal Reserve Bank of Kansas City, serving until December 31, 1938. Since this office was placed on an honorarium basis on January 1, 1937, Thomas resumed his law practice in Seward, Nebraska, but continued to serve as a class C director of the Kansas City Fed until December 31, 1941. Thomas died on April 22, 1952, in Seward, Nebraska.

BIBLIOGRAPHY

New York Times. 1933. June 4, p. II–9.
Who's Who in America, 1936–1937. Vol. 19. Chicago: A.N. Marquis.

JAMES KIMBLE VARDAMAN, JR.
(1894–1972)

Yale L. Meltzer

James Kimble Vardaman, Jr., who served as a governor of the Federal Reserve board from 1946 to 1958, was born on August 28, 1894, in Greenwood, Mississippi. When he was nine years old, his father, James K. Vardaman, Sr., was elected governor of Mississippi, serving from 1904 to 1908. Subsequently, his father was elected to the U.S. Senate and served as the senator from Mississippi from 1913 to 1919.

James K. Vardaman, Jr., studied at the U.S. Naval Preparatory School at Annapolis, Maryland (1910–1911), and then attended the University of Mississippi (1911–1912). In 1914, Millsaps College in Jackson, Mississippi, conferred upon him the LL.B. degree, and in that same year he was admitted to the bar.

Vardaman was a practicing attorney in Jackson, Mississippi, from 1914 until April 1917. When the United States declared was on Germany, he entered the U.S. Army as a second lieutenant with the 335th Field Artillery. He served in France and rose to the rank of captain by the time he was discharged from the army in 1919.

After leaving the army, he moved to Missouri. Setting up an office in St. Louis, he became a representative for banking syndicates and became involved with securities. It was at this time that he met Harry Truman. Vardaman became more and more politically active and helped Truman in his political campaigns. In addition, Vardaman became increasingly involved in banking activities.

In 1926 he became a loan officer at the Liberty-Central Trust Company. In 1933 he was appointed regional manager of the Reconstruction Finance Corporation (RFC) for the St. Louis district. After serving for four years in that position, he became president of the Tower Grove National Bank and Trust Company of St. Louis as part of a change of management required by the Federal Reserve. The bank improved its operations during his term of office, but he resigned after a sharp disagreement he had with the bank's board of directors.

Although Vardaman had served for twenty years in the U.S. Army Reserve, he transferred to the U.S. Naval Reserve, where he was given the rank of lieutenant commander on September 13, 1939. In July 1941 he was called to active duty and was made an officer in charge of the Naval Intelligence Office at St. Louis, remaining in that position until April 1942. He was sent overseas as security officer on the staff of Admiral Harold R. Stark, who was in charge of U.S. naval forces in Europe. In November 1942 Vardaman commanded a landing party on the Algerian coast as part of the U.S. invasion of North Africa. After other assignments in North Africa, he was made chief of staff officer to the commander, Advanced Base Group, Tunisia, for the launching of the invasion of Sicily.

In spite of being injured in July 1943, he continued to plan and conduct the campaign for General George S. Patton's army, which led to the fall of Messina. For this heroism, Vardaman received the Legion of Merit and the Silver Star.

In January 1945 he was assigned to the Pacific theater of operations as executive officer on the staff of Lieutenant General Simon Bolivar Buckner, commander of the 10th Army. He served with the 24th Corps on Leyte and participated in the invasion of Okinawa. On April 21, 1945, he was promoted to captain.

By now Truman was president of the United States, and Vardaman was called to Washington, D.C., to become naval aide to the president. He assumed this position in May 1945 and in July accompanied President Truman to the Potsdam Conference. In August 1945 Vardaman was promoted to the rank of commodore.

On January 21, 1946, President Truman appointed Vardaman to the Board of Governors of the Federal Reserve system, an appointment greeted with considerable opposition in the Senate. This opposition was clear and strong in statements made by business opponents in the hearings before the Subcommittee of the Senate Committee on Banking and Currency on March 22, 1946, under the chairmanship of Senator George L. Radcliffe. Nevertheless, the subcommittee recommended confirmation by a vote of 4–0. The full Senate Committee on Banking and Currency voted in Vardaman's favor 9–1, and the full U.S. Senate confirmed his appointment. On April 4, 1946, Vardaman took his oath of office and joined the Federal Reserve board under the chairmanship of Marriner Eccles.*

Vardaman, President Truman's first appointment to the Federal Reserve board, was watched closely. His first position was to oppose the policy under chairman Eccles of requiring 100 percent margin on the purchase of common stock. Vardaman felt that this policy was too restrictive. Eventually his view prevailed, and in February 1947, margin requirements were reduced to 75 percent.

At the Federal Reserve board, Vardaman favored a general policy of wage and price controls. In February 1951 he was drawn into the controversy then raging between the majority at the Federal Reserve board and the U.S. Treasury over the management of the national debt. The Truman administration wanted to peg the rate on U.S. Treasury bonds, and thus the national debt, at 2½ percent. Secretary John Snyder was strongly committed to a general policy of maintaining high prices on U.S. government securities, a policy opposed by Thomas B. McCabe,* who had succeeded Eccles as chairman of the Federal Reserve board. McCabe felt that the 2 ½ percent rate would be too inflationary.

President Truman gave solid support to Treasury Secretary Snyder's position.

The broad position of the Truman administration was, in fact, that the threat of unemployment posed a greater danger to the country than the threat of inflation. On the Federal Reserve board, Vardaman was a strong supporter of Snyder and President Truman. The impasse was finally settled on March 3, 1951, when Snyder and McCabe issued a joint statement that nonmarketable U.S. Treasury bonds would have a 2 ¾ percent interest rate. This was considered a great victory for Vardaman, Snyder, and Truman. As a result, President Truman accepted McCabe's resignation as chairman on March 15, 1951, effective that same month, and William McChesney Martin, Jr.,[*] then assistant secretary of the Treasury, succeeded McCabe as chairman of the Federal Reserve board.

During World War II, Federal Reserve operations had been subordinated to helping the U.S. Treasury borrow money at low interest rates to aid the war effort. The possible inflationary effect had been tempered by price controls, the encouragement of putting money in savings accounts by the public, and the sale of U.S. savings bonds to the public. After the war, however, prices rose sharply in 1947 and 1948, and the Federal Reserve was criticized for not having used open market operations enough to curb inflationary pressures. With the outbreak of hostilities in Korea in 1950, there was another surge in inflationary pressures as the Korean War was financed by credit. The famous U.S. Treasury–Federal Reserve Accord of 1951 was achieved primarily through the efforts of William McChesney Martin, Jr., while he was still at the U.S. Treasury. Under this accord, it was agreed that Federal Reserve policies should no longer be subordinated to U.S. Treasury financing. Vardaman was certainly a factor in the rapprochement between the U.S. Treasury and the Federal Reserve.

Under Martin, the Federal Reserve became more aggressive and politically strong than it had been under Eccles and McCabe. This change took place during Vardaman's tenure as a governor of the Federal Reserve board. During Vardaman's tenure, the board became increasingly involved with economic stabilization; it emphasized price stability and in general pursued a restrictive policy on growth in the money supply.

Also, during Vardaman's tenure under chairman Martin, the Federal Reserve succeeded in operating more agressively than it had under the chairmanships of Eccles and McCabe. From the end of 1951 to mid–1953 the United States achieved a high level of production and employment, together with relatively stable commodity prices. During this period, the Federal Reserve pursued a policy of slight restraint through the use of open market operations. From mid–1953 to the end of 1954, the United States went into a recession, and the Federal Reserve used open market operations and a lowering of legal reserve requirements to fight it. Unfortunately, the Eisenhower administration was simultaneously cutting federal expenditures.

From the end of 1954 to mid–1957, the U.S. economy expanded. During this period, an economic boom developed, and the Federal Reserve moved against the wind by raising interest rates. There was an increase in inflation, but the Federal Reserve was exerting control.

From mid–1957 to mid–1958, the United States had its third post–World War

II recession. The Federal Reserve first used open market operations to bring the country out of the recession, followed by a reduction in the discount rate and the legal reserve requirements. An economic recovery started in mid–1958 and continued, and the Federal Reserve then moved to a policy of monetary restraint. It was during this expansionary period that Vardaman decided to leave the Fed. He resigned as a governor of the Federal Reserve board on November 30, 1958, effective December 1, 1958.

In addition to being active in banking, Vardaman was active in civic and cultural areas. His interest in cultural activities and related activities took numerous forms. For example, he was the vice-president of the St. Louis Grand Opera Association, a member of the board of the St. Louis Symphony Society, and a director of the St. Louis National Horse Show.

On September 23, 1917, Vardaman married Beatrice Middleton Lane. They had one son.

James Kimble Vardaman, Jr., died on July 28, 1972.

BIBLIOGRAPHY

Federal Reserve System Board of Governors. 1946–1959. *Annual Report*.
————. 1989. Correspondence with Yale L. Meltzer.
U.S. Congress. House. Subcommittee on Fiscal Affairs of the Committee on the District of Columbia. 1956. *Hearings to Amend Title II of the Act of August 30, 1954, entitled "An Act to Authorize and Direct the Construction of Bridges over the Potamac River and for Other Purposes."* H.R. 7228. 84th Cong., 2d sess., May 9.
U.S. Congress. Senate. Subcommittee of the Committee on Banking and Currency. 1946. *Hearings on the Nomination of James Kimble Vardaman, Jr.* 79th Cong., 2d sess., March 22.
U.S. Department of the Treasury. Secretary of the Treasury. 1947–1959. *Annual Report*. Washington, D.C.: Government Printing Office.

PAUL ADOLPH VOLCKER, JR. (1927–)

Robert Stanley Herren

Paul Adolph Volcker, Jr., who served as chair of the Board of Governers of the Federal Reserve system from 1979 10 1987, was born on September 5, 1927 to Paul Adolph and Alma Louise Kleppel Volcker in Cape May, New Jersey. He had three older sisters: Ruth, Louise, and Virginia. Paul, Sr., a civil engineer, became city manager of Teaneck, New Jersey, where Volcker spent his early years. Most people considered Paul to be a shy boy who kept his thoughts to himself.

In high school Paul played varsity basketball while earning an excellent academic record. In 1945 he entered Princeton University against the advice of his father, who wanted Paul, Jr., to attend his alma mater, Rensselaer Polytechnic Institute. At Princeton, Volcker continued his basketball career; his 6-foot, 7-inch frame overcame his lack of athletic ability to earn him a position on the varsity basketball team. He was attracted to economics because it appeared to be more precise than other social sciences, and he wanted to use the logical structure of economics to aid in solving public policy problems; his father had instilled in him the virtue and importance of public service. His economic professors at Princeton taught classical economics; his favorite teachers included Friedrick Lutz and Oscar Morgenstern. He again achieved high grades with little apparent effort. He graduated in 1949 summa cum laude with a B.A. in economics.

Volcker continued his education at Harvard's Littauer Graduate School of Public Administration (now the Kennedy School of Government) where he first encountered Keynesian economists; he took one course from Alvin Hansen, whom economists often regard as the leading U.S. popopulizer and interpreter of Keynes. Although Volcker highly regarded his Harvard instructors, he never became a Keynesian. He earned an M.A. degree in 1951. Volcker spent the 1951–1952 academic year on a Rotary Foundation fellowship at the London School of Economics, ostensibly researching postwar British monetary policy for his doctoral dissertation. Volcker later conceded that he found things other than economic research to do in London; he never completed the dissertation.

During the 1950s, Volcker began both a family and his lifetime work in banking and in public service. On September 11, 1954, Volcker married Barbara Marie Bahnson of Jersey City, New Jersey. They honeymooned in Poco Moon Shine, Maine, a fishing camp where Barbara says "the highlight of the evening was to go down to the garbage dump and watch the black bears eat the garbage." (Volcker remains an avid fisherman, although Barbara has not joined him on any more fishing trips.) Their daughter, Janice, was born in 1955 and their son, James, in 1958. Although his work schedule prevented Volcker from spending much time with his children, they know him as a loving father.

Volcker entered the banking world during the summers of 1949 and 1950 when he worked at the New York Federal Reserve Bank as a research assistant. After his year in London and a brief stint as a junior management assistant in the Treasury Department, Volcker returned to the New York Fed in the research division headed by Robert Roosa. Between 1953 and 1957, his responsibilities included preparing the monthly summary of money market conditions, analyzing government securities markets, and reporting on foreign financial developments.

Recognizing Volcker's expertise, Chase Manhattan Bank in 1957 hired him to direct its research on domestic financial institutions and markets. Volcker represented the bank's president, David Rockefeller, at many meetings on the Commission of Money and Credit, where he expanded his contacts with influential financial leaders.

In January 1962 the revolving door between private banking and governmental service spun once again when Robert Roosa, now under secretary for monetary affairs (Treasury Department), appointed Volcker director of Treasury's Office of Financial Analysis. Volcker became deputy under secretary for monetary affairs in November 1963. Working closely with Roosa, he dealt with both domestic and foreign monetary problems. He acquired international experience as he met with foreign finance ministers and central bankers. His peers recognized his excellence. In 1965, Treasury Secretary Douglas Dillion awarded him the Treasury Department's Exceptional Service Award, and Volcker earned the Arthur S. Flemming Award, awarded to the ten most outstanding young federal service employees.

Chase Manhattan Bank again lured Volcker back into the private sector in late 1965 when he became director of forward planning and a vice-president. He remained with Chase Manhattan until 1969 when the new secretary of Treasury, David M. Kennedy, appointed Volcker to be the under secretary for monetary affairs with specific responsibilities concerning international monetary developments, an appointment that placed Volcker more into the public spotlight than his previous work because structural problems existed within the Bretton Woods system. Initially Volcker, always the conservative, did not favor floating exchange rates and even preferred to confine to academic circles plans that would permit wider bands of fluctuations around parities. Volcker reasoned that if the United States reduced its inflation and if other nations' inflation rates slightly increased, the pressure on the dollar would ease. During the next two years, proponents of flexible exchange rates debated with those, such as Volcker, who wished to maintain the status quo of fixed exchange rates. Events dealt the status quo advocates a losing hand.

In July 1971 Volcker changed his mind about the need for the devaluation of the dollar. Treasury economists were now forecasting that the United States would run a current account deficit for 1971, the first time in the century. Indeed, in 1971, the deficit on official reserves transactions increased to $30 billion, and foreign central banks accumulated huge amounts of dollar reserves. Volcker reluctantly acknowledged that the United States would have to suspend gold convertibility to obtain a realignment of currencies because other governments would match any changes in the dollar-gold price.

Volcker participated in the Camp David meetings that resulted in Nixon's New Economic program, announced on August 15, 1971. Although Volcker obtained the closing of the gold window, he clearly did not agree with other aspects of Nixon's program. He disliked the import surcharge because it interfered with free trade. He was ambivalent toward imposing wage-price controls. He did not want long-lasting wage-price controls because he believed that they harmed economic efficiency. On the other hand, under orders from Secretary of Treasury John Connally, Volcker aided in formulating a wage-price freeze proposal. Volcker believed that a three-month freeze could stop inflationary expectations, thereby giving tighter monetary and fiscal policies a better chance to stem inflation. The government in the following months did not adopt Volcker's ideas; fiscal and monetary policies were expansionary, and wage-price controls lingered into 1974.

Volcker soon traveled to London and Paris to begin negotiations concerning realignment of currencies. The shock of the August announcement, market forces, and the U.S. willingness to negotiate an increase in the price of gold led to the Group of Ten's Smithsonian Agreement (December 18, 1971). The realignment of currencies included a devaluation of the dollar (the price of gold increased from $35 per ounce to $38) and a revaluation of both the Japanese yen and West German mark; the United States rescinded its import surcharge but retained dollar inconvertibility.

Although Volcker hoped that exchange rate stability had returned, the Smithsonian Agreement placed a temporary bandage on serious flaws of the international monetary system. Working under a new secretary of Treasury, George Shultz, Volcker directed the staff work for a U.S. proposal for full-scale monetary reform. Volcker, no fan of freely floating exchange rates, incorporated as many elements of stability as possible into the proposed reform. He attempted to develop a system that included equal pressures on both surplus and deficit countries to adjust currencies; he recognized that one weakness of the Bretton Woods system was the asymmetrical pressure for deficit countries to devalue but no similar pressure for surplus countries to revalue. The United States presented this proposal in Shultz's speech at the International Monetary Fund's meeting in September 1972. While negotiations dragged on, events once again forced U.S. action.

By February 1973 markets were indicating that further changes in exchange rates were needed. George Shultz sent Volcker on a secret mission to discuss with leaders of other governments the alternatives of a further dollar devaluation or a completely clean dollar float. Volcker, knowing that Europeans believed that Japan should revalue its currency the most, flew first to Tokyo to meet Prime Minister Kakuei Tanaka and then to Europe where he met with British Prime Minister Edward Heath and finance ministers of Britain, France, Italy, and West Germany. Within a week, Volcker traveled over 31,000 miles, lost his hat in Japan, and ran out of both cigars and clean shirts, but he obtained agreement for another 10 percent devaluation of the dollar. This so-called Volcker agreement lasted less than a month as foreign exchange markets continued to place downward pressure on the dollar. The final breakdown of the fixed exchange rate system was near. The International Monetary Fund's (IMF) Jamaica Conference (January 1974) acknowledged that the world was on a floating exchange rate system. While many more negotiations were necessary to work out details for the new system, Volcker's role ended when he resigned from the Treasury later in 1974.

During his five years in the Treasury Department, Volcker participated in making fundamental changes in the international monetary system. Although he preferred a fixed exchange rate system, events forced him to accept and to aid in its dismantling. This episode indicates his strong sense of pragmatism—his refusal to cling to ideological positions in the face of overwhelming evidence supporting change. His foreign missions won him respect from governmental officials around the world for being an honest broker and for being discrete; his ability to travel unnoticed prompted a Japanese foreign minister to call him the ninja ("invisible warrior") banker. Volcker had established close working relationships with many central bankers and with finance ministers, including Valèry Giscard d'Estaing (France) and Helmut Schmidt (West Germany), who later became heads of state.

Fed officials, led by Arthur Burns,[*] promised Volcker the presidency of the New York Federal Reserve Bank when the incumbent, Alfred Hayes, retired. Volcker returned to Princeton as a visiting fellow (1974–1975). He became president of the New York Fed in August 1975.

His year at Princeton removed him from his firefighting duties of moving from one policy crisis to the next and provided him with time to reflect on recent developments in monetary theory. Volcker developed his own brand of practical monetarism. He stated that the positive, lasting contributions of monetarists include emphasis on the distinction between real and nominal interest rates, insights concerning lags between policy actions and their impact on the economy with resulting limitations on fine-tuning, and their stress on the role of price expectations in the economy. Moreover, Volcker interpreted the Fed's adoption (congressionally mandated) of announcing annual targets for monetary aggregates to have provided discipline for Federal Reserve debates. He noted, however, that using his approach of practical monetarism does not solve the debates about which monetary aggregate is most important or about where the monetary targets should be set.

Volcker contended that the Fed's procedure of targeting the federal funds rate could increase instability in financial markets, but he was not sure that targeting reserves would improve monetary control. In addition, he argued that unstable money demand resulted in velocity's being unpredictable; thus, exclusive reliance on targeting monetary aggregates could be dangerous. Central bankers needed to avoid an ideological inflexibility; instead, they must use judgment to change policies in response to economic disturbances. For Volcker, money mattered, but it was not the only thing that mattered.

Volcker often discussed the need for improved international economic co-operation. He realized that recycling petrodollars presented a major challenge to the world's financial markets. Although he admitted that the floating exchange rate system had not slowed the growth in trade, he still preferred more stability in exchange rates. He noted that generally exchange rates moved to changes in purchasing power parities and that even large changes in exchange rates were not always effective in adjusting persistent imbalances in nations' current accounts. Volcker favored "quiet mutual contingency planning"—allowing a "few leading nations" to reach a consensus concerning ranges of tolerable exchange rate fluctuations. Although he knew that intervention in foreign exchange markets could not substitute for responsible domestic policies, he thought such actions would result in a greater commitment to a more stable international order.

As president of the New York Fed, Volcker participated in the monetary policy decision-making process between 1975 and 1979. The recession of 1974–1975 reduced inflation at the expense of much higher unemployment and may have cost President Gerald Ford the 1976 election. During 1977 real output rose, unemployment fell, and inflation remained relatively stable. Inflation accelerated in 1978–1979 as the Organization of Petroleum Exporting Countries again raised oil prices and monetary and fiscal policies expanded the economy beyond full employment (natural real gross national product [GNP]). By spring 1979 Volcker favored tighter money; opposing Fed chairman G. William Miller,[*] he twice voted for monetary restraint.

As inflation continued to rise throughout the summer of 1979, President Carter decided to change his economic policy team in a dramatic attempt to regain market (both domestic and international) confidence in his program. He removed Secretary of Treasury Michael Blumenthal and appointed Miller in Blumenthal's place. Miller gladly accepted this move; he was never comfortable with the Fed's need for consensus and with its intellectual give and take.

Carter now needed a Federal Reserve chair. Several members of Carter's administration, particularly Anthony Solomon, Treasury under secretary for monetary affairs, recommended Volcker. Carter, however, was inclined to nominate someone from the private banking community; indeed, he reportedly offered the job to Volcker's former mentor, David Rockefeller, and to A. W. Clausen, president of Bank of America. After both men declined the position, Carter turned to Volcker. Everyone agreed that Volcker possessed the technical ability to conduct monetary policy and that both domestic and foreign financial leaders respected him. Several presidential advisers objected to Volcker; they considered him too arrogant and not a team player. They were concerned that his anti-inflationary zeal would result in a too tight monetary policy during the 1980 presidential campaign. In his interview with President Carter, Volcker emphasized his commitment to fight inflation and to maintain the Fed's independence. Carter nominated Volcker on July 25, 1979; Volcker was sworn in on August 6, 1979.

For several reasons, Volcker was reluctant to accept this position. Barbara Volcker suffers from severe arthritis and diabetes; she did not want to return to Washington because her doctors were in New York City. The Volckers decided that they would become a two-city family, with Barbara remaining in New York. Setting up a second household intensified the financial strain on the Volckers— Paul was taking a pay cut from $116,000 to $57,000—so Barbara returned to work as a bookkeeper in an architectural firm. Volcker did not live in a luxurious palace in Washington; in 1986, *Newsweek* described him living "like a struggling graduate student" using "green milk crates for end tables" with "a 10-inch black-and-white television set" in a small apartment cluttered with fishing tackle and cigar butts.

Volcker accepted the job to continue the public service mission that his father had instilled in him. He believed that being chair of the Federal Reserve board provided him with his best opportunity to fight inflation and that he was the best person to win the battle. Leaders of many governments and financial experts throughout the world applauded Volcker's appointment. Volcker was as famous for his discrete competence in solving crises as he was infamous for smoking cheap cigars, wearing rumpled clothing, and complaining about high restaurant prices.

Volcker's first move on the board was to raise the discount rate by 0.5 percent. He instructed the Fed staff to gather information concerning a proposal to use bank reserves rather than the federal funds rate as the operating target in controlling monetary aggregates. He and other Fed anti-inflationary hawks, such as Henry Wallich, [*] were not convinced that targeting reserves rather than the federal funds rate would improve control of monetary aggregates. Instead they supported this change as a method to obtain a tighter monetary policy. They knew that every incremental increase in the funds rate was vigorously resisted within the Fed and often resulted in a split vote. Volcker wanted the public to perceive that interest rate increases resulted from market pressures and not from the board's actions, and he wanted to reestablish the Fed's credibility in fighting inflation.

On September 29 Volcker and Treasury Secretary Miller met with West German officials in Hamburg. The next day Volcker went to Belgrade for the annual joint meeting of the World Bank and IMF. The West Germans and other foreign leaders told him that the United States needed to get its inflation under control before they would continue to support the dollar. These conversations reinforced Volcker's conviction that the Fed needed to tighten monetary policy. Before the meetings ended, Volcker returned to Washington where he called an emergency Federal Open Market Committee (FOMC) meeting.

On Saturday October 6, 1979, the FOMC members discussed ways to break the public's inflationary expectations; they realized that dramatic action was necessary. Unanimously they approved raising the discount rate from 11 percent to 12 percent. They also imposed an 8 percent reserve requirement on managed liabilities and placed less day-to-day emphasis on restraining fluctuations of the federal funds rate and more emphasis on using nonborrowed reserves as an instrument in targeting monetary aggregates. This ''Saturday Night Special'' (Volcker announced these decisions at 6:00 P.M.) began a momentous era as the Fed began to allow larger fluctuations in the federal funds rate while focusing more on restraining growth of monetary aggregates.

During the first five months of this experiment, money supply growth slowed; however, the continued rise of nominal interest rates was politically unacceptable to the Carter administration. On March 14, 1980, President Carter used the authority of the Credit Control Act of 1969 to authorize the Fed to implement ''special measures of credit restraint.'' Although Volcker disliked direct credit controls as at best effective only temporarily, he publicly backed Carter's program. However, he had bargained vigorously that the credit controls be only a minor part of Carter's anti-inflationary program, which would emphasize reduction of the budget deficit.

In one sense, the program worked too well; people restrained their use of credit cards and paid off existing balances with demand deposits; the money supply (M1) contracted during April and May. Moreover, real GNP also declined (9.6 percent annual rate) during the second quarter of 1980. Volcker allowed the Fed to change course by terminating the special measures and expanding money supply growth. Although the Fed again tightened monetary growth in September, money growth in 1980 was above target (fourth year in a row), and the growth had been unusually erratic. Clearly such performance did not inspire confidence that the Fed had improved its ability to stop inflation.

During 1980 the Fed also faced major challenges concerning the regulatory structure of the financial industry where rising inflation during the 1970s increased disintermediation and incentives for loophole mining. Regulators instituted several temporary palliatives but postponed fundamental reform.

With regard to regulatory reform, Volcker acted as a conservative bureaucrat protecting his turf. He desired to stem the exodus of member banks leaving the Federal Reserve system in part to maintain the scope of Federal Reserve's regulatory responsibilities. In the Depository Institutions Deregulation and Monetary Control Act of 1980, the Fed obtained authority to impose uniform reserve requirements on transaction accounts at all depository institutions while all depository institutions obtained access to the discount window and other Fed services. Volcker argued that such provisions were necessary to improve monetary control.

The Fed's tighter monetary policy that it started in the fall of 1980 continued through the summer of 1982, with a resulting recession. Unemployment rose over 10 percent, and bankruptcies increased, especially in construction and farming. To many, Volcker became public enemy number 1; indeed, the Secret Service began to protect him as the hostility toward him increased. All of Volcker's associates state that he felt the pain that recession was inflicting on people and businesses. However, he and his allies on the FOMC were convinced that adherence to a tight monetary policy was necessary to squeeze inflationary expectations out of the U.S. economy.

In addition to defending its policies from traditional enemies of tight money, Volcker's Fed also received criticism from economic conservatives. Traditional monetarists viewed disinflation as occurring too rapidly and not giving the affected sectors enough time to adjust; they favored a more gradual policy. On the other hand, the emerging tribe of supply-side economists contended that their policies, primarily reducing marginal income tax rates, would increase aggregate supply sufficiently to reduce inflation without a tight money policy, which they considered unnecessary and dangerous.

The newly elected Reagan administration contained both camps of conservative critics, with each fighting for control over economic policy. The Fed initially enjoyed proper but not close relations with Reagan's economic policymaking team. Volcker had a weekly breakfast with Treasury Secretary Donald Regan, often saw the Council of Economic Advisers (CEA) chair, and the Board of Governors usually met with the entire CEA every other week. Volcker's well-known ability to talk at great length without revealing his plans frustrated administration officials, who wanted more explicit statements regarding monetary policy. Regan's Treasury Department soon began to criticize the Fed for its inability to maintain constant money supply growth. Norman Ture and Paul Craig Roberts, supply-side economists in Treasury, vigorously opposed a tighter monetary policy; they preferred to allow the economy to grow out of inflation. Regan often joined in this criticism of Volcker and the Fed. On the other hand at the White House, Murray Weidenbaum, CEA chair, and David Stockman, budget director, generally supported Federal Reserve policies.

Events of late 1981 placed even more pressure on the Fed to change policies. Both real GNP and income velocity of money sharply decreased. The introduction of new types of deposit accounts (e.g., NOW) and shifts from one type of financial asset to other types played havoc with the predictability of monetary aggregates, especially M1. Thus, the Fed was attempting to maintain credibility for its disinflation policy while monetary growth was erratic.

Dissatisfaction with the Fed's policies erupted early in 1982. Reagan and his staff publicly complained that the erratic money growth was a major source of instability in the economy. Volcker responded that maintaining stable money growth was almost impossible in the short run. Moreover, he continued his campaign against structural budget deficits, which he believed raised both nominal and real interest rates and he reemphasized that the Federal Reserve must remain independent to defeat inflation.

The continuing high interest rates distressed members of Congress. In the House, conservative supply sider Jack Kemp (R, New York) and liberal majority leader James Wright (D, Texas) both called for Volcker's resignation. Congressman Henry Reuss (D, Wisconsin), chair of the Joint Economic Committee, threatened to introduce legislation to dismember the Fed if it did not reduce interest rates. Senator Edward Kennedy (D, Massachusetts) argued for reimposition of credit controls accompanied by monetary expansion. In June the House and Senate Budget Committees passed resolutions that stated the FOMC should reevaluate monetary targets if Congress significantly reduced the budget deficit. Although Volcker realized that this was an idle threat, the Fed resented any challenge to its independence. Volcker conducted a long-running debate with Congress concerning budget deficits and monetary policy. Many members of Congress wanted Volcker to commit to an easier monetary policy if Congress reduced the budget deficit. Volcker refused to commit the Fed. Instead, he emphasized the need for deficit reduction, preferably spending cuts, to provide the Fed with more flexibility in its policy options. He noted that deficit reduction would make it easier for the Fed to loosen monetary policy; however, the Fed's precise response to deficit reduction would depend on the current situation. Volcker's noncommittal stance did not satisfy Congress, which continued to harass the Fed; in August over thirty Senate Democrats introduced a bill that mandated the Fed to reduce real interest rates to 4 percent. Volcker met this escalating criticism in his usual unflappable manner. He testified before Congress, met with administration officials, and made numerous speeches using his patented brand of "Fed-speak": reasoned, rational comments that provided no details about his plans.

Unperturbed outwardly, Volcker internally was uncertain about when to loosen monetary policy. He and other Fed officials wanted to ensure a permanent fall in inflationary expectations; they were looking for the correct time to change official policy. The Fed began an easier monetary policy in July 1982 but continued to talk a tough anti-inflationary policy. Finally, in October 1982, the Fed announced that the FOMC had voted for an easier money policy, for a retreat from using nonborrowed reserves as an instrument to target money supply, and for a deemphasis on M1. Volcker's gamble ultimately succeeded as the Fed jump-started the long-running economic expansion of the 1980s without reigniting inflation.

During the summer of 1982, Volcker devoted much time to the debt crisis of developing countries. For many years, he had monitored the situation and had privately urged banks to reduce their lending. He deferred public action because he believed that overall the situation was sustainable. Volcker and the rest of the world were shocked into reality in August 1982 when the Mexican government announced a moratorium on its foreign debt.

Volcker supported expansion of the IMF's reserve fund. In March 1982, well before the Mexican moratorium, he circulated his ideas through policy circles. The Reagan administration policymakers, especially Treasury Secretary Regan, rejected Volcker's plan because of their ideological preference for allowing private markets to solve problems. Mexico's announcement in August caught most administration officials by surprise, and they were forced to adopt the only available plan: Volcker's. Because the administration had allowed a crisis to develop, Volcker first had to arrange a temporary financing package. Working with other central banks, Volcker arranged a $1.5 billion package (the Fed's share was $750 million) through the Bank of International Settlements in Switzerland. He then spent the rest of the "Mexican weekend" (August 13–15) at the Treasury Department formulating an emergency package that ultimately totaled $4 billion, with the United States contributing about $3 billion of Fed loans, a (discount) purchase of Mexican oil, and emergency food credits.

Volcker now had to obtain congressional approval of the agreement. The administration and Volcker needed to persuade a hesitant Congress to increase the U.S. commitment to IMF at a time when domestic social welfare programs were suffering. To some, this plan represented a camouflaged bailout of large commercial banks that had used poor judgment in making loans. Volcker led the fight by testifying before Congress and by privately obtaining support from congressional leaders. After much debate, Congress enacted the necessary legislation.

Volcker was also struggling to keep Mexico from scuttling the agreement. The Mexican president in his State of the Union speech objected to the IMF austerity program; U.S. bankers panicked. Volcker and his long-time friend (and fishing partner) Jacques de Larosiere, the IMF managing director, firmly informed Mexico that its government would have to reduce spending, raise taxes, rescind exchange controls, and slow wage growth. Finally, in late October, Mexico agreed to the IMF program.

The Mexican bailout was followed by numerous other crises as developing countries lined up for debt rescheduling. In each case, Volcker retained his reputation as a masterful crisis manager as he combined his widesweeping net of contacts with his legendary persuasive abilities to patch together deal after deal. Rescheduling the debt was only a temporary solution however; it did not solve fundamental problems.

Most articles written about Volcker during the first half of 1983 were concerned with whether President Reagan would appoint him for a second four-year term as chair of the Board of Governors. Most writers speculated that Reagan did not want to reappoint Volcker, a nominal Democrat whom Carter had appointed. Volcker's continued advocacy for fiscal restraint, including tax hikes, irritated supply siders in the Treasury Department. Moreover, many people clearly identified Volcker with recession. Reagan's political advisers feared that Volcker, in his zeal to prevent inflation, would follow a too tight monetary policy prior to the 1984 elections; they contended that he was not a team player. Among President Reagan's advisers, Don Regan most vigorously opposed Volcker.

On the other hand, both domestic and international financial communities strongly supported Volcker for his role in reducing inflation, his resolve in maintaining an independent central bank, and his active involvement in attempts to solve the international debt crisis. Within the administration, Volcker maintained good relationships with Martin Feldstein (CEA chair) and David Stockman. Furthermore, the anti-Volcker faction did not possess a consensus candidate to replace him. Supply siders favored Preston Martin,* vice-chair of the Fed; however, the business community did not support this Californian and many considered him to be too inexperienced. The person most often mentioned was Alan Greenspan.* Although Reagan's political operatives considered him a "Ford person" (Greenspan had been CEA chair, 1974–1976) and Greenspan lacked Volcker's international experience and contacts, the domestic business community respected him. Greenspan, however, publicly praised Volcker's actions as chair and recommended that Reagan reappoint Volcker. In addition, many congressional leaders now supported Volcker. Howard Baker (R, Tennessee), Senate majority leader, vociferously had criticized Volcker during 1982; by 1983 Baker recommended Volcker's reappointment because Volcker had convinced financial markets that he was willing to take tough actions in battling inflation. Paul Laxalt (R, Nevada), reportedly President Reagan's closet friend in the Senate, expressed similar support. Even many Democrats, such as William Proxmire (D, Wisconsin), praised Volcker and urged Reagan to reappoint him. Not having a clear alternative to Volcker and not wanting to risk the fragile recovery by upsetting financial markets, Reagan nominated Volcker for reappointment as chair (June 18, 1983). By a vote of 84 to 16, Congress confirmed Volcker's nomination on July 27, 1983.

Volcker again was ambivalent about accepting the position. His wife preferred that he return to New York City; Volcker often worried that he was asking his family to make too large a sacrifice. On the other hand, he told associates that he would like to deal more adequately with the international debt problems. Ultimately Volcker could not resist the temptation of guiding monetary policy for another four years.

During the next four years, Volcker's goal was to expand the money supply rapidly enough so that recovery would continue without increasing inflation; he desired low-inflationary growth with the emphasis on "low inflationary." Reagan and his advisers also wanted low-inflationary growth, but they emphasized "growth." President Reagan continued to appoint governors sympathetic to supply-side views that the economy had ample room to grow without reigniting inflation. In technical terms, Volcker believed that the natural rate of real GNP was lower (and the natural rate of unemployment was higher) than that argued by supply siders. In open market policy, Volcker's dominance of the Board of

Governors was supplemented by several anti-inflationary hawks among the Federal Reserve bank presidents. In January 1986 the confirmation of two new Reagan appointees placed Volcker potentially in the minority on the Board of Governors but not on the FOMC. Volcker's potential opponents included Preston Martin, Martha Seger,* often a supply-side supporter, Manuel Johnson,* whose appointment Jack Kemp pushed, and Wayne Angell,* an economics professor and farmer, who obtained Senate majority leader Robert Dole's (R, Kansas) support for easier farm credit. Not only did Volcker's critics on the board often disagree with the substance of his monetary policy, they also disliked his management style. They considered him to be arrogant, autocratic, and too secretive, particularly in the international sphere.

The showdown arrived on February 24, 1986, when the Board of Governors voted 4 to 3, with Volcker in the minority, to lower the discount rate by ½ percent. Volcker objected to the discount rate cut, which would weaken the dollar. He asked that the vote not be recorded immediately; several hours later, Angell changed his vote to allow Volcker time to arrange with Japan and West Germany coordinated discount rate reductions. (Several writers have speculated that James Baker influenced Angell to switch his vote to prevent Volcker from resigning.) In early March Volcker convinced Japanese and West German central banks to lead a coordinated discount rate reduction.

Throughout March the media speculated about Volcker's future as chair. Apparently Martin, whose term as vice-chair was expiring, asked the White House for a commitment to appoint him chair when Volcker's term expired in 1987. When the White House refused to make such a commitment, Martin resigned on March 22 (effective April 30, 1986).

Martin's resignation removed the most immediate threat to Volcker's authority. Although rebellion against Volcker's autocratic procedures surfaced continually, Johnson and Angell voted with Volcker frequently enough that their supporters believed the system and Volcker had co-opted them. In reality, Volcker's well-renowned pragmatism maintained his control as he allowed faster monetary growth during 1986 and paid more attention to factors emphasized by other board members such as capacity utilization (Johnson) and prices in commodity auction markets (Angell).

During the battle for reappointment, Volcker had indicated that he believed that he had unfinished work in the international sphere. Although his primary worry was the global debt problem, he was troubled by the dollar's continued appreciation and the resulting increase in net imports. Volcker, who generally preferred stability of exchange rates, believed this appreciation resulted from higher real interest rates that arose from an expansionary fiscal–contractionary monetary policy mix. His preferred solution was to reduce the budget deficit, thereby increasing the Fed's flexibility to expand the money supply. Volcker's insistence that even tax increases would be preferable to the current situation continued to annoy many in the Reagan administration.

In January 1985 James Baker became Treasury secretary when he and Donald Regan switched jobs. Although the dollar had fallen by about 11 percent during the spring and early summer of 1985 without governmental intervention, Baker decided in mid-summer to begin secret negotiations with other Group of Five (G–5) nations to bring down the dollar. On September 22, the G–5 finance ministers and central bankers announced the formal agreement to depreciate the dollar in an orderly manner. During the next five months, the dollar significantly declined, although probably because of fundamental reasons rather than from intervention. Concerned by the inflationary consequences of the dollar's rapid depreciation, Volcker on February 19, 1986, stated that he believed that the dollar "may have fallen enough." To prevent further depreciation, Volcker worked with Japanese and West German central banks to coordinate discount rate reductions.

The Treasury Department interpreted central bank cooperation as a signal to promote its plan for establishing a set of unannounced broad exchange rate zones for each country—a plan similar to one that Volcker first proposed in 1972. Although Volcker approved of putting more stability back in the system, the Japanese and West Germans opposed this plan. Negotiations went slowly until February 21 and 22, 1987, when the G–5 finance ministers agreed to keep exchange rates at about current levels. Although Volcker had spent much time with Baker and with other countries' central bankers, he knew that government intervention in foreign currency markets constituted only a limited, temporary solution; only fundamental changes in trade balances could reduce pressure for further dollar depreciation. In numerous speeches, Volcker stated that he preferred Japan and West Germany to expand their domestic economies, thereby reducing reliance on exports to the United States for their economic growth. Moreover, he stressed the need to support free trade policies and resist increased protectionism.

The exchange rate negotiations involved other developed, industrialized nations; Volcker also had to deal with the Third World debt crisis. The IMF-imposed austerity programs resulted in lower inflation and reduced budget deficits but also often in reduced economic growth and sometimes even recession. As the debtor nations voiced increasing opposition to these austerity measures, Baker (with Volcker's private help) developed "A Program for Sustained Growth." Announced at the annual IMF–World Bank meeting in October 1985, the program proposed replacing IMF austerity with loans to debtor countries that made structural reforms promoting economic growth. However, the plan depended on commercial banks' extending new loans and many banks were reluctant to make new loans to debtor countries. Volcker often pressured banks to increase their loan commitments. Although some observers saw improvement, crises continued to arise; it became evident that Volcker had not developed a permanent solution, although his support of market-oriented reforms and free trade moved the debate in the correct direction.

The revolution engulfing depository institutions continued to overwhelm regulators. Fast-moving developments provided Volcker with many opportunities to excel as a crisis manager and to work toward overall structural reform.

The bailout of Continental Illinois National Bank in May-July 1984 exemplifies Volcker's approach toward commercial banks experiencing severe financial difficulties. Continental possessed a small local deposit base because of Illinois's restrictive branch banking legislation. Acquiring funds through aggressive use of managed liabilities, it had rapidly expanded its loan portfolio from $12 billion in 1976 to $34 billion in 1982, with most new loans going to the energy industry. As the decline in oil prices caused many of Continental energy loans to fail, businesses and other banks began to withdraw their funds. Volcker believed that if Continental failed, a national banking panic would ensue because over 2,000 correspondent banks had deposits at Continental (with 179 having deposits of more than 50 percent of their capital). When no other bank was willing to merge with Continental, government officials decided to bail out Continental and protect all of its depositors. The Fed loaned Continental over $5 billion until the FDIC worked out a $4.5 billion rescue effort. Although Volcker considered this bailout to be essential in maintaining confidence in the banking system, others criticized his efforts as sending to large banks and their large depositors an improper signal that regardless of how poorly large banks were managed, the government would always be there to bail them out. Moreover, some analysts noted that for several years, Volcker had been aware of Continental's severe financial problems. Although he often privately urged Continental leaders to take drastic remedial actions, he did not order them to do so. In other words, Volcker's critics acknowledged that he was a master of managing crises but pointed out that his procrastination often contributed to the crisis occurring.

With regard to structural reform, Volcker possessed two objectives. First, he did not want the Fed to lose any regulatory authority. To protect the Fed, Volcker delayed for several years the findings of a presidential task force that favored stripping the Fed of its regulatory powers to create one superagency to regulate depository institutions. Second, he desired to restrict the amount of risky activities that commercial banks could undertake. Although Volcker favored allowing commercial banks to underwrite municipal revenue bonds, distribute mutual funds, and other discount brokerage services, he vigorously opposed allowing commercial banks to underwrite corporate securities and to engage in real estate development. Volcker, however, favored several drastic changes in the regulatory structure: nationwide banking, closing the loophole on nonbank banks, basing capital requirements on the risk structure of assets, and paying interest on reserves. Because the Fed was only one player out of many in the financial services regulation game, Volcker achieved much less influence than he commanded in the domestic monetary policy arena.

Once again the approaching end of Volcker's four-year term set off massive speculation concerning whether President Reagan would nominate him for another term. Many officials in the Reagan administration disliked Volcker's skepticism about the economy's ability to grow rapidly without reigniting inflation and his unwillingness to support further deregulation of depository institutions and financial markets. On the other hand, some Reagan officials, such as Treasury Secretary James Baker and Howard Baker, chief of staff after Regan's departure, supported Volcker. With political turmoil resulting from the Iran-contra scandal threatening to cause additional instability in financial markets, many saw Volcker's ability as a crisis manager to be essential in upcoming months. Moreover, the anti-Volcker faction did not have an alternative candidate who inspired confidence in financial markets; the only person seriously considered was Alan Greenspan, whose views on policy issues were similar to Volcker's.

Because his wife wanted him to return to New York, Volcker decided that he would accept another term only if President Reagan strongly supported him. On June 1 Reagan, without enthusiasm, asked Volcker to remain as chair; Volcker resigned. The next day Reagan nominated Alan Greenspan to replace Volcker who remained at the Fed until the Senate confirmed Greenspan.

Leaving the Fed allowed Volcker to rejoin his wife in New York City and to see more of his son, Jimmy. Volcker soon agreed to serve, without pay, as chair of the privately funded National Commission on Public Service, which was studying methods to make government service more attractive. Volcker received many offers from the private sector, especially from bond trading companies. Finally in March 1988, he became chair and part owner of James D. Wolfensohn, a firm that specializes in international financial services; in this job, Volcker believed that he would play a key role in the firm's development and not be just an ornament. He also accepted a part-time appointment at Princeton University as professor of international economic policy and agreed to serve as a consultant to the World Bank on international debt.

The news media continue to record his thoughts on economic policies and his views on public service. Volcker stated that the federal government is losing its ability to attract the best people because of unrealistically low pay scales compared to similar jobs in the private sector and because the increased number of political appointees reduces the authority and responsibility for senior civil servants; the problem is most serious for people with special skills, such as engineers, lawyers, and central bankers. As Fed chair, Volcker often agonized that his dedication for public service was hurting his family financially. He ultimately persuaded the Commission on Public Service to recommend higher salaries and increased responsibility for many government employees.

Volcker is a complex, multifaceted individual. He was a shy boy, and many consider him a shy man who possesses unbounded self-confidence. Many consider him aloof, but he displays an ironic, and often self-deprecating, sense of humor. Once he dressed up as the Jolly Green Giant (in reference to his height) to attend a Washington costume party. He has enjoyed a stable family life with a supportive wife. Although he did not spend much time with his children, they regard him as a loving father, who now is far more attentive to his grandchildren. Ultimately the picture that emerges is one of a strong-willed man of high integrity whose preference was for public service.

Volcker's two most significant accomplishments at the Fed were to improve the status of the Fed and to reduce inflation. Under his leadership, the Fed assumed unprecedented dominance of macroeconomic policy. His critics argue that Volcker's disinflation occurred too rapidly, resulting in more economic suffering and dislocation than necessary; they preferred a gradualist disinflation policy. Indeed, some argue that Volcker's policy was an accident because the Fed experienced difficulties in controlling monetary aggregates and in estimating velocity. On the other hand, some analysts contend that Volcker believed the U.S. public would not tolerate a long, protracted battle against inflation and thus felt compelled to conquer inflation rapidly. Volcker came to represent the nation's commitment to fight inflation. The economic expansion from late 1982 through the remainder of the 1980s was a direct outcome of the disinflationary monetary policies of 1981–1982. Volcker's critics complained that he would not allow enough economic expansion, but Volcker was probably correct when he argued that the inflationary episodes of the 1960s and 1970s had demonstrated the dangers of too rapid monetary growth.

His battle against inflation tied his hands with respect to international initiatives. The Fed could engage in only limited foreign exchange intervention and recommend that the U.S. budget deficit be reduced to relieve pressure on real interest rates and thereby on the dollar. He effectively resolved international debt crises in the short term; however, these short-term palliatives did not cure fundamental long-term problems.

To accomplish goals, the Fed chair must be a political operative who obtains support from members of Congress, presidential staff, reserve banks, and commercial banks, among others. Volcker mastered the art of finding support for his (often controversial) policies. His tenure as chair stretched through a turbulent economic period. His guidance of monetary policy may have been imperfect, but it is not clear that anyone else could have done a better job.

BIBLIOGRAPHY

Greider, William. 1987. *Secrets of the Temple: How the Federal Reserve Runs the Country*. New York: Simon and Schuster.

Kettl, Donald F. 1986. *Leadership at the Fed*. New Haven: Yale University Press.

Neikirk, William R. 1987. *Volcker: Portrait of the Money Man*. New York: Congdon & Weed.

Niskanen, William A. 1988. *Reaganomics: An Insider's Account of the Policies and the People*. New York: Oxford University Press.

"Paul Adolph Volcker." 1973. *Current Biography, 1973*, pp. 425–28.

Solomon, Robert. 1982. *The International Monetary System, 1945–1981*. New York: Harper & Row.

Volcker, Paul A. 1977. "Monetary Policy Coordination." In Robert A. Mundell and

Jacques J. Polak, eds., *The New International Monetary System*. New York: Columbia University Press.

———. 1977–1978. "The Challenges in International Economic Policy." *New York Federal Reserve Bank Quarterly Review* (Winter): 1–6.

———. 1978a. *The Rediscovery of the Business Cycle*. New York: Free Press.

———. 1978b. "The Role of Monetary Targets in an Age of Inflation." *Journal of Monetary Economics* 4 (April): 329–39.

———. 1978–1979. "The Political Economy of the Dollar." *New York Federal Reserve Bank Quarterly Review* (Winter): 1–12.

———. 1988. *Public Service: The Quiet Crisis*. Washington, D.C.: American Enterprise Institute.

HENRY WALLICH (1914–1988)

David J. Leahigh

Henry Christopher Wallich, a governor of the Federal Reserve from 1974 to 1986, was born on June 10, 1914, in Berlin, Germany, the son of a banker. He had, by his own admission, a rather checkered academic career. He spent one term at Munich University, where he claims he spent more time on the tennis court than in the library. While he never lost his love for tennis, he did turn his attention to more academic matters when he went to Oxford for a year. By this time, the Nazis had come to power in Germany, so rather than return home, Wallich went to Buenos Aires, Argentina, to work for an exporting firm there.

In 1935 he moved to New York, taking a position with Chemical Bank. Shortly afterward, in 1936, he joined the brokerage firm of Hackney, Hopkinson, and Sutphen as a securities analyst. While working for this firm, he also attended classes at New York University. Despite not having a university degree, Wallich was persuaded to apply to Harvard for the Ph.D. economics program in 1939. The university gave him credit for his time at Oxford and work experience, in essence waiving the degree requirements, and admitted him to the program in 1940.

In the summer of 1941, Wallich went to work for the New York Federal Reserve Bank as its Latin American expert. While there, he did some research on Latin American economies and international monetary reform. This early research was to color Wallich's views on the international economy for many years, including his years on the Board of Governors. In 1944 he became U.S. citizen. He eventually moved up to become chief of the Foreign Research Division at the New York Fed from 1946 to 1951. During this time, in 1950, he married Mable Inness Brown, with whom he had one son and two daughters. In 1951 he left the New York Fed and was appointed professor of economics at Yale University. He maintained his association with Yale until his appointment to the board in 1974, being named Yale's Seymour H. Knox Professor in 1970.

He never lost his urge for public service, however, and throughout the 1950s served in a variety of capacities for the federal government. In 1954 he served as an adviser to President Dwight D. Eisenhower on trade policy. In this capacity he argued for a liberalization of U.S. trade policy. In 1958 he came back to Washington to be the head of the Treasury Department's tax analysis staff. In this function, he advocated accelerated depreciation for business investment. This idea was shelved until the 1960s and the Kennedy administration. In 1959 he was appointed to the President's Council of Economic Advisers. One of his ideas during this time period was an interest rate experiment that later came to be known as Operation Twist. As with his ideas on depreciation, this policy did not come to fruition until the Kennedy administration.

With the arrival of the Kennedy administration in 1961, Wallich returned to Yale. About the same time he was asked to join the editorial staff of the *Washington Post*. He remained on the staff until 1965, when he left the *Post* to become a columnist for *Newsweek* magazine to write commentaries on the economy. He rotated the assignment with Paul Samuelson and Milton Friedman. Wallich later wrote of that experience, "I felt that I represented common sense tempering the voice of genius."

In 1969 Wallich answered the call of public service yet again, this time as a senior consultant to the Treasury Department. His service in that capacity, and on other commissions, led to his nomination by President Richard Nixon for a position on Board of Governors of the Federal Reserve. On March 8, 1974, Wallich was sworn in as a member of the board, a position he held until poor health forced him to resign on December 15, 1986. He died September 15, 1988.

In many ways during the latter part of his term, Wallich was the most publicly visible member of the board except for the chairman, Volcker,* giving lectures and appearing repeatedly before congressional committees. He was also a strong voice within the board's private discussions, not afraid to speak his mind. He summarized his tenure on the board in 1982 saying, "I usually found myself in a minority of one." This may well be a result of his experience in post–World War I Germany with the hyperinflation of that era. Indeed, Paul Volcker, in his introduction to *International Monetary Cooperation: Essays in Honor of Henry C. Wallich*, noted Wallich's persistence in pointing out the dangers of inflation and his consistent voting record in favor of price stability. This emphasis on monetary restraint is best illustrated in the records of the Federal Open Market Committee from late 1979 into the early 1980s. On several occasions during this period, Wallich was the lone dissenter from the committee's action, advocating invariably tighter monetary policies. In fact, the minutes of the meeting of October 5–6, 1981, indicate that he favored lower growth rates in the monetary aggregates. He took this stance despite strong evidence at the time of an economy in recession.

He refused to be swayed by popular currents in economic policy. For instance, while he was strongly anti-inflation, he was very critical of purely monetarist solutions to the problem, such as Milton Friedman's monetary growth rules. Nor was he much taken with the idea of supply-side economics, which received so much play in the early 1980s. But he was willing to change his mind when the facts demanded it. His experiences in the 1930s and 1940s with international economic issues led him to become a staunch advocate of fixed exchange rates, which he believed seemed to promote the stability necessary for the expansion of international trade. But by the late 1960s, events in the exchange markets led him to doubt whether fixed rates promoted the necessary stability. His position on the exchange markets became one of nonintervention except to smooth out temporary fluctuations.

Interestingly, given his wide-ranging background in finance and economics and the role the Fed plays in regulating commercial banking, Wallich was less sure of his expertise in that area. He expressed few opinions in this area that stood out as clearly as his views on inflation.

Wallich brought several qualities with him to every position he held: his desire to engage in public service, an adherence to his basic intellectual principles, a preciseness of thought based on those principles, and an ability to communicate his ideas to a wide range of audiences from the academic community through journal articles to laymen through his *Newsweek* commentaries.

BIBLIOGRAPHY

Volcker, Paul, ed. 1987. *International Monetary Cooperation: Essays in Honor of Henry C. Wallich*. Princeton, N.J.: International Finance Section, Department of Economics, Princeton University.

Wallich, Henry C. 1982a. *Monetary Policy and Practice: A View from the Federal Reserve Board*. Lexington, Mass.: Lexington Books.

———. 1982b. "Some Uses of Economics." Banca Nazionale del Lavoro *Quarterly Review* 141 (June): 119–45.

Who Was Who in America, 1989. Vol. 9. Chicago: Marquis Who's Who.

PAUL MORITZ WARBURG
(1868–1932)

Robert Stanley Herren

Paul Moritz Warburg, a member of the original Federal Reserve Board of Governors from 1914 to 1918, was born on August 10, 1868, in Hamburg, Germany to Moritz and Charlotte Warburg. His Jewish family had been in the banking business for many years; his great-grandfather in 1798 had founded M. M. Warburg and Company, which soon became a prominent merchant banking firm in Europe. Paul and three of his four brothers—Felix (1871–1937), Fritz (1879–1962), and Max (1867–1946)—would all ultimately become partners in the family bank; his other brother, Aby (1866–1929), became a renowned art historian.

Paul's education and early work experience superbly prepared him for a career in banking. After graduating from the Real Gymnasium in Hamburg in 1886, he worked first for an exporting firm in Hamburg and then for shipping and banking houses in both London and Paris. In 1895 he returned to Hamburg to become a partner in the family banking house. In the same year, he married Nina J. Loeb, daughter of Solomon Loeb, one of the founding partners of the New York investment banking firm Kuhn, Loeb and Co.; he met Nina at the wedding of his brother, Felix, to Frieda Schiff, daughter of Jacob Schiff, senior partner in Kuhn, Loeb and Co.

Warburg remained a partner in the rapidly expanding family firm until 1907, although his active involvement ended in 1902 when he moved his family, which now included son James Paul (1896) and daughter Bettina (1900), to New York City, where he became a partner in his father-in-law's firm. During his first few years with Kuhn, Loeb and Co., his major responsibilities involved arranging loans for the governments of Argentina, Brazil, China, Cuba, Japan, and Mexico.

Soon after arriving in the United States, Warburg became convinced that the American banking system had several serious flaws. He wrote a memo outlining a plan, based on his European experiences, to correct these defects. After circulating this memo within his firm and to other bankers in New York City, he discovered that many American bankers preferred to pretend that problems in the U.S. banking system did not exist. For example, James A. Stillman, president of the National City Bank of New York, told Warburg that Warburg had incorrectly concluded that European banking methods were superior to American methods when in fact American methods were superior.

The panic of 1907 shattered the complacency of bankers such as Stillman and threw Warburg into active involvement in the monetary reform process. Warburg believed years of educational work would be necessary before meaningful reform occurred. In November 1907, he published a paper, "A Plan for a Modified Central Bank," which indicated his belief that the United States needed a central bank—as centralized as U.S. politics and values would allow (reprinted in Warburg 1930, 2:29–36). According to Warburg, this central bank must have discretionary control over discounting real bills because reliance on a self-regulating banking system was a prescription for further banking panics.

Warburg became involved in the monetary reform movement on many fronts. He participated in academic forums, as well as in the political arena. He presented papers at American Economic Association meetings and regularly communicated with leading economists, such as James Laughlin, O. M. W. Sprague, and Edwin Seligman. His debate with professional economists revolved around the correct interpretation of the real bills doctrine and its suitability to central banking in the United States. His studies of European banking systems had convinced him that a central bank should have the authority to issue paper currency when it discounted commercial paper (real bills). He realized that a mechanical adherence to discounting real bills could result in inflation but argued that a discretionary policy could avoid inflation while providing an elastic currency to prevent temporary credit crunches from becoming full-blown financial panics. While he did not convince everyone to accept his views, professional economists did respect his ideas.

Besides attempting to convince economists about the validity of his proposed reforms, Warburg diligently worked to educate the general public, including the banking community. In 1908 he convinced the *Banking Law Journal* to poll bankers concerning the need for bank reform to demonstrate the existence of broad support for a central bank. In 1911 he aided in founding the National Citizens League, an organization formed to arouse public sentiment in favor of banking reform. He recommended that Laughlin, professor of economics at the University of Chicago, head the league to emphasize that banking reform had national support and was not just the idea of Wall Street bankers. Laughlin proved to be a vigorous advocate of monetary reform, although he did not agree with all aspects of Warburg's plans.

Warburg also participated in drafting legislation for monetary reform. In 1907, he met Senator Nelson W. Aldrich (R, Rhode Island) who chaired the National Monetary Commission, created by Congress in 1908 (and dissolved in 1911). Warburg wrote the commission's report on central banking in Europe. In November 1910 he participated in a secret meeting arranged by Senator Aldrich at Jekyll Island, Georgia, to draft a monetary reform bill. The resulting bill, after some slight modifications, became the Aldrich bill; its basic features were similar to Warburg's united reserve bank plan, which he had published in March 1910. The bill's national reserve association was based on a clearinghouse principle. It made no provision for government participation; Warburg's original plan included some government participation—one-fifth of the national board of directors.

Although many of its provisions were eventually incorporated into the Federal Reserve Act, Congress never seriously debated the Aldrich bill because Democrats won control of the House in 1910. The elections of 1912 changed the political equation as Democrats won control of both Congress and the White House. This electoral change reduced Warburg's role in drafting legislation because, like most other contemporary bankers, he leaned toward the Republicans. He continued to write about monetary reform and to testify concerning various legislative proposals. Significantly, his professional approach toward monetary reform and his willingness to accept majority governmental control over the proposed reserve system impressed even his political opponents, so he continued to maintain cordial relationships with the Wilson administration and with many congressional Democrats.

President Woodrow Wilson signed the Federal Reserve Act on December 23, 1913; his next task was to appoint the Federal Reserve Board. In April 1914 Wilson's aide, Colonel House, approached Warburg about whether he would be willing to accept an appointment to the board. Warburg "had become convinced that no one with the interests of the country genuinely at heart would be justified in refusing to give the best that was in him to the perfection of the great work about to be undertaken" (Warburg 1930, 1:143). Wilson officially nominated Warburg for a four-year term on June 10, 1914. Warburg immediately caused a political ruckus when he refused to testify at his confirmation hearings because he thought he was "singled out" for a "humiliating procedure"; the Senate committee had already favorably reported Charles Hamlin,[*] W. P. G. Harding,[*] and A. C. Miller[*] without their testimony. Warburg later related: "The deadlock continued for four weeks during which the President urged me to give in, while I urged him to withdraw my name. Much to my mortification, the controversy became one of the main topics of the newspapers. . . . When the Great War broke out, I waived my own feelings and . . . appeared before the committee" (1930, 1:147) The Senate confirmed Warburg for a four-year term. Warburg resigned from all directorships and trusteeships (one estimate had his annual income in the $500,000 range) to become a member of the board (a $12,000 job), which took office on August 10, 1914.

Most historians contend that Wilson appointed Warburg to provide a link between the New York City banking community and the Federal Reserve Board and to convince (Republican) bankers that the populist wing of the Democratic party would not be controlling monetary policy. Warburg viewed his role as one of guiding the evolution of "the dwarfed and limping system originally sanctioned by Congress" and to free it from "its original deadly strait jacket."

The Federal Reserve Act had widely dispersed and vaguely defined the lines of authority within the system. Warburg and several other appointive members (Frederic Delano,* Harding, Miller) constantly became embroiled in controversy with the ex officio members (secretary of Treasury and comptroller of the currency), the district banks, and Congress over the board's role within the system.

Warburg, Delano, Harding, and Miller ignited a political firestorm in 1915 when they discussed the possibility of merging Federal Reserve districts. The Federal Reserve Act had provided for "not less than eight nor more than twelve" districts; Congress also established an Organization Committee, which decided on twelve reserve banks. Warburg's group wanted districts large enough so that each district bank would have enough capital to meet its responsibilities; Warburg believed that the large number of district banks, some of them poorly capitalized, actually increased the role of the well-capitalized New York City district bank, an ironic situation because Congress had established the district reserve system to reduce the influence of Wall Street bankers. Nevertheless, politicians around the country and in Congress, the board's ex officio members (who had been members of the Organization Committee), and district bank officials immediately protested even discussing the issue (no formal plan of reorganization was ever submitted); some described Warburg's group as "dark conspirators, banded together to destroy the Reserve System with a view to paving the way for the ultimate establishment of a central bank" (Warburg, 1930, 1:425). Warburg's aim was to make the existing system effective; he realized that contemporary U.S. politics precluded a true central bank. In November 1915 the U.S. attorney general ruled that the board could not reduce the number of district banks; in April 1916 he ruled that the board could not change the location of bank reserve cities.

These rulings effectively ended one organizational dispute, but board members were already involved in another: the independence of the board from the Treasury Department. Secretary of Treasury William McAdoo always considered the board to be a subservient adjunct to the Treasury Department and constantly tried to reduce the status of board members. Although today some of the dispute over the social status of board members may appear petty, Warburg's group considered themselves to be nonpartisan neutral experts who possessed responsibility for running the monetary system for the public good; the higher their status was, the more independent of political influences they could be.

The first governor, Hamlin, had previously served in Treasury under McAdoo and was personally loyal to him. Although the other appointed members personally liked Hamlin, they advocated regular rotation in the offices of governor and vice-governor to preserve the "prestige and independence of the Board." Amid much controversy, President Wilson in August 1916 appointed Harding as governor and Warburg as vice-governor. However, the entry of the United States into World War I forced the Federal Reserve system to work closely with the Treasury Department in wartime financing; the issue regarding the relationship between the Fed and Treasury Department would remain contentious for many decades.

The war resulted in Warburg's leaving the Federal Reserve Board in 1918. His critics argued that a naturalized citizen (1911) of German birth whose brothers were prominent in the German banking industry should not be on the Federal Reserve board. Warburg's resignation letter (May 27, 1918) to President Wilson reveals much about the strength of Warburg's character.

I did not swear that "I absolutely and entirely renounce and abjure all allegiance and fidelity to any foreign potentate and particularly to Wilhelm II, Emperor of Germany", etc. until I was quite certain that I was willing and anxious to cast my lot unqualifiedly and without reserve with the country of my adoption and to defend its aims and ideals. . . .

I have considered it the greatest privilege to serve my country. . . . I do not abandon lightly a work, half done, in which I am deeply and genuinely interested. But my continuation in office under present conditions might make the Board a target of constant attack by unscrupulous or unreasoning people, and my concern to save any embarrassment to you and to the Board. . . .

In writing you this letter, I have been prompted solely by my sincere conviction that the national welfare must be our only concern. Whatever you may decide to be best for the country will determine my future course. We are at war, and I remain at your orders. (Warburg 1930, 1:802–4)

President Wilson decided to accept his resignation; Paul Warburg returned to private life on August 10, 1918.

Warburg's life remained hectic. He served, at various times, as a director of First National Bank of Boston, Baltimore and Ohio Railroad, Union Pacific Railroad, and Western Union Telegraph Company, in addition to other firms. He and his wife continued to support a wide array of cultural and charitable activities; for example, he was a director of Julliard School of Music, trustee of the National Child Labor Committee, and trustee of Tuskegee College.

His business energies centered around his conviction that American banking must be willing to take international financial responsibilities, especially to support Europe. In addition to advocating U.S. government financing of reconstruction in Europe, Warburg organized (1921) the International Acceptance Bank for that purpose; in 1929, this bank merged with the Bank of the Manhattan Co. In 1924 Warburg organized a consortium of large New York City banks to finance trade credits to Germany. These efforts enjoyed some short-run success but failed in the long run.

In general, Warburg wanted to see the improvement of international relations, with a special interest in strengthening cultural relations between the United States and Germany. In 1930 he helped established the Carl Schurz Memorial Foundation to encourage German-American cultural cooperation. He provided significant financial contributions to the Warburg Library in Hamburg and to the Academy of Political Science in Berlin.

Warburg retained an active interest in monetary policy. From 1921 to 1926 he served as a member of the Advisory Council of the Federal Reserve Board.

He remained in touch with friends, such as Benjamin Strong, within the system; indeed, it had been Warburg who, in the summer of 1914, had convinced a reluctant Strong to accept the presidency of the New York Federal Reserve Bank. He continued to write about monetary policy. His massive 1930 work (two volumes, over 1,700 pages) included proposals for future reforms and collected many of his previous speeches and articles. He also wanted to "correct" the historical record that he believed was being misinterpreted in work by people such as Carter Glass and Parker Willis; for example, he included a 200-page comparison of the Aldrich bill with the Federal Reserve Act. To promote economic research, he provided both financial support and leadership to the Institute of Economics, founded in 1922, and to Brookings Institution after it merged with the Institute of Economics in 1927.

He attracted national attention in March 1929 when he warned about the disaster facing the economy due to wild stock speculation because increases in stock prices were unrelated to underlying economic factors. Improper lending practices by banks caused this orgy of speculation; he predicted that unless they were restrained, the result would be a depression throughout the United States. After the October 1929 stock market crash, he argued that the economy could recover quickly if the Fed provided banks with funds to loan to productive enterprises and if Congress would remove artificial barriers to trade, such as tariffs.

In addition to being concerned about the condition of the U.S. economy, Warburg was distressed by economic and political events in Germany. The weakening of the German economy and withdrawals of foreign funds endangered the family firm in Germany. Paul and Felix Warburg provided some infusion of much-needed capital, although Paul remained pessimistic about the political future in Germany.

On the other hand, his wife and children continued to provide emotional support. His son, James, worked with him from 1921 to 1932; he was a financial adviser of President Franklin Roosevelt and, after 1935, a prolific author. His daughter, Bettina, was a psychiatrist practicing in New York City.

On January 24, 1932, Paul Moritz Warburg died in his home in New York City. History remembers him for his activities in monetary reform, as a member of the Federal Reserve Board, and as a prominent and wealthy U.S. banker for the first three decades of the twentieth century. A contemporary, writing in the *Nation* magazine (February 3, 1932, p. 132), remembered him:

No one in a similarly influential position excelled Mr. Warburg in his feeling of responsibility to the public. Never was there a man who recognized more keenly the principle that wealth, like nobility, obliges. His generosity was without stint; his philanthropy ranged all over the world, and it was always intelligent, constructive, and farsighted. A patron of the arts, he never ceased to do what he could to advance the cultural development of the United States. There is hardly an office in this country which he could not have filled with distinction. As it was, his modesty made him shun proffered public contacts for which many another would have sought in vain. A leader among American Jews, it can truthfully be said of him that he set for his race in America an unsurpassable example of public service.

BIBLIOGRAPHY

Farrer, David. 1975. *The Warburgs: The Story of a Family*. New York: Stein and Day.
"Paul M. Warburg." 1932. *Nation*, February 3, p. 132.
Rosenbaum, E., and Sherman, A. J. 1979. *M. M. Warburg and Co., 1798–1938, Merchant Bankers of Hamburg*. New York: Holmes and Meier Publishers.
Warburg, James. 1964. *The Long Road Home: The Autobiography of a Maverick*. New York: Doubleday.
Warburg, Paul M. 1910. *The Discount System in Europe*. Washington, D.C.: Government Printing Office.
———. 1914. *Essays on Banking Reform*. Proceedings of the Academy of Political Science. January.
———. 1923. "The Federal Reserve Banks and the Open Market for Acceptances." *Harvard Business Review* (April): 257–68.
———. 1930. *The Federal Reserve System, Its Origin and Growth: Reflections and Recollections*. 2 vols. New York: Macmillan.
West, Robert Craig. 1977. *Banking Reform and the Federal Reserve, 1863–1923*. Ithaca, N.Y.: Cornell University Press.

DAVID C. WILLS (1872–1925)

Paul J. Kubik

David Crawford Wills was born in Pittsburgh, Pennsylvania, on August 11, 1872, and raised there. Immediately following his graduation in 1889 from Allegheny High School, Wills began his career in banking, a career that would eventually carry him to a post as a member on the Federal Reserve Board during the years 1920 and 1921. His first position was as a messenger for the Mechanics National Bank of Pittsburgh. While he was with the Mechanics Bank, Wills married Bessie A. Smith of Belleville, Pennsylvania, on May 23, 1895. In 1902 Wills became an auditor with the Mellon National Bank of Pittsburgh and in 1904 a cashier for the Diamond National Bank, also in Pittsburgh. In 1907 Wills organized and became president of the Citizen's National Bank of Bellevue, Pennsylvania, a position he held until 1914.

Wills's public service began in 1914 when he received an appointment as chairman of the board of directors and Federal Reserve agent at the Federal Reserve Bank of Cleveland. Wills was the first chairman, serving for six years. On September 29, 1920, he was appointed to the Federal Reserve Board by President Woodrow Wilson to fill the vacancy left open by the retirement of Henry A. Moehlenpah,* whose term had expired on August 9. Wills's appointment to the board was one step in the attempt by Republican presidents to place Republicans on the board. Wills, a Republican, was succeeded by John R. Mitchell,* a Republican banker from Minneapolis who was appointed by President Warren Harding.

Wills was appointed to the board during a congressional recess under a provision in section 10 of the original Federal Reserve Act providing the president with the "power to fill all vacancies that may happen on the Federal Reserve Board during the recess of the Senate by granting commissions which shall expire thirty days after the next session of the Senate convenes." The Senate reconvened on December 4, 1920. This set the expiration of Wills's term at January 3, 1921. The Federal Reserve Act provision, however, was inconsistent with the U.S. Constitution, which provides that commissions made during a congressional recess shall expire at the close of the next session of the Senate.

PIERRE CORNEILLE
From an engraving after a portrait by J. Gigoux

Racine they could scarcely bring themselves to speak with patience. "*Bérénice*," wrote Sainte-Beuve in a characteristic sally, "peut être dite une charmante et mélodieuse faiblesse dans l'œuvre de Racine, comme la Champmeslé le fut dans sa vie." In spite of Stendhal's timely championship of "the great and good Corneille," Corneille himself fared no better. "I admire his characters," said Taine, "but from a distance: I should not care to live with any of them." "C'est beau, admirable, sublime, ce n'est ni humain, ni vivant, ni réel," said Brunetière.

That was the verdict of the nineteenth century. Corneille was widely recognized as "the Father of French Tragedy," but he had become the professor's poet, a "classic" whose proper place was not the playbill, but the examination syllabus. Racine has long since come into his own in France, but it has been left to the younger French critics of our own day to discover in this staid classic, whose *Horace* delights or was supposed to delight the populace at the free matinée on Armistice Day, a much more exciting figure. According to one of the latest of his critics, Corneille's world is not a world of flourishes and lofty feelings. It is a world of corruption and intrigue inhabited by doddering, time-serving fathers and criminal stepmothers plotting the ruin of their children who are drawn with a ferocity that is worthy of Racine.[1]

There is, perhaps, a danger of exaggerating the sensational element in Corneille and the reason is not hard to discover. Contemporary admirers are a little too anxious to profit by the popularity of Racine and to discover similarities between the two writers, though it is clearly the differences which ought to detain us. One of the most important of these differences is brought out in the first chapter of M. Jean Schlumberger's valuable study when he speaks of the contrast between

"an heroic art and an art which aims at entertainment or pure knowledge, an art which builds up an exemplary picture of man and an art which destroys this picture by analysis and excessive refinement."[2]

It is a curious fact that few French critics manage to be fair to both poets and that their "rivalry," which is merely of historical interest, still influences critical opinion. Stendhal spoilt his defence

[1] Robert Brasillach, *Pierre Corneille*, Paris, 1938.
[2] *Plaisir à Corneille: Promenade anthologique*, Paris, 1936, p. 9.

of Corneille by declaring roundly that he was "immensely above Racine"; and it is one of the drawbacks of M. Schlumberger's study that he is inclined to diminish Racine's greatness in order to make his defence of Corneille more convincing. This is surely a mistake. No one seriously believes that he is as great a poet as Racine, but they are not "rivals" and they are not interchangeable. Without Corneille there would be a gap in French literature which Racine could never have filled.

Racine belongs to an age of transition from the old order to the new, from the old social solidarity to the new individualism. His impact on French poetry produced what was virtually a change of direction—a movement away from all that Corneille had stood for —and for this reason he seems to me to be much more the predecessor of Baudelaire than the successor of Corneille.[1] Corneille is not in himself a difficult poet, but an appreciation of his poetry has been made difficult by changing circumstances. He is more than most other great poets the test of a catholic taste in poetry, because to enjoy him it is necessary to realize that poetry may be "sublime" *and* "human, living and real." He wrote heroic plays and it is as an heroic poet that he stands or falls. A criticism of his work is primarily an elucidation of this uncomfortable term. M. Schlumberger's suggestion that an appreciation of Corneille involves an appreciation of Hugo and Claudel seems to me a strategic error, and Croce's invitation to us to discard Corneille's four most famous tragedies and to discover the true Corneille—Corneille the Poet—in the final plays simply shirks all the difficulties.

2

Corneille's achievement becomes more comprehensible when we consider it in relation to his own age. The reign of Louis XIII opened appropriately with an assassination. France was governed by a despotism, but an uneasy despotism. The first part of the century is dominated by Richelieu. The spectacle of Richelieu entering La Rochelle at the head of the King's troops to celebrate the Mass of thanksgiving for the fall of the town is a symbol of the

---

[1] There is perhaps a parallel here between Racine and Donne which seems more striking when one considers the recent history of their reputations in their own countries.

contradictions of the age and of its strange mixture of piety and opportunism. It was an age of rival factions and incredible intrigues, an age that delighted in great exploits and violent actions. France had been shaken to the core by the religious wars of the previous century; and though the worst of them were over, the country was still split in two by the conflict between Catholic and Protestant. It was also a period of intense religious revival in which the chief figures were St. François de Sales and St. Vincent de Paul. Although it has seemed to later generations that theology and philosophy parted company in the seventeenth century, Corneille's contemporaries saw no conflict between the old religion and the "new philosophy." Descartes and the theologians were at one in their interest in psychology and their preoccupation with moral problems; and Pascal and Bossuet were both admirers of the Cartesian philosophy.

In Corneille's poetry all these different and sometimes contradictory elements found a place. The interest that he shows in family feuds in the *Cid*, in political intrigue in *Cinna* and religious dissensions in *Polyeucte*, is clearly a reflection of events that were going on around him. The relation of a great poet to his time, however, is primarily a matter of temper, and it was left to Sainte-Beuve to define it in a sympathetic moment in his description of the famous *journée du guichet* in *Port-Royal*:

"It is the same struggle, the same triumph; if *Polyeucte* moves us and carries us away it is because something of the kind is and remains possible to human nature when assisted by grace. I will go further than this. If the genius of Corneille was capable of producing *Polyeucte* at this time, it was because there was still something in his surroundings (whether Corneille himself was aware of it or not) which matched its spirit and achieved the same miracles."[1]

The fact that internally France was in a state of turmoil undoubtedly produced a considerable effort towards consolidation.[2]

[1] *Port-Royal*, II, Paris, 1848, p. 115. The *journée du guichet* was the day when Arnauld was refused admission to the Abbey by his daughter, the abbess, to prevent interference with his children's religious vocation. Sainte-Beuve's words are still more significant when one recalls what a large part of Corneille's work was occupied with conflicts between parents and children.

[2] The propaganda for absolute monarchy, which is prominent in all Corneille's plays, seems to be a sign of the political uneasiness of the times and of the "effort towards consolidation."

In spite of its contradictions, Corneille's age was in many ways an age of reconstruction. A sense of effort, a striving towards a moral end, seems to me to be the deepest thing in his poetry. It is well expressed in a characteristic couplet from one of Auguste's last speeches in *Cinna*:

> Je suis maître de moi comme de l'univers;
> Je le suis, je veux l'être.

In the first line we notice that the personal problem is related to the social one, and in the second that the statement is significantly followed by the aspiration.

A direct preoccupation with morality and the constant recurrence of words denoting moral qualities like *honneur*, *gloire*, *grand cœur* and *mâle assurance* are usually a sign of literary decadence—a sign that society is becoming self-conscious about qualities that it is in the process of losing. With Corneille this is not so. Much of his work—particularly the heroic element—is sixteenth-century in feeling, but it also marks the transition from the wild and extravagant sixteenth century to the reasonable seventeenth century. In his poetry, as surely as in Pope's, the words represent "robust moral certitudes" which were the product of centuries of civilization and the common heritage of the people. France was engaged in setting her house in order, in trying to work out a fresh code after the upheavals of the previous century, and this produces a literature of great vitality. Corneille's heroes are not, as they are sometimes said to be, mere abstractions or metaphysical entities, but the embodiment of all that was best in the middle class from which the poet came. They are human beings realizing their aspirations in *action*. It is the integrity of this middle class—*la solide vertu*, as Horace calls it—which gives his poetry its personal idiom and its peculiar strength. For this reason Corneille's poetry, in spite of a certain narrowness, possesses a maturity of outlook which makes the lesser Elizabethans in England seem crude and immature by comparison.

The political triumphs of the latter part of Louis XIII's reign made possible the *external* stability of the reign of Louis XIV. They also account for some of the main differences in the poetry of the two periods. M. Schlumberger suggests that Corneille's work is the product of an age in which civilization was threatened and

Racine's the product of an age of security, an age which encouraged disinterested speculation without the necessity of translating thought into action. Racine's elegance, as we shall see, belonged to a civilization which had reached its zenith, but a civilization which had within it the seeds of its own dissolution. Corneille's verse sometimes appears clumsy in comparison; but it is a clumsiness which comes from living in a difficult age and not the clumsiness of a man who is not the master of his medium. Racine's age did not possess the same internal stability and its moral fibre was less fine. I think that one might defend the view that Racine made greater poetry out of a poorer philosophy.

When we compare

> Il est doux de revoir les murs de la patrie
> *(Sertorius)*

with

> Dans le fond des forêts votre image me suit
> *(Phèdre)*

or

> Tous les monstres d'Égypte ont leurs temples dans Rome
> *(Polyeucte)*

with

> Dans l'Orient désert quel devint mon ennui!
> *(Bérénice)*

or

> . . . sur mes passions ma raison souveraine
> Eût blâmé mes soupirs et dissipé ma haine
> *(Polyeucte)*

with

> Il n'est plus temps. Il sait mes ardeurs insensées.
> De l'austère pudeur les bornes sont passées
> *(Phèdre),*

we may think that though Racine's lines are finer, they are not obviously more "poetical." It is clear, however, that the lines are the product of two very different sensibilities. Corneille limits and defines and finally sets a particular feeling against its background. Racine's method is a process of infinite suggestion; the lines seem to expand in the mind, to set up waves of feeling which become more and more subtle and elusive. In the first line *patrie* has a precise geographical connotation and limits the emotion to a definite area.

In the second there is no barrier; *fond* suggests an infinite extension which has no limit and no term. In the third line—a description of the perverse Eastern cults which are tolerated in Rome while Christianity is persecuted—Corneille deliberately strips the East of the glamour with which Racine's *Orient désert* invests it. The squalor and degeneracy of the East are set against the moral integrity which Rome so often suggests in Corneille's poetry. In the last example, the "barrier" is purely a moral one; but the *raison souveraine* (which is deliberately placed after *passions*) is so vividly apprehended by the poet that it gives us a sense of physical repression. In Racine's couplet, on the contrary, the "limit" is only mentioned in order to tell us that it has long since been exceeded.

The differences become still more pronounced when we compare longer passages:

> Quoique pour ce vainqueur mon amour s'intéresse,
> Quoiqu'un peuple l'adore et qu'un roi le caresse,
> Qu'il soit environné des plus vaillants guerriers,
> J'irai sous mes cyprès accabler ses lauriers.
>
> > (*Le Cid.*)

> Je le vis, je rougis, je pâlis à sa vue;
> Un trouble s'éleva dans mon âme éperdue;
> Mes yeux ne voyaient plus, je ne pouvais parler,
> Je sentis tout mon corps et transir et brûler.
>
> > (*Phèdre.*)

The speakers in these passages are both victims of a conflict between what might provisionally be called "duty" and "inclination." In Racine, Phèdre's personality crumbles and disintegrates at once; the emotion of the passage is split up into its component parts, but though there is analysis there is no synthesis. Chimène's character is different. She is not passive, but active. The two conflicting impulses are balanced against one another and the conflict is resolved by the will acting in obedience to a principle. There is nothing specious about it; the solution springs necessarily from the *données*.

The great passage from which Racine's lines are taken will be discussed in more detail in another place. I must now record that the four lines from the *Cid* seem to me to be one of the glories of Corneille's poetry. The first three lines have an extraordinary lyrical élan which is intensified by the obvious sexual connotation of *intéresse, adore, caresse,* and the suggestion of "action" and "vitality" contained in *vainqueur* and *guerriers.* This feeling of expansion, this sense of personal liberation which comes from the momentary identification of Chimène with Rodrigue and his exploits, is suddenly checked by something altogether impersonal in the last line. The spreading foliage of the cypresses, with their sinister hint of darkness and death, comes down like a pall and stifles the "life" which is now concentrated in *lauriers.* The final effect of the passage, however, is not negative. The emotion of the first three lines is skilfully transformed so that the last line has behind it the force of the whole passage. It will be seen that there is no casuistry and no argument here: Corneille's method is a purely poetic one and depends on the opposition of *cyprès* and *lauriers* and the triumphant use of the word *accabler.* The image in the last line is fully adequate to the emotion; it stands out against the sober background of Corneille's verse and glows with a sombre splendour.

I hope that these comparisons have given some indication of the structure of Corneille's world. It is a finite world whose geographical boundaries are marked with such clarity that we sometimes have a feeling of almost physical oppression in reading him. His conception of the nature of man is defined with the mathematical precision of Descartes' *Traité des passions de l'âme* which gives his poetry its certainty and forthrightness. He is only interested in a few aspects of human nature and therefore only master of a limited range of emotion.[1] Within these limits he is a great writer, but when he ventures outside them the results are disastrous. He is, it need hardly be said, a more pedestrian writer than Racine, and the hard, metallic clang of his verse is in strong contrast to Racine's sensuous, flexible rhythms. There are no surprises in his poetry, none of those sudden glimpses into a subconscious world of primitive instinct that we get in Racine. For Corneille's aim was to bring that world of primitive instinct under the dominion of reason before reason was overthrown by it and society reduced to a state of chaos. Corneille's vocabulary was no smaller than Racine's, but it is

---

[1] It is this tendency to select, to isolate emotion, which is responsible for the sense of remoteness from common experience that we sometimes have in reading Corneille, and it may have inspired the criticisms of Taine and Brunetière given above.

probable that his language has less power of suggestion than that of any other great French poet. Words are scientific terms which mean exactly what they say. He did not possess Racine's gift of revealing mysterious depths with the most commonplace words as, for example, when Hippolyte says:

> Je me suis engagé trop avant.
> Je vois que la raison cède à la violence.

Corneille's four most famous plays are really variations on the same theme. They show the Cornelian hero in relation to the code of chivalry, to patriotism, to politics and finally to religion. In the later plays there is no doubt that Corneille was sometimes inclined to play the showman and to write without any inner compulsion and it is this, perhaps, which has led critics to say that his characters are artful mechanical contrivances without contact with living experience. The simplicity of his psychology and the ease with which he could define his position have undoubtedly lent currency to this view. In a remarkable passage in the Epistle Dedicatory to *la Place Royale* he wrote:

"It is from you that I learnt that the love of an *honnête homme* must always be voluntary; that we must never allow our love to reach the point at which we cannot stop loving; that if we do, love becomes a tyranny whose yoke must be shaken off; and, finally, that the person whom we love is under a much greater obligation to us when our love is the result of our own choice and of her merit than when it is the result of a blind impulse and is forced on us by some influence of birth which we are unable to resist."

This is a statement of principle which underlies the whole of Corneille's work, and our opinion of him as a poet depends on whether it is a living principle which produced vital poetry or an assumed position which led to a frigid formalism. It is plain that we have here a conception of love which is completely opposed to the one that dominates the poetry of Racine and of almost every great French poet who has since written. Hostile critics have always maintained that Corneille's was an artificial system deliberately imposed on living experience. Its authenticity can only be fully tested by an examination of Corneille's verse, but there are two reservations, both more or less theoretical, which should be made. The first is that the view of passion contained in Racine's poetry has become so much a part of our consciousness that we are no longer capable of approaching Corneille with an open mind. And the second is that although the code of honour on which the *Cid* is based may no longer seem valid, the quality of the poetry it once inspired is not affected by changed moral standards.

3

Corneille's poetry has been variously described as a conflict between "love and honour," as a "drama of the will" or as mere stoicism. All these views have been challenged at one time or another; but though it is true that a great poet's work can never be summed up in a single formula, these views may serve as pointers in examining his work so long as they are not too rigidly interpreted. "Love and honour" was a favourite theme in the literature of chivalry and it is interesting to see how Corneille extends its significance. The central fact in the *Cid* is a duel—the single combat between two "men of honour." It has not been sufficiently remarked that far from being a picturesque incident, the duel is a symbol of the whole play and indeed of all Corneille's poetry:

D. RODRIGUE:
    A moi, Comte, deux mots.
LE COMTE:
                Parle.
D. RODRIGUE:
           Ote-moi d'un doute.
    Connais-tu bien don Diègue?
LE COMTE:
                Oui.
D. RODRIGUE:
           Parlons bas; écoute.
    Sais-tu que ce vieillard fut la même vertu,
      La vaillance et l'honneur de son temps? le sais-tu? . . .
LE COMTE
              Que m'importe?
D. RODRIGUE:
    A quatre pas d'ici je te le fais savoir.

LE COMTE
> Jeune présomptueux!

D. RODRIGUE:
>   Parle sans t'émouvoir.
> Je suis jeune, il est vrai; mais aux âmes bien nées
> La valeur n'attend point le nombre des années. . . .

LE COMTE:
> Retire-toi d'ici.

D. RODRIGUE:
>   Marchons sans discourir.

LE COMTE
> Es-tu si las de vivre?

D. RODRIGUE
>   As-tu peur de mourir?

In this admirable scene we hear the thrust and parry of the rapiers—the hiss of steel in

> Sais-tu que c'est son sang? le sais-tu?

and we hear it all through the play. It is the duel that is evoked at the height of the drama in Chimène's

> Dedans mon ennemi je trouve mon amant;
> Et je sens qu'en dépit de toute ma colère,
> Rodrigue dans mon cœur combat encor mon père:
> Il l'attaque, il le presse, il cède, il se défend,
> Tantôt fort, tantôt faible, et tantôt triomphant;
> Mais, en ce dur combat de colère et de flamme,
> Il déchire mon cœur sans partager mon âme. . . .

The thrust and parry of the duel merges into the movement of consciousness, into the conflict between *amour* and *devoir* and this gives the play its unity. These passages reflect the movement of all Corneille's verse—a simple movement befitting a simple psychology. We feel it again, for example, in these lines from *Polyeucte* where the "duel" is purely an interior one:

POLYEUCTE:
> C'est peu d'aller au ciel, je vous y veux conduire.

PAULINE
> Imaginations!

POLYEUCTE:
>   Célestes vérités!

PAULINE:
    Étrange aveuglement!
POLYEUCTE
        Éternelles clartés!

It is possible now to see how Corneille extends the significance of love and honour. The movement of his verse is not a destructive movement and the conflict does not end, as it usually does in tragedy, in the destruction of the characters. Nor is it true to say, as Lemaître and other French critics have said, that Corneille's poetry is simply a glorification of will and power for their own sake. There is always a definite aim in view, a process in which new values are forged, the human material reshaped and given a fresh direction. Honour is not merely a symbol of reason, it stands for the principle of order which has to be imposed on the chaos of unruly desires, on the whole of the instinctive life which Corneille constantly refers to as *les sens*. The real theme of his poetry, therefore, is not a simple clash between duty and inclination, but the subordination of one set of values to another which leads to the creation of a fresh order.

The background of Corneille's drama is aristocratic, the life of the court. In each of his major works the even flow of this life is disturbed by a shock—by a duel in the *Cid*, a conspiracy in *Cinna*, a conversion in *Polyeucte*. The effect of the shock and the conflict thus set up is to reveal the Cornelian hero to himself in a new way. The court life is seen to be conventional and unreal; and it is only when the convention is disturbed that the characters come into contact with the vital experience which is hidden beneath the outer husk, and that the mechanical code of honour is transformed into something living.

Corneille's drama, particularly the *Cid*, is always a drama of initiation. Fresh claims are made on human nature and it undergoes a change. In the opening scene of the *Cid* Chimène says to her *confidente*:

    Dis-moi donc, je te prie, une seconde fois
    Ce qui te fait juger qu'il approuve mon choix.

It is the voice of a child asking to be told over again that her father approves of her young man. In the second act she says to the Infanta:

    Maudite ambition, détestable manie,
    Dont les plus généreux souffrent la tyrannie!

This time it is the voice of the mature woman criticizing the values she is called upon to accept; and the alexandrine registers the change with remarkable delicacy.

The sudden contact with life produces in the Cornelian heroes a peculiar self-knowledge:

> Je *sais* ce que je suis, et que mon père est mort,

cries Chimène.

> Mon père, je suis femme, et je *sais* ma faiblesse,

says Pauline. This clairvoyance—this insight into their own feelings—gives Corneille's characters a poise, a centrality which are perhaps unique in European drama. The hero is always in imminent danger of being betrayed by the uprush of *les sens* which threaten to overturn reason and plunge him into chaos and disaster.

> La surprise des sens n'abat point mon courage,

says one of them, and it is precisely these *surprises* which are the condition of heroic virtue, of the *grand cœur*:

> Une femme d'honneur peut avouer sans honte
> Ces surprises des sens que la raison surmonte;
> Ce n'est qu'en ces assauts qu'éclate la vertu,
> Et l'on doute d'un cœur qui n'a point combattu.

The theme of the *Cid* is the clash between two generations, the dilemma of youth thrown into a world made by its parents and called upon to accept its standards. It is one of the signs of Corneille's maturity that these standards are never accepted passively; his attitude towards them is always critical. Honour is in constant danger of becoming inhuman and mechanical unless it is accompanied by a profound humanity which is always referred to by the word *généreux*. When Don Diègue says:

> Nous n'avons qu'un honneur, il est tant de maîtresses!
> L'amour n'est qu'un plaisir, l'honneur est un devoir.

the cynical slickness of the lines and the facile epigram are certainly ironic. *Honneur* and *devoir* are turned into counters which no longer correspond to any moral experience. For Don Diègue expresses something which is incompatible with the Cornelian view of life.

The combat does not destroy *les sens*, it dominates them in order to incorporate them into a definite hierarchy—a hierarchy which would be ruined if they were predominant, but which would be hollow and incomplete without them, as the world of Don Diègue and the Horaces is hollow and incomplete.

The criticism in *Horace* is of a far more drastic order. The play becomes in the person of Camille—one of Corneille's most extraordinary creations—a harsh and angry indictment of the whole system:

> Rome, l'unique objet de mon ressentiment!
> Rome, à qui vient ton bras d'immoler mon amant!
> Rome qui t'a vu naître, et que ton cœur adore!
> Rome enfin que je hais parce qu'elle t'honore!
> Puissent tous ses voisins ensemble conjurés
> Saper ses fondements encor mal assurés!

The heavy, monotonous verse suggests the terrible machine remorselessly sacrificing humanity to an empty phantom. It is not easy to decide how far Corneille ever accepted his own sanctions, but it seems clear that they were only acceptable as a means to a richer and fuller life, not as an end in themselves.

The struggle towards a new synthesis produces some of Corneille's finest and subtlest verse:

> Ma raison, il est vrai, dompte mes sentiments;
> Mais quelque autorité que sur eux elle ait prise,
> Elle n'y règne pas, elle les tyrannise;
> Et quoique le dehors soit sans émotion,
> Le dedans n'est que trouble et que sédition.
> Un je ne sais quel charme encor vers vous m'emporte;
> Votre mérite est grand, si ma raison est forte:
> Je le vois encor tel qu'il alluma mes feux,
> D'autant plus puissamment solliciter mes vœux,
> Qu'il est environné de puissance et de gloire . . .
> Mais ce même devoir qui le vainquit dans Rome,
> Et qui me range ici dessous les lois d'un homme,
> Repousse encor si bien l'effort de tant d'appas,
> Qu'il déchire mon âme et ne l'ébranle pas.[1]

[1] This speech occurs in a meeting between Pauline and Sévère, the admirer whom she had been obliged to give up in obedience to her father's wish for her to marry Polyeucte, and who now returns from the wars covered in glory and the Emperor's favourite.

This passage with its inversions, its verbs deliberately piled at the end of the lines, is a remarkable example of the pitiless self-inquisition to which the Cornelian heroes are subjected. There is a deliberate and calculated clumsiness about the verse which admirably expresses the immense effort that the speaker is making to dominate her feelings. The passage gets its life from the constant alteration of tone, the change from a note of defiance and determination to the half-whispered reflection of lines 6–8. The merits of Sévère are carefully catalogued and balanced against the claims of reason until one has the feeling that Pauline is being gradually engulfed in a vast stream which threatens to dislodge her at any moment. In the line

> D'autant plus puissamment solliciter mes feux

the hiss of the s's suggests the voluptuous element, the tug of *les sens*. Then, at the moment when she seems lost, there is a sudden shifting of the tension in the victorious

> Repousse encor si bien l'effort de tant d'appas,
> Qu'il déchire mon âme et ne l'ébranle pas.

The Cornelian "will" is not an abstract principle. The *déchire* and the *ne l'ébranle pas* are both deeply *felt* and express a genuine tension between two conflicting tendencies. The antithesis, so far from being an artificial literary device, is dynamic and corresponds to a deep division in Pauline's mind. When we compare Corneille's lines with Racine's

> . . . la raison cède à la violence

we see that while in Racine the accent falls on the destructive word *cède*, in Corneille it falls unmistakably on the words expressing opposition and resistance—*repousse* and *ne l'ébranle pas*. The will to resist temptation and the "inclination" for one's lover are sources of energy and vitality. Man cannot live without the energy derived from *amour*, but neither can he resist dissolution and collapse if it is allowed to become predominant. The conflict thus becomes a method of psychological revelation.

The dramatic assertion of the will is, as I have already suggested, one of the most striking characteristics of Corneille's poetry; and it seems to me that it is here rather than in the famous *Qu'il mourût!* that we detect the authentic heroic note. It is a note that we hear not once, but many times in every play. It does not lower the tension or resolve the conflict, but produces a marked increase of life and vitality that enables the Cornelian hero to "carry on."

From this we may turn to Pauline's speech at the beginning of Act III:

> Que de soucis flottants, que de confus nuages
> Présentent à mes yeux d'inconstantes images!
> Douce tranquillité, que je n'ose espérer,
> Que ton divin rayon tarde à les éclairer!
> Mille agitations, que mes troubles produisent,
> Dans mon cœur ébranlé tour à tour se détruisent:
> Aucun espoir n'y coule où j'ose persister;
> Aucun effroi n'y règne où j'ose m'arrêter.
> Mon esprit, embrassant tout ce qu'il s'imagine,
> Voit tantôt mon bonheur, et tantôt ma ruine,
> Et suit leur vaine idée avec si peu d'effet,
> Qu'il ne peut espérer ni craindre tout à fait.
> Sévère incessamment brouille ma fantaisie:
> J'espère en sa vertu, je crains sa jalousie;
> Et je n'ose penser que d'un œil bien égal
> Polyeucte en ces lieux puisse voir son rival.

"This is half-way to poetry," remarks a university lecturer patronizingly.[1] It seems to me to be a good deal more than that. It seems to me to be not only dramatically effective, but something to which we can hardly refuse the title of great poetry. The same writer complains that "the metaphors and images are confused," but the confusion does not seem to me to lie in Corneille's imagery. For the success of the passage depends very largely on the skill with which the poet presents "a whole of tangled feelings." The focal point of the passage is the image of the conflicting feelings dissolving into and destroying one another. The words *soucis flottants, confus nuages, inconstantes images* suggest a state of complete instability which is accompanied by a desperate longing for the elusive stability promised by *douce tranquillité, persister, arrêter*; but there is no security anywhere. Whatever Pauline tries to cling on to dissolves into mere *fantaisie*. For here the words "seem to do what they say" as surely as in the finest English poetry of the same period. Pauline's mind is battered into a state of immobility. She

---

[1] *Poetry in England and France*, by Jean Stewart, London, 1931, p. 52.

c

is acutely aware of what she feels, but in the midst of the tumult of warring impulses she is passive and unable to act. Only a dumb determination to "hang on" persists and gives the poetry its vitality. The tension does not depend, as it does in Racine, on the sickening sense of complete collapse, but on a contrast between the rigid immobility—the numbness between the metal walls of the alexandrine—which prevents action, and the swirl of the rapidly changing feelings.

Although the passages I have discussed come from different plays, they illustrate the stages in the evolution of Corneille's characters which scarcely varies from one play to another. It is evident that this evolution is as different from the one we find in Racine as it could well be. In Racine there is a violent conflict, but it does not end in the creation of fresh moral values or the renewal of life; it ends in the reversal of all moral values. Corneille is inferior to Racine as a psychologist, but he seems to me to reveal a greater range of what is commonly described as "character." Racine concentrates the whole of his attention on the moral crisis and there is nothing in his work which is comparable to the moral growth that takes place in Corneille's characters. We can, I think, sum up the differences between the two by saying that Corneille's characters are people *qui se construisent* and Racine's people *qui se défont*. The "shock," of which I have already spoken, shatters the complacency of Corneille's characters and reveals their own perplexity and confusion to them. But it also reveals the goal towards which they must strive, and by their immense determination they overcome this perplexity and confusion and achieve a new unity.[1] Racine's characters, on the other hand, start their career as unified or apparently unified beings, and the drama lies in the dissolution of that inner unity.

The final change in Corneille's characters, when it does come, appears as a flash of illumination which transcends all the separate acts of the individual and the different phases of the drama which lead up to it. One is Auguste's sudden realization of his place in the existing order:

> Je suis maître de moi comme de l'univers;
> Je le suis, je veux l'être.

[1] The Germans would call them *zielbewusst* or "goal-conscious." It is this more than anything else which gives their creator's outlook its maturity.

Another is the description of a conversion in *Polyeucte*:

> Je m'y trouve forcé par un secret appas;
> Je cède à des transports que je ne connais pas. . . .

I should be shirking a difficulty if I failed to mention the celebrated encounter between Rodrigue and Chimène in Act III. Sc. iv. This scene—too long to set out here—seemed to Corneille's age to be a masterpiece of pathos. M. Schlumberger cannot resist the temptation to quote it and Brasillach subjects it to an enthusiastic analysis. My own opinion is that Corneille was not a master of pathos and that though the scene contains good passages, the most admired parts are tiresome and embarrassing. They are an example of what happens when Corneille ventures outside his limited field. It must, of course, be remembered that his verse was written to be declaimed and that lines which are embarrassing in the study may sound well enough on the stage, and I have myself seen a good company "carry" what appear to be the weaker parts of this scene. It is one of the shortcomings of the grand manner that it does allow the poet to "fake" emotion, to rely on the sweep of the alexandrine when there is no correspondence between his personal sensibility and the emotion that he is staging.

4

The *Cid* has always been Corneille's most popular play and it possesses the peculiar beauty which belongs to the first work of a great writer's maturity; but the plays which followed also possess a vision, a complexity, that we do not find in the *Cid*. It has been pointed out that the discovery of Rome was an event of the first importance in Corneille's development, but its importance is not always understood. Corneille wrote of Rome at several different periods of her history and his attitude towards her varied, but the most impressive of the Roman plays is perhaps *Cinna*. The *Cid* is the most individualistic, the most "romantic," of his works. It does not possess, that is to say, any coherent view of society. There is simply the life of the Court with its etiquette and conventions. *Cinna* is far from being a faultless play, but there does emerge from it a definite conception of society, something which can, I think, not unreasonably be called a social order. We must not expect to find in French drama the sort of picture of contemporary life that we get in the English drama of the same period. French tragedy was essentially the product of an intellectual aristocracy. There was no place for *le peuple* whom Corneille regarded as creatures of instinct in whose life reason played little part. The social order which emerges from *Cinna* is therefore concerned with the problems of the ruling class, for it is assumed—not unnaturally— that reconstruction starts from above. The advance in Corneille's art is apparent from the great speech of Auguste who in the second act significantly displaces Cinna as the hero:

> Cet empire absolu sur la terre et sur l'onde,
> Ce pouvoir souverain que j'ai sur tout le monde,
> Cette grandeur sans borne et cet illustre rang,
> Qui m'a jadis coûté tant de peine et de sang,
> Enfin tout ce qu'adore en ma haute fortune
> D'un courtisan flatteur la présence importune,
> N'est que de ces beautés dont l'éclat éblouit,
> Et qu'on cesse d'aimer sitôt qu'on en jouit.
> L'ambition déplaît quand elle est assouvie,
> D'une contraire ardeur son ardeur est suivie;
> Et comme notre esprit, jusqu'au dernier soupir,
> Toujours vers quelque objet pousse quelque désir,
> Il se ramène en soi, n'ayant plus où se prendre,
> Et monté sur le faîte, il aspire à descendre.
> J'ai souhaité l'empire, et j'y suis parvenu;
> Mais en le souhaitant, je ne l'ai pas connu:
> Dans sa possession j'ai trouvé pour tous charmes
> D'effroyables soucis, d'éternelles alarmes,
> Mille ennemis secrets, la mort à tout propos,
> Point de plaisir sans trouble, et jamais de repos.

It is one of the finest examples of Corneille's handling of the grand style. Without any rhetoric, the *ampleur* of the style and the regular thud of the end-rhymes contrive to suggest a stable order. For there are two voices speaking here—the voice of the lonely, harassed individual debating whether or not to give up his throne, and what one may call the public voice. It is no longer simply a matter of coming to terms with oneself or of satisfying accepted standards of honour, but of playing a part in society. *Cinna* is a drama of adjustment. The individual experience has to fit in with the experience of the community and the drama is only complete when this is accomplished. In *Cinna*, therefore, there is a blending of the political and the moral problems. It is not simply that all political problems are seen to involve a moral problem, but that in transforming moral problems into political problems Corneille gives them a wider context and immensely increases the import of his poetry. It is this which makes his approach extremely actual to-day. In the great political discussion at the beginning of Act II one is aware of a straightening out of the emotions, and order, which is so often discussed and so rarely defined, becomes something almost tangible.

Although Corneille's contemporaries thought of him as the author of *Cinna*, many modern critics consider that *Nicomède*—a much later work—is the finest of the political plays. It is not, perhaps, surprising that the Latin mind with its passion for the "well made play" should be more aware of *Cinna's* faults than its virtues, and no doubt some writers have suspected that the defence of absolute monarchy implied a defence of the monstrous injustices associated with it. *Cinna*, however, is not important as a defence of a particular system of government, but for the passion for order which inspires it. The very violence with which the *individual* conspirators are swept into that order shows that Corneille was fully conscious of these difficulties—conscious of them *as a poet*. For his poetry marks the end of an epoch and he may have felt that the order for which he had fought was doomed to destruction by its inherent rigidity and its inability to provide a bulwark against chaos.

Nicomède is an extraordinary ironic *tour de force* which deserves to be better known in England. "Tenderness and passion have no part in it," said Corneille in his Dedication. "My chief aim has been to paint Rome's politics in her relations with other states." He sets his "cool and efficient hero"—the language of the best-seller is somehow appropriate—against the background of political intrigue and proceeds, very skilfully, to "debunk" the large pretensions of Rome and her predatory designs on smaller countries. Nicomède's ruthless sardonic humour gives the play its peculiar flavour.

Ostensibly he is trying to bolster up his father and make him resist the demands of Rome; but there is an undercurrent of resentment which spares neither Prusias' inefficiency nor his senile passion for his second wife.[1]

PRUSIAS:
> Quelle bassesse d'âme,
> Quelle fureur t'aveugle en faveur d'une femme?
> Tu la préfères, lâche! à ces prix glorieux
> Que ta valeur unit au bien de tes aïeux! . . .

NICOMÈDE:
> Je crois que votre exemple est glorieux à suivre . . .
>
> Pardonnez-moi ce mot, il est fâcheux à dire,
> Mais un monarque enfin comme un autre homme expire . . .

He carefully points the contrast between the office of king and its present occupant. *Expire*, with its suggestions of the funeral cortège, the vast mausoleum with the appropriate inscriptions, reveals the fatuity of the person who will be buried there. The wit reaches its peak in the last act after Prusias' attempted flight:

ATTALE:
> J'ai couru me ranger auprès du Roi mon père . . .
> . . . ce monarque étonné . . .
>
> Avait pris un esquif pour tâcher de rejoindre
> Ce Romain, dont l'effroi peut-être n'est pas moindre.
> (*Prusias entre*)

PRUSIAS:
> Non, non; nous revenons l'un et l'autre en ces lieux
> Défendre votre gloire, ou mourir à vos yeux.

Prusias is a richly comic creation and has a definite place in Corneille's survey of seventeenth-century society. In the *Cid* and in *Horace* he exposed an "honour" which had become mechanical and inhuman. Through Félix in *Polyeucte* and Prusias in *Nicomède* he makes the essential criticisms of middle-class complacency, of the moral corruption which prevents the attainment of Cornelian honour.[2]

[1] *cf*. Prusias' remark to his son: "J'ai tendresse pour toi, j'ai passion pour elle."

[2] Thus Félix, who decides to sacrifice his son-in-law in order to save his career, remarks naively:

A word must be said about a more debatable side of Corneille's work—the religious side. Some critics have denied that he is properly speaking a religious poet at all, while others have described *Polyeucte*, which is certainly his greatest play, as a masterpiece of religious poetry. It must be recorded with gratitude that it is refreshingly free from the incorrigibly romantic attitude towards sin that we find in certain living Catholic writers; but in spite of its subject it is neither more nor less religious than any of Corneille's other works. What is religious in all Corneille's best work is not the subject or the setting, but his sense of society as an ordered whole and of man as a member of this hierarchy. If he tried to round off the picture in *Polyeucte* by presenting the natural order in the light of the supernatural, it seems to me that he failed. It is significant that in this play the fable was modified to fit the usual Cornelian formula and we are left with the feeling that the religion was not inevitable, but that any other *motif* might have produced an equally great play. Corneille's world remains a circumscribed world and his religion does not extend the field of his experience as it clearly ought to have done.[1]

> Te dirai-je un penser indigne, bas et lâche?
> Je l'étouffe, il renaît; il me flatte, et me fâche.
> L'ambition toujours me le vient présenter,
> Et tout ce que je puis, c'est de le détester.
> Polyeucte est ici l'appui de ma famille;
> Mais si, par son trépas, l'autre épousait ma fille,
> J'acquerrais bien par là de plus puissants appuis,
> Qui me mettraient plus haut cent fois que je ne suis.
> Mon cœur en prend par force une maligne joie;
> Mais que plutôt le ciel à tes yeux foudroie,
> Qu'à des pensers si bas je puisse consentir,
> Que jusque-là ma gloire ose se démentir!

[1] *cf.* "The museum of masterpieces is there and none of us will ever grow weary of visiting it. It is superfluous and would be impertinent to insist on this point. Nor can it be denied that in the works of the classic writers the author also expresses himself as a man, sometimes in spite of himself, and sometimes by means of that indirect method of which I have just spoken. It is simply a matter of drawing attention to a point which is of capital importance: according to the classic writer's conception and the canons governing classic art, the author, the man and the Christian are three separate persons, so that in his work the fundamental interior unity of the human being, which was the centre of 'all the different parts' of which man 'is composed,' is destroyed." (Charles Du Bos, *Approximations*, 6ième série, Paris, 1934, p. 255.) See, too, Mauriac, *Journal*, III ("La Grâce dans *Polyeucte*").

It should be apparent by now in what sense Corneille is an heroic poet. It has nothing to do with declamation and bombast (though there is plenty of both in his work), or with the misleading theory that his characters are "supermen." It simply means that by a combination of insight and will power the moral values which Corneille derived from close contact with his class are raised in his plays to a high level of poetic intensity. He was a great poet because he expressed something that is permanent in human nature and because he had behind him the whole weight of what was best in contemporary society. One has only to compare him for a moment with Dryden to see the difference. For Dryden's age was not an heroic age and in trying to write heroic plays he was simply going against the spirit of his time. His drama is an example of the false sublime, of the stucco façade which ill conceals the viciousness and corruption beneath.

5

Corneille's later plays have been the subject of considerable controversy. Contemporary apologists like M. Schlumberger take up their stand against the traditional view which regards the later plays, in Lytton Strachey's words, as "miserable failures." Pierre Lièvre's introduction to his admirable edition of the plays[1] is an eloquent plea that Corneille's work should be treated as a whole, as a steady development from the early comedies to the final tragedies. I confess that I find it difficult to accept this view. Plays like *Rodogune* and *Pompée*, which belong to the third period that lasts from 1644 to 1669, contain fine things, but compared with Corneille's best work they seem to me to show a pronounced falling off. There is, perhaps, a greater breadth of characterization, but the poetry is less impressive. The fact that Corneille never stood still and never repeated himself may be the reason for the difficulty. With *Polyeucte* the Cornelian hero is complete and there is no room for further development along those lines. The poet loses interest in his hero who degenerates into a mechanical warrior —*Attila* provides the worst example—and concentrates on the

---

[1] *Théâtre complet* (Bibliothèque de la Pléiade), 2 vols., Paris, 1934. (This is much the most satisfactory edition for "the common reader.")

people who surround him. The main interest of the plays of this period lies in the amazons like Rodogune, Cornélie and the two Cléopâtres. This produces an alteration in the quality of the verse. Corneille develops the vein of rhetoric which is already visible in the *Cid*:

> Paraissez, Navarrois, Mores et Castillans,
> Et tout ce que l'Espagne a nourri de vaillants;
> Unissez-vous ensemble, et faites une armée,
> Pour combattre une main de la sorte animée . . .

In *Rodogune* this becomes the staple of the whole play:

> Serments fallacieux, salutaire contrainte,
> Que m'imposa la force et qu'accepta ma crainte,
> Heureux déguisements d'un immortel courroux,
> Vains fantômes d'État, évanouissez-vous.

There is a natural tendency to rhetoric in French poetry, to use words as mere labels and to rely for the "poetry" on the drive of the alexandrine. Certainly there is no lack of drive in *Rodogune*, but there is a loss of subtlety and a marked coarseness of texture in the verse.[1]

Although M. Schlumberger has apparently abandoned the view that the last plays of all are the crown of Corneille's work, he still

---

[1] As a vehicle for invective Corneille's later verse has a strange impressiveness, but it should be noticed that invective is often used as a substitute for something different. In *Pertharite*, Rodelinde, speaking of her son says to her suitor:

> Puisqu'il faut qu'il périsse, il vaut mieux tôt que tard;
> Que sa mort soit un crime, et non pas un hasard;
> Que cette ombre innocente à toute heure m'anime,
> Me demande à toute heure une grande victime;
> Que ce jeune monarque, immolé de ta main,
> Te rende abominable à tout le genre humain . . .
> Je t'épouserai lors, et m'y viens d'obliger,
> Pour mieux servir ma haine, et pour mieux me venger,
> Pour moins perdre de vœux contre ta barbarie,
> Pour être à tous moments maîtresse de ta vie,
> Pour avoir l'accès libre à pousser ma fureur,
> Et mieux choisir la place à te percer le cœur.

There are two things that strike us in this passage. One is that moral values are no longer *directly* apprehended and that the poet is using declamation to keep up appearances. The other is that his psychological insight has become blunted. The characters no longer analyse their feelings and turn instead to the denunciation of their enemies. It is in this sense that invective is a clever substitute for the great qualities that have been lost.

C*

gives *Pulchérie* and *Suréna* a high place in it. In these plays there is a return to the old Cornelian formula which was to some extent abandoned in the plays of the middle period. He sees in them a tenderness and serenity which he does not find in any of Corneille's other work. This may be so, but one cannot help wondering whether they deserve all the praise they get. Consider, for example, the opening speech of *Pulchérie*:

> Je vous aime, Léon, et n'en fais point mystère:
> Des feux tels que les miens n'ont rien qu'il faille taire.
> Je vous aime, et non point de cette folle ardeur
> Que les yeux éblouis font maîtresse du cœur,
> Non d'un amour conçu par les sens en tumulte,
> A qui l'âme applaudit sans qu'elle se consulte,
> Et qui ne concevant que d'aveugles désirs,
> Languit dans les faveurs, et meurt dans les plaisirs:
> Ma passion pour vous, généreuse et solide,
> A la vertu pour âme, et la raison pour guide,
> La gloire pour objet, et veut sous votre loi
> Mettre en ce jour illustre et l'univers et moi.

According to Croce this passage marks the summit of Corneille's poetry and, with a lofty assumption of philosophical detachment, he proceeds to commend Pulchérie's attitude to physical love. It is not difficult to see why these lines appeal to one whose criterion is evidently "simple, sensuous and passionate." It is by no means a negligible piece of verse, but it owes its charm to a subtle flavour of dissolution. The difficulty that one feels might be expressed by saying that honour wins altogether too easily. It is clear from the looseness of texture, the slackness of the versification, that we are a long way from the poet of *Polyeucte*. It is the work of an old man, of a great poet in decline. Nor can one share Croce's enthusiasm for the content. For who but a survival of nineteenth-century romanticism can feel any sympathy for the bloodless spinster high-mindedly giving up her love to contract a "chaste" alliance with her father's aged counsellor?[1]

---

[1] The same weariness, the same tendency to take a voluptuous pleasure in suffering, are apparent in his last play, *Suréna:*

> Je veux, sans que la mort ose me secourir,
> Toujours aimer, toujours souffrir, toujours mourir.
>
> .   .   .
>
> Que tout meure avec moi, Madame; que m'importe
> Qui foule après ma mort la terre qui me porte?

What is to be the final estimate? "Corneille," answers M. Schlumberger, "does not ask the supreme questions, neither does he answer them. If I give him a high place in my æsthetic, there remains a vast region of myself in which I feel the need of other poets besides him." It is clear that he lacks many of the qualities that we have come to expect of poetry. Certain fundamental truths were grasped with the clarity and the tenacity of genius; he was a penetrating critic of the evils of the existing order; but his own vision was partial and incomplete and the order towards which he was striving seems somehow indistinct. Yet his central experience —his sense of society as an ordered whole and of man as a part of that hierarchy—has an important place in European literature and without him it would be incomplete. Of all the great masters Corneille is the most limited, but that he is a master we cannot doubt.

MOLIERE

"C'est une étrange entreprise que de faire rire les honnêtes gens"
—La Critique de l'École des Femmes

I. MOLIÈRE AND HIS AGE

1

T H E seventeenth century in France is curiously deceptive. On the surface it app?ars to be simple and uniform. In reality it was complex and multiform. We are faced not with one age, but with several ages; not with a static society, but with a society in a continual process of evolution. The different ages overlap, merge into one another, so that conventional divisions into historical periods are of little assistance. We need fresh standards, and a useful approach is suggested by a passage in M. Pierre Maillaud's admirable book on France:

"Throughout the Classical Age," he writes, "the fundamental object of philosophy, literature, and art remains the study of Man, of his nature, of his passions, of his motives, of his social habits and oddities: man as an individual to whom the existing social order provides only an artistic background, and not man against an existing order, for there is no sign of political reformism among its writers."[1]

The single-minded concentration of the masters of the Classical Age on their subject is one of the main sources of their greatness. When it is looked at as a whole, the work of the philosophers, the moralists and the poets of the seventeenth century is seen to be one of the most searching examinations of human nature that has ever been made. Its completeness depends paradoxically on the acceptance by individual writers of the limitations of their art, on their concentration not simply on man, but on certain facets of his character; and the facets that they chose to reveal were largely determined by social and political changes and by changes in sensibility which were going on beneath the surface of society. We never meet Man in their writings; we meet instead the Rational Man, the Sceptical Man, the Social Man or the Natural Man. Labels are always danger-

[1] *France* (The World To-day), Oxford, 1942, p. 55.

44

MOLIÈRE
From a drawing by Ronjat, after the painting attributed
to Pierre Mignard

ous, but as long as we realize that there was room for innumerable variations within the individual approach they help us to understand the relations between a particular writer's conception of man and the age in which he wrote. With these reservations, the century can be divided broadly into three ages and the ages named after the three greatest French dramatists—Corneille, Molière, Racine.

Corneille wrote at a time when France had been disrupted by the wars of religion and was trying to set her house in order. His theme is the Man of Honour, the imposition of order—a moral order—on the chaos of human desires. Racine stands at the other extreme. He belonged not to an age of reconstruction, but to an age which had reached its zenith and was beginning to disintegrate from within. His interest lies in the Man of Passion, in the collapse of order before the swirls of unruly desires. Molière occupies a position midway between the two extremes. The centre of his world is the Natural Man and he studies the way in which perverted natural instincts may become a danger to the community. He believed more deeply, perhaps, in his age than either Corneille or Racine. He was the laureate of *la bonne Régence*, of an age when society seemed for a moment to have reached stability, when, in spite of conflicting "philosophies," its structure was not threatened and there was time to examine man's "social habits and oddities," to laugh over his extravagances.

Although a precise clear-cut conception of man emerges from the work of each of the three poets, the change from the Age of Corneille to the Age of Molière, or from the Age of Molière to the Age of Racine, was not the result of any violent upheaval. The changes were gradual, the shades and subtleties almost infinite. They can be detected in a shifting of the focus, in the sounding of a fresh note which was not always perceptible to contemporary readers. Indeed, the cross-currents of the century were so complex that not only the passing of one age but the beginning of the next was sometimes manifested in the work of the same writer. We can see now that in *Nicomède*, which was written in 1651, eight years after the last of the four great tragedies and after a series of imitations of his own style, Corneille not only wrote a masterpiece, but a masterpiece in a new manner. Prusias is an ironic figure in which the possibilities of Félix in *Polyeucte* are exploited and he points the way straight to the Age of Molière.

Yet when Molière tried to do the same thing in 1658 the result was a failure. *Dom Garcie de Navarre* did not fail because Molière was writing against the grain of the age, as one feels that Racine was in *Alexandre le Grand* where the Cornelian phrases stick out jaggedly among the smooth alexandrines. It failed because *Nicomède* was so far in advance of its time that in 1658 Molière was not sufficiently mature to benefit from its discoveries. It was only in the *Misanthrope*, for which Molière significantly lifted some of the best passages from *Dom Garcie*, that *Nicomède* bore its full fruit, and lines which had sounded hollow and unreal in Dom Garcie's mouth are in perfect harmony with Alceste's character. The *Misanthrope* is the meeting-point of three ages. It is the finest flower of the Age of Molière, but it looks back in a healthy sense to the Age of Corneille and forward to the Age of Racine. Compare Auguste's

> Je suis maître de moi comme de l'univers;
> Je le suis, je veux l'être.

with Alceste's

> Je veux qu'on soit sincère, et qu'en homme d'honneur
> On ne lâche aucun mot qui ne parte du cœur.

and you see at once that the times have changed. You notice that the "Man of Honour" has ceased to be a man of *action* and become a man of *words*—an apostle of plain speaking. You notice, too, that there is no genuine volition behind Alceste's *Je veux*. He is incapable of imposing a positive discipline first on himself, then on society, as Auguste does. When faced with the obstacles which Corneille's characters successfully overcome, he simply abdicates:

> Je n'y puis plus tenir, j'enrage, et mon dessein
> Est de rompre en visière à tout le genre humain.

His determination crumbles at once and his energy dissolves in an explosion of useless rage which drives him towards a negative goal —the abandonment of society and the hunt for

> un endroit écarté
> Où d'être homme d'honneur on ait la liberté.

These lines are a forcible illustration of the nature of the changes which had taken place. The heroic age is past; the Cornelian Man of

Honour has become a figure of fun, a windbag who leads an eccentric life outside society. Rodrigue turns into Alceste, Polyeucte into Orgon. The true representatives of the Age of Molière are the *honnêtes hommes* with their reasonable, tolerant outlook, their solid, unheroic virtues. Alceste is a comic figure, but a comic figure of a new kind, for he is already endowed with the power of introspection, the deadly lucidity of the heroes of Racine, and his

> Mes sens par la raison ne sont plus gouvernés,
> Je *cède* aux mouvements d'une juste colère.

recalls at once Hippolyte's

> Je me suis engagé trop avant.
> Je vois que la raison *cède* à la violence.

In Molière's characters, the energy and drive which in Corneille bring order out of chaos are transformed into a fanaticism which potentially at least is as dangerous to society as the "violence" of Racine.

"In Molière," wrote Sainte-Beuve in one of his memorable over-statements—"in Molière as in Montaigne we meet nature, but nature without any appreciable mixture of what belongs to the *order of Grace*; he was not touched at any period of his life, any more than Montaigne was, by Christianity."[1] Discussions of the relative value of the three writers are fruitless, but Sainte-Beuve's *mot* helps to explain the popularity of Molière in this country— the country of Shakespeare—and the sad neglect of Corneille and Racine. The English reader is disconcerted by the world of France's two greatest tragic poets. He does not know what to make of the booming voices extolling *honneur* and *gloire* and exhorting him to acts of heroic virtue. He is no more at home in Racine's world which threatens to dissolve at any moment and to engulf its inhabitants in their own furious passions.

Molière presents a very different picture. He has his roots deep in the earth and he introduces the English reader to a world where he is on firm ground, a solid, opaque world built in the normal dimensions and filled with the ceaseless noise and bustle of the *quartier*:

[1] *Port-Royal* III, Paris, 1848, p. 198.

> Ces carrosses sans cesse à la porte plantés,
> Et de tant de laquais le bruyant assemblage.

We find it very difficult to visualize the physical appearance of Racine's characters. The whole of the drama is concentrated into the world within; passion glows like a single white-hot filament in the surrounding darkness; and clothes are only mentioned to show that even the flimsiest garment is an intolerable constraint to the vibrating nerves, the tormented bodies:

> Que ces vains ornements, que ces voiles me pèsent!

Molière's characters not only wear clothes like other people, the clothes are a part of the characters. The subtle, flexible style, which faithfully registers the accent of the individual voice—the whine of Orgon, the ranting of Harpagon, the childlike lisp of Agnès— possesses vivid pictorial qualities which place the characters compellingly before our eyes: Tartuffe in his peculiar monkish habit calling on his servant to tighten the hair shirt and Alceste, unforgettable as "l'homme aux rubans verts." "Il a au cœur la tristesse," said Sainte-Beuve of Molière; but though a sombre note runs through some of his greatest plays, our abiding impression is not one of sadness. There is an immense *joie* in the created world, in the world of *pourpoints, collets, rubans* and *canons*.

As Molière's genius ripens, the panorama of a whole age unfolds before us. He does not confine himself to any one section of the community like Corneille with his warriors or Racine with his princes and princesses. His vision has greater width than theirs; his work is a *comédie humaine* which embraces society from top to bottom, a society of courtiers, *marquis*, doctors, lawyers, prudes, peasants, lacqueys, of amorous old men and lecherous young women.

2

The face which looks down at us from the Mignard portrait of Molière is an impressive one. There is a hint of melancholy and even of suffering in the eyes, but it is not this alone that makes the portrait so arresting. It is rather the expression of wisdom, of a wisdom derived from human experience in which *tristesse* blends with an obvious zest for life that is apparent in the full, sensual lips. When we survey Molière's career as a writer, it is indeed a combination of wisdom, immense determination and an enormous love of life which seems to distinguish it.

"One of the clearest signs of the character of the man and of his creative power," writes M. Maurice Blanchot in an excellent note on Molière, "is his sudden impatient and imperious grasp of things. We are aware in Molière of a power of attack which is apparent not merely in his taste for satire, which is something much more general, so that as soon as he is in contact with his subject he takes possession of it and goes straight for the essential . . . Molière shows the same hot-headedness as his own Misanthrope."[1]

It is not difficult to see why this should be so. It is easy to explain too much in terms of heredity and environment, but there can be little doubt that Molière's early life played a part of capital importance in the development of the qualities which M. Blanchot describes and which give his work its immense vitality.

Jean-Baptiste Poquelin, who later became known as Molière, was born in Paris on 15th January 1622, in a house at the corner of the Rue Saint-Honoré and the Rue des Vieilles Étuves which was popularly known as the Maison des Singes from the decorations on the pillars. He came on both sides of solid, middle-class parents and was in the fullest sense of the term *un bourgeois de Paris*. His father, Jean Poquelin, was a *marchand-tapissier* or upholsterer and his mother was Marie Cressé, the daughter of another *marchand-tapissier*. Molière's father was a person of some importance in his profession, and in 1631 he obtained a charge as *tapissier du roi*, a position which has been compared to that of a high official in the Office of Works in our own time.

Molière's childhood and youth are obscured by a mass of legend and speculation. His biographers cannot agree whether or not he was a pupil of the famous Gassendi, and literary critics cannot agree about the influence or supposed influence of that philosopher on his work. A few facts, however, are undisputed. From 1635 to 1641 he was a pupil of the Jesuits at Clermont. It was the custom at

[1] *Faux pas*, Paris, 1943, p. 307.

Jesuit schools for masters and boys to collaborate in the adaptation and production of Latin plays on public occasions, and Molière like Corneille before him may well have acquired his taste for the theatre in this way.

Clermont was a decidedly "smart" school and Molière made one important "contact" there. He met the famous Prince de Conti who became his friend and patron during his years in the provinces. Conti went to Clermont in 1637 and at fifteen he took his "degree." "A little monster of learning," observes one of Molière's biographers.[1] He was soon to become a monster of another kind. For some years he was one of the most notorious *libertins* of the day. Then, with the violence and suddenness which were characteristic of the century, he was converted and, swinging to the other extreme, became a leading *dévot*, renounced the arts, withdrew his patronage from Molière and joined the Compagnie du Saint-Sacrement. "Cet amour de la comédie," observes Allier drily, "était le moindre péché d'un homme qui s'était roulé dans toutes les ordures et qui s'était rongé de débauches."[2]

Molière's father had contrived to have his charge at Court made hereditary and it was in his capacity as *valet-tapissier du roi* that in 1642 the young Molière accompanied Louis XIII on his journey to Narbonne, saw the Midi for the first time and only returned to the capital at the end of the year.

The meeting with Madeleine Béjart the following year was a turning-point in Molière's career. She was the daughter of Joseph Béjart, an official in the Department of Forestry. The Béjarts were a large, picturesque and somewhat disreputable family living on the edge of Bohemia. They had one thing in common—a passion for the theatre. At eighteen Madeleine was writing verses to the dramatist Rotrou. At nineteen she was the mistress of the Comte de Modène and at twenty the birth of a daughter, so far from being considered a scandal, was celebrated by a handsome christening at which the Comte's paternity was publicly acknowledged. The child's godparents were her natural grandmother and the legitimate son of her own illegitimate father.

In one of those peculiar distinctions at which the French excel, Ramon Fernandez has described Molière's relations with Madeleine

[1] John Palmer, *Moliere: His Life and Works*, London, 1930, p. 16.
[2] *La Cabale des dévots*, Paris, 1902, p. 393.

as an "amitié sexuelle autant que morale."[1] No doubt he is right, but the rest is speculation. What is certain is that her influence on his future as a writer was decisive. After a struggle with his father he abandoned his charge at Court, entered into partnership with Madeleine and founded the Illustre Théâtre. The enterprise was not a success and in 1646 Molière with Madeleine and the company set out on a tour of the French provinces where he spent the next twelve years as an actor-playwright. Critics have drawn fanciful pictures of the weary actors trapesing from place to place with their stage properties and putting up in barns, and one writer has hinted salaciously at happy promiscuity in the warm hay. Life under such conditions was very different from Corneille's uneventful youth at Rouen or Racine's monkish, cloistered childhood among the "solitaries" at Port-Royal and his visit to his uncle's comfortable rectory at Uzès, where he waited impatiently for the *bon bénéfice* which never turned up. It left a lasting impression on Molière's work, for it was during the *wanderjahre* that he came into close contact with the people and acquired the habit of acute, humorous observation of his fellow-men.

The formative influences were the old French farces, the Commedia dell'Arte and direct experience. His earliest plays, in which faithless wives plant the horned cap well and truly over the ears of their elderly husbands or send the unfortunate husbands to market trussed up in sacks like pigs, in which *coups de bâton* and *pots de chambre* abound, are pure slapstick. They do not seem particularly funny to-day, but they treat of themes which are deeply rooted in the consciousness of the race and which appeal directly to primitive instincts—laughter, mockery, hatred, envy. They may seem far from the famous *réalisme comique* of his greatest work, but in reality there is a direct connection between the two. Although Molière abandoned these crude methods, he retained many of his early themes and his appeal was always to natural human feelings which are stifled beneath the conventions of civilization. The light-hearted farce of *la Jalousie du barbouillé* and *l'Étourdi* develops into the grim farce of parts of the *École des femmes* and *George Dandin*. One of the chief means of getting a laugh in the early farces was repetition. In the mature comedies the repetition of phrases like *Le pauvre homme!* and *Sans dot!* which reminds one

[1] *La Vie de Molière* (Vies des Hommes Illustres No. 32), Paris, 1929, p. 19.

of a gramophone needle which has got stuck in the same groove, becomes a skilful device for revealing the characters' state of mind. The whole trend of Molière's art was away from the comedy of situation to the comedy of character. We can see how the comic exaggerations of his early work are transformed into the strange manias which possess Arnolphe, Orgon and Alceste, and a German critic has coined the word *durchpsychologisierung*[1] to describe the process.

3

In 1658 Molière and his troupe returned to Paris. The following year he produced the *Précieuses ridicules*. It is generally recognized that this play is a landmark in his work. The farces are a thing of the past. Molière has found his vocation. The *Précieuses ridicules* is a brilliantly satirical picture of one section of French society and the two disguised *marquis* show how much Molière had profited from the traditional French farces. The play has, however, a deeper purpose which can be illustrated by two brief extracts. When one of the *précieuses* remarks:

"Mais de grâce, monsieur, ne soyez pas inexorable à ce fauteuil qui vous tend les bras il y a un quart d'heure; contentez un peu l'envie qu'il a de vous embrasser"

—we are not being asked to laugh at a simple misuse of language. The distortion of language reflects a psychological distortion. For words and gestures which express human emotions are used of inanimate things. There is an inclination to rob words of a certain sexual connotation by misapplying them to things and to lower people by raising things. This intention becomes more apparent when we turn back to Cathos' words in the preceding scene:

"Pour moi, mon oncle, tout ce que je vous puis dire, c'est que je trouve le mariage une chose tout à fait choquante. Comment est-ce qu'on peut souffrir la pensée de coucher contre un homme vraiment nu?"

The *précieuses* may be only a pair of silly, affected girls playing at being "high society," but the trend is evident, and it leads to the

[1] There is no English equivalent. It means to fill in the characters' psychology, to "psychologize" the characters.

attitude towards marriage which is attacked in *les Femmes savantes*. There is a flight from natural human feelings, a morbid horror of what is *vraiment nu*. Preciosity is seen to be a form of defence mechanism, a method of neutralizing the life of our normal instincts by robbing them of their vitality. It leads straight to psychological perversion, to the obsessions which are studied with marvellous insight in Molière's greatest plays.

It must not be thought that Molière's work is merely a gallery of eccentrics. His starting-point is always the individual man or woman, but his characters are all representative, are all rooted in the society of their time, and he goes on to make an anatomy of this society in which some of the deepest as well as some of the most controversial problems are debated. The *Précieuses ridicules* with its frontal attack on preciosity was his first serious essay in social criticism and its effectiveness is proved by the storm that it created. The main line runs thence through the two *Écoles*, reaches its summit in his three greatest plays—*Tartuffe*, *Dom Juan* and *le Misanthrope*—and moves on to its logical conclusion in *George Dandin* and *le Malade imaginaire*. In these plays he examined the position of women, the state of religious belief, and the nature and place of medicine in society. It was because his vision transcended the limits of his age that his characters are symbols of universal significance which belong to all time.

II. *L'ÉCOLE DES FEMMES*

The year 1662 was an important one in Molière's life. It was the year of his marriage to Armande Béjart. This event has been a gift to the gossip-writer and to critics who delight in discovering autobiographical references in his plays. We cannot say with any certainty who Armande Béjart was but it seems probable that she was a younger sister of Molière's friend and partner, Madeleine Béjart. Molière's enemies took a different view and it was not long before they were accusing him "d'avoir épousé la fille et d'autrefois avoir couché avec la mère." At the time of his marriage Molière was forty and his wife eighteen. It is not altogether surprising that enemies and critics alike should have regarded *l'École des maris* and *l'École des femmes* as attempts to solve personal problems—the problems of the middle-aged man who marries a young girl—and already in his own time people were saying that in begetting his own wife Molière had begun her education even earlier than Arnolphe.

A great imaginative writer naturally draws on his own experience for his work, but there is no evidence for the view that in the *École des maris* Molière was attempting to explore the prospects of his forthcoming marriage or that Arnolphe in the *École des femmes* is "a portrait of the artist." In both plays the emphasis falls on *école*, on education for marriage. The *École des maris* is a charming comedy in which Molière contrasts two different ways of bringing up young women—the narrow, jealous method of Sganarelle which leads to deception and disaster, and the tolerant and reasonable spirit of Ariste who lets Léonor go her own way, marries her with her own consent and no doubt lived happily ever after.

L'École des femmes is not among Molière's supreme achievements, but it marks an immense step forward. For here in essentials and for the first time we find the mature Molière. The maturity is nowhere more apparent than in the transformation of Sganarelle into Arnolphe, the first of the great comic characters. When Arnolphe declares:

> J'ai suivi sa leçon sur le sujet d'Agnès,
> Et je la fais venir dans ce lieu tout exprès,
> Sous prétexte d'y faire un tour de promenade,
> Afin que les soupçons de *mon esprit malade*
> Puissent sur le discours la mettre adroitement,
> Et, lui sondant le cœur, s'éclaircir doucement.

he not only sounds a fresh note, he also looks forward to Cléante's warning to Alceste:

> Non, tout de bon, quittez toutes ces incartades.
> Le monde par vos soins ne se changera pas;
> Et puisque la franchise a pour vous tant d'appas,
> Je vous dirai tout franc que *cette maladie*
> Partout où vous allez, donne la comédie.

The critical words are *mon esprit malade* and *cette maladie*. For all Molière's principal comic characters are *malades*. More than any other great comic writer of the time he realized that comedy is essentially a serious activity. His work is a study of some of the chief social maladies not merely of his own, but of all time, seen against the background of a stable order. In this play it is jealousy, in *Tartuffe* religious mania and in *le Malade imaginaire* the cult of ill-health. The ravages of the *maladie* are very extensive. It undermines the natural human faculties and encloses the victim in a private world of his own disordered imagination. One of the fundamental traits of the *malade* is a fanatical desire to impose the standards of this private world on society, as Alceste tries to "change the world" and Arnolphe tries to bring up Agnès according to his own unbalanced theories:

> Dans un petit couvent, loin de toute pratique,
> Je la fis élever selon ma politique,
> C'est-à-dire ordonnant quels soins on emploierait
> Pour la rendre idiote autant qu'il se pourrait.

This sinister declaration, this open attempt to destroy a woman's natural faculties, shows to what extent the *malade* has become a menace to the community. The remedy lies in collective action, in the destruction of the anti-social tendencies by laughter and the introduction of sane values into the comic world. This brings us to the *honnête homme* who makes his first appearance in the *École des femmes*. Chrysalde is not of the stature of Cléante or Philinte, and his view that it doesn't matter whether you are a *cocu* or not as long as you take your misfortune like a gentleman is crude in comparison with their urbane, polished discourses on *la juste nature* and *la parfaite raison*; but in spite of his shortcomings he does stand for a norm of tolerance and good sense.

I have never felt convinced by the theory of certain French critics that Molière's characters are in some sense abstractions, that he shows us the Jealous Man, the Hypocrite, the Misanthrope or the Miser, while a modern novelist like Balzac shows us a particular miser in a particular French province in the nineteenth century. There is a clear distinction between Shakespearean comedy and Jonson's "comedy of humours." It seems to me that Molière is closer to Shakespeare than he is to Jonson, and that so far from probing more deeply into human nature than Molière, Balzac bears a striking resemblance to Jonson. Classical comedy certainly imposed limitations, but what is remarkable is that in spite of these limitations Molière managed to present such a comprehensive study of the complexities and contradictions of human nature. Argan is not merely a *malade imaginaire*, he is mean and cruel and cheerfully prepared to sacrifice his daughter's happiness in order to secure free medical advice for himself. In the *Femmes savantes* what really interests us in Armande is not her ridiculous intellectual pretensions, but the angry frustration of the sexually acquisitive woman.

The *École des femmes* is primarily a study of jealousy, but Arnolphe is no more a simple case than Molière's other characters. The originality of Molière's approach is well brought out by Ramon Fernandez when he suggests that the point of the play lies in the transformation of the *homme-père* into the *homme-mari*. It is true that Arnolphe loves his ward as a husband while she can only love him as a father, but this is not the whole of the problem. It must not be thought that the prominence given to cuckoldry is a light-hearted borrowing from traditional French farce or that Molière's treatment of it has anything in common with Wycherley's in his crude adaptation of the play. Arnolphe's anxiety to "create" a wife who will be faithful to him springs from a primitive but deep-seated fear of being a cuckold. There is no need to dwell on the psychological implications of this fear which is so pervasive that it turns jealousy into a form of sexual mania. When Arnolphe declares:

> Je veux pour espion, qui soit d'exacte vue,
> Prendre le savetier du coin de notre rue.
> Dans la maison toujours je prétends la tenir,
> Y faire bonne garde, et surtout en bannir
> Vendeuses de ruban, perruquières, coiffeuses,
> Faiseuses de mouchoirs, gantières, revendeuses,
> Tous ces gens qui sous main travaillent chaque jour
> A faire réussir les mystères d'amour.

the crux of the passage lies in the lurid *mystères d'amour*, and the words gain their effect from the contrast with the normal life of the *quartier* which Molière evokes with his characteristic skill. For in Arnolphe's disordered imagination the whole of this world is undermined by the subterranean activities of the purveyors of love, as the whole of his personality is undermined by his mania. When in another place he cries:

> Et cependant je l'aime, après ce lâche tour,
> Jusqu'à ne me pouvoir passer de cet amour.
> Sot, n'as-tu point de honte? Ah! je crève, j'enrage,
> Et je souffletterais mille fois mon visage.

there is no mistaking the voice. It is the voice of all Molière's great comic characters, the voice of impotent, exasperated denunciation of a world which they cannot "change" and in which they have no place.

The voice also explains one of the secrets of Molière's art. "His characters," wrote Paul Bourget, "are, so to speak, composed in two layers. The first consists of the peculiarities which make them ridiculous, the second of the authentic human material. . . . At certain moments in the play, the first layer bursts apart and reveals the second."[1]

Although this comment suggests that there is something a little mechanical about the construction of Molière's characters and underestimates, perhaps, the extent to which their peculiarities are rooted in their personality, it underlines one important factor. In the central passages in the comedies there is a sudden eruption of subterranean instincts into the world of everyday experience, and it is this that gives Molière's work its special resonance. At such moments the mind of the spectator is suspended between two impulses—pity and laughter—which superficially appear to exclude one another, and comedy is felt to be a continual oscillation between what one writer has lately called *la vie tragique* and *la vie triviale*. It is not, however, an alternation between tragic and comic emotions. The two are fused into a single new emotion which differs from them both and is proper to comedy. Life is suddenly perceived under a twofold aspect and this is the core of the comic poet's experience.

It is not the tranquil homilies of Chrysalde which place Arnolphe's *maladie* in its true perspective, but the simple words of Agnès, as she speaks of her love for Horace:

> Il jurait qu'il m'aimait d'une amour sans seconde,
> Il me disait des mots les plus gentils du monde,

---

[1] *Œuvres complètes: II. Critique, études et portraits*, Paris, 1900, p. 271.

Des choses que jamais rien ne peut égaler,
Et dont, toutes les fois que je l'entends parler,
La douceur me chatouille et là-dedans remue
Certain je ne sais quoi dont je suis toute émue.

In these lines, in which we seem to catch the very tone of the girl's voice and which derive much of their force from the contrast with Arnolphe's overwrought declarations, we see the healthy, natural human feelings asserting themselves, expressing themselves in spite of a lack of adequate concepts on the part of the speaker. It is the ruin of Arnolphe's horrifying *politique*.

III. *TARTUFFE*

1

" When Molière wrote his *Tartuffe*," said a contemporary, "he read the first three acts to the king. This play pleased His Majesty who spoke much too well of it not to arouse the jealousy of Molière's enemies and above all of the *cabale des dévots*. M. de Péréfixe, Archbishop of Paris, placed himself at their head and spoke to the king against this comedy. The king, who was continually under pressure on all sides, told Molière that one must not annoy the *dévots* who were implacable and that he ought not to perform his *Tartuffe* in public. His Majesty thought it sufficient to speak to Molière in this way without ordering him to suppress the play. It is for this reason that Molière took the trouble to read it aloud to his friends."

This, broadly speaking, is the story of one of the bitterest of all the literary controversies of the seventeenth century. *Tartuffe* was given its première on 12th May 1664. Five days later the storm broke with a frontal attack in the *Gazette de France* which declared roundly that the play was "extremely harmful to religion and likely to have a most dangerous effect." It was useless for Molière to change the title to *l'Hypocrite*, to protest that he was only attacking the *faux dévots* or to say that one of the functions of the theatre was to correct human vices. The pious world was thoroughly roused. The denunciation in the *Gazette de France* was followed by other attacks. In a tract called *le Roy glorieux au monde*, Pierre Roullé, the parish priest of Saint-Barthélmy, described Molière as "un homme, ou plutôt un démon vêtu de chair et habillé en homme, et le plus signalé impie et libertin qui fût jamais dans les siècles passés." Bourdaloue, who at this time was the fashionable preacher at Notre-Dame, took part in the battle, and years after Molière's death Bossuet spoke of him with a depth of bitterness which shows how profoundly the *bien pensants* had been shaken.

The heaviest blow of all came from the Archbishop of Paris who forbade the faithful to be present at a performance of *Tartuffe* under pain of excommunication. Although the King, who was clearly on Molière's side, was advised by an eminent canon lawyer that the ban was probably invalid, he did not intervene. For five years the play led an underground existence in constantly altering versions.[1] It was read, apparently with approval, before the Papal Nuncio and his suite, in the salons and at the home of Ninon de Lenclos; but it was not until 1669, when the King had composed his differences with the Holy See, that he removed the obstacles and *Tartuffe* was played to packed houses while Molière's enemies retired discomforted.

Tartuffe was closely bound up with the religious situation in the seventeenth century and we must glance at one of the chief manifestations—the Compagnie du Saint-Sacrement or, as its enemies called it, *la cabale des dévots*—if we are to appreciate the play to the full. In May 1627, a devout nobleman, Henri de Levis, duc de Ventadour and a peer of the realm, had conceived the idea of founding a pious association for the furtherance of the Catholic religion in France. From modest beginnings the redoubtable Compagnie du Saint-Sacrement arose with affiliated branches which extended all over the country. Its membership was large and varied. It included bishops, prelates, simple parish priests, members of the aristocracy—some of them among the most famous names in France—and, inevitably, a vast number of pious busybodies. Its activities were manifold. It did good work in the mission field, in the fields of prison reform, social welfare and what is now called the *protection de la jeune fille*. Not all its activities were equally

[1] The original version had only three Acts.

creditable. It undoubtedly developed into a powerful religious secret society with an efficient police system, denouncing and persecuting heretics, informing husbands of the debauchery and infidelity of wayward wives and interfering in the dioceses of lazy bishops. Its ultimate downfall and destruction were brought about by its campaign against duelling which annoyed the nobility and led to the personal intervention of Mazarin.

The *Compagnie* was formally suppressed in 1660, but its power remained virtually intact for some years to come and there is no doubt that it was largely reponsible for keeping *Tartuffe* off the stage for five years. That such a society should have been founded at all, that it should have reached such dimensions and have fought so bitterly against Molière, is an illuminating comment on the religious situation in the seventeenth century. Although the Catholic Church in France had emerged victorious from the wars of religion, the faith had been deeply disturbed by the upheavals of the sixteenth century.

"Let us have no illusions about the state of religious belief in this seventeenth century which people always choose to see in a blaze of glory . . ." wrote Sainte-Beuve. "Madame du Deffand says somewhere that she cannot think of anyone in the seventeenth century except M. de La Rochefoucauld who really was a free-thinker. This remark merely shows how ill each age knows the one that immediately preceded it. When we examine the seventeenth century from a particular angle, we perceive unbelief running all the way through it *in a direct unbroken tradition.* The reign of Louis XIV is thoroughly undermined by it."[1]

Debauchery and unbelief were rife. There was certainly plenty to occupy the faithful, but their methods were not always happily chosen nor were their aims invariably to be commended. We may admire a St. Vincent de Paul (whose attitude towards the *Compagnie* was highly circumspect) or a Bérulle, but the grim spirit of persecution and spying which distinguished the *dévots*, and their suspicious attitude towards anything which could be interpreted as an attack on religion, were a clear sign of weakness. They felt that the Church was threatened, but the methods used to meet the threat betray not merely a sense of impotency, but an absence of true spirituality on the part of those who practised them.

---

[1] *Port-Royal*, III, pp. 229–30 (italics Sainte-Beuve's).

2

Although these events took place nearly three hundred years ago, *Tartuffe* has remained a battleground. The debate, which began with Bourdaloue and Bossuet, echoes down the centuries, disturbing peaceful academic backwaters and ruining the objectivity of literary critics. Sainte-Beuve propounded a tempting theory that the play was a subtle apologia for *la morale des honnêtes gens* and Brunetière, while still a champion of free-thought, published a long essay on "La Philosophie de Molière" in which he demonstrated gleefully that Molière was an exponent of "la philosophie de la nature" and the forerunner of the materialist philosophers of the eighteenth century.[1] To-day *Tartuffe* is still a scandal to the devout and a stick with which the free-thinkers try to belabour the *bien pensants*. Ramon Fernandez has alleged mischievously that Orgon is a representative Christian, and M. François Mauriac leaves us with the impression that, in the eyes of the author of *Destins*, only Molière's Christian death excuses him for having written *Tartuffe*.

The doctrinaire approach has done much to prevent a true appreciation of one of the greatest masterpieces of the French theatre. The misunderstandings and misrepresentations have been so grave that the time has come to declare roundly that there is no attack, direct or indirect, on religion in the play, that there is little to support Sainte-Beuve's theory and nothing at all to excuse Brunetière's fanciful views of Molière's philosophy. Molière was not a deeply religious man certainly, but in spite of constant persecution by the *dévots* there is no reason for supposing that he was anything but a believing Christian. In *Tartuffe* he dealt with one of the burning questions of the time; but though he could not resist baiting the *dévots*, he approached a serious question with the seriousness and detachment of a great artist.[2]

Tartuffe is first and foremost a sociological study of the corrosive

[1] A few years later a converted Brunetière repeated the same arguments in another of those interminable volumes on the history of French literature, but his satisfaction had disappeared and Molière's "philosophy" was the subject for schoolmasterly reproach.

[2] He was partly to blame for the trouble. His provocative reference to "les célèbres originaux du portrait que je voulais peindre" was an opportunity for his enemies and a temptation to literary critics to forget the text in order to indulge in fruitless detective work.

influence, not of religion, but of a decadent religiosity on the life of the community, and as such it seems to me to be unsurpassed in European literature. Molière does not study its effect on the community as a whole; he selects a particular unit—the family. He draws, with that incomparable colour and vitality which have placed him among the great European masters, a prosperous middle-class French family in the reign of Louis XIV. There are the middle-aged husband and his young and rather worldly second wife, the two children of his first marriage—the headstrong Damis and the timid, wilting Marianne who is in love with Valère—the crusty puritanical mother-in-law, the urbane and reasonable brother-in-law and the magnificent *bonne*.

Brunetière declared that Orgon is as much the centre of the play as Tartuffe and there is a good deal of truth in this observation. Tartuffe himself is a superbly comic creation; he possesses the same life and vitality as the Wife of Bath or Falstaff and his character is perhaps more varied. He is a composite figure. He represents all the main varieties of contemporary religious abuse and is the channel through which they infect the sane, balanced life of the family and almost bring it to disaster. This is also the real reason for the attacks on Molière. The abuses that Molière was attacking were so widespread and were perceived with such clarity that nearly all the devout felt that the blows were aimed at them, and instead of searching their hearts, they tried to allay their sense of guilt by violent attacks on their critic.

Tartuffe is a good deal more besides. "Tartuffe," wrote Edmond Jaloux, in a valuable note on the play,

"Tartuffe is greedy, lazy, licentious and self-seeking, but he is only these things at certain times and, so to speak, spasmodically. He has no intention of hiding his real self behind the mask of hypocrisy. *It is his real self that is hypocritical. . . .* We can be sure that when he is alone in his room, he is far from laughing over the gullibility of the good Orgon, but that he piously says his rosary, not without interrupting his devotions from time to time to sigh regretfully over Elmire."[1]

Tartuffe is not a purely religious figure. He is a scoundrel, the eternal "confidence man." Since the society which produced him was in the main a Christian one, nothing was more natural than to choose religion as the means of cheating the gullible Orgon

[1] *L'Esprit des livres*, 1ère série, Paris, 1923, pp. 6 and 7 (italics mine).

out of his possessions and seducing his wife. In other ages he employs other means. Tartuffe is the sham clergyman who collects for a non-existent charity, or the sham soldier who sells bogus news about your son who has been reported missing at the front; but he is also the soap-box orator and the editor of the small sectarian paper, whether political or religious; he is even the political leader with his smooth assurances and promises. For the crux of the matter is that, in spite of his viciousness, Tartuffe is in his way genuine—genuine in that his hypocrisy is an integral part of his character—and deceives himself as well as other people. It is, indeed, his soft corruption—admirably brought out by Molière in the language used by Tartuffe and Orgon—which makes him such a menace to the community.

Our starting-point is the description of Tartuffe which Orgon gives his brother:

Ha! si vous aviez vu comme j'en fis rencontre,
Vous auriez pris pour lui l'amitié que je montre.
Chaque jour à l'église il venait, d'un air doux,
Tout vis-à-vis de moi se mettre à deux genoux.
Il attirait les yeux de l'assemblée entière
Par l'ardeur dont au Ciel il poussait sa prière;
Il faisait des soupirs, de grands élancements,
Et baisait humblement la terre à tous moments;
Et, lorsque je sortais, il me devançait vite
Pour m'aller à la porte offrir de l'eau bénite.
Instruit par son garçon, qui dans tout l'imitait,
Et de son indigence et de ce qu'il était,
Je lui faisais des dons; mais, avec modestie,
Il me voulait toujours en rendre une partie.
"C'est trop, me disait-il, c'est trop de la moitié;
Je ne mérite pas de vous faire pitié."
Et quand je refusais de le vouloir reprendre,
Aux pauvres à mes yeux, il allait le répandre.
Enfin le Ciel chez moi me le fit retirer,
Et, depuis ce temps-là, tout semble y prospérer . . .
Mais vous ne croiriez point jusqu'où monte son zèle:
Il s'impute à péché la moindre bagatelle;
Un rien presque suffit pour le scandaliser,
Jusque-là qu'il se vint l'autre jour accuser
D'avoir pris une puce en faisant sa prière,
Et de l'avoir tuée avec trop de colère.

This passage, with its brilliantly comic ending, is a masterly portrait of a type who is always with us. It is also an excellent example of the vivid pictorial qualities of Molière's style and his power of seizing on the essential gestures of his characters—the *air doux*, "se mettre à *deux* genoux," the sighs, the humble kissing of the ground, the offering of holy water. Molière's characters are in no sense caricatures. He has a firm hold on the world of common experience which makes his slight deviations from it the more effective and explains why his characters are so convincing and so durable. Molière's irony is a two-edged weapon. In this passage he is able to attack the exaggerated and unhealthy devotion of the day in Tartuffe and, at the same time, by presenting Tartuffe through Orgon's eyes, to show exactly how he himself is corrupted by it. Orgon was undoubtedly a deeply religious man before meeting Tartuffe. The change is, therefore, from a deep but healthy piety to an unhealthy devotion which is apparent in the tone of cringing admiration in which he speaks of Tartuffe. This is how Dorine describes Tartuffe's influence on him:

> Nos troubles l'avaient mis sur le pied d'homme sage,
> Et pour servir son prince il montra du courage;
> Mais il est devenu comme un homme hébété,
> Depuis que de Tartuffe on le voit entêté.
> Il l'appelle son frère et l'aime dans son âme
> Cent fois plus qu'il ne fait mère, fils, fille et femme.
> C'est de tous ses secrets l'unique confident
> Et de ses actions le directeur prudent . . .

The focal word is *hébété*. Instead of enriching the personality by building on the natural, human qualities, this sort of religiosity has the reverse effect. It corrodes and undermines what is sane and healthy, and this is the basis of Molière's criticism. Dorine's views are reinforced by Orgon's naïve admission:

> Oui, je deviens tout autre avec son entretien:
> Il m'enseigne à n'avoir affection pour rien,
> De toutes amitiés il détache mon âme,
> Et je verrais mourir frère, enfants, mère et femme,
> Que je m'en soucierais autant que de cela.

Cléante makes the appropriate rejoinder:

> Les sentiments humains, mon frère, que voilà!

It draws attention to the obvious point—*les sentiments humains* which suffer such violence and perversion. Orgon is a type who is well known to us. He is what a contemporary writer has called in another context a *rat de bénitier*; but in his case the malady has become radical and dangerous. His attitude is not one of Christian resignation; it is the reverse of Christian. It simply cuts straight across all Christian teaching and is entirely contrary to charity.

This absurd and dangerous devotion produces one of the great comic scenes of the play:

ORGON:
> Tout s'est-il, ces deux jours, passé de bonne sorte?
> Qu'est-ce qu'on fait céans? comme est-ce qu'on s'y porte?

DORINE:
> Madame eut avant-hier la fièvre jusqu'au soir,
> Avec un mal de tête étrange à concevoir.

ORGON
> Et Tartuffe?

DORINE:
> Tartuffe? Il se porte à merveille,
> Gros et gras, le teint frais, et la bouche vermeille.

ORGON:
> Le pauvre homme!

DORINE:
> Le soir, elle eut un grand dégoût
> Et ne put au souper toucher à rien du tout,
> Tant sa douleur de tête était encor cruelle!

ORGON
> Et Tartuffe?

DORINE:
> Il soupa, lui tout seul, devant elle,
> Et fort dévotement il mangea deux perdrix
> Avec une moitié de gigot en hachis.

ORGON:
> Le pauvre homme!

DORINE:
> La nuit se passa tout entière
> Sans qu'elle pût fermer un moment la paupière;
> Des chaleurs l'empêchaient de pouvoir sommeiller,
> Et jusqu'au jour près d'elle il nous fallut veiller.

ORGON:
> Et Tartuffe?

D

DORINE:

    Pressé d'un sommeil agréable,
Il passa dans sa chambre au sortir de la table,
Et dans son lit bien chaud il se mit tout soudain,
Où sans trouble il dormit jusques au lendemain.

ORGON:

    Le pauvre homme!

From the time of the earliest comedies, the repetition of words and phrases had been one of the commonest of Molière's comic devices. He developed it until it became, as it is here, a subtle method of probing the minds of his characters. For Orgon's folly is not merely described: the identity of word and action is complete. His inability to understand what is said to him reveals the grotesque effects of his perverse devotion. He does not notice that Tartuffe's gluttony cuts straight across his austere principles. He does not see that his own indifference to the physical welfare of his family is incompatible with his solicitude for Tartuffe's well-being, that his preoccupation with Tartuffe—with the superficial appearance of piety—is actually becoming, in theological language, an obstacle to his salvation. Orgon's state of mind, indeed, bears a marked resemblance to Alceste's during his *emportement* against the customs of society. He has entered a world of private mania and his contact with the actual world is only intermittent. This is apparent from his failure to understand what is being said to him. In Dorine's description of Tartuffe devouring partridges and swilling wine the words do not register because there is a gulf between Orgon and the world of common experience. He sees only the miserable, ragged, indigent Tartuffe of the first meeting which for psychological reasons has fixed itself in his subconscious mind, refusing to allow the real Tartuffe to enter the world of private fantasy.

The effects of his inhibition are far-reaching. They lead to a decline which is at once intellectual, moral and emotional. He does not scruple to break his promise to allow his daughter to marry Valère, and plays the part of the tyrannical father in order to force her to marry Tartuffe. He makes over his possessions to Tartuffe without considering the claims of his family, turns a secret entrusted to him by a friend into an absurd *cas de conscience* and finishes by betraying the confidence to Tartuffe. In other words, he is hypnotized by Tartuffe and this leads to a complete disruption of all values.

In order to exhibit to the full the ravages of false religion, Molière provides his principal characters with two foils—Cléante and Dorine—who both represent his own point of view. Cléante has been the subject of considerable controversy and dons have debated his religious views in learned footnotes.[1] Brunetière considered that the part was superfluous, but one suspects that this was because his religious opinions were contrary to the professor's theories about "the philosophy of Molière." Allier and Michaut felt that Cléante is the pivot of the play and that he represents Molière's own religious position. It seems to me that the second view is in the main the true one, but the part is perhaps more important than these critics allow. Cléante is like Philinte in the *Misanthrope*, the urbane, cultured man of the world, tirelessly expounding the philosophy of the *juste milieu*:

> Les hommes, la plupart, sont étrangement faits!
> Dans la juste nature on ne les voit jamais;
> La raison a pour eux des bornes trop petites;
> En chaque caractère ils passent ses limites;
> Et la plus noble chose, ils la gâtent souvent
> Pour la vouloir outrer et pousser trop avant.

This is the voice of true civilization, of a society in which it was natural to speak of measure and proportion. But if this were all, Cléante might still be, as Brunetière alleged, a *porte-parole* who was designed to mislead the public about Molière's personal opinions and who was not essential to the action of the play. His importance lies precisely in the fact that in the pattern of the play he stands for the incorruptible intellect cutting remorselessly through Orgon's mental confusions, stripping away the subterfuges of the *dévots* and revealing them in their true light. His eulogy of *la juste nature* is followed immediately by a frontal attack on hypocrisy:

> Je ne suis point, mon frère, un docteur révéré,
> Et le savoir chez moi n'est pas tout retiré.
> Mais, en un mot, je sais, pour toute ma science,
> Du faux avec le vrai faire la différence.
> Et, comme je ne vois nul genre de héros
> Qui soient plus à priser que les parfaits dévots,

---

[1] "Une petite question indiscrète: ce Cléante fait-il ses Pâques? je le crois. Certainement, cinquante ans plus tard il ne les fera plus!" (Sainte-Beuve, *Port-Royal*, III, p. 215 *n.*)

Aucune chose au monde et plus noble et plus belle
Que la sainte ferveur d'un véritable zèle,
Aussi ne vois-je rien qui soit plus odieux
Que le dehors plâtré d'un zèle spécieux,
Que ces francs charlatans, que ces dévots de place,
De qui la sacrilège et trompeuse grimace
Abuse impunément et se joue à leur gré
De ce qu'ont les mortels de plus saint et sacré;
Ces gens qui, par une âme à l'intérêt soumise,
Font de dévotion métier et marchandise,
Et veulent acheter crédit et dignités
A prix de faux clins d'yeux et d'élans affectés;
Ces gens, dis-je, qu'on voit d'une ardeur non commune
Par le chemin du Ciel courir à leur fortune,
Qui, brûlants et priants, demandent chaque jour,
Et prêchent la retraite au milieu de la cour,
Qui savent ajuster leur zèle avec leurs vices,
Sont prompts, vindicatifs, sans foi, pleins d'artifices,
Et pour perdre quelqu'un couvrent insolemment
De l'intérêt du Ciel leur fier ressentiment . . .

Cléante does not make any great claims for himself. He is not, he assures Orgon, *un docteur révéré*. He does not pretend to be a deeply spiritual man, but is content to admire the devotion of the saints from a respectful distance. He merely claims to be able to distinguish true devotion from false, and this passage leads up to the famous plea for a decent, human piety:

On ne voit point en eux ce faste insupportable,
Et leur dévotion est humaine, est traitable . . .

Cléante's intellectualism is important because intellectual confusion—an inability to distinguish true piety from the sham which is so effectually denounced here—is at the root of Orgon's own corruption. It is left to Dorine to deal with some of the other consequences of this perversity. She is very different from Cléante, but it is a sign of Molière's wide and generous humanity that her role is not less important. She is the peasant, the voice of the earth. She is guided not by careful distinctions or elaborate arguments, but by sound instinct, by a natural wisdom which belongs to her class. The clue to her part in the play is the description of the prude in the first scene:

Il est vrai qu'elle vit en austère personne;
Mais l'âge dans son âme a mis ce zèle ardent,
Et l'on sait qu'elle est prude à son corps défendant.
Tant qu'elle a pu des cœurs attirer les hommages,
Elle a fort bien joui de tous ses avantages;
Mais, voyant de ses yeux tous les brillants baisser,
Au monde, qui la quitte, elle veut renoncer,
Et du voile pompeux d'une haute sagesse
De ses attraits usés déguiser la faiblesse.
Ce sont là les retours des coquettes du temps.
Il leur est dur de voir déserter les galants.
Dans un tel abandon, leur sombre inquiétude
Ne voit d'autre recours que le métier de prude,
Et la sévérité de ces femmes de bien
Censure toute chose et ne pardonne à rien;
Hautement d'un chacun elles blâment la vie
Non point par charité, mais par un trait d'envie,
Qui ne saurait souffrir qu'une autre ait les plaisirs
Dont le penchant de l'âge a sevré leurs désirs.

This passage is an example of Molière's style at its best. It shows
the vitality with which he could hit off the portraits of the types
who surrounded him. It is also a brilliant exposition of his views on
the life of the senses and an illustration of the way in which these
views are dissolved into the play. In spite of their difference of
approach, Cléante and Dorine are complementary. A healthy piety
—a devotion that is *humaine* and *traitable*—is perfectly compatible
with the normal life of the senses. Dorine's attack on the false prude
is very similar in intention to Cléante's on the *faux dévots*. She
attacks the prude because her austerity is not genuine, because it
does not spring from true spirituality but from sexual frustration.
The "zèle ardent" is the result of a debilitated body, a body worn
out by the empty coquetry of her youth which is criticized by
implication. The positives and negatives are balanced with considerable felicity: *zèle ardent, corps défendant*; *attraits usés, sombre
inquiétude*; *l'âge a sevré leurs désirs*. In Molière's world the life of
the senses, when properly developed, is the stable element which
binds humanity together; but the prude through her lack of moderation has transformed herself into an empty shell; her sexual frustration has changed into a bitter censorious devotion that cuts
her off from the rest of humanity, and we seem, in the last phrase,

to hear Time's scythe cutting remorselessly through the withered *désirs*.

The same sturdy common sense is apparent in Dorine's *rapports* with her master. When Orgon, speaking of the marriage of his daughter with Tartuffe, remarks:

> Cet hymen de tous biens comblera vos désirs,
> Il sera tout confit en douceurs et plaisirs.
> Ensemble vous vivrez, dans vos ardeurs fidèles,
> Comme deux vrais enfants, comme deux tourterelles . . .

we not only detect the senile whining note of the *dévot*, we see that the *désirs* and *plaisirs*, which in Dorine are healthy and vigorous, have become twisted and perverted. There is something about those *désirs* and those *ardeurs fidèles* which makes the flesh creep. Dorine has already stated the proper view:

> . . . laissons sa noblesse . . .
> Sachez que d'une fille on risque la vertu,
> Lorsque dans son hymen son goût est combattu,
> Que le dessein d'y vivre en honnête personne
> Dépend des qualités du mari qu'on lui donne,
> Et que ceux dont partout on montre au doigt le front
> Font leurs femmes souvent ce qu'on voit qu'elles sont.

The feeble and *fainéante* Marianne, who talks of retiring to a convent or of committing suicide if she is made to marry Tartuffe, produces a violent reaction in Dorine:

> Fort bien. C'est un recours où je ne songeais pas;
> Vous n'avez qu'à mourir pour sortir d'embarras.
> Le remède sans doute est merveilleux. J'enrage
> Lorsque j'entends tenir ces sortes de langage.

The whole of Molière's belief in life is crowded into these four lines, his intense belief that life is good, that the senses are good provided that one follows *la juste nature* and avoids the inhibitions of a narrow puritanism or frittering one's life away in a series of empty *affaires*.

3

Tartuffe himself does not make his appearance until the third Act, but the way has been well prepared. We have already seen the

ravages that he has caused in the family and when he does appear
the relation between a false piety and an unhealthy sexuality is
very clearly brought out. His entry is one of the high lights of the
play:

> Laurent, serrez ma haire avec ma discipline,
> Et priez que toujours le Ciel vous illumine.
> Si l'on vient pour me voir, je vais aux prisonniers
> Des aumônes que j'ai partager les deniers.

The accent falls ostensibly on the disciplining of unruly desires;
but instead of being genuinely disciplined, these desires are driven
underground, are "prisoners" and prisoners of a very dangerous
and subversive nature. With an absurdly exaggerated gesture, he
throws his handkerchief over Dorine's breasts:

TARTUFFE:

> Couvrez ce sein que je ne saurais voir;
> Par de pareils objets les âmes sont blessées,
> Et cela fait venir de coupables pensées.

The description of the breasts as "de pareils objets" at
once strikes a perverse, unhealthy note and Dorine's reaction is
characteristic:

> Vous êtes donc bien tendre à la tentation,
> Et la chair sur vos sens fait grande impression?
> Certes, je ne sais pas quelle chaleur vous monte;
> Mais à convoiter, moi, je ne suis point si prompte,
> Et je vous verrais nu du haut jusques en bas,
> Que toute votre peau ne me tenterait pas.

This onslaught strikes exactly the right note. It is a gust of fresh
air which for a moment dissipates the stuffy erotic mist that surrounds Tartuffe. The language possesses the crude, racy vitality
of the peasant living in close contact with the earth. Dorine is a
symbolical figure. Her voice is a primitive voice; it represents the
primitive folk-element which is present in nearly all the greatest
art down to the seventeenth century, and it is the absence of this
element from the slick, cynical comedies of Molière's English contemporaries which makes them shallow and empty and explains
the thinness and poverty of their language.[1] Dorine joins hands with

[1] Compare *l'École des femmes* with Wycherley's English adaptation of it—
The Country Wife.

Shakespeare's peasants. She stands for the norm on which a great civilization was founded. It was because Molière himself believed so firmly in the life of the senses that sexual intrigue, which is a deviation from the norm, is given such prominence in his work.

Tartuffe's encounter with Dorine is followed by the magnificent scene in which he attempts the seduction of Elmire. What is strikingly original in these scenes is the way in which Molière explores the connection between a debased religion and the sexual instinct. The handling of his medium is triumphantly successful, and the verse has a subtlety and brilliance which are not surpassed in any of his other plays:

> Que le Ciel à jamais par sa toute bonté
> Et de l'âme et du corps vous donne la santé,
> Et bénisse vos jours autant que le désire
> Le plus humble de ceux que son amour inspire!

The key-words are *âme*, *corps* and *santé*. For the scene is precisely a conflict between *âme* and *corps*. The *santé* for which Tartuffe prays is something very different from norm represented by Dorine. Tartuffe's own gestures, which are described in the sinister stage directions: "Il lui met la main sur le genou," "Maniant le fichu d'Elmire," are indeed a denial of true *santé*. This is the real Tartuffe, the disgusting, libidinous old man pawing the wife of his protector while aspiring to the hand of the daughter. It leads to the first of the great speeches:

> L'amour qui nous attache aux beautés éternelles
> N'étouffe pas en nous l'amour des temporelles.
> Nos sens facilement peuvent être charmés
> Des ouvrages parfaits que le Ciel a formés.
> Ses attraits réfléchis brillent dans vos pareilles;
> Mais il étale en vous ses plus rares merveilles.
> Il a sur votre face épanché des beautés
> Dont les yeux sont surpris et les cœurs transportés;
> Et je n'ai pu vous voir, parfaite créature,
> Sans admirer en vous l'auteur de la nature,
> Et d'une ardente amour sentir mon cœur atteint,
> Au plus beau des portraits où lui-même il s'est peint.
> D'abord j'appréhendai que cette ardeur secrète
> Ne fût du noir esprit une surprise adroite,

Et même à fuir vos yeux mon cœur se résolut,
Vous croyant un obstacle à faire mon salut.
Mais enfin je connus, ô beauté toute aimable,
Que cette passion peut n'être point coupable,
Que je puis l'ajuster avecque la pudeur,
Et c'est ce qui m'y fait abandonner mon cœur.

These lines sometimes remind one of the speech beginning
"Good morning to the day" in *Volpone*, but the resemblance is a
superficial one. Molière's method is very different from Jonson's.
He does not create a fantastic world by exaggeration and distortion; his method is more directly satiric, more realistic, and his
aims are perhaps more varied. The Christian believes that human
beauty is a reflection of the Divine beauty, and that it is because of
the limitations of human language and human concepts that he
must describe God in human terms. In this passage and in the
passages that follow the process is inverted. Tartuffe contrives by
an adroit mingling of the clichés of devotional and erotic writing
to transform Elmire into a being who is partly saint and partly
mistress and whom he proceeds to invoke. When he says

Nos sens facilement peuvent être charmés
Des ouvrages parfaits que le Ciel a formés

or

D'abord j'appréhendai que cette ardeur secrète
Ne fût du noir esprit une surprise adroite

or

J'aurai toujours pour vous, ô suave merveille,
Une dévotion à nulle autre pareille

we detect in the alternation of the hissing s's and the liquid l's and
m's the sudden intake of the breath, the sudden catching back of
the saliva as desire rises. For the movement of sexual desire, which
he refers to furtively as *cette ardeur secrete* and *un feu discret*, follows
the movement of the invocation like an insidious undercurrent,
wrapping itself round and round the strange fantastic Elmire whom
he has created, fretting and nibbling at her in the attempt to undermine her resistance and stifle her scruples.

It is both invocation and argument; content and movement are
welded into one. The problems presented are specious and are
D*

"solved" by a series of sleights of hand, by the pretence of sudden illumination:

> ... même à fuir vos yeux mon cœur se résolut,
> Vous croyant un obstacle à faire mon salut.
> Mais enfin je *connus*, ô beauté toute aimable,
> Que cette passion peut n'être point coupable ...

It is the undercurrent of sexual desire, which is carefully maintained, that gives the passage and indeed the whole scene its unity. When Elmire objects that such language is unbecoming in a *dévot*, Tartuffe repeats the same formulas with more vehemence:

> Ah! pour être dévot, je n'en suis pas moins homme;
> Et lorsqu'on vient à voir vos célestes appas,
> Un cœur se laisse prendre, et ne raisonne pas.
> Je sais qu'un tel discours de moi paraît étrange;
> Mais, Madame, après tout, je ne suis pas un ange,
> Et, si vous condamnez l'aveu que je vous fais,
> Vous devez vous en prendre à vos charmants attraits.

The famous line

> Ah! pour être dévot, je n'en suis pas moins homme ...

is one of the focal points of the play. It is a restatement, from another point of view, of Cléante's

> Les hommes, la plupart, sont étrangement faits!
> Dans la juste nature on ne les voit jamais ...

Tartuffe is indeed a man, but a man whose natural instincts have been warped and perverted because he has strayed from the norm. For this reason he is an object of satire, is one of the varieties of perversion which are studied in this and in the other plays.

There is one other aspect of this scene which calls for comment. It is not merely an attack on religious hypocrisy in general; it is directed in particular against the casuists and the famous method known as *la dévotion aisée*. When Molière makes Tartuffe say of his passion for Elmire

> ... je puis l'ajuster avecque la pudeur

he is attacking precisely the same abuse as Pascal in *les Provinciales* —the method of juggling with conscience which had become fashionable and which was attributed to the Jesuits. This line of attack is only concluded in the second scene between Tartuffe and Elmire:

ELMIRE:
Mais comment consentir à ce que vous voulez,
Sans offenser le Ciel, dont toujours vous parlez?
TARTUFFE:
Si ce n'est que le Ciel qu'à mes vœux on oppose,
Lever un tel obstacle est à moi peu de chose,
Et cela ne doit pas retenir votre cœur.
ELMIRE:
Mais des arrêts du Ciel on nous fait tant de peur!
TARTUFFE:
Je puis vous dissiper ces craintes ridicules,
Madame, et je sais l'art de lever les scrupules.
Le Ciel défend, de vrai, certains contentements;
(*C'est un scélérat qui parle.*)
Mais on trouve avec lui des accommodements.
Selon divers besoins, il est une science
D'étendre les liens de notre conscience,
Et de rectifier le mal de l'action
Avec la pureté de notre intention.

The trite, banal rhythm provides the appropriate comment on this form of intellectual perversion. The last five lines, however, are not merely a caricature of the methods of the casuists; there is a serious purpose behind them. For Molière these methods, as surely as the piety of Orgon and the hypocrisy of Tartuffe, are a deviation from the norm. What he does is to demonstrate that this sort of intellectual and moral dishonesty leads straight to crime. So far from being a forerunner of eighteenth-century materialism, he seems to me in this play to be a serious critic of an abuse which went a very long way towards undermining the authority of the Church in France and preparing the way for the secularization of French culture. There is something ominous about the lines which follow:

Enfin votre scrupule est facile à détruire:
Vous êtes assurée ici d'un plein secret,
Et le mal n'est jamais que dans l'éclat qu'on fait.
Le scandale du monde est ce qui fait l'offense,
Et ce n'est pas pécher que pécher en silence.

In this whispered confidence we have a sinister vision of a great and gracious civilization whose foundations are already threatened by the subversive activities of warring *cabales*, whose moral fibre is profoundly undermined by people who in all seriousness could sponsor such views.

For the sake of completeness one must turn back a few pages to the scene where Elmire explains to her husband why she did not want her stepson to reveal the first assault on her virtue:

> Est-ce qu'au simple aveu d'un amoureux transport
> Il faut que notre honneur se gendarme si fort?
> Et ne peut-on répondre à tout ce qui le touche
> Que le feu dans les yeux et l'injure à la bouche?
> Pour moi, de tels propos je me ris simplement,
> Et l'éclat là-dessus ne me plaît nullement.
> J'aime qu'avec douceur nous nous montrions sages,
> Et ne suis point du tout pour ces prudes sauvages
> Dont l'honneur est armé de griffes et de dents
> Et veut au moindre mot dévisager les gens;
> Me préserve le Ciel d'une telle sagesse!

The attitude behind these lines has been variously interpreted. Some writers have regarded Elmire as a mean opportunist, others as an ally of her brother, as an upholder of the golden mean. Their importance seems to me to lie in the fact that this is the reverse of the heroic attitude, that the reference to "le feu dans les yeux et l'injure à la bouche" is a deliberate parody of the Cornelian honour which marks the passing of an age. It is the attitude of an astute, sensible middle-class woman who is responsible for outwitting Tartuffe.

With the unmasking of Tartuffe at the end of Act IV Molière arrives at the last stage of his journey, but before following him further it is worth glancing at what has already been accomplished. The study is clearly a twofold one. There is a psychological study of the influence of a false conception of religion on the character of a group of individuals, and the sociological study of its consequences or possible consequences for a middle-class family. The group divides roughly into two parties. In Tartuffe, Orgon and Madame Pernelle religion produces a marked deterioration of character and fosters weaknesses which are inherent in their personalities. In Cléante and Dorine it produces the reverse effect; it causes the healthy organism to react vigorously, to apply itself to the expulsion of the intruder and to the mitigation of the damage already caused. The reactions of Elmire are of a severely practical nature like Dorine's. She is not interested in theory, but simply in averting the catastrophe which threatens her home and her children. Her role is, therefore, to expose Tartuffe, and there is no conflict between her skilful action and her disparaging comments on honour. The two children are caught between the contending parties. Damis is headstrong and simply wants to see Tartuffe thrown out, and Cléante has to try to exercise a moderating influence on him. Marianne is inclined to give in and it needs all Dorine's vitality to prop her up, to stimulate a healthy reaction to the situation.

Although Tartuffe has been unmasked the tribulations of the family are by no means over. It is now threatened with complete ruin through the foolish actions committed by Orgon under the influence of Tartuffe. The last scene, where the Exempt steps in and marches him off to prison, has been regarded as a *deus ex machina* and a graceful tribute to King Louis. One editor, indeed, has even suggested that the Exempt's speech is so ill-written that it must be an interpolation. These arguments seem to me to miss the point. The conclusion is perfectly logical and in spite of *négligences*, which are by no means uncommon in Molière's work, the last long speech is completely convincing. Not simply a single family, but the whole of society is menaced by the extravagances of the *dévots*, and salvation is only to be found in a vigorous community life under a discerning monarch. This is precisely what Louis XIV was for Molière. Whatever may be said of the rest of the speech, no one can mistake the immense confidence behind

Nous vivons sous un Prince ennemi de la fraude.

It not only carries immediate conviction; it is not too much to say that the whole weight of the play is behind this single line. No one criticized contemporary abuses more vigorously than Molière, and no one was more conscious of the dangers of the various abuses which threatened to cloud men's minds, warp their senses and seduce them from *la juste nature*. No one was more conscious than he that the majority of his fellows were indifferent to the maxims of "Reason," but this did nothing to undermine his own belief in the fundamental decency and sanity of the existing order. We may feel that he judged it too lightly, but that is not relevant in a study of *Tartuffe*. What matter are the brilliance and penetration of the play and the unity and coherence of the poet's vision.

IV. *DOM JUAN*

1

Financially, the suppression of *Tartuffe* was a serious blow to Molière. He was already at work on *le Misanthrope*, but in order to keep his company together it was imperative to produce a new play at once. *Dom Juan* had its première in February 1665. The theme was a popular one in the seventeenth century and the new play was a success. It is not surprising—particularly when one recalls that a fresh attack on the *dévots* was provocatively put into the mouth of Dom Juan himself—that it should have added fuel to the flames, and though it escaped the drastic fate of *Tartuffe* it, too, became a battle-ground and has continued to be the subject of acrimonious controversy down to our own time.

In the nineteenth century earnest free-thinkers hailed *Dom Juan* as "un intrépide représentant de la libre pensée," and the play as a text-book which had anticipated their own views by two hundred years and stated them with a power and persuasiveness to which they could scarcely pretend. It was incredible, they thought, that anyone who was not blinded by superstition could still doubt that Dom Juan was Molière's own spokesman. If one is determined to have a "message" at all costs, *Dom Juan* can be used to prove almost anything. It would not be difficult, for example, to make out a case for a Marxist Molière born out of due time by pretending that he was really on the side of "the people" against the corrupt aristocrat and writing off the supernatural as a concession to popular superstition.

The truth seems to me to be rather different. *Dom Juan* is a companion piece to *Tartuffe* in which Molière subjects the problem of extreme incredulity to the same searching examination as the problem of extreme credulity in the earlier play. He was an artist, not a pamphleteer trying to make proselytes, but there is nothing in the play to suggest that he intended to hold his principal character up to admiration. His attacks are directed against both the *libertins* and the *dévots*:

"Vous savez ce que vous faites, vous, et, si vous ne croyez rien, vous avez vos raisons; mais il y a certains petits impertinents dans le monde, qui sont libertins sans savoir pourquoi, qui font les esprits forts parce qu'ils croient que cela leur sied bien . . ."

"L'hypocrisie est un vice à la mode, et tous les vices à la mode passent pour vertus. . . . Tous les autres vices des hommes sont exposés à la censure, et chacun a la liberté de les attaquer hautement; mais l'hypocrisie est un vice privilégié, qui de sa main ferme la bouche à tout le monde et jouit en repos d'une impunité souveraine."

The first of these comments belongs to Sganarelle, the second to Dom Juan; but though there is bitter personal feeling behind the onslaught on hypocrisy, there is no reason to doubt that Sganarelle's remarks about *certains petits impertinents* are meant to be taken at their face value. Molière drew for his material in this play on the *libertins* as surely as he had drawn on the *dévots* in *Tartuffe*.

"The lack of prudence which Molière displays in *Dom Juan*," writes M. Blanchot, "is like a series of uncontrolled movements which are provoked by annoyances that have become too persistent. In trying to drive off the hornets buzzing round his head which infuriate him, he strays to the edge of the forbidden zone. His impatience carries him further than he realized, and by an impulse which is contrary to his natural inclination, he identifies himself with an extreme example of the spirit of rebellion and anti-conformity."

"In his greatest plays," continues the same critic, "Molière does not show the slightest interest in speculative questions. His morality is in no sense based on indulgence and compromise. If it tends to relax the bonds of convention and make rules more flexible, it is not on account of a taste for something which is flat and flabby. On the contrary, it springs from Molière's hostility to artificial restrictions, to conventions which stifle the growth of genuine vitality and put the brake on his natural impatience."[1]

M. Blanchot makes two important points here. Molière's exasperation may have led him too far at times—this must remain a

[1] *op. cit.*, p. 308.

matter of opinion—but it is a sign of his immense vitality and a great positive force in his work. The second point is his complete lack of interest in speculative problems which is well illustrated by Sganarelle's opening speech:

"Quoi que puisse dire Aristote et toute la Philosophie, il n'est rien d'égal au Tabac; c'est la passion des honnêtes gens, et qui vit sans tabac n'est pas digné de vivre. Non seulement il réjouit et purge les cerveaux humains, mais encore il instruit les âmes à la vertu, et l'on apprend avec lui à devenir honnête homme. Ne voyez-vous pas bien, dès qu'on en prend, de quelle manière obligeante on en use avec tout le monde, et comme on est ravi d'en donner à droit et à gauche, partout où l'on se trouve?"

This passage provides a clue to the whole play. It strikes, to be sure, a farcical note but the intention is serious. Molière is pointing the contrast between the claims of abstract thought, of "Philosophy," and the simple pleasure-life symbolized by "Tobacco." For he was not interested in the philosophical system on which the *libertins* based their outlook any more than he was interested in the particular doctrines on which the *dévots* founded their claims to interfere with other people's business or the theories of medicine which led doctors to behave in such a peculiar and dangerous manner. He was interested in the concrete and particular, in the attitude of mind and the conduct of those who took it upon themselves to upset the simple, tobacco-loving *honnêtes gens* or to bleed perfectly healthy people to death with their appalling *saignées*.

This attitude is maintained consistently throughout the play and frequently brings Molière to the edge of what M. Blanchot calls *les gouffres interdits*. Sganarelle's "defence" of religion is one of the best examples:

SGANARELLE:

Mon raisonnement est qu'il y a quelque chose d'admirable dans l'homme, quoi que vous puissiez dire, que tous les savants ne sauraient expliquer. Cela n'est-il pas merveilleux que me voilà ici, et que j'aie quelque chose dans la tête qui pense cent choses différentes en un moment et fait de mon corps tout ce qu'elle veut? Je veux frapper des mains, hausser le bras, lever les yeux au ciel, baisser la tête, remuer les pieds, aller à droit, à gauche, en avant, en arrière, tourner . . .

(Il se laisse tomber en tournant)

DOM JUAN:
  Bon! voilà ton raisonnement qui a le nez cassé.

This was one of the scenes which most scandalized the devout
in the seventeenth century as it no doubt elated the sceptics in the
nineteenth century. There are no real grounds for scandal or, apart
from its intrinsic funniness, for elation. Molière is not ridiculing
the simple soul whose outlook is deliberately contrasted with Dom
Juan's. He is tilting at *raisonnement*, at abstract thought as such, and
when we reach the end of the play we find that none of the fashionable systems has escaped without a "broken nose."

I think that we should add that every form of dogmatism, everything which could be called a "system," was fundamentally abhorrent to Molière because he saw that they all led to the fanaticism
and intolerance which he was always criticizing in his plays. In
Dom Juan the main onslaught appears to be directed against the
libertins, or what Lenin was contemptuously to describe much
later as "the bourgeois free-thinkers' movement"; but Arnolphe's
politique and Orgon's religious mania were both manifestations of
"philosophy" and hateful for the same reasons. They are the
"artificial restrictions . . . which stifle the growth of genuine vitality
and put the brake on his natural impatience." The attack in *Dom
Juan* is a twofold one because, as Stendhal pointed out, Don
Juanism can exist only in a society which is riddled with hypocrisy.
It is dislike of hypocrisy that explains one of Dom Juan's most
striking traits—a psychological need to outrage public opinion.
Molière would probably have been the first to admit that one of the
principal evils of hypocrisy was the fact that it drove the Natural
Man to abandon measure and proportion and to "stray to the edge
of the forbidden zone," to become a victim of the exaggerations
against which Molière himself was fighting.[1]

It must be emphasized, however, that Molière was primarily
concerned with states of mind, with the repressive impulses which
inspired the followers of "Philosophy" and regarded the particular
tenets of the warring sects as a matter of very minor importance.
These impulses are still with us and that is one of the reasons why
Molière's work has lost none of its vitality in the two and a half
centuries which have passed since it was written. If he had lived

[1] See Stendhal's interesting discussion of the play at the beginning of the
story called "Les Cenci" in *Chroniques et nouvelles*.

in the twentieth century, we can be sure that he would have been among the most ruthless and amusing critics of Marxism, Fascism and the other forms of political despotism which are so clearly at variance with *la parfaite raison* and such an intolerable nuisance to the pleasure-loving *honnête homme.* Whether he would have escaped as lightly as he did at the hands of the *dévots* is another matter.

2

In *Dom Juan* Molière abandoned the usual pattern; there are no *honnêtes hommes* to prod us in the ribs or pluck our sleeve when the author is about to speak; but it seems clear that we are intended to sympathize with at least four characters in whom Dom Juan's career arouses horror and disgust—Done Elvire, Dom Carlos, Dom Louis and "le Pauvre"—and they provide a more varied commentary than the usual spokesmen. They stand, broadly speaking, for the virtues of Faith, Hope, Charity, Chivalry and Simplicity which are outraged by Dom Juan.

Molière took his Dom Juan from legend and transformed him into a serious study which has little in common with the heroes of contemporary plays on the subject or with the Don Juan of the Romantic Movement. The result is a superb example of *durch-psychologisierung!*

Sganarelle provides a useful hint towards the interpretation of his character when he remarks in the opening scene:

"Mais un grand seigneur méchant homme est une terrible chose."

This comment is echoed by Dom Juan's father towards the end of the play when he says:

"Apprenez enfin qu'un gentilhomme qui vit mal est un monstre dans la nature, que la vertu est le premier titre de noblesse, que je regarde bien moins au nom qu'on signe qu'aux actions qu'on fait, et que je ferais plus d'état du fils d'un crocheteur qui serait honnête homme, que du fils d'un monarque qui vivrait comme vous."

Dom Juan's high estate is a factor of the greatest importance in the interpretation of his character. He is essentially an aristocrat, a member of the ruling class. It is his rank that gives him his immense power for evil-doing, for harming the simple people for whom Sganarelle speaks. Dom Louis' indictment follows the same lines, but he looks at his son from a different angle. There is genuine fear behind Sganarelle's "un grand seigneur méchant homme est une terrible chose"; but Dom Louis is primarily concerned with his son's abuse of his privileges. In his world privileges imply duties, but instead of setting a good example Dom Juan has outraged all the canons of this world and not least the code of chivalry by using his great position to do evil, has become in fact "un monstre dans la nature." When Dom Louis goes on to observe: "La vertu est le premier titre de noblesse" and "Je regarde bien moins au nom qu'on signe qu'aux actions qu'on fait," he is asserting standards of honesty and decency which Molière himself would have been the first to endorse, as he would assuredly have endorsed the primacy of "virtue" over "rank."

Earlier in the opening scene Sganarelle has observed to Gusman:

"Tu vois en Dom Juan, mon maître, le plus grand scélérat que la terre ait jamais porté, un enragé, un chien, un diable, un Turc, un hérétique, qui ne croit ni Ciel, ni Enfer, ni loup-garou, qui passe cette vie en véritable bête brute, un pourceau d'Épicure, un vrai Sardanapale, qui ferme l'oreille à toutes les remontrances qu'on lui peut faire et traite de billevesées tout ce que nous croyons. Tu me dis qu'il a épousé ta maîtresse: crois qu'il aurait plus fait pour sa passion, et qu'avec elle il aurait encore épousé toi, son chien et son chat. Un mariage ne lui coûte rien à contracter; il ne se sert point d'autres pièges pour attraper les belles, et c'est un épouseur à toutes mains. Dame, demoiselle, bourgeoise, paysanne, il ne trouve rien de trop chaud ni de trop froid pour lui; et si je te disais le nom de toutes celles qu'il a épousées en divers lieux, ce serait un chapitre à durer jusques au soir. Tu demeures surpris et changes de couleur à ce discours; ce n'est là qu'une ébauche du personnage, et, pour en achever le portrait, il faudrait bien d'autres coups de pinceau."

This is written with all Molière's incomparable comic verve, but the intention is serious. It is a portrait of Dom Juan as he appears to "the little man," but Sganarelle possesses a shrewd common sense. He sees very clearly that Dom Juan's amorous exploits and his unbelief are inseparable and are the key to his character. The main emphasis, however, properly falls on the distance between "him" and "us." "All that *we* hold with is just a lot of mumbo-jumbo to *him*. Thorough old ram too. Fair goes off his head at the sight of a skirt. Makes no difference whether it's a decent girl or a tart: they're all the same to him. A gent who goes on like that's a menace to the lot of us. We're none of us safe when he's around."

All this, adds Sganarelle, is only "une ébauche du personnage," and it is precisely the "bien d'autres coups de pinceau" that the rest of the play provides. Molière worked on a large canvas in *Dom Juan*. The unities of time and place were properly jettisoned to enable him to exhibit the principal character in all his complexity. The play is singularly rich in local colour, and outside Shakespeare it is difficult to think of anything comparable to the peasant scenes or some of the exchanges between Sganarelle and Dom Juan. It is rich, too, in incidents, but each incident—each *coup de pinceau*— is carefully selected to illustrate a particular trait of Dom Juan's character. It is only when we have studied his treatment of Elvire, the peasants, "le Pauvre," his tailor, his reactions to his father and to the Commander that we can be said to know the character, to have the finished portrait in front of us.

The scene in which Sganarelle appears disguised as a doctor shows how closely knit the play is. There is an extremely funny moment when he tries to excuse himself for hiding behind a bush when his master is attacked by remarking: "Je crois que cet habit est purgatif"; but it is not merely an attack on doctors. Its intention is to illustrate the completeness of Dom Juan's scepticism:

DOM JUAN:
Et quels remèdes encore leur as-tu ordonnés?
SGANARELLE:
Ma foi, monsieur, j'en ai pris par où j'en ai pu attraper; j'ai fait mes ordonnances à l'aventure, et ce serait une chose plaisante si les malades guérissaient et qu'on m'en vînt remercier.
DOM JUAN:
Et pourquoi non? Par quelle raison n'aurais-tu pas les mêmes privillèges qu'ont tous les autres médecins? Ils n'ont pas plus de part que toi aux guérisons des malades, et tout leur art est pure grimace. Ils ne font rien que recevoir la gloire des heureux succès, et tu peux profiter comme eux du bonheur du malade, et voir attribuer à tes remèdes tout ce qui peut venir des faveurs du hasard et des forces de la nature.
SGANARELLE:
Comment, monsieur! vous êtes aussi impie en médecine?

DOM JUAN:
C'est une des grandes erreurs qui soit parmi les hommes.

SGANARELLE:
Quoi! vous ne croyez pas au séné, ni à la casse, ni au vin émétique?

DOM JUAN:
Et pourquoi veux-tu que j'y croie?

SGANARELLE:
Vous avez l'âme bien mécréante. Cependant vous voyez depuis un temps que le vin émétique fait bruire ses fuseaux. Ses miracles ont converti les plus incrédules esprits, et il n'y a pas trois semaines que j'en ai vu, moi qui vous parle, un effet merveilleux.

DOM JUAN:
Et quel?

SGANARELLE:
Il y avait un homme qui depuis six jours était à l'agonie; on ne savait plus que lui ordonner, et tous les remèdes ne faisaient rien; on s'avisa à la fin de lui donner de l'émétique.

DOM JUAN:
Il réchappa, n'est-ce pas?

SGANARELLE:
Non, il mourut.

DOM JUAN:
L'effet est admirable.

SGANARELLE:
Comment! il y avait six jours entiers qu'il ne pouvait mourir, et cela le fit mourir tout d'un coup. Voulez-vous rien de plus efficace?

DOM JUAN:
Tu as raison.

Molière strikes a fresh note in this scene. There had been criticism of doctors in his earlier plays, but the seriousness behind this criticism is something new. I shall have more to say about this later; for the moment I merely wish to point out how carefully Molière's plays must be read in order to be sure that we have understood the tone and intention of a particular scene. Although Molière does not seem to me to identify himself with his principal character, Dom Juan is clearly the most intelligent character in the play and Molière does not scruple to use him as his mouthpiece when making his most radical criticisms of contemporary abuses.

Sganarelle is one of Molière's most remarkable creations and he is one of the key-figures in the play. He is to some extent a chorus commenting on the action, but he is also a symbolical figure who seems at times to represent poor erring humanity. He disapproves of many of his master's actions and though he is in the main too cowardly to stand up to him, he does criticize him openly on occasion. On such occasions he resembles the King's fool and enjoys the same sort of immunity. One of the things which most outraged the *dévots* was that Molière should have entrusted the defence of Christianity to a buffoon. Sganarelle is certainly no theologian; he thinks that belief in heaven and hell and in *le moine bourru* or *le vin émétique* is equally important; but from an artistic point of view, it is precisely his inadequacy as a theologian which gives his simple, muddled *raisonnement* the stamp of truth. The discussion on medicine quoted above leads logically to the discussion of religious belief. "What do you believe in?" asks Sganarelle later in the same scene.

DOM JUAN:

Je crois que deux et deux sont quatre, Sganarelle, et que quatre et quatre sont huit.

SGANARELLE:

La belle croyance et les beaux articles de foi que voilà! Votre religion, à ce que je vois, est donc l'arithmétique?

The laugh does not seem to me to be at the expense of religion, but of Dom Juan. For Sganarelle's method is the only one for dealing with this solemn, humourless profession of unbelief.

Dom Juan is the rootless intellectual aristocrat whose powers are bent on destruction. When he remarks:

"Quoi qu'il en soit, je ne puis refuser mon cœur à tout ce que je vois d'aimable; et, dès qu'un beau visage me le demande, si j'en avais dix mille, je les donnerais tous. Les inclinations naissantes, après tout, ont des charmes inexplicables, et tout le plaisir de l'amour est dans le changement"

—it sounds at first like a passage from an early work by M. André Gide, but this impression is misleading. Dom Juan is a *libertin* and he must be seen in his historical setting. M. Blanchot rightly describes him as "une image extrême de la rébellion et de l'anti-conformisme." The *libertins* mark a break with tradition. They inaugurate what M. Denis de Rougemont calls the "secularization of the myth."[1] Love is stripped of its glamour, ceases to be some-

[1] See pp. 165–70 below.

thing sacrosanct as it had been in the past and becomes a purely biological function. Dom Juan's feeling for women—it is this that makes him a representative *libertin*—is shorn of any emotional attraction and has far more in common with the *volupté* of the eighteenth century than with the *amour* of the seventeenth. He is really an eighteenth-century figure and the immediate ancestor of Casanova and Valmont.[1]

The destructiveness of Dom Juan's mind is apparent in the peasant scene:

"Jamais je n'ai vu deux personnes être si contents l'un de l'autre et faire éclater plus d'amour.... Oui, je ne pus souffrir d'abord, de les voir si bien ensemble; le dépit alarma mes désirs, et je me figurai un plaisir extrême à pouvoir troubler leur intelligence et rompre cet attachement dont la délicatesse de mon cœur se tenait offensée."

At the root of his corruption and his nihilism is intellectual pride. He is the eternal gambler who cannot bear to admit defeat. He is not really interested in the two peasant girls, but he cannot tolerate the thought that either of them should prefer another man to himself, any more than he could tolerate the idea that Done Elvire might prefer fidelity to her vows to marriage with him. He might have said of her life in the religious community as he says here of Charlotte and Pierrot:

"Je ne pus souffrir d'abord, de les voir si bien ensemble; le dépit alarma mes désirs."

It is a revealing phrase which tells us a lot about his psychology. His actions are not governed by the positive *désirs*, but by the negative *dépit*, the irritation caused by a happiness in which he has no part, by the thought that anyone can be happy without being dependent on him. This is strikingly illustrated by his encounter with "le Pauvre":

DOM JUAN:
Il ne se peut donc pas que tu ne sois bien à ton aise?
LE PAUVRE:
Hélas! monsieur, je suis dans la plus grande nécessité du monde.

[1] The new attitude was certainly fostered by the philosophical materialism implicit in Descartes' *Traité des passions de l'âme*.

DOM JUAN:

Tu te moques: un homme qui prie le Ciel tout le jour ne peut pas manquer d'être bien dans ses affaires.

LE PAUVRE:

Je vous assure, monsieur, que le plus souvent je n'ai pas un morceau de pain à mettre sous les dents.

DOM JUAN:

Voilà qui est étrange, et tu es bien mal reconnu de tes soins. Ah! ah! je m'en vais te donner un louis d'or tout à l'heure, pourvu que tu veuilles jurer.

LE PAUVRE:

Ah! monsieur, voudriez-vous que je commisse un tel péché?

DOM JUAN:

Tu n'as qu'à voir si tu veux gagner un louis d'or ou non. En voici un que je te donne, si tu jures. Tiens, il faut jurer.

LE PAUVRE:

Monsieur! . . .

DOM JUAN:

ᵛA moins de cela tu ne l'auras pas.

SGANARELLE:

Va, va, jure un peur, il n'y a pas de mal.

DOM JUAN:

Prends, le voilà; prends, te dis-je; mais jure donc.

LE PAUVRE:

Non, monsieur, j'aime mieux mourir de faim.

DOM JUAN:

Va, va, je te le donne pour l'amour de l'humanité.

The speech opens in a tone of raillery and Dom Juan pretends to be incredulous when he hears that anyone who spends his life in prayer is "dans la plus grande nécessité." He is prepared to relieve the Pauvre's material needs, but only at the price of upsetting the harmony of this life, this world from which he is excluded. The hermit's refusal to swear in order to win the *louis d'or* is incomprehensible to him. When he persists in his refusal, a note of perplexity and irritation creeps into Dom Juan's voice. The refusal is a challenge to his pride and he is faced with defeat through his failure to trouble this life. The firmness of the "Non, monsieur, j'aime mieux mourir de faim" shows him that he has met his match and to save his face he gives the money with the sardonic: "Va, va, je te le donne pour l'amour de l'humanité" and at once tries to retrieve his position by going to the rescue of Dom Carlos who has been attacked by bandits:

"Mais que vois-je là? Un homme attaqué par trois autres? La partie est trop inégale, et je ne dois pas souffrir cette lâcheté."

The accent falls on "*Je* ne dois pas souffrir." He will compensate himself by making someone far grander than "le Pauvre" dependent on him. It remains to add that Sganarelle's "Va, va, jure un peu, il n'y a pas de mal" reveals the touch of a master. It is weak and wayward humanity always ready to compromise principles in the interests of immediate necessity.

The encounter with the Statue is really the final stage in the revelation of Dom Juan's character. When the Statue nods, he is plainly disconcerted and says hurriedly:

"Allons, sortons d'ici."

Sganarelle emphasizes his discomfort:

"Voilà des mes esprits forts, qui ne veulent rien croire."

The words seem intended to reduce his master to the level of "certains petits impertinents . . . qui font les esprits forts parce qu'ils croient que cela leur sied bien."

Dom Juan has certainly been badly shaken and his irritation is evident from the next scene:

"Quoi qu'il en soit, laissons cela: c'est une bagatelle, et nous pouvons avoir été trompés par un faux jour, ou surpris de quelque vapeur qui nous ait troublé la vue."

When Sganarelle retorts:

"Eh! monsieur, ne cherchez point à démentir ce que nous avons vu des yeux que voilà."

Dom Juan loses his temper and threatens to beat him unless he drops the matter altogether.

Dom Juan's pride is the decisive factor in his downfall. The Statue has made a breach in his philosophy. As a thoroughgoing pragmatist he cannot deny the evidence of his senses, but his pride prevents him from admitting that what he has seen is proof of any supernatural intervention. He is certainly not lacking in physical courage, and in spite of the warnings of the Statue, of Done Elvire and the phantom, he simply persists in his refusal to repent and goes stoically down to damnation:

"Il y a bien quelque chose là-dedans que je ne comprends pas; mais, quoi que ce puisse être, cela n'est pas capable, ni de convaincre mon esprit, ni d'ébranler mon âme. . . ."

Molière's contemporaries were profoundly shocked by the final scene where fire comes down from heaven and the earth opens and swallows Dom Juan. They said that the clumsy stage properties made this representation of the Divine wrath ridiculous and unseemly and were, indeed, intended to do so. This criticism seems to me to reveal a complete misunderstanding of Molière's purpose. The number of different spokesmen that he used enabled him to show Dom Juan's character in a constantly changing light, but the general effect depends very largely on the contrast between the haughty, disdainful aristocrat and the delightful and ridiculous Sganarelle. *The last episode is seen through Sganarelle's eyes.* For him the annihilation of the arrogant Dom Juan is at once bewildering, terrifying and comic, and his final words: "Mes gages, mes gages, mes gages," which had to be omitted from seventeenth-century productions, strike exactly the right note. It is not, as contemporary critics alleged, impious farce, but a very serious and sombre farce.

V. *LE MISANTHROPE*

1

Le Misanthrope is by common consent the greatest of Molière's plays, but attempts to discover the nature of its peculiar excellence have sometimes led critics into unprofitable paths. The Romantic critics found in it the main support for their theory of "the tragic Molière"; Ramon Fernandez, the stern champion of "philosophical criticism," has spoken of "cette comédie où le principe même de la comédie est mis en péril"[1]; and a German writer has used it to

---

[1] *op. cit.*, p. 189.

propound a theory of "the diabolical element in great comedy."[1]
These theories have one factor in common. They suggest that the
Misanthrope is in some way "deeper," more "profound," more
"serious" than Molière's other works, overlooking perhaps the
fact that comedy is essentially a serious activity.[2] Compare it with
Tartuffe and the dangers of such a criterion are at once apparent.
It is not difficult to see in what sense the *Misanthrope* and *Tartuffe*
are more "serious" than *les Femmes savantes* or *l'Avare*, but we
should be on very uncertain ground in claiming that the *Misanthrope* is more serious than *Tartuffe*. Indeed, it would be less difficult
to prove the contrary. *Tartuffe* has obvious affinities with primitive
comedy. The most striking of them is the sacrificial element.
Tartuffe is the scapegoat whose chastisement provides a release
for the audience's primitive desires and emotions, and Molière
knew very well what he was about when he underlined the sexual
propensities of his victim. The play appeals to some of the deepest,
though not the most admirable, of human instincts, and it has a
ferocity which is unparalleled in Molière's work. "My opinion of
Tartuffe," wrote Baudelaire in his diary, "is that it is not a comedy,
but a pamphlet." This is an over-statement, but it helps us to understand the limitations of that masterpiece and the superiority of the
Misanthrope.

The *Misanthrope* in the seventeenth century was the connois-
seur's play and a contemporary described it with felicity as "une
pièce qui fait rire dans l'âme." Its pre-eminence lies not in greater
depth or profundity, but in a greater variety of tone, a wider social
reference, more complex and more delicate shades of feeling. It is
one of the most personal of Molière's plays. *Tartuffe* was a magnificent onslaught on a narrow, vindictive puritanism which had all
but succeeded in driving comedy from the stage. The *Misanthrope*
was written during a personal crisis and is certainly coloured by

---

[1] Curt Sigmar Gutkind in *Molière und das Komische Drama* (Halle, 1928).
It is only fair to add that the point is not unduly stressed and that the chapter
on the *Misanthrope* seems to me to be the best study of the play that I have
come across in any language.

[2] How little this has been understood in France, where the distinction
between tragedy and comedy is much more definite than in England, can be
seen from Brunetière's "*Le Misanthrope* and *Tartuffe* are already middle-class
tragedies which Molière tried in vain to fit into the framework of comedy."
("Les Époques de la Comédie de Molière" in *Études critiques sur l'histoire
de la littérature française*, VIII, 3ième éd., Paris, 1922, pp. 116–17.)

Molière's own domestic difficulties. We must be careful not to read too much into the play, but those critics who have found its laughter "sad" are on the right track; there is no doubt that personal suffering helped to give Molière the astonishing insight into the human heart which he displays in the *Misanthrope* and which contributes to its richness and maturity.[1]

2

"He did not set out to write a comedy full of incidents," said Visé in a commentary which is believed to have been published with Molière's approval, "but simply a play in which he could speak against the manners of the age."

There is one striking difference between the *Misanthrope* and Molière's other plays. He does not confine himself to the study of the psychology of an individual seen against the background of a stable society. His irony is turned on society as well as on Alceste, and the play ends, as we shall see, not with the restoration of order, but with something that is very like a mark of interrogation.

The theme is presented by means of a triple conflict—the conflict between Alceste and social convention, Alceste and justice, Alceste and Célimène. It is the constant shifting of the focus from one to the other and the way in which Molière plays on our divided sympathies that give the *Misanthrope* its variety, so that it calls for a greater effort of attention from the reader than any of the other comedies.

Mr. L. C. Knights has suggested that a close examination of the tone and intention of each line in the first scene is the best way of discovering how the play as a whole should be read.[2] The opening scene is so carefully constructed and the theme stated with such clarity and force that almost everything which follows is a development of hints and suggestions contained in it.

PHILINTE:
    Qu'est-ce donc? Qu'avez-vous?
ALCESTE (*assis*):
                        Laissez-moi, je vous prie.

---

[1] When the play was originally produced, Alceste was played by Molière, Célimène by his wife, Éliante by his mistress and Arsinoé by Mlle du Parc who had repulsed his advances!

[2] In *Determinations*, London, 1934, p. 118.

PHILINTE:
> Mais encor, dites-moi, quelle bizarrerie . . .

ALCESTE:
> Laissez-moi là, vous dis-je, et courez vous cacher.

PHILINTE:
> Mais on entend les gens, au moins, sans se fâcher.

ALCESTE:
> Moi, je veux me fâcher, et ne veux point entendre.

PHILINTE:
> Dans vos brusques chagrins je ne puis vous comprendre,
> Et, quoique amis, enfin, je suis tout des premiers . . .

ALCESTE (se levant brusquement):
> Moi, votre ami? Rayez cela de vos papiers.
> J'ai fait jusques ici profession de l'être;
> Mais après ce qu'en vous je viens de voir paraître,
> Je vous déclare net que je ne le suis plus,
> Et ne veux nulle place en des cœurs corrompus.

The play opens as usual on a note which sounds uncommonly like farce, but the intention is serious. There is something wrong with Alceste and most of the play is devoted to discovering what it is. It makes his behaviour so unreasonable that he becomes incomprehensible to the tolerant and reasonable Philinte. The violent tone is characteristic of Alceste and an understanding of it leads to an understanding of the *motifs* behind it. The *cacher* and the *brusques chagrins* are important clues—the unobtrusive stage direction, *se levant brusquement*, illustrates the close connection between word and gesture in Molière—and their recurrence in the play emphasizes the closeness of its texture.

The dialogue that follows explains the origin of Alceste's *chagrin*, but before examining it in detail, I wish to jump eighty lines and look at the next use of the word:

ALCESTE:
> Mes yeux sont trop blessés, et la cour et la ville
> Ne m'offrent rien qu'objets à m'échauffer la bile;
> J'entre en une humeur noire, en un chagrin profond,
> Quand je vois vivre entre eux les hommes comme ils font . . .

PHILINTE:
> Ce chagrin philosophe est un peu trop sauvage.
> Je ris des noirs accès où je vous envisage . . .

It is clear that for Alceste the *humeur noire* and the *chagrin profond* are a matter of deadly seriousness, but it is also clear from the change of tone and the ironical *chagrin philosophe* that they have a different value for Philinte, for the ordinary, reasonable man. It is characteristic of the peculiar ambiguity of the play, and of Philinte's place in it, that we feel doubtful at this point whether the *chagrin* is or is not a laughing matter. There is still room for doubt when he goes on four lines later:

> Non, tout de bon, quittez toutes ces incartades.
> Le monde par vos soins ne se changera pas;
> Et puisque la franchise a pour vous tant d'appas,
> Je vous dirai tout franc que cette maladie,
> Partout où vous allez, donne la comédie . . .

Philinte drops the tone of easy banter and proceeds to give a serious warning. The *chagrin* is now described as *cette maladie* and we are meant to take the word at its face value, but it is still a *maladie* which in the eyes of the world *donne la comédie*. There is a conflict of values. The *chagrin* has a different significance for different individuals. The doubt lies in deciding what importance should be attached to the respective valuations of Alceste, Philinte and *le monde*. Are they all right or all wrong, or partly right and partly wrong?

This doubt is really the crux of the whole play, and it is interesting to glance at the use of this and similar words—the *désert* and the *endroit écarté*—in other contexts:

> 1. Têtebleu! ce me sont de mortelles blessures
>   De voir qu'avec le vice on garde des mesures;
>   Et parfois il me prend des mouvements soudains
>   De fuir dans un *désert* l'approche des humains.
>   (I. i.)
> 2. C'est que jamais, morbleu! les hommes n'ont raison,
>   Que *le chagrin contre eux* est toujours de saison . . .
>   (II. iv.)
> 3. Elle tâche à couvrir d'un faux voile de prude
>   Ce que chez elle on voit *d'affreuse solitude*.
>   (*Célimène of Arsinoé*, III. iii.)

4. Allez-vous en la voir, et me laissez enfin
   Dans ce petit coin sombre, avec *mon noir chagrin.*
   (v. i.)

5. Pourvu que votre cœur veuille donner les mains
   Au dessein que j'ai fait de fuir tous les humains,
   Et que dans mon *désert*, où j'ai fait vœu de vivre,
   Vous soyez, sans tarder, résolue à me suivre . . .
   (v. iv.)

6. Trahi de toutes parts, accablé d'injustices,
   Je vais sortir d'un *gouffre* où triomphent les vices,
   Et chercher sur la terre *un endroit écarté*,
   Où d'être homme d'honneur on ait la liberté.
   (v. iv.)

It is tempting but dangerous to compare Alceste's *chagrin* with Pascal's vision of *l'abîme*[1] or even with Baudelaire's *spleen*, because in doing so we run the risk of serious misinterpretation. Alceste is painfully conscious of his perplexity and frustration, but it is evident from these examples that his attitude is a *personal* one. It does not spring from a vision which transcends the deceptive appearances of everyday life. It is largely negative, is directed *contre* [*les hommes*]; and in the fourth example, where he caricatures himself, he seems for a moment to be aware that there is something a little absurd about his *chagrin*. There is a burlesque note, too, in the fifth and sixth examples. Alceste strikes a pose. He renounces the world and goes off to play at being a "man of honour" in the "desert." Now the "desert" is both objective and subjective, and it has certain affinities with Arsinoé's *affreuse solitude* which are suggested by a passage in M. Mauriac's interesting essay on the play:

"In a world where a decent man and a Christian has so many reasons if not for protest, at least for examining his own conscience, Alceste only attacks the most harmless practices, those 'lies' which do not take anyone in but which are necessary if social life is to go on at all. He is indignant over slanders which only affect people indirectly, which do not penetrate the hidden vices and merely provoke laughter. In a world where injustice is rife, where crime is everywhere, he is up in arms against trivialities. He feels no horror for what is really horrible—beginning with himself. All his attacks are directed to things outside himself; he

[1] See Sainte-Beuve's interesting, but to my mind misleading, discussion of Pascal and Molière in *Port-Royal*, III, pp. 201 *et seq.*

only compares himself with other people in order to demonstrate his own superiority."[1]

M. Mauriac's criticism of Alceste seems to me to be unduly severe and there is, perhaps, a tendency to simplify the issues; but it does illuminate one side of his character. A good deal of his *chagrin contre les hommes* springs from a psychological need to distract his attention from his own sense of frustration, from "what is horrible" in his own nature, and in this he is representative of the society that he is attacking. For all the characters on whom Molière turns his irony are in a greater or lesser degree aware of their own interior emptiness, of an *affreuse solitude* from which they are trying to escape. This explains their restless activity, their desperate preoccupation with gossip and *galanterie*. While the struggle to escape from themselves by losing themselves in the world of minor social events is one of the principal themes of the play, it must be emphasized that Molière's study of their vacancy and fatuity is not a tragic one. The *Misanthrope* is pre-eminently a comedy; it is not a *tragédie bourgeoise* in the manner of *l'Éducation sentimentale*.

3

It is time to turn to a consideration of the individual characters and their place in the pattern of the play, and to the sources of Alceste's *chagrin*. His first long speech is a denunciation of social convention:

> Je vous vois accabler un homme de caresses,
> Et témoigner pour lui les dernières tendresses;
> De protestations, d'offres et de serments
> Vous chargez la fureur de vos embrassements;
> Et quand je vous demande après quel est cet homme,
> A peine pouvez-vous dire comme il se nomme;

[1] *Journal*, II, Paris, 1937, pp. 147–8.
As a corrective to this, compare Stendhal's view of Alceste: "His mania for hurling himself against whatever appears odious, his gift for close and accurate reasoning and his extreme probity would soon have led him into politics or, what would have been much worse, to an objectionable and seditious philosophy. Célimène's salon would at once have been compromised and soon have become a desert. And what would a coquette find to do in a deserted salon?" (*Racine et Shakespeare*, II ed., P. Martino, Paris, 1925, p. 177.)

Votre chaleur pour lui tombe en vous séparant,
Et vous me le traitez, à moi, d'indifférent.
Morbleu! c'est une chose indigne, lâche, infâme,
De s'abaisser ainsi jusqu'à trahir son âme;
Et si par un malheur j'en avais fait autant,
Je m'irais, de regret, pendre tout à l'instant.

The tone of nervous exasperation, the taste for extremes, signified by *accabler, dernières tendresses, fureur de vos embrassements,* and the piled up adjectives rising to a crescendo—*indigne, lâche, infâme* —is peculiar to Alceste, and there is an obvious disproportion between the language used and the "most harmless practices" which he is attacking. He uses precisely the same tone in speaking of his lawsuit and his love affair:

Quoi! contre ma partie on voit tout à la fois
L'honneur, la probité, la pudeur, et les lois;
On publie en tous lieux l'équité de ma cause,
Sur la foi de mon droit mon âme se repose;
Cependant je me vois trompé par le succès:
J'ai pour moi la justice, et je perds mon procès!
Un traître, dont on sait la scandaleuse histoire,
Est sorti triomphant d'une fausseté noire!
Toute la bonne foi cède à sa trahison!
Il trouve, en m'égorgeant, moyen d'avoir raison!
Le poids de sa grimace, où brille l'artifice,
Renverse le bon droit et tourne la justice!

.   .   .

J'ai ce que sans mourir je ne puis concevoir;
Et le déchaînement de toute la nature
Ne m'accablerait pas comme cette aventure.
C'en est fait . . . Mon amour . . . Je ne saurais parler.

The uniformity of tone shows that he reacts in precisely the same way to three different situations, that he places the same valuation on his campaign against convention, his lawsuit and his love affair. There is certainly a connection between the three, but they are very far from being of the same importance. His cult of sincerity is a fetish. If his principles were adopted, social intercourse would come to an end, and it is perhaps because he is a threat to a brittle society that his attitude is unpopular. There is more to be

E

said for his other preoccupations. Philinte admits that he has a grievance over the unfortunate lawsuit, and Célimène confesses that she has treated him badly. But though they sympathize with him, they are at one in protesting against the violence of his denunciation and the extravagance of his remedies. "I agree with all you say," remarks Philinte,

> ... je tombe d'accord de tout ce qu'il vous plaît:
> Tout marche par cabale et par pur intérêt;
> Ce n'est plus que la ruse aujourd'hui qui l'emporte,
> Et les hommes devraient être faits d'autre sorte.
> *Mais est-ce une raison que leur peu d'équité*
> *Pour vouloir se tirer de leur société ?*[1]

In short, Alceste's attitude betrays a confusion of values, an extraordinary lack of discrimination, which alone would make him ludicrous. Minor mishaps are the pretext for wild generalizations about human nature; the perfidy of a shallow, frivolous society woman assumes the proportions of a universal catastrophe in his disordered imagination, and his denunciation peters out in a strangled cry:

> C'en est fait . . . Mon amour . . . Je ne saurais parler.

The more we study his pronouncements, the more evident it becomes that his attitude is the reverse of disinterested. When he declares:

> Je veux qu'on soit sincère, et qu'en homme d'honneur
> On ne lâche aucun mot qui ne parte du cœur

we may feel that though this is a counsel of perfection, it is not altogether unreasonable. A few lines later, however, his real objections to the insincere enthusiasm with which people greet one another emerge very clearly:

> Je refuse d'un cœur la vaste complaisance
> Qui ne fait de mérite aucune différence;
> Je veux qu'on me distingue, et, pour le trancher net,
> L'ami du genre humain n'est point du tout mon fait.

There is a strong element of vanity in his protests. He is determined that people shall be made to distinguish *him* from his fellows,

---

[1] Italics mine.

and the lines betray a sense of insecurity, a need of psychological affirmation. When Philinte suggests in the first scene that he should visit some of the judges who will try his suit, he refuses angrily:

> Non; j'ai résolu de n'en pas faire un pas.
> J'ai tort ou j'ai raison.

The second line is a curious illustration of the rigidity of Alceste's mind which prevents any compromise with society; but it is interesting for another reason. It has not always been understood by contemporary readers who have felt that his attitude is commendable and have compared it favourably with Célimène's assiduous "touting" in *her* lawsuit. Now it must be remembered that in the seventeenth century the practice of visiting one's judges was universal and was not regarded as being in any way improper. The explanation of Alceste's refusal is to be found in his reaction to Philinte's suggestion that he should appeal against the decision when he loses his case:

> Non; je veux m'y tenir.
> Quelque sensible tort qu'un tel arrêt me fasse,
> Je me garderai bien de vouloir qu'on le casse:
> On y voit trop à plein le bon droit maltraité,
> Et je veux qu'il demeure à la postérité
> Comme une marque insigne, un fameux témoignage
> De la méchanceté des hommes de notre âge.
> Ce sont vingt mille francs qu'il m'en pourra coûter;
> Mais pour vingt mille francs j'aurai droit de pester
> Contre l'iniquité de la nature humaine,
> Et de nourrir pour elle une immortelle haine.

These are not the words of a fighter or a reformer. Alceste is convinced that there has been a miscarriage of justice; but instead of trying to set it right, he is delighted at the loss of his suit because he feels that it gives him a *right* to fulminate against human nature, and this right seems cheap at twenty thousand francs. This is characteristic of his general behaviour. He is always on the lookout for some abuse that he can attack or someone with whom he can pick a quarrel, and the slightest excuse is sufficient to set the machinery of excited denunciation in motion. "Quoi!" cries the horrified Philinte,

Quoi! vous iriez dire à la vieille Émilie
Qu'à son âge il sied mal de faire la jolie,
Et que le blanc qu'elle a scandalise chacun?

ALCESTE:
Sans doute.

PHILINTE:
A Dorilas, qu'il est trop importun,
Et qu'il n'est, à la cour, oreille qu'il ne lasse
A conter sa bravoure et l'éclat de sa race?

ALCESTE:
Fort bien.

This suggests that his attitude is to a certain extent *voulu*. While it is true that denunciation is a form of self-indulgence, a substitute for *action*, this does not exhaust the question. It is noticeable that in most of the plays the *honnête homme* treats this heated denunciation as the danger point. It is the point at which the normative influence of society ceases to be effective and the comic character's hysterical mood may well lead to some desperate act. It is for this reason that Philinte's warnings are nearly always directed against Alceste's *tone* and not against what he says. Now Alceste's violence deserves a closer examination than it has perhaps received. In some of the lines lifted from *Dom Garcie de Navarre* Alceste denounces Célimène's perfidy:

Que toutes les horreurs dont une âme est capable
A vos déloyautés n'ont rien de comparable;
Que le sort, les démons, et le Ciel en courroux
N'ont jamais rien produit de si méchant que vous.

Again:

Je ne suis plus à moi, je suis tout à la rage:
Percé du coup mortel dont vous m'assassinez,
Mes sens par la raison ne sont plus gouvernés,
Je cède aux mouvements d'une juste colère. . . .

At such moments we have the illusion that we are listening to a Cornelian *tirade*, but it is an illusion. Alceste is not, even at these moments, a tragic figure. His denunciation, though undeniably serious, belongs peculiarly to comedy, and there is an interesting passage at the beginning of the play which helps us to appreciate why this is so:

Non, je ne puis souffrir cette lâche méthode
Qu'affectent la plupart de vos gens à la mode;
Et je ne hais rien tant que les contorsions
De tous ces grands faiseurs de protestations,
Ces affables donneurs d'embrassades frivoles,
Ces obligeants diseurs d'inutiles paroles,
Qui de civilités avec tous font combat,
Et traitent du même air l'honnête homme et le fat.

What is striking about these lines is a curious air of unreality, the sense that we are watching a Punch-and-Judy show. This is no accident. The violence and the jerkiness have a different function here. The focal word is *contorsions* and it colours the rest of the passage. The element of caricature is deliberate. This is not abstract denunciation of real people; it is society as it appears to Alceste. We feel ourselves looking at it through his eyes and seeing a world of grinning, gesticulating marionnettes, going through their grotesque performance as some unseen showman pulls the strings. For Alceste's violence leads to a state of hysteria—Molière's word for it is *emportement*—in which the actual world is transformed into a comic nightmare, reminding us a little oddly of a Disney cartoon. The nightmare is in Alceste's mind, and the contrast between his distorted outlook and unreasonable behaviour and the humdrum world in which he lives makes him at once a comic and a moving figure. Our response to this passage, and indeed to the whole play, is a balance between two impulses which superficially appear to exclude one another—the impulse to laugh at Alceste's absurdity and the impulse to pity the obvious waste of his gifts. The art of the comic writer depends on preserving this nice balance between two apparently contradictory emotions, on the continual switch from one set of feelings to another and back again without ever allowing the balance to tip over to the extremes of tragedy or farce. There are moments when he takes us to the brink of tragedy. George Dandin will go to the edge of the water and will stand there gazing at his own reflection, wondering whether to throw himself in or not; but in the end he will turn his back on it and return slowly homewards, will return to the cultivation of his farm and to the problem of finding a *modus vivendi* with his impossible wife—as Molière himself did. In the same way, Alceste reaches the point at which reason totters, but he too will retreat into the world of words and harmless denunciation. It is not the least of the dramatist's achievements that he establishes this feeling of confidence in his audience and convinces us that it will be so.

It is the failure to understand this that has led to many of the attempts to turn the *Misanthrope* into a tragedy. Fernandez, for example, has suggested that in the course of the play Alceste's character undergoes a radical change and that the man who departs for the "desert" as the curtain falls is no longer the same man as the fiery reformer of Act I. The change is supposed to lie in the collapse of the will. It is an entertaining theory, but I can find no evidence for it in the text of the play. It is true that Alceste is always using expressions of great determination—"Je veux qu'on me distingue," "Je veux m'y tenir"—but, as I have already suggested, there is no real volition behind the words which are a sort of smoke screen used to hide a complete absence of determination. The Alceste of Act v is identical with the Alceste of Act I. His *physical* exile is the logical outcome of the *psychological* exile—the retreat into a private world—which is studied with such profound insight in the course of the play.

I stress this point because Fernandez' theory seems to me to rest on a misunderstanding of Molière's method of presentation in this play. Alceste is constructed partly by direct statement and partly by his action on other characters. Certain essential traits are presented in the opening scene and driven home by deliberate repetition all through the play. Once he has sketched the outlines, Molière proceeds to fill in the details. A series of impressions of Alceste as he appears to other characters is superimposed one on another. These impressions add to our knowledge both of Alceste and of the other characters. They are not always in agreement and sometimes, as we shall see, they qualify or contradict one another. This is a point of considerable importance and it is one of the things that force the reader to follow the dialogue with such minute care, to decide what weight must be attributed to the constant shift and change of tone.

This brings us to a consideration of Philinte's role in the play. In one of the central passages he declares:

> Il faut, parmi le monde, une vertu traitable;
> A force de sagesse on peut être blâmable;

La parfaite raison fuit toute extrémité,
Et veut que l'on soit sage avec sobriété.
Cette grande roideur des vertus des vieux âges
Heurte trop notre siècle et les communs usages;
Elle veut aux mortels trop de perfection:
Il faut fléchir au temps sans obstination,
Et c'est une folie à nulle autre seconde
De vouloir se mêler de corriger le monde.
J'observe, comme vous, cent choses tous les jours,
Qui pourraient mieux aller, prenant un autre cours;
Mais, quoi qu'à chaque pas je puisse voir paraître,
En courroux, comme vous, on ne me voit point être;
Je prends tout doucement les hommes comme ils sont,
J'accoutume mon âme à souffrir ce qu'ils font;
Et je crois qu'à la cour, de même qu'à la ville,
Mon flegme est philosophe autant que votre bile.

We recognize this passage, which recalls Cléante's plea for a devotion which is *humaine* and *traitable*, as the familiar statement of Molière's positives. It is also a good example of the patterned movement of his verse. It is not a mere catalogue of "the great abstractions." There are life and warmth in his *sagesse, parfaite raison* and *sobriété*. They have behind them centuries of European civilization which is vividly felt. The *roideur des vieux âges* underlines the peculiar and disabling rigidity of Alceste's outlook and, at the same time, reflects a delicate appreciation of the graciousness of contemporary civilization which exists in spite of human imperfection. The passage closes on a personal note; precept merges into practice and one becomes aware of the urbanity and good sense of the civilized man. Philinte's tone is intended to act as a foil to Alceste's, to moderate his transports. When Alceste cries

Et parfois il me prend des mouvements soudains
De fuir dans un désert l'approche des humains,

Philinte replies:

Mon Dieu, des mœurs du temps mettons-nous moins en peine,
Et faisons un peu grâce à la nature humaine.

The sharp *soudains-humains* creates a sense of physical constriction and the relief provided by *peine-humaine* is palpable. The *grâce* and the *douceur* prolong the process on the logical plane. It is not without significance, however, that Philinte's attempts to moderate Alceste's transports are seldom successful. The very gentleness of tone seems to heighten his exasperation, and he reserves some of his bitterest shafts for his friend. In these exchanges his tactics vary and he is decidedly *rusé*. When he retorts:

> Mais ce flegme, monsieur, qui raisonne si bien,
> Ce flegme pourra-t-il ne s'échauffer de rien?

raisonne is balanced against *s'échauffer*. He feels instinctively that *flegme* puts the brake on his *emportement* and he tries to discredit it by suggesting that it is an excuse for tolerating injustice. There is a curious eagerness to brush aside obstacles. The verse stumbles and almost comes to a halt over the repeated *flegme*, then moves breathlessly forward to the word *s'échauffer* which is sufficient to set the machinery of denunciation in motion.

"Je sais," he begins with icy politeness in another place,

> Je sais que vous parlez, monsieur, le mieux du monde;
> En beaux raisonnements vous abondez toujours;
> Mais vous perdez le temps et tous vos beaux discours.
> La raison, pour mon bien, veut que je me retire:
> Je n'ai pas sur ma langue un assez grand empire;
> De ce que je dirais je ne répondrais pas,
> Et je me jetterais cent choses sur les bras.

In order to keep up the appearance of rational behaviour, he pretends that his proposal to retire to the desert is a reasoned one, but there is a world of difference between the *beaux raisonnements* attributed to Philinte and Alceste's *raison*. "Reason" ceases to be universal and becomes a private and very misleading label that he attaches to the demon which is driving him into the desert. The last three lines are double-edged. It is because he is unreasonable and not because society is unreasonable that he is likely to find himself in trouble if he remains where he is.

I have already spoken of the peculiar ambiguity of the play and of Philinte's place in it. In the *Misanthrope* there is a skilful modification of the pattern of Molière's comedies which becomes more subtle and more varied. Although Philinte is certainly Molière's spokesman in many places and certainly helps to provide the background of reason and sanity which contributes largely to the poise of the play, his role is a shifting one. We do not feel, as we do with Cléante, that the whole of the play is behind his words, and the explanation is to be found in Éliante's observations on Alceste in Act IV. Sc. i:

> Dans ses façons d'agir il est fort singulier;
> Mais j'en fais, je l'avoue, un cas particulier,
> Et la sincérité dont son âme se pique
> A quelque chose en soi de noble et d'héroïque.
> C'est une vertu rare au siècle d'aujourd'hui,
> Et je la voudrais voir partout comme chez lui.

Éliante is the only wholly sympathetic character in the play. It would not be accurate to say that she represents Molière's own point of view more completely than Philinte, but her role is of the first importance. In the *Misanthrope*, as in *Tartuffe*, Molière felt the need of two spokesmen; but the function of Éliante and Philinte goes beyond that of Dorine and Cléante. Dorine and Cléante complete one another, but Éliante qualifies the role of Philinte and it is this that gives the play a mellowness which is unique in Molière's work. For Éliante's words display a fresh attitude towards the comic hero. Arnolphe, Harpagon and Orgon (in spite of his conversion to a *dévotion traitable*) are and remain completely unsympathetic; but Alceste awakens the sympathies of the audience to a degree which is exceptional in seventeenth-century and indeed in all comedy.

Éliante minimizes Alceste's peculiarities and by placing the emphasis on his "rare virtue" she corrects Philinte. Alceste is not a buffoon in the same sense as Molière's other comic characters. There is always a foundation of good sense behind his criticisms and, in spite of their exaggeration, this is true of his attacks on convention. In the scene where Oronte's sonnet is criticized, which is significantly placed immediately after the exposition of the principal theme of the play in Scene i, his good taste and sound judgment obviously compare favourably with Philinte's flattery.[1] There is a less obvious but more impressive example towards the

---

[1] For a more orthodox interpretation of Philinte's role and of this scene, see Michaut's chapter on the play in *les Luttes de Molière* (Paris, 1925). Although I do not feel able to accept this interpretation, I should like to commend Michaut's writings on Molière which are the best kind of literary scholarship and are of inestimable value to the literary critic.

E*

end of the play when, after commiserating with Alceste on the loss of his lawsuit, Philinte proceeds to expound the virtues of his own philosophy:

> Tous ces défauts humains nous donnent dans la vie
> Des moyens d'exercer notre philosophie;
> C'est le plus bel emploi que trouve la vertu;
> Et si de probité tout était revêtu,
> Si tous les cœurs étaient francs, justes et dociles,
> La plupart des vertus nous seraient inutiles . . .

Philinte's logic may be unexceptionable, but is not the attitude that he is defending in danger of becoming abstract and unreal? Is there not a gap between life and thought, a gap which can only be closed by the more human and more generous approach of Éliante? Does not his attitude overlook the fact that the ordinary man is not a mere logician and that "the exercise of our philosophy" cannot impose order on the tangled feelings and desires which Molière perceived as clearly as Racine? The neat maxims which appealed so much to the reasonable seventeenth century are useless in solving the central problem of the play—the conflict between what Gutkind calls with true Teutonic violence "the pert, frivolous, fickle, coquettish young widow and Alceste, the heavy-blooded man who is eaten up by his passion and who is fighting for his love."[1]

The conclusion seems to me to be unmistakable. In this play Molière criticizes his own standards. The urbanity and moderation of the *honnête homme* are felt to be insufficient. When Éliante speaks of "quelque chose en soi de noble et d'héroïque," she is referring to the potentialities of Alceste's character; but these potentialities are prevented from realizing themselves by his lack of balance and his impatience of all restraint. His virtues are converted into negation, into the *haines vigoureuses* of one passage and the *immortelle haine* of another; his violence leads him away from the world of common experience into a world of private mania where, deprived of the normative influence of society, he thunders against wildly exaggerated abuses in the void. This makes him a comic figure, but it is the consciousness of his potential virtues and of his profound humanity which gives the play its peculiar resonance.

[1] *op. cit.*, p. 125.

4

The triple conflict represents the three points of contact between Alceste and society. The continual switching from one to the other and back again enables Molière to present both Alceste and society in a perpetually changing light until, as the play moves towards its climax, the three blend and give it its cumulative force. The direct conflict with convention underlines Alceste's absurdity and prevents comedy from turning into tragedy; the lawsuit redresses the balance and seems at times to justify his violence; the affair with Célimène is the richest and most serious of all and in a way contains them both. Alceste's rage over convention and his lawsuit is the point at which he separates himself from his fellow men and his love affair is the point at which he rejoins them. It stands for normality; it is the side of his character by which (in Mauriac's words) "il nous devient fraternel." "Je m'étonne, pour moi," remarks Philinte:

> Je m'étonne, pour moi, qu'étant, comme il le semble,
> Vous et le genre humain si fort brouillés ensemble,
> Malgré tout ce qui peut vous le rendre odieux,
> Vous ayez pris chez lui ce qui charme vos yeux;
> Et ce qui me surprend encore davantage,
> C'est cet étrange choix où votre cœur s'engage.
> La sincère Éliante a du penchant pour vous,
> La prude Arsinoé vous voit d'un œil fort doux:
> Cependant à leurs vœux votre âme se refuse,
> Tandis qu'en ses liens Célimène l'amuse,
> De qui l'humeur coquette et l'esprit médisant
> Semble si fort donner dans les mœurs d'à présent.

Alceste replies at once, with his curious mixture of arrogance and perspicacity, that he has no illusions about the shortcomings of Célimène:

> Non, l'amour que j'ai pour cette jeune veuve
> Ne ferme point mes yeux aux défauts qu'on lui treuve,
> Et je suis, quelque ardeur qu'elle m'ait pu donner,
> Le premier à les voir, comme à les condamner.
> Mais, avec tout cela, quoi que je puisse faire,
> Je confesse mon faible, elle a l'art de me plaire;

> J'ai beau voir ses défauts, et j'ai beau l'en blâmer,
> En dépit qu'on en ait, elle se fait aimer;
> Sa grâce est la plus forte, et sans doute ma flamme
> De ces vices du temps pourra purger son âme.

Célimène's importance is twofold. She is the complete representative of the society that Alceste and through him Molière is attacking. When some of her retainers tell Alceste that he should blame her and not them for the spiteful remarks that she is making about acquaintances and friends, he retorts acutely:

> Non, morbleu! c'est à vous; et vos ris complaisants
> Tirent de son esprit tous ces traits médisants.

Part of his problem is to "convert" Célimène, to carry her away from the vicious circle in which she lives; but the problem remains unsolved because of Alceste's eccentricity, because he can only convert her by transporting her into his own world, by carrying her off with him into the "desert" to which he eventually retires. What distinguishes him from Molière's other characters is an extraordinary insight into his own feelings. There are moments when he suddenly forgets his grievances against society, drops the tone of violent denunciation and sees himself as he really is—not a reformer, but a man sadly perplexed by his passion for a woman who is unworthy of him. It is at such moments that we become aware of his immense superiority over the brittle society that is trying to laugh him out of criticisms which are felt to be a threat to it:

PHILINTE:
> Pour moi, si je n'avais qu'à former des désirs,
> La cousine Éliante aurait tous mes soupirs.
> Son cœur, qui vous estime, est solide et sincère,
> Et ce choix plus conforme était mieux votre affaire.

ALCESTE:
> Il est vrai: ma raison me le dit chaque jour;
> Mais la raison n'est pas ce qui règle l'amour.

In the last two lines *raison* is used in its normal sense, which is not the sense of

> La raison, pour mon bien, veut que je me retire.

Célimène stands for the tangled feelings and desires which, as I have already suggested, the seventeenth century tried in vain to enclose in its neat formulas. It is at this point that the "systems" of both Alceste and Philinte break down. The obstinate fanaticism of the one and the philosophical maxims of the other are alike impotent to solve the problems of life. For in this play Molière explores regions in which conventional formulas have no validity, and the insight with which he does so gives the *Misanthrope* its exceptional place in French comedy. Nor must we overlook the irony of *solide et sincère* which is echoed later in the play by Alceste's

> Enfin, quoi qu'il en soit, et sur quoi qu'on se fonde,
> Vous trouvez des raisons pour souffrir tout le monde.

Alceste, Célimène and Éliante form a triangle. Alceste places himself at a point outside society; Célimène is entirely absorbed in it; Éliante occupies an intermediate position. She is of society, but is wholly uncontaminated by it. *Alceste's contact with the world of common experience is seen to be intermittent.* He is continually rebounding from its polished surface into the world of his private mania. The victory of either Alceste or Célimène in the tug-of-war would fail to solve the problem. For Alceste the only solution, the only way back to the norm of sanity and common sense, lies in marriage with Éliante and he refuses it. This is true of nearly all the characters in their different ways. They are all looking for something *solide et sincère*, for some philosophy on which to base their lives, but they meet with disappointment at every turn. Custom, justice and love prove equally hollow and unreal and they suddenly find themselves face to face with the void.

A large part of the play is thus taken up with the tug-of-war between Alceste and Célimène as each tries to draw the other into his or her own sphere. Célimène is shallow and frivolous but she too is dimly conscious of her shortcomings, and it is only because she is not beyond redemption that she provides Alceste with an adequate foil. From time to time the glitter and polish of the exchanges between them are disturbed by a deeper note:

ALCESTE:
> Mais moi, que vous blâmez de trop de jalousie,
> Qu'ai-je de plus qu'eux tous, madame, je vous prie?

CÉLIMÈNE:
> Le bonheur de savoir que vous êtes aimé.

This note only occurs at rare intervals. Célimène's normal tone bears a marked similarity to Philinte's. She answers Alceste's over-wrought declarations either in a mood of light banter or with mild surprise which lowers the tension:

ALCESTE:
> Morbleu! faut-il que je vous aime!
> Ah! que si de vos mains je rattrape mon cœur,
> Je bénirai le Ciel de ce rare bonheur!
> Je ne le cèle pas, je fais tout mon possible
> A rompre de ce cœur l'attachement terrible;
> Mais mes plus grands efforts n'ont rien fait jusqu'ici
> Et c'est pour mes péchés que je vous aime ainsi.

CÉLIMÈNE:
> Il est vrai, votre ardeur est pour moi sans seconde.

ALCESTE:
> Oui, je puis là-dessus défier tout le monde.
> Mon amour ne se peut concevoir, et jamais
> Personne n'a, madame, aimé comme je fais.

CÉLIMÈNE:
> En effet, la méthode en est toute nouvelle,
> Car vous aimez les gens pour leur faire querelle;
> Ce n'est qu'en mots fâcheux qu'éclate votre ardeur,
> Et l'on n'a jamais vu un amour si grondeur.

ALCESTE:
> Mais il ne tient qu'à vous que son chagrin[1] ne passe.
> A tous nos démêlés coupons chemin, de grâce,
> Parlons à cœur ouvert, et voyons d'arrêter . . .

This illustrates very well the constant change of tone. Alceste begins in a mood of deadly seriousness. The turns and twists of the dialogue reflect the turns and twists of the trapped animal— "the heavy-blooded man who is eaten up by his passion and who is fighting for his love"—to escape the *attachement terrible*, and recalls ironically Philinte's

> Cependant à leurs vœux votre âme se refuse,
> Tandis qu'en ses liens Célimène l'*amuse*.

For Alceste's struggle is no laughing matter, and the gravity of Célimène's

> Il est vrai, votre ardeur est pour moi sans seconde

[1] This use of the word *chagrin* illustrates the way in which, as I have already said, Alceste's love affair "contains" the conflict with convention and justice.

shows that she is impressed in spite of herself, is faced with something which is outside her experience. But when Alceste continues in the same tone, her mood changes and she comments lightheartedly on the "new method" of making love. The reference to his notorious ill-humour not only lowers the tension of the scene, it brings Alceste back to his usual level—the comic figure who is at odds with society. The relief, however, is only momentary, and the scene closes with something that sounds like a cry for mercy. "Coupons chemin, de grâce"—Alceste's arrogance vanishes and he knows that he has been defeated in the encounter.

5

With Act II. Sc. ii the work of exposition is complete. The stage is cleared and Molière brings his batteries to bear on the procession of vain, empty, frivolous courtiers who have nothing better to do than engage Célimène in malicious chatter or attend some small function at Court.

ACASTE:
        A moins de voir Madame en être importunée,
        Rien ne m'appelle ailleurs toute la journée.
CLITANDRE:
        Moi, pourvu que je puisse être au petit couché,
        Je n'ai point d'autre affaire où je sois attaché.

It is noticeable that almost every word uttered by these people about their friends or in the bitter exchanges between themselves is double-edged. It returns like a boomerang to the speaker. Acaste remarks complacently:

        Parbleu! je ne vois pas, lorsque je m'examine,
        Où prendre aucun sujet d'avoir l'âme chagrine.

The implication is that the game of self-deception is so successful, that he is so shallow and empty, that he is incapable of perceiving his shortcomings or experiencing the torment which infects Alceste. This becomes clearer in the brilliant portrait of the fop which emerges innocently as the speech continues:

Pour le cœur, dont sur tout nous devons faire cas,
On sait, sans vanité, que je n'en manque pas,
Et l'on m'a vu pousser, dans le monde, une affaire
D'une assez vigoureuse et gaillarde manière.
Pour de l'esprit, j'en ai sans doute, et du bon goût
A juger sans étude et raisonner de tout,
A faire aux nouveautés, dont je suis idolâtre,
Figure de savant sur les bancs du théâtre,
Y décider en chef, et faire du fracas
A tous les beaux endroits qui méritent des Has.
Je suis assez adroit; j'ai bon air, bonne mine,
Les dents belles surtout, et la taille fort fine.
Quant à se mettre bien, je crois, sans me flatter,
Qu'on serait mal venu de me le disputer.
Je me vois dans l'estime autant qu'on y puisse être,
Fort aimé du beau sexe, et bien auprès du maître.
Je crois qu'avec cela, mon cher Marquis, je crois
Qu'on peut, par tout pays, être content de soi.

The small, flat words contrast with the solemnity of the performance. When he uses a word like *vigoureuse* the thin, mincing lilt of the line robs it of its power and gives it a grotesque air. When we come to the *juger sans étude*, there is a note of fatuity which is heightened by the eulogy of his teeth and his waist which are given the same importance as his skill as a critic. And with a final pirouette he turns to survey the admiring world of his peers. The brittle, artificial style reflects the poverty of experience of all these people.

One of the best demonstrations of the vigour and subtlety of Molière's style occurs in the great scene between Célimène and Arsinoé which is one of the high-lights of the play. Thus Célimène:

Oui, oui, franche grimace;
Dans l'âme elle est du monde, et ses soins tentent tout
Pour accrocher quelqu'un, sans en venir à bout.
Elle ne saurait voir qu'avec un œil d'envie
Les amants déclarés dont une autre est suivie;
Et son triste mérite, abandonné de tous,
Contre le siècle aveugle est toujours en courroux.
Elle tâche à couvrir d'un faux voile de prude
Ce que chez elle on voit d'affreuse solitude,
Et, pour sauver l'honneur de ses faibles appas,
Elle attache du crime au pouvoir qu'ils n'ont pas.

Cependant un amant plairait fort à la dame,
Et même pour Alceste elle a tendresse d'âme;
Ce qu'il me rend de soins outrage ses attraits,
Elle veut que ce soit un vol que je lui fais,
Et son jaloux dépit, qu'avec peine elle cache,
En tous endroits, sous main, contre moi se détache.

The more one studies Molière's style, the more impressed one is by its concrete particularity. It is possible to argue, as some critics have done, that his prose is superior to his verse and that the alexandrine was on occasion too rigid an instrument for his purpose. This may be true, but it can be seen in this play that the verse registers the changing expressions of his characters with remarkable vividness and that, without seeming to do so, the words do an immense amount of work. Words almost invariably issue in action and the actions of the characters mirror conflicting feelings. There was nothing absurd or discreditable about the *métier de prude* in the seventeenth century. A prude was simply an austere and rather puritanical woman; it was only later that the word acquired its present-day suggestion of affectation and insincerity. Molière's prudes, however, are all "false prudes" and they are used as negative symbols—as symbols of a hypocritical rejection of the life of the senses in which Molière himself believed so firmly. So it is here. *Grimace* sets the tone of the passage and it is sufficient to give us a picture of the stiff, puritanical old maid, trying to hide her lack of success behind a mask; but it is a *franche grimace*, a mask which hides nothing and simply draws attention to her hypocrisy. For in spirit she belongs to the world of Célimène and Acaste, accepts its values and does her best to "hook" or "angle" for a husband. We see the prude stretching out her hand furtively, but she misses the mark. She is left looking enviously at the procession of gallants who pass her by, without so much as a glance, in the train of some other beauty. She is the withered old maid—this is the cruel sense of *triste mérite*—completely abandoned in a world, in an age, in which favours are only too lightly distributed. The *faux voile de prude* reinforces the *franche grimace*, makes it more explicit, more pictorial. It is a veil which she puts between herself and the world, a veil which she uses vainly to cover the *affreuse solitude*, the terrible, consuming sexual frustration of the ageing spinster. But her deception extends further than that. It is used to conceal her intrigues and it is also a weapon which she uses to attack other women who are more successful than herself. The hand which is stretched out, pathetically, to "hook" a gallant is now stretched out to stab Célimène as a relief to her bitterness. The image of the "veil" is caught up and developed in the encounter between Célimène and Arsinoé which follows. Célimène is pretending to quote some unfavourable comments on Arsinoé's deportment which she has overheard in someone's drawing-room:

> A quoi bon, disaient-ils, cette mine modeste,
> Et ce sage dehors que dément tout le reste?
> Elle est à bien prier exacte au dernier point;
> Mais elle bat ses gens et ne les paye point.
> Dans tous les lieux dévots elle étale un grand zèle;
> Mais elle met du blanc et veut paraître belle.
> Elle fait des tableaux couvrir les nudités;
> Mais elle a de l'amour pour les réalités.

The procedure is the same as in the earlier passage. We see life going on simultaneously on different sides of a "veil," the contrast between the public and private life of a false prude. The *mine modeste* is the mask which hides, or is intended to hide, an interior disorder. She is exact in carrying out her religious duties; we see her sink to her knees and rise to her feet in church; but behind the locked doors of her house, the pious gestures merge into the savage rise and fall of the whip as she thrashes her servants. She gives alms, but has no money to pay her servants their just wages. She is the centre of attention at the cenacle where the pious meet, ostentatiously crossing herself; but in the fastness of her boudoir the pious gestures are replaced by the hand painting the face in a vain effort to repair its *triste mérite*. The last two lines are one of the glories of the play. The prude solemnly hangs a veil over some heavy classical painting of nude figures to hide them from a shocked world, but it is another subterfuge, another attempt to hide her own frustration. The *réalités* convey an extraordinary sense of hot, guilty intimacy, a morbid brooding over the intimate details of sexual relations, and the spiteful Célimène is only too conscious of the bitterness of the shaft.

I have dwelt on these passages not only because of their intrinsic merits, but also because the image of the "veil" and the "mask" explains the intention behind the play. It is to an even greater extent than *Tartuffe* a comedy of unmasking, but the unmasking is a game in which author and characters all take part. Alceste tries to abolish conventional politeness because he feels that it encourages insincerity and prevents him from seeing into the human heart. He attacks his opponent in the lawsuit because he is accepted at his face value and is able to secure an unjust decision:

> Au travers de son *masque* on voit à plein le traître;
> Partout il est connu pour tout ce qu'il peut être,
> Et ses roulements d'yeux et son ton radouci
> N'imposent qu'à des gens qui ne sont point d'ici.

In another place:

> . . . on devrait châtier sans pitié
> Ce commerce honteux de *semblants d'amitié*.

Célimène is busy stripping the mask from Arsinoé and from other members of her circle in order to reveal their hypocrisy and absurdity, but at the end of the encounter with Arsinoé she makes a far more damaging admission than she realizes:

> Madame, on peut, je crois, louer et blâmer tout,
> Et chacun a raison suivant l'âge ou le goût.
> Il est une saison pour la galanterie;
> Il en est une aussi propre à la pruderie.
> On peut, par politique, en prendre le parti,
> Quand de nos jeunes ans l'éclat est amorti:
> Cela sert à couvrir de fâcheuses disgrâces.
> Je ne dis pas qu'un jour je ne suive vos traces:
> L'âge amènera tout, et ce n'est pas le temps,
> Madame, comme on sait, d'être prude à vingt ans.

For here Molière himself takes a hand. The fragile prettiness of the verse reflects the fragile values by which Célimène lives. She accepts them absolutely and uncritically, and the future holds out little for her beyond Arsinoé's own fate.

The characters enter wholeheartedly into the game of unmasking which reaches its climax with the reading of Célimène's letter in the last Act; but as with Arsinoé they only do it as a distraction, as a means of "veiling" their own interior emptiness from themselves. Now the game is of the utmost seriousness when played by

Alceste and Célimène. They are doubtful about their feelings for one another. Alceste *thinks* that he is madly in love with Célimène, but the very violence of his protestations betrays an element of doubt. He is not at all sure that she loves him, and he sets to work to find out because it distracts him from his doubts about his own feelings. The play enters on its last phase when Arsinoé undertakes to prove to Alceste that Célimène is not in love with him:

> Oui, toute mon amie, elle est et je la nomme
> Indigne d'asservir le cœur d'un galant homme,
> Et le sien n'a pour vous que de feintes douceurs.

Alceste bridles at this:

> Cela se peut, madame: on ne voit pas les cœurs;
> Mais votre charité se serait bien passée
> De jeter dans le mien une telle pensée.

The "on ne voit pas les cœurs" is a defence mechanism: it describes exactly what Alceste wants to know and directs his attention uncomfortably back to his own doubts. The damage is done in spite of his protests:

> Non; mais sur ce sujet, quoi que l'on nous expose,
> Les doutes sont fâcheux plus que toute autre chose;
> Et je voudrais, pour moi, qu'on ne me fît savoir
> Que ce qu'avec clarté l'on peut me faire voir.

Arsinoé gleefully undertakes the job—on condition that he goes home with her:

> Là je vous ferai voir une preuve fidèle
> De l'infidélité du cœur de votre belle;
> Et si pour d'autres yeux le vôtre peut brûler,
> On pourra vous offrir de quoi vous consoler.

She is extremely successful in giving Célimène away, but not in replacing her. In the last two acts Molière rings the changes so rapidly, the feelings are so complex, that one is doubtful whether "comic," "moving" or "horrible" is the proper description of some of the scenes.

" The whole misfortune of Alceste," writes M. Mauriac, "of that Alceste who is in all of us, lies in a psychological need of the absolute that we bring to love which is the most relative of human feelings.

Alceste angrily brushes aside all false appearances; he is determined to advance on firm ground into this *pays du Tendre* which is essentially the home of fickleness and change; and it is precisely because it is the home of fickleness and change that it is the domain of Célimène."[1]

Alceste's

> Non; j'ai résolu de n'en pas faire un pas.
> J'ai tort ou j'ai raison,

of which I have already spoken, has its parallel in the story of his love affair. When he remarks

> Plus on aime quelqu'un, moins il faut qu'on le flatte:
> A ne rien pardonner le pur amour éclate,

his *pur amour* is the absolute love described by Mauriac, the absolute necessity of fixing his love in a formula and compelling the loved one to conform to it. It is here that he fails with Célimène. He feels that he is in the *domaine du mouvant*, that the ground is shifting under his feet, threatening to plunge him into chaos at any moment. When he discovers the letter to Oronte, he loses all control over himself; the whole universe rocks:

> . . . le déchaînement de toute la nature
> Ne m'accablerait pas comme cette aventure.

Éliante comes to the rescue with her moderate and reasonable

> Avez-vous, pour le croire, un juste fondement?

recalling the *solide et sincère* and the desperate hunt for a sound foundation of earlier scenes. This produces an extraordinary reaction in Alceste who suddenly sees in her a refuge against the devouring doubt. "You must avenge me, madame," he cries. "Avenge you, but how?"

> En recevant mon cœur.
> Acceptez-le, madame, au lieu de l'infidèle ;
> C'est par là que je puis prendre vengeance d'elle.

When we recall that Éliante is Alceste's one chance of salvation, we can appreciate the grimness of Molière's irony here.

It becomes clearer as the play draws towards its conclusion that

---

[1] *Journal*, II, pp. 151–2.

Célimène is a means to an end, that Alceste's chief preoccupation is deliverance from his own obsession, is a need to achieve a startling success to rehabilitate himself in the eyes of the world and to make himself feel that he is rooted in society:

> Ah! rien n'est comparable à mon amour extrême,
> Et, dans l'ardeur qu'il a de se montrer à tous,
> Il va jusqu'à former des souhaits contre vous.
> Oui, je voudrais qu'aucun ne vous trouvât aimable,
> Que vous fussiez réduite en un sort misérable,
> Que le Ciel, en naissant, ne vous eût donné rien,
> Que vous n'eussiez ni rang, ni naissance, ni bien,
> Afin que de mon cœur l'éclatant sacrifice
> Vous pût d'un pareil sort réparer l'injustice,
> Et que j'eusse la joie et la gloire, en ce jour,
> De vous voir tenir tout des mains de mon amour.

This shows to what extent Alceste lives in a private world, how impossible it is to prevent the "quelque chose en soi de noble et d'héroïque" from being swamped and destroyed by his eccentricities. For he is obliged to invent a situation, in which he can repair imaginary injustices by imaginary sacrifices, to convince himself not merely of the reality of his own feelings, but of his very existence.

While Alceste is hunting desperately to discover some sure foundation in the *domaine du mouvant*, Célimène is clinging no less tenaciously to her shifting, changing world. For her whole existence depends on maintaining a state of doubt—doubt about her own feelings, doubt in the minds of her retainers about her feelings for them. When Alceste and Oronte deliver their ultimatum— "Choose between us two"—it is she who assumes the role of a trapped animal, or perhaps of the trapped butterfly, struggling desperately to avoid a commitment:

> Mon Dieu! que cette instance est là hors de saison,
> Et que vous témoignez, tous deux, peu de raison!
> Je sais prendre parti sur cette préférence,
> Et ce n'est pas mon cœur maintenant qui balance:
> Il n'est point suspendu, sans doute, entre vous deux,
> Et rien n'est si tôt fait que le choix de nos vœux.
> Mais je souffre, à vrai dire, une gêne trop forte
> A prononcer en face un aveu de la sorte:

Je trouve que ces mots, qui sont désobligeants,
Ne se doivent point dire en présence des gens;
Qu'un cœur de son penchant donne assez de lumière,
Sans qu'on nous fasse aller jusqu'à rompre en visière;
Et qu'il suffit enfin que de plus doux témoins
Instruisent un amant du malheur de ses soins.

Finally, when she can no longer avoid making a choice, she
discovers that she does not love Alceste enough to follow him into
his desert, and his vanity is too great to allow of any compromise:

La solitude effraye une âme de vingt ans;
Je ne sens point la mienne assez grande, assez forte,
Pour me résoudre à prendre un dessein de la sorte . . .

6

I have already spoken of the differences between the *Misanthrope*
and Molière's other plays. When the curtain comes down on the
École des femmes, *Tartuffe*, *l'Avare* and *les Femmes savantes*, the
audience is left in no doubt about the author's intentions. It is able
to "determine . . . exactly what attitude is broken down and what
takes its place." In *Tartuffe* religious mania is satirized, a criminal
is brought to book and the play closes with the triumph of society.

The same cannot be said of the *Misanthrope*. Molière has richly
fulfilled his intention of speaking *contre les mœurs du siècle*; but
the doubt, which is an integral part of our experience, persists.
We are, perhaps, able to determine what attitude is broken down,
but it is less easy to decide what takes its place. It is idle to pretend
that order is re-established and that a chastened buffoon is brought
back to the norm of sanity. At the close of the play society, in the
persons of Célimène and her retainers, leaves by one exit and
Alceste abandons society by another, leaving an empty stage. The
line that echoes in the mind is not profession of belief, but a profession of complete disbelief, is not Philinte's

La parfaite raison fuit toute extrémité,

but Alceste's

Mais la raison n'est pas ce qui règle l'amour.

Indeed, so far from ending in another triumph for *la parfaite raison*, it is *la parfaite raison* which dissolves into Alceste's

Mes sens par la raison ne sont plus gouvernés.

Ramon Fernandez seems to put his finger on the point when, in the course of his stimulating but highly erratic study of Molière, he remarks that Molière lived in an age of intellectual scepticism. For when one considers the play as a whole, it is difficult not to feel that Molière had come to share Alceste's own scepticism. The *honnête homme* no doubt contributes to the poise of each of the plays in which he appears, but his urbane, polished discourses never succeed in converting anyone; and even in *Tartuffe* conversion is brought about by a sudden change of situation—the intervention of the "great Prince"—and not by Cléante. In the *Misanthrope*, more than in any of the other plays, the *honnête homme* is a symbolical figure and Molière is particularly careful to avoid the appearance of imposing a solution. The most that he does is to suggest that a blending of the virtues of Philinte and Éliante may have some bearing on the complicated situation which he has created. In no other play does he reveal such variety and complexity of feelings, but in no other does he show such reluctance to judge the individual or so marked a tendency to call in question all accepted standards and formulas. It is a masterly exploration of the motives behind social behaviour; feelings are tracked down, as surely as in Racine, to the moment of their formation; but judgment on them is suspended. There is in truth no formal ending to the play. The cartharsis lies in the clarifying of our feelings, in the perception that social adjustment is a personal matter where in the last resort no facile slogan or philosophical system can help us; and the "message," if we must have one, is that we must have the courage to create our own "order," whatever the cost, instead of yielding to the temptation of an easy escape.

VI. THE LAST PHASE

1

Le Misanthrope was produced in 1666, but though it was on the whole well received it was not the brilliant success that Molière had hoped. He seems to have divined the reasons and he was not slow to take the hint. He wrote fifteen plays after the *Misanthrope*, but though *George Dandin*, *l'Avare*, *le Bourgeois Gentilhomme*, *les Femmes savantes* and *le Malade imaginaire* are clearly the work of a master at the height of his powers and possess all Molière's wit and gaiety and his zest for demolishing middle-class complacency, there is for the most part an unmistakable change in the quality. He must have perceived that in the *Misanthrope* he had written something which was "above the heads" of many of his audience. In the last plays we have the impression that he is deliberately avoiding the depths which he had explored in *Tartuffe* and the *Misanthrope*, that he is keeping near the surface, and the introduction of a ballet into some of the plays seems to me to be the sign of a desire to please his audience and to ensure that his plays were a popular success.

George Dandin, which was produced in 1668, is one of the most curious of Molière's works. It is the story of a *déclassement*, of the decent, prosperous peasant who has married into a family which is socially above him. The sub-title of the play is "le Mari confondu," and though Molière exposes the snobbish pretentiousness of the urban middle classes with all his old skill, it is privilege which wins in the end. There is a bitterness and a depth of feeling beneath the brittle gaiety of the play which suggest that Molière drew heavily on his personal experience. Outwardly George Dandin bears very little resemblance to his creator, but it is worth noticing that he is a completely sympathetic figure and that the satirical quality which we find in the portraits of Arnolphe and Argan is absent. When he declares in the closing lines of the play:

"Ah! je la quitte maintenant, et je n'y vois plus de remède. Lorsqu'on a, comme moi, épousé une méchante femme, le meilleur parti qu'on puisse prendre, c'est de s'aller jeter dans l'eau la tête la première"

—it is the greyness of death and despair which suddenly, incongruously, breaks through into the comic world.

In the *Femmes savantes* Molière deals effectively with intellectual pretentiousness. Philaminte is a brilliant study of the *bas bleu*, of the woman who two hundred years later will develop into the nineteenth-century "progressive" and, later still, into the suffragette and the apostle of sex reform. The attack on the pedants is deadly, but it leaves us with the impression that Molière is, perhaps, playing down to his audience. In the exposure of the folly and conceit of Trissotin and Vadius we miss the assertion of positive standards that we find in the scene in the *Misanthrope* in which Alceste disposes of Oronte's sonnet and provides us with an excellent piece of literary criticism. It is only in the character of Armande, of which I have already spoken, that Molière forgets his resolution and lets himself go.

L'Avare, which had been produced four years earlier, leaves us with a similar impression. Harpagon is a monster, but Molière takes care to make him a comic monster, and the comment on his horses by one of the servants turns something which is potentially horrible into pure comedy:

"Vos chevaux, monsieur? Ma foi, ils ne sont point du tout en état de marcher. Je ne vous dirai point qu'ils sont sur la litière: les pauvres bêtes n'en ont point, et ce serait fort mal parler; mais vous leur faites observer des jeûnes si austères, que ce ne sont plus rien que des idées ou des fantômes, des façons de chevaux."

The high light of *l'Avare* is the great scene at the end of Act IV, where Harpagon discovers the loss of his money, which is one of the most impressive that Molière ever wrote:

HARPAGON (*Il crie "Au voleur!" dès le jardin, et vient sans chapeau*):
Au voleur! au voleur! à l'assassin! au meurtrier! Justice, juste Ciel! Je suis perdu, je suis assassiné, on m'a coupé la gorge, on m'a dérobé mon argent. Qui peut-ce être? Qu'est-il devenu? Où est-il? Où se cache-t-il? Que ferai-je pour le trouver? Où courir? Où ne pas courir? N'est-il point là? N'est-il point ici? Qui est-ce? Arrête. Rends-moi mon argent, coquin. . . . (*Il se prend lui-même le bras.*) Ah! c'est moi. Mon esprit est troublé, et j'ignore où je suis, qui je suis, et ce que je fais. Hélas! mon pauvre argent, mon pauvre argent, mon cher ami! on m'a privé de toi; et puisque tu m'es enlevé, j'ai

perdu mon support, ma consolation, ma joie; tout est fini pour moi, et je n'ai plus que faire au monde! Sans toi, il m'est impossible de vivre. C'en est fait, je n'en puis plus; je me meurs, je suis mort, je suis enterré. N'y a-t-il personne qui veuille me ressusciter, en me rendant mon cher argent, ou en m'apprenant qui l'a pris? Euh? que dites-vous? Ce n'est personne. Il faut, qui que ce soit qui ait fait le coup, qu'avec beaucoup de soin on ait épié l'heure; et l'on a choisi justement le temps que je parlais à mon traître de fils. Sortons. Je veux aller quérir la justice, et faire donner la question à toute ma maison: à servantes, à valets, à fils, à fille, et à moi aussi. Que de gens assemblés! Je ne jette mes regards sur personne qui ne me donne des soupçons, et tout me semble mon voleur. Eh! de quoi est-ce qu'on parle là? De celui qui m'a dérobé? Quel bruit fait-on là-haut? Est-ce mon voleur qui y est? De grâce, si l'on sait des nouvelles de mon voleur, je supplie que l'on m'en dise. N'est-il point caché là parmi vous? Ils me regardent tous, et se mettent à rire. Vous verrez qu'ils ont part, sans doute, au vol que l'on m'a fait. Allons vite, des commissaires, des archers, des prévôts, des juges, des gênes, des potences et des bourreaux. Je veux faire pendre tout le monde; et si je ne retrouve mon argent, je me pendrai moi-même après.

Harpagon's voice is heard before he appears on the stage, and the long-drawn-out vowel sounds of *Au voleur!* give the impression of a dirge. There is a sudden change to the short i's as he arrives on the stage, and the dirge becomes an hysterical scream. The conjunction of "on m'a coupé la gorge, on m'a dérobé mon argent" betrays a complete confusion of values and marks the point at which the real world changes into the world of the comic nightmare. The confusion of mind grows with "Où courir? Où ne pas courir?" The disintegration of language and the tendency of words to lose their rational meaning reflect the disintegration of the world of common experience in Harpagon's mind. The scene takes on a sinister, macabre aspect when he suddenly grasps his own arm, thinking that he has caught the thief—"Rends-moi mon argent, coquin." There follows one of those lucid moments which always come to Molière's great comic characters at the height of the *délire* and which intensify its effect: "Ah! c'est moi. Mon esprit est troublé." This moment, when the comic character suddenly sees himself from the standpoint of the normal person, is one of the clearest signs of Molière's genius. The glimpse is only momentary and the tone sinks to a senile, blubbering wail: "Hélas! mon pauvre argent, mon pauvre argent, mon cher ami, on m'a privé de toi. . . ." The money has clearly usurped the place of family and friends, and we recall that his cruelty to his children is one of the miser's most hateful traits. The seriousness of his condition is heightened by the fantasy of

"Je me meurs, je suis mort, je suis enterré. N'y a-t-il personne qui veuille me ressusciter, en me rendant mon cher argent . . ."

The irony lies in the fact that it is his money which is destroying him, eating up his life; its return can only enclose him more firmly in a private world, and this is what happens at the end of the play.

Harpagon is clearly the victim of persecution mania, and he imagines that he is surrounded by a vast number of people who are all guilty in some way of the theft of his money. He strikes the macabre note again when he proceeds to address the silent, motionless figures of the nightmare.

"Que de gens assemblés . . . De grâce, si l'on sait des nouvelles de mon voleur, je supplie que l'on m'en dise."

Suddenly the silent throng seems to come to life:

"Ils me regardent tous, et se mettent à rire"

—he imagines himself in the midst of a laughing, jeering crowd of thieves.

The passage reaches its climax in the immense exaggeration of:

"Allons vite, des commissaires, des archers, des prévôts, des juges, des gênes, des potences et des bourreaux. Je veux faire pendre tout le monde; et si je ne retrouve mon argent, je me pendrai moi-même après."

His private misfortune becomes a universal catastrophe. In his delirium, he assembles the shadow armies of justice to execute the phantoms that he imagines in front of him and proposes to commit suicide afterwards.

No one can doubt the impressiveness of this scene, but it knocks the rest of the play sideways.[1]

[1] It is well known that the play is an adaptation of Plautus's *Aulularia*, but Gutkind's comparison between this passage and the original on which it was based emphasizes the brilliance of the achievement. (V. *op. cit.*, p. 38.)

2

In 1665 Molière suffered a serious breakdown in health and placed himself under the care of M. de Mauvillain. He became more or less of an invalid, was shortly afterwards put permanently on a milk diet and was never really out of the doctors' hands until his death in 1673. It seems at first surprising that a writer who so consistently poked fun at doctors, who in *Dom Juan* had denounced their art as *pure grimace* and professed a belief in nature's power to bring about her own cures without the aid of medicine, should have entrusted himself to doctors at all and should have been on excellent terms with his own physician. The explanation is probably to be found in a scene of the *Malade imaginaire* where Béralde declares:

"Ce ne sont point les médecins qu'il [Molière] joue, mais le ridicule de la médecine."

It was the same argument that he had used when he was accused of attacking religion in *Tartuffe* and it seems to me to be equally convincing.

The outcome of Molière's illness was obvious. He was a man of wide culture and took a lively interest in every aspect of social life. It was only natural that his personal contact with doctors should have stimulated his interest in medicine, and that he should have introduced what was after all one of the "burning questions" of the day into his plays.

The doctor, in his tall pointed hat and long black cloak riding round on a mule to visit his patients, was one of the stock figures of seventeenth-century comedy which had inherited it from the Commedia dell' Arte. He makes his appearance in Molière's early plays, but he bears only a superficial resemblance to the doctors in *l'Amour médecin* and *le Malade imaginaire*. The doctor in *la Jalousie du barbouillé*, for example, is none other than the stage Pedant who was a perennial figure of fun in the old farces. It is his long pompous speeches with their endless Latin tags which make him funny; the fact that he is a doctor is a matter of secondary importance. It is far otherwise in the last plays where Molière treats the abuses of the profession with the same seriousness that he had treated other abuses in his earlier plays.

Medical science has advanced so rapidly since the seventeenth century that we are in danger of missing the implications of Molière's criticism and of mistaking his plays about doctors for good-humoured skits. They are far from being that. The conference of doctors in *l'Amour médecin* and the consultation in *le Malade imaginaire* are in no way burlesque. They erred if anything on the side of leniency. The state of the profession was something which is scarcely credible to us to-day. A gullible public was impressed by the elaborate ceremonial and the air of learning assumed by the profession, and treated the pronouncements of doctors with the same uncritical respect that we give to those of scientists in our own time. Their confidence, however, was rudely shaken by a series of scandals. In 1666 Paris had been profoundly shocked by a series of notorious bedside disputations at which eminent doctors had differed violently over the nature of the illness and its treatment while the unfortunate patients lay dying. Desfourgerais, one of the King's physicians, was openly accused by Bussy Rabutin of practising abortion. Guénot, another of them, who had a passion for antimony, was charged with having killed his wife, daughter, nephew, two sons-in-law and a host of other patients with his famous remedy. He attended Mazarin in his last illness, and it is reported that when he was caught in a traffic jam on his way home, a carter who recognized him shouted cheerfully to the assembled crowd: "Way, there, for his honour. It's the good doctor who killed the Cardinal." Still another of the royal physicians, Vallot, was a few years later publicly credited with the death of Queen Henrietta of England.

"Public opinion as to the value of medicine," wrote Palmer, "wavered between blind faith and nervous mockery. Louis XIV might laugh at a travesty of his physicians in ordinary, but he was obliged to entrust his life into their hands, and they got him at last. . . .

"Louis XIV was tortured and misused by a succession of doctors whose proceedings would have been incredible to posterity—had they not left a minute record of their grotesque proceedings. The curious may still read the *Journal de la Santé du Roi* in which Vallot, Daquin and Fagon in turn exhibit with a dreadful complacency the wonders of their science. It is clear from the *Journal* that the King, apart from the fact that he suffered from worms—a circumstance which made the royal appetite the wonder and envy of the realm—had a magnificent constitution, and could only with the greatest difficulty be reduced and kept by his doctors in the condition of a chronic invalid. He should never have needed a doctor, but he was seldom out of their hands. Finally, they contrived, by a course of purging, bleeding, blistering and sweating which would have killed any ordinary man in his prime, to remove him from the world in the seventy-second year of his reign with all his organs still sound as a bell but naturally a little fatigued from the constant 'refreshment'— it is the favourite word of Daquin—which had been lavished on them for over forty years. The royal dentists had by this time removed his teeth and perforated his palate so that he could no longer masticate or even taste his food. Nothing in the comedies of Molière concerning the doctors of the period exceeds the fantastical reality as disclosed in this professional record and in none of his attacks upon contemporary prejudices does he keep more strictly to the sober facts of the case."[1]

Such is the background of Molière's attack on the doctors. Although doctors appear frequently in the plays written after 1664 and *Dom Juan* and *l'Amour médecin* both contain some very pertinent criticisms of the profession, it is to his last play—*le Malade imaginaire*—that we must turn for the fullest and most searching examination of the place of medicine in society. M. Diafoirus and his appalling son are among the most brilliant of Molière's minor characters. The father boasts of his son's conservatism:

"... il s'attache aveuglément aux opinions de nos anciens ... jamais il n'a voulu comprendre ni écouter les raisons et les expériences des prétendues découvertes de notre siècle, touchant la circulation du sang et autres opinions de la même farine."

In the course of his incredibly gauche proposal of marriage to Argan's daughter, the son invites the company

"... à venir voir l'un de ces jours, pour vous divertir, la dissection d'une femme sur quoi je dois raisonner."

These comments are deadly, but in this play the focus shifts from the doctors to the patient. The play is, indeed, a remarkable illustration of the way in which Molière not only used, but also transmuted his personal experience in his work. It is, as Palmer

---

[1] *op. cit.*, pp. 350-1. (I am indebted to this writer's chapter on "The Impious in Medicine" for most of the facts in this account of seventeenth-century medicine.)

points out, the story of the death of Molière; and the way in which
he puts himself into the play as the imaginary invalid is a singular
example of the courage of a great writer. The play bears a marked
resemblance to *Tartuffe*. In the earlier play he had studied the effects
of extreme credulity in religion; in his last play he studies the same
phenomenon in medicine. Argan's cult of ill-health and his faith
in medical charlatans is similar to Orgon's cult of a debased religiosity and his naïve trust in the religious charlatan, and it has the
same corrosive effect on his personality. When he explains his
reasons for wishing to marry his daughter to the young Diafoirus
by saying

"Ma raison est que, me voyant infirme et malade, comme je suis, je
veux me faire un gendre et des alliés médecins, afin de m'appuyer de bons
secours contre ma maladie, d'avoir dans ma famille les sources des
remèdes qui me sont nécessaires, et d'être à même des consultations et
des ordonnances"

—we see at once that he is living in a world of fantasy, that his
supposed illness insulates him as effectively from the world of
common experience as Orgon's religion or Harpagon's avarice.

The heart of the play, however, is the scene between Argan and
his brother:

BÉRALDE:
    J'entends, mon frère, que je ne vois point d'homme qui soit moins
    malade que vous, et que je ne demanderais point une meilleure con-
    stitution que la vôtre. Une grande marque que vous vous portez
    bien, et que vous avez un corps parfaitement bien composé, c'est
    qu'avec tous les soins que vous avez pris, vous n'avez pu parvenir
    encore à gâter la bonté de votre tempérament, et que vous n'êtes
    point crevé de toutes les médecines qu'on vous a fait prendre . . .
ARGAN:
    . . . Que faire donc, quand on est malade?
BÉRALDE:
    Rien, mon frère.
ARGAN:
    Rien?
BÉRALDE:
    Rien. Il ne faut que demeurer en repos. La nature, d'elle-même,
    quand nous la laissons faire, se tire doucement du désordre où elle
    est tombée. C'est notre inquiétude, c'est notre impatience qui gâte

tout, et presque tous les hommes meurent de leurs remèdes, et non pas de leurs maladies.

ARGAN:

Mais il faut demeurer d'accord, mon frère, qu'on peut aider cette nature par de certaines choses.

BÉRALDE:

Mon Dieu! mon frère, ce sont pures idées, dont nous aimons à nous repaître; et, de tout temps, il s'est glissé parmi les hommes de belles imaginations, que nous venons à croire, parce qu'elles nous flattent et qu'il serait à souhaiter qu'elles fussent véritables . . . lorsqu'il [le médecin] vous parle de rectifier le sang, de tempérer les entrailles et le cerveau, de dégonfler la rate, de raccommoder la poitrine, de réparer le foie, de fortifier le cœur, de rétablir et conserver la chaleur naturelle, et d'avoir des secrets pour étendre la vie à de longues années; il vous dit justement le roman de la médecine.

This sounds like Molière's usual methods applied to medicine, or rather to what he calls *le roman de la médecine*; and while this is true, we perceive that he strikes a fresh note in this scene. Béralde is Molière's spokesman as surely as Cléante in *Tartuffe*; but it must be remembered that though Molière was never tempted to indulge in the extravagances of Orgon or to join the *dévots*, he was a very sick man when he wrote *le Malade imaginaire*. It seems to me that the scene between Béralde and Argan is not the usual exchange between the author and his victim, but a dialogue of the artist with himself. For Molière is both Béralde and Argan. Béralde stands for the normal, healthy impulses in Molière's own character and his zest for life; Argan is the sick Molière, is a projection of corrupt tendencies which he may have felt were present in him or of what he may have regarded as a temptation. The whole scene is a dramatic struggle between sickness and health. We see Molière turning his own weapons against himself; we see Molière in his prime ironically chiding the sick Molière, telling him that he must get a grip on himself, that he mustn't brood over his ailment, that there's precious little wrong with him, that all he needs to do is to empty his medicine bottles down the drain, send the doctors away and give nature a chance.

The projection of this personal conflict into the play gives it its special poignancy, and the climax is reached in the final exchanges between Béralde and Argan:

F

BÉRALDE:

... j'aurais souhaité de pouvoir un peu vous tirer de l'erreur où vous êtes, et, pour vous divertir, vous mener voir sur ce chapitre quelqu'une des comédies de Molière.

ARGAN:

C'est un bon impertinent que votre Molière avec ses comédies, et je le trouve bien plaisant d'aller jouer d'honnêtes gens comme les médecins.

BÉRALDE:

Ce ne sont point les médecins qu'il joue, mais le ridicule de la médecine ...

ARGAN:

Par la mort non de diable! si j'étais que des médecins, je me vengerais de son impertinence; et quand il sera malade, je le laisserais mourir sans secours. Il aurait beau faire et beau dire, je ne lui ordonnerais pas la moindre petite saignée, le moindre petit lavement, et je lui dirais: "Crève, crève! cela t'apprendra une autre fois à te jouer à la Faculté." ...

BÉRALDE:

Il sera encore plus sage que vos médecins, car il ne leur demandera point de secours.

ARGAN:

Tant pis pour lui, s'il n'a point recours aux remèdes.

BÉRALDE:

Il a ses raisons pour n'en point vouloir, et il soutient que cela n'est permis qu'aux gens vigoureux et robustes, et qui ont des forces de reste pour porter les remèdes avec la maladie; mais que, pour lui, il n'a justement de la force que pour porter son mal.

The sequel was a tragic one. A week after the first production of *le Malade imaginaire*, Molière was obviously ailing. Armande and his friend Baron begged him not to play that night. The reply was characteristic of the man:

"What do you expect me to do? There are fifty poor workers who have only their daily wage to live on. What will become of them if the performance does not take place? I could not forgive myself for failing to support them for a single day if it were humanly possible to do so."[1]

During the performance he became seriously ill, but he went on to the end of the play. When he left the stage he collapsed and had to be carried to his lodging. His last words to Armande and Baron

[1] Grimarest quoted by Mauriac, *Trois grands hommes devant Dieu*, Paris, 1930, p. 50.

recall Béralde's: "Il n'a justement de la force que pour porter son mal":

"When my life was evenly divided between pleasure and pain, I thought myself happy; but now that I am weighed down by suffering without being able to count on a moment's comfort or relief, I see that the time has come to throw in my hand. I cannot hold out any longer against the pain which never leaves me a second's respite."[1]

A few minutes later he was dead. There was no time for "la moindre petite saignée" or "le moindre petit lavement."

3

I have made extensive use of the word *malade* in discussing the characteristics of Molière's art, but though this is his own word it needs to be used with great circumspection. I do not wish to give the impression that I regard the plays as case-books or as studies in abnormal psychology which anticipate the methods and findings of the modern novelist. The eccentricities and social abuses which he criticizes are placed in their true perspective. They are seen to be flaws in an otherwise healthy organism. For Molière believed in his age in a way that is impossible for the contemporary writer. In spite of the wealth of detail with which they described the life of their time, the great French novelists who came after Constant and Stendhal—Balzac, Flaubert and Proust—do not seem to me to be the heirs of Molière. They are much closer to Racine. Their work is in the main a study of *une maladie des sentiments* which sometimes bears a superficial resemblance to Molière's approach, but their concentration on one aspect of their characters is so complete that the *sentiment* tends to dissolve into the *maladie*. Flaubert's description of Frédéric Moreau at the end of *l'Education sentimentale* might well serve as an epigraph for them all: "La véhémence du désir, la fleur même de la sensation était perdue." This limits their value as social criticism and, indeed, as criticism of any kind. For the more we read them, the more evident it becomes that their sensibility only touches life at comparatively few points. They do not show the human being with his foibles and his passions—the character-

[1] *ibid.*, p. 46.

istics which alternately join him to and divide him from society —in relation to an existing order as Molière does. They are only interested in him in so far as he is the product of his immediate environment and his feelings are conditioned and corrupted by it. The accent should, therefore, fall on the breadth and variety of Molière's vision of man and society, on his sense of society as a coherent whole, on his fundamental sanity and on that wisdom which belongs peculiarly to the great European masters.

JEAN RACINE

"Dans Racine, je vois la passion toute pure et sans contre-poids. Ni le devoir, ni la religion, ni la politique ne balancent la passion un seul moment. De là que Racine est si vrai et si grand et si terrible."

—ANDRÉ SUARÈS : *Xénies*

I. THE SOCIAL SCENE

1

WHEN Corneille, very old, very lonely and very grand, nodded his head solemnly over a performance of *Britannicus* and complained that the author dwelt too much on the *faiblesses* of human nature, he spoke for a large body of influential people. They were shocked by the violence of Racine's tragedies and by the poet's apparent indifference to the ideal of "honour" which had had a long and successful run on the seventeenth-century stage. It was difficult for Corneille himself to be fair to the young man who was taking his place in the affections of the coming generation and who made little attempt to conceal his contempt for all that Corneille had stood for. And a man of Racine's temperament was not likely to forget or forgive Corneille's patronizing comment on his early work: "Young man," he had said, "you have no gift for the theatre."

Corneille's admirers stood loyally by him and professed to discover a new and subtle beauty in his later work, but it may be doubted whether their applause was altogether successful in reassuring him. For in his later plays the familiar voice of the old poet had become harsh and strained, and the ideals which had been a magnificent inspiration in the *Cid* and *Polyeucte* had grown a little hollow.

At bottom the problem was not a personal one; it arose from the clash between two generations rather than from the clash between two temperaments. "In spite of the success which still greeted his work," wrote Pierre Lièvre, "people began to feel that the atmosphere of the century was no longer the same."[1] It would be difficult to put the matter better or more fairly. Although Corneille and Racine lived in the same century, they belonged to different ages.

[1] *Corneille: Théâtre Complet* (Bibliothèque de la Pléiade), I, p. 12.

Corneille's work marks the end of the old age and Racine's the beginning of a new. Corneille did not see—perhaps did not wish to see—that he stood on the threshold of a new age bringing fresh problems which demanded fresh solutions.

The mistake has been a common one, and Racine's true role has not always been appreciated by his critics. The nineteenth century saw clearly that his poetry was the direct expression of the life of his time, but when Sainte-Beuve declared that this poetry was the product of "le commerce paisible de cette société où une femme écrivait *la Princesse de Clèves*," we may conclude that his reading of the age was at fault.[1] It was Sainte-Beuve and Taine who created the "tender Racine," the neat and accomplished craftsman whose poetry reflected the elegance of the Court of King Louis—an elegance which seemed a little faded to those who were accustomed to the revolutions of the nineteenth century and whose ears were too familiar with the thud of Hugo's rhetoric to appreciate the subtler Racine.

In our own time we may flatter ourselves that we have reached a truer estimate of Racine's genius. The "tender Racine" of the nineteenth-century myth has been swept away to be replaced by the "implacable Racine" whose ferocity delights our age as it shocked Racine's own. Yet the old error reappears in another form. Jean Giraudoux, who has done full justice to Racine's ferocity, tells us that there is not a sentiment in his work which is not a literary sentiment and that it contains no trace of the great movements of his time which have left their mark on the letters of Madame de Sévigné.[2]

Racine's great gifts—his honesty and integrity, his clarity and critical detachment—are so badly needed at the present time that it is worth while insisting on a neglected aspect of his genius. So far from being the laureate of Versailles, he was (whether consciously or not) the critic of an age of false stability. He exposed the corruption of the Court in *Britannicus* and more pointedly in *Athalie*; but as a rule he did not refer directly to political events. He was more concerned with "the atmosphere of the century," with the

---

[1] As a corrective to the genteel, anaemic society described by Sainte-Beuve and Taine, see the valuable collection of documents in Félix Gaiffe's *l'Envers du grand siècle*, Paris, 1924, *passim*.

[2] *Racine*, Eng. tr., Cambridge, 1938, p. 7.

changes that were taking place in the moral life of the people. Because the seventeenth century in France was one of the greatest centuries in European literature, it does not follow that the social order which produced this literature was sound or healthy. "Louis XIV made a mess—but there was *Phèdre*," wrote Mr. E. M. Forster.[1] In spite of its outward magnificence, the age of Louis XIV was beginning to disintegrate from within, and in order to appreciate the nature of the process we must go behind Racine's poetry and look at the conditions in which he wrote and perhaps at the man himself.

"The seventeenth century," writes an historian, "is peculiarly baffling because it appears on the surface so simple. It is simple because the *Mémoires* dealing with the upper classes are as excellent as they are numerous: it is difficult because the peasant and the tradesman of the period are elusive persons who will not stand and deliver any information about themselves."[2] We may think that though this is part of the difficulty, it is only a part. The difficulty does not lie least in the nature of the sources. Madame de Sévigné and Saint-Simon were essentially *individualists*. Their aim was not to write a history of their times. It was, in Saint-Simon's own words (which are as true of the letter-writer as of the memoir-writer), to give an account of their own lives which included "tout ce qui a un rapport particulier à moi et aussi un peu en général et superficiellement une espèce de relation des événements de ces temps, principalement des choses de la Cour."[3] They were almost exclusively concerned with personalities and events which had a strict bearing on their own lives and feelings. They have left us a picture of unsurpassed vividness of what happened to them and what interested them. We follow the trial of Fouquet with breathless interest in the *Letters* and we share Madame de Sévigné's hopes and fears; we know from the *Mémoires* exactly how Fénelon looked when he made a public retraction after the condemnation of some of his writings by the Holy See; we see every gesture and we almost catch the intonation of his voice; but it was no part of the writers' intention to indicate the precise significance or the causes of those events.

[1] "The New Disorder" in *Horizon*, IV, No. 24, December, 1941.
[2] Hugon, *Social France in the Seventeenth Century*, London, 1911, p. 7.
[3] *Mémoires* (ed. Chéruel et Régnier), I, Paris, 1889, p. 28.

Another thing that makes the seventeenth century difficult to understand is the preponderance of Versailles which was in reality a vast façade, a symbol of outward splendour that hid an interior deterioration. The stage is so crowded with Kings, Princes, Bishops and Ambassadors that we do not at first notice the absentees or grasp the meaning of the intrigues which are recounted with such wealth of detail. It is only later that we perceive the significance of the spectacle and the way in which these events fit into the complete pattern of the century. Nothing appears to matter except Madame de Sévigné's emotion on becoming a grandmother, or the mixture of vexation and amusement with which she learns that her son has contracted a disgraceful malady, or the disputes over whose turn it was to hold His Majesty's nightshirt.

It is only occasionally that the even flow in the *Letters* is disturbed by a deeper note which betrays the weariness, the sadness, of what Paul Bourget called in a different context *une civilisation vieillissante.* "Il semble qu'il n'y ait plus qu'à nous faire enterrer," she writes in a letter to Madame de La Fayette. And when she remarks in another letter: "The balls at Saint-Germain are of a deadly sadness," we seem to catch a prophetic glimpse of the courtiers, their faces weary and drawn beneath their make-up, as they revolve mechanically round the doddering monarch.[1]

Saint-Simon belongs to a later generation than Madame de Sévigné. The process of decay had become more evident when he wrote his great work, and though he, too, relies for the most part on indirect criticism, his indictment is more radical. His *Mémoires* are often biased and inaccurate; a great deal of his bitterness is that of an able man whose abilities found no outlet in a period of corruption and incompetence; but the bitterness is not merely personal. The remorselessness with which he strips away the gorgeous clothing to reveal the ugliness of his victims; the satisfaction with which he lifts the veil to show a noble lady relieving herself in church and the way in which he rakes the muck-heap in his hunt for a suitable epithet to point the contrast between the pretence

[1] *cf.*   Enfin je me dérobe à la joie importune
De tant d'amis nouveaux que me fait la fortune;
Je fuis de leurs respects l'inutile longueur,
Pour chercher un ami qui me parle du cœur.
(*Bérénice*, Act i. Sc. iv.)
See, too, Funck-Brentano, *La Cour du Roi Soleil*, Paris, 1937, pp. 194–200.

and the reality, give an extraordinary feeling of the atmosphere of his times. In spite of the difference of style, his findings differ little from Racine's; and his final summing-up of the age—particularly the contrast between the confusion of the time and the order of his art—might serve as an epigraph for the tragedies.

"Since at the time of which I have written," he says, "particularly towards the end, everything was falling into a state of decadence, confusion and chaos which has grown steadily worse until the most complete and universal ignorance has extended its empire everywhere; and since these Memoirs stand for order, law, truth and fixed principles, it follows that [if given to the public] this mirror of truth would cause a general uproar."[1]

"La Cour," he wrote in another place, "fut un autre manège de la politique du despotisme." This sentence goes to the roots of the trouble. The spiritual life of France was being strangled, the old social solidarity of the people was being undermined by a ruthless despotism. The policy of Louis XIV was to make France safe for dictatorship. The nobility was deprived of its functions and replaced by a bureaucracy to prevent it from becoming a challenge to the royal omnipotence.

The ruling classes were encouraged to pursue a life of reckless extravagance because a ruined nobility and a ruined bourgeoisie would be dependent on royal favours. The Court served another purpose. It not only impressed the world with the magnificence of the reign, but it also kept the nobility dancing attendance on the King's person instead of retiring to their estates where they might have become centres of independence and disaffection. The same policy was pursued, though with less success, in religion. Louis XIV tried to establish the Gallican Church in order to make his authority over the clergy absolute. He persecuted the Jansenists (in spite of their Gallican leanings) not because they could have threatened his power, but because to the despot any independent movement seemed a potential menace.

The results of this policy are clear, but they only became clear in the cataclysm which overtook France in the next century. The structure of society was disrupted. Men were cut off from their estates; they ceased to be human beings and were transformed into artificial people who were compelled to submit to an artificial code

---

[1] *op. cit.*, XIX, p. 222.

F*

of manners which fettered their minds as well as their bodies. They were made to live under the royal supervision to prevent them from finding time to plot against the régime in the fastness of their châteaux, so that the Court life served much the same purpose as the cult of marching in the Third Reich. All criticism was mercilessly suppressed with scarcely a pretence of justice. The courtiers became so used to playing a game that they lost their power of criticism unless they happened to be very exceptional people. Racine and Saint-Simon were accomplished courtiers, but because they were great men they managed to distinguish between their real and their artificial selves. Saint-Simon had to wait until after his death for the publication of his life work, and Racine's championship of a dissident minority, and possibly his outspoken criticism of the condition of the peasants, brought disgrace which is said to have hastened his death.

2

On the surface the middle classes present the same homogeneous appearance as the aristocracy. Paris seems at first to be a smart Renaissance city; we hear little of the murders and crimes that went on in its streets or of the unspeakably squalid life of many of its inhabitants or their strange vices.[1] We see only the prosperous bourgeois living in their solid houses, the stuffy, richly draped rooms with their heavy furniture where they entertained their friends to vast meals with elaborate ceremony. Their only interests seem to be their business, the marriage of their children and their prospects of obtaining an appointment at Court.

The reality was very different. The relations between the aristocracy and the middle classes were close and intricate. It was the middle classes which produced most of the great imaginative writers whose work showed the direction in which society was moving. For the middle classes were far less self-contained than they appeared to be. They were, as their name suggests, a fluctuating body and we can detect three main groups. There were the patricians who tended to rise out of their class, to intermarry with the aristocracy or like the writers to move in Court circles by virtue of their calling. At the other end of the scale were the provincials

[1] V. Gaiffe, *op. cit.*, chapter IV.

who were drifting towards the peasantry and who, living dim, ignorant and impoverished on their farms, were the constant butt of seventeenth-century wit. In between these two extremes came the bourgeois proper—the doctors, lawyers and merchants. They were prosperous, respectable and pious and had for many years been the backbone, the true moral core, of France.

Corneille and Racine were both products of the middle classes, but they belonged to different groups. Corneille was the laureate of the bourgeoisie whose moral integrity he had celebrated in his greatest plays. Racine was the pure patrician and his poetry has all the characteristics of patrician art—the characteristics that we shall find two hundred years later in the work of the Symbolists. It is subtle, refined, individualist, is the art of a civilization which has reached its zenith and is leaning towards its decline.

"Your goodness in asking me to tell you about my doings," wrote the Cardinal de Retz to his patroness, "fills me with such gratitude and such tenderness that I cannot help giving you an account of all my thoughts; and I experience an unbelievable pleasure in searching for them in the depths of my mind and in submitting them to your judgment."

It is this *plaisir incroyable* that a writer experiences in analysing his own feelings, this conviction of the immense importance of his findings for others, which more than anything stamps an art as patrician. The focus was shifting from the bourgeoisie to the patrician. The writer no longer thought of himself as a member of a closely knit community; he had become an isolated individual whose task was not to praise but to dissect society. His was the voice of a society which was menaced, but which was not yet fully aware of its danger.

It is commonly assumed that the art of the seventeenth century was the art of an *élite* in which the people had no part. It is true that apologists of Louis XIV have little to say of the famines, slaughter and campaigns which ravaged the country; and the sufferings of the peasantry, the most robust and worst-treated class in France, seem no more than a distant echo in the writings of an elegant civilization. The truth is less simple.[1] It is a curious fact

---

[1] Contemporaries had a good deal to say about them. La Bruyère described them as "animaux farouches . . . répandus par la campagne, noirs, livides et tout brûlés du soleil, attachés à la terre qu'ils fouillent et qu'ils remuent avec une opiniâtreté invincible," and whose sufferings "saisissent le cœur." V. Gaiffe, chapter VII.

that Corneille is far more "class-conscious" than Racine. In his poetry the people are treated as creatures of mere instinct, are always seen *collectively*. When properly led they may be a source of strength to the existing order and when left to their own devices they may overthrow it. Corneille's *confidents* are colourless people whose only function is to act as a foil to the heroes and heroines, to make the remark that will set the machinery of the great *tirades* in motion. In Racine they possess a distinct personality. They have that simplicity which belongs peculiarly to the peasantry—a simplicity which is derived from contact with the soil. They may, like Narcisse and Œnone, corrupt their masters through their own primitive cunning or they may be corrupted by them; but usually they represent a norm of sanity in a disordered world. It is they who, in lines which have a different *timbre* from the subtle speeches of their masters, warn them when they are about to set out on some dubious enterprise to satisfy selfish desires. The contrast between the two styles can be seen in the dialogue between Bérénice and Phénice:

PHÉNICE:
>   Que je le plains! Tant de fidélité,
> Madame, méritait plus de prospérité.
> Ne le plaignez-vous pas?

BÉRÉNICE:
>   Cette prompte retraite
> Me laisse, je l'avoue, une douleur secrète.

PHÉNICE:
> Je l'aurais retenu.

BÉRÉNICE:
>   Qui? moi? le retenir?
> J'en dois perdre plutôt jusques au souvenir.
> Tu veux donc que je flatte une ardeur insensée?

PHÉNICE:
> Titus n'a point expliqué sa pensée.
> Rome vous voit, madame, avec des yeux jaloux;
> La rigueur de ses lois m'épouvante pour vous.
> L'hymen chez les Romains n'admet qu'une Romaine.
> Rome hait tous les rois, et Bérénice est reine.

In Phénice's words we detect the accent of the old French *bonne*, and she speaks with that wisdom and directness which belong to simple people.

We can go further than this. We can say that Racine's popularity is largely due to his power of discovering a common humanity beneath the refinements of civilization, of speaking of passion as directly to the flower-seller as to the intellectual. "For," said Mauriac in a reply to some tendentious criticism,

". . . Racine had to go as far afield as Epirus and Troezene in search of his Hermione and his Phèdre to enable the shoe-stitcher or the char-woman, as well as the idle rich, to recognize themselves in these princesses whose rank spared them the necessity of any other form of occupation. It must be emphasized that if the scales are weighted in Racine, they are weighted in favour of the people. A Hermione or a Roxane are of their very nature much closer to the people than they are to the world of fashion. . . . Hermione, with her moments of respect for Pyrrhus, her sudden changes from a tone of the utmost familiarity to formulas drawn from the protocol[1], shows the extent to which the royal princess is sub-merged beneath the abandoned woman. On the other hand, the poorest worker conceals a Racinian princess. What little working girl has not murmured more than once in her life phrases which echo almost word for word some line from Racine: 'Je ne t'ai point aimé, cruel? Qu'ai-je donc fait?' "[2]

Racine is not the preserve of a small intellectual *élite*. He belongs to the French people as Shakespeare belongs to the English. When one watches the French people going about their daily occupations, when one sees the *concierges* and the old women in carpet slippers trudging along the banks of the Seine with their shopping-bags, mothers and nurses sewing and talking while their children play in the Luxembourg, the schoolgirls passing with their vivid gestures, their shrill voices coming through the autumn gardens or whispering together with a gleam—at once "tender" and "implacable"—in their eyes, one knows that these are Racine's countrymen and not Shakespeare's, that they are the raw material of Racine's heroines and his *confidentes*.

We cannot speak of Corneille with the same confidence. His characters have the timelessness of great art; they command our admiration, but we admire them from a respectful distance. They are experts in morality who sometimes remind us of a prize team playing an exhibition match or showing how easy it really is to

[1] "ses alternatives de tutoiement passionné et de formules protocolaires."
[2] *Journal*, II, pp. 117–18.

overcome the obstacles which always bring us crashing to the ground. It is an impressive performance certainly and we realize, as we watch their feats with growing discouragement, that we shall never "make the grade." Then our discouragement changes to a different feeling. For in our hearts we know that we do not really want to "make the grade." We turn, with a guilty sigh and a sense of great relief, to Racine. These princes and princesses are, after all, people like ourselves, are "our sort." They fail ingloriously at all the obstacles; they invariably yield to every temptation, and "honour" is soundly beaten every time. They are more than companions; they are accomplices whose voices insinuate themselves into our conscience asking why we worry over the obstacles, why we bother to resist instead of keeping our eye on the "prey."[1]

Of all the great French classics Racine is the most seductive as he is the most subversive. That his plays are considered fit instruction for the young while Baudelaire is banished from the academic syllabus can only be a source of amused surprise to anyone who understands his work; and that his reconciliation with Port-Royal should have been brought about through *Phèdre* is simply the best of all literary jokes.

3

French literature in the seventeenth century cannot be fully appreciated unless we know something of the religious dissensions of the time and unless full weight is given to the fact that Corneille was a pupil of the Jesuits and Racine a pupil of Port-Royal.

There were two main divisions within the Church—the Ultra-montanes led by the Jesuits, and the Jansenists whose headquarters were at the Abbey of Port-Royal-des-Champs. There is no need to enter into the details of the doctrinal controversy. From a literary point of view only one difference seriously concerns us. The teaching of the Jesuits laid great stress on the importance of free-will, on the co-operation of the human will with Divine grace in the work of the Redemption. Man had fallen, but his nature was not completely ruined by the Fall, for his sin had been redeemed by the

---

[1] "Corneille nous assujettit à ses caractères et à ses idées, Racine se conforme aux nôtres . . ." (La Bruyère).

sacrifice of Christ. This was in essence a Christian optimism. It encouraged men to hope and to place confidence in their own actions. It was bound up with Ultramontanism. The Jesuits opposed all attempts to set up a local national church and to divide Christians into tiny, hostile groups. They saw the Church as a divine society which stretched beyond national frontiers, as a great hierarchy with the Pope as its earthly head. This led them to stress the basic identity of the individuals of whom this society was composed, to see man as a member of the Christian community rather than as an individual. This view encouraged corporate worship and curbed the vagaries of religious experience. It stood for authority and discipline; it was essentially a reasonable, moderate outlook.

The most important aspect of Jansenism was its view of grace and original sin. The Jansenists claimed that their teaching on original sin was derived from Augustine through Jansenius; but in practice it approximated to the Lutheran belief that man's nature had been completely ruined by the Fall and to the denial of free-will. Man was reduced to the state of a helpless individual who could not accomplish any good action without the direct intervention of grace.

Jansenism had Gallican leanings which emphasized man's isolation and minimized the normative influence of the Christian society. It was in essentials a pessimistic doctrine which placed man at the mercy of his passions and this accounts for the streak of fatalism which runs all through Racine's poetry. It was also a highly introspective religion, and whatever the intentions of Jansenist theologians, it undoubtedly exalted the importance of the individual conscience at the expense of external authority.

It can now be seen that the relation between religion and literature was a close and unusual one. The seventeenth century in France, as in England, was a period in which civilization was undergoing revolutionary changes. The old world was crumbling and a new world was emerging. There were curious cross-currents in France where, more than in England, two orders faced one another. They cannot be measured in terms of years and any attempt to do so would be misleading. All that can be said is that the century was divided by opposing but coexisting tendencies. We cannot say that the change took place in a given year; we can only say that from about 1667 onwards one of the tendencies appears to become less and the other more pronounced. One is represented by Bossuet and Corneille, the other by Pascal and Racine, for Corneille is the literary counterpart of Bossuet as Racine is of Pascal. It sometimes happens that a phase of human experience only receives its final, its consummate, expression when that phase is passing away. Thus one of the most complete defences of Catholicism was written in the century that followed the Reformation. Sainte-Beuve called Bossuet "l'âme la moins combattue qui fût au monde," and Pascal is the father of that spiritual unrest which has become so common in the modern world. His was a religion of tormented and uneasy consciences; he saw men as lonely individuals who were hopelessly lost in the universe without grace, and his work is filled with brooding about sin and doubt. The force of Corneille's criticism of Racine quoted at the beginning of this study will now be apparent. Racine's Jansenism encouraged him to dwell on man's fallen state and to represent him as incapable of resisting the impulses of his animal nature. Jansenism thus begins to assume the appearance of "modern religion," and it is not difficult to see why it fitted in well with the disintegrating forces that were at work in the latter part of the century.

II. THE MAN

It has been shown that social and religious changes in the seventeenth century had a considerable influence on literature, and before going on to a detailed study of Racine's poetry, it is necessary to ask what sort of man he was and what part heredity and early environment played in the formation of the poet.

He was born of an ardent Jansenist family at the little town of La Ferté-Milon in the Valois country about 22nd December 1639. His family belonged to the professional classes on both sides. His grandfather, Jean Racine, who had begun life as a clerk in the Salt Office, had married into the Desmoulins family. He later became a man of some note in his native town, rose to be Comptroller of the Salt Office, and was ennobled by the King.

Jean Racine had eight children by Marie Desmoulins, but only two have left any trace of themselves: the eldest, Jean Racine the younger, who was the father of the poet; and a daughter, Agnès, who entered Port-Royal as a schoolgirl at the age of twelve, never left the Abbey and became first Prioress and then Abbess. It was this daughter who, as Sœur Agnès de Sainte-Thècle, later made such desperate efforts to persuade the poet, when he was on the threshold of his career, to give up the theatre and return to the fold.

In 1639 Jean Racine the younger married Jeanne Sconin whose father was an important person at La Ferté-Milon: Royal Commissioner, Crown Attorney and President of the Salt Office. They had two children, the poet and his sister Marie who was born in 1641. The mother died at the birth of the daughter, and two years later the father, too, died at the early age of twenty-eight.

The grandparents divided the children. Racine was brought up by his grandfather and Marie Desmoulins, and his sister by the Sconins. The wordly Sconins did not mix well with the devout Desmoulins and the two children saw little of one another.

M. Masson-Forestier (a descendant of Racine's sister Marie), going a good deal further than Taine ever ventured, has argued that the district in which Racine was born and the intermarriage of the Racines and the Sconins account for most of the attributes of Racine's poetry. In the seventeenth century, he said, the wooded valley of La Ferté-Milon was a peat bog; the Ourcq, which to-day is a limpid stream, was a rapid and dangerous river. The town was surrounded by vast forests, and there was little cultivation. The townspeople were energetic, devout and somewhat gloomy; the life that they were forced to lead was narrow and inhibited.[1]

The same authority, probing into the histories of the two families, goes on to say that the Sconins were by nature violent and brutal, with Scandinavian and perhaps Frankish blood in their veins. The Racines were naturally gentle and devout, Latin by temperament and clerical.

According to M. Masson-Forestier, this explains the elegance and ferocity of Racine's plays. The theory no doubt sounds a little fanciful; but though we may discount the influence of the countryside, the intermingling of the Sconins and the Racines does to some extent illuminate the contradictions and conflicting impulses that we shall find both in Racine's character and in his poetry.

[1] *Autour d'un Racine ignoré*, Paris, 1910.

A year before Racine's birth the town of La Ferté-Milon and, adds M. François Mauriac in a characteristic sentence, perhaps "la maison où l'on s'occupait chastement à lui donner la vie,"[1] became the refuge of the Jansenists who had been driven from the Abbey of Port-Royal. Although they left La Ferté-Milon a few months after the poet's birth, they had made a lasting impression on their hosts, and Racine was brought up in an atmosphere in which the piety of *ces messieurs de Port-Royal* had already become legendary.

Racine stayed with his grandparents until, at the age of ten, he was sent to school at Beauvais, a sister house of Port-Royal. At the age of fifteen he became a pupil at Port-Royal itself. His biographers have pointed out that this fact is exceptional because as a rule Port-Royal only took children between the ages of nine and ten.

In 1656 the Abbey school was disbanded and for three years Racine was Port-Royal's solitary pupil. It would be difficult to exaggerate the influence on his character of his upbringing there during the formative years. He had, as tutors, four of the most distinguished scholars of the time—Lancelot, Nicole, Antoine Lemaître and Hamon, men who had withdrawn from the world at the height of their fame to devote themselves to the life of prayer. "Comme instruction," wrote Jules Lemaître, "c'est unique, c'est magnifique, et plus que princier. Comme enseignement religieux, c'est intense."[2]

There were, indeed, two elements in Racine's education: an immense love of the pagan classics coupled with an intense religious training, a profound love of the profane coupled with a no less profound sense of the presence of God—of the Jansenist God. Since he was the only pupil at Port-Royal, he was of necessity left a good deal to himself. His tutors spoke of him as the *petit Racine*, and he was a child in a world of grown-ups, of serious men devoting their lives to prayer and to the study of the Fathers of the Church.

"His greatest pleasure," wrote Louis Racine in his memoirs of his father, "was to bury himself in the woods in the grounds of the Abbey with a volume of Sophocles or Euripides whose work he knew almost by

[1] *la Vie de Jean Racine* (Le Roman des Grandes Existences), Paris, 1928, p. 10.
[2] *Jean Racine*, Paris, 1908, p. 9.

heart. He had an amazing memory. He happened to come upon a Greek novel about the loves of Theagena and Charides. He was devouring it when the sacristan, Claude Lancelot, seized the book and burnt it. He managed to obtain another copy which met with the same fate. Then a third, and to avoid any more trouble he learnt it by heart before taking it to the sacristan with the words: 'You can burn this like the others'."[1]

The words "learnt by heart" must not be taken too literally. The novel is six hundred pages long, but Racine's interest in it was significant. The first book deals with a young man who was loved too well by his stepmother. "Phèdre et Hippolyte sous d'autres noms," observes Jules Lemaître.[2]

It was at Port-Royal that Racine wrote his first verses, an elegant and somewhat frigid exercise that need not detain us here. What is of importance is that when he left Port-Royal in October 1658 he was, as Lemaître puts it, "à la fois un adolescent très pieux et un adolescent fou de littérature."[3] When we recall the relations between the *bien pensants* and the men of letters in the seventeenth century, the contrast between the atmosphere of devotion in which Racine was brought up and the nature of his reading, the significance is unmistakable.

In 1658 the eighteen-year-old Racine went to the Collège d'Harcourt in Paris to do a year's philosophy. It is thought that he lived in furnished rooms near Sainte-Geneviève. He had already become firm friends with his cousin, the Abbé Le Vasseur, and with the poet, La Fontaine.

A year later he was installed at the Hôtel de Luynes, Quai des Grands Augustins, the house of his uncle, Nicolas Vitart, the Intendant of the Duc de Luynes. Nicolas Vitart had himself been a pupil of Port-Royal, but it does not seem to have affected him deeply. At this time he was prosperous, worldly, and his main interests were literature—particularly *vers galants*—and the theatre.

The atmosphere of the Vitarts' house was very different from that of Port-Royal. They were cheerful and easy-going and untouched by the sombre Jansenism of the Racines and Desmoulins. There was plenty of company, and Racine has left a list of the attractive girls whom he met there and of a number of men of

---

[1] "Mémoires sur la vie de Jean Racine" in *Œuvres de J. Racine* (ed. Paul Mesnard), I, Paris, 1865, pp. 211–12.

[2] *op. cit.*, p. 2   [3] *ibid.*, p. 30.

letters and theatrical celebrities to whom the Abbé Le Vasseur introduced him.

There is no doubt that Racine enjoyed his freedom after the years spent at Port-Royal. He could see everyone, read everything without fear of interruptions from sacristans, say everything. In a letter to Le Vasseur we catch a glimpse of a Racine who was already a little different from the pious infant of Port-Royal. Commenting on these lines from a Latin poem by a doctor named Quillet:

> Nimirum crudam si ad laeta cubilia portas
> Perdicem, incoctaque agitas genitalia coena,
> Heu! tenue effundes semen . . .

he observes:

"But it matters little to me how I write to you as long as I have the pleasure of conversing with you, just as I should find it very difficult to wait for my supper to digest on the night of my wedding. I am not patient enough to observe so many formalities."

"Sentez-vous, au milieu d'un badinage assez libre," asks Jules Lemaître in an amusing commentary, "la réserve d'un bon jeune homme encore intact, et proche encore des pieux enseignements de ses maîtres?"[1] No doubt we do, but it is also clear that Racine's latent sensuality was already coming to the surface in the freedom of Paris. There is as yet no conflict between passion and morality, but there are already indications that morality will not put up much resistance when the conflict comes.

Racine's first literary success came at the age of twenty. He wrote an ode in the artificial style of the time called *la Nymphe de la Seine à la reine* to mark the occasion of the King's marriage. Vitart showed it to Chapelain and Perrault, who were impressed. Chapelain mentioned it to Colbert and "this minister sent the poet 100 *louis* on behalf of the King, and shortly afterwards granted him a State pension of 600 *livres* a year as a man of letters."

It was an encouraging beginning and it bore fruit. In 1660 Racine completed a tragedy called *Amasis* which has not survived. A year later he is engaged on another tragedy on the *Loves* of Ovid. Reports of his activities must have reached Port-Royal and we hear the first rumblings of the storm.

[1] *ibid.* p. 38.

The initiative was taken by Port-Royal. Arrangements were made with Racine's relatives at La Ferté-Milon to have him taken away from Paris. It was decided that he should pay a prolonged visit to his uncle, Canon Sconin, at Uzès in Languedoc. The uncle held out hopes of securing a *bon bénéfice* for his nephew. Racine had never showed any signs of a vocation, but he was without any means save his State pension and he may have thought that, after all, tragedies could be written as easily in Languedoc as in Paris. He set out for Uzès without demur. The journey was a considerable undertaking in those days. There were twelve travellers in the party and they rode together as far as Lyons where they spent two days visiting the city and the neighbourhood. The second stage was a two days' sail down the Rhône. After spending a night at Vienne and another at Valence, they proceeded across country by way of Avignon to Uzès, which is on the road to Nîmes.

A letter written by Racine to La Fontaine on 11th November 1661 gives some vivid and amusing impressions of the journey which bring home to us the immense difference between Paris and *la province*:

"It was at Lyons that I first discovered that I could no longer understand the language of the country or make myself understood; but heaven knows, things were much worse at Valence where I asked one of the maids for a chamber-pot and she put a bed-warmer under my bed. You can well imagine what the sequel to this unfortunate story might have been, and what happens to a sleepy man who uses a bed-warmer if he's taken short in the night. But it's worse still at Uzès. I swear I need an interpreter as much as a Muscovite would in Paris. I am just beginning to see that this queer language is mixed with Spanish and Italian; and, as I have quite a good knowledge of both those languages, I sometimes use them to understand what's said to me and to make myself understood. But even so I often get completely lost, as I did yesterday. I wanted some tin-tacks to make a few alterations in my room, so I sent my uncle's valet into town and told him to buy me two or three hundred. When he got back, he blithely handed me three boxes of matches."[1]

In the same letter we catch a glimpse of the country and its inhabitants:

"I can't help telling you something of the beauties of the country. I had heard them very well spoken of in Paris, but I assure you without

[1] Mesnard, VI, pp. 413–14.

any exaggeration that the number and quality far exceed what I had been told. There isn't a village girl or a cobbler's daughter who doesn't put the Fouillous and the Menevilles completely in the shade. If the country-side itself had more delicacy and fewer rocks, it would be a veritable paradise. All the women are dazzling and know how to make the most of themselves in the most natural way imaginable. As for their person: *Color verus, corpus solidum et succi plenum.*"

Then, recalling the purpose of his visit to Uzès, he adds:

"But hush! It was the first thing that I was warned about, so I'll say no more about it. Besides, I should be profaning the pious house of a priest like the one I am in. *Domus mea domus orationis.* That is why you must not expect me to say anything more about such things. They said to me: 'Be blind.' If I can't quite manage that, I must at least be dumb. For, as you know, I must be clerical with the clergy just as I was a wolf with you and the other wolves of your society. *Adiousias.*"[1]

He seems on the whole to have taken kindly to the life at his uncle's home:

"I spend all my time with my uncle, with St. Thomas and Virgil [he writes to Vitart on 17th January 1662]; I copy out long extracts from theological works and a certain number from poetical works. That's how I pass my time; and I must say that I am not bored, especially when I have a letter from you which keeps me company for two whole days."[2]

The study of Augustine and Aquinas did not interfere with his passionate study of the classics or with the writing of *vers galants*. It was during his stay at Uzès that he put the finishing touches on a poem called *les Bains de Vénus*, which has been lost, and began work on *les Frères ennemis*, the first of his tragedies to survive.

His life was not marked by any external incident of special interest or importance; but though he behaved with the correctness of a *jeune abbé*,[3] we can see from his letters that the real Racine was emerging from the chrysalis:

"I had a visit this afternoon which wasted all the time that I had meant to spend writing to you [he writes to the Abbé Le Vasseur on 16th May 1662]. It was a young man who lives here. He is well favoured but passionately in love. You must realize that in these parts there are no half-hearted love affairs; they are all carried to excess. The townspeople,

---

[1] Mesnard, VI, pp. 415–16.   [2] *ibid.*, VI, p. 438.
[3] "He [my uncle] makes me dress in black from top to toe" (letter to Vitart of 17th January 1662).

who are easy-going enough in other ways, commit themselves far more deeply where their *inclinations* are concerned than the people of any other country in the world."[1]

This suggests already the world of Racine's own poetry, and it would not be easy to find a better description of his characters than "toutes les passions y sont démesurées." Nor should we overlook the detachment of "fort bien fait, mais passionément amoureux" and the appearance of the sinister word *inclinations*.

He was to go a good deal further in revealing his tastes in a letter that he wrote to Vitart a fortnight later:

"I'll tell you another little story which though not important is strange enough. A young girl of Uzès, who lived quite close to us, poisoned herself yesterday by swallowing a great handful of arsenic in order to revenge herself on her father who had given her a heavy dressing-down. She had time to make her confession and did not die until a couple of hours afterwards. Everyone thought that she was pregnant and had been driven by shame to this mad course. But, when her body was opened, it was seen that never was maid more maid than she. Such is the character of these people who push their passions to the last extremity."[2]

It was the sort of story that could scarcely fail to interest the future author of *Andromaque*, though one feels that he might have found it still more attractive if the suicide had been caused by disappointed love. It is a striking revelation of the man and the writer. The cool detachment of the earlier letters has been replaced by something which looks very like cruelty. There is not, as Lemaître observes, the slightest edifying reflection. The facts are stated baldly and it is their baldness which makes them striking. "Mais on l'ouvrit toute entière, et jamais fille ne fut plus fille." Here, already, are signs of Racine's extraordinary economy and precision of language; here too is that extreme curiosity, that desire to penetrate and lay bare the final secrets whether they are psychological or physiological. Here is the skilful mingling of the two which will be a notable characteristic of *Phèdre*.

There are other letters which sound a more personal note. On 30th April 1662 he had written to the Abbé Le Vasseur:

"You know very well that a wounded heart always needs someone to whom it can go for sympathy. If I were one of that sort, I would never

[1] Mesnard, VI, p. 468.　　　　[2] *ibid.*, p. 473.

confide in anyone but you. But I am still free, thank goodness, and if I left this place tomorrow, my heart would still be as much my own as when I arrived. There is, however, one rather amusing little story on the subject that I must tell you. There's an attractive girl here and she has a nice figure. I had only seen her from a distance of five or six yards and had always thought her pretty. Her complexion appeared fresh and sparkling; her eyes big and dark; her throat and all the rest which is so freely displayed in these parts was as white as snow. I felt rather attracted to her, felt something not unlike an *inclination*; but I only saw her in church, for, as I have already explained, I keep pretty much to myself—rather more in fact than my cousin had advised. Well, I wanted to be sure that I hadn't made any mistake about her, so I waited until an opportunity occurred and went up and spoke to her. All this happened less than a month ago and I only wanted to see what sort of an answer I should get. I began to chat about things of no importance, but as soon as I opened my mouth I thought that I was going to dry up altogether. I saw that her face was covered with blotches as though she had just got over an illness. That made me change my ideas a bit; but I didn't stop talking and she answered me very sweetly and politely. To tell the truth, I think I must have struck one of her bad days. For she is considered very good-looking in this town and I know lots of young men who rave about her. She is also considered a good girl and one of the most cheerful hereabouts. Still, I am rather relieved at our meeting, which has put a stop to my tender feelings, because I am trying to behave rather more sensibly and not to let myself be carried away by anything that comes along. I am starting my noviciate. . . ."[1]

It is an amusing story, but there is a vein of seriousness running through it. Racine is no longer altogether the detached and ironical observer, and his concern for his natural susceptibility is genuine. There is a difference between the light-hearted banter at the beginning of the passage and "J'en avais toujours quelque idée assez tendre et assez *approchante d'une inclination.*" There is a genuine feeling of relief behind "Je fus bien aise de cette rencontre, qui me servit du moins à me délivrer de quelque *commencement d'inquiétude,*" which is very different from the sententious reference to his noviciate. For the unfortunate girl's blotches were a better protection than Racine's vocation.

Meanwhile, the negotiations for the *bon bénéfice* were not going well. On 30th May Racine remarked bitterly in a letter to Vitart:

---

[1] Mesnard, VI, pp. 457–8.

"The monks here are the greatest fools alive and, what is more, ignorant fools. They never open a book and I take care to keep out of their way completely. To tell the truth, I have developed a sort of horror for this slothful monkish life which I can scarcely hide."[1]

On 4th July he wrote to Le Vasseur:

"There is no fresh news here. My affairs don't seem to be making much progress which reduces me to despair."[2]

He added significantly:

"I am looking round for a subject for a play and should like to set to work on it, but I have too many reasons to feel moody where I am now. One needs to have one's mind free from the sort of preoccupations that fill mine at present."

In the meantime the situation over Racine's living was becoming very delicate. His uncle spoke at one time of resigning his own living in favour of his nephew:

"... I haven't dared to broach the subject of resigning his living again [Racine writes to Vitart on 25th July], because I don't want him to think me self-seeking. Still, he must realize that I haven't come all this way for nothing; but so far I have been so docile and so frank with him that he thinks that I should be content to go on living with him as we are now without having any designs on his living, and I certainly hope that he will always have the same good opinion of me."[3]

We do not know how the problem was solved, but in the summer of 1663 Racine left Uzès on excellent terms with his uncle. As soon as he was back in Paris, he settled down to the life of a man of letters. *Les Frères ennemis* was produced in July 1664, exactly a year after his return, and *Alexandre le Grand* followed in 1665.

Racine was sometimes inclined to lament his lost career as a monk, but he had little cause to do so. His two and a half years' stay at Uzès had not been altogether in vain. A living eventually materialized and Racine found himself endowed with the income of the Priory of Sainte-Madeleine de l'Épinay in Anjou. When a change in public opinion compelled him to give up his priory in 1673, he had no difficulty in obtaining another sinecure. He became treasurer of France for the town of Moulins where he never set foot in his life.

[1] *ibid.*, p. 472.   [2] *ibid.*, p. 485.   [3] *ibid.*, p. 495.

His relations with the Church were not always so happy. Port-Royal was naturally horrified by his new vocation and it did not intend to let him go without a fight. In August 1665 his aunt, Sœur Agnès, wrote to tell him how deeply grieved she was by the news that he had "plunged more deeply than before into the society of those persons who are abominable in the sight of all who, in however feeble a degree, are truly pious; they are people against whom the church door is closed."[1]

A more formidable attack came from a different quarter. "A poet," wrote Nicole, the celebrated Jansenist theologian, "is a public poisoner and a writer for the stage should be considered as guilty of the murder of innumerable souls." The tears of Sœur Agnès could be ignored, but not the redoubtable Nicole. His attack drew a devastating retort from Racine.

"And so [he wrote] the man who writes a novel or a comedy is a Public Poisoner? And the man who writes the *Provincial Letters* is a Saint! Sir, I pray you, tell me what difference you see between the two of them. M. Pascal—no less than any of us—was a writer of comedies. What takes place, after all, in a comedy? You put on the stage a sly fellow of a servant, or a miserly old cit, or an extravagant marquis. It is certain that M. Pascal aimed higher than this. He chose his *dramatis personæ* in the convents and at the Sorbonne. And sometimes he put on the stage this order of monks and sometimes that, but all of them were Jesuits. How many different parts he made them play! Sometimes he shows us an affable Jesuit, and sometimes a bad Jesuit and always a ridiculous Jesuit. Admit then, sir, that since your comedies and ours are so surprisingly alike, ours cannot be entirely criminal."

This was something that could not be forgiven. The *Lettres provinciales* were among the sacred books of Port-Royal, and Racine's reply caused a rupture which lasted for nearly twelve years.

The Langres portrait of Racine is an extremely revealing piece of work. We can see at a glance that this elegant young man, with the full-bottomed wig falling over his shoulders, is a courtier to his finger-tips. It does not need any great acumen to perceive that the face, with its sensitive, highly strung expression, is the face of an artist. The portrait can tell us a good deal more besides. The sitter,

[1] Mesnard, VI, p. 510.

one feels, is proud and disdainful, and the tiny moustache seems to emphasize the superciliousness of his general expression. It is a handsome face certainly, the face of a remarkably sensual man, but the sensuality is not tempered by the kindliness and good nature which make the Molière of the Mignard portrait a genial figure. There is a hard, determined look in the eyes which gives the face its suggestion of cruelty. The man behaved exactly as anyone who has studied his portrait intently would expect. He was interested in one thing and one thing only—his career. He was determined to be a success at all costs. He was completely merciless in his treatment of his enemies and sacrificed his friends ruthlessly if they seemed likely for a moment to stand in his way.

One need have no sympathy with Jansenism to feel that Racine's treatment of Port-Royal is difficult to defend on human grounds, though it is easy to see that the new threat to his career from his pious friends must have driven the haughty, irritable dramatist into a frenzy of exasperation. His treatment of Molière is less excusable and far more shocking. It was Molière who brought him to the stage when the royal tragedians had been hesitating for months over the production of his first play. It was Molière, too, who produced *Alexandre le Grand* at the Palais Royal in December 1665. No trouble or expense was spared to make the production a success. Molière himself did not act, probably as a concession to Racine who admired Montfleury and could not therefore admire Molière as a tragic actor. Madeleine Béjart was also omitted from the cast to make way for Marquise du Parc—the most beautiful and the least intelligent of Molière's actresses—because Racine was already passionately in love with her.

The première was something of an occasion; but though Monsieur, Madame, the great Condé and the Princess Palatine were present, the play was not the success that Racine had hoped. He jumped to the conclusion that this was due to faulty production and, without a word of warning to Molière, he arranged for a fresh production to be staged by a rival company at the Hôtel de Bourgogne. On 18th December, exactly a fortnight after the original production, the play was performed simultaneously at both theatres. The comment of La Grange, Molière's manager, is a model of restraint. "The troupe," he wrote in his Register, "was surprised to discover that the same tragedy was being played at the Théâtre de l'Hôtel de Bourgogne. As the new arrangement had been made with the connivance of M. Racine, the company did not feel bound to pay him his share as author, since he had used them so ill as to give his play to another theatre."

"Trahison fameuse qui rompt à jamais une amitié," observes M. Pierre Brisson.[1] Racine, however, seems to have taken the breach with Molière as lightly as the breach with Port-Royal. But though he did not mind sacrificing his friend to his career, he had no intention of losing his mistress, and it was not long before she was induced to follow him to the Hôtel de Bourgogne. *Andromaque*, the first of his major works, with the fascinating Mlle du Parc in the chief part, was produced in 1667 and *les Plaideurs*, a witty attack on lawyers, a year later. But the year 1668 ended tragically. Marquise du Parc died in mysterious circumstances. It was whispered that her death was caused by an abortion and that Racine was the father of the child, though this was probably only malicious gossip of the kind that accused Molière of marrying his own illegitimate daughter.

Racine took the blow hardly, but he did not allow it to affect his work as a writer. *Britannicus*, one of his three greatest plays, was produced in 1669 and *Bérénice*, with his new mistress, Mlle de Champmeslé, in the name part, followed the next year. *Bajazet* was produced in 1672, *Mithridate* in 1673, *Iphigénie* in 1674 and *Phèdre* in 1677.

III. THE WORLD OF TRAGEDY

1. The Moral Obstacle Race

We have seen something of the situation in which Racine's poetry was written and we know something of the man who wrote it. When we turn to the poetry, it is possible to discover evidence

[1] *Les deux visages de Racine*, Paris, 1944, p. 20.
This may be an over-statement. It is said that Molière later defended *les Plaideurs* against the ill-judgment of the town and that Racine once snubbed a detractor of the *Misanthrope* by retorting that it was impossible for Molière to write a bad play. But Racine's conduct was too much even for the good-natured Molière, and their relations seem to have been no more than "polite" for the rest of their lives.

not only of a searching criticism of contemporary France, but also of a highly personal outlook in almost every line. When we compare some characteristic lines from Corneille and Racine, we begin to understand the changes that were taking place in French civilization. When, for example, we compare Corneille's

> Contre mon propre honneur mon amour s'intéresse

with Racine's

> Je n'ai pour lui parler consulté que mon cœur

we see that in the first line there is a conflict between a principle and a feeling, a struggle to fit the experience of the individual into the framework of the community life. The speaker contemplates the situation with a certain detachment; he is able to stand back and examine his love, to weigh the two values—the claims of society and personal interest—calmly and objectively. In Racine's line *honneur* has not simply disappeared; it has been carefully eliminated. The clear-cut lines of *amour* are transformed into something more complex. The word *cœur* stands for the shadowy world of the unconscious, that region of tangled desires which Racine explored with such marvellous insight and which becomes the centre round which all things revolve. This is made clearer by a second comparison. When a character in Corneille's *Sertorius* remarks

> Il est doux de revoir les murs de la patrie

we are in a clearly defined territory—a country governed by its proper laws and its moral code. There is a perfect correspondence between the emotion and its object, and the line expresses the sentiment of the *honnête homme* for his fatherland. But when Néron's mother exclaims:

> Ai-je mis dans sa main le timon de l'État
> Pour le conduire au gré du peuple et du sénat?
> Ah! que de la patrie il soit, s'il veut, le père;
> Mais qu'il songe un peu plus qu'Agrippine est sa mère

the scene is altered. The individual becomes the centre of the picture. Law and morality are swept away. *Patrie* is set against the vast disorder of Agrippine's own emotions and becomes a plaything to be exploited in the selfish interests of the ruler. These lines reveal a fundamentally different attitude towards the life of the community. Corneille's hero has a definite place in the community; and the recognition of its moral code determines his personal feelings and imposes a discipline which constitutes a positive value. Racine's characters have no place in the social order; they are outsiders who have lost their bearings as completely as Frédéric Moreau or any other nineteenth-century hero. It is one of the paradoxes of despotism that the attempt to impose complete uniformity on the common life defeats its own end, encourages a revolutionary individualism, and promotes a subterranean hostility between the individual and the artificial group which it tries to set up in place of the natural community of the people.

This change is a subtle one and is clearly seen in the way in which the two poets handle words. When Corneille uses a word like *légitime* or *gloire*, it has a fixed, unchanging meaning. Actions are right or wrong, good or bad; there is no middle course. The Cornelian hero always knows what line of conduct he must adopt in any given circumstances; the well-tried tests never let him down. Racine's use of words reveals a far wider range of experience; words have no fixed meaning, but are constantly acquiring fresh overtones; and though he appears to employ the same vocabulary as Corneille, he succeeds in presenting a situation which is diametrically opposed to that in Corneille's plays. Racine sets his personal stamp on words as surely as any other great poet. It would be possible, for example, to write an essay on the different meanings that the word *loi* has for him, and in the course of this study we shall see that the development in the meaning of the word corresponds to a development in Racine's experience as a whole. There is a marked contrast between Corneille's *devoir* and Racine's *loi*. *Devoir* implies an obligation, but it is not a mere abstraction; there is a wealth of living human feeling behind it and its power lies precisely in the fact that the obligation is freely accepted by the Cornelian hero in virtue of his place in the community. It is a sign that he recognizes a valid relationship with the community and with his fellow-men as members of it. *Loi* also implies an obligation, but save in Racine's later plays, the emphasis falls on the repressive nature of the obligation. There is nothing human and living about *loi*. It is a dry, legal abstraction imposed by force from without, and so far from being recognized, the one desire of Racine's characters is to circumvent it.

Another example is their use of the word *honneur*. When Corneille speaks of *honneur*, he means the attitude of heroic virtue which enables the hero to dominate the life of instinct and accomplish actions which order the whole of his being instead of destroying it by placing him at the mercy of conflicting desires. Now when Œnone persuades Phèdre to pretend to Thésée that it was Hippolyte who tried to seduce her instead of her trying to seduce him by saying:

> ... pour sauver notre *honneur* combattu,
> Il faut immoler tout, et même la *vertu*

it is evident that *honneur* means primarily "keeping up appearances." The implications of this change are far-reaching. *Honneur* has ceased to be a reality and become an attitude to be maintained—an attitude to which the positive value implied by *vertu* is unhesitatingly sacrificed. Conduct itself, therefore, becomes a series of postures which no longer correspond to any moral feeling; it follows from this that there is a complete divorce between the public and private life of the individual which leads to thoroughgoing moral anarchy. "When," wrote Taine, "Hippolyte speaks of the forest where his youth was spent, we must understand the avenues of Versailles."[1] Those critics who are still disposed to think of Racine as the laureate of Versailles might consider the significance of "palaces" in his poetry. When he describes his characters wandering alone and without any sense of direction in the vast empty palaces:

> Errante et sans dessein, je cours dans ce palais
> ... errant dans le palais sans suite et sans escorte

—does he not point the contrast between the disorder of the individual life and an order of society which had ceased to be a true order and degenerated into mere formalism? The word "palace" has a curious ambiguity in his poetry. Palaces and temples —using the words in a wide sense—played a large part in his personal life. He had been brought up in the sheltered seclusion of the Abbey of Port-Royal, but the freedom of the Court turned out to be an illusion too. The "palaces" are, therefore, at once a symbol

[1] *Nouveaux essais de critique et d'histoire*, 3 ième éd., Paris, 1880, p. 188.

of refuge and prison; and though it is to the "temple" that he will
return (in the person of a converted and repentant Abner) in his
last play, it will only be at the close of a long struggle and in a
spirit of profound disillusionment. In the secular plays the "palace"
is the sign of the rootless existence of the individual, and it is not
surprising that it sometimes assumes the aspect of a prison where
the individual is kept by the "Sovereign." Thus we read in *Bajazet*:

> Songez-vous que je tiens les portes du palais,
> Que je puis vous l'ouvrir, ou fermer pour jamais,
> Que j'ai sur votre vie un empire suprême,
> Que vous ne respirez qu'autant que je vous aime?

It is not suggested that Racine's world is a world in which there
are no moral values. On the contrary, they are often perceived by
his characters with the same clarity as Corneille's; but instead of
conforming to them, their one desire is to impugn their validity
or to evade their obligations. This explains why the plays abound
in words like *artifice* and *stratagème*. In a remarkable passage
Andromaque explains to her *confidente* that she is going to marry
Pyrrhus in order to save her son's life:

> Pyrrhus en m'épousant s'en déclare l'appui.
> Il suffit: je veux bien m'en reposer sur lui.
> Je sais quel est Pyrrhus. Violent, mais sincère,
> Céphise, il fera plus qu'il n'a promis de faire.
> Sur le courroux des Grecs je m'en repose encor:
> Leur haine va donner un père au fils d'Hector.
> Je vais donc, puisqu'il faut que je me sacrifie,
> Assurer à Pyrrhus le reste de ma vie;
> Je vais, en recevant sa foi sur les autels,
> L'engager à mon fils par des nœuds immortels.
> Mais aussitôt ma main, à moi seule funeste,
> D'une infidèle vie abrégera le reste,
> Et, sauvant ma vertu, rendra ce que je doi
> A Pyrrhus, à mon fils, à mon époux, à moi.
> Voilà de mon amour l'innocent stratagème;
> Voilà ce qu'un époux m'a commandé lui-même.

Andromaque knows very well that her plan is an evasion of the
promise given "at the altars"; but she also knows that in spite of
his shortcomings, Pyrrhus will carry out his part of the bargain

scrupulously. She counts on his "sincerity," on his doing "more than he promised," and tries to excuse her own action by describing it as "un *innocent* stratagème." The word *innocent* is skilfully used to confuse the real issue, and to conceal the profound immorality of her action, by pretending that she is acquitting herself of her obligations to Pyrrhus, her husband and her son.

The desire of Racine's characters to evade their obligations is also symbolized by the back door escape from the palace. In *Andromaque* Oreste has been sent as ambassador by the Greeks to hasten the marriage of Pyrrhus and Hermione. Instead, he proposes to carry off Hermione and leave by a secret door:

> Je sais de ce palais tous les détours obscurs:
> Vous voyez que la mer en vient battre les murs;
> Et cette nuit, sans peine, une secrète voie
> Jusqu'en votre vaisseau conduira votre proie.

The criticism implied is a destructive criticism; the only standards of conduct are the prescriptions of the Court, but they are hollow and unreal. The individual cheerfully throws over this remnant of morality and discipline in the pursuit of his "prey," in response to the promptings of his "heart." Yet these "secret ways" and "innocent stratagems" do not solve any problems; they merely create fresh ones. They lead the characters to a boat tossing on the stormy seas—the stormy seas of passion—which significantly "beat against the palace walls."

2. L'Amour

"We simply regard love as a passion of the same nature as all the other human passions, that is to say, its effect is to derange our reason and its aim to provide pleasure. The Germans, on the other hand, regard love as something sacred and religious, as an emanation of the divinity itself, as the fulfilment of man's destiny on earth, as a mysterious and all-powerful link between two souls which only exist for one another. According to the first of these views, love is common to man and beast; according to the second, it is common to man and God."
—BENJAMIN CONSTANT: *Réflexions sur le théâtre allemand*

"The English, whatever they were in the Elizabethan era, are not an amorous race. Love with them is more sentimental than passionate.

G

They are of course sufficiently sexual to reproduce their species, but they cannot control the instinctive feeling that the sexual act is disgusting. They are more inclined to look upon love as affection or benevolence than as passion. They regard with approval its sublimations which dons describe in scholarly books, and with repulsion or with ridicule its frank expression. English is the only modern language in which it has been found necessary to borrow from the Latin a word with a depreciatory meaning, the word uxorious, for a man's devoted affection for his wife. That love should absorb a man has seemed to them unworthy. In France a man who has ruined himself for women is usually regarded with sympathy and admiration; there is a feeling that it was worth while; and the man who has done it feels a certain pride in the fact; in England he would be thought and will think of himself as a damned fool. That is why *Antony and Cleopatra* has always been the least popular of Shakespeare's greater plays. Audiences have felt that it was contemptible to throw away an empire for a woman's sake. Indeed if it were not founded on an accepted legend they would be unanimous in asserting that such a thing was incredible."[1]

—SOMERSET MAUGHAM: *The Summing Up*, pp. 142–3

i

Corneille would no doubt have been deeply distressed had he known that one day the *faiblesses* which shocked him in *Britannicus* would be given statutory recognition as the *crime passionnel*, that multitudes would flock to the Comédie Française to salute Racine as its first great laureate, and rise to their feet with claps and cheers when the great passages were declaimed on the stage.

The French preoccupation with love has sometimes appeared to foreigners to be an amiable but eccentric trait. It reminds us of the illustrations in those old-fashioned editions of Maupassant's stories, showing a demure young lady in a long black dress with an innocent-looking muff and a wicked-looking veil who is plunged suddenly, hopelessly, into a fatal passion by a chance encounter in a shop or a discreet squeeze in the bus, and who suffers all the agonies of disappointed love until the story ends with shots in a taxi and a grim paragraph in the *Ami du Peuple*.

[1] The fact that Titus sacrifices Bérénice to an empire is probably the reason why English critics are inclined to rate *Bérénice* more highly than most French critics.

In English, expressions like "love at first sight" or "a broken heart" are not taken altogether seriously. It is thought unreasonable and unseemly to allow one's life to be ruined by such things, and love is reduced to the unlovely terminology of the Divorce Court: "Intimacy took place." In France it is far otherwise. There is a wealth of human experience behind the simple phrases: *une inclination aveugle*—sudden, blind, helpless passion; *chagrin d'amour*—the overwhelming despair of the person who has loved and lost; the passion of *une femme au déclin de l'âge*—the terrifying, destructive love of the woman on the threshold of middle age, and its counterpart in men—the *démon de midi* which plays such havoc with human happiness.[1]

In no other country has love been studied with such passionate interest. The study has not been confined to the scholarly disquisitions of dons or even to the works of poets and novelists. The greatest French moralists have written of it with the same care and seriousness as of the other great human problems, and with far more enthusiasm. The nature and growth of sexual passion, the various kinds and degrees of love, the difference between love and friendship, love and gallantry, love and ambition, have been carefully analysed and diligently classified and the findings enshrined in a number of imperishable maxims. The works of Descartes, La Rochefoucauld and Pascal, La Bruyère and a host of lesser writers are a mine of *practical* wisdom on this absorbing subject. The soothing tone of the moralist banishes a dull *malaise* by telling you exactly what you feel, and the philosopher explains why you feel as you do. You disregard their "tips" at your peril. If you mistake a momentary *froideur* for *indifférence*, you will probably miss your chance and be condemned to lifelong unhappiness. On the other

[1] No one who has lived in France can suppose that this is an exaggeration or can doubt that for the French *l'amour* is the most absorbing, the most exciting, thing in life. I well remember the sense of hushed expectancy which descended on the company when a visitor to the family in which I was living entered with the remark: "Madame X a quitté son mari." "Tiens, Madame X. Je ne l'aurais jamais cru." "Mais si, Thérèse, tu sais . . ." The record of this family in love was by no means unremarkable. I recall one *coup de foudre* and three serious cases of *chagrin d'amour*. Two of the victims languished silently, but the third almost came to an untimely end. A sixteen-year-old girl, who had fallen wildly in love with an Indian student, threw herself from a third-story window in a fury of despair, turned a complete somersault in mid-air and landed, miraculously, on her feet on the soft earth underneath and escaped with a severe shaking.

hand, if you mistake a passing *inclination* for a *grande passion* you will certainly end up in the Divorce Court.

"Il est difficile de définir l'amour," said La Rochefoucauld: "ce qu'on en peut dire est que, dans l'âme, c'est une passion de régner; dans les esprits, c'est une sympathie; et dans les corps, ce n'est qu'une envie cachée et délicate de posséder ce que l'on aime après beaucoup de mystères."

The same astringent, slightly acid note is perceptible in his other maxims:

"Si on juge de l'amour par la plupart de ses effets, il ressemble plus à la haine qu'à l'amitié."

"Il y a des gens qui n'auraient jamais été amoureux s'ils n'avaient jamais entendu parler de l'amour."

La Bruyère is a more genial and sometimes a more penetrating guide:

"L'amour naît brusquement, sans autre réflexion, par tempérament ou par faiblesse: un trait de beauté nous fixe, nous détermine . . ."

He is a master of the phrase that echoes in the memory long after one has closed the book, distilling its essence slowly like lavender which perfumes a whole wardrobe:

"C'est faiblesse que d'aimer; c'est souvent une autre faiblesse que de guérir."

"L'amour commence par l'amour; et l'on ne saurait passer de la plus forte amitié qu'à un amour faible."

"L'amour qui naît subitement est le plus long à guérir."

These maxims are not a cure for love—the moralists all agree that it is incurable—their aim is to enable the *malade* to probe and understand his *maladie*.

The most striking thing about the great French moralists is the continuity of their work. The maxims are not isolated discoveries made by solitary individuals experimenting in their own laboratories. They not only have behind them layers and layers of civilization; they are a product of the collective experience of the race, so that we detect the voice of civilization itself in the single maxim. It is interesting to watch the evolution of this collective experience, to see the different writers stretching their hands out to one another across the ages, to listen to the new voice taking up the old theme and adding something to it.

"L'amitié peut subsister entre des gens de différents sexes, exempte même de toute grossièreté," said La Bruyère . . . "Cette liaison n'est ni passion ni amitié pure: elle fait classe à part."

It was left for a later writer to find the perfect definition of this friendship—*l'amitié amoureuse.*

When La Rochefoucauld urbanely remarks:

"On a bien de la peine à rompre quand on ne s'aime plus"

the voice that answers him is the anguished voice of Benjamin Constant:

". . . telle est la bizarrerie de notre cœur misérable, que nous quittons avec un déchirement horrible ceux près de qui nous demeurions sans plaisir."

And when he observes in still another maxim:

"La jalousie naît toujours avec l'amour; mais elle ne meurt pas toujours avec lui"

it is the figure of the seedy, asthmatic Proust that he conjures up, brooding darkly in his cork-lined room over the infidelities of the dead Albertine.

Stendhal distinguishes four kinds of love: *l'amour-passion, l'amour-goût, l'amour-physique, l'amour de vanité.* But it was Jules Lemaître who coined the perfect word for the first of the four in his study of Racine—*l'amour-maladie.*

ii

It is for these reasons that the French interest in love seems to me to be one of the signs of the intense psychological realism of a great people. It is with love that the greatest French poet of the seventeenth century is concerned from one end of his secular plays to the other. Although there is much that is undeniably original in his study of sexual passion and some dangerous secrets are given away, Racine has his roots deep in the past, and his conception of love is largely derived from a much older tradition. He reveals impulses which lay buried—and buried for good reason—in the unconscious memory of the race. In his fascinating book, *l'Amour et l'Occident*,[1] M. Denis de Rougemont has shown that Racine can only be fully appreciated when we know something of the "myth" which received its classic formulation in the twelfth-century *Roman de Tristan* and has pervaded European literature ever since. It is worth giving a brief account of his findings before going on to study the texts of the plays.

"My Lords, will it please you to hear a fine tale of love and death?"

The opening sentence of Bédier's *Roman de Tristan et Iseut*[2] provides us with the first clue to the myth—the connection between love and death. It will be recalled that Tristan went on a mission to Ireland to find a bride for his uncle, King Mark of Cornwall. Tristan slays the dragon and is given the King of Ireland's daughter, Iseut la Blonde, as a reward. He announces that he does not intend to marry Iseut himself, but proposes to take her to England to be the wife of his uncle. The pair set out for Tintagel. During the sea voyage, Iseut's maid accidentally gives Tristan and her mistress the "love potion" which Iseut's aunt had prepared for King Mark and his bride. Tristan and Iseut are overcome by a violent and fatal passion for one another which they proceed to satisfy at once. Nevertheless, Tristan decides to keep his promise, but though he hands Iseut over to his uncle, they do not cease to be lovers. The rest of the legend is taken up with their adventures: their three years' wandering in the forest, their repentance and Iseut's return to King Mark, Tristan's exile and his marriage to Iseut aux Blanches Mains in France, which remains *un mariage blanc*. Finally, when Tristan lies dying in France, he persuades his brother-in-law to fetch Iseut la Blonde from England for a last meeting. His wife overhears their plan to put up a white sail on the ship if Iseut is with him and a black one if she is not. The boat comes in sight. In a fit of jealousy Tristan's wife tells him that the sail is black. Tristan collapses and dies. Iseut la Blonde arrives, kisses the dead Tristan, lies down beside him and dies too.

[1] Paris, 1939. See especially Books I–IV. (An abridged edition of this book has been published in English under the title of *Passion and Society*. My references are to the French edition and the renderings are my own.)

[2] *Le Roman de Tristan et Iseut*, traduit et restauré par Joseph Bédier, Paris, 1900.

"As long as one is free to stick to the facts and to express them openly and directly," writes M. de Rougemont, "there can be no myth. On the contrary, the myth makes its appearance when it would be either dangerous or impossible to admit openly certain facts about religion, society and emotional relationships which we are anxious to preserve or which we could not allow to be destroyed. For example, we have no need of myths to express scientific truths . . . *But we do need a myth to express the obscure and inadmissible fact that passion is linked with death.*"[1]

M. de Rougemont goes on to analyse certain symbols which recur in all the early versions of the Tristan legend. The two most important are the *philtre* (the "love potion") and the "obstacle." When Tristan announces that he is taking Iseut back to England to marry his uncle she is a little piqued, not because she is in love with him but because it is customary for the hero who slays the dragon to marry the King's daughter himself. She also has a grudge against him because it was he who three years earlier had slain her own uncle, Morholt the Giant, who had terrorized the Kingdom of Cornwall. When they drink the love potion, we are told:

"Non, ce n'était pas du vin: c'était la passion, c'était l'âpre joie et l'angoisse sans fin, et la mort."[2]

The legend makes it clear that the love of Tristan and Iseut is a "sin," but it is also made clear in their meeting with the hermit that they are under a spell, that they cannot help themselves. The hermit says:

> Amors par force vos demeine!
> Combien durra vostre folie?
> Trop avez mené ceste vie.

When they are urged to repent and separate, they excuse themselves by saying that they are not in love with one another:

> Q'el m'aime, c'est par la poison
> Ge ne me pus de lié partir,
> N'ele de moi . . .

Thus Tristan, and Iseut supports him:

> Sire, por Dieu omnipotent,
> Il ne m'aime pas, ne je lui,
> Fors par un herbé dont je bui
> Et il en but: ce fu pechiez.

[1] p. 8 (italics in the text). [2] Bédier, *op. cit.*, p. 75.

The symbol of the "obstacle" is not less interesting. Tristan might have refused to hand Iseut over to Mark and they could have gone away together and married. Instead, he hands her over; she marries Mark, and her passion for Tristan leads to adultery. When Tristan is exiled, he marries Iseut aux Blanches Mains whom he does not love and thus of his own free will creates another "obstacle."

M. de Rougemont adopts the psycho-analytical explanation of these symbols, and he seems to me to prove his case up to the hilt. The "love potion" is an "alibi." "C'est ce qui permet aux malheureux amants de dire: 'Vous voyez que je n'y suis pour rien, vous voyez que c'est plus fort que moi.' "[1] It stands for the irresistible nature of sexual passion which excuses every excess, every breach of divine or human law because it deprives the lovers of free-will and they cease to be answerable for their own actions. They are right in protesting that they are not in love with one another: they are in love with love. The hidden motive of their love—the motive that society for its own safety cannot admit—is the death-wish. The object of desire is not another human being, but death. It follows from this that love is regarded as being essentially anti-social and disruptive. It is also of its nature unhappy or, as M. de Rougemont puts it, it is *l'amour réciproque malheureux.*

"Happiness in love has no history [he continues] ... Without the husband, there would be nothing left for the two lovers to do but to marry. Now one simply cannot imagine Tristan marrying Iseut. She is the sort of woman that one doesn't marry. For if one did, one would stop loving her because she would no longer be the woman that in fact she is. Mrs. Tristan—just imagine it!"[2]

And of course we can't imagine anything so prosaic as "Mrs. Tristan"! They would not love one another unless there were an obstacle which threatened to separate them and maintain their unhappiness. The obstacle is, therefore, an irritant, a stimulant that prevents their love from dying or the effects of the love potion from wearing off.[3] That the principal obstacle should be marriage underlines the essentially anti-social nature of passion and the myth becomes a symbol of a subterranean attack on society and its

---

[1] *l'Amour et l'Occident*, p. 39.   [2] *ibid.*, pp. 2, 35.

[3] In some versions of the legend the effects of the love potion last only for three years; but though Tristan and Iseut repent at the end of that time and she returns to Mark, they soon start all over again!

institutions. The other obstacle—Tristan's marriage—has a twofold significance. It is intended to stimulate the first Iseut's desire for him, but the fact that the marriage is not consummated also makes it a symbol of suicide and another manifestation of the death-wish. There is a further point which is not perhaps sufficiently brought out in M. de Rougemont's analysis. Although the love of Tristan and Iseut is clearly seen to be "sinful," the anonymous authors of the legend do everything possible to work up their audience's sympathy for the lovers. Their love may be sinful, but that does not prevent divine protection and miraculous intervention from saving them at moments of great danger, such as Tristan's leap from the chapel or Iseut's trial by ordeal, when she succeeds by a trick. The barons, who repeatedly warn the King of the love between his wife and nephew and who evidently stand for society trying to safeguard its institutions, are invariably described as *barons félons*; and the King's retainers who act as spies and informers against the lovers all come to a violent end at the hands of Tristan or his friends. I think that this must be ascribed to the influence of the code of chivalry. Love and marriage were always regarded as incompatible, and passionate love meant adultery. The barons thus become the symbols of the "bourgeois respectability" of a later day, and are the enemy. The lesson is obvious. Love may be sinful, unhappy and anti-social, but it is also sacrosanct, and though the lovers are doomed from the first this does not prevent them from enjoying special favours until the moment of their doom.

M. de Rougemont goes on to trace the fortunes of the "myth" in French life and literature from the twelfth century down to our own times. He discusses its revival in the seventeenth century, its "profanation" in the eighteenth and nineteenth centuries and its final degradation in the twentieth century, when he argues that in the popular film it is a potent factor in the modern attack on marriage.

It is, however, the seventeenth century that interests us here. Corneille's work is well described as *le mythe combattu* and Racine's as *le mythe déchaîné* and finally as *le mythe puni*. For the potency of the "myth" in Racine's plays is unmistakable. In almost every play we are confronted, in varying forms, with the "love potion" and the "obstacle." There is an obvious parallel between the mission of Tristan and the mission of Oreste in *Andromaque*. Tristan has been sent to find a wife for the King, falls in love with her himself and

G*

seduces her. Oreste arrives in Epirus as the Ambassador of Greece on a special mission to see that Pyrrhus keeps his promise to marry Hermione. Instead, he murders Pyrrhus and attempts to carry off Hermione. In other plays the obstacle is a "law" which separates the lovers, or a "vow" which binds one of them to a third party, or even a blood-relationship which would make their love "incestuous."[1] In *Britannicus* the lovers are separated by the claims of the Emperor, in *Bérénice* by the "claims of State," in *Mithridate* by the rivalry of father and son, and in *Iphigénie* by the need to propitiate the gods by a sacrifice. It is, however, *Phèdre* that provides the perfect illustration of M. de Rougemont's thesis. The "obstacle" is twofold: it is "incest" which stands between Phèdre and Hippolyte, and the "law" imposed by Thésée which separates Hippolyte and Aricie. The "love potion" is disguised as Venus and its origins are plain in the celebrated lines:

> Ce n'est plus une ardeur dans mes veines cachée;
> C'est Vénus toute entière à sa proie attachée.

For in blaming Venus for her guilty passion, Phèdre uses precisely the same argument as Tristan and Iseut when they visit the hermit. It is this that enables her to plead: "Vous voyez que je n'y suis pour rien, vous voyez que c'est plus fort que moi."

The passion that Racine's characters feel for one another is clearly of the same nature as the passion of Tristan and Iseut. Their habit of describing lovers and mistresses as their "prey" is evidently the reappearance of the "death-wish." Their love is heavy with doom and we know from the first that death is the only outcome. Racine's originality, as we shall see, lies largely in his concentration on the "paroxysm" and in the light that he throws on the state of mind of his characters when the crisis is reached.

iii

Although there is undoubtedly an element of complicity in Racine's study of sexual passion, his approach to the problem was a serious one and he did not indulge, as hostile critics have alleged, in the analysis of violent passion merely for its own sake.

---

[1] Compare the incident in the legend where King Mark finds the lovers asleep in a cabin in the forest fully dressed and with Tristan's sword between them. The King removes the sword and places his own there in its place, so that it becomes a symbol of the "law" which the lovers have transgressed.

In making sexual passion the mainspring of human action, he anticipated some of the more revolutionary findings of contemporary psychologists. It did not narrow the scope of his work; it enabled him to make one of the most searching examinations of human nature in French literature; and as I have already suggested, it was precisely his interest in love that helped him to break down the barriers between the different classes and to concentrate on emotions which are common to human nature as a whole without distinction of class or creed.

There is a passage in *Bajazet* which provides a good illustration of the sombre power of Racine's study of man and also serves to remind us that he lived in the same century as John Donne. Atalide is proposing to surrender her lover to Roxane and to commit suicide:

> Roxane s'estimait assez récompensée,
> Et j'aurais en mourant cette douce pensée
> Que, vous ayant moi-même imposé cette loi,
> Je vous ai vers Roxane envoyé plein de moi;
> Qu'emportant chez les morts toute votre tendresse,
> Ce n'est point un amant en vous que je lui laisse.

We must not misunderstand the word *tendresse*—"that terrible little word," as a French critic once called it. It is not the same as love; it is the capacity for love, a capacity which is transformed from potency to act as soon as a suitable object presents itself.[1] In Racine's poetry love is always what Corneille called *une inclination aveugle*, a blind urge for possession which not only prefers the death of the beloved to allowing him to fall into the clutches of a rival, but which sees consummation not in union with, but in the pursuit and destruction of its "prey." The tragic dilemma lies in the fact that lacking *tendresse*, man is deprived of something vital without which he ceases to be man and becomes an impotent shell. With it he is inexorably dedicated to destruction and death.

In a passage which I set at the head of this chapter, the great Benjamin Constant declared that the effect of love is to *égarer notre raison* and its aim to *procurer des jouissances*. Racine is almost exclusively concerned with its effect, and the *jouissances* invariably elude his characters. The word *égarer* was carefully chosen by Constant and it was a favourite word of Racine's, a word that goes a

[1] *cf.* "*L'amour* où je voulais amener sa *tendresse*" (*Britannicus*).

long way towards illuminating the central experience of his poetry. The rhythm of passion is also the rhythm of the plays and it always follows the same course. The movement is indeed almost physiological, and it is well illustrated by Néron's speech in *Britannicus*, Act II. Sc. ii:

Excité d'un désir curieux,
Cette nuit je l'ai vue arriver en ces lieux,
Triste, levant au ciel ses yeux mouillés de larmes,
Qui brillaient au travers des flambeaux et des armes;
Belle, sans ornements, dans le simple appareil
D'une beauté qu'on vient d'arracher au sommeil.
Que veux-tu? Je ne sais si cette négligence,
Les ombres, les flambeaux, les cris et le silence,
Et le farouche aspect de ses fiers ravisseurs,
Relevaient de ses yeux les timides douceurs.
Quoi qu'il en soit, ravi d'une si belle vue,
J'ai voulu lui parler, et ma voix s'est perdue:
Immobile, saisi d'un long étonnement,
Je l'ai laissé passer dans son appartement.
J'ai passé dans le mien. C'est là que, solitaire,
De son image en vain j'ai voulu me distraire:
Trop présente à mes yeux je croyais lui parler;
J'aimais jusqu'à ses pleurs que je faisais couler.
Quelquefois, mais trop tard, je lui demandais grâce;
J'employais les soupirs, et même la menace.
Voilà comme, occupé de mon nouvel amour,
Mes yeux, sans se fermer, ont attendu le jour . . .
Soit que son cœur, jaloux d'une austère fierté,
Enviât à nos yeux sa naissante beauté,
Fidèle à sa douleur, et dans l'ombre enfermée,
Elle se dérobait même à sa renommée;
Et c'est cette vertu, si nouvelle à la cour,
Dont la persévérance irrite mon amour.
Quoi, Narcisse! tandis qu'il n'est point de Romaine
Que mon amour n'honore et ne rende plus vaine,
Qui, dès qu'à ses regards elle ose se fier,
Sur le cœur de César ne les vienne essayer,
Seule dans son palais la modeste Junie
Regarde leurs honneurs comme une ignominie,
Fuit, et ne daigne pas peut-être s'informer
Si César est aimable, ou bien s'il sait aimer?
Dis-moi, Britannicus l'aime-t-il?

Racine's critics have pointed out that Néron is only seen in this play on the threshold of his career of crime and that he is far milder than the monster of history. Now it was no part of Racine's purpose to tone down Néron's character out of respect for contemporary susceptibilities or to present posterity with an exact picture of the historical Nero. His Néron is the blasé representative of an ageing civilization and a vehicle for Racine's criticism of the ruling class. The passage is an admirable example of the beauty and subtlety of his poetry. It can be seen that the language is psychological. Racine does not describe the physical appearance of people or things for its own sake; he only does so in order to reveal the state of mind of an observer. His descriptions of things are therefore general, and his descriptions of feelings concrete and particular. We do not see Junie herself; we only see her through Néron's eyes. He himself does not see her as an individual; his attention is concentrated on his own feelings and Junie is merely the "prey" who will provide him with fresh sensations. His interest is selective and limited to those features which appeal directly to his sexual desires or, as he puts it, "irrite mon amour." Only general terms are used to describe her such as "yeux mouillés de larmes," "belle, sans ornements," "timides douceurs" and "naissante beauté."

Néron's own feelings, however, are complex. The "désir curieux" contains an element of refined corruption, but it also suggests the devious, winding course of his desires. The absence of all ornament is a symbol of simplicity and purity which are distinguished from the tricks and disingenuousness of the ladies of the Court. The flickering torches reflect the stirrings of Néron's feelings and may recall the décor of the Court orgies. The "arms" and the "soldiers" emphasize the softness and helplessness of the victim and are also a sign of Néron's power over her. This power is purely physical and the victim remains remote and inaccessible, which only serves to titillate Néron's jaded senses. His corruption is underlined by his sudden shyness; but there is no real volition behind "J'ai voulu lui parler"; the shyness is a perverse archness and is contrasted with the genuine timidity of Junie.

The success of the passage depends to a large extent on the way in which the movement of feeling is woven into the movement of the procession of soldiers with their captive. It determines the tempo and it gives the passage its internal coherence. The procession passes with great rapidity, and the rapidity—the shift and change of exciting, stimulating feelings blending with the measured tread of the guards—reflects the rapid growth of Néron's "interest." But as Junie disappears from view with her captors, whose *farouche* vitality makes Néron even more conscious of his need for stimulation, there is a sudden slowing down of the tempo.

Immobile, saisi d'un long étonnement

provides the speaker with a *soulagement*, a vicarious satisfaction. He goes into his own room where the solitude increases the effect of his impressions and he indulges in a form of *delectatio morosa*. The solitude is invaded by sexual fantasies which torment him. He tries to brush them aside, but they return with renewed force. The tempo quickens as momentary satisfaction changes to the irritation of exasperated desires. The *austère fierté* and the *vertu* are both attractive and irritating; attractive because they offer a fresh, inviolate "prey"; irritating because they represent a formidable obstacle in the way of satisfaction—a moral obstacle.

Néron is not restrained by moral scruples of his own, but by a code which is recognized by the intended victim and which he himself does not recognize. This turns the chase into a moral obstacle race. In nearly all the plays, Racine's principal characters start at a point *inside* the moral code of society, but they are driven by their own furious passions *outside* society altogether. This is Néron's journey, and, in the other plays, by the time they have reached the state of paroxysm the characters are in the same position. Néron's starting-point is the *désir curieux* which leads him to the moral barriers represented by *austère fierté* and *vertu*. He knows that he cannot break them down and will have to circumvent them by the removal of Britannicus. The line

Dis-moi, Britannicus l'aime-t-il?

is the point at which he has arrived. He is now ready to commit murder, is indeed a potential murderer. For these stories always end with murder or suicide or both, and the characters never have any difficulty in finding people to tell them that the moral code not only does not matter, but does not exist once the heart is engaged.

Mais l'amour ne suit point ces lois imaginaires

cries Roxane, and she speaks for all Racine's heroines. Passion is the reality, "law" but the shadow. Passion sweeps aside law, reason and morality as it hurries humanity down the dizzy slope to destruction. The conviction that passion is absolutely irresistible is common to all the characters, and it appears to be a matter for rejoicing or lamentation according to their personal outlook. Roxane proclaims the fact triumphantly in a line of immense vitality:

> Viens m'engager ta foi: le temps fera le reste.

But some of Racine's finest lines express a different view—a tragic sense that it is too late, that all the supports have been removed:

> Il n'est plus temps. Il sait mes ardeurs insensées.
> De l'austère pudeur les bornes sont passées.

> Je me suis engagé trop avant.
> Je vois que la raison cède à la violence.

There is nothing genteel, nothing bloodless, about these feelings. Racine is at some pains to emphasize the physical side of love. In the great speech in Act IV, Sc. ii of *Britannicus* Agrippine remarks:

> une loi moins sévère
> Mit Claude dans mon *lit*, et Rome à mes genoux.

The bed sticks out in Racine's poetry. It is the ultimate goal towards which all these frenzied lovers strive; and neither the silken canopies nor the coroneted sheets can hide the violence of the drama that will be enacted there, or its appalling consequences:

> Ses gardes, son palais, son *lit*, m'étaient soumis,
> Je lui laissai sans fruit consumer sa tendresse.

Thus Agrippine, and she, too, speaks for all Racine's heroines. One of the most striking figures in the plays is the predatory female who for all her air of modesty and virtue pursues the reluctant male and sucks out his vitality.

Although the conflict, in which "law" is swept away or conveniently relaxed in order to smooth the heroine's path to an incestuous couch, springs from a profound hostility between the individual and society, it is not until we reach *Phèdre* and *Athalie* that the issue becomes a specifically moral one. The characters in the final plays are in a sense destroyed by their own guilty consciences, but those in the earlier plays are the victims of a catastrophe of a different nature. When, for example, Oreste declares:

> Je pensai que la guerre et la gloire
> De soins plus importants rempliraient ma mémoire;
> Que, mes sens reprenant leur première vigueur,
> L'amour achèverait de sortir de mon cœur,

it is clear that he is not concerned with the relative values of *gloire* and *amour*. Sexual passion is not regarded as wrong in itself, as it is in *Phèdre*, or as the occasion of wrongful actions; it is seen to be something very like a physical disturbance, a disease which corrodes and undermines the native health and "vigour" of the human organism.

In a comment on the line:

> Leur haine ne fera qu'irriter sa tendresse,

Jacques Rivière pointed out that it formulates the basic principle of Racine's psychology. There is no conflict between principle and feeling or between reason and emotion, but the naked friction of one set of feelings on another which ends by destroying both.

"There is nothing in his mind," said Rivière of Oreste, "which, properly speaking, acts as a dam against the wave of love except a contrary feeling which you can call anger, resentment, hate or what you like, but which at bottom is of the same nature and the same stuff as the passion against which it is pitted."[1]

Once the paroxysm has begun, nothing can stop it. The essence of the process is not that the characters are completely at the mercy of their passions and that reason is impotent; it is rather that they recognize paroxysm as their habitual state and resent any intervention of reason. When Oreste is reminded of the reason for his presence in Epirus, he cries impatiently

> Je suis las d'écouter la raison.

When he himself proceeds to give reasons for not killing Pyrrhus, Hermione retorts savagely:

> Ah! c'en est trop, Seigneur!
> Tant de raisonnements offensent ma colère.

[1] *Moralisme et littérature*, p. 28.

The appeal to "reason" provokes an immediate and violent reaction, not merely because it frustrates personal desires, but because it stands for a way of life which is fundamentally antipathetic to the inhabitants of Racine's world. Why this is so is explained in a remarkable utterance of Pyrrhus:

> Oui, mes vœux ont trop loin poussé leur *violence*
> Pour ne plus s'arrêter que dans l'indifférence.
> Songez-y bien: il faut désormais que mon cœur,
> S'il n'aime avec *transport*, haïsse avec *fureur*.
> Je n'épargnerai rien dans ma juste colère:
> Le fils me répondra des mépris de la mère . . .

The words "Il faut désormais que mon cœur . . ." betray a profound psychological need on the part of the speaker to live at a certain pitch of intensity, to maintain the paroxysm which is native to him. He is faced with three alternatives: "love," "hate," "indifference." Now "indifference" is ruled out precisely because it is a *neutral* state. It leaves no room for the "transports" of love or the "fury" of hatred and would lower the pitch of intensity in a manner that is inconceivable to Racine's characters, would bring them back to a norm of sanity which would be as distasteful as it would be precarious. Although "indifference" may seem to be of "the same nature and the same stuff" as love and hatred, Racine's characters instinctively perceive that it is the product of "reason," and reason is felt to be the enemy of life and spontaneity. For moderation in any form is impossible and abhorrent; the suggestion that they should even listen to reason is felt to be an intolerable affront which at once raises the paroxysm to its maximum intensity. There is no mistaking the place where the emphasis falls in a line that I have already quoted:

> Tant de raisonnements *offensent* ma colère.

When Hermione is finally thrown over by Pyrrhus, she says of him:

> Ah! je l'ai trop aimé pour ne le point haïr.

There is no middle course. They love or hate with the whole force of their being. Hatred is its own justification, and it seems natural in such a world to describe the wrath which proposes to visit the refusal of the mother on the head of an infant son as a *juste colère*.

In another place Oreste remarks:

> Détestant ses rigueurs, rabaissant ses attraits,
> Je défiais ses yeux de me troubler jamais.
> Voilà comme je crus étouffer ma tendresse.
> En ce calme trompeur j'arrivai dans la Grèce . . .

"Calm" is always unnatural and deceptive, is never more than a pause between the paroxysms, an uneasy truce between the combatants. For *tendresse* lasts as long as life; it cannot be "stifled"; it is either gratified or it turns into hatred, and the transports of love and the fury of hatred both lead to the same doom.

So they live, tragic or triumphant, in a perpetual state of oscillation between two extremes, never knowing from one moment to the next at which pole they will find themselves.

> S'il ne meurt aujourd'hui, je puis l'aimer demain

says Hermione of her feelings for Pyrrhus. And when she herself is described as

> Toujours prête à partir, et demeurant toujours,

the line suggests very well the restless movement of the whole play and of all Racine's work.

Much has been written of Racine's "elegance," of his "politeness" and of his fondness for the *formules protocolaires*, but their purpose has not always been appreciated. When Bajazet makes difficulties over accepting Roxane's offer of marriage, she replies in a tone of the utmost correctness:

> Je vous entends, Seigneur; je vois mon imprudence,
> Je vois que rien n'échappe à votre prévoyance.
> Vous avez pressenti jusqu'au moindre danger
> Où mon amour trop prompt vous allait engager.

The studied politeness and the biting contempt with which she contrasts his *prévoyance* (which is a product of "reason") and her own *imprudence*, her own *amour trop prompt*, shows that she is making an immense effort to control her feelings which are clearly on the verge of eruption. Her very restraint heightens the dramatic intensity of the scene and we can imagine the spectators beginning to feel warm under their collars, wriggling happily in their seats and whispering to one another: "Tu vois. Elle va éclater."

Twenty lines later it happens. The *Seigneur* and the whole protocol go by the board, and Roxane denounces Bajazet with a savage proletarian invective:

> Ne m'importune plus de tes raisons forcées.
> Je vois combien tes vœux sont loin de mes pensées;
> Je ne te presse plus, ingrat, d'y consentir.
> Rentre dans le néant dont je t'ai fait sortir . . .
> Mais je m'assure encore aux bontés de ton frère:
> Il m'aime, tu le sais; et malgré sa colère,
> Dans ton perfide sang je puis tout expier,
> Et ta mort suffira pour me justifier.
> N'en doute point, j'y cours, et dès ce moment même.

"Ça y est. La voilà partie," whisper the spectators; but almost at once there is another change of tone—a change this time to a warm familiarity, to a tone of supplication:

> Bajazet, écoutez, je sens que je vous aime:
> Vous vous perdez. Gardez de me laisser sortir.
> Le chemin est encore ouvert au repentir.
> Ne désespérez point une amante en furie.
> S'il m'échappait un mot, c'est fait de votre vie.

What is interesting in these lines is Roxane's consciousness that she is suspended between "love" and "hatred," and her attempt to persuade her disdainful lover to prevent her from swinging to the other pole which will lead to death and disaster. Bajazet's clumsy reference to his brother's love for Roxane:

> Peut-être que ma mort . . .
> Vous rendra dans son cœur votre première place,

drives her back at once to the *tutoiement passionné*:

> Dans son cœur? Ah! crois-tu, quand il le voudrait bien,
> Que si je perds l'espoir de régner dans le tien,
> D'une si douce erreur si longtemps possédée,
> Je puisse désormais souffrir une autre idée,
> Ni que je vive enfin, si je ne vis pour toi?
> Je te donne, cruel, des armes contre moi,
> Sans doute, et je devrais retenir ma faiblesse.
> Tu vas en triompher. Oui, je te le confesse,

J'affectais à tes yeux une fausse fierté.
De toi dépend ma joie et ma félicité.
De ma sanglante mort ta mort sera suivie.
Quel fruit de tant de soins que j'ai pris pour ta vie!

We can see now that Racine's elegance is a surface elegance which does nothing to mitigate the violence of the tumult which goes on beneath. His aim is to probe feelings which are properly speaking anterior to all civilization and which a supreme degree of civilization covers but cannot extinguish.[1] His polished elegance is a method of penetrating the defences of his sophisticated audience— that complicated system of inhibitions which is the product of centuries of civilization—and of evoking the response that he wants. There can be little doubt that it was his skill in revealing the primitive man beneath the civilized man which disconcerted his contemporaries and provoked the bitter attacks on his work by conservative critics. For the creation of Roxane reminded them uncomfortably of the exploits of an Anne de Gonzague or a Madame Murat, reminded them too pointedly of what lay only just beneath the surface of their splendid society. It was the triumph of Racine's art not simply to lay bare these feelings, but to give them a social reference, to show that they were bound to be in a state of constant eruption in a civilization which in some respects had become a façade. It was the tragedy of a people who were deprived of an order that could provide a proper outlet for their immense vitality; a force which was of necessity turned inward against itself to become a source of waste and destruction.

"A scene in Corneille," wrote Giraudoux, "is an official rendez-vous where one comes to discuss in hopes of a settlement. In Racine, it is the explanation which closes for the time a series of negotiations between wild beasts"; and a few pages later he speaks of Racine's characters confronting one another "on a footing of awful

---

[1] Racine's characters are conscious not only of the opposition between "love" and "reason," but of the fact that love is *anterior* to reason. In the quotation from *Britannicus* which follows, *amour* and *raison* really mean "passion" and "civilization." (The third line should be compared with Oreste's declaration on p. 176 above.)

NÉRON:
    Si jeune encor, se connaît-il lui-même?
    D'un regard enchanteur connaît-il le poison?
NARCISSE:
    Seigneur, l'amour toujours n'attend pas la raison.

equality, of physical and moral nudity."[1] The morality of Racine's world is the morality of the jungle, but the violence is intensified and not diminished by the characters' exceptional powers of insight, their extremely sensitive consciousness of their most intimate feelings which belonged to a people of whom the poet constantly uses the word *sensible*. This insight can be seen in the lines:

> Déjà même je crois entendre la réponse
> Qu'en secret contre moi votre haine prononce,

where the movement of feeling is seized before it becomes articulate. When exceptional insight into human feelings exists without a true social order, it can only work destructively. Racine's use of the words *menacé* and *atteint* is no less revealing than his fondness for the word *sensible*. His characters are only too conscious that their inner stability is threatened, and *atteint* shows how successful their enemies are in destroying it. For they use their gifts to torture themselves and each other. They possess like their creator a remarkable streak of cruelty, and their clairvoyance makes them immensely vulnerable for one another. It enables them to perceive, without possibility of error, the weakness of their opponents, to track life to its source, to strike and kill with deadly accuracy. Their desire to annihilate and their complete absence of pity are apparent in some lines from *Andromaque* in which Hermione recalls Pyrrhus' exploits in the Trojan war:

> Du vieux père d'Hector la valeur abattue
> Aux pieds de sa famille expirante à sa vue,
> Tandis que dans son sein votre bras enfoncé
> *Cherche un reste de sang que l'âge avait glacé.*

After planning the assassination of Pyrrhus, Hermione sends her *confidente* to Oreste with this message:

> Va le trouver: dis-lui qu'il apprenne à l'ingrat
> Qu'on l'immole à ma haine, et non pas à l'État.
> Chère Cléone, cours. Ma vengeance est perdue
> S'il ignore en mourant que c'est moi qui le tue.

The words *désordre* and *inutile* also recur all through the plays, and they reveal more clearly than anything the nature of the

[1] *op. cit.*, pp. 24, 27.

tragedy—the sense of helpless confusion in a world that offers the individual no help, no constructive principle for the ordering of his life. *Honneur* and *gloire* had lost their meaning; all that remained was an enemy to torture and destroy.

>Je crains de me connaître, en l'état où je suis,

cries one. Of another we are told:

>Il peut, Seigneur, il peut, dans ce *désordre* extrême
>Épouser ce qu'il hait, et punir ce qu'il aime.

In *Iphigénie* it is said:

>Il fallut s'arrêter, et la rame *inutile*
>Fatigua vainement une mer immobile.

The *inutile* suggests the hopelessness of the struggle, and the *fatigua* underlines the fact that the effort, instead of strengthening and purifying character as it does in Corneille, has the reverse effect and produces a state of exhaustion which undermines character. There is only one answer:

>Puisqu'après tant d'efforts ma résistance est vaine,
>Je me livre en aveugle au destin qui m'entraîne.

In this world passion is destiny. It is at once the source of life and of death. "Songez," said Roxane to her lover, "Songez"

>Que vous ne respirez qu'autant que je vous aime.

No one is in any doubt about the outcome, which is accepted not merely with resignation but with satisfaction:

>Je trouvais du plaisir à me perdre pour elle.

In making sexual passion the supreme value in a world of dissolving values, the last refuge of the man who has lost faith in all else, Racine anticipates the writers of a later age. He also anticipates them in revealing that man deliberately attaches himself to the principle of death and destruction, that it is indeed the death-wish which is the deepest and most secret thing in passion.

3. The Pattern of the Plays

I have never felt convinced by the view that Corneille's work represents a steady process of development from the early comedies to the final tragedies, but it is a claim which can be made with some confidence in the case of Racine. His poetry, indeed, is only fully intelligible when it is seen as a whole, as a logical progression from the early imitations of Corneille to *Phèdre* and *Athalie*.

His first play, *les Frères ennemis*, is a mechanical affair of little intrinsic value which need not detain us; but the second, *Alexandre le Grand*, cannot be altogether disregarded. It was in some ways an interesting experiment. It was written as a tribute to the King whom the poet presents in the guise of a Cornelian hero. Its interest lies in the way in which Racine's personal sensibility peeps out from behind phrases lifted bodily from Corneille. When Alexandre declares:

> ... au seul nom d'un roi jusqu'alors *invincible*,
> A de nouveaux exploits mon cœur devint *sensible*,

we feel at once that there is something wrong, that there is a contrast between the heroic vocabulary and the lack of a corresponding drive in the texture of the verse. *Invincible* is a borrowing from Corneille, but "mon cœur devint *sensible*" bears Racine's own stamp. The invincibility of the Cornelian hero might arouse the admiration of an opponent, but it would never provoke the reaction attributed to Alexandre in these lines, and the confusion runs all through the play. Alexandre's use of the heroic vocabulary is false and embarrassing; he has none of the "toughness" of the Cornelian hero and he is also without the sensitiveness of Racine's characters. He is nothing more than a ventriloquist's doll mouthing the big words in his thin, piping voice.

Andromaque is the first of the great masterpieces. It occupies the same place in Racine's work as the *Cid* in Corneille's, and it possesses the same peculiar beauty. But in spite of its beauty, an occasional roughness in the texture, which disappears in the later plays, and a certain note of harshness make it difficult of access when read for the first time. I have already drawn heavily on this play because it is the perfect illustration of some of Racine's special interests, but I cannot leave it without some further comments. One of the most striking things about it is the range of tone and mood displayed in the character of Hermione—the soft, caressing

> Le croirai-je, Seigneur, qu'un reste de tendresse
> Vous fasse ici chercher une triste princesse?

the perfidious

> Enfin, qui vous a dit que malgré mon devoir
> Je n'ai pas quelquefois souhaité de vous voir?

the haughty

> Seigneur, je le vois bien, votre âme prévenue
> Répand sur mes discours le venin qui la tue . . .

the indignant surprise of

> Qui vous l'a dit, Seigneur, qu'il me méprise?

the coarse brutality of

> Et tout ingrat qu'il est, il me sera plus doux
> De mourir avec lui que de vivre avec vous,

and what Mauriac calls the *tutoiement passionné* of

> Je ne t'ai point aimé, cruel? Qu'ai-je donc fait?

"C'est une certaine candeur violente de créature encore intacte," wrote Jules Lemaître of Hermione. Although Andromaque gives her name to the play, it is Hermione and Oreste who occupy the centre of the stage. For the play is a consummate study of youthful passion.[1] Racine chose a moment which comes once and once only in a life, and his study has the finality of great art.

The play is important for another reason. It illustrates Racine's approach to a Cornelian situation, and a comparison with the *Cid* helps us to understand in what sense Racine's impact produced a change of direction in French drama. There is an obvious conflict between Oreste's personal interests and the claims of State or, to use the Cornelian formula, between "love" and "honour." The startling innovation is not that "honour" is completely routed, but

---

[1] But compare: "Je parle d'Hermione comme d'une femme et non comme d'une jeune fille ce qui est contraire aux données de la pièce, mais conforme à son esprit. Le rôle n'est virginal à aucun moment." (Brisson, *op. cit.*, p. 37.)

that Oreste appears to be unaware that its claims even exist. He admits that he never had the slightest intention of carrying out his mission, but undertook it purely in the hope that it would give him a last opportunity of making a conquest of Hermione and of carrying her off. The violent conflict which eventually destroys him is not provoked by the irreconcilable claims of "love" and "honour," but by his failure to win Hermione. As the Ambassador of Greece, he hesitates, quite understandably, before making up his mind to assassinate the sovereign to whom he is accredited; but when it is done, it is not remorse for his crime that drives him mad. It is the realization that his elaborate "stratagems," which have culminated in murder, have been in vain and that Hermione is irrevocably lost to him.[1]

Although Britannicus gives his name to Racine's next tragedy, it is not primarily a study of youthful passion or even of youthful despotism. The young lovers do not occupy the centre of the stage; they are mainly interesting in that they are the pretext for Néron's crime. *Britannicus* is a more complex play than *Andromaque*. It is the first play in which Racine deals directly with political problems, and there are some lines in Act IV which show that he already understands very clearly the nature of dictatorship. Narcisse is advising his master against a policy of clemency:

> Mais, Seigneur, les Romains ne vous sont pas connus.
> Non, non, dans leurs discours ils sont plus retenus.
> Tant de précaution affaiblit votre règne:
> Ils croiront, en effet, mériter qu'on les craigne.
> Au joug depuis longtemps ils se sont façonnés.
> Ils adorent la main qui les tient enchaînés.

Britannicus points the way to *Athalie*, but the study of despotism is much more limited in scope than it is in Racine's last play. The despot only uses his absolute powers in an attempt to rid himself of one wife and to secure another. His crime is essentially a *crime d'amour*, but Racine's treatment of the connection between love and politics breaks fresh ground in his work. Néron's personal vanity is outraged by Junie's refusal, but he also feels that her refusal is an affront to his position as emperor:

---

1 His apology to Hermione, when announcing the murder of Pyrrhus, for not being able to find a place to stab him himself, is a characteristic touch.

> Du sang dont vous sortez rappelez la mémoire;
> Et ne préférez point, à la solide gloire
> Des honneurs dont César prétend vous revêtir,
> La gloire d'un refus, sujet au repentir.

The *solide gloire* which Néron dangles vainly before Junie's eyes is something much less estimable than Cornelian glory, but it shows the extent to which "love" and "ambition" are interrelated in the "police state." In *Britannicus* love is sought not merely for its own sake, but as a means to an end. Its exploitation is seen to be one of the most effective ways of obtaining political power, and the brazen Agrippine admits it frankly:

> Je souhaitai son lit, dans la seule pensée
> De vous laisser au trône où je serais placée.

The royal bed is the symbol of political domination. The banishment or escape of one of the partners from the bed is the sign of a change in the political "line-up":

> Je vois de votre cœur Octavie effacée,
> Prête à sortir du lit où je l'avais placée.

In *Bajazet* Roxane uses her dictatorial powers to try to force her "brother-in-law" to marry her, but it is not a political play in the same sense as *Britannicus*. Racine said in his Preface that it was based on an incident which took place in Turkey in 1638 and that he had heard the story from the Comte de Cézy who was French Ambassador to the Ottoman Empire at the time. No one has succeeded in tracing a copy of the account which Racine purported to have read, and some of his editors have suggested that the story is a *superchérie*. It may well be that Racine invented it in order to forestall criticism of the content of the play. There is no doubt that it was the setting of the seraglio which fired his imagination, and in the creation of Roxane he went a good deal further in his study of violent passion than in any of the preceding plays. *Bajazet* is interesting for another reason. It is strikingly like *Phèdre* with the religious *motif* omitted. In essentials it is the same story—the story of a woman whose "guilty" passion destroys "innocent" lovers.

The innocent couple whose happiness is threatened by the

claims of State but who eventually escape destruction is the theme of both *Mithridate* and *Iphigénie*. Neither of these plays is among Racine's supreme achievements, but *Mithridate* is a new departure. Xipharès says of his father's love for Monine:

> En ce malheur je tremblai pour ses jours;
> Je redoutai du roi les cruelles amours.
> Tu sais combien de fois ses jalouses tendresses
> Ont pris soin d'assurer la mort de ses maîtresses.

The *cruelles amours* and the *jalouses tendresses* show the direction in which Racine was moving. Mithridate, as Racine presents him, is a comparatively harmless and rather pathetic figure; but we have the impression that his creator was itching to give his audience a powerful study of sadism and was only prevented from doing so by the *bienséances*. The weakness of the play lies mainly in the contrast between Mithridate's reputation and the poor, jealous old man who actually appears on the stage.

These, then, are the lines along which Racine's work was developing, but it remains to point out a further change which took place after *Andromaque* and which goes deeper than any of those I have already mentioned. *Andromaque* is a consummate study of youthful passion certainly, but it is a play which could only have been written at a particular moment in a poet's development. In the plays which followed, the focus shifts from youth to middle age. Racine's greatest plays are not studies of innocence; they are studies of crises in the lives of middle-aged women who are certainly not *intactes*. As his genius ripened, characters like Agrippine, Roxane, Phèdre and Athalie and, to a lesser extent, the middle-aged warrior in *Mithridate* who returns home after his armies have been defeated and his country laid waste by a "useless campaign," became the symbols of a spiritual crisis through which society was passing. When played by a distinguished actress, the great *tirades*—Agrippine's encounter with Néron in *Britannicus* Act IV. Sc. ii, Phèdre's confession of her jealousy and Athalie's dream—have an impressiveness which is unique in the European theatre.[1]

---

[1] Racine's genius was in many ways a feminine one and this is apparent in the immense superiority of his female characters. Oreste is the only one of his men who can be compared with the greatest of his women.

4. *Bérénice*

Bérénice, like *Andromaque*, has a special place in the Racinian canon, and a few words must be said about it before passing on to a detailed discussion of *Phèdre* and *Athalie*. The play was in the nature of a "command performance." Louis XIV's sister-in-law, the charming and tragic Henriette d'Angleterre, suggested to Corneille and Racine that they should write plays on the love of Titus and Bérénice. The two poets set to work each unaware that the suggestion had been made to the other. Their plays were both produced in the autumn of 1670 and the competition led to a signal defeat for the ageing Corneille. It is probable that Henriette would have regretted her mischievous suggestion had she been there to see the result. But she was not. She had died during the previous summer either of a gastric ulcer or of appendicitis.

It is said that Henriette herself provided Racine with the material as well as the subject of his play, that Titus and Bérénice are none other than Louis XIV and Henriette. "She only meant the King to love her as a sister-in-law," wrote Madame de La Fayette in her *Histoire de Madame Henriette d'Angleterre*,[1] "but I fancy that he loved her differently. And she, I think, believed that she merely returned his fraternal affection; yet, perhaps, she gave him something more. At all events, since they were both infinitely lovable and both of an amorous disposition, since they met day after day in a continual round of pleasure and festivity, there were onlookers who thought that they possessed for one another the attraction and charm which precede a *grande passion*."

In spite of its success on the seventeenth-century stage, *Bérénice* has not worn well. It was felt in the next century by Vauvenargues to be inferior to Racine's finest work. This view was shared by Sainte-Beuve—we remember his *mot* about the "charmante et mélodieuse faiblesse"—and is held among living French critics by M. Pierre Brisson. It is curious that Lemaître, whose book did so much to dispose of the "tender Racine," should have declared that *Bérénice* is "the most Racinian of the plays because it is the most tender."[2] It seems to me on the contrary to be the least success-

[1] *Mémoires de Madame de La Fayette*, publiés avec préface, notes et tables par Eugène Asse, Paris, 1890, p. 36.
[2] *op. cit.*, p. 204.

ful of the mature tragedies precisely because Racine was obliged to handle a theme which was eminently unsuited to his genius. It is the only one of his plays in which "honour" triumphs over "love," and his palpable disbelief in the values invoked drove him to strange lengths in order to impose on others convictions which he himself did not hold. It is this that makes the verse seem hollow and inflated. At bottom it is a curious *tour de force*. Racine hovers on the verge of a highly refined and very personal sentimentality, and only his extreme virtuosity prevents him from succumbing to it.

"It is not necessary to have blood and corpses in a tragedy," he wrote in his Preface; "it is sufficient if the action is great, if the characters are heroic, the passions aroused, and if the whole play makes us feel that majestic sadness which is the pleasure proper to tragedy."

We may suspect that heroism and *tristesse majestueuse* are incompatible and that it was the attempt to combine them which makes the verse of the play so instructive. Titus is no hero; he is a prig who dwells voluptuously on his own weaknesses which he manages both to excuse and to boast about:

> Tu ne l'ignores pas: toujours la renommée
> Avec le même éclat n'a pas semé mon nom.
> Ma jeunesse, nourrie à la cour de Néron,
> S'égarait, cher Paulin, par l'exemple abusée,
> Et suivait du plaisir la pente trop aisée.

It is not surprising after this to find that *honneur* and *gloire* are invoked with great frequency. When Titus declares:

> Bérénice a longtemps balancé la victoire;
> Et si je penche enfin du côté de ma *gloire*,
> Crois qu'il m'en a coûté, pour vaincre tant d'amour,
> Des combats dont mon cœur saignera plus d'un jour,

or

> Forcez votre amour à se taire;
> Et d'un œil que la *gloire* et la raison éclaire
> Contemplez mon devoir dans toute sa rigueur.
> Vous-même contre vous fortifiez mon cœur:
> Aidez-moi, s'il se peut, à vaincre sa faiblesse,
> A retenir des pleurs qui m'échappent sans cesse,

or

> Plaignez ma *grandeur* importune.
> Maître de l'univers, je règle sa fortune;
> Je puis faire les rois, je puis les déposer:
> Cependant de mon cœur je ne puis disposer

—we feel that though he is giving up Bérénice in obedience to the claims of State, he is not concerned with the common good or even with the sufferings of Bérénice; he is completely taken up with his own feelings. All these passages begin with a reference to *gloire* or *grandeur*, which are *public* virtues, but they all lead back to his *private* feelings, to his "bleeding heart" or the "tears" which are shed with such abundance throughout the play.[1] The same morbid concern for his own feelings is apparent in the references in other places to his *cruel sacrifice* and his *cruelle constance*. The word *gloire* has no moral content; it simply means reputation or what people will think of him if he prefers love to an empire. There is something repellent about this selfish and self-centred preoccupation with his reputation which makes him oblivious to everyone's sufferings but his own. The rhetorical tone in which *gloire* is invoked betrays a note of falseness which runs all through the play and which we may feel sure was no part of the poet's intention. The weaknesses of Racine's hero point to an element of uncertainty in the poet's mind and this is brought home by the way in which the verse, after a few flourishes, simply peters out. Thus in the line

> Des combats dont mon cœur saignera plus d'un jour

the *saignera* is evidently an attempt to heighten feelings which are in danger of flagging.

These weaknesses become still more pronounced in Bérénice's

> Ah! Seigneur, songez-vous en vous-même
> Combien ce mot cruel est affreux quand on aime?
> Dans un mois, dans un an, comment souffrirons-nous,
> Seigneur, que tant de mers me séparent de vous?

[1] *cf.* "The whole play is inundated with tears. Bérénice weeps; Antiochus weeps; Arsace and Phénice weep because they see them weeping. As for Titus, he doesn't weep, he streams. . . . It is a veritable deluge. There is not a dry eye in the play. There is not a handkerchief, not a carpet, not a scene, not a couplet, not even a sigh which isn't drenched in tears." (Brisson, *op. cit.*, pp. 73, 76.)

Que le jour recommence et que le jour finisse
Sans que jamais Titus puisse voir Bérénice,
Sans que de tout le jour je puisse voir Titus?

This passage is an example of the hollow, inflated verse of which
I have spoken. There is an obvious attempt on the part of the speaker
to create a "big scene" and every resource is used to heighten the
effect, from the over-statement of

Combien ce mot *cruel* est *affreux* quand on aime . . .

to the emphasis on time and space, and the sentimental reflections
on the sun rising and the sun setting.

As the play progresses, the impression becomes stronger that
the characters are not characters at all, but dummies who declaim
the arbitrary sentiments which the poet puts into their mouths. In
place of a detached analysis of emotion, they look at themselves
from without. Their one concern is the effect of their high-flown
sentiments on the audience; they do not consider the intrinsic
rightness or wrongness of their actions and feelings, but only what
people will think if they choose some other course, or how much
people will be impressed by their *cruel sacrifice*. It is on a note of
smug self-satisfaction that the play ends, when Bérénice urges the
unfortunate Antiochus (who at least is honest about his feelings)
to take a leaf out of her book:

Sur Titus et sur moi réglez votre conduite:
Je l'aime, je le fuis; Titus m'aime, il me quitte.
Portez loin de mes yeux vos soupirs et vos fers.
Adieu, servons tous trois d'exemple à l'univers
De l'amour la plus tendre et la plus malheureuse
Dont il puisse garder l'histoire douleureuse.

There is something disconcerting about the complacency of a
woman who can hold her own conduct up as a model not merely to
a few friends but to the "universe," and who is so convinced of
the importance to history of her own emotions.

IV. *PHÈDRE*

"L'entraînement de notre misérable nature humaine n'a jamais été plus mis à nu." Sainte-Beuve's shrewd comment on *Phèdre* explains very well the change that was taking place in Racine's approach to contemporary problems. In his earlier plays he had revealed himself as the critic of an age of false stability. He had recorded the disintegration of a society whose spiritual life was threatened by a ruthless despotism; he had probed the maladies of the individual soul, had exposed the brittleness of honour and morality in the conflict with sexual passion; but his own attitude had remained one of detachment. He had not troubled about a constructive solution of the problems that he had handled and was undisturbed by the indifference to moral sanctions displayed by his own characters. *Phèdre* belongs to a transitional period in his life. It reveals a deepening of experience; it is richer and more complex than any of its predecessors and the sustained magnificence of the poetry is not surpassed even in *Athalie*. Jules Lemaître called it the first stage in his conversion, and it does show a concern for moral values which is new in Racine's poetry. It is shot through and through with the doctrines of predestination and original sin. Destiny broods darkly over the play and the *motifs* of *race* and *sang* are constantly recurring. Phèdre and Hippolyte are the children of parents who were themselves the victims of guilty passion, and Jansenist theology is enlisted to show the hopelessness of the struggle against heredity and fate without the intervention of grace.

Racine uses the design which had become familiar in his other plays—the triangle in which A pursues B who is desperately in love with C. His contemporaries found it difficult to understand why he had so far departed from tradition as to give Hippolyte a lover, and his frivolous reply that it was to prevent Hippolyte from being suspected of what were discreetly known as "Italian tastes" could scarcely satisfy them. This innovation enabled Racine not only to contrast two forms of love, but also to throw fresh light on the tragic nature of sexual passion. He emphasizes the difference between "innocent" and "guilty" love, and the Christian view of sin and temptation is apparent in the lines:

> Grâces au ciel, mes mains ne sont point criminelles.
> Plût aux dieux que mon cœur fût innocent comme elles!
>
> Le jour n'est pas plus pur que le fond de mon cœur.
> Et l'on veut qu'Hippolyte, épris d'un feu profane . . .

It is still more strongly marked in Phèdre's

> Ne pense pas qu'au moment que je t'aime,
> Innocente à mes yeux je m'approuve moi-même,
> Ni que du fol amour qui trouble ma raison
> Ma lâche complaisance ait nourri le poison,

which suggests already that Phèdre's guilty conscience plays its part in her downfall. It is noticeable, however, that though sin and temptation are among the principal *motifs* of the play, Phèdre's knowledge that her love is sinful does not increase her powers of resistance; the knowledge that this is so and the sense that she is heading for disaster are part of her temptation.

Racine had become so obsessed by the Jansenist sense of the inherent sinfulness of sexual love that even Hippolyte's love for Aricie is described as *un fol amour*, as an aberration of his *sens égarés*. It leads to disaster as surely as Phèdre's incestuous passion, but to assume that he is destroyed merely because he abandons the role assigned to him by tradition is to underrate the subtlety of Racine's interpretation. The view underlying the play is that once a "limit" has been passed, once weakness or wickedness has entered into the human heart, it can never be cast out again and nothing can stop its ravages. This is felt strongly by Phèdre and Hippolyte, who both realize too late that the limit has been passed:

> Il n'est plus temps. Il sait mes ardeurs insensées.
> De l'austère pudeur *les bornes sont passées.*
>
> Quiconque a pu franchir *les bornes légitimes,*
> Peut violer enfin les droits les plus sacrés.

This applies to the "innocent" as well as to the "guilty." Hippolyte is described more than once as *l'insensible Hippolyte,* and it is precisely his "insensibility" which provides the best protection against the consequences of the furious passions which are unleashed among those who surround him. The stoic ideal, however, is a negative one and Hippolyte is fully conscious of its inadequacy.

H

As soon as his father is reported to be dead, he moves away from it towards something more positive and more human. His feelings for Aricie lead to a relaxation of his father's prohibition against her marrying and when he tells her:

> La Grèce me reproche une mère étrangère.
> Mais, si pour concurrent je n'avais que mon frère,
> Madame, j'ai sur lui de véritables *droits*
> Que je saurais sauver du caprice des *lois*

—there is a distinction between *droits* and *lois*, between natural human "rights" and inhuman "laws." The distinction is a vital one and it is apparent in all Racine's work. In his earlier plays he had exposed the hollowness of an order which had ceased to be a true order and had degenerated into mere "legalism," into the external observance of empty formulas. In *Phèdre* the criticism becomes more searching. The dilemma lies in the fact that though "laws" are incapable of providing a constructive solution of the problems which confronted Racine's contemporaries, they were the only barrier against anarchy. Once a "law," however capricious, was set aside, the way was open to confusion and disorder. This is brought home by the tragic accents of Phèdre's declaration:

> Moi, régner! Moi, ranger un État sous ma *loi*,
> Quand ma faible raison ne règne plus sur moi,
> Lorsque j'ai de mes sens abandonné l'empire,
> Quand sous un joug honteux à peine je respire . . .

The choice lies between legalism and disaster, between an "insensibility," which excludes natural "rights," and a "shameful yoke." In a tragic world the person who desires no more than his natural rights follows the road to destruction. Thésée forbade Aricie to marry because she came of contaminated "blood." Hippolyte's relaxation of his father's prohibition is tantamount to an infringement of "law" which at once involves him in the intrigues that are going on in his entourage. The maxim, as always in Racine, is that there is not and indeed cannot be a middle course which offers security and honour.

One of the most interesting things about the imagery of this play is the symbolism of light and darkness. M. Denis de Rougemont speaks of the opposition between "la Norme du Jour et la

Passion de la Nuit," between the normal feelings of the "daylight" world and the dark passions which are unleashed "in the night."[1] In the minds of Phèdre and Hippolyte, "daylight" is associated with "innocence" and "night" with "guilt." This explains Phèdre's desperate longing to regain her lost "innocence" and Hippolyte's battle to protect his "innocence" by an assumed "insensibility." In the speeches of both characters we are aware at times of an immense effort—a moral effort—to escape from *la nuit infernale*, to prevent it from swallowing up the "innocent" everyday life. When Phèdre discovers that Hippolyte is in love with Aricie, she cries:

> Tous les *jours* se levaient *clairs* et sereins pour eux.
> Et moi, triste rebut de la nature entière,
> Je me cachais au *jour*, je fuyais la *lumière*.
> La mort est le seul dieu que j'osais implorer,

which shows that she has abandoned all hope, is resigned to "night" and "death." "Je voulais," she declares in another place

> Je voulais en mourant prendre soin de ma gloire,
> Et dérober au *jour* une flamme si *noire*.

Flamme is normally a symbol of light, a guide in darkness. When used to describe love it is also a symbol of life, but in making *flamme noire*, a fresh significance is given to it. Light is turned into darkness, life itself into death. There is a great deal in the play about Thésée's exploits in the pagan hell where he has gone to help a friend to carry off Pluto's spouse. It seems at first as though these references are a concession to legend, are mere classical ornament; but when we look at the texts we find that they have a different significance and are closely connected with Racine's interest in darkness. There may be a contrast between the pagan hell from which a man might escape, and the real hell of spiritual and emotional torment from which there is no escape. But there is something more besides. Ismène tells Aricie that Thésée

> a vu le Cocyte et les rivages *sombres*,
> Et s'est montré vivant aux infernales *ombres*.

And Aricie replies:

---

[1] *op. cit.*, p. 13.

> Croirai-je qu'un mortel, avant sa dernière heure
> Peut pénétrer des morts la *profonde* demeure?

Thésée himself refers to the exploit in similar terms:

> Moi-même, il m'enferma dans des cavernes *sombres*,
> Lieux *profonds* et voisins de l'empire des *ombres*.

The word *ombres* is one of the focal words of the play because it is at once a symbol of "imprisonment" and "refuge." When, for example, Phèdre cries:

> Dieux! que ne suis-je assise à *l'ombre des forêts*!

the cool, leafy green of the forests offers a prospect of escape from her trouble; but though it brings a moment of release from the torments of passion, it is an illusion. It is the struggle of the trapped animal to escape, but there is no escape from the *interior* torment which pursues the victim into the shady refuge:

> Dans *le fond des forêts* votre image me suit;
> La *lumière* du jour, les *ombres* de la nuit,
> Tout retrace à mes yeux les charmes que j'évite,
> Tout vous livre à l'envi le rebelle Hippolyte.

It may well have been of these lines that Taine was thinking when he remarked that when Hippolyte speaks of the forests where his youth was spent, we must substitute the avenues of Versailles. It is a strange assumption which scarcely contributes to a true interpretation of the play. In Racine's lifetime a large part of France was covered by real forests and one of them actually extended to the outskirts of La Ferté-Milon. France was not a vast Versailles, a country of trim gardens and shady walks. It was a country in which a few towns were surrounded by belts of forest, a country in which a high degree of civilization was surrounded by the darkness of the uncivilized provinces. Now this corresponds exactly to the view of human nature that we find in Racine's plays. Human nature was highly reasonable and well-balanced up to a point, but men were becoming increasingly aware of the psychological hinterland, the hidden motives which played a decisive part in human actions. The philosophers, the moralists and the dramatists made common cause in the attempt to penetrate into this psychological jungle. No one was more clearly aware than Racine of what to-day is called the unconscious, and his aim was to probe the obscure regions of the mind which are constantly suggested by the phrases *l'empire des ombres, le fond des forêts*, and others which are equally significant. The ambiguity which surrounds "forests" heightens the tragic urgency of the poetry and is characteristic of the whole play. All the chief characters are the victims of two conflicting impulses— the impulse to conceal their true motives from themselves, to force them into the subconscious and seal them off by using the phrases *le fond des forêts* or *l'empire des ombres*, and the impulse to bring them out into the open by confession. The subtlety and insight with which Racine exposes this tangle of conflicting feelings has never been surpassed in French literature.

The first of these impulses is illustrated by Aricie's declaration of her love for Hippolyte:

> Non que, par les yeux seuls lâchement enchantée,
> J'aime en lui sa beauté, sa grâce tant vantée,
> Présents dont la nature a voulu l'honorer,
> Qu'il méprise lui-même, et qu'il semble ignorer.
> J'aime, je prise en lui de plus nobles richesses,
> Les vertus de son père, et non point les faiblesses.
> J'aime, je l'avoûrai, cet orgueil généreux
> Qui jamais n'a fléchi sous le joug amoureux.
> Phèdre en vain s'honorait des soupirs de Thésée:
> Pour moi, je suis plus fière, et fuis la gloire aisée
> D'arracher un hommage à mille autres offert,
> Et d'entrer dans un cœur de toutes parts ouvert.
> Mais de faire fléchir un courage inflexible,
> De porter la douleur dans une âme insensible,
> D'enchaîner un captif de ses fers étonné,
> Contre un joug qui lui plaît vainement mutiné:
> C'est là ce que je veux, et c'est là ce qui m'irrite.
> Hercule à désarmer coûtait moins qu'Hippolyte,
> Et vaincu plus souvent, et plus tôt surmonté,
> Préparait moins de gloire aux yeux qui l'ont dompté.

The impress of Jansenism is clearly visible in these lines. Aricie's declaration that she is not attracted by Hippolyte's physical beauty is perfectly sincere; she does not know that an unconscious fear of physical love is making her hide her real feelings. There is a certain satisfaction in the reference to his beauty which is already suspect, and Aricie's true feelings become abundantly clear as the passage develops. The minx peeps out from behind the solemn puritan. She is the familiar figure of the predatory female pursuing the reluctant male.

> Il oppose à l'amour un cœur inaccessible:
> Cherchons pour l'attaquer quelque endroit plus sensible,

cries Phèdre, and Aricie's sentiments are no different. She is spurred on by the love of the hunt, by the desire of making a conquest of someone who is reputed to be insensible to feminine charms. *Gloire* is something very different from the Cornelian glory; in its present context it means no more than success in the chase—the satisfaction of outdistancing one's "rival." Aricie does not think of the pursuit in terms of a goal or of "domestic happiness" any more than the equally demure Atalide in *Bajazet*; she thinks of it in terms of "romance." It is not merely possession that she desires; she wants to dominate Hippolyte, to make him feel the *douleur* of love, to captivate a warrior with "chains" so that all resistance becomes vain. It is characteristic of these "hunts" that they always end in the destruction of the unhappy male. The female is bent on domination and subjection, and the innocent-looking word *fléchi* has a sinister inflection. We cannot shut our eyes to it. This passage is an episode in the sex-war, the eternal rivalry of Man and Woman.

As Racine's genius ripened, he became a pastmaster of the art of revealing the true feelings of his characters which were concealed beneath the elaborate psychological subterfuges constructed by them, and this highly personal form of ambiguity became a persistent feature of his style.

The "innocent" lovers try to hide their feelings, but the "guilty" lover feels impelled to confide in someone. The role of Phèdre seems at first to be one long confession, but in reality there are three distinct confessions and all of them serve different purposes. The confession to Œnone is made partly to rid herself of a crushing sense of guilt and partly to obtain practical assistance in her attempts to win Hippolyte. The confession to Hippolyte himself is intended to break down his resistance. Only the final confession to Thésée is disinterested, is a belated attempt to expiate a wrong.

The nature of the conflict between the need to confess and the

desire to conceal can be seen in the symbolical utterance which
precedes the great speech in Act I. Sc. iii:

> Que ces vains ornements, que ces voiles me pèsent!
> Quelle importune main, en formant tous ces nœuds,
> A pris soin sur mon front d'assembler mes cheveux?
> Tout m'afflige et me nuit, et conspire à me nuire.

The constraint suggested by *nœuds* is so intense that the confession
brings with it a sense of *physical* deliverance:

> Mon mal vient de plus loin. A peine au fils d'Egée
> Sous les lois de l'hymen je m'étais engagée,
> Mon repos, mon bonheur, semblait être affermi,
> Athènes me montra mon superbe ennemi.
> Je le vis, je rougis, je pâlis à sa vue;
> Un trouble s'éleva dans mon âme éperdue;
> Mes yeux ne voyaient plus, je ne pouvais parler,
> Je sentis tout mon corps et transir et brûler.
> Je reconnus Vénus, et ses feux redoutables,
> D'un sang qu'elle poursuit tourments inévitables.
> Par des vœux assidus je crus les détourner:
> Je lui bâtis un temple, et pris soin de l'orner;
> De victimes moi-même à toute heure entourée,
> Je cherchais dans leurs flancs ma raison égarée,
> D'un incurable amour remèdes impuissants!

The abrupt statement with which the speech opens has a curiously
steadying effect. It gathers up the diffused emotions of the whole
scene and fixes them on a single point: the definition of Phèdre's
mal. We feel her groping dimly in the subterranean depths of her
mind. The word *mal*—the realization that she is a sick woman—is
a talisman which sets complicated mental processes in movement
and the guilty secret seems to burst out of her.

The poet presents a picture of ordinary, everyday married life
which is shattered by a guilty passion. The alexandrines, with the
verb pushed to the end of the second line, express perfectly the
moral effort made by Phèdre to submit to the marriage "law," and
they also reinforce the apparent stability of her happiness. It
must be remembered that she is *une femme au déclin de l'âge*;
her love for her young and handsome stepson offers a last chance
of romantic happiness. *Superbe*, with its suggestion of "glamour"

and "romance," is pitted against the humdrum, domestic associations of *engagée* and *affermi* which offer, or once offered, spiritual security. The sudden change of tense—*Athènes me montra*—gives an extraordinary sensation of the "enemy" being hurtled into the attack on conventional married life. The immediate surface reactions, the rapid changes of colour, are carefully noted; the physiological reactions are the prelude to a profound psychological disturbance. There is an inward movement (admirably expressed by *trouble* with its suggestion of limpid water clouding over) and Racine begins to probe the deeper levels. The happiness, which seemed solid and well founded, crumbles at once and the clear-cut lines of *affermi* dissolve into the paroxysm suggested by one of Racine's favourite words—*éperdue*. The psychological disturbance is so violent that it provokes a fresh physical reaction indicated by *brûler* and *transir*. The simple, homely words—*trouble, rougis, brûler, transir*—express Phèdre's state of mind and the complicated interplay of the physiological and the psychological elements with an almost terrifying clarity. It is a sign of Racine's art that *brûler* and *transir*, which are normally associated with the contrary extremes of heat and cold, are here combined to convey the absolute mental and emotional paralysis which overtakes Phèdre.

The analysis has now been pushed to the utmost possible limit —to the point at which it is no longer possible to differentiate between the various sensations—and the result is a form of psychological black-out. It is remarkable how the masterly compression of Racine's verse and the rapidity with which the changes of feeling follow one another contribute to the sense of complete spiritual and moral collapse that we get from the passage as a whole. This impression is heightened by the return to lucidity in l. 9, and Phèdre's realization that she is doomed. The introduction of Venus is not a piece of classical decoration, but an example of the way in which Racine adapts the classics. Venus is not something external to man as she was for the Greeks, but a projection of his own passion which by this means becomes invested with super-human, with irresistible force.[1] Once Venus appears the issue is

---

[1] This explains the tragic irony in the latter part of the speech. Phèdre tells Œnone that in order to escape from Hippolyte, she demanded his banishment:

Je pressai son exil, et mes cris éternels
L'arrachèrent du sein et des bras paternels.

virtually decided. She is contrasted with the humdrum married life, and by a skilful shifting of the emphasis the *feux redoutables* are flung against *bonheur . . . affermi.* It is significant that she attaches herself to the "blood" which is the seat of the primeval passions that Racine uncovers. The reference to the sacrifice is a stroke of irony. Phèdre is engaged in a superstitious game, but is herself the real "victim." The feverish, futile slaughter of the animals indicates her growing desperation. *Entourée* contains a sinister hint that she is being engulfed by passion, by "blood"; *raison* dissolves into *égarée* which refers back to *éperdue*, intensifying the sickening sense of dissolution that we experience in listening to the lines. The whole is clinched by the despairing *remèdes impuissants.*

"All that she is, all that she says, thinks and does only half belongs to her," writes M. Pierre Brisson of the role of Œnone. "Her mind is the invisible emanation of those dark impulses in Phèdre's nature which Phèdre herself is least capable of perceiving."[1]

I think that we can go further than this. Œnone is a symbol rather than an independent person. She is personification of part of Phèdre's mind, a projection of her worse self, always counselling actions which can only lead to disaster, always revealing Phèdre's motives to herself in a way that increases her *trouble.*

> Je t'ai tout avoué; je ne m'en repens pas,

says Phèdre at the end of this speech. But the "confession," far from bringing relief, has precisely the reverse effect. For, writes M. Brisson, "she succumbs to the most corrupting of all sins: the sin of knowledge."[2]

This passage seems to me to be a complete answer to the usual criticisms of Racine's style. It is part of his greatness that the apparent limitations of his medium became one of the main sources of his

---

The remedy failed, and another reference to Venus tells us why it failed:

> Ce n'est plus une ardeur dans mes veines cachée:
> C'est Vénus toute entière à sa proie attachée.

Physical exile could not possibly relieve a *mal* which is essentially an interior one, which belongs to "blood" and entrails, and the disproportion between the evil and the remedy simply intensifies the paroxysm.

[1] *op cit.,* p. 165.   [2] *ibid.,* p. 152.
H*

strength. The alexandrine was not for him, as one feels that it sometimes was for Corneille, a constraint; it was a positive discipline which made possible an extremely *ordered* presentation of emotion. The nineteenth-century view that the great monologues were carefully rehearsed speeches which failed to carry conviction seems to me to be untenable. They are not frigid recitals of old emotions; it is in the retelling that feelings come to life and assume their proper place in the pattern of the plays as psychological events. All the great monologues turn out on examination to be definitions of particular states of mind. In the present case it is the definition of Phèdre's *mal*, and we notice that the passage moves with a mathematical precision from one point to another, as the *mal* is analysed into its component parts. *Éperdue* and *égarée* are stages on the way which follow one another logically. When we look at the passage as a whole—it is forty-eight lines long altogether —we find that Phèdre's state of mind has undergone a change and that just as there are stages within the passage, so the passage itself represents a complete stage in the unfolding of the play.

I have used the word "analysis" to describe the process, but it may be doubted whether the term is altogether exact. There is a sharp distinction between the method of the great imaginative writers of the seventeenth century—it applies in the main to Madame de La Fayette as well as to Racine—and the method of the modern novelist. The characters of Constant and Stendhal consciously and deliberately take their minds to pieces, and in more recent authors the analysis is sometimes pushed to the point at which emotion is destroyed. In Racine there is properly speaking no such thing as analysis. The plays record, to be sure, a process of progressive and destructive self-knowledge, yet it is the result not of carefully calculated analysis, but of intuition, of a sudden insight into their own feelings, of repressed feelings becoming conscious and causing the collapse of personality.

The passage also illustrates the peculiar virtues of Racine's language. The conventional vocabulary has sometimes appeared to English readers to be colourless and inexpressive; but Racine's style is not only perfectly adequate to his experience, it is an instrument of extraordinary delicacy in revealing emotional states. His method is entirely different from that of English poets. English poetry is remarkable for the richness and variety of its imagery and for its accumulation of sense-perceptions. In Racine's poetry there are comparatively few images and no accumulation; there is often simply bare *statement*. He owes nearly everything to the *precision* with which his language renders the obscurest sensations and to his exquisite sensibility. The simple, conventional words seem somehow to penetrate into the furthest layers of the mind, to catch and fix emotion at the moment of its formation.

I think that we may add that Racine's genius is also the genius of the French language. In English and still more in German literature—particularly in the *weltschmerz* of the Romantics—there almost always remains an unanalysed residue in the feelings presented which makes a whole poem or a whole play vague and misty. In the great French masters there is no mist and no blur. It is because they realized the limitations of language that they have achieved an extraordinary degree of clarity and depth in the presentation of emotional states. It is, perhaps, for this reason that the Romantic Movement in France has seemed to many good critics to have been a betrayal of the French tradition.

From this we can turn to the famous *déclaration* in Act II. Sc. v:

> Oui, Prince, je languis, je brûle pour Thésée.
> Je l'aime, non point tel que l'ont vu les enfers,
> Volage adorateur de mille objets divers
> Qui va du dieu des morts déshonorer la couche;
> Mais fidèle, mais fier, et même un peu farouche,
> Charmant, jeune, traînant tous les cœurs après soi,
> Tel qu'on dépeint nos dieux, ou tel que je vous voi.
> Il avait votre port, vos yeux, votre langage,
> Cette noble pudeur colorait son visage,
> Lorsque de notre Crète il traversa les flots,
> Digne sujet des vœux des filles de Minos.
> Que faisiez-vous alors? Pourquoi sans Hippolyte
> Des héros de la Grèce assembla-t-il l'élite? . . .
> Par vous aurait péri le monstre de la Crète,
> Malgré tous les détours de sa vaste retraite.
> Pour en développer l'embarras incertain,
> Ma sœur du fil fatal eût armé votre main.
> Mais non, dans ce dessein je l'aurais devancée:
> L'amour m'en eût d'abord inspiré la pensée.
> C'est moi, Prince, c'est moi dont l'utile secours
> Vous eût du Labyrinthe enseigné les détours.

> Que de soins m'eût coûtés cette tête charmante!
> Un fil n'eût point assez rassuré votre amante.
> Compagne du péril qu'il vous fallait chercher,
> Moi-même devant vous j'aurais voulu marcher;
> Et Phèdre, au Labyrinthe avec vous descendue,
> Se serait avec vous retrouvée, ou perdue.

One's first impression is that Phèdre has deliberately abandoned any further attempt to conceal the nature of her feelings for Hippolyte and that the ambiguity of her speech is a trick to make him listen to her. There is nothing here of the minx's satisfaction over catching a man who is reputed to be indifferent to all women. Her attitude is that of an experienced woman who is determined to find her way to the bed of a young man who has never known woman; and for this reason she dwells, a little enviously perhaps, on his *noble pudeur*. Her feelings are frankly sexual and there is a rapt ecstatic note in her description of his physical beauty, in the soft, caressing

> Charmant, jeune, traînant tous les cœurs après soi,

or in the weary sigh that one detects in

> Que de soins m'eût coûtés cette tête charmante!

While there is no doubt that Phèdre does wish to seduce Hippolyte, these impressions are only partly correct. The speech is far more than an impassioned declaration of love, and Phèdre's tactics are far from being carefully and deliberately calculated. In reality, the confession is torn from her in spite of herself and it is this that gives it its peculiar intensity. The more we study the passage, the more conscious we become that Phèdre is speaking in a trance in which she betrays her innermost feelings. She is aware of what she is doing, but is powerless to stop herself.[1]

The Labyrinth of the Minotaur is evoked because it is the perfect expression of Phèdre's feelings. It is a far more complex image than the "palaces" of the earlier plays and its *détours* have a deeper significance. The Labyrinth is at once objective and subjective. Phèdre would like to see Hippolyte trapped by the Minotaur— trapped and helpless—so that she can rescue him and win his love.

[1] *cf.*   Que dis-je? Cet aveu que je te viens de faire,
                    Cet aveu si honteux, le crois-tu volontaire?

It is a romantic dream, but it is also an astonishing piece of psychological realism. We are all familiar with the extravagances of the psycho-analytical critics, but this seems to me to be one of the very few instances in great literature where the Freudian symbols offer a complete explanation of the unconscious motives of the poet and his characters. There is no need to dwell on the meaning of the "descent," the guiding "thread" or the more obvious significance of the Labyrinth itself, beyond remarking that the whole passage is an allegory of the sexual act, an allegory which is driven home by the extraordinary urgency of

> C'est moi, Prince, c'est moi dont l'utile secours
> Vous eût du Labyrinthe enseigné les détours,

where the focus of the picture suddenly becomes sharp and the general erotic associations at the beginning of the passage crystallize, concentrating attention on a particular relationship between two individuals.

It is precisely in the use of symbols that Phèdre's state of mind resembles a trance or dream. The Labyrinth is the labyrinth of our hidden desires, a region beyond the range of normal human intercourse and therefore outside conventional tabus. It is the labyrinth in which Phèdre herself is a prisoner, but it offers a prospect of gratifying illicit desires. She is anxious to see Hippolyte trapped in the same prison; she wants to make him fall in love with her or possibly to show him that, without knowing it, he is already in love with her. The obstacle is not only his "insensibility"; it is also his relationship with her which is a tabu that can only be evaded in the Labyrinth, in the place which is "beyond good and evil."[1] Phèdre sees that their problem is a common one which can only be solved in partnership, and her excitement is, perhaps, heightened by the thought that it is a partnership of guilt. It is only by working together that they can overcome their difficulties and find their way out of the Labyrinth which is also paradoxically the only place where desire can be satisfied. They are joined by a bond which must bring either ecstatic happiness or complete destruction:

---

[1] The Labyrinth also seems to me to be a symbol of the poet's own unconscious desire to escape from convention, from the constraint of the "palaces" of earlier plays, just as Abner's return to the Temple in *Athalie* is a symbol of Racine's return to the life of convention and respectability.

> Et Phèdre, au Labyrinthe *avec vous* descendue,
> Se serait *avec vous* retrouvée, ou perdue.

This extraordinary fantasy provides Phèdre with a vicarious satisfaction, but the ultimate goal eludes her. The *perdue* marks the passing of the trance and the return to the actual world with its shattering sense of disillusionment, which is underlined by Hippolyte's shocked but prosaic

> Dieux! qu'est-ce que j'entends? Madame, oubliez-vous
> Que Thésée est mon père, et qu'il est votre époux?

and by the exchange which follows:

PHÈDRE:

> Et sur quoi jugez-vous que j'en perds la mémoire,
> Prince? Aurais-je perdu tout soin de ma gloire?

HIPPOLYTE:

> Madame, pardonnez. J'avoue, en rougissant,
> Que j'accusais à tort un discours innocent.
> Ma honte ne peut plus soutenir votre vue,
> Et je vais . . .

PHÈDRE:

> Ah! cruel, tu m'as trop entendue.
> Je t'en ai dit assez pour te tirer d'erreur.
> Hé bien! connais donc Phèdre et toute sa fureur.
> J'aime. Ne pense pas qu'au moment que je t'aime,
> Innocente à mes yeux je m'approuve moi-même,
> Ni que du fol amour qui trouble ma raison
> Ma lâche complaisance ait nourri le poison.
> Objet infortuné des vengeances célestes,
> Je m'abhorre encor plus que tu ne me détestes.
> Les dieux m'en sont témoins, ces dieux qui dans mon flanc
> Ont allumé le feu fatal à tout mon sang,
> Ces dieux qui se sont fait une gloire cruelle
> De séduire le cœur d'une faible mortelle.

The effectiveness of the scene as a whole lies in the contrast between these two speeches. The line

> Ah! cruel, tu m'as trop entendue,

with its immensely effective switch from the *formules protocolaires* back to the *tutoiement passionné*, seems to me to be one of those miracles which only Racine could have accomplished. There is a whole civilization behind its singular richness. Hippolyte was certainly intended to "understand" Phèdre's indirect advances, but he was no less certainly intended to accept or reject them in accordance with the seventeenth-century code which governed such matters. His blunt retort crashes through all the reticences. The secret is out and the game of refined pretence is useless. The real disaster, however, is the psychological effect of Hippolyte's bluntness. He has given a name to "un amour qui n'ose pas dire son nom," and in doing so he has destroyed Phèdre's powers of resistance. It is this that provokes the bitter reproach of "Tu m'as *trop entendue.*" He tries, to be sure, to repair his *gaucherie,* but the damage is done. Phèdre herself can no longer bear the thought that he might after all not have "understood"; she is driven to intervene in spite of herself, and it is this that makes the brief exchange between the two great speeches one of the most dramatic moments in the play.

Although there is no lowering of the tension, it is clear that Phèdre is speaking on a different plane. The world of erotic fantasy with its Labyrinth has disappeared. She looks at her love with the eyes of an ordinary moral citizen and condemns the rapture of a moment ago as a "fol amour qui trouble ma raison." The references to *raison, innocente* and *lâche complaisance* imply a belief in a clearly defined moral order, but—this is the tragedy—it can no longer do anything to enable Phèdre to dominate her emotions.

"Her mind," writes M. Brisson with his usual acumen, "judges and betrays her at the same time, *inflames her passion at the very moment at which it appears to be fighting against it.* Through a reversal of the normal process, which is of profound significance, it is the mind of Phèdre which contaminates the flesh. No figure of the universal theatre gives away such dangerous secrets as hers, none comes closer to the eternal abyss."[1]

In all Racine's plays, reason is powerless to resist the swirls of passion. Phèdre's attempt to shift the blame for her downfall on to the gods is the purest Jansenist doctrine and it shows the weaknesses of that line as a guide to living. At the same time, it does nothing to mitigate its votaries' sense of guilt. The honesty and

[1] *op. cit.,* pp. 153–4 (italics mine).

lucidity with which Phèdre faces the implications of her conduct and her recognition of the code which she has outraged are characteristic of seventeenth-century literature.

The movement of the play is essentially a destructive movement. The human personality is shattered by its own passions and the play closes with its total dislocation. The false report of Thésée's death raises Phèdre's hopes for a moment; in spite of her rebuff by Hippolyte, she is led on by the thought that her love is no longer illicit and may be satisfied. The violence of passion is increased by the simultaneous discovery that Thésée is living and that Hippolyte is in love with Aricie. The terrible clarity with which these discoveries are registered in Phèdre's mind throw a good deal of light on the tragic process. When she says

> Mon époux est vivant, et moi je brûle encore!

the activity implied by *brûler* is felt to be *morally* wrong and *physically* destructive. It puts an immense strain on the human personality which rapidly disintegrates. The violence of the "fire," which eats up life, is contrasted with the decorous domestic feelings which should be felt by a wife of Phèdre's age for her husband and which alone are compatible with "living." The exasperation and frustration of unrequited passion have seldom been more powerfully expressed than in the line:

> Hippolyte est sensible, et ne sent rien pour moi!

It is a wonderful example of Racine's gift of condensation. The fondness of the seventeenth century for the word *sensible* was, as we know, characteristic of a society which was acutely conscious of its most intimate feelings. Racine's sense of language enabled him to set his stamp on the word and enrich its meaning. For Phèdre becomes so acutely *sensible* that the disappointment of her hopes of physical satisfaction makes the sense of bodily frustration unbearable. Her brooding over the intimate details of the satisfaction enjoyed by other people plunges her into a fresh orgy of sexual fantasy:

> Ah! douleur non encore éprouvée!
> A quel nouveau tourment je me suis réservée!
> Tout ce que j'ai souffert, mes craintes, mes transports,
> La fureur de mes feux, l'horreur de mes remords,

Et d'un refus cruel l'insupportable injure,
N'était qu'un faible essai du tourment que j'endure.
Ils s'aiment! Par quel charme ont-ils trompé mes yeux?
Comment se sont-ils vus? Depuis quand? Dans quels lieux?
Tu le savais. Pourquoi me laissais-tu séduire?
De leur furtive ardeur ne pouvais-tu m'instruire?
Les a-t-on vu souvent se parler, se chercher?
Dans le fond des forêts allaient-ils se cacher?
Hélas! ils se voyaient avec pleine licence.
Le ciel de leurs soupirs approuvait l'innocence;
Ils suivaient sans remords leur penchant amoureux;
Tous les jours se levaient clairs et sereins pour eux.
Et moi, triste rebut de la nature entière,
Je me cachais au jour, je fuyais la lumière.
La mort est le seul dieu que j'osais implorer.

The poignancy of this passage lies in the sense of frustration and waste.[1] The activity signified by *craintes, fureur* and *horreur* has been in vain; the reward has gone to another. The situation has undergone a change since the reflections on the Labyrinth in Act II, and this passage only yields its full flavour when it is seen in relation to the earlier one. The first passage derives its power from its sense of hot, guilty intimacy; the second from an agonizing sense of exclusion from intimacy which is heightened by the knowledge of other people's enjoyment of it. Hippolyte and Aricie are united in a real forest (as distinct from the fanciful Labyrinth) and are beyond Phèdre's reach. The darkness of the forest prevents her from seeing them, and their actions can only be the subject of unhealthy imaginings. One of the most curious things about the passage is the use of the words *innocence, licence* and *penchant*. The idea of love has become for Phèdre inseparable from the idea of sin. The ardour of Hippolyte and Aricie is therefore *furtive*, and though the logical sense of *licence* is innocent, there is clearly a suggestion—perhaps an unconscious suggestion—of moral licence. Nor can we have any doubts about the implications of *se chercher*. It is a reflection on Phèdre's state of mind that though she associates love with sin, she is particularly fascinated by the lovers who (she implies) are innocent in the sense that this is "the first time" and who provide a "thrill" to the jaded senses of the ageing Amazon.

[1] *cf.*   J'ai langui, j'ai séché dans les feux, dans les larmes.

The words *licence* and *penchant* are deliberately ambiguous. They suggest freedom, but it is a freedom for others; it brings Phèdre a vicarious satisfaction and at the same time intensifies her sense of personal inhibition. The line

> Ils suivaient sans remords leur penchant amoureux

reveals the subtle temptation, which is always present to the minds of Racine's heroines, to throw off all restraint—to throw off the veneer of civilization and give full rein to instincts that are by no means civilized. The word *remords* is of particular interest. It stands for the moral barrier which ought to have arrested Phèdre's downward course; but it is no barrier for the innocent lovers who are free to follow the incline which is fatal to Phèdre. Instead of arresting her downfall, "remorse" has merely poisoned her pleasure and incensed her against the others. The most painful thing in the passage is Phèdre's sense of *physical* separation, and the short, staccato questions:

> Comment se sont-ils vus? Depuis quand? Dans quels lieux?

convey very well the vibration of nerves which have reached an intolerable degree of sensitiveness. The feeling of physical separation is heightened and complicated by her consciousness of *moral* ostracism. The last six lines refer back to the lines in an earlier passage in which she reproaches the gods:

> Ces dieux qui se sont fait une gloire cruelle
> De séduire le cœur d'une faible mortelle.

For the same gods, who have turned her into a moral outcast, look down benevolently on the loves of Hippolyte and Aricie. There is an immense despair behind

> Tous les jours se levaient clairs et sereins pour eux.
> Et moi, triste rebut de la nature entière,
> Je me cachais au jour, je fuyais la lumière.
> La mort est le seul dieu que j'osais implorer.

Phèdre looks longingly at the darkening skies in the vain hope that the miracle will take place, that grace will intervene to save her; but there are no miracles in this world. When she describes herself as "triste rebut de la nature entière," moral and physical exclusion is implied which brings a sudden numbing sense of the annihilation of all feeling, the dissolution of all moral values. There is a genuine nostalgia in Phèdre's reference to the "innocence" which is denied her and in her reference to the symbols of grace—*clairs, sereins, jour, lumière*—but the absence of any supernatural aid drives her to her final crime. We can now perceive more clearly the force of a remark of M. Brisson's which I have already quoted: "Her mind judges and betrays her at the same time, inflames her passion at the very moment at which it appears to be fighting against it." For Phèdre's attempts to control her emotions simply exasperate her feelings and in this way contribute largely to the destruction of her moral scruples. The paroxysm does not reach its full intensity until the next *tirade* and it is, significantly, Œnone who provokes the final crisis.

ŒNONE:
  Quel fruit recevront-ils de leurs vaines amours?
  Ils ne se verront plus.
PHÈDRE:
     Ils s'aimeront toujours!
  Au moment que je parle, ah! mortelle pensée!
  Ils bravent la fureur d'une amante insensée.
  Malgré ce même exil qui va les écarter,
  Ils font mille serments de ne se point quitter.
  Non, je ne puis souffrir un bonheur qui m'outrage,
  Œnone. Prends pitié de ma jalouse rage.
  Il faut perdre Aricie. Il faut de mon époux
  Contre un sang odieux réveiller le courroux.
  Qu'il ne se borne pas à des peines légères:
  Le crime de la sœur passe celui des frères.
  Dans mes jaloux transports je le veux implorer.
  Que fais-je? Où ma raison se va-t-elle égarer?
  Moi, jalouse! Et Thésée est celui que j'implore!
  Mon époux est vivant, et moi je brûle encore!
  Pour qui? Quel est le cœur où prétendent mes vœux?
  Chaque mot sur mon front fait dresser mes cheveux.
  Mes crimes désormais ont comblé la mesure.
  Je respire à la fois l'inceste et l'imposture.
  Mes homicides mains, promptes à me venger,
  Dans ce sang innocent brûlent de se plonger.

The focal word is *insensée*. For Phèdre has now lost all control over herself; but it does not affect her lucidity. In the middle of her *égarement* she realizes with horror what she is doing, but she cannot help herself. "Moi, jalouse!" she cries with a horrified astonishment, but there is at the same time a moral resignation in

> Mes crimes désormais ont comblé la mesure.

When, at the close of the scene, she turns on Œnone and denounces her evil advice, it is in reality her own worse self that she is denouncing:

> Puisse le juste ciel dignement te payer;
> Et puisse ton supplice à jamais effrayer
> Tous ceux qui, comme toi, par de lâches adresses,
> Des princes malheureux nourrissent les faiblesses,
> Les poussent au penchant où leur cœur est enclin,
> Et leur osent du crime aplanir le chemin;
> Déstestables flatteurs, présent le plus funeste
> Que puisse faire aux rois la colère céleste!

The moral is obvious. The activity of the senses—the *sens égarés*—does not lead for Phèdre, as it should, to life and companionship, but to exile and death. "Fuyons," she cries,

> Fuyons dans la nuit infernale.

The "clear" and "serene" skies grow dark. Phèdre recoils from "life" and turns to face "death." She is resigned to the final crime, but she is also resigned to the doom which must follow it, to *la nuit infernale*.

With the confession of her jealousy, the evolution of Phèdre's character is virtually complete. Although the brief confession to Thésée is in a sense an expiation, its main function is to round off the play:

> Déjà jusqu'à mon cœur le venin parvenu
> Dans ce cœur expirant jette un froid inconnu;
> Déjà je ne vois plus qu'à travers un nuage
> Et le ciel, et l'époux que ma présence outrage;
> Et la mort, à mes yeux dérobant la clarté,
> Rend au jour, qu'ils souillaient, toute sa pureté.

In these lines physical extinction, with its deliberate emphasis on the heart as the seat of the passions, is seen to be the consummation of the interior disintegration of Phèdre's personality. The removal of the corrupt element is supposed to lead to the restoration of a sane order. The skies appear to clear; purity seems once more to be supreme. That, at least, is what happens in theory, and there is little doubt that Racine intended to give this impression. The play, however, has a deeper significance, a significance that Racine may well have had unconscious reasons for wishing to conceal. Shortly before Phèdre makes her first appearance, Théramène describes her as

> Une femme mourante, et qui cherche à mourir.

In nearly all Racine's plays, passion leads logically to death; but in *Phèdre* the connection between passion and death is much closer and much more complex. The connection is underlined by the incest *motif*. *Phèdre* appears to be the only play in which the theme of incest is introduced, but it would be more accurate to say that it is the only play in which it is *openly* introduced. For, as Jean Giraudoux once suggested, the passions in all Racine's plays are surrounded by an atmosphere of incest. He also made another interesting suggestion. He suggested that in Racine passion is always *contagious*, and the point is worth developing. In the other plays the principal character suffers from a fatal passion which infects those who surround him or her, so that each of them develops the same passion for a third person. Oreste infects Hermione who becomes infatuated with Pyrrhus who in turn is infatuated with Andromaque. Roxane infects Bajazet who falls in love with Atalide. Phèdre infects the "insensible" Hippolyte who becomes desperately in love with Aricie.

This leads to another point. The connection between the poet and his characters in *Phèdre* is closer than in any of the other plays with the possible exception of *Athalie*. Phèdre and Hippolyte are both portraits not of the artist, but of certain sides of the artist's character. Phèdre stands for the guilty Racine of the past, the Racine who seduced Mlle du Parc and later Mlle de Champmeslé, the actress who created the part of Phèdre; Hippolyte stands for the new Racine, the pure young man that he would like to have been. This seems to me to be the true explanation of Phèdre's desperate concern with "purity" and the concentration on light and darkness of which I have already spoken. "It is her nature, which is in love with innocence," writes M. Blanchot, "that carries her irresistibly towards the Amazon's son, towards the man who is intact, the Thésée without a blemish for whose impossible resurrection she hopes in vain."[1] The solution is, indeed, impossible, unthinkable. Phèdre, we remember, is

Une femme mourante, *et qui cherche à mourir.*

It may well be, as M. de Rougemont suggests,[2] that Racine set out to punish his own guilty passion in this play, but the curse which Phèdre persuades Thésée to lay on Hippolyte is the outward sign of the internal ravages of her love for him. For the play is nothing less than a *suicide pact.* The Past infects the Present and, in a sense, the Future; the old Racine infects the new, dragging him inexorably down into the abyss. "Phèdre," says M. Blanchot, "can only achieve consummation in the abyss. She demands ruin. Hers is a nature on which nothing can be built. Her kingdom is annihilation. . . . She may withdraw into the shadows in order to give back to the day its light, but the day that she leaves behind her is an empty shattered day."[3] When we consider *Phèdre* from this angle, we have less difficulty in understanding the twelve years' silence. The doom hanging over the kingdom, of which I spoke in my opening chapter, has fallen. Human society is obliterated and only the eternal values remain intact. There is nothing left except to rebuild the human kingdom from the start with fresh material.

Phèdre is therefore not Racine's last word on contemporary problems. In spite of the part played by religion, he was primarily

---

[1] *op. cit.,* p. 87.

[2] "Under cover of his 'classical subject,' Racine contrives to punish himself twice over in *Phèdre.* In the first place, he punishes himself by making the 'obstacle' an incestuous passion, that is to say, an obstacle that one no longer even has the right to want to overcome. Public opinion, to which Racine is very sensitive, is always on Tristan's side against King Mark, is always on the side of the seducer against the husband whom he deceives; but it is never on the side of incestuous lovers. In the second place, Racine punishes himself by introducing other people between Phèdre and her passion and by refusing to allow it to be reciprocated by Hippolyte. Now *Phèdre* was written for Champmeslé who played the part of the queen. Hippolyte is none other than Racine as he would like to be—insensible to mortal charms. . . . By confusing Phèdre with the woman he loves, he takes his revenge on the object of his passion and, at the same time, he proves to himself that this passion must be condemned *without appeal.*" (*op. cit.,* pp. 193–4. Italics in the text.)

[3] *ibid.,* pp. 88, 89.

concerned with the fate of the individual and made little attempt to see the individual in relation to society as a whole. The order which is "restored" is a metaphysical order and is defined in terms of "the great abstractions." This is partly for the reasons given above and partly for other reasons. For though there is much in this play about "innocence" and "purity," Racine's negatives are far more convincing than his positive values. One feels that there is something timid and shrinking about the "virtue" which prompts Aricie to ask coyly whether Hippolyte's intentions are "honourable" before deciding to run away with him, and Hippolyte himself to reply sententiously:

> Arrachez-vous d'un lieu funeste et profané,
> Où la vertu respire un air empoisonné.

For a detailed application of these principles to the religious and political situation of Racine's day, we have to wait for *Athalie*, his last and in some respects his greatest play.

V. *ATHALIE* AND THE DICTATORS

1

The twelve years' silence that followed the production of *Phèdre* is one of the most curious and intriguing of all literary problems. The critic is confronted with the spectacle of a great poet, who was at the height of his powers, deliberately turning his back on the art which had made him famous and refusing not merely to write, but to take any further interest in literature. The decision was the outcome of a personal crisis; and since the crisis had a decisive influence on *Athalie*, no account of Racine's final period is satisfactory without some discussion of the events which led to it.

Phèdre was produced at the beginning of February 1677, and was a complete failure. The failure was not due to any flaw in that incomparable poem or to mere caprice on the part of the public. It was skilfully engineered by Racine's enemies. It is doubtful whether any other French writer of the same eminence has aroused more antipathy than Racine. He had been the constant victim of professional jealousy and malicious intrigue, but this time matters were carried to unprecedented lengths. As soon as it became known that he was at work on *Phèdre*, the Duchesse de Bouillon commissioned a wretched hack named Pradon to write a play on the same theme and both plays were produced simultaneously. Similar tactics had been employed with *Iphigénie*, but this time nothing was left to chance. The Duchess bought up most of the seats for the first six nights at both theatres, and while Pradon's work was played to a house filled to capacity with her minions dutifully applauding the feeblest lines, Racine's was played before empty benches.

This prank is said to have cost the Duchess 15,000 *livres*. It was not, perhaps, an exorbitant price to pay for the destruction of the greatest French poet of the century, and its success was complete. Racine was haughty and irritable and bitterly resented any criticism of his work. He had had a good deal to put up with, but in the past he had generally outmatched his enemies. The Prefaces to the tragedies contain biting comments on the folly and ignorance of critics. Their miserable, halting epigrams provoked devastating retorts which were sometimes out of all proportion to the offence and in which we detect a savage pleasure in the infliction of pain.

The collapse of *Phèdre* was followed by the usual bitter exchange of epigrams, but the poet's heart does not seem to have been in the battle. This time he capitulated. He turned his back on his enemies, proceeded to compose his differences with Port-Royal and his mind turned once more to the possibility of the priesthood. He talked indeed of becoming a Carthusian, but allowed himself to be dissuaded from this extreme course by his confessor who counselled marriage. The elegant courtier, who had been the lover of two of the most celebrated actresses of the day, chose what must seem a strange companion. "L'amour ni l'intérêt n'eurent part de ce choix," wrote Louis Racine of his father's marriage to Catherine de Romanet.[1] His wife was a staid, middle-class lady; she was plain and devout, proved an excellent wife and mother, but had little sensibility for the arts. It is generally believed that she never read her husband's works, either from lack of interest or on account of religious scruples. The marriage was celebrated on 1st June 1677,

[1] Mesnard, I, p. 268.

less than four months after the disaster, and for the next twelve years Racine divided his time between his duties as *père de famille* and recording the victories of Louis XIV in his capacity as official historian.

These facts have been variously interpreted by writers of widely differing views. Some have attributed the silence to religious scruples, others to disgust with the literary coteries, and others still to the fact that for the time being Racine had nothing more to say. It is probable that all these interpretations contain a measure of truth, but none of them alone can provide an explanation of all the facts. The reasons for the decision must be sought in an unusual *combination* of circumstances. I think that it can be said that the brutality of the attack on *Phèdre* provided the shock which was needed to set in motion certain latent psychological factors which might otherwise have remained inactive.

It must be remembered that at the time of his marriage Racine was in his thirty-eighth year. It is an age at which surprising things can happen. Men who have led disorderly lives sometimes feel the need of stability or of committing themselves *irrevocably* to a particular course of action; and this need often assumes the choice between two extreme courses leading in opposite directions. It thus happens that some men—particularly men of letters approaching their fortieth year—who have been indifferent Christians or unbelievers all their lives suddenly undergo a violent conversion, while others make a final break with religion. Some who have led irreproachable domestic lives fall a victim to the *démon de midi*, while others still, who like Racine have been profligates, become the model husbands of plain women. It is also the age at which men who have led stormy, quarrelsome lives suddenly yearn for peace and quietness and simply give in.

"La piété fut en lui le fruit de l'agenouillement," said M. Mauriac of Racine's conversion.[1] No one to-day doubts the sincerity of Racine's beliefs, but conversion does not exclude the human element. The way is often prepared by factors which seem to have little to do with religion, and conversion is nearly always coloured by the milieu of the convert. When he looked back on his secular plays, Racine may well have wondered where his work was leading him, whether there was not after all something in Nicole's descrip-

[1] *La Vie de Jean Racine*, p. 156.

tion of playwrights as "public poisoners"; and it is not surprising that he should have turned in his perplexity and his search for security to the religion of his youth. He was no doubt influenced by other considerations as well. He had been brought up in an atmosphere of the most rigid puritanism, but his was an exceptionally sensual nature which had been indulged to the full since the break with Port-Royal. In spite of his preoccupation with "sin" and "temptation" in *Phèdre*, that play is not the simple drama of good and evil which Racine contrived to suggest in his Preface. There is an unmistakable element of complicity in the magnificent study of sexual mania, a boldness in the exploration of erotic fantasy which points to a deep-seated conflict in the poet's mind. Racine had hovered between God and Eros, and perhaps the weariness of the old *roué* and the ugly circumstances of the death of Mlle du Parc played their part in his final choice. It must never be forgotten that he was a man of violent extremes. His Jansenist upbringing had left an indelible impress on his personality and a complete break with religion was impossible. It was only natural that the imperious claims of Port-Royal should have reasserted themselves at a time when his career as a dramatist seemed to be foundering, and that his conversion should have taken the form of a return to the strict Jansenism of his childhood. There was nothing in Catholic teaching to prevent him from continuing his work as a poet, but in the Jansenist interpretation of that teaching there was a great deal.

His conversion produced a change of direction; his outlook became positive instead of negative. Although there does not seem at first to be any evidence in his plays to support the view that he had nothing more to say, it is difficult to believe that the new outlook and his growing sense of responsibility for his writings could have been reconciled with the production of more plays in the manner of *Phèdre*, or that the change could have been accomplished without some break in his work. A writer who has passed through a crisis of this sort clearly needs time to settle down before he can translate his new approach to contemporary problems into poetry. The distance that Racine travelled can only be appreciated after a close comparison between *Phèdre* and *Athalie*. In spite of Lemaître's description of *Phedre* as "the first stage in Racine's conversion," *Athalie* is not a development of tendencies which are present in *Phèdre*; it is a new departure in his work. Those critics who have lamented the effects of his conversion and the loss of the masterpieces which might otherwise have been written between *Phèdre* and *Athalie* were, perhaps, short-sighted. It is certain that without the conversion there would have been no *Athalie*, and no one who has studied the play attentively will feel that the twelve years' silence was altogether a waste of time.

Whether Racine would have turned his conversion to such good account without some form of outside stimulus may be doubted. Fortunately the stimulus was provided in a way that could scarcely remain without effect. In 1689 he was invited by Madame de Maintenon to devote his leisure moments to writing "some sort of moral or historical poem from which love was to be completely banished." It did not matter, she said, whether the poem conformed to the rules or not provided that it "helped her with her plans for amusing the young ladies of Saint-Cyr while at the same time improving their minds."[1]

Racine carried out his instructions to the letter. I have sometimes felt tempted to describe *Esther* as "slight," but the term is not exact. It is not of the same calibre as the great tragedies, but it is clearly the work of a master whose powers were in no way diminished and who has done exactly what he set out to do. The brutality of the Bible story is discreetly toned down and the play has a freshness—one might almost call it a fragrance—which is unique in Racine's poetry. It is not a religious play in the same sense as *Athalie*; it does not possess the richness and complexity of that work; but it expresses the awakening of the *jeunes filles* to the realities of the life about them. The combination of freshness and gravity that one feels in the lines:

> Jeunes et tendres fleurs par le sort agitées
> Sous un ciel étranger comme moi transplantées,

[1] Love was apparently not one of the subjects in which the young ladies needed instruction. "For," wrote Madame de La Fayette, "anyone who thinks that the three hundred girls who stay there until they are twenty and who have a court filled with people whose passions are awakened on their very doorstep, particularly when the King's authority does not make itself felt; anyone, I repeat, who thinks that girls and young men can be so close to one another without jumping over the walls is scarcely reasonable." (*op. cit.*, p. 213.)

The anonymous author of a pamphlet published in Holland was more explicit, describing Saint-Cyr as "little better than a seraglio which an aged sultana was preparing for a new Ahasuerus."

gives the play its special charm. It is the only one of Racine's plays which deserves the misused epithet "tender."

Racine was himself responsible for the production of the play. He rehearsed the young ladies of Saint-Cyr with the same care with which years before he had rehearsed Marquise du Parc and Mlle de Champmeslé. *Esther* was performed before the King and his Court with such success that Madame de Maintenon repeated her invitation. Racine could never resist success and the new invitation was accepted with alacrity. He devoted the whole of his great powers to *Athalie*, but the result was very different from its predecessor. The play was performed on three occasions only, during January and February 1691, in Madame de Maintenon's room without music or décors, and when it was printed it attracted little attention. It is said that Madame de Maintenon considered it unsuitable for Saint-Cyr and this point of view is certainly understandable. She may also have been prompted by other considerations, by the attack on absolute monarchy in Act IV. Sc. ii, and by the author's open sympathy with the Jansenist cause. Her reasons are not, perhaps, of great importance. For Racine success was success, and failure was failure. Once more he turned his back on the theatre and this time there was no recall. He devoted himself more assiduously than ever to his duties as *père de famille*, as the King's historian and as the agent of Port-Royal at the Court.

Mauriac speaks in one of his essays of the disproportion which exists between Racine and his work. "When we say that we are fond of Racine," he writes, "we mean that we are fond of Racine's tragedies. We know very little of the man who wrote them and that is a sign of his pre-eminence. For when posterity remembers a lot about the private lives of great writers, it often forgets about their most important books."[1] I think that we must add that what we do know we do not like. There is nothing very sympathetic about the young Racine angling for his *bon bénéfice*, quarrelling with Port-Royal and ruthlessly sacrificing his friends to his determination to be a success at all costs. But there is something peculiarly repellent about the middle-aged Racine, the Jansenist spy, the fond parent weeping copiously when one of his daughters took the veil, or the prig who, learning that his former mistress lay dying, could write to his son: "The day before yesterday I heard from M. Rost

[1] *Journal*, III, pp. 203–4.

RACINE
From a lithograph after a portrait by Santerre

that the Chamellay (*sic*) was at death's door. He appeared to be greatly distressed, but there is another thing which is much more distressing and which did not seem to worry him at all—I mean the obstinacy with which this unhappy woman refuses to renounce the stage."[1]

2

Incest naturally seems to most of us to be a more amusing subject for a play than the factions between Biblical tribes, and the present writer is probably not alone in coming to *Athalie* only after reading and re-reading nearly all Racine's other plays. Yet it would be a pity to allow one's distaste for a play with "a religious subject" and a discouraging sub-title—"Tragédie tirée de l'Écriture sainte" —to prevent one from studying a work which has a peculiar relevance for our own time. Racine's last play is not simply a searching criticism of the religious and political situation in France at the close of the seventeenth century; it is an attempt to state his problem in terms of religion and to find a solution.

The subject of the play is the struggle between a religious order based on *loi*—a word that assumes an intense positive significance in *Athalie*—and a pagan order based on force and bolstered up by ignoble superstition. The high lights are the extraordinary study of the personality of the "dictator" and her immediate entourage, and the frontal attack on absolute monarchy in Act IV. Although the play ends with the "liberation" of the people from despotism and the restoration of "law," the poet himself seems to have perceived clearly that it was no more than a temporary and precarious restoration. *Athalie* is a religious play in the fullest sense of the term; it is not like *Polyeucte* a great play which happened to have a religious subject. Yet we cannot help feeling that it is the quality not of the poet's *faith*, but of his *doubt*, which makes it so arresting. Racine does not offer us a social panacea or a facile solution. In his last play he looks wistfully back to the time when, as he imagined, a sane order was an established fact. He believes that this order has been preserved in a fragmentary state by one section of the community, and he considers the means of extending it to

1 Mesnard, VII, pp. 243–4. (Letter of 16th May 1698.)

the rest of society. He comes to the conclusion that the only guarantee of "law" lies in the union of Throne and Altar, but it is apparent all through the play that he had very little confidence either in bringing about this union or in its effectiveness if it were achieved. For this reason his order remains potential; it is never actually realized in the life of the community *as a whole* as it is in Corneille's greatest plays.

Athalie has long been regarded as a *pièce à clef.* When it was published, one of Racine's allies, the Père Quesnel, remarked with satisfaction that it contained portraits "où l'on n'a pas besoin de dire à qui ils ressemblent." Attempts have been made by French critics to discover the "key," but this sort of detective work is likely to prove unprofitable and misleading. *Athalie* is not, as Sainte-Beuve alleged, "a simple and powerful story"; still less is it a gallery of contemporary portraits or a "philosophical play" in which ghostly characters debate abstract problems. The characters are poetic creations, are the vehicles of a poetic criticism of the contemporary situation which is pre-eminently concrete and particular. Racine may well have had Bossuet in mind when he drew his portrait of Joad, but Joad's importance has nothing to do with his resemblance to Bossuet or to the Old Testament model. It lies solely in the fact that he represents a particular element in the pattern of the play.

One of the most interesting characters in the play is Athalie's general. Abner, whom the High Priest calls "l'un des soutiens de ce tremblant État," occupies an intermediate position between the two warring orders. He tries to combine fidelity to the true religion with loyalty to the person whom he believes, until the last Act, to be his lawful sovereign. It is not, perhaps, unduly fanciful to see him as the representative of Racine's own point of view, to see in his struggle a reflection of the difficulties experienced by Racine in trying to work out the relation of the individual to the social order. It is into his mouth that the great opening speech is placed:

> Oui, je viens dans son temple adorer l'Éternel.
> Je viens, selon l'usage antique et solennel,
> Célébrer avec vous la fameuse journée
> Où sur le mont Sina la loi nous fut donnée.
> Que les temps sont changés! Sitôt que de ce jour
> La trompette sacrée annonçait le retour,

Du temple, orné partout de festons magnifiques,
Le peuple saint en foule inondait les portiques;
Et tous, devant l'autel avec ordre introduits,
De leurs champs dans leurs mains portant les nouveaux fruits,
Au Dieu de l'univers consacraient ces prémices.
Les prêtres ne pouvaient suffire aux sacrifices.
L'audace d'une femme, arrêtant ce concours,
En des jours ténébreux a changé ces beaux jours.
D'adorateurs zélés à peine un petit nombre
Ose des premiers temps nous retracer quelque ombre.
Le reste pour son Dieu montre un oubli fatal,
Ou même, s'empressant aux autels de Baal,
Se fait initier à ses honteux mystères,
Et blasphème le nom qu'ont invoqué leurs pères.
Je tremble qu'Athalie, à ne vous rien cacher,
Vous-même de l'autel vous faisant arracher,
N'achève enfin sur vous ses vengeances funestes,
Et d'un respect forcé ne dépouille les restes.

I think it will be agreed that this opening speech is an impressive example of the grand manner. We are carried along by the sweep of the verse, the rich, open vowel-sounds, the trumpets and the pageantry. We cannot help being impressed by the certainty with which the great positive values are apprehended, the physical sense of them crowding in and enveloping us. The accent falls on four words: *Éternel, solennel, loi, ordre*. They may seem at first to be abstractions, but the *festons magnifiques*, the *foule qui inondait les portiques* and the *nouveaux fruits* transform them into the concrete embodiment of a vividly apprehended way of life. "The chief or rather the only character in *Athalie*," said Sainte-Beuve, "is God." It is a highly plausible view. We seem to feel all through the play a presence which is mysteriously shaping the destinies of the characters until it becomes something almost tangible, and the *Éternel-solennel* recurs like a theme in music. The poet evokes a stable order, a world in which "law" is supreme and its claims paramount. It is "law" which brings Abner to the Temple on the feast day; its significance is reinforced by the traditional associations of *antique*, and the offering of the firstfruits stresses its connection with the life of the common people living on the soil. It is the recognition of "law" which creates "order" and guarantees the calm and peaceful life. The point is emphasized by the homely picture of the priests shepherding the faithful into the Temple in an "orderly fashion."

All this is true, but the more we consider it, the more evident it becomes that the tragic force of the passage lies in the contrast between the order which has been lost, or which the poet believes to have been lost, and the present chaos; between the imagined splendour of the past and the very real distress and division of the present. A shadow falls across the scene transforming the *beaux jours* into *jours ténébreux*. The harsh, rending sounds of *audace* and *arracher* slash across the tranquil picture of the past which quivers and disintegrates. *Ombre* becomes the focal word. The rhyme points the contrast with *nombre,* and the reference back to *trompettes, annonçait* and *inondait* changes the splendour of the past into the insubstantial shapes of a dream.

For Racine the present is the reality and the past no more than a tantalizing dream. When he compares the crowds who once flocked to the Temple with the scattered wavering remnant of the faithful who remained, he was almost certainly thinking of the persecution of Port-Royal in his own time, and this accounts for the intensely personal feeling behind the lines. When he wrote *Athalie*, he was openly identified with the Jansenist cause and he must have been aware of the parallel between the *peuple saint* in his play and the Jansenist community. He felt that the task of preserving the true faith and restoring "law" belonged to Jansenism. In the play the Temple is the last stronghold of religion in a pagan world, is the place from which the saviour (Joas) will emerge. This was the role that Racine hoped that Port-Royal would play, but it is already apparent that the solution is not a very promising one. There was nothing in the past history of Jansenism which was comparable to the past of the *peuple saint*, and this emphasizes Racine's own scepticism. He must have realized that the movement had no past and no future and that there was not the slightest prospect of its producing a "saviour." It is a striking fact that in this, the opening speech which sets the tone of the rest of the play, it is the note of doubt which predominates. Abner is Racine's spokesman, and Abner is a doubter. His words remind us irresistibly of Auguste's great speech in *Cinna*.[1] For here, as surely as in *Cinna*, there are two voices—the voice of the orthodox believer reaffirm-

[1] See pp. 36–7 above.

ing his faith in God and the divine order, and the voice of the doubter who, in spite of his faith, does not believe for a moment that his prayer will be answered. All through the speech we overhear the dialogue between scepticism and belief going on in a muttered undertone inside the elegant periods. Sainte-Beuve's theory that God is the only character in *Athalie* fits in very well with his view of the play, but this view is open to serious criticism. It is not the presence of God that we feel so much as the presence of a god who is a cross between the jealous tribal god of the Old Testament and the remote god of the Jansenists. For the reality of Jansenism is not the presence of God, but the tormented and uneasy conscience of the individual as he stumbles blindly through the doomed world.

We have already seen that "temples" and "palaces" had played an important part in Racine's life and in his poetry. In his last play he elaborates and develops the image. The Temple of the Jews and the palace of Athalie stand for the two orders that face one another; they are the symbols of religion and secularism, of the Church and the world. There can be little doubt that Abner's return to the Temple symbolizes the return of the prodigal but repentant Racine to the bosom of Port-Royal. When Abner remarks nervously:

> J'attendais que, le temple en cendre consumé,
> De tant de flots de sang non encore assouvie,
> Elle [Athalie] vînt m'affranchir d'une importune vie . . .

he seems to reflect Racine's well-founded fear that Port-Royal would one day be destroyed by the royal power.[1] Racine also seems to identify himself to some extent with Joas whose childhood in the Temple strongly resembled his own. He is exposed to the same temptations. Athalie tries to entice him into making what Racine may have felt to have been his own mistake:

> Venez dans mon palais, vous y verrez ma gloire.

The secular "glory" of her palace is contrasted, in a magnificent line, with the sanctity of the Temple:

> Lieu terrible où de Dieu la majesté repose.

Sainte-Beuve's description of *Athalie* as "a simple and powerful story" seems to me to have been based on an incomplete analysis of

---

[1] The Abbey was closed by royal decree in 1705 and destroyed in 1710.

I

the religious elements in the play. They are not simple, but complex. There is the hard "official" religion—the religion of the orthodox—which is represented by the High Priest, and the uneasy "personal" religion which breaks through in the speeches of Abner and still more in the choruses.

The nostalgic note which is discernible in the opening speech becomes more pronounced as the play proceeds. In the lines:

> O divine, ô charmante loi!
> O justice, ô bonté suprême!
> Que de raisons, quelle douceur extrême
> D'engager à ce Dieu son amour et sa foi!

the hard, precise connotations of *loi, justice* and *raison* dissolve into the fragile, exotic beauty of *charmante* and *douceur*; and the action of *engager* becomes submerged in a voluptuous, mystical ecstasy. In the description of David praising God, the process is the same:

> Au lieu des cantiques *charmants*
> Où David t'exprimait ses *saints ravissements,*
> Et bénissait son Dieu, son seigneur, et son père,
> Sion, chère Sion, que dis-tu quand tu vois
> Louer le dieu de l'impie étrangère,
> Et blasphémer le nom qu'ont adoré tes rois?

The warrior-king is obscured by the mystic king lost in his *saints ravissements.*

The pronouncements of the High Priest are in a different style. His is a militant religion. He chides Abner and the Jews for their weakness and want of faith and glories in a God of vengeance:

> Faut-il, Abner, faut-il vous rappeler le cours
> Des prodiges fameux accomplis en nos jours?
> Des tyrans d'Israël les célèbres disgrâces,
> Et Dieu trouvé fidèle en toutes ses menaces;
> L'impie Achab détruit, et de son sang trempé
> Le champ que par le meurtre il avait usurpé;
> Près de ce champ fatal Jézabel immolée,
> Sous les pieds des chevaux cette reine foulée,
> De son sang inhumain les chiens désaltérés,
> Et de son corps hideux les membres déchirés . . .

The High Priest represents the tough, practical element in the "party" whose sinister methods are more apparent to us than they were to Racine. He does, indeed, go into a trance at one moment in the play, but his principal work is to bring about the destruction of his enemies by turning their own weapons of violence and cunning against them, by inciting the faithful to carry the struggle into the pagan stronghold

> . . . réveillant la foi dans les cœurs endormie,
> Jusque dans son palais cherchons notre ennemie.

In this work, he assures them, they will have God's help:

> Dieu sur ses ennemis répandra sa terreur.
> Dans l'infidèle sang baignez-vous sans horreur.[1]

The practical element is visible in the staccato order that he gives to his assistants:

> Qu'à l'instant hors du temple elle soit emmenée;
> Et que la sainteté n'en soit plus profanée,

and perhaps in the short, brutal announcement of one of his lieutenants:

> Mathan est égorgé.

The skill with which Racine wove these diverse strands into the texture of his play gives it its subtle and varied beauty and its tragic urgency. The quality of the play also helps us to appreciate the complexity of the problem which confronted the poet. The High Priest and Abner are both concerned in their different ways with the restoration of "law" in the world. The High Priest stands not only for officialdom, but also for the institutional element in religion which is the necessary corollary to the personal element of the choruses. Racine may not have cared much for what Joad stood for, but he saw clearly that his peculiar and somewhat repellent gifts were necessary if the goal was to be reached, and he may well have regretted that Port-Royal did not possess a champion of this calibre to stand up to the royal persecution. It is significant that the High Priest is always regarded as a means to an end. With the

---

[1] Stendhal declared, characteristically, that the play was "souverainement immorale en ce qu'elle autorise le prêtre à se soulever contre l'autorité et à massacrer les magistrats." (V. Martino, *Stendhal*, Paris, 1934, p. 48.)

crowning of Joas and the death of Athalie, his work as a "resistance leader" is done and he becomes at once a figure of less importance. We may conclude that in the new order which was supposed to emerge from the existing state of anarchy he would have been a minor functionary, a sort of ecclesiastical policeman who would have kept an eye on the machinery. For the new order was to be centred not merely in the somewhat dubious figure of the Priest-King, but in that perpetual hope—the "new generation," the child of tender years whom Racine, unable to deceive himself, describes sadly as

> Triste reste de nos rois,
> Chère et dernière fleur d'une tige si belle,
> Hélas! sous le couteau d'une mère cruelle
> Te verron-nous tomber une seconde fois?

"The subject of the play is Joas who is recognized as king and enthroned," wrote Racine in the Preface to *Athalie*, "and strictly speaking I should have called it *Joas*. But as most people have only heard it spoken of as *Athalie*, I did not see any point in publishing it under a different title; and besides, Athalie plays a very important part in it and it is her death that brings the play to a close."

We may wonder whether Racine altogether believed what he said in his Preface. He was inclined to use the Prefaces to tell the public what it ought to think about the plays. He may have considered it politic to emphasize the religious aspect of *Athalie* as he had emphasized the moral aspect of *Phèdre* in the Preface to that play. Racine's religion was remarkable for its intense preoccupation with sin, and he did not allow his search for a constructive solution of the problem to diminish his passionate interest in evil, in the forces that were undermining the religious order. In *Athalie*, as in the other plays, one of his principal interests is the disintegration of the personality of his "heroine." Athalie herself clearly belongs to the tragic sisterhood of the other plays. There is a world of difference between the simple Biblical character who is struck down by the servants of an avenging God, and the complex "modern woman" who is studied with such marvellous psychological insight.

Athalie is presented as a ruthless, inhuman monster who has usurped the throne of the rightful king and who did not stop at murder in order to achieve her aims. She has broken with the historic faith and slaughtered its priests. For, like all despots, she has found religion the most serious obstacle to the rule of force, and superstition the most potent ally. She has carried all before her, and at the opening of the play she is faced only with a remnant of the faithful who, led by the High Priest, is openly hostile to the usurper. She prepares to "liquidate" this remnant by the usual methods, but— to the surprise of friends and enemies alike—she hesitates. Her methods of violence have failed to create an *interior* unity and her own personality cannot resist the destructive forces that she herself has unleashed. From the beginning of the play she is seen under two different aspects. Josabet describes her on the day of the attempted murder of Joas:

> Un poignard à la main, l'implacable Athalie
> Au carnage animait ses barbares soldats.

This image, which has burnt itself into the imagination of the faithful, is suddenly replaced by a different one. In his opening speech Abner declares:

> Enfin depuis deux jours la superbe Athalie
> Dans un sombre chagrin paraît ensevelie.

Then her henchman Mathan says of her:

> Ami, depuis deux jours je ne la connais plus.
> Ce n'est plus cette reine éclairée, intrépide,
> Élevée au-dessus de son sexe timide,
> Qui d'abord accablait ses ennemis surpris,
> Et d'un instant perdu connaissait tout le prix.
> La peur d'un vain remords trouble cette grande âme:
> Elle flotte, elle hésite; en un mot, elle est femme.

The hard indomitable qualities implied in *superbe, implacable, intrépide* dissolve into the *sombre chagrin*, the *vain remords*: instead of action there is hesitation and indecision. Athalie herself completes the evidence. In the middle of one of her furious outbursts she is suddenly overcome by a sense of her own loneliness:

> Et moi, reine sans cœur, fille sans amitié.

When confronted with the child who she does not know is Joas she says:

Quel prodige nouveau me trouble et m'embarrasse?
La douceur de sa voix, son enfance, sa grâce,
Fait insensiblement à mon inimitié
Succéder . . . Je serais sensible à la pitié?

It is of the essence of despotism that the ruler builds up a system which is based on the suppression of the natural human virtues, a system which rapidly develops into an unending process of repression and destruction. In *Athalie* the personal tragedy of the despot lies in the fact that it is the return of natural human weaknesses which actually leads to the collapse of the system. The despot is a human being, and the remains of her humanity prove to be her undoing.

It is important to realize that *Athalie* is not the study of an isolated individual in the same sense as Racine's other plays. He sets Athalie in her proper milieu, and one of the most impressive things in the play is the study of the progressive moral deterioration of her entourage and its influence on her policy. The bearing which this point has on our present perplexities is obvious and it is worth examining Racine's handling of it in detail. To do so, we must compare Mathan's speech in Act III. Sc. iii, with the High Priest's attack on absolute monarchy in Act IV. Sc. iii.

Ami, peux-tu penser que d'un zèle frivole
Je me laisse aveugler par une vaine idole,
Pour un fragile bois que malgré mon secours
Les vers sur son autel consument tous les jours?
Né ministre du Dieu qu'en ce temple on adore,
Peut-être que Mathan le servirait encore,
Si l'amour des grandeurs, la soif de commander,
Avec son joug étroit pouvait s'accommoder.
Qu'est-il besoin, Nabal, qu'à tes yeux je rappelle
De Joad et de moi la fameuse querelle,
Quand j'osai contre lui disputer l'encensoir,
Mes brigues, mes combats, mes pleurs, mon désespoir?
Vaincu par lui, j'entrai dans une autre carrière,
Et mon âme à la cour s'attacha toute entière.
J'approchai par degré de l'oreille des rois,
Et bientôt en oracle on érigea ma voix.
J'étudiai leur cœur, je flattai leurs caprices,
Je leur semai de fleurs le bord des précipices.

Près de leurs passions rien ne me fut sacré;
De mesure et de poids je changeais à leur gré.
Autant que de Joad l'inflexible rudesse
De leur superbe oreille offensait la mollesse,
Autant je les charmais par ma dextérité,
Dérobant à leurs yeux la triste vérité,
Prêtant à leurs fureurs des couleurs favorables,
Et prodigue surtout du sang des misérables . . .

Mathan is a brilliantly ironical creation. He stands alone among Racine's characters, and to find anything comparable in French tragedy we have to turn to Félix in *Polyeucte* and Prusias in *Nicomède*. For by using his observation of the political scene, Racine created something which was a perfect vehicle for his criticism of the French Court. Mathan is the measure of the corruption of the life of the time; the weaknesses of human nature are set in their true perspective, enabling Racine to lay bare the roots of the evil.

The passage depends for its effect on the contrast between the hard, virile qualities suggested by *joug étroit, inflexible rudesse*, and the sinister, subterranean suggestions of *flattais, étudiais, mollesse, dextérité*. The worms "consuming" the idol indicate the moral softness of the sovereign and look forward to *offensait la mollesse*. Mathan alludes, with cynical humour, to his own softness when he declares that he was unable to submit to the discipline of the *joug étroit*. The image of the worms eating the wood of the idol is reinforced by *étudiais leur cœur*, for Mathan's method of insinuating himself into the confidence of the sovereign is identical with that of the worms and, by implication, the sovereign becomes a *vaine idole* —at any rate in the eyes of the "enlightened." The rhyme links *caprices* and *précipices*. For it is the unbridled passion that cannot submit to the *joug étroit* which contains the germ of dissolution. The fact that Mathan's defection to Baal was caused by some trivial dispute with Joad over the censer is the final damaging admission which sets his peculiar career and his unpleasant personality in their proper light.

From this we turn to the High Priest's warning to Joas:

Loin du trône nourri, de ce fatal honneur,
Hélas! vous ignorez le charme empoisonneur.
De l'absolu pouvoir vous ignorez l'ivresse,
Et des lâches flatteurs la voix enchanteresse.

Bientôt ils vous diront que les plus saintes lois,
Maîtresses du vil peuple, obéissent aux rois;
Qu'un roi n'a d'autre frein que sa volonté même;
Qu'il doit immoler tout à sa grandeur suprême;
Qu'aux larmes, au travail, le peuple est condamné,
Et d'un sceptre de fer veut être gouverné;
Que s'il n'est opprimé, tôt ou tard il opprime.
Ainsi de piège en piège, et d'abîme en abîme,
Corrompant de vos mœurs l'aimable pureté,
Ils vous feront enfin haïr la vérité,
Vous peindront la vertu sous une affreuse image.
Hélas! ils ont des rois égaré le plus sage.

I have already suggested that the theme of *Athalie* is not the study of the destructive forces at work in an otherwise stable order, but a conflict between two separate orders. One of them is wholly corrupt and must be destroyed as a preliminary step towards the restoration of "law." The other contains the possibility of a stable order, but stability can only be achieved provided that certain conditions are fulfilled. Joad's admirably "democratic" speech is a courageous criticism of the Court of Louis XIV. It is a description of the manner in which sovereignty degenerates into dictatorship and is of exceptional interest at the present time; but it only becomes fully intelligible when read in the light of Mathan's pronouncement. It is a statement of the problem from a different angle. Its intention is wholly constructive; it is a serious warning against dangers which may lead to a repetition of the disasters that overtook the *peuple saint* under the rule of Athalie. There is the same contrast between the *plus saintes lois* and the subterranean associations of *charme empoisonneur, voix enchanteresse, piège* and *abîme*. The effect, however, is to correct Mathan by restoring the values that he deliberately undermined. The *amour des grandeurs* is stigmatized as *ce fatal honneur*; the "passions" and the "caprices" are seen to possess a *charme empoisonneur* which inevitably corrodes what is best in civilization, which leads to an *ivresse* that is incompatible with *pureté* or *vérité*. Mathan's is the *voix enchanteresse*; he is one of the *lâches flatteurs* concealing the dangers, removing the *frein* from the supreme will of the sovereign. This time the situation is looked at objectively and the words are given a different value. The substitution of *frein* for *joug étroit* is an example. In other words, the elaborate subterfuge, the flowers strewn on the edge of the precipice, the *couleurs favorables* which hide truth, are cleared away and the full rottenness of the situation is exposed and judged.

It is interesting to notice that Athalie and her minions (like some of the most notorious of their modern exemplars) are *apostates*. They have abandoned one set of beliefs and set up an alien system in its place. It is characteristic of these substitute-religions, as we know to our cost, that they bear a close resemblance to the thing that they replace. At bottom, Athalie is a woman in whom the habits of mind of a Jansenist have survived the repudiation of the faith, and this is true of her entourage. They have a dogmatic system; they have above all the same uneasy consciences as the Jansenists,[1] and they are painfully aware of human weaknesses; but in their system the normal values are turned upside down and it is this that leads to disaster. It is true that there is no "love interest" in *Athalie*, but Athalie's infidelity is not less corrosive than Roxane's passion for her "brother-in-law" or Phèdre's for her stepson. Her collapse is an interior collapse, and though she is actually killed by the Levites, her physical death is simply the consummation of the process.

3

Athalie's great speech in Act II. Sc. v, is the centre of the play and must be examined in detail. For convenience sake it can be divided into three movements. The first is from l. 6 to l. 26; the second from l. 27 to l. 48; and the third from l. 50 to l. 88.

> Prêtez-moi l'un et l'autre une oreille attentive.
> Je ne veux point ici rappeler le passé,
> Ni vous rendre raison du sang que j'ai versé.
> Ce que j'ai fait, Abner, j'ai cru le devoir faire.
> Je ne prends point pour juge un peuple téméraire.

---

[1] In the speech from which I have already quoted, Mathan says:
> Toutefois, je l'avoue, en ce comble de gloire,
> Du Dieu que j'ai quitté l'importune mémoire
> Jette encore en mon âme un reste de terreur;
> Et c'est ce qui redouble et nourrit ma fureur.
> Heureux si, sur son temple achevant ma vengeance,
> Je puis convaincre enfin sa haine d'impuissance,
> Et parmi les débris, le ravage et les morts,
> A force d'attentats perdre tous mes remords!

I*

from one end of the play to the other. Jehu was an object of hatred and fear, a physical as well as a psychological danger. Athalie tries desperately to convince herself that she has reduced him to impotence so that he cannot repeat his treatment of her mother in her own case. Then the final picture of Athalie herself:

> Il me laisse en ces lieux souveraine maîtresse.
> Je jouissais du fruit de ma sagesse.

The material triumph is consolidated by *souveraine* and *sagesse*, a word with profoundly religious associations.

I have spoken of the difference between the intention and the effect of the passage. When it is studied closely, it is seen to be an elaborate pantomime in which Athalie recounts her triumphs over phantom armies. These phantoms have a deep psychological significance because they are an attempt to exteriorize fears to which Athalie cannot give a name. She tries to reassure herself by describing a victory over imaginary enemies in place of her own collapse in the face of real enemies whom she cannot overcome. The *effect* of the passage is, therefore, to create in the spectator's mind an impression of a precarious peace.

> Mais un trouble importun vient, depuis quelques jours,
> De mes prospérités interrompre le cours.
> Un songe (me devrais-je inquiéter d'un songe?)
> Entretient dans mon cœur un chagrin qui le ronge.
> Je l'évite partout, partout il me poursuit.
> C'était pendant l'horreur d'une profonde nuit.
> Ma mère Jézabel devant moi s'est montrée,
> Comme au jour de sa mort pompeusement parée.
> Ses malheurs n'avaient point abattu sa fierté;
> Même elle avait encor cet éclat emprunté
> Dont elle eut soin de peindre et d'orner son visage,
> Pour réparer des ans l'irréparable outrage.
> *Tremble*, m'a-t-elle dit, *fille digne de moi.*
> *Le cruel Dieu des Juifs l'emporte aussi sur toi.*
> *Je te plains de tomber dans ses mains redoutables,*
> *Ma fille.* En achevant ces mots épouvantables,
> Son ombre vers mon lit a paru se baisser.
> Et moi, je lui tendais les mains pour l'embrasser.

Mais je n'ai plus trouvé qu'un horrible mélange
D'os et de chairs meurtris, et traînés dans la fange,
Des lambeaux pleins de sang et des membres affreux,
Que des chiens dévorants se disputaient entre eux.

The opening lines of the second movement betray the insecurity of Athalie's "peace." The material success begins at once to crumble. The punctuation gives the impression of a series of strangled gasps. There is a conflict between Athalie's desire to conceal her dream and a desperate desire to confide in someone, to be reassured.

The crux of the passage, and perhaps of the play, is the word *songe,* and Athalie's voice sinks to a terrified whisper:

Un songe (me devrais-je inquiéter d'un songe?)

Her fear is powerfully augmented by the word *ronge*. Subterranean influences undermining normal life are one of the principal *motifs* of the play. The worms "consume" the wooden idols; the trickery of Mathan undermines sovereignty; and the dream undermines Athalie's peace of mind.

The celebrated line:

C'était pendant l'horreur d'une profonde nuit

focuses our whole attention on the dream, gathers up the emotion of the previous twenty lines and concentrates it on a single point. It is a wonderful example of Racine's power of condensation and of his dramatic sense. This line robs the material triumphs, sedulously catalogued in the first movement, of all their reality. For the rest of the play it is the dream world which is the reality, the shadow world of the supernatural which breaks through Athalie's psychological armour and destroys her. The terror and darkness suggested by the long, slow syllables of the *profonde nuit* extend over everything. The *calme profond*, for which Athalie had been fighting desperately, changes into another sort of *calme*—a silence in which terror reigns.

In place of the image of the proud and successful Athalie that was built up in the first movement, there arises a different figure. Jezabel is not merely Jezabel; she is Athalie herself. The description of Jezabel has a profoundly ironic significance—ironic because the subterfuge of Athalie's self-portrait is deliberately stripped away. The *pompeusement parée* refers to the insignia of royalty—the external symbols—on which Athalie herself has insisted. The décor is seen to be a disguise for her true feelings:

> Même elle avait encor cet éclat emprunté
> Dont elle eut soin de peindre et d'orner son visage,
> Pour réparer des ans l'irréparable outrage.

The unreal, painted figure is Athalie in her precarious and unreal security. The *sagesse* of l. 26 is not wisdom at all, but trickery. The hopeless despair behind the *irréparable outrage* gives the passage its tragic note.

The grim story of Jezabel's violent death is evoked more than once in this play. Joad dwells on it with a savage glee because he feels that it is the weak spot in Athalie's defences. Athalie herself refers to it because it has never ceased to prey on her mind until it has finally become a presage of her own death, and this explains the reference to Jehu in the first part of the speech.

Racine certainly intended the dream to be accepted as a supernatural warning, but its working is subjective. We must remember that Racine's Catholicism was a religion of intense subjective manifestations. The figure of Jezabel has much the same significance in this play as Venus in *Phèdre*. Once the fearful warning:

> Le cruel Dieu des Juifs l'emporte aussi sur toi

—which looks forward to Athalie's last despairing cry

> Dieu des Juifs, tu l'emportes!

—has been uttered, Athalie is a beaten woman. Her character disintegrates in precisely the same way as that of the other Racinian heroines.

The process of disintegration is described with consummate power in seven lines. One of the things that makes the passage effective is the *speed* of the process of disintegration. The painted Jezabel is presented in six lines; in six lines a sickening feeling of collapse is suggested by the poet. Then there is a pause; the painted figure hangs suspended in the darkness illuminated by a harsh, crude light which reveals its battered appearance. The warning is uttered; the *fille digne de moi* links the fate of mother and daughter, and the *digne* heightens the macabre comedy of the scene. Then the figure leans dramatically towards Athalie; Athalie raises her arms to embrace it or to assure herself of its reality or perhaps even to obtain some sort of support from it. Suddenly the figure crumples up leaving only a mass of torn and bloody flesh over which the mongrels fight. It is the outward and visible sign of the interior psychological collapse of Racine's heroine which is presented with a *hardiesse* that is without parallel in the whole of his work. It can now be seen how little truth there is in the theory that Racine's great monologues are frigid recitals of past events. His greatness does not lie least in the fact that the change which takes place in the personality of his characters actually happens before our eyes.

The third movement is no less important than the others, but it does not call for the same detailed analysis and is too long to set out in full here. It begins with a continuation of the dream:

> Dans ce désordre à mes yeux se présente
> Un jeune enfant couvert d'une robe éclatante . . .
> Mais, lorsque revenant de mon trouble funeste
> J'admirais sa douceur, son air noble et modeste,
> J'ai senti tout à coup un homicide acier
> Que le traître en mon sein a plongé tout entier . . .

The word *désordre* is of the utmost importance because of its many implications. The physical disorder to which it refers is the symbol of psychological disorder, but it is also out of this disorder that the new order will emerge. The child in his white robe is set against the bloody confusion of mangled flesh to emphasize the contrast between "innocence" and "corruption," "order" and "disorder." He may also be intended to suggest the Christ-Child because there is evidently a contrast between the disorder of the old world and the order of the new world of Christianity. Nor should we overlook the implication that the new world, for all its gentle beginnings, was a revolution that destroyed what was corrupt in the old. The dagger, for example, is probably a foreboding of Athalie's own death, but it is also symbolical of the stealthy way in which her destruction was brought about, and of the secret beginnings of Christianity.

The most important lines in the third movement are those describing Athalie's meeting in the Temple with the High Priest and Joas whom she recognizes as the child of the dream:

> Le grand prêtre vers moi s'avance avec fureur.
> Pendant qu'il me parlait, ô surprise! ô terreur!
> J'ai vu ce même enfant dont je suis menacée,
> Tel qu'un songe effrayant l'a peint en ma pensée ...
> Il marchait à côté du grand prêtre.

At this point the two worlds—the dream world and the real world —merge and consolidate against Athalie. The spectacle of the High Priest and Joas making common cause against her suggests better than anything the experience that we get from the last three acts of the play. We have a sense, which at times becomes almost oppressive, of the hostile forces closing in and paralysing Athalie; but we also have a sense of liberation, a sense of the new order symbolized by Joas taking shape and growing until it transcends the narrow religion of the High Priest.

4

Although the play closes with the triumph of religion and the reconstruction of the *tremblant État*, Racine was at some pains in his Preface to remind us that this triumph was only a temporary one. For many years Joas was a model king, but he ended his reign by killing the High Priest of the time in the Temple in a fit of anger.[1] In spite of its satisfactory ending, *Athalie* is shot through and through with an unmistakable note of pessimism. Its nature becomes clear from Joad's vision of the ultimate downfall of Joas, the Babylonian captivity and the foundation of the Catholic Church:

> Comment en un plomb vil l'or pur s'est-il changé?
> Quel est dans le lieu saint ce pontife égorgé?
> Pleure, Jérusalem, pleure, cité perfide,
> Des prophètes divins malheureuse homicide!
> De son amour pour toi ton Dieu s'est dépouillé.
> Ton encens à ses yeux est un encens souillé ...

> Quelle Jérusalem nouvelle
> Sort du fond du désert brillante de clartés,
> Et porte sur le front une marque immortelle?
> Peuples de la terre, chantez.
> Jérusalem renaît plus charmante et plus belle.

[1] This may have been a personal allusion to Racine's own excesses which followed his model childhood at Port-Royal.

There is a striking contrast between the language used to describe the disasters and the language used to describe the foundation of the Church. The images of destruction are precise and concrete; the images of reconstruction vague and abstract. The dull lead smothers the glittering gold; the priest is killed in the sanctuary; the incense is "soiled." From these ruins there emerges a strange "repository" Church. The homely "lead" and the "soiled" incense emphasize the curious prettiness of the "Jérusalem nouvelle brillante de *clartés*" and of the "plus *charmante* et plus *belle*," which makes the Church seem beautiful at the expense of strength. It is probable that the imagery was suggested by church decorations, but this merely underlines the fact that the poet was obliged to rely on second-hand images to describe the triumph of religion. For the "new order" is somehow unreal, and its very unreality seems to reflect the poet's own disillusionment and the defeat of his hopes.

I think that we must conclude that Racine had come to feel that his great hope—the creation of a Christian society on the ruins of the society analysed in the secular plays—was not destined to be realized. The history of the past hundred and fifty years has abundantly justified his pessimism. It is true that France rid herself of the evils against which Joad solemnly warned Joas in the attack on absolute monarchy; but the cost to Europe as well as to France herself was appalling. For the remedy was to a large extent destroyed with the evil, and the suffering that this involved has not yet finished. Nor can we overlook the immense responsibility of the Roi Soleil for the fact that the same evil later took root in a neighbouring country.

Comment en un plomb vil l'or pur s'est-il changé?

It is a question on which we should all do well to meditate in a spirit of profound humility.

EPILOGUE

In an earlier chapter I suggested, with reservations, that the seventeenth century can be divided broadly into three ages and those ages named after France's three greatest dramatists. When I stand back and survey the three portraits from a distance, I am more conscious of the difficulties of this division and more aware of the continuity of the French tradition. Their work seems at first to be a study of three different people—the Man of Honour, the Natural Man and the Man of Passion—but the impression is perhaps misleading. The real theme of the seventeenth century is the fortunes of the struggle between Reason and Passion seen at three different moments, and the Man of Honour, the Natural Man and the Man of Passion are really three facets of the same person. It is, indeed, the story of the rise and fall of Reason in France; and we discover with surprise that at the end of the century the three dramatists, starting from three different places, converge on a single point, share the same disbelief in Reason.

Corneille set out in his earlier plays to establish the dominion of Reason; in the period of comparative calm which followed, Molière shows us the dominion of Reason as an accomplished fact and proceeds to satirize any deviations from it which threaten the balance of society. *Le Misanthrope*, however, does more than look forward to Racine. When Alceste declares impatiently

> Mais la raison n'est pas ce qui règle l'amour

he is not merely looking forward to Hermione's

> Tant de raisonnements offensent ma colère.

The *authors* of both plays are saying the same thing, are proclaiming their growing scepticism about the ability of Reason to solve the human problems that face it. What is really startling, however, is the discovery that, in his declining years, Corneille seems to have become a convert to the same way of thinking. We have seen that in *Pulchérie* "honour" wins too easily; but it is not a complaint that can be made against *Suréna*, the last play of all, which was produced in 1674. When Suréna remarks

> . . . l'amour, jaloux de son autorité
> Ne reconnaît ni roi, ni souveraineté

is he not echoing words used only two years earlier by Roxane—

> Mais l'amour ne suit point ces lois imaginaires?

And Eurydice's injunction to her lover to marry some other princess for political reasons, but not to love her—

> Il faut qu'un autre hymen me mette en assurance.
> N'y portez, s'il se peut, que de l'indifférence

—recalls Atalide's boast

> Je vous ai vers Roxane envoyé plein de moi . . .
> Ce n'est point un amant en vous que je lui laisse.

In this last play Corneille's characters proclaim their love with a shamelessness which is worthy of the most abandoned of Racine's heroines. Reason is scarcely mentioned. "Duty" has become a political subterfuge which enables members of the ruling party to impose their will and break up the *mariages d'amour* of their rivals. Suréna and Eurydice only mention it to brush it rudely aside as an intolerable obstacle to their desires. The ideal of service and the acceptance of the political *mariage de raison* have gone by the board. Instead, they prefer to settle down to a leisurely enjoyment of the pleasures of *chagrin d'amour*:

> Je veux qu'un noir chagrin à pas lents me consume,
> Qu'il me fasse à longs traits goûter son amertume.

Thus Eurydice; and when she tries, not very convincingly, to persuade Suréna that it is his duty to marry another princess and give the State children who will emulate his own exploits on the field of battle, he disposes very briefly of her argument:

> Quand nous avons perdu le jour qui nous éclaire,
> Cette sorte de vie est bien imaginaire,
> Et le moindre moment d'un bonheur souhaité
> Vaut mieux qu'une si froide et vaine éternité.

Racine, one feels, can hardly have missed the point of that. He must have perceived the connection between Suréna's *imaginaire* and Roxane's *lois imaginaires*, must secretly have applauded Suréna's sentiments and reflected that his former "rival" had made splendid progress since his condemnation of *Britannicus* for dwelling too much on the *faiblesses* of human nature.

If *Suréna* falls a long way below Corneille's finest work it is not because "honour" wins too easily; it is because the characters, after ridding themselves of their troublesome scruples, no longer have the courage to seize the *bonheur souhaité*, to ensure the triumph of their passions. The only one of them who displays the true Cornelian fire is Suréna's sister, Palmis, who, when she sees the wilting Eurydice collapse and die very suddenly on the stage, brings the play to a close by declaring, in lines worthy of Corneille at his best:

> Suspendez ces douleurs qui pressent de mourir,
> Grands dieux! et dans les maux où vous m'avez plongée,
> Ne souffrez point ma mort que je ne sois vengée!

The death of Racine brings the *grand siècle* to a close. It is more than the end of an age; it is the end of a whole phase of human experience. With Racine the French classical theatre reached the summit of perfection; no further development along the same lines was possible. This did not prevent the eighteenth century from trying to continue the work of its predecessors; but in spite of the undoubted achievement of Marivaux and Beaumarchais, the attempt was a failure. The immense vitality of the seventeenth century depended, as I have tried to show, on its ambivalent attitude towards authority, on its attitude of acceptance-and-resistance. In the seventeenth century "the rules" were a constant subject of lively debate; it was not until the next century that the doctrines of classicism ceased to be controversial and were universally and passively accepted. This acceptance, and the divorce between reason and passion, explain the lifelessness of the eighteenth-century theatre. The work of the dramatists, as we can see from Voltaire's tragedies, became a boring imitation of "the Ancients." *Gloire*, which had had an immense glamour for the seventeenth century, degenerated into a counter; *passion* was no more than a frigid pose. The *philosophes*, using the methods which they had learnt from their distinguished predecessors, proceeded to apply them to the dissection of a dying society. They divided Man neatly into two, into a being who possessed the intelligence of a highly civilized person and the body of a highly trained animal. There was no longer any conflict between reason and emotion. For emotion was largely eliminated and replaced by sensation. The mind was simply an instrument for providing the body with agreeable sensations. The result was a drastic impoverishment of life which is amply reflected in eighteenth-century literature until the Revolution upset the balance and provided poetry with fresh and exciting material.

Racine's work was an end, but it was also a beginning, though what it began only becomes apparent a hundred and fifty years after his death. Professor Willey has shown that the materialism implicit in the Cartesian philosophy created a "climate of opinion" which was fundamentally hostile to poetry, but this is not the whole of the story.[1] The Cartesian philosophy did more than ruin traditional metaphysics. It marked the transition from a classical metaphysic to the idealist systems which have dominated modern literature.[2] I am not suggesting that Descartes had a direct influence on Racine, but it seems to me that a philosophy which makes the mind reflecting on its own processes—the *Cogito ergo sum*—its starting-point, and the preoccupation of the imaginative writer with what happens inside the individual mind, are manifestations of the same tendency and of a change which took place in the human mind during the seventeenth century. The work of Corneille and Molière was pre-eminently a study of man in society, of the Social Man. Now one of Racine's most startling innovations was not merely to shift the drama from the outer to the inner world, to transform the Social Man into the Individual Man; it was to make the inner drama his *exclusive* preoccupation, so that all his greatest characters might echo the words he used in one of his occasional poems: "Il y a deux hommes en moi." In his plays there is not, as there was in Corneille's and Molière's, a conflict between the claims of the individual and the claims of society; they reflect the disintegration of society within the consciousness of the individual. When Alceste turns his back on society and throws over the *bienséances* to set out in search of the *endroit écarté*, he performs a symbolical act. There are grounds for thinking that his creator felt tempted, at any rate for a moment, to follow his example; but he thought better of it and returned in his later work to his normal manner. It was

[1] *The Seventeenth-Century Background*, London, 1934, chapters V, VI and X.

[2] See Remy de Gourmont's interesting discussion of the connection between idealism in philosophy and the Symbolist Poets in *l'Idéalisme* (Paris, 1893), where he remarks (p. 27): "Le symbolisme est l'expression esthétique de l'idéalisme."

left to Racine to make the gesture a reality; the *endroit écarté* was both psychological and physical, and it can be argued that in Racine psychological and physical exile is an accomplished fact. In his greatest work he pushes the exploration of the human mind far beyond anything which had previously been attempted in France, and it was no doubt this tendency which prompted M. Pierre Brisson to say of Phèdre that "no other figure of the universal theatre gives away such dangerous secrets as hers."

In the eighteenth century, Racine's work was continued up to a point in the comedies of Marivaux. The strength and weakness of Marivaux would make an absorbing study, but this is not the place to undertake it. All that I can do is to point out that in Marivaux's comedies feelings become more and more rarefied and elusive until they seem to evaporate altogether like a delicate perfume. His work is a strange mixture of acute psychological insight and a special kind of verbiage for which the French coined the word *marivaudage*. It is the verbiage which chiefly interests us here. *Le Jeu de l'amour et du hasard* is a delightful comedy, but the very words of the title reveal its weakness and the poverty of the age which produced it. Its weakness is that the attitude behind it is altogether *trop voulu*. *L'amour* is not a powerful and dangerous emotion which continually threatens the balance of society, as it had done in the seventeenth century; it is an interesting state of mind, is no more than a "game." The characters are always asking themselves not simply "What do I feel?" but "How should I feel if I found myself in this or that situation?" In other words, the drama does not arise from a clash between powerful feelings or a conflict between a principle and a feeling, but from an absence of feeling, a *plein repos* which is very different from the state which Pascal analysed. Their dissatisfaction leads them to make use of *le hasard*, to invent artificial situations and then "see what it feels like." The two principal characters in *le Jeu de l'amour et du hasard* decide that it would be altogether too commonplace and uninteresting to meet, see whether they like one another and, if they do, marry. They hit independently on the same idea of disguising themselves as their servants and their servants as themselves. After a great deal of fun and misunderstanding, the couples find that they like each other very well, and marry. I think we must conclude from this that the seventeenth century had explored certain feelings so thoroughly that they were exhausted.

Now when a distinguished artist—and there is no doubt about Marivaux's distinction—is driven to manufacture artificial obstacles in order to create new feelings or to titillate old ones, there is clearly something wrong. His verbiage is not, as it sometimes appears to be, merely a playful *badinage* which is deliberately written to entertain the audience. It is a sign of sterility and it also marks the limit to which psychological investigation can be pushed *on the stage* without degenerating into a mere *jeu de mots*.

Marivaux, therefore, marks the transition from dramatic poetry to the short poem and the novel of our own times. The true heirs of Racine are not Marivaux and Voltaire, but the authors of the *Fleurs du mal* and the incomparable *Adolphe*. For Racine carried the dialogue of the mind with itself to the point where the debate could only be continued in private and in exile. No dramatist could push the exploration of the split personality further than Racine did in *Phèdre* or improve on the supreme technical accomplishment that he displayed in the role of Œnone; but it is the same voice that we hear when we listen to the cloistered Adolphe bitterly upbraiding himself for his treatment of Ellénore and to the dialogue between the anonymous travellers as they gaze in horror at the corpse dangling on the end of the gibbet on the shores of Cythère:

Ridicule pendu, tes douleurs sont les miennes!

It was probably only his immense respect for *les bienséances* which prevented Racine from saying precisely the same thing when he contemplated the dead Phèdre and brooded darkly over the *nuit infernale* which had swallowed her up.

TABLE OF DATES

BIBLIOGRAPHICAL NOTE

In addition to the works referred to in the text, the following may be consulted:

BOURGET, P., *Œuvres complètes, II, Critique*, Paris, 1900 ("Réflexions sur le Théâtre").

BRISSON, P., *Molière, sa vie dans ses œuvres*, Paris, 1942.

BROWN, A. M., M.D., *Molière and his Medical Associations*, London, 1897.

DESJARDINS, P., *La Méthode des classiques français*, Paris, 1904.

DUCLAUX, MARY, *The Life of Racine*, London, 1925.

FERNANDEZ, R., *Itinéraire français*, Paris, 1943.

GHÉON, H., *L'Art du théâtre*, Montreal, 1944.

GUIZOT, M., *Corneille et son temps*, Paris, 1852.

LANSON, G., *Corneille* (Les Grands Écrivains Français), Paris, 1898.

MAULNIER, T., *Racine*, Paris, 1936.

MICHAUT, G., *La Bérénice de Racine*, Paris, 1907; *La Jeunesse de Molière*, Paris, 1922; *Les Débuts de Molière à Paris*, Paris, 1923.

MORNET, D., *Histoire de la littérature française classique* (1660–1700), Paris, 1940.

SAINTE-BEUVE, C.-A., *Portraits littéraires* I (Corneille, Racine, "La Reprise de *Bérénice*"); *Portraits littéraires* II (Molière); *Nouveaux lundis*, VII ("Corneille: *le Cid*"); *Histoire de Port-Royal* II (Corneille); *Histoire de Port-Royal* III (Molière); *Histoire de Port-Royal* VI (Racine). (It is instructive to compare the studies of Corneille and Racine in the *Portraits littéraires* with the much more sympathetic approach in *Port-Royal*.)

SAINT-ÉVREMOND, C. DE, *Œuvres complètes*, I (ed. Planhol), Paris, 1927. ("Défense de Quelques Pièces de M. Corneille")

STRACHEY, LYTTON, *Landmarks in French Literature*, London, 1912; *Books and Characters*, London, 1922.

VALÉRY P., *Variété V, Sur Phèdre Femme*, Paris, 1944.

VAUVENARGUES, MARQUIS DE, *Œuvres complètes*, I, Paris, 1821 ("Réflexions sur Quelques Poètes").

VEDEL, V., *Deux classiques français vus par un critique étranger: Corneille et son temps—Molière*, Paris, 1935.

ADDENDA

The bibliography has been enlarged to include some important works which have appeared, or have come to my notice, since this book was first published.

Except where the contrary is stated, books in English and French are published in London and Paris respectively.

GENERAL

ADAM, A., *Histoire de la littérature française au XVIIe siècle*, 5 vols., Domat, 1948–56 (Corneille, I, pp. 469–544, IV, pp. 200–37; Molière, III, pp. 181–403; Racine, IV, pp. 255–377, V, pp. 39–57).

BÉNICHOU, P., *Morales du Grand Siècle* (*Bibliothèque des Idées*), Gallimard, 1948, 231 pp. (Outstanding.) *L'Écrivain et ses travaux*, José Corti, 1967, 362 pp. ('Le Mariage du Cid', pp. 171–206; Racine, pp. 207–323).

BRAY, R., *La Formation de la doctrine classique en France*, Nizet, 1927, vi + 389 pp.

KRAILSHEIMER, A. J. *Studies in Self-interest from Descartes to La Bruyère*, Oxford: Clarendon Press, 1962, xiv + 222 pp. (Corneille, pp. 47–60; Molière, pp. 152–72).

LANCASTER, H. C., *A History of French Dramatic Literature in the Seventeenth Century*, 9 vols., Baltimore: Johns Hopkins Press, 1929–42.

MAURIAC, F., *Journal, II*, Grasset, 1937, 230 pp. (Molière, pp. 146–54; Racine, pp. 115–9, 141–5). *Journal, III*, Grasset, 1940, 218 pp. ('La Grâce dans *Polyeucte*', pp. 105–10; Molière, pp. 91–9; Racine, 202–11).

MAURON, C., *Des Métaphores obsédantes au mythe personnel*, José Corti, 1962, 380 pp. (Corneille, pp. 243–69; Molière, pp. 270–90).

MAY, G., *Tragédie cornélienne, tragédie racinienne: Étude sur les sources de l'intérêt dramatique* (Illinois Studies in Comparative Literature, Vol. XXXII, No. 4.) Urbana: University of Illinois Press, 1948, 255 pp. (Corneille, pp. 6–115; Racine, pp. 116–191).

MORNET, D., *Histoire de la littérature française classique, 1660–1700*, Armand Colin, 1940, 427 pp.

NELSON, R. J., *Corneille and Racine, Parallels and Contrasts.* New Jersey: Prentice-Hall, 1966, 176 pp.

PÉGUY, C., *Victor-Marie, Comte Hugo,* Gallimard, 1934, 241 pp. (Corneille and Racine, *passim*).

POULET, G., *Études sur le temps humain,* Edinburgh: The University Press, 1949, 407 pp. (Corneille, pp. 125–37; Molière, pp. 116–24; Racine, pp. 138–53).

REYNOLD, G., *Le XVIIe siècle: le Classique et le Baroque,* Montreal: Éditions de l'Arbre, 1944, 280 pp.

SAINTE-BEUVE, C. A. *Histoire de Port-Royal* (Bibliothèque de la Pléiade), 3 vols., Gallimard, 1953–55 (Corneille, I, pp. 174–201; Molière, II, pp. 246–88; Racine, pp. 535–602). *Portraits littéraires,* I (Corneille, pp. 29–50; Racine, pp. 69–112; 'La Reprise de *Bérénice',* pp. 113–27). *Portraits littéraires,* II (Molière, pp. 1–63); *Nouveux lundis,* VII ('Corneille: *Le Cid',* pp. 199–306).

SCHÉRER, J., *La Dramaturgie classique en France,* Nizet, 1954, 427 pp.

STAROBINSKI, J., *L'Oeil vivant,* Gallimard, 1961, 262 pp. (Corneille, pp. 29–68; Racine pp. 69–90).

STEINER, G., *The Death of Tragedy,* Faber, 1961, viii + 356 + Index xii pp.

VEDEL, V., *Deux classiques français vus par un critique étranger: Corneille et son temps—Molière:* Translated from the Danish, Champion, 1935, 520 pp.

CORNEILLE

BOORSCH, J., 'Remarques sur la Technique dramatique de Corneille', pp. 101–62 of *Studies by Members of the French Department of Yale University* (Yale Romanic Studies, XVIII) Ed. A. Feuillerat, New Haven: Yale University Press, 1941, vii + 496 pp.

BRASILLACH, R., *Corneille,* Fayard, 1938, 496 pp.

COUTON, G., *La Vieillesse de Corneille (1658–1684),* Deshayes, 1949, v + 381 pp. *Corneille et la Fronde,* Clermont-Ferrand: Imprimerie G. de Bussac, 1951, 114 pp. *Corneille* (Connaissance des Lettres), Hatier, 1958, 224 pp. (Good introduction.)

CROCE, B., *Ariosto, Shakespeare and Corneille,* Eng. tr., D. Ainslie, Allen and Unwin, 1920, viii + 440 pp. (Corneille, pp. 337–430).

DESJARDINS, P., *La Méthode des classiques français,* Armand Colin, 1904, ii + 277 pp. (Corneille, pp. 1–164. Excellent.)

DORT, B., *Pierre Corneille dramaturge* (Les Grands Dramaturges, 16), L'Arche, 1957, 157 pp. (Marxist view of Corneille.)

DOUBROVSKY, S., *Corneille et la dialectique du héros* (Bibliothèque des Idées), Gallimard, 1963, 588 pp. (Important.)

HERLAND, L., *Corneille par lui-même*, Éditions du Seuil, 1956, 192 pp. *Horace ou Naissance de l'homme,* Éditions de Minuit, 1952, 213 pp.

LANSON, G., *Corneille* (Les Grands Écrivains Français), Hachette, 1898, 207 pp. (Still worth reading.)

NADAL, O., *Le Sentiment de l'amour dans l'oeuvre de Pierre Corneille* (Bibliothèque des Idées), Gallimard, 1948, 418 pp. (Probably the most valuable of recent studies of Corneille.)

NELSON, R. J., *Corneille, His Heroes and Their Worlds.* University of Pennsylvania Press, 1963, 322 pp.

SCHLUMBERGER, J., *Plaisir à Corneille,* Gallimard, 1936, 276 pp.

STEGMANN, A., *L'Héroisme cornélien,* 2 vols., Armand Colin, 1968, Vol. I, 246 pp., Vol. II, 760 pp.

YARROW, P. J., *Corneille,* Macmillan, 1963, x + 325 pp.

MOLIÈRE

BORDONOVE, G., *Molière génial et familier,* Laffont, 1967, 541 pp.

BRAY, R., *Molière homme de théâtre,* Mercure de France, 1954, 308 pp.

BRISSON, P., *Molière sa vie dans ses oeuvres,* Gallimard, 1942, 319 pp. (Entertaining.)

CAIRNCROSS, J., *Molière bourgeois et libertin,* Nizet, 1963, 192 pp.

DESCOTES, M., *Les Grands rôles du théâtre de Molière,* Presses Universitaires de France, 1960, 268 pp.

DUSSANE, B., *Un Comédien nommé Molière,* Plon, 1936, 285 pp.

FERNANDEZ, R., *La Vie de Molière* (Vies des Hommes Illustres, No. 32), Gallimard, 1929, 241 pp. (Important.)

GOSSMAN, L., *Men and Masks.* A Study of Molière, Oxford University Press, 1963, xii + 310 pp. (One of the most penetrating of recent studies.)

GUICHARNAUD, J., *Molière: Une Aventure théâtrale* (Bibliothèque des Idées), Gallimard, 1963, 548 pp.

GUTKIND, C. J., *Molière und das Komische Drama,* Halle: Niemeyer, 1928, 183 pp. (Valuable.)

JASINSKI, R., *Molière et le Misanthrope,* Armand Colin, 1951, 327 pp.

JOUVET, L., *Molière et la comédie classique* (Coll: 'Pratique du Théâtre'), Gallimard, 1965, 300 pp. (Extracts from a course in acting given by this great artist at the Paris Conservatoire in 1939–40. Of immense value for an understanding of Molière as dramatist.)

MAURIAC, F., *Trois grands hommes devant Dieu,* Éditions de la Capitole, 1930, 185 pp. ('Molière le Tragique', pp. 13–51).

MAURON, C., *Psychocritique du genre comique,* José Corti, 1964, 188 pp. (Stimulating.)

MICHAUT, G., *La Jeunesse de Molière,* Hachette, 1922, 255 pp. *Les Débuts de Molière à Paris,* Hachette, 1923, 253 pp. *Les Luttes de Molière,* Hachette, 1925, 249 pp. (They should be read with circumspection, but remain one of the indispensable contributions to the study of Molière.)

MOORE, W. G., *Molière, A New Criticism,* Oxford: Clarendon Press, 1949, 136 pp.

MORNET, D., *Molière l'homme et l'oeuvre* (Connaissance des Lettres), Boivin, n.d. (1943), 200 pp.

PALMER, J., *Molière His Life and Work,* Bell, 1930, viii + 431 pp.

SIMON, A., *Molière par lui-même,* Éditions du Seuil, 1957, 192 pp. (Stimulating.)

RACINE

BARTHES, R., *Sur Racine,* Éditions du Seuil, 1963, 171 pp.

BRERETON, G., *Jean Racine, A Critical Biography,* Cassell, 1951, xii + 362 pp.

BRISSON, P., *Les Deux visages de Racine,* Gallimard, 1944, 268 pp.

BUTLER, P., *Classicisme et baroque dans l'oeuvre de Racine,* Nizet, 1959, 349 pp.

CAHEN, J. B., *Le Vocabulaire de Racine,* Droz, 1946, 251 pp.

CLARK, A. F. B., *Jean Racine* (Harvard Studies in Comparative Literature, Vol. XVI), Cambridge (Massachusetts): Harvard University Press, 1939, xiv + 354 pp. (Good general study.)

DESCOTES, M., *Les Grands rôles du théâtre de Racine.* Presses Universitaires de France, 1957, 208 pp.

FERGUSSON, F., *The Idea of a Theatre,* Princeton University Press, 1949, 240 pp. ('*Bérénice:* the Action and Theater of Reason,' pp. 42–67).

FRANCE, P., *Racine's Rhetoric,* Oxford: Clarendon Press, 1965, 256 pp.

FUBINI, M., *Jean Racine e la critica delle sue tragedie*, Turin: Sten, 1925, 291 pp.

GIRAUDOUX, J., *Littérature*, Grasset, 1941, 268 pp. (Racine, pp. 27–55. The famous essay.)

GOLDMANN, L., *Le Dieu caché* (Bibliothèque des Idées), Gallimard, 1955, 454 pp. Eng. tr., P. Thody: *The Hidden God*, Routledge and Kegan Paul, 1964. (Racine, pp. 347–451). *Jean Racine dramaturge* (Les Grands Dramaturges, 13), L'Arche, 1956, 159 pp. (Marxist view of Racine.)

GRACQ, J., *Préférences*, New. ed., José Corti, 1961, 253 pp. ('A Propos de *Bajazet*', pp. 183–202. Remarkable essay.)

GUÉGUEN, P., *Poésie de Racine*, Éditions du Rond Point, 1946, 343 pp. (An illuminating and enjoyable study. Unfortunately out of print and difficult to consult.)

HOOG, A., *La Littérature en Silésie*, Grasset, 1944, 311 pp. ('Notre Mère Phèdre', pp. 21–78).

HUBERT, J. D., *Essai d'exégèse racinienne: Les secrets témoins*, Nizet, 1956, 278 pp.

JASINSKI, R., *Vers le vrai Racine*, 2 vols., Armand Colin, 1958, I. xxviii + 491 pp. II. 563 pp. (Ingenious, but somewhat far-fetched attempt to identify all the 'originals' of Racine's characters.)

JOUVET, L., *Tragédie classique et théâtre du XIXe siècle*. ('Pratique du Théâtre') Gallimard. 1968, 272 pp. (See comments on same author's books on Molière above.)

KNIGHT, R. C., *Racine et la Grèce*, Boivin, 1950, 467 pp.

LAPP, J. C., *Aspects of Racinian Tragedy*, Oxford University Press, 1955, xii + 195 pp. (Good study of Racine's symbolism.)

LEMAÎTRE, J., *Jean Racine*, Calmann Lévy, 1908, 328 pp.

MASSON-FORESTIER, *Autour d'un Racine ignoré*, Mercure de France, 1910, 442 pp. (Biased, but influential work.)

MAULNIER, T., *Racine*, Gallimard, 1936, 269 pp. *Lecture de Phèdre*, Gallimard, 1943, 162 pp. *Langages*, Éditions du Conquistador, 1946, 279 pp. (Admirable studies of the first three tragedies.)

MAURIAC, F., *La Vie de Jean Racine* (Le Roman des Grandes Existences), Plon, 1928, 255 pp.

MAURON, C., *L'Inconscient dans l'oeuvre et la vie de Racine*, Gap: Éditions Ophrys, 1957, 350 pp. *Phèdre*, José Corti, 1968, 188 pp. (Amusing psychoanalytical studies.)

MICHAUT, G., *La Bérénice de Racine*, Société Française d'Imprimerie et de Librairie, 1907, xiii + 355 pp.

MOREAU, P., *Racine, l'homme et l'oeuvre* (Connaissance des Lettres), Hatier-Boivin, 1943, 174 pp.

MORNET, D., *Jean Racine*, Aux Armes de France, 1943, 224 pp. *Andromaque de Jean Racine*, Étude et Analyse, Mellottée, 1947, 309 pp. (Useful study of Racine's antecedents.)

MOURGUES, O. DE, *Racine or The Triumph of Relevance*, Cambridge University Press, 1967, iv + 171 pp. (Good monograph.)

ORCIBAL, J., *La Genèse d'Esther et d'Athalie*, Vrin, 1950, 152 pp.

PICARD, R., *La Carrière de Jean Racine* (Bibliothèque des Idées), Gallimard, 1956, New ed., 1961, 708 pp.

POMMIER, J., *Aspects de Racine*, Nizet, 1954, xxxviii + 465 pp.

RIVIÈRE, J. and FERNANDEZ, R., *Moralisme et littérature*, Corrêa, 1932 ,203 pp. (Rivière on Racine, pp. 26–41.)

SCHMID, R., *Der Dramatische Stil bei Racine*, Aarau: H. R. Sauerländer, 1958, 149 pp. (Perceptive study of Racine's dramatic technique.)

SEGOND, J., *Psychologie de Jean Racine*, Les Belles Lettres, 1940, 225 pp.

SPITZER, L., *Romanische Stil- und Literaturstudien*, Vol. II, Marburg (Lahn): N.G. Elwert'sche Verlagsbuchlandlung, 1931, 301 pp. ('Die Klassische Dämpfung in Racines Stil', pp. 135-268. One of the best studies of Racine's language.) *Linguistics and Literary History*, Princeton University Press, 1948, viii + 236 pp. ('Le Récit de Théramène', pp. 87-134. Remarkable and controversial essay on the baroque element in Racine.)

STRACHEY, G. L., *Landmarks in French Literature*, Williams and Norgate, 1921, 256 pp. (Racine, pp. 89–110). *Books and Characters*, Chatto and Windus, 1922, 306 pp. (Racine, pp. 3–37).

TAINE, H., *Nouveaux essais de critique et d'histoire*, 3rd ed., Hachette, 1880, (Racine, pp. 171–223).

VALERY, P., *Variété V*, Gallimard, 1945, 325 pp. ('Sur Phèdre Femme', pp. 185–96).

VARIOUS *Europe*, No. 453, January, 1967. (Special number for the tercentenary of *Andromaque*. Interesting articles, particularly those dealing with the recent Racine controversy in France.) *Racine* (Modern Judgements) Edited by R. C. Knight, Macmillan, 1969, 239 pp. (Contains a number of valuable essays most of which were not easy to obtain.)

VAUNOIS, L., *L'Enfance et la jeunesse de Racine,* del Duca, 1964, 253 pp.

VINAVER E., *Racine et la poésie tragique,* Nizet, 1951, 253 pp. Eng. tr., P. M. Jones, Manchester University Press, 1955.

VOSSLER, K., *Jean Racine,* Munich: Hueber, 1926, 189 pp.

WEINBERG, B., *The Art of Jean Racine,* University of Chicago Press, 1963, 355 pp.

INDEX

Once made aware of this fact, President Wilson granted Wills a new commission, which expired March 4, 1921. The Federal Reserve Act was subsequently amended by an act of June 3, 1922, so as to be consistent with the Constitution on this matter.

At the conclusion of his term, Wills returned to his former post at the Federal Reserve Bank of Cleveland and remained there until his death on October 22, 1925, the victim of a failed appendicitis operation. Wills left behind a legacy of responsible public service and activity in his community. He was a trustee for Westminster College in New Wilmington, Pennsylvania, the first president of the Pittsburgh chapter of the American Institute of Banking, a member of the Executive Council of the American Bankers Association, and a bible school teacher at the First United Presbyterian Church.

Wills was a member of the Federal Reserve Board from September 29, 1920, to March 4, 1921. In this period, the Federal Reserve system was in the midst of executing its first significant independent policy actions. Until late 1919, Federal Reserve officials had been completely involved with setting up the system itself and then with the execution of Treasury-designed wartime policies. Throughout World War I the Federal Reserve followed Treasury direction, maintaining its discount rate schedule at low levels to keep Treasury financing costs at a minimum. In December 1919 the Treasury Department, believing the success of the final bond issue of the war to be secure, allowed the Federal Reserve to operate independently. The immediate response of the system to its new-found freedom was to raise discount rates to 4 ¾ percent. In January 1920 the rate was increased dramatically to 6 percent and in June of the same year to 7 percent. The chief advocate of higher rates was Benjamin Strong, governor of the Federal Reserve Bank of New York. During his tenure at the New York bank, Strong dominated Federal Reserve policy.

The purpose of the rate increase was to reduce the volume of credit (not the supply of money) and limit the inflation and speculation that had developed in the brief postwar boom. The environment that Federal Reserve officials were forced to operate in at the conclusion of the war was different from the one that the system was intended to operate in. Not only was the gold standard inoperative, but there was also a tremendous amount of government debt outstanding. Federal Reserve officials believed that this debt, since it was not directly linked to output, was inflationary. Accordingly, their move was against the perceived excessive volume of credit. Changing the discount rate was the only policy option open to Federal Reserve officials since reserve requirements were fixed in this period and open market operations were yet to be developed as a significant coordinated policy tool; no other actions were possible.

Wills's influence on the policy stance of the system during his tenure on the Federal Reserve Board was certainly minimal. The increase in rates to 7 percent occurred before his appointment. This rate was maintained unchanged during his tenure on the board and for several months after his departure. There is no indication that he strongly opposed the restrictive policies of the system during his tenure. His temporary appointment to the board was not based on his understanding of credit policy as much as his political views.

BIBLIOGRAPHY

Cyclopedia of American Biography. 1918–1931. Supp. ed. New York: Press Compilers Association.
New York Times. 1925. October 23, p. 23.
Who Was Who in America, 1897–1942. Vol. 1. Chicago: Marquis Who's Who.

ROY ARCHIBALD YOUNG
(1882–1960)

Vibha Kapuria-Foreman

Born in Marquette, Michigan, in 1882, Roy Archibald Young grew to be the man most small boys imagine they will become. Through honesty, hard work, and a sparkling social manner, Young rose from an entry position as bank messenger to become governor of the Federal Reserve Bank of Minneapolis in less than twenty years; at the time of his appointment in 1919, he was easily the youngest governor in the system. Within another eight years, he was appointed governor of the Federal Reserve Board, the highest banking position in the nation.

An Episcopalian of Scots-Irish heritage, Young was most often described by friends and associates as an individual devoted to his work, a man possessed of an outstanding capacity for mastering any task undertaken. He was widely reputed to be a fine story teller with an exceptionally pleasant manner and the ability to make and keep friends for life.

Young's professional history stands as testimony to these qualities. Upon graduation from high school in Marquette in 1900, Young began his working life employed by Western Union. Soon after he accepted his first position in banking as a messenger for the First National Bank of Marquette. Over the following decade, he rose through the ranks in various commercial banks in the upper peninsula of Michigan.

In 1913, a year after his marriage to Amy Bosson, Young attained the rank of vice-president of the Citizen's National Bank of Houghton. While there, he earned the admiration and respect of John W. Black, a prominent businessman. When Black was appointed to the board of directors of the Federal Reserve Bank of Minneapolis by President Woodrow Wilson in 1917, he recommended Young for a position at the Minneapolis Fed. Young subsequently became assistant to bank governor Theodore Wold.

When Wold retired in October 1919, Young was appointed to the post of governor. He remained governor of the Minneapolis Federal Reserve Bank until 1927 and directed its operations through some of the most difficult and turbulent years in the upper Midwest. His tenure as governor coincided with the beginning of a prolonged agricultural depression in the region. The decline of the agricultural sector brought with it an era of mounting distress for the banks of the area. The growing integration of the regional economy had led to a loss of customers by rural banks to their urban counterparts. Simultaneously, the agricultural depression made it more difficult for the rural banks to find profitable investments. Thus, the beginning of the end of rural unit banks had arrived.

Young remained in charge of the Minneapolis Fed throughout this period of deflation, depression, and the breakdown of credit. His adept handling of reserve bank policy during this prolonged crisis was an important factor in his appointment to the post of governor of the Federal Reserve system in 1927.

Young was a professional banker rather than an owner who ran a bank. The fourth governor of the Fed, he was the first to have come up through the ranks and also the first to have been appointed from within the Federal Reserve system. His predecessors had all begun at the top of the system, either as members of the board or by direct appointment as governors.

In July 1927 the reserve system underwent a crisis regarding the authority of the Federal Reserve Board over the operations of the regional reserve banks. Young was then at Minneapolis, and his stance in this struggle for power between the board and the reserve banks was indicative of his view of the decision-making authority of individual reserve banks. He supported the right of the regional reserve banks to set discount rates on the basis of local conditions and independently of the Federal Reserve Board.

During the first few months of 1927, the United States experienced a large inflow of gold. By summer, credit conditions in Europe had become extremely tight. England was struggling to remain on the gold standard, and Italy and France were attempting to adopt it. If U.S. interest rates had continued unchanged, autumn would have brought a severe strain on these countries' exchange rates. Europe normally experienced its largest annual need for gold to purchase American goods in autumn, and this seasonal demand was expected either to deplete gold reserves or require an increase in interest rates. Either would have crippled the gradual recovery of European economies and threatened international economic stability.

In the United States, the economy had been in recession since the last quarter of 1926, but recovery appeared to have begun. The stock exchange was active, and stock prices were rising; the wholesale price index had risen for the first time in two years. The timing of Fed actions indicates it was foreign considerations rather than domestic events that determined Fed policy (Wicker 1966, p. 114).

In July a meeting took place in New York between Benjamin Strong of the New York Federal Reserve Bank; Montagu Norman of the Bank of England; Hjalmar Schacht, president of the German Reichsbank; and Charles Rist, deputy governor of the Bank of France (Wicker 1966, p. 110). This meeting, and the subsequent changes in discount rates, led many to perceive that the formulation of U.S. monetary policy was dominated by European interests. In late July and early August the Federal Reserve banks of Kansas City, St. Louis, Boston, and New York announced decreases in their discount rates from 4 percent to 3 ½ percent. Strong, as head of the New York Reserve Bank, initiated policies that the board subsequently endorsed. The board then moved to force all reserve banks to pursue these policies. Young later reported that the decline in discount rates was occasioned by a desire to assist business at home and aid foreign countries in maintaining the gold standard. Adolph C. Miller[*] had expressed concern to the board about the inflationary impact of this action, but Young later argued that they were well aware of this possibility and had chosen what they perceived to be the lesser of two evils (Young 1928c).

At that time, however, the Reserve Bank of Chicago under James McDougal refused to lower its discount rate. Young of the Reserve Bank of Minneapolis supported this position. McDougal apparently believed that a decrease in the discount rate was unnecessary. In response, Daniel Crissinger[*] was able to marshal a slim majority on the Federal Reserve Board and force the Chicago Reserve Bank to lower its discount rate. Some sections of the press doubted the legality of this action and questioned the wisdom of forcing the issue in the absence of a national emergency. The vote reasserted the board's commitment to centralized money management but also rekindled fears about the eastern elite's control of Fed policy.

This decrease in the discount rate was successful in reversing the flow of gold, but Miller, as revealed in a letter to Herbert Hoover in 1934, accused Strong of having made a monumental error (Kettl 1986, p. 34). The 1927 incident made the Fed appear to be a tool of foreigners and created a serious rift in the unity of the Federal Reserve system. It was perceived by some commentators as the cause of Crissinger's resignation and by others to have fueled the stock market boom.

Young argued later that this policy aided domestic producers because it saved exporters from the ''hazards arising from unstable foreign exchanges'' and helped enable their customers to buy their products. In 1927, however, the Federal Reserve Bank of Minneapolis was the last to lower the discount rate. There is some discrepancy between what Young did while governor of the Minneapolis Fed and what he said about the earlier actions of the Fed once he became its governor. Although he defended the actions of the board during the spring and summer of 1927, he deplored board activism and clearly opposed it. Thus, when Young was appointed governor of the Federal Reserve Board in October 1927, it was widely perceived that President Calvin Coolidge preferred a weak board. In addition, Young's appointment appeared to reflect an attempt by the president to allay the fears of western bankers about the monopolization of board policy by eastern interests. Analysts concluded that Young would support the independence of reserve banks and avoid overruling them except in an economic emergency.

Before the Banking Act of 1935, the position of governor was a relatively weak one. The Federal Reserve Act of 1913 had vested the Federal Reserve Board with quite limited power. The board was to be a general board of management, and the regional banks were granted virtual autonomy. Their relative power can be gauged through an examination of the salary structure of the 1920s. Members of the Federal Reserve Board earned $12,000 per annum, while the governors of the individual reserve banks earned much more. Young had earned $25,000 at Minneapolis, and Strong was paid a $50,000 salary while governor of the Federal Reserve Bank of New York.

The board was legislatively enjoined to accommodate the needs of commerce and industry. The framers of the Federal Reserve Act had envisaged decentralized control of the banking system; the presence of bankers and government officials on the board had been a compromise between interests that were mutually suspicious.

Before 1935 the chairman of the Federal Reserve Board was referred to as governor, the title assigned to the heads of the regional reserve banks. The secretary of the Treasury and the comptroller of the currency were ex officio members of the board. Although the governor was the executive head of the Federal Reserve Board, the secretary of the Treasury chaired its meetings, and the governor was in charge only when the secretary chose not to attend. Thus, Young's move to Washington involved not only a loss of salary but also of power and authority.

During the first year of Young's tenure, the board was dominated by Benjamin Strong, who had influence due to the preeminence of New York among the nation's financial markets and also because of the strength of his personality and ideas. His well-established relationships with the New York financial community, various government officials, politicians, and the governors of foreign central banks added to his dominance. He was deeply interested in employing the influence of the Fed in the international arena, and he played a leading role in shaping its policies even when Young was nominally in charge—this despite the fact that he was not a member of the Federal Reserve Board. Indeed, some scholars blame the Great Depression on the crisis of leadership that occurred after Strong's death in October 1928 (Friedman and Schwartz 1963; Kettl 1986).

Young entered this milieu as an outsider. He did not wear the old school tie, and he was not a member of the eastern elite. He was a federalist with an abiding interest in the maintenance of regional autonomy. Even if he had been able to wrest leadership of the board, it is highly doubtful he would have exercised it to affect changes in reserve bank policies.

Young was a practical banker with demonstrated ability and a wealth of experience in dealing with the particulars of banking. He had learned his profession on the job and from within; he was not a theorist. He thought in terms of short-term credit needs, not long-term trends. Young was both intellectually and temperamentally unsuited to handle issues regarding the manipulation of the domestic economy and its relations with the world. In fact, he was suspicious of any attempt to harness the potential and power of the Federal Reserve system to influence the course of economic activity.

Young perceived the role of the Federal Reserve board to be limited to overseeing the general health of the banking system. In an address to the American Bankers Association in October 1928, Young argued that the Federal Reserve system had to use all its expertise and facilities to ensure the viability of the banking system (Young 1928b). In his opinion, the paramount responsibility of the system was the conservation of its reserves on a proper gold basis.

Young envisaged the role of the reserve banks as involving the issuance of currency, rediscounting, the settlement of international transactions, acting as the central clearinghouse for checks and drafts, and providing information regarding its policies and operation. He steadfastly resisted any attempt to extend the responsibilities of the system beyond these traditional functions. He argued that it would be unfortunate if the Federal Reserve system were made responsible for matters not directly related to banking. Among such matters Young included two major items: moderating the swings in business conditions and stabilizing the price level. Thus, he clearly believed that the Federal Reserve system should not conduct monetary policy and deplored attempts to charge it with that function.

He argued against such an interventionist policy partly because it was not an element of the Federal Reserve system's legislated mandate. In addition, the system did not possess adequate information and authority to stabilize the economy and prevent inflationary and deflationary periods. He appears to have agreed with Strong's assertion that inflation and deflation were best prevented by strict adherence to the gold standard. Young averred that a healthy banking system was the best guarantor of economic stability and would ensure strong, steady economic development. Finally, he maintained that overseeing the banking structure was enough of a mandate for the Federal Reserve system. Any increase in responsibility would merely serve to overtax the abilities of the system. Thus, in March 1928 Young testified before the House Committee on Banking and Currency against a bill directing the Federal Reserve Board to utilize its powers to foster the stability of the purchasing power of the dollar.

Even in the credit market, a legitimate concern of the central bank, Young perceived the appropriate function of the Fed as exercising a stabilizing, not a controlling, influence. He forcefully disagreed with the theory of managed credit, arguing that the instruments available to the Federal Reserve system, such as open market operations and rediscounting, were inadequate for controlling credit.

Further, Young did not believe in an activist role for the Federal Reserve system. He was a staunch conservative who insisted that economic conditions should and do affect reserve policy, rather than the converse. It was not the Federal Reserve system's responsibility to initiate economic or credit policy aimed at shaping the economic environment. Rather, its role was to accommodate the needs of business and industry.

Finally, within the Federal Reserve system itself, the board had an essentially passive role, which Young heartily endorsed. The individual reserve banks, steeped as they were in knowledge of local conditions, would propose appropriate policies. The board's province was limited to their endorsement.

From May to November 1927 the Federal Reserve system offset gold exports by purchasing government securities. Through this action, a policy aimed at aiding European countries was prevented from exerting a tightening influence on the money market. However, the stock market boom continued unabated, and the board became increasingly concerned about the inflationary effects of this policy even as it was having the intended effect in Europe (Young 1928a).

In November the Federal Reserve system ceased buying securities and allowed the outflow of gold to exercise a restraining influence. In addition, the system began to sell securities in order to bring pressure to bear on member banks. This attempt to reduce stock market loans indirectly was largely unsuccessful.

In January 1928 President Calvin Coolidge announced that there was no cause for concern over the volume of speculative activity. This startling public statement dismayed members of the board, who perceived the volume of investment in the stock market to be excessive and were attempting to reduce it. Young questioned Secretary Andrew Mellon about the president's statement and was told that Coolidge had not discussed the matter with his secretary of the Treasury.

In any event, concerns about the stock market could not yet be allowed to dictate board policy because the economy had not sufficiently recovered from the recession of 1926–1927. Thus, the Federal Reserve Board was presented with a dilemma: allow stock market speculation to continue unchecked and prepare the banking system for the inevitable correction or raise discount rates and in all probability destroy the still-fragile recovery.

The board was further hampered by the existence of some disagreement among its members regarding their authority to attempt to limit stock market loans in the absence of a clear and present danger to the banking system. Loans to stock market speculators were profitable and appeared safe. The fact that 1928 was an election year complicated the situation. The president and members of his cabinet publicly argued that the strength of the stock market reflected the health of the economy, an argument based more on political expedience than fact.

Young reported that although he was certain member banks were not borrowing from the reserve system in order to invest in the stock market, by February it was clear that both the low discount rate and high open market rate were encouraging member banks to borrow from reserve banks rather than curtailing their investments. When the Chicago reserve bank requested an increase in the discount rate to 4 percent, the board reluctantly agreed. Other reserve banks also raised their rates but with no perceptible impact on stock speculation. Lending continued to expand, and bank indebtedness to the reserve system continued to increase.

Early in March in testimony before the Senate Committee on Banking and Currency, Young declared that he did not fear for the safety and liquidity of brokers' loans. He estimated that only $2.25 billion of the $54 billion of outstanding credit in the United States was invested in brokers' loans. He argued that although bank credit appeared to have increased too rapidly, there was no indication it was at the expense of the needs of agriculture and industry. Further, he could not envisage any additional corrective measures the Federal Reserve system might legitimately pursue. Finally, he stated that he could not suggest any legislative measures that would correct the credit situation.

On March 26 the Open Market Investment Committee voted to resume sales of government securities. In April the Boston Reserve Bank requested and received permission to raise its discount rate to 4 ½ percent, citing local conditions as the motivation for this change. Other reserve banks slowly followed suit.

In its intended effect, this policy of tightening credit was only partially successful. By June member banks still owed the Federal Reserve system over $1 billion. According to Young, most of this borrowing was centered in large cities, and it was obvious that some banks could not get out of debt through a straightforward reorganization of their investments.

In an unintended way, the policy failed by succeeding all too well. Loans by member banks employed for stock market speculation decreased, especially in the New York area. This decline, however, was more than offset by increased lending by nonmember banks and nonbank sources. The volume of credit poured into the stock market by alternate sources was much larger than the reduction in bank lending and dwarfed the amount lent by banks for commercial purposes. Indeed, there were indications that businesses and individuals were withdrawing funds from banks in order to invest in the stock market.

Some commentators argued that the very policy of restraint that the Federal Reserve system had adopted in an attempt to stem the tide of speculative activity had, by raising interest rates, fueled the flow of funds to the stock market. Others proposed that the board abandon its gradualist approach and resort to a sharp increase in the discount rate to break the bull market (*Annalist* 1928, pp. 87–88). It was apparent that none of the actions of the reserve banks had succeeded in dampening the speculative boom.

In July the New York Federal Reserve Bank increased its discount rate from 4 ½ percent to 5 percent. A few days later the Open Market Investment Committee recommended a cessation in the sale of securities since the value of securities in the special investment account had decreased to $75 million. Also, the impact of the policy of restraint pursued for the previous six months could clearly be seen in the tightening of the money market. Given these considerations, the board promptly agreed to this recommendation.

The press became increasingly concerned about stock market speculation during this period. Some argued that the fault lay not with the Federal Reserve Board but with the changes in banking practices that had been promoted through its establishment. The Federal Reserve Act made credit more cheaply and freely available while providing banks with an illusion of insurance against failure. This in turn encouraged speculation. Thus there were many calls for radical revisions in the Federal Reserve system.

Others believed that the Federal Reserve Board was not doing enough to restrain speculation. They contented that the gradual increases in the discount rate would harm business without administering the shock necessary to stem the speculative fever. Thus, they clamored for sharper increases and more thorough follow-up measures to restrain stock speculation (*Bankers Magazine* 1928, pp. 186–87).

Over the next few months, Young found himself pulled between the ever-present and clearly conflicting demands of business and the stock market. In July business was booming. The index of industrial production would rise by 4½ percent during the third quarter of 1928. By August, therefore, the Federal Reserve Board began to concern itself with the potential impact of high interest rates on industry. In addition, there was the expected autumnal increase in the need for money to be considered. The board entertained the option of open market purchases of government securities but instead chose to meet this seasonal demand by buying acceptances.

Young informed the Open Market Investment Committee of the board's permission to acquire a maximum of $100 million in securities but emphasized the board's preference for acceptances. A majority on the board believed that the manner in which money was introduced into the economy could determine its ultimate destination. They took the view that money injected through the purchase of acceptances would be introduced much more slowly, and therefore much less of it would be employed for speculative purposes (Wicker 1966, p. 127).

In September Young declared himself satisfied with the operation of the Federal Reserve system. He asserted that the Fed was not worried about the state of the money market and expressed faith in its self-correcting mechanism; those who engaged in improper speculation would suffer the consequences during the inevitable period of correction. By October, however, he had begun to favor a check on the abnormal growth of credit. He voiced concern about the threat to the banking system from the enormous expansion of loans to stock speculators. Nevertheless, he argued that the Federal Reserve system stood powerless to effect significant change. It was unable to support any one class of loans; it could not control the uses to which its credit was put.

By November the Federal Reserve Board had become cautiously optimistic. There had been a continued decrease in bank credit, especially to traders in securities. Call money rates had risen to 8 percent. Thus, Young pronounced the policy a success. He stated that the slight increase in the cost of borrowing apparently had not had the detrimental impact on business conditions previously feared, and he forecast continued growth and prosperity. In light of this, the reserve banks ceased buying acceptances in December. Thereafter member bank indebtedness again began to increase as call money rates rose to 10 percent.

Adolph Miller pointed to the growing gap between the discount rate and the call money rate and argued that it provided an incentive to member banks to borrow from the reserve system in order to lend for purposes of speculation. He proposed that banks be required to explain how they intended to deal with this situation if it should arise. All the board members except Young approved (Wicker 1966, p. 125). Young believed that the bull market would collapse without any further action by the Fed. He perceived that the Federal Reserve system had done all it properly could to inhibit stock speculation and now needed to concentrate its resources on protecting the banking system when the correction occurred.

In January 1929 Miller formulated a policy of direct pressure, which he proposed that the board adopt. This involved directing a letter to all reserve banks informing them of the board's concern about the volume of stock speculation and warning them that rediscounting might be denied to banks lending on securities. The letter was distributed to the reserve banks February 2 and made public February 7.

Miller did not believe continued increases in the discount rate would accomplish the desired objective. With call money rates as high as 12 percent, it was apparent the discount rate would have to rise to an unprecedented level to curb stock market speculation. In addition, this policy of direct pressure could discriminate between banks lending to speculators and those lending to commercial enterprises. Miller and Charles Hamlin[*] were the sponsors and the strongest supporters of this policy. Young doubted the efficacy of moral suasion but was willing to attempt it (Friedman and Schwartz 1963, p. 267). He favored raising the discount rate only as a last resort.

In the letter released February 7 (*Annalist* 1929a, pp. 309–10), the board asserted that the large volume of credit devoted to speculative pursuits was endangering commerce and industry. Although disavowing any desire or authority to be the arbiter of the appropriate volume or value of investments in the stock market, the board declared itself compelled to restrain the use of Federal Reserve credit for speculative purposes. The statement asserted further that a "member bank is not within its reasonable claims for rediscount facilities at its Federal Reserve Bank when it borrows either for the purpose of making speculative loans or for the purpose of maintaining speculative loans."

This policy of direct pressure was roundly criticized from within and without the Federal Reserve system. Members of the press argued that the reserve board's warning represented an assumption of unwarranted authority. As with every previous attempt to enforce discipline deliberately, there was some question of the legality of the board's actions. This threat to refuse rediscounting to member banks holding paper that until now had been eligible for this service was seen by many as capricious and unfair.

At this time, the New York Federal Reserve Bank requested permission to increase its discount rate to 6 percent, arguing that such a rate increase was the only effective means available for quelling stock speculation. This disagreement about appropriate policies between the Federal Reserve Board and the New York bank was a constant source of conflict for the first six months of 1929. The result was a board bogged down in inaction.

Between February 14 and May 26 the directors of the New York Federal

Reserve Bank repeatedly voted to raise their discount rate and demanded permission from the Federal Reserve Board to do so. Permission was always denied, although Harrison's private lobbying of the board was gradually successful in changing the votes of some members. Young finally voted in favor of a discount rate increase in mid-May, but Miller, Hamlin, and Edward Cunningham[*] remained obdurate, and George James[*] and Comptroller of the Currency John Pole voted with them (Wicker 1966, p. 138; Friedman and Schwartz 1963, p. 259). The sentiment in favor of a discount rate increase would not muster a majority until August.

While Young traveled in April and May to the western reserve districts for the first time since becoming governor, these skirmishes continued. The board persisted in curbing the attempts at independent action by the New York Federal Reserve Bank while endeavoring to exercise the policy of direct pressure. The New York bank continued to appeal for the authority to employ a more flexible policy in its dealings with member banks, a policy involving liberal rediscounting and increasing discount rates whenever necessary.

In April Treasury officials, in an attempt to reassure the public, stated that the heavy margin requirement for loans to investors would serve to prevent a financial crisis by insuring the viability of these loans. In May Young cited evidence that individuals and businesses were liquidating savings accounts to invest in the stock market. This caused an increase in bank indebtedness to the Federal Reserve system and made discount rate increases inevitable. It was obvious the actions of the Federal Reserve system had failed to reduce speculation.

Stock market speculators apparently doubted the board's willingness to maintain its firm stand, for good reason. In September 1928 Young had stated that he would be satisfied if member banks owed the Federal Reserve system approximately $1 billion in rediscounts after January 1929. However, in January, when rediscounts were well below the limit specified, the board did not act to increase bank indebtedness. Instead it inaugurated the policy of direct pressure.

The pursuit of this policy gave no indication of firmness. In March, when this policy had been in operation for over a month, Charles E. Mitchell, a director of the New York Reserve Bank and president of the National City Bank, announced that his bank was willing to extend an additional $25 million in call loans in order to "prevent a dangerous crisis in the money market" (*Annalist* 1929b, p. 587). Such open defiance of stated board policy by an officer of the New York Federal Reserve Bank did not augur well for the success of the policy and appeared to confirm the weakness of board control over the banking system.

Earlier in March Young had stated that the Fed would resort to the "orthodox and traditional" method of a rate increase if the policy of direct pressure was unsuccessful. Such experimentation was widely interpreted as a sign that the board was not seriously interested in restraining speculation. Finally, in April Young said he had been unable to observe any signs of inflation. All these incidents made the board appear vacillating and weak. The continued rise in stock prices indicated that stock market speculators were neither intimidated nor impressed by board threats.

Although direct action continued to be the only policy employed to check the speculative hysteria, in June this approach was scaled back. Miller reported that this slackening occurred not only because the policy had succeeded but also due to fears that it might lead to a stock market collapse (Miller 1935, p. 451).

In August, with an eye to the anticipated seasonal increase in the demand for funds, George Harrison, governor of the New York Federal Reserve bank, requested that the Federal Reserve Board adopt a tightening policy of increasing the discount rate to 6 percent accompanied by an easing policy of purchasing acceptances. Young raised the issue at the Governors Conference and received a favorable recommendation. The board subsequently voted to allow the New York Reserve Bank to raise its discount rate while lowering its bill rate. Thereafter, the Federal Reserve system acquired $300 million in acceptances to fulfill the demands of commerce and industry while continuing to exert pressure on the stock market.

Surprisingly, there were no public addresses or statements by Young between June 1929 and March 1930. Following the crash of October 24, 1929, the New York Federal Reserve Bank purchased well over $100 million in government securities. It was supported in this attempt to ease the money market by a Federal Reserve Board policy that stressed liberal rediscounting.

There was, however, some disagreement between Harrison and the Fed regarding the New York bank's assumption of initiative in this matter. Thus, when the Open Market Investment Committee, under Harrison's leadership, requested permission to buy an additional $200 million in government securities to reduce the indebtedness of member banks, the board refused. When the request was repeated two weeks later permission was finally granted with Young's support (Friedman and Schwartz 1963, pp. 364–65).

During the same period, the board approved requests from the New York Federal Reserve Bank for successive decreases in the discount rate to 5 percent and then 4 ½ percent. In January the bill rate was decreased substantially, but a request for a further decrease in the discount rate to 4 percent was denied despite Young's favorable vote. This request was finally granted in February.

In March Young proposed authorizing the New York Federal Reserve Bank to purchase a maximum of $50 million in securities. The board approved. In the same month the discount rate was lowered to 3 ½ percent. Soon after the Open Market Investment Committee was reorganized and became the Open Market Policy Conference. The governors of all twelve reserve banks became members. Although the composition of the executive committee remained unchanged, its decision-making authority was scaled back.

Over the next few months, the New York bank continued to press for a more rapid decrease in the discount rate and substantial purchases of government securities. Miller consistently argued and voted against rate reductions and was frequently able to delay their adoption. The new composition of the Open Market

Committee also made the pursuit of securities purchases by the reserve system more difficult.

A majority of the governors believed that it was not the responsibility of the reserve banks to attempt to pull the economy out of the recession. Some argued that reserve banks should conserve their resources rather than inject them into the money market. Others were swayed by Miller's argument that money was already too cheap. Many of the bankers feared another speculative boom would result from easily available funds despite Young's assurance that this was unlikely. It was widely argued in the financial press that the 1928–1929 speculative hysteria had resulted from the actions of the reserve system during 1927. Faith in the reserve system on the part of bankers and economists was diminishing, and public support was almost nonexistent.

In an address in 1930 before the American Automobile Association broadcast on NBC radio, Young summarized the Federal Reserve Board's attempts to reduce stock speculation over the previous two years. He outlined the steps the reserve system had undertaken in the aftermath of the crash in order to prevent a total collapse of the banking system. A third of his speech, however, was devoted to a defense of the Federal Reserve system.

He asserted that the system had not been hesitant or slow and had "moved as rapidly as the mechanics would permit and . . . as rapidly as the situation [had] justified" (Young 1930, p. 4). In May Young again defended the reserve system, praising member banks for the promptness with which they had offset the withdrawal of funds by nonbanking lenders and thus averted "a panic and a collapse of our credit machinery." He argued that misplaced faith in the Federal Reserve system might, in part, have permitted member banks to be less than prudent and thus encouraged the crash. He emphasized that membership in the reserve system does not guarantee deposits and pleaded for the assumption of greater responsibility by banks.

In August Young resigned as governor of the Federal Reserve Board. In his letter to President Herbert Hoover, he stated that he was resigning in order to accept a more lucrative position. He had been unable to abandon his post while credit conditions in the country were strained, but he now considered himself able to look toward his own financial concerns since it was "evident that the credit structure of the country [was] in an easy and exceptionally strong position" (*Bankers Magazine* 1930, p. 398). Young's resignation was promptly accepted. He immediately accepted appointment as governor of the Federal Reserve Bank of Boston and entered this position on September 1, 1930.

Congressman Louis McFadden, chairman of the House Committee on Banking and Currency, alleged that Young and Platt, the vice-governor, had been forced off the board to make room for Eugene Meyer[*]. Young was called to testify and stated that he had not accepted a bribe to quit the reserve board governorship He asserted that only the higher salary and the condition of "my personal finances" had impelled his resignation.

As governor of the Federal Reserve Bank of Boston, Young continued to exercise influence over Federal Reserve policy through his membership on the Open Market Executive Committee. He may even have had greater impact upon open market operations than he did as governor of the Federal Reserve Board. Over the next few years he joined with McDougal in opposing the open market purchases of government securities that Harrison consistently recommended.

At Harrison's urging, the Federal Reserve Board adopted a program permitting reserve banks to ease the bill rate and, if they considered such action necessary, the discount rate while purchasing government securities. Endorsement of this policy was provided in Open Market Committee meetings during April and June 1931. Young voted against this proposal; he argued that requiring banks to hold more money would accomplish nothing. Although authorization for purchases had been granted, the amount acquired was well short of the amount permitted due to Harrison's concern about international developments. Thus, the policy was temporarily abandoned in July. In August, when Harrison requested permission to purchase an additional $300 million in securities, all governors except Eugene Black* of Atlanta voted against the proposal.

In January 1931 Young testified before the House Ways and Means Committee concerning the potential impact of the veteran's cash bill, a proposal for a $3.5 million cash payment to veterans to be financed by the sale of government bonds. He argued that such a payment would have a tremendous inflationary impact. Further, since the bond market was near saturation, interest rates would have to be increased in order to sell additional government bonds and would induce a fall in bond prices. This would cause a depreciation in the value of outstanding federal bonds and force the Federal Reserve system to raise the discount rate further in order to protect its position. Such actions would carry business ''further back than the stimulation has brought us forward.''

Young expressed the belief that the sale of government securities to the public would necessitate their withdrawal of funds from the already weakened banking system. Given the large number of bank failures, it would be foolhardy to place such additional pressure on the banking system. The liquidation of deposits for these purchases and the depreciation of bank assets as bond prices declined would serve to precipitate even more bank failures.

Compelled by this concern for the financial status of banks, Young consistently opposed open market purchases of securities during the rest of the year. He did not believe that the accumulation of reserves by banks would lead to the seepage of money to other parts of the country. He doubted the effectiveness of such a policy for affecting economic conditions since there was no indication that the increased liquidity of banks would induce them to increase lending or investment. He asserted his belief in the inevitability of further bank failures and argued that these, in turn, would require banks to borrow from the Federal Reserve system. The program of purchasing securities would place Federal Reserve banks in a difficult situation when these demands were eventually made.

The Banking Act of 1935 not only changed the name of the Federal Reserve Board to the Board of Governors of the Federal Reserve system but also changed the titles and increased the salaries of its members. The Federal Open Market Investment Committee underwent another reorganization; the twelve governors of the Federal Reserve banks were replaced by seven members of the board and five representatives of the reserve banks. Young lost his seat on the Open Market Committee and his role in national events as a result of this reorganization.

He continued as president of the Federal Reserve Bank of Boston until his retirement from government service in 1942. Thereafter, he became president of the Merchants National Bank of Boston. He remained at this post until his retirement from work in January 1954. During that same period he became a director of the American Woolen Company, the Calumet and Hecla Consolidated Copper Company, and the Fedders-Quigan Corporation for Saving, all in Boston, and the Madeira School in Greenaway, Virginia. He was a trustee of the Deaconess Hospital in Boston and a Knight First Class of the Royal Order of St. Olav (Norway).

After a lingering illness, he died on December 31, 1960, leaving behind his wife and two daughters, Jane B. Young and Martha B. Youngquist.

BIBLIOGRAPHY

Annalist. 1928. 32, no. 809 (July): 87–88.

———. 1929a. 33, no. 838 (February): 309–10.

———. 1929b. 33, no. 845 (March): 587.

Bankers Magazine. 1928. 117, no. 2 (August): 186–87.

———. 1930. 121, no. 3 (September): 398.

Federal Reserve System Board of Governors. 1927–1942. *Annual Reports.*

Friedman, M., and Anna Schwartz. 1963. *A Monetary History of the United States, 1867–1960.* Princeton: Princeton University Press.

Kettl, D. F. 1986. *Leadership at the Fed.* New Haven: Yale University Press.

Miller, A. C. 1935. "Responsibility for Federal Reserve Policies: 1927–1929." *American Economic Review* 25, no. 4: 442–58.

Wicker, E. R. 1966. *Federal Reserve Monetary Policy, 1917–1933.* New York: Random House.

Young, R. A. Addresses and Statements, 1927–30. Library, Board of Governors of the Federal Reserve System, Washington, D.C.

———. 1928a. "The Present Credit Situation." Addresses and Statements. Library, Board of Governors of the Federal Reserve System, Washington, D.C.

———. 1928b. "The Banker's Responsibilities." *Bankers Magazine* 117, no. 6 (December 1928): 973–76.

———. 1928c. "Peace and World Prosperity." Proceedings of the Academy of Political Science 13, no. 2, pt. III, pp. 320–25.

———. 1930. "Credit and Its Present Relation to Business." Address before the American Automobile Association broadcast on NBC Radio, March 20. Addresses and Statements. Library, Board of Governors of the Federal Reserve System, Washington, D.C.

INDEX

ABOUT THE EDITOR AND CONTRIBUTORS

DR. EARL W. ADAMS is Andrew Wells Robertson Professor, and chairs the Economics Department at Allegheny College in Pennsylvania. He has taught at Amherst College, the University of Pittsburgh, and the University of Massachusetts. He was a Woodrow Wilson Fellow at Johns Hopkins, and received his Ph.D. from the Massachusetts Institute of Technology.

DR. REXFORD AHENE is Associate Professor of Economics at Lafayette College in Pennsylvania. Professor Ahene lectures in international business and economic development. Author of a real estate evaluation monograph, he is also the editor of a book on investment in Africa as well the author of economic articles in academic journals.

DR. OGDEN O. ALLSBROOK, JR., is an Associate Professor of Economics at the University of Georgia. His research and teaching interests lie in the fields of monetary and fiscal policy. He has published widely in academic journals and has edited two books in the area of defense economics.

DR. WILLIAM J. BARBER is the Andrews Professor of Economics at Wesleyan University in Connecticut. Author of numerous articles and books, his research and teaching interests lie in the areas of fiscal and monetary theory and policy.

JULI CICARELLI is a journalist writing in the fields of women's studies, volunteer motivation, and economics. Her publications include several biographies in the area of economics.

DR. GREGORY A. CLAYPOOL is an Associate Professor in the Department of Accounting and Finance at Youngstown State University in Ohio. Voted Youngstown State University's Outstanding Accounting Educator of the Year in 1988, his research interests include professional ethics and accounting education and history.

DR. MICHAEL CONNELL is Assistant Professor of Economics at Lafayette College in Pennsylvania. Dr. Connell's teaching and research interests lie in the areas of law and economics and macroeconomic policy.

DR. JOHN P. CULLITY is Professor of Economics at Rutgers–the State University, and research associate at the Center for International Business Cycle Research at Columbia University. He has published widely in books and in academic and nonacademic journals.

DR. DAVID E. R. GAY is Professor of Economics at the University of Arkansas in Fayetteville. Dr. Gay lectures and has published extensively in the fields of finance and monetary economics.

DR. KATHIE S. GILBERT is Professor of Economics and Finance at Mississippi State University at State College. Dr. Gilbert lectures and writes in the area of monetary economics.

DR. THOMAS HAVRILESKY is Professor of Economics at Duke University. He has written extensively on the theory and practice of monetary and fiscal policy.

DR. ROBERT STANLEY HERREN is an Associate Professor of Economics at North Dakota State University. He has previously taught at the University of Mississippi and at Vanderbilt University. He has published numerous works in various areas of economics.

DR. ANNE R. HORNSBY is Professor and Chair of the Economics Department at Spelman College in Atlanta, Georgia. Her teaching and research interests lie in the fields of monetary economics and economic development.

DR. VIBHA KAPURIA-FOREMAN is an Assistant Professor of Economics at The Colorado College in Colorado Springs. She is a graduate from the University of Delhi, India, and the University of Pittsburgh, Pennsylvania.

DR. BERNARD S. KATZ is Associate Professor of Economics at Lafayette College in Pennsylvania. Dr. Katz lectures and writes primarily in the field of international economics. He is the author of *Biographical Dictionary of the Council of Economic Advisers* (Greenwood Press, 1988, coedited with Robert Sobel) and is also the editor of several volumes covering a spectrum of subjects on economics. Dr. Katz is currently working on three forthcoming books from Praeger, *The Oil Market in the 1980s: A Decade of Decline*, *Economic Transformation of Eastern Europe*, and *Investment in Africa*.

PAUL J. KUBIK is an Assistant Professor of Economics at Arkansas State University. His research and teaching interests lie in the fields of economic history and economic development. He has published in both academic and nonacademic journals.

PENNY KUGLER is a faculty member at Central Missouri State University, Warrensburg. Ms. Kugler was awarded the College of Business and Economics Outstanding Faculty Award in 1990.

DR. PHILIP LANE is Professor of Economics at Fairfield University in Connecticut. Professor Lane lectures in finance and monetary theory.

PROFESSOR DAVID J. LEAHIGH lectures in the Finance Program at Kings College in Pennsylvania.

PROFESSOR JEAN-CLAUDE LEON lectures in the Department of Economics and Business at the Catholic University of America in Washington, D.C. Dr. Leon has written articles and essays on various economic subjects in academic journals.

DR. MARIE McKINNEY is Associate Professor of Economics at Framingham State College in Massachusetts. Dr. McKinney has published in books and journals and lectures in the area of microeconomics.

DR. THOMAS R. McKINNON is currently Professor of Economics in the Center for Economic Education at the University of Arkansas in Fayetteville. Dr. McKinnon's main academic and educational interests are in the areas of finance and monetary economics.

PROFESSOR NEELA D. MANAGE lectures in the Department of Economics at Florida Atlantic University in Boca Raton. Dr. Manage writes in the areas of finance and monetary economics.

DR. JAMES N. MARSHALL is Professor of Economics at Muhlenberg College in Pennsylvania. He is the author of numerous essays, book reviews, and papers in economics and finance. His biography on William J. Fellner is forthcoming.

PROFESSOR YALE L. MELTZER is an Assistant Professor of Economics at the City University of New York (College of Staten Island). Lecturer in money and banking, he is the author of numerous books and articles in several fields in economics.

PROFESSOR ROBERT METTS lectures in the Department of Economics at the University of Nevada at Reno. Dr. Metts's research and publishing interests range from European integration to domestic monetary policy.

ANNETTE E. MEYER, an Associate Professor of Economics at Trenton State College, New Jersey, lectures and publishes in the fields of public finance and fiscal policy. Her monograph, *Evolution of United States Budgeting* was published by Greenwood Press in 1989.

PROFESSOR GEOFREY T. MILLS is Assistant Dean of the School of Business at the University of Northern Iowa. In addition to his administrative functions, Professor Mills lectures and writes in finance and economics.

DR. MARY MURPHY is an Assistant Professor at Lafayette College in Pennsylvania. Dr. Murphy lectures and writes on corporate finance and financial markets.

DR. THOMAS J. PIERCE is a Professor of Economics at California State College, San Bernardino. His research and teaching interests are in the areas of macroeconomic theory and monetary economics. He is the author of numerous articles in the general area of economics.

RONALD ROBBINS is the head research librarian at Lafayette College in Pennsylvania. Mr. Robbins has published several biographies and is the editor of a volume on classical economic treatises.

PROFESSOR CYNTHIA SALTZMAN lectures in the School of Management at Widener University in Pennsylvania. Professor Saltzman lectures and writes in the fields of finance and monetary policy.

DR. GEORGE G. SAUSE is an Emeritus Professor of Economics at Lafayette College in Pennsylvania where, in addition to money and banking, he taught courses in macroeconomics and public finance. He is the author of a book on money and banking and a number of articles on a variety of economic subjects.

DR. SHIVA SAYEG is an Assistant Professor of Economics at Lafayette College in Pennsylvania. Dr. Sayeg's teaching and research interests lie in the areas of international economics as well as money and banking.

DR. JAMES W. SCHMOTTER is Associate Dean of Administration at Cornell University, Ithaca, New York. Dr. Schmotter has written biographies of outstanding economists and has lectured in finance and macroeconomics.

PROFESSOR JANE M. SIMMONS is Professor of Marketing in the Williamson School of Business Administration at Youngstown State University in Ohio. Her research and teaching interests lie in the fields of advertising and public relations.

PROFESSOR NANCY M. THORNBORROW is the Lynn White, Jr., Professor of Economics at Mills College in California. Her research and teaching interests lie in the fields of labor and macroeconomics. She has published numerous articles in academic journals and books.

PROFESSOR DANIEL VENCILL is Professor of Economics and former Department Chair at San Francisco State University, California. His research and teaching interests are in the fields of monetary theory and the history of economic thought. His publications include numerous biographical essays and articles on forensic economics and labor market topics.

DR. DONALD R. WELLS is Professor of Economics and Department Chair at Memphis State University. His major area of research is the history of U.S. and Canadian banking. He has published in the *Cato Journal* and other academic journals.

DR. JACK B. WHITE is a Professor in the Department of Finance and Economics at Georgia Southern College in Statesboro, Georgia. Professor White lectures and has written extensively in the areas of finance and monetary economics.

DR. ROBERT C. WINDER is a Professor of Finance at Christopher Newport College in Virginia. Professor Winder's writings have ranged from biographical essays to theoretical studies in the areas of finance and macroeconomics.